PEARSON CUSTOM
COMPUTER SCIENCE

COMS W1001
Introduction to Information Science
Columbia University

Pearson Custom Publishing

New York   Boston   San Francisco
London   Toronto   Sydney   Tokyo   Singapore   Madrid
Mexico City   Munich   Paris   Cape Town   Hong Kong   Montreal

Senior Vice President, Editorial and Marketing: Patrick F. Boles
Executive Marketing Manager: Nathan Wilbur
Sponsoring Editor: Debbie Coniglio
Development Editor: Kelly Weaver
Operations Manager: Eric Kenney
Database Product Manager: Jennifer Berry
Art Director: Renée Sartell
Cover Designer: Kristen Kiley

Cover Art: "Blend," courtesy of Getty Images/Jason Reed; "Binary Data Flowing," courtesy of iStockphoto/Andrey Solovyev; "Beech Forest," courtesy of iStockphoto; "Small Plant," courtesy of iStockphoto/Florea Marius Catalin; "Network," courtesy of iStockphoto/Andrey Prokhorov.

Printed in the United States of America.

Please visit our web site at *www.pearsoncustom.com*

Attention Bookstores: For permission to return any unsold stock, contact us at *pe-uscustomreturns@pearson.com*.

**Pearson
Custom Publishing**
is a division of

www.pearsonhighered.com

ISBN 10: 0558462707
ISBN 13: 9780558462703

Important Information Regarding Supplemental Materials for Your Book

Your custom book comes with additional student resources, designed to aid you, including source code, development environments, etc. These materials are available to you via the following website, searchable by author last name and title:

http://www.pearsonhighered.com/cs_custom

Before completing a project, it is sometimes necessary to download and open data files. These files provide the starting point for the project and the data with which to work. Check with your Instructor for the best way to download these files, or use the following instructions.

Downloading Procedures for the Student Data Files in the Pearson Custom Publishing Program in Computer Science

1. From an open Web browser go to: http://www.pearsonhighered.com/cs_custom. Note: You may want to bookmark the appropriate page, as it contains links to additional products that you may be using in class.

2. Click on the appropriate title of your Computer Science text. This is where you will find all of the data files to complete the projects.

3. Because you have a Custom book, the chapter references in these data files may not match up with the chapter order in your book. This can be solved by browsing through the posted folders and matching the file name to the appropriate topic covered in your book.

4. When you find the file that you need, you may open to view the file immediately, or you may save the file to a specific location on you hard drive. We recommend saving the files to your desktop to find them easily.

Any resources not found on http://www.pearsonhighered.com/cs_custom can be found at www.mycodemate.com.

MyCodeMate

MyCodeMate is a book-specific Web resource that provides tutorial help and evaluation of student programs. In addition to Student Data Files, your book may reference specific programs available through the www.mycodemate.com website. If your professor ordered an access card to accompany your book, you have access to the materials available through MyCodeMate. If you do not have an access card, you can purchase a subscription online at www.mycodemate.com.

The additional student resources through http://www.pearsonhighered.com/cs_custom and www.mycodemate.com are provided to assist you in learning and practicing the concepts covered in your Custom book. When these resources are mentioned in a chapter, please refer back to these instructions to access and download the correct content.

Contents

1

Introduction

In this chapter we consider the scope of computer
science, develop a historical perspective, and
establish a foundation
from which to launch our study.

1 The Role of Algorithms
2 The Origins of Computing Machines
3 The Science of Algorithms

4 Abstraction
5 An Outline of Our Study
6 Social Repercussions

Computer science is the discipline that seeks to build a scientific foundation for such topics as computer design, computer programming, information processing, algorithmic solutions of problems, and the algorithmic process itself. It provides the underpinnings for today's computer applications as well as the foundations for tomorrow's applications.

We will investigate a wide range of topics including most of those that constitute a typical university computer science curriculum. We want to appreciate the full scope and dynamics of the field. Thus, in addition to the topics themselves, we will be interested in their historical development, the current state of research, and prospects for the future. Our goal is to establish a functional understanding of computer science—one that will support those who wish to pursue more specialized studies in the science as well as one that will enable those in other fields to flourish in an increasingly technical society.

1 The Role of Algorithms

We begin with the most fundamental concept of computer science—that of an algorithm. Informally, an **algorithm** is a set of steps that defines how a task is performed. For example, there are algorithms for cooking (called recipes), for finding your way through a strange city (more commonly called directions), for operating washing machines (usually displayed on the inside of the washer's lid or perhaps on the wall of a laundromat), for playing music (expressed in the form of sheet music), and for performing magic tricks (Figure 1).

Before a machine such as a computer can perform a task, an algorithm for performing that task must be discovered and represented in a form that is compatible with the machine. A representation of an algorithm is called a **program.** For the convenience of humans, computer programs are usually printed on paper or displayed on computer screens. For the convenience of machines, programs are encoded in a manner compatible with the technology of the machine. The process of developing a program, encoding it in machine-compatible form, and inserting it into a machine is called **programming.** Programs, and the algorithms they represent, are collectively referred to as **software,** in contrast to the machinery itself, which is known as **hardware.**

The study of algorithms began as a subject in mathematics. Indeed, the search for algorithms was a significant activity of mathematicians long before the development of today's computers. The goal was to find a single set of directions that described how all problems of a particular type could be solved. One of the best known examples of this early research is the long division algorithm for finding the quotient of two multiple-digit numbers. Another example is the Euclidean algorithm, discovered by the ancient Greek mathematician Euclid, for finding the greatest common divisor of two positive integers (Figure 2).

Figure 1   An algorithm for a magic trick

Effect: The performer places some cards from a normal deck of playing cards face down on a table and mixes them thoroughly while spreading them out on the table. Then, as the audience requests either red or black cards, the performer turns over cards of the requested color.

Secret and Patter:

Step 1.   From a normal deck of cards, select ten red cards and ten black cards. Deal these cards face up in two piles on the table according to color.

Step 2.   Announce that you have selected some red cards and some black cards.

Step 3.   Pick up the red cards. Under the pretense of aligning them into a small deck, hold them face down in your left hand and, with the thumb and first finger of your right hand, pull back on each end of the deck so that each card is given a slightly *backward* curve. Then place the deck of red cards face down on the table as you say, "Here are the red cards in this stack."

Step 4.   Pick up the black cards. In a manner similar to that in step 3, give these cards a slight *forward* curve. Then return these cards to the table in a face-down deck as you say, "And here are the black cards in this stack."

Step 5.   Immediately after returning the black cards to the table, use both hands to mix the red and black cards (still face down) as you spread them out on the tabletop. Explain that you are thoroughly mixing the cards.

Step 6.   As long as there are face-down cards on the table, repeatedly execute the following steps:

6.1. Ask the audience to request either a red or a black card.

6.2. If the color requested is red and there is a face-down card with a concave appearance, turn over such a card while saying, "Here is a red card."

6.3. If the color requested is black and there is a face-down card with a convex appearance, turn over such a card while saying, "Here is a black card."

6.4. Otherwise, state that there are no more cards of the requested color and turn over the remaining cards to prove your claim.

Figure 2   The Euclidean algorithm for finding the greatest common divisor of two positive integers

Description: This algorithm assumes that its input consists of two positive integers and proceeds to compute the greatest common divisor of these two values.

Procedure:

Step 1. Assign M and N the value of the larger and smaller of the two input values, respectively.

Step 2. Divide M by N, and call the remainder R.

Step 3. If R is not 0, then assign M the value of N, assign N the value of R, and return to step 2; otherwise, the greatest common divisor is the value currently assigned to N.

Once an algorithm for performing a task has been found, the performance of that task no longer requires an understanding of the principles on which the algorithm is based. Instead, the performance of the task is reduced to the process of merely following directions. (We can follow the long division algorithm to find a quotient or the Euclidean algorithm to find a greatest common divisor without understanding why the algorithm works.) In a sense, the intelligence required to solve the problem at hand is encoded in the algorithm.

It is through this ability to capture and convey intelligence (or at least intelligent behavior) by means of algorithms that we are able to build machines that perform useful tasks. Consequently, the level of intelligence displayed by machines is limited by the intelligence that can be conveyed through algorithms. We can construct a machine to perform a task only if an algorithm exists for performing that task. In turn, if no algorithm exists for solving a problem, then the solution of that problem lies beyond the capabilities of machines.

Identifying the limitations of algorithmic capabilities solidified as a subject in mathematics in the 1930s with the publication of Kurt Gödel's incompleteness theorem. This theorem essentially states that in any mathematical theory encompassing our traditional arithmetic system, there are statements whose truth or falseness cannot be established by algorithmic means. In short, any complete study of our arithmetic system lies beyond the capabilities of algorithmic activities.

This realization shook the foundations of mathematics, and the study of algorithmic capabilities that ensued was the beginning of the field known today as computer science. Indeed, it is the study of algorithms that forms the core of computer science.

2 The Origins of Computing Machines

Today's computers have an extensive genealogy. One of the earlier computing devices was the abacus. Its history has been traced as far back as the ancient Greek and Roman civilizations. The machine is quite simple, consisting of beads strung on rods that are in turn mounted in a rectangular frame (Figure 3). As the beads are moved back and forth on the rods, their positions represent stored values. It is in the positions of the beads that this "computer" represents and stores data. For control of an algorithm's execution, the machine relies on the human operator. Thus the abacus alone is merely a data storage system; it must be combined with a human to create a complete computational machine.

In more recent years, the design of computing machines was based on the technology of gears. Among the inventors were Blaise Pascal (1623–1662) of France, Gottfried Wilhelm Leibniz (1646–1716) of Germany, and Charles Babbage (1792–1871) of England. These machines represented data through gear positioning, with data being input mechanically by establishing initial gear positions. Output from Pascal's and Leibniz's machines was achieved by observing the final gear positions. Babbage, on the other hand, envisioned machines that would print results of computations on paper so that the possibility of transcription errors would be eliminated.

Figure 3   An abacus (photography by Wayne Chandler)

As for the ability to follow an algorithm, we can see a progression of flexibility in these machines. Pascal's machine was built to perform only addition. Consequently, the appropriate sequence of steps was embedded into the structure of the machine itself. In a similar manner, Leibniz's machine had its algorithms firmly embedded in its architecture, although it offered a variety of arithmetic operations from which the operator could select. Babbage's Difference Engine (of which only a demonstration model was constructed) could be modified to perform a variety of calculations, but his Analytical Engine (the construction for which he never received funding) was designed to read instructions in the form of holes in paper cards. Thus Babbage's Analytical Engine was programmable. In fact, Augusta Ada Byron (Ada Lovelace), who published a paper in which she demonstrated how Babbage's Analytical Engine could be programmed to perform various computations, is often identified today as the world's first programmer.

The idea of communicating an algorithm via holes in paper was not originated by Babbage. He got the idea from Joseph Jacquard (1752–1834), who, in 1801, had developed a weaving loom in which the steps to be performed during the weaving process were determined by patterns of holes in paper cards. In this

Augusta Ada Byron

Augusta Ada Byron, Countess of Lovelace, has been the subject of much commentary in the computing community. She lived a somewhat tragic life of less than 37 years (1815–1852) that was complicated by poor health and the fact that she was a nonconformist in a society that limited the professional role of women. Although she was interested in a wide range of science, she concentrated her studies in mathematics. Her interest in "compute science" began when she became fascinated by the machines of Charles Babbage at a demonstration of a prototype of his Difference Engine in 1833. Her contribution to computer science stems from her translation from French into English of a paper discussing Babbage's designs for the Analytical Engine. To this translation, Babbage encouraged her to attach an addendum describing applications of the engine and containing examples of how the engine could be programmed to perform various tasks. Babbage's enthusiasm for Ada Byron's work was apparently motivated by his hope that its publication would lead to financial backing for the construction of his Analytical Engine. (As the daughter of Lord Byron, Ada Byron held celebrity status with potentially significant financial connections.) This backing never materialized, but Ada Byron's addendum has survived and is considered to contain the first examples of computer programs. The degree to which Babbage influenced Ada Byron's work is debated by historians. Some argue that Babbage made major contributions whereas others contend that he was more of an obstacle than an aid. Nonetheless, Augusta Ada Byron is recognized today as the world's first programmer, a status that was certified by the U.S. Department of Defense when it named a prominent programming language (Ada) in her honor.

manner, the algorithm followed by the loom could be changed easily to produce different woven designs. Another beneficiary of Jacquard's idea was Herman Hollerith (1860–1929), who applied the concept of representing information as holes in paper cards to speed up the tabulation process in the 1890 U.S. census. (It was this work by Hollerith that led to the creation of IBM.) Such cards ultimately came to be known as punched cards and survived as a popular means of communicating with computers well into the 1970s. Indeed, the technique lives on today, as witnessed by the voting issues raised in the 2000 U.S. presidential election.

The technology of the time was unable to produce the complex gear-driven machines of Pascal, Leibniz, and Babbage in a financially feasible manner. But with the advances in electronics in the early 1900s, this barrier was overcome. Examples of this progress include the electromechanical machine of George Stibitz, completed in 1940 at Bell Laboratories, and the Mark I, completed in 1944 at Harvard University by Howard Aiken and a group of IBM engineers (Figure 4). These machines made heavy use of electronically controlled mechanical relays. In this sense they were obsolete almost as soon as they were built, because other researchers were applying the technology of vacuum tubes to construct totally electronic computers. The first of these machines was apparently the Atanasoff-Berry machine, constructed during the period from 1937 to 1941 at Iowa State College (now Iowa State University) by John Atanasoff and his assistant, Clifford Berry. Another was a machine called Colossus, built under the direction of Tommy Flowers in England to decode German messages during the latter part of World War II. (Actually, as many as ten of these machines were apparently built, but military secrecy and issues of national security kept their existence from

Figure 4   The Mark I computer (photo courtesy of Addison-Wesley)

becoming part of the "computer family tree.") Other, more flexible machines, such as the ENIAC (electronic numerical integrator and calculator) developed by John Mauchly and J. Presper Eckert at the Moore School of Electrical Engineering, University of Pennsylvania, soon followed.

From that point on, the history of computing machines has been closely linked to advancing technology, including the invention of transistors and the subsequent development of integrated circuits, the establishment of communication satellites, and advances in optic technology. Today, small handheld computers have more computing power than the room-size machines of the 1940s and can exchange information quickly via global communication systems.

A major step toward popularizing computing was the development of desktop computers. The origins of these machines can be traced to the computer hobbyists who began to experiment with homemade computers shortly after the development of the large research machines of the 1940s. It was within this "underground" of hobby activity that Steve Jobs and Stephen Wozniak built a commercially viable home computer and, in 1976, established Apple Computer, Inc. (now Apple Inc.) to manufacture and market their products. Other companies that marketed similar products were Commodore, Heathkit, and Radio Shack. Although these products were popular among computer hobbyists, they were not widely accepted by the business community, which continued to look to the well-established IBM for the majority of its computing needs.

In 1981, IBM introduced its first desktop computer, called the personal computer, or PC, whose underlying software was developed by a newly formed company known as Microsoft. The PC was an instant success and legitimized the desktop computer as an established commodity in the minds of the business community. Today, the term *PC* is widely used to refer to all those machines (from various manufacturers) whose design has evolved from IBM's initial desktop computer, most of which continue to be marketed with software from Microsoft. At times, however, the term *PC* is used interchangeably with the generic terms *desktop* or *laptop*.

The miniaturization of computers and their expanding capabilities have brought computer technology to the forefront of today's society. Computer technology is so prevalent now that familiarity with it is fundamental to being a member of modern society. Home computers have become integrated with entertainment and communication systems. Cellular telephones, digital cameras, and audio/video players are now combined with computer technology in single hand-held units called personal digital assistants (PDAs) that communicate via radio broadcast technology. Computing technology has altered the ability of governments to exert control; had enormous impact on global economics; led to startling advances in scientific research; revolutionized the role of data collection, storage, and applications; and has repeatedly challenged society's status quo. The result is a proliferation of subjects surrounding computer science, each of which is now a significant field of study in its own right. Moreover, as with mechanical engineering and physics, it is often difficult to draw a line between these fields

Babbage's Difference Engine

The machines designed by Charles Babbage were truly the forerunners of modern computer design. If technology had been able to produce his machines in an economically feasible manner and if the data processing demands of commerce and government had been on the scale of today's requirements, Babbage's ideas could have led to the computer revolution in the 1800s. As it was, only a demonstration model of his Difference Engine was constructed in his lifetime. This machine determined numerical values by computing "successive differences." We can gain an insight to this technique by considering the problem of computing the squares of the integers. We begin with the knowledge that the square of 0 is 0, the square of 1 is 1, the square of 2 is 4, and the square of 3 is 9. With this, we can determine the square of 4 in the following manner (see the diagram below). We first compute the differences of the squares we already know: $1^2 - 0^2 = 1$, $2^2 - 1^2 = 3$, and $3^2 - 2^2 = 5$. Then we compute the differences of these results: $3 - 1 = 2$, and $5 - 3 = 2$. Note that these differences are both 2. Assuming that this consistency continues (mathematics can show that it does) we conclude that the difference between the value $(4^2 - 3^2)$ and the value $(3^2 - 2^2)$ must also be 2. Hence $(4^2 - 3^2)$ must be 2 greater than $(3^2 - 2^2)$, so $4^2 - 3^2 = 7$ and thus $4^2 = 3^2 + 7 = 16$. Now that we know the square of 4, we could continue our procedure to compute the square of 5 based on the values of 1^2, 2^2, 3^2, and 4^2. (Although a more in-depth discussion of successive differences is beyond the scope of our current study, students of calculus may wish to observe that the preceding example is based on the fact that the derivative of $y = x^2$ is a straight line with a slope of 2.)

x	x^2	First difference	Second difference
0	0		
		1	
1	1		2
		3	
2	4		2
		5	
3	9		2
		7	
4	16		2
5			

and computer science itself. Thus, to gain a proper perspective, our study will not only cover topics central to the core of computer science but will also explore a variety of disciplines dealing with both applications and consequences of the science. Indeed, an introduction to computer science is an interdisciplinary undertaking.

3 The Science of Algorithms

Conditions such as limited data storage capabilities and intricate, time-consuming programming procedures restricted the complexity of the algorithms utilized in early computing machines. However, as these limitations began to disappear, machines were applied to increasingly larger and more complex tasks. As attempts to express the composition of these tasks in algorithmic form began to tax the abilities of the human mind, more and more research efforts were directed toward the study of algorithms and the programming process.

It was in this context that the theoretical work of mathematicians began to pay dividends. As a consequence of Gödel's incompleteness theorem, mathematicians had already been investigating those questions regarding algorithmic processes that advancing technology was now raising. With that, the stage was set for the emergence of a new discipline known as *computer science*.

Today, computer science has established itself as the science of algorithms. The scope of this science is broad, drawing from such diverse subjects as mathematics, engineering, psychology, biology, business administration, and linguistics. Indeed, researchers in different branches of computer science may have very distinct definitions of the science. For example, a researcher in the field of computer architecture may focus on the task of miniaturizing circuitry and thus view computer science as the advancement and application of technology. But, a researcher in the field of database systems may see computer science as seeking ways to make information systems more useful. And, a researcher in the field of artificial intelligence may regard computer science as the study of intelligence and intelligent behavior.

Thus, an introduction to computer science must include a variety of topics, which is a task that we will pursue in the following chapters. In each case, our goal will be to introduce the central ideas in the subject, the current topics of research, and some of the techniques being applied to advance knowledge in the area. With such a variety of topics, it is easy to lose track of the overall picture. We therefore pause to collect our thoughts by identifying some questions that provide a focus for its study.

- Which problems can be solved by algorithmic processes?
- How can the discovery of algorithms be made easier?
- How can the techniques of representing and communicating algorithms be improved?
- How can the characteristics of different algorithms be analyzed and compared?
- How can algorithms be used to manipulate information?
- How can algorithms be applied to produce intelligent behavior?
- How does the application of algorithms affect society?

Note that the theme common to all these questions is the study of algorithms (Figure 5).

Figure 5   The central role of algorithms in computer science

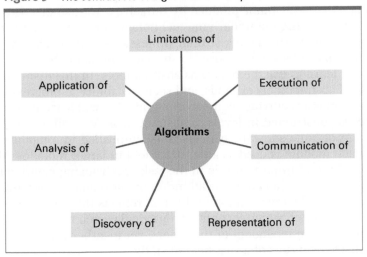

4 Abstraction

The concept of abstraction so permeates the study of computer science and the design of computer systems that it behooves us to address it in this preliminary chapter. The term **abstraction,** as we are using it here, refers to the distinction between the external properties of an entity and the details of the entity's internal composition. It is abstraction that allows us to ignore the internal details of a complex device such as a computer, automobile, or microwave oven and use it as a single, comprehensible unit. Moreover, it is by means of abstraction that such complex systems are designed and manufactured in the first place. Computers, automobiles, and microwave ovens are constructed from components, each of which is constructed from smaller components. Each component represents a level of abstraction at which the use of the component is isolated from the details of the component's internal composition.

It is by applying abstraction, then, that we are able to construct, analyze, and manage large, complex computer systems, which would be overwhelming if viewed in their entirety at a detailed level. At each level of abstraction, we view the system in terms of components, called **abstract tools,** whose internal composition we ignore. This allows us to concentrate on how each component interacts with other components at the same level and how the collection as a whole forms a higher-level component. Thus we are able to comprehend the part of the system that is relevant to the task at hand rather than being lost in a sea of details.

We emphasize that abstraction is not limited to science and technology. It is an important simplification technique with which our society has created a lifestyle that would otherwise be impossible. Few of us understand how the various conveniences of daily life are actually implemented. We eat food and wear clothes that we cannot produce by ourselves. We use electrical devices without understanding the underlying technology. We use the services of others without knowing the details of their professions. With each new advancement, a small part of society chooses to specialize in its implementation while the rest of us learn to use the results as abstract tools. In this manner, society's warehouse of abstract tools expands, and society's ability to progress increases.

Abstraction is a recurring theme in our study. We will learn that computing equipment is constructed in levels of abstract tools. We will also see that the development of large software systems is accomplished in a modular fashion in which each module is used as an abstract tool in larger modules. Moreover, abstraction plays an important role in the task of advancing computer science itself, allowing researchers to focus attention on particular areas within a complex field. In fact, the organization of this text reflects this characteristic of the science. Each chapter, which focuses on a particular area within the science, is often surprisingly independent of the others, yet together the chapters form a comprehensive overview of a vast field of study.

5 An Outline of Our Study

This text follows a bottom up approach to the study of computer science, beginning with such hands-on topics as computer hardware and leading to the more abstract topics such as algorithm complexity and computability. The result is that our study follows a pattern of building larger and larger abstract tools as our understanding of the subject expands.

We begin by considering topics dealing with the design and construction of machines for executing algorithms. We look at how information is encoded and stored within modern computers, and we investigate the basic internal operation of a simple computer. Although part of this study involves technology, the general theme is technology independent. That is, such topics as digital circuit design, data encoding and compression systems, and computer architecture are relevant over a wide range of technology and promise to remain relevant regardless of the direction of future technology.

We study the software that controls the overall operation of a computer. This software is called an operating system. It is a computer's operating system that controls the interface between the machine and its outside world, protecting the machine and the data stored within from unauthorized access, allowing a computer user to request the execution of various programs, and coordinating the internal activities required to fulfill the user's requests.

We study how computers are connected to each other to form computer networks and how networks are connected to form internets. This study leads to topics such as network protocols, the Internet's structure and internal operation, the World Wide Web, and numerous issues of security.

We will introduce the study of algorithms from a more formal perspective. We investigate how algorithms are discovered, identify several fundamental algorithmic structures, develop elementary techniques for representing algorithms, and introduce the subjects of algorithm efficiency and correctness.

We consider the subject of algorithm representation and the program development process. Here we find that the search for better programming techniques has led to a variety of programming methodologies or paradigms, each with its own set of programming languages. We investigate these paradigms and languages as well as consider issues of grammar and language translation.

We will introduce the branch of computer science known as software engineering, which deals with the problems encountered when developing large software systems. The underlying theme is that the design of large software systems is a complex task that embraces problems beyond those of traditional engineering. Thus, the subject of software engineering has become an important field of research within computer science, drawing from such diverse fields as engineering, project management, personnel management, programming language design, and even architecture.

We look at ways data can be organized within a computer system. We introduce techniques traditionally used for organizing data in a computer's main memory and then trace the evolution of data abstraction from the concept of primitives to today's object-oriented techniques. We consider methods traditionally used for organizing data in a computer's mass storage and investigate how extremely large and complex database systems are implemented.

We explore the subject of graphics and animation, a field that deals with creating and photographing virtual worlds. Based on advancements in the more traditional areas of computer science such as machine architecture, algorithm design, data structures, and software engineering, the discipline of graphics and animation has seen significant progress and has now blossomed into an exciting, dynamic subject. Moreover, the field exemplifies how various components of computer science combine with other disciplines such as physics, art, and photography to produce striking results.

We learn that in order to develop more useful machines computer science has turned to the study of human intelligence for leadership. The hope is that by understanding how our own minds reason and perceive, researchers will be able to design algorithms that mimic these processes and thus transfer these capabilities to machines. The result is the area of computer science known as artificial intelligence, which leans heavily on research in such areas as psychology, biology, and linguistics.

We close our study by investigating the theoretical foundations of computer science—a subject that allows us to understand the limitations of algorithms (and thus machines). Here we identify some problems that cannot be solved algorithmically (and therefore lie beyond the capabilities of machines) as well as learn that the solutions to many other problems require such enormous time or space that they are also unsolvable from a practical perspective. Thus, it is through this study that we are able to grasp the scope and limitations of algorithmic systems.

Our goal is to explore to a depth that leads to a true understanding of the subject. We want to develop a working knowledge of computer science—a knowledge that will allow you to understand the technical society in which you live and to provide a foundation from which you can learn on your own as science and technology advance.

6 Social Repercussions

Progress in computer science is blurring many distinctions on which our society has based decisions in the past and is challenging many of society's long-held principles. In law, it generates questions regarding the degree to which intellectual property can be owned and the rights and liabilities that accompany that ownership. In ethics, it generates numerous options that challenge the traditional principles on which social behavior is based. In government, it generates debates regarding the extent to which computer technology and its applications should be regulated. In philosophy, it generates contention between the presence of intelligent behavior and the presence of intelligence itself. And, throughout society, it generates disputes concerning whether new applications represent new freedoms or new controls.

Although not a part of computer science itself, such topics are important for those contemplating careers in computing or computer-related fields. Revelations within science have sometimes found controversial applications, causing serious discontent for the researchers involved. Moreover, an otherwise successful career can quickly be derailed by an ethical misstep.

The ability to deal with the dilemmas posed by advancing computer technology is also important for those outside its immediate realm. Indeed, technology is infiltrating society so rapidly that few, if any, are independent of its effects.

This text provides the technical background needed to approach the dilemmas generated by computer science in a rational manner. However, technical knowledge of the science alone does not provide solutions to all the questions involved. With this in mind, this text includes several sections that are devoted to social, ethical, and legal issues. These include security concerns, issues of software ownership and liability, the social impact of database technology, and the consequences of advances in artificial intelligence.

Moreover, there is often no definitive correct answer to a problem, and many valid solutions are compromises between opposing (and perhaps equally valid) views. Finding solutions in these cases often requires the ability to listen, to recognize other points of view, to carry on a rational debate, and to alter one's own opinion as new insights are gained. Thus, each chapter of this text ends with a collection of questions under the heading *Social Issues* that investigate the relationship between computer science and society. These are not necessarily questions to be answered. Instead, they are questions to be considered. In many cases, an answer that may appear obvious at first will cease to satisfy you as you explore alternatives. In short, the purpose of these questions is not to lead you to a "correct" answer but rather to increase your awareness, including your awareness of the various stakeholders in an issue, your awareness of alternatives, and your awareness of both the short- and long-term consequences of those alternatives.

We close this section by introducing some of the approaches to ethics that have been proposed by philosophers in their search for fundamental theories that lead to principles for guiding decisions and behavior. Most of these theories can be classified under the headings of consequence-based ethics, duty-based ethics, contract-based ethics, and character-based ethics. You may wish to use these theories as a means of approaching the ethical issues presented in the text. In particular, you may find that different theories lead to contrasting conclusions and thus expose hidden alternatives.

Consequence-based ethics attempts to analyze issues based on the consequences of the various options. A leading example is utilitarianism that proposes that the "correct" decision or action is the one that leads to the greatest good for the largest portion of society. At first glance utilitarianism appears to be a fair way of resolving ethical dilemmas. But, in its unqualified form, utilitarianism leads to numerous unacceptable conclusions. For example, it would allow the majority of a society to enslave a small minority. Moreover, many argue that consequence-based approaches to ethical theories, which inherently emphasize consequences, tend to view a human as merely a means to an end rather than as a worthwhile individual. This, they continue, constitutes a fundamental flaw in all consequence-based ethical theories.

In contrast to consequence-based ethics, duty-based ethics does not consider the consequences of decisions and actions but instead proposes that members of a society have certain intrinsic duties or obligations that in turn form the foundation on which ethical questions should be resolved. For example, if one accepts the obligation to respect the rights of others, then one must reject slavery regardless of its consequences. On the other hand, opponents of duty-based ethics argue that it fails to provide solutions to problems involving conflicting duties. Should you tell the truth even if doing so destroys a colleague's confidence? Should a nation defend itself in war even though the ensuing battles will lead to the death of many of its citizens?

Contract-based ethical theory begins by imagining society with no ethical foundation at all. In this "state of nature" setting, anything goes—a situation in which individuals must fend for themselves and constantly be on guard against aggression from others. Under these circumstances, contract-based ethical theory proposes that the members of the society would develop "contracts" among themselves. For example, I won't steal from you if you won't steal from me. In turn, these "contracts" would become the foundation for determining ethical behavior. Note that contract-based ethical theory provides a motivation for ethical behavior—we should obey the "contracts of ethics" because we would otherwise live an unpleasant life. However, opponents of contract-based ethical theory argue that it does not provide a broad enough basis for resolving ethical dilemmas since it provides guidance only in those cases in which contracts have been established. (I can behave anyway I want in situations not covered by an existing contract.) In particular, new technologies may present uncharted territory in which existing ethical contracts may not apply.

Character-based ethics (sometimes called virtue ethics), which was promoted by Plato and Aristotle, argues that "good behavior" is not the result of applying identifiable rules but instead is a natural consequence of "good character." Whereas consequence-based ethics, duty-based ethics, and contract-based ethics propose that a person resolve an ethical dilemma by asking, "What are the consequences?," "What are my duties?," or "What contracts do I have?," character-based ethics proposes that dilemmas be resolved by asking "Who do I want to be?" Thus, good behavior is obtained by building good character, which is typically the result of sound upbringing and the development of virtuous habits.

It is character-based ethics that underlies the approach normally taken when "teaching" ethics to professionals in various fields. Rather than presenting specific ethical theories, the approach is to introduce case studies that expose a variety of ethical questions in the professionals' area of expertise. Then, by discussing the pros and cons in these cases, the professionals become more aware, insightful, and sensitive to the perils lurking in their professional lives and thus grow in character. This is the spirit in which the questions regarding social issues at the end of each chapter are presented.

Social Issues

The following questions are intended as a guide to the ethical/social/legal issues associated with the field of computing. The goal is not merely to answer these questions. You should also consider why you answered as you did and whether your justifications are consistent from one question to the next.

1. The premise that our society is *different* from what it would have been without the computer revolution is generally accepted. Is our society *better* than it would have been without the revolution? Is our society worse? Would your answer differ if your position within society were different?

2. Is it acceptable to participate in today's technical society without making an effort to understand the basics of that technology? For instance, do members of a democracy, whose votes often determine how technology will be supported and used, have an obligation to try to understand that technology? Does your answer depend on which technology is being considered? For example, is your answer the same when considering nuclear technology as when considering computer technology?

3. By using cash in financial transactions, individuals have traditionally had the option to manage their financial affairs without service charges. However, as more of our economy is becoming automated, financial institutions are implementing service charges for access to these automated systems. Is there a point at which these charges unfairly restrict an individual's access to the economy? For example, suppose an employer pays employees only by check, and all financial institutions were to place a service charge on check cashing and depositing. Would the employees be unfairly treated? What if an employer insists on paying only via direct deposit?

4. In the context of interactive television, to what extent should a company be allowed to retrieve information from children (perhaps via an interactive game format)? For example, should a company be allowed to obtain a child's report on his or her parents' buying patterns? What about information about the child?

5. To what extent should a government regulate computer technology and its applications? Consider, for example, the issues mentioned in Questions 3 and 4. What justifies governmental regulation?

6. To what extent will our decisions regarding technology in general, and computer technology in particular, affect future generations?

7. As technology advances, our educational system is constantly challenged to reconsider the level of abstraction at which topics are presented. Many questions take the form of whether a skill is still necessary or whether students should be allowed to rely on an abstract tool. Students of trigonometry are no longer taught how to find the values of trigonometric functions using tables. Instead, they use calculators as abstract tools to find these values. Some argue that long division should also give way to abstraction. What other subjects are involved with similar controversies? Do modern word processors eliminate the need to develop spelling skills? Will the use of video technology someday remove the need to read?

8. The concept of public libraries is largely based on the premise that all citizens in a democracy must have access to information. As more information is stored and disseminated via computer technology, does access to this technology become a right of every individual? If so, should public libraries be the channel by which this access is provided?

9. What ethical concerns arise in a society that relies on the use of abstract tools? Are there cases in which it is unethical to use a product or service without understanding how it works? Without knowing how it is produced? Or, without understanding the byproducts of its use?

10. As our society becomes more automated, it becomes easier for governments to monitor their citizens' activities. Is that good or bad?

11. Which technologies that were imagined by George Orwell (Eric Blair) in his novel *1984* have become reality? Are they being used in the manner in which Orwell predicted?

12. If you had a time machine, in which period of history would you like to live? Are there current technologies that you would like to take with you? Could your choice of technologies be taken with you without taking others? To what extent can one technology be separated from another? Is it consistent to protest against global warming yet accept modern medical treatment?

13. Suppose your job requires that you reside in another culture. Should you continue to practice the ethics of your native culture or adopt the ethics of your host culture? Does your answer depend on whether the issue involves dress code or human rights? Which ethical standards should prevail if you continue to reside in your native culture but conduct business with a foreign culture?

14. On the basis of your initial answers to the preceding questions, to which ethical theory presented in Section 6 do you tend to subscribe?

Additional Reading

Goldstine, J. J. *The Computer from Pascal to von Neumann*. Princeton: Princeton University Press, 1972.

Kizza, J. M. *Ethical and Social Issues in the Information Age*. New York: Springer-Verlag, 1998.

Mollenhoff, C. R. *Atanasoff: Forgotten Father of the Computer*. Ames: Iowa State University Press, 1988.

Neumann, P. G. *Computer Related Risks*. Boston, MA: Addison-Wesley, 1995.

Quinn, M. J. *Ethics for the Information Age*, 2nd ed. Boston, MA: Addison-Wesley, 2006.

Randell, B. *The Origins of Digital Computers*. New York: Springer-Verlag, 1973.

Spinello, R. A. and H. T. Tavani. *Readings in CyberEthics*. Sudbury, MA: Jones and Bartlett, 2001.

Swade, D. *The Difference Engine*. New York: Viking, 2000.

Tavani, H. T. *Ethics and Technology: Ethical Issues in an Age of Information and Communication Technology*. New York: Wiley, 2004.

Woolley, B. *The Bride of Science, Romance, Reason, and Byron's Daughter*. New York: McGraw-Hill, 1999.

2

Operating Systems

In this chapter we study operating systems, which are software packages that coordinate a computer's internal activities as well as oversee its communication with the outside world. It is a computer's operating system that transforms the computer hardware into a useful tool. Our goal is to understand what operating systems do and how they do it. Such a background is central to being an enlightened computer user.

An **operating system** is the software that controls the overall operation of a computer. It provides the means by which a user can store and retrieve files, provides the interface by which a user can request the execution of programs, and provides the environment necessary to execute the programs requested.

Perhaps the best known example of an operating system is Windows, which is provided in numerous versions by Microsoft and widely used in the PC arena. Another well-established example is UNIX, which is a popular choice for larger computer systems as well as PCs. In fact, UNIX is the core of two other popular operating systems: Mac OS, which is the operating system provided by Apple for its range of Mac machines, and Solaris, which is a product of Sun Microsystems. Still another example of an operating system found on both large and small machines is Linux, which was originally developed noncommercially by computer enthusiasts and is now available through many commercial sources, including IBM.

1 The History of Operating Systems

Today's operating systems are large, complex software packages that have grown from humble beginnings. The computers of the 1940s and 1950s were not very flexible or efficient. Machines occupied entire rooms. Program execution required significant preparation of equipment in terms of mounting magnetic tapes, placing punched cards in card readers, setting switches, and so on. The execution of each program, called a **job,** was handled as an isolated activity—the machine was prepared for executing the program, the program was executed, and then all the tapes, punched cards, etc. had to be retrieved before the next program preparation could begin. When several users needed to share a machine, sign-up sheets were provided so that users could reserve the machine for blocks of time. During the time period allocated to a user, the machine was totally under that user's control. The session usually began with program setup, followed by short periods of program execution. It was often completed in a hurried effort to do just one more thing ("It will only take a minute") while the next user was impatiently starting to set up.

In such an environment, operating systems began as systems for simplifying program setup and for streamlining the transition between jobs. One early development was the separation of users and equipment, which eliminated the physical transition of people in and out of the computer room. For this purpose a computer operator was hired to operate the machine. Anyone wanting a program run was required to submit it, along with any required data and special directions about the program's requirements, to the operator and return later for the results. The operator, in turn, loaded these materials into the machine's mass storage where a program called the operating system could read and execute them one at a time. This was the beginning of **batch processing**—the execution of jobs by collecting them in a single batch, then executing them without further interaction with the user.

In batch processing systems, the jobs residing in mass storage wait for execution in a **job queue** (Figure 1). A **queue** is a storage organization in which objects (in this case, jobs) are ordered in **first-in, first-out** (abbreviated FIFO and pronounced "FI-foe") fashion. That is, the objects are removed from the queue in the order in which they arrived. In reality, most job queues do not rigorously follow the FIFO structure, since most operating systems provide for consideration of job priorities. As a result, a job waiting in the job queue can be bumped by a higher-priority job.

In early batch processing systems, each job was accompanied by a set of instructions explaining the steps required to prepare the machine for that particular job. These instructions were encoded, using a system known as a job control language (JCL), and stored with the job in the job queue. When the job was selected for execution, the operating system printed these instructions at a printer where they could be read and followed by the computer operator. This communication between the operating system and the computer operator is still seen today, as witnessed by PC operating systems that report such errors as "disk drive not accessible" and "printer not responding."

A major drawback to using a computer operator as an intermediary between a computer and its users is that the users have no interaction with their jobs once they are submitted to the operator. This approach is acceptable for some applications, such as payroll processing, in which the data and all processing decisions are established in advance. However, it is not acceptable when the user must interact with a program during its execution. Examples include reservation systems in which reservations and cancellations must be reported as they occur; word processing systems in which documents are developed in a dynamic write and rewrite manner; and computer games in which interaction with the machine is the central feature of the game.

To accommodate these needs, new operating systems were developed that allowed a program being executed to carry on a dialogue with the user through

Figure 1 Batch processing

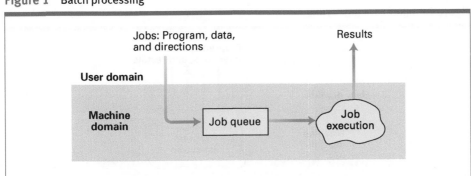

remote terminals—a feature known as **interactive processing** (Figure 2). (A terminal consisted of little more than an electronic typewriter by which the user could type input and read the computer's response that was printed on paper. Today terminals have evolved into more sophisticated devices called workstations and even into complete PCs that can function as standalone computers when desired.)

Paramount to successful interactive processing is that the actions of the computer be sufficiently fast to coordinate with the needs of the user rather than forcing the user to conform to the machine's timetable. (The task of processing payroll can be scheduled to conform to the amount of time required by the computer, but using a word processor would be frustrating if the machine did not respond promptly as characters are typed.) In a sense, the computer is forced to execute tasks under a deadline, a process that became known as **real-time processing** in which the actions performed are said to occur in real-time. That is, to say that a computer performs a task in real time means that the computer performs the task in accordance with deadlines in, its (external real-world) environment.

If interactive systems had been required to serve only one user at a time, real-time processing would have been no problem. But computers in the 1960s and 1970s were expensive, so each machine had to serve more than one user. In turn, it was common for several users, working at remote terminals, to seek interactive service from a machine at the same time, and real-time considerations presented obstacles. If the operating system insisted on executing only one job at a time, only one user would receive satisfactory real-time service.

The solution to this problem was to design operating systems that provided service to multiple users at the same time: a feature called **time-sharing.** One means of implementing time-sharing is to apply the technique called **multiprogramming** in which time is divided into intervals and then the execution of each job is restricted to only one interval at a time. At the end of each interval, the current job is temporarily set aside and another is allowed to execute during the next interval. By rapidly shuffling the jobs back and forth in this manner, the illusion of several jobs executing simultaneously is created. Depending on the types of jobs being executed, early time-sharing systems were able to provide acceptable real-time processing to as many as 30 users simultaneously. Today, multiprogramming

Figure 2 Interoctive processing

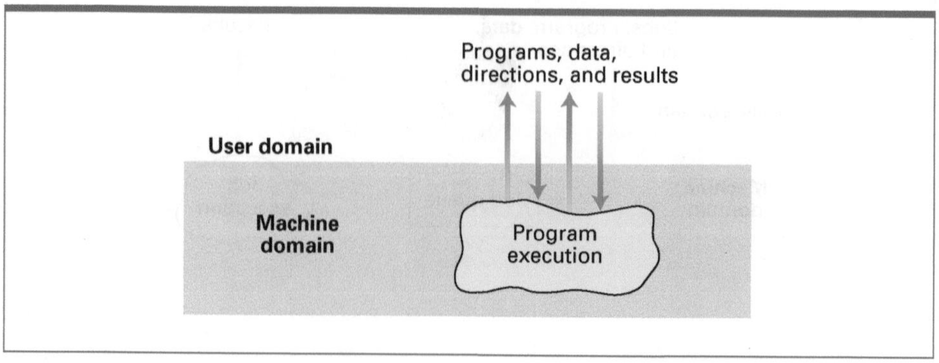

techniques are used in single-user as well as multiuser systems, although in the former the result is usually called **multitasking.** That is, time-sharing refers to multiple users sharing access to a common computer, whereas multitasking refers to one user executing numerous tasks simultaneously.

With the development of multiuser, time-sharing operating systems, a typical computer installation was configured as a large central computer connected to numerous workstations. From these workstations, users could communicate directly with the computer from outside the computer room rather than submitting requests to a computer operator. Commonly used programs were stored in the machine's mass storage devices and operating systems were designed to execute these programs as requested from the workstations. In turn, the role of a computer operator as an intermediary between the users and the computer begin to fade.

Today, the existence of a computer operator has essentially disappeared, especially in the arena of personal computers where the computer user assumes all of the responsibilities of computer operation. Even most large computer installations run essentially unattended. Indeed, the job of computer operator has given way to that of a system administrator who manages the computer system—obtaining and overseeing the installation of new equipment and software, enforcing local regulations such as the issuing of new accounts and establishing mass storage space limits for the various users, and coordinating efforts to resolve problems that arise in the system—rather than operating the machines in a hands-on manner.

In short, operating systems have grown from simple programs that retrieved and executed programs one at a time into complex systems that coordinate time-sharing, maintain programs and data files in the machine's mass storage devices, and respond directly to requests from the computer's users.

But the evolution of operating systems continues. The development of multiprocessor machines has led to operating systems that provide time-sharing/multitasking capabilities by assigning different tasks to different processors as well as by sharing the time of each single processor. These operating systems must wrestle with such problems as **load balancing** (dynamically allocating tasks to the various processors so that all processors are used efficiently) as well as **scaling** (breaking tasks into a number of subtasks compatible with the number of processors available).

Moreover, the advent of computer networks in which numerous machines are connected over great distances has led to the necessity for software systems to coordinate the network's activities. Thus the field of networking is in many ways an extension of the subject of operating systems—the goal being to develop a single network-wide operating system rather than a network of individual operating systems.

Still another direction of research in operating systems is the development of systems for small hand-held computers such as PDAs. Here the challenges of limited data storage capabilities and power conservation requirements have forced developers to re-examine the manner in which operating systems carry out their assignments. Successes in this endeavor are marked by systems such as VxWORKS, developed by Wind River Systems and used in the Mars Exploration Rovers named Spirit and Opportunity; Windows CE (also known as Pocket PC) developed by Microsoft; and Palm OS developed by PalmSource, Inc. especially for use in PDAs.

Questions & Exercises

1. Identify examples of queues. In each case, indicate any situations that violate the FIFO structure.
2. Which of the following activities require real-time processing?

    a. Printing mailing labels
    b. Playing a computer game
    c. Displaying letters on a monitor screen as they are typed at the keyboard
    d. Executing a program that predicts the state of next year's economy
    e. Playing an MP3 recording

3. What is the difference between real-time processing and interactive processing?
4. What is the difference between time-sharing and multitasking?

2 Operating System Architecture

To understand the composition of a typical operating system, we first consider the complete spectrum of software found within a typical computer system. Then we will concentrate on the operating system itself.

A Software Survey

We approach our survey of the software found on a typical computer system by presenting a scheme for classifying software. Such classification schemes invariably place similar software units in different classes in the same manner as the assignment of time zones dictates that nearby communities must set their clocks an hour apart even though there is no significant difference between the occurrence of sunrise and sunset. Moreover, in the case of software classification, the dynamics of the subject and the lack of a definitive authority lead to contradictory terminology. For example, users of Microsoft's Windows operating systems will find groups of programs called "Accessories" and "Administrative Tools" that include software from what we will call the application and utility classes. The following taxonomy should therefore be viewed as a means of gaining a foothold in an extensive, dynamic subject rather than as a statement of universally accepted fact.

Let us begin by dividing a machine's software into two broad categories: **application software** and **system software** (Figure 3). Application software consists of the programs for performing tasks particular to the machine's utilization. A machine used to maintain the inventory for a manufacturing company will contain different application software from that found on a machine used by an electrical engineer. Examples of application software include spreadsheets,

Figure 3 Software classification

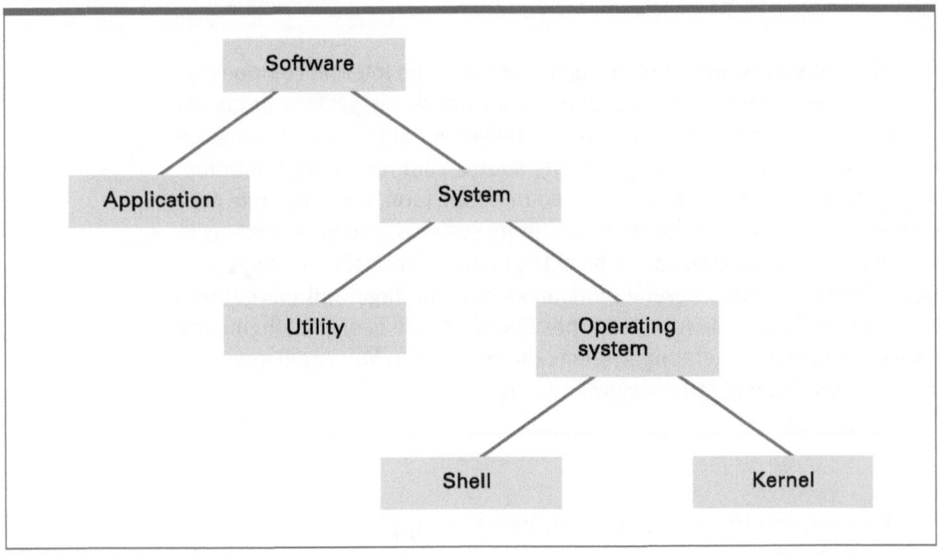

database systems, desktop publishing systems, accounting systems, program development software, and games.

In contrast to application software, system software performs those tasks that are common to computer systems in general. In a sense, the system software provides the infrastructure that the application software requires, in much the same manner as a nation's infrastructure (government, roads, utilities, financial institutions, etc.) provides the foundation on which its citizens rely for their individual lifestyles.

Within the class of system software are two categories: one is the operating system itself and the other consists of software units collectively known as **utility software.** The majority of an installation's utility software consists of programs for performing activities that are fundamental to computer installations but not included in the operating system. In a sense, utility software consists of software units that extend (or perhaps customize) the capabilities of the operating system. For example, the ability to format a magnetic disk or to copy a file from a magnetic disk to a CD is often not implemented within the operating system itself but instead is provided by means of a utility program. Other instances of utility software include software to compress and decompress data, software for playing multimedia presentations, and software for handling network communication.

Implementing certain activities as utility software, allows system software to be customized to the needs of a particular installation more easily than if they were included in the operating system. Indeed, it is common to find companies or individuals who have modified, or added to, the utility software that was originally provided with their machine's operating system.

Linux

For the computer enthusiast who wants to experiment with the internal components of an operating system, there is Linux. Linux is an operating system originally designed by Linus Torvalds while a student at the University of Helsinki. It is a non-proprietary product and available, along with its source code and documentation, without charge. Because it is freely available in source code form, it has become popular among computer hobbyists, students of operating systems, and programmers in general. Moreover, Linux is recognized as one of the more reliable operating systems available today. For this reason, several companies now package and market versions of Linux in an easily useable form, and these products are now challenging the long-established commercial operating systems on the market. You can learn more about Linux from the website at http://www.linux.org.

Unfortunately, the distinction between application software and utility software can be vague. From our point of view, the difference is whether the package is part of the computer's "software infrastructure." Thus a new application may evolve to the status of a utility if it becomes a fundamental tool. When still a research project, software for communicating over the Internet was considered application software; today such tools are fundamental to most PC usage and would therefore be classified as utility software.

The distinction between utility software and the operating system is equally vague. In particular, anti-trust lawsuits in the United States and Europe have been founded on questions regarding whether units such as browsers and media players are components of Microsoft's operating systems or utilities that Microsoft has included merely to squash competition.

Components of an Operating System

Let us focus now on components that are within the domain of an operating system. In order to perform the actions requested by the computer's users, an operating system must be able to communicate with those users. The portion of an operating system that handles this communication is often called the **shell.** Older shells communicate with users through textual messages using a keyboard and monitor screen. More modern shells perform this task by means of a **graphical user interface** (**GUI**—pronounced "GOO–ee") in which objects to be manipulated, such as files and programs, are represented pictorially on the monitor screen as icons. These systems allow users to issue commands by pointing to these icons using a hand-held device called a mouse and pressing a button on the mouse (a process called clicking). These GUIs are often called **WIMP** (Windows, Icons, Menus, and Pointers) interfaces in reference to the components on which they are based. Whereas today's GUIs use two-dimensional image projection systems, three-dimensional interfaces that allow human users to communicate with computers by means of 3D projection systems, tactile sensory devices, and surround sound audio reproduction systems are subjects of current research.

Although an operating system's shell plays an important role in establishing a machine's functionality, this shell is merely an interface between a user and the real heart of the operating system (Figure 4). This distinction between the shell and the internal parts of the operating system is emphasized by the fact that some operating systems allow a user to select among different shells to obtain the most compatible interface for that particular user. Users of the UNIX operating system, for example, can select among a variety of shells including the Bourne shell, the C shell, and the Korn shell. Moreover, early versions of Microsoft Windows were constructed by essentially replacing the text-based shell that was currently used with the operating system called MS-DOS with a GUI shell—the underlying operating system remained MS-DOS.

An important component within today's GUI shells is the **window manager,** which allocates blocks of space on the screen, called windows, and keeps track of which application is associated with each window. When an application wants to display something on the screen, it notifies the window manager, and the window manager places the desired image in the window assigned to the application. In turn, when a mouse button is clicked, it is the window manager that computes the mouse's location on the screen and notifies the appropriate application of the mouse action.

In contrast to an operating system's shell, the internal part of an operating system is called the **kernel.** An operating system's kernel contains those software components that perform the very basic functions required by the computer installation. One such unit is the **file manager,** whose job is to coordinate the

Figure 4   The shell as the interface between users and the operating system's kernel

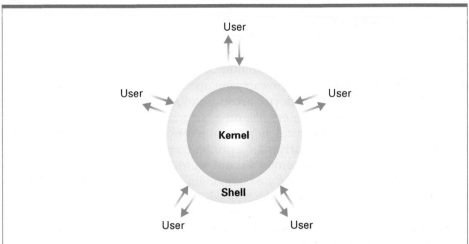

use of the machine's mass storage facilities. More precisely, the file manager maintains records of all the files stored in mass storage, including where each file is located, which users are allowed to access the various files, and which portions of mass storage are available for new files or extensions to existing files. These records are kept on the individual storage medium containing the related files so that each time the medium is placed on-line, the file manager can retrieve them and thus know what is stored on that particular medium.

For the convenience of the machine's users, most file managers allow files to be grouped into a bundle called a **directory** or **folder.** This approach allows a user to organize his or her files according to their purposes by placing related files in the same directory. Moreover, by allowing directories to contain other directories, called subdirectories, a hierarchical organization can be constructed. For example, a user may create a directory called `MyRecords` that contains subdirectories called `FinancialRecords`, `MedicalRecords`, and `HouseHold-Records`. Within each of these subdirectories could be files that fall within that particular category. (Users of a Windows operating system can ask the file manager to display the current collection of folders by executing the utility program Windows Explorer.)

A chain of directories within directories is called a **directory path.** Paths are often expressed by listing the directories along the path separated by slashes. For instance, `animals/prehistoric/dinosaurs` would represent the path starting at the directory named `animals`, passing through its subdirectory named `prehistoric`, and terminating in the sub-subdirectory `dinosaurs`. (For Windows users the slashes in such a path expression are reversed as in `animals\prehistoric\dinosaurs`.)

Any access to a file by other software units is obtained at the discretion of the file manager. The procedure begins by requesting that the file manager grant access to the file through a procedure known as opening the file. If the file manager approves the requested access, it provides the information needed to find and to manipulate the file. This information is stored in an area of main memory called a **file descriptor.** It is by referencing the information in this file descriptor that individual operations are performed on the file.

Another component of the kernel consists of a collection of **device drivers,** which are the software units that communicate with the controllers (or at times, directly with peripheral devices) to carry out operations on the peripheral devices attached to the machine. Each device driver is uniquely designed for its particular type of device (such as a printer, disk drive, or monitor) and translates generic requests into the more technical steps required by the device assigned to that driver. For example, a device driver for a printer contains the software for reading and decoding that particular printer's status word as well as all the other hand-shaking details. Thus, other software components do not have to deal with those technicalities in order to print a file. Instead, the other components can merely rely on the device driver software to print the file, and let the device driver take care of the details. In this manner, the design of the other software units can be independent of the unique characteristics of particular devices. The result is a generic operating system that can be customized for particular peripheral devices by merely installing the appropriate device drivers.

Still another component of an operating system's kernel is the **memory manager,** which is charged with the task of coordinating the machine's use of main memory. Such duties are minimal in an environment in which a computer is asked to perform only one task at a time. In these cases, the program for performing the current task is placed at a predetermined location in main memory, executed, and then replaced by the program for performing the next task. However, in multiuser or multitasking environments in which the computer is asked to address many needs at the same time, the duties of the memory manager are extensive. In these cases, many programs and blocks of data must reside in main memory concurrently. Thus, the memory manager must find and assign memory space for these needs and ensure that the actions of each program are restricted to the program's allotted space. Moreover, as the needs of different activities come and go, the memory manager must keep track of those memory areas no longer occupied.

The task of the memory manager is complicated further when the total main memory space required exceeds the space actually available in the computer. In this case the memory manager may create the illusion of additional memory space by rotating programs and data back and forth between main memory and mass storage (a technique called **paging**). Suppose, for example, that a main memory of 1024MB is required but the computer only has 512MB. To create the illusion of the larger memory space, the memory manager reserves 1024MB of storage space on a magnetic disk. There it records the bit patterns that would be stored in main memory if main memory had an actual capacity of 1024MB. This data is divided into uniform sized units called **pages,** which are typically a few KB in size. Then the memory manager shuffles these pages back and forth between main memory and mass storage so that the pages that are needed at any given time are actually present in the 512MB of main memory. The result is that the computer is able to function as though it actually had 1024MB of main memory. This large "fictional" memory space created by paging is called **virtual memory.**

Two additional components within the kernel of an operating system are the **scheduler** and **dispatcher,** which we will study in the next section. For now we merely note that in a multiprogramming system the scheduler determines which activities are to be considered for execution, and the dispatcher controls the allocation of time to these activities.

Getting It Started

We have seen that an operating system provides the software infrastructure required by other software units, but we have not considered how the operating system gets started. This is accomplished through a procedure known as **boot strapping** (often shortened to **booting**) that is performed by a computer each time it is turned on. It is this procedure that transfers the operating system from mass storage (where it is permanently stored) into main memory (which is essentially empty when the machine is first turned on). To understand the boot strap process and the reason it is necessary, we begin by considering the machine's CPU.

A CPU is designed so that its program counter starts with a particular predetermined address each time the CPU is turned on. It is at this location that the CPU expects to find the beginning of the program to be executed. Conceptually, then, all that is needed is to store the operating system at this location. However, for technical reasons, a computer's main memory is typically constructed from volatile technologies—meaning that the memory loses the data stored in it when the computer is turned off. Thus, the contents of main memory must be replenished each time the computer is restarted.

In short, we need a program (preferably the operating system) to be present in main memory when the computer is first turned on, but the computer's volatile memory is erased each time the machine is turned off. To resolve this dilemma, a small portion of a computer's main memory where the CPU expects to find its initial program is constructed from special nonvolatile memory cells. Such memory is known as **read-only memory (ROM)** because its contents can be read but not altered. As an analogy, you can think of storing bit patterns in ROM as blowing tiny fuses, although the technology used is more advanced. More precisely, most ROM in today's PCs is constructed with flash memory technology (which means that it is not strictly ROM because it can be altered under special circumstances).

In a general-purpose computer, a program called the **bootstrap** is permanently stored in the machine's ROM. (A program stored in ROM is called **firmware,** reflecting the fact that it consists of software permanently recorded in hardware.) This, then, is the program that is initially executed when the machine is turned on. The instructions in the bootstrap direct the CPU to transfer the operating system from a predetermined location in mass storage into the volatile area of main memory (Figure 5). Once the operating system has been placed in main memory, the bootstrap directs the CPU to execute a jump instruction to that area of memory. At this point, the operating system takes over and begins controlling the machine's activities. The overall process of executing the bootstrap and thus starting the operating system is called **booting** the computer.

You may ask why computers are not provided with enough ROM to hold the entire operating system so that booting from mass storage would not be necessary. The answer is that devoting large blocks of main memory in general-purpose computers to nonvolatile storage is not efficient with today's technology. On the other hand, most special-purpose computers, such as those in household appliances, have all of their software permanently stored in their main memories where it is readily available each time the device is turned on. Such systems are known as **turnkey** systems because they are ready to function with the flip of a switch or the turn of a key. With the rapid advances that are being made in memory technology, it may soon be that many of the steps in the booting

Figure 5 The booting process

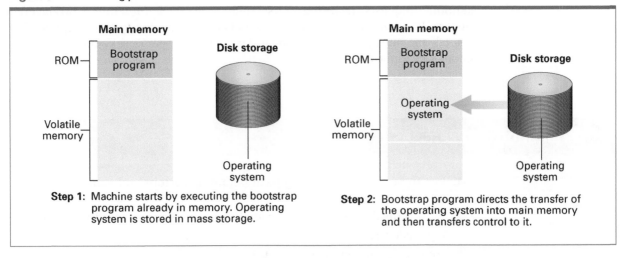

Step 1: Machine starts by executing the bootstrap program already in memory. Operating system is stored in mass storage.

Step 2: Bootstrap program directs the transfer of the operating system into main memory and then transfers control to it.

process will become obsolete, and that general-purpose computers will approach turnkey status.

In closing we should point out that understanding the bootstrap process as well as the distinctions between an operating system, utility software, and application software allows us to comprehend the overall methodology under which most general-purpose computer systems operate. When such a machine is first turned on, the bootstrap process loads and activates the operating system. The user then makes requests to the operating system regarding the utility or application programs to be executed. As each utility or application is terminated, the user is

BIOS

In addition to the bootstrap, the ROM in a PC contains a collection of software routines for performing fundamental input/output activities such as receiving information from the keyboard, displaying messages on the computer screen, and reading data from mass storage. Being stored in ROM, these routines can be used by the bootstrap to perform I/O activities before the operating system becomes functional. For example, they are used to communicate with the computer user before the boot process actually begins and to report errors during bootstrapping. Collectively these routines form a basic input/output system (BIOS, pronounced "BYE–os"). Thus the term *BIOS* actually refers only to a portion of the software in a computer's ROM, although the term is widely used today in reference to the entire collection of software stored in ROM and sometimes to the ROM itself.

put back in touch with the operating system, at which time the user can make additional requests. Learning to use such a system is therefore a two-layered process. In addition to learning the details of the specific utility or application desired, one must learn enough about the machine's operating system to navigate among the applications.

Questions & Exercises

1. List the components of a typical operating system and summarize the role of each in a single phrase.
2. What is the difference between application software and utility software?
3. What is virtual memory?
4. Summarize the booting procedure.

3 Coordinating the Machine's Activities

In this section we consider how an operating system coordinates the execution of application software, utility software, and units within the operating system itself. We begin with the concept of a process.

The Concept of a Process

One of the most fundamental concepts of modern operating systems is the distinction between a program and the activity of executing a program. The former is a static set of directions, whereas the latter is a dynamic activity whose properties change as time progresses. This activity is known as a **process.** Associated with a process is the current status of the activity, called the **process state.** This state includes the current position in the program being executed (the value of the program counter) as well as the values in the other CPU registers and the associated memory cells. Roughly speaking, the process state is a snapshot of the machine at a particular time. At different times during the execution of a program (at different times in a process) different snapshots (different process states) will be observed.

In a typical time-sharing/multitasking environment many processes are normally competing for the computer's resources. It is the task of the operating system to manage these processes so that each process has the resources (peripheral devices, space in main memory, access to files, and access to a CPU) that it needs, that independent processes do not interfere with one another, and that processes that need to exchange information are able to do so.

Process Administration

The tasks associated with coordinating the execution of processes are handled by the scheduler and dispatcher within the operating system's kernel. The scheduler maintains a record of the processes present in the computer system, introduces new processes to this pool, and removes completed processes from the pool. Thus when a user requests the execution of an application, it is the scheduler that adds the execution of that application to the pool of current processes.

To keep track of all the processes, the scheduler maintains a block of information in main memory called the **process table.** Each time the execution of a program is requested, the scheduler creates a new entry for that process in the process table. This entry contains such information as the memory area assigned to the process (obtained from the memory manager), the priority of the process, and whether the process is ready or waiting. A process is **ready** if it is in a state in which its progress can continue; it is **waiting** if its progress is currently delayed until some external event occurs, such as the completion of a mass storage operation, the pressing of a key at the keyboard, or the arrival of a message from another process.

The dispatcher is the component of the kernel that overseas the execution of the scheduled processes. In a time-sharing/multitasking system this task is accomplished by **multiprogramming;** that is, dividing time into short segments, each called a **time slice** (typically no more than 50 milliseconds), and then switching the CPU's attention among the processes as each is allowed to

Figure 6   Multiprogramming between process A and process B

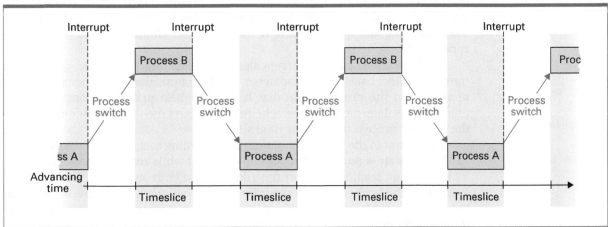

Interrupts

The use of interrupts for terminating time slices, as described in the text, is only one of many applications of a computer's interrupt system. There are many situations in which an interrupt signal is generated, each with its own interrupt routine. Indeed, interrupts provide an important tool for coordinating a computer's actions with its environment. For example, both clicking a mouse and pressing a key on the keyboard generate interrupt signals that cause the CPU to set aside its current activity and address the cause of the interrupt.

To manage the task of recognizing and responding to incoming interrupts, the various interrupt signals are assigned priorities so that the more important tasks can be taken care of first. The highest priority interrupt is usually associated with a power failure. Such an interrupt signal is generated if the computer's power is unexpectedly disrupted. The associated interrupt routine directs the CPU through a series of "housekeeping" chores during the milliseconds before the voltage level drops below an operational level.

execute for one time slice (Figure 6). The procedure of changing from one process to another is called a **process switch** (or a **context switch**).

Each time the dispatcher awards a time slice to a process, it initiates a timer circuit that will indicate the end of the slice by generating a signal called an **interrupt.** The CPU reacts to this interrupt signal in much the same way that you react when interrupted from a task. You stop what you are doing, record where you are in the task (so that you will be able to return at a later time), and take care of the interrupting entity. When the CPU receives an interrupt signal, it completes its current machine cycle, saves its position in the current process and begins executing a program, called an **interrupt handler,** which is stored at a predetermined location in main memory. This interrupt handler is a part of the dispatcher, and it describes how the dispatcher should respond to the interrupt signal.

Thus, the effect of the interrupt signal is to preempt the current process and transfer control back to the dispatcher. At this point, the dispatcher selects the process from the process table that has the highest priority among the ready processes (as determined by the scheduler), restarts the timer circuit, and allows the selected process to begin its time slice.

Paramount to the success of a multiprogramming system is the ability to stop, and later restart, a process. If you are interrupted while reading a book, your ability to continue reading at a later time depends on your ability to remember your location in the book as well as the information that you had accumulated to that point. In short, you must be able to re-create the environment that was present immediately prior to the interruption.

In the case of a process, the environment that must be re-created is the process's state, which as already mentioned, includes the value of the program counter as well as the contents of the registers and pertinent memory cells. CPUs designed for multiprogramming systems incorporate the task of saving this information as part of the CPU's reaction to the interrupt signal. These CPUs also tend to have machine-language instructions for reloading a previously saved state. Such features simplify the task of the dispatcher when performing a process switch and exemplify how the design of modern CPUs is influenced by the needs of today's operating systems.

In closing, we should note that the use of multiprogramming has been found to increase the overall efficiency of a machine. This is somewhat counterintuitive since the shuffling of processes required by multiprogramming introduces an overhead. However, without multiprogramming each process runs to completion before the next process begins, meaning that the time that a process is waiting for peripheral devices to complete tasks or for a user to make the next request is wasted. Multiprogramming allows this lost time to be given to another process. For example, if a process executes an I/O request, such as a request to retrieve data from a magnetic disk, the scheduler will update the process table to reflect that the process is waiting for an external event. In turn, the dispatcher will cease to award time slices to that process. Later (perhaps several hundred milliseconds), when the I/O request has been completed, the scheduler will update the process table to show that the process is ready, and thus that process will again compete for time slices. In short, progress on other tasks will be made while the I/O request is being performed, and thus the entire collection of tasks will be completed in less time than if executed in a sequential manner.

Questions & Exercises

1. Summarize the difference between a program and a process.
2. Summarize the steps performed by the CPU when an interrupt occurs.
3. In a multiprogramming system, how can high-priority processes be allowed to run faster than others?
4. If each time slice in a multiprogramming system is 50 milliseconds and each context switch requires at most a microsecond, how many processes can the machine service in a single second?
5. If each process uses its complete time slice in the machine in Question/Exercise 4, what fraction of the machine's time is spent actually performing processes? What would this fraction be if each process executed an I/O request after only a microsecond of its time slice?

4 Handling Competition Among Processes

An important task of an operating system is the allocation of the machine's resources to the processes in the system. Here we are using the term *resource* in a broad sense, including the machine's peripheral devices as well as features within the machine itself. The file manager allocates access to files as well and allocates mass storage space for the construction of new files; the memory manager allocates memory space; the scheduler allocates space in the process table; and the dispatcher allocates time slices. As with many problems in computer systems, this allocation task may appear simple at first glance. Below the surface, however, lie several subtleties that can lead to malfunctions in a poorly designed system. Remember, a machine does not think for itself; it merely follows directions. Thus, to construct reliable operating systems, we must develop algorithms that cover every possible contingency, regardless of how minuscule it may appear.

Semaphores

Let us consider a time-sharing/multitasking operating system controlling the activities of a computer with a single printer. If a process needs to print its results, it must request that the operating system give it access to the printer's device driver. At this point, the operating system must decide whether to grant this request, depending on whether the printer is already being used by another process. If it is not, the operating system should grant the request and allow the process to continue; otherwise, the operating system should deny the request and perhaps classify the process as a waiting process until the printer becomes available. After all, if two processes were given simultaneous access to the computer's printer, the results would be worthless to both.

To control access to the printer, the operating system must keep track of whether the printer has been allocated. One approach to this task would be to use a flag, which in this context refers to a bit in memory whose states are often referred to as *set* and *clear,* rather than 1 and 0. A clear flag (value 0) indicates that the printer is available and a set flag (value 1) indicates that the printer is currently allocated. On the surface, this approach seems well-founded. The operating system merely checks the flag each time a request for printer access is made. If it is clear, the request is granted and the operating system sets the flag. If the flag is set, the operating system makes the requesting process wait. Each time a process finishes with the printer, the operating system either allocates the printer to a waiting process or, if no process is waiting, merely clears the flag.

However, this simple flag system has a problem. The task of testing and possibly setting the flag may require several machine instructions. (The value of the flag must be retrieved from main memory, manipulated within the CPU, and finally stored back in memory.) It is therefore possible for a task to be interrupted after a clear flag has been detected but before the flag has been set.

In particular, suppose the printer is currently available, and a process requests use of it. The flag is retrieved from main memory and found to be clear, indicating that the printer is available. However, at this point, the process is interrupted and another process begins its time slice. It too requests the use of the printer. Again, the flag is retrieved from main memory and found still clear because the previous process was interrupted before the operating system had time to set the flag in main memory. Consequently, the operating system allows the second process to begin using the printer. Later, the original process resumes execution where it left off, which is immediately after the operating system found the flag to be clear. Thus the operating system continues by setting the flag in main memory and granting the original process access to the printer. Two processes are now using the same printer.

The solution to this problem is to insist that the task of testing and possibly setting the flag be completed without interruption. One approach is to use the interrupt disable and interrupt enable instructions provided in most machine languages. When executed, an interrupt disable instruction causes future interrupts to be blocked, whereas an interrupt enable instruction causes the CPU to resume responding to interrupt signals. Thus, if the operating system starts the flag-testing routine with a disable interrupt instruction and ends it with an enable interrupt instruction, no other activity can interrupt the routine once it starts.

Another approach is to use the **test-and-set** instruction that is available in many machine languages. This instruction directs the CPU to retrieve the value of a flag, note the value received, and then set the flag—all within a single machine instruction. The advantage here is that because the CPU always completes an instruction before recognizing an interrupt, the task of testing and setting the flag cannot be split when it is implemented as a single instruction.

A properly implemented flag, as just described, is called a **semaphore,** in reference to the railroad signals used to control access to sections of track. In fact, semaphores are used in software systems in much the same way as they are

Microsoft's Task Manager

You can gain insight to some of the internal activity of a Microsoft Windows operating system by executing the utility program called Task Manager. (Press the Ctrl, Alt, and Delete keys simultaneously.) In particular, by selecting the Processes tab in the Task Manager window, you can view the process table. Here is an experiment you can perform: Look at the process table before you activate any application program. (You may be surprised that so many processes are already in the table. These are necessary for the system's basic operation.) Now activate an application and confirm that an additional process has entered the table. You will also be able to see how much memory space was allocated to the process.

in railway systems. Corresponding to the section of track that can contain only one train at a time is a sequence of instructions that should be executed by only one process at a time. Such a sequence of instructions is called a **critical region.** The requirement that only one process at a time be allowed to execute a critical region is known as **mutual exclusion.** In summary, a common way of obtaining mutual exclusion to a critical region is to guard the critical region with a semaphore. To enter the critical region, a process must find the semaphore clear and then set the semaphore before entering the critical region; then upon exiting the critical region, the process must clear the semaphore. If the semaphore is found in its set state, the process trying to enter the critical region must wait until the semaphore has been cleared.

Deadlock

Another problem that can arise during resource allocation is **deadlock,** the condition in which two or more processes are blocked from progressing because each is waiting for a resource that is allocated to another. For example, one process may have access to the computer's printer but be waiting for access to the computer's CD player, while another process has access to the CD player but is waiting for the printer. Another example occurs in systems in which processes are allowed to create new processes (an action called **forking** in the UNIX vernacular) to perform subtasks. If the scheduler has no space left in the process table and each process in the system must create an additional process before it can complete its task, then no process can continue. Such conditions, as in other settings (Figure 7), can severely degrade a system's performance.

Figure 7   A deadlock resulting from competition for nonshareable railroad intersections

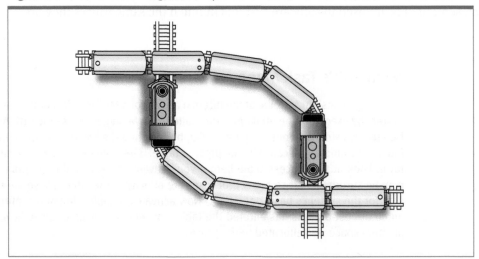

Analysis of deadlock has revealed that it cannot occur unless all three of the following conditions are satisfied:

1. There is competition for nonshareable resources.
2. The resources are requested on a partial basis; that is, having received some resources, a process will return later to request more.
3. Once a resource has been allocated, it cannot be forcibly retrieved.

The point of isolating these conditions is that the deadlock problem can be removed by attacking any one of the three. Techniques that attack the third condition fall into the category known as deadlock detection and correction schemes. In these cases, the occurrence of deadlock is considered so remote that no effort is made to avoid the problem. Instead, the approach is to detect it should it occur and then correct it by forcibly retrieving some of the allocated resources. Our example of a full process table might fall in this class. If deadlock should occur due to a full table, routines within the operating system (or perhaps a human administrator using his or her powers as "super user") can remove (the technical term is **kill**) some of the processes. This releases space in the process table, breaking the deadlock and allowing the remaining processes to continue their tasks.

Techniques that attack the first two conditions are known as deadlock avoidance schemes. One, for example, attacks the second condition by requiring each process to request all its resources at one time. Another scheme attacks the first condition, not by removing the competition directly but by converting nonshareable resources into shareable ones. For example, suppose the resource in question is a printer and a variety of processes require its use. Each time a process requests the printer, the operating system could grant the request. However, instead of connecting the process to the printer's device driver, the operating system would connect it to a device driver that stores the information to be printed in mass storage rather than sending it to the printer. Thus each process, thinking it has access to the printer, could execute in its normal way. Later, when the printer is available, the operating system could transfer the data from mass storage to the printer. In this manner, the operating system would make the nonshareable resource appear shareable by creating the illusion of more than one printer. This technique of holding data for output at a later but more convenient time is called **spooling.**

We have introduced spooling as a technique for granting several processes access to a common resource—a theme that has many variations. For example, a file manager could grant several processes access to the same file if the processes are merely reading data from the file, but conflicts can occur if more than one process tries to alter a file at the same time. Thus, a file manager may allocate file access according to the needs of the processes, allowing several processes to have read access but allowing only one to have write access. Other systems may divide the file into pieces so that different processes can alter different parts of the file concurrently. Each of these techniques, however, has subtleties that must be resolved to obtain a reliable system. How, for example, should those processes with only read access to a file be notified when a process with write access alters the file?

Questions & Exercises

1. Suppose process A and process B are sharing time on the same machine, and each needs the same nonshareable resource for short periods of time. (For example, each process may be printing a series of independent, short reports.) Each process may then repeatedly acquire the resource, release it, and later request it again. What is a drawback to controlling access to the resource in the following manner:

   Begin by assigning a flag the value 0. If process A requests the resource and the flag is 0, grant the request. Otherwise, make process A wait. If process B requests the resource and the flag is 1, grant the request. Otherwise, make process B wait. Each time process A finishes with the resource, change the flag to 1. Each time process B finishes with the resource, change the flag to 0.

2. Suppose a two-lane road converges to one lane to pass through a tunnel. To coordinate the use of the tunnel, the following signal system has been installed:

   A car entering either end of the tunnel causes red lights above the tunnel entrances to be turned on. As the car exits the tunnel, the lights are turned off. If an approaching car finds a red light on, it waits until the light is turned off before entering the tunnel.

   What is the flaw in this system?

3. Suppose the following solutions have been proposed for removing the deadlock that occurs on a single-lane bridge when two cars meet. Identify which condition for deadlock given in the text is removed by each solution.

   a. Do not let a car onto the bridge until the bridge is empty.
   b. If cars meet, make one of them back up.
   c. Add a second lane to the bridge.

4. Suppose we represent each process in a multiprogramming system with a dot and draw an arrow from one dot to another if the process represented by the first dot is waiting for a (nonshareable) resource being used by the second. Mathematicians call the resulting picture a **directed graph.** What property of the directed graph is equivalent to deadlock in the system?

5 Security

Since the operating system oversees the activities in a computer, it is natural for it to play a vital role in maintaining security as well. In the broad sense, this responsibility manifests itself in multiple forms, one of which is reliability. If a flaw in the file manager causes the loss of part of a file, then the file was not secure. If a defect in the dispatcher leads to a system failure (often called a system crash) causing the loss of an hour's worth of typing, we would argue that our work was not secure. Thus the security of a computer system requires a well-designed, dependable operating system.

The development of reliable software is not a subject that is restricted to operating systems. It permeates the entire software development spectrum and constitutes the field of computer science known as software engineering. In this section, then, we focus on security problems that are more closely related to the specifics of operating systems.

Attacks from the Outside

An important task performed by operating systems is to protect the computer's resources from access by unauthorized personnel. In the case of computers used by multiple people, this is usually approached by means of establishing "accounts" for the various authorized users—an account being essentially a record within the operating system containing such entries as the user's name, password, and privileges to be granted to that user. The operating system can then use this information during each **login** procedure (a sequence of transactions in which the user establishes initial contact with a computer's operating system) to control access to the system.

Accounts are established by a person known as the **super user** or the **administrator.** This person gains highly privileged access to the operating system by identifying himself or herself as the administrator (usually by name and password) during the login procedure. Once this contact is established, the administrator can alter settings within the operating system, modify critical software packages, adjust the privileges granted to other users, and perform a variety of other maintenance activities that are denied normal users.

From this "lofty perch," the administrator is also able to monitor activity within the computer system in an effort to detect destructive behavior, whether malicious or accidental. To assist in this regard, numerous software utilities, called **auditing software,** have been developed that record and then analyze the activities taking place within the computer system. In particular, auditing software may expose a flood of attempts to login using incorrect passwords, indicating that an unauthorized user may be trying to gain access to the computer. Auditing software may also identify activities within a user's account that do not conform to that user's past behavior, which may indicate that an unauthorized user has gained access to that account. (It is unlikely that a user who traditionally uses only word processing and spreadsheet software will suddenly begin to access highly technical software applications or try to execute utility packages that lie outside that user's privileges.)

Another culprit that auditing systems are designed to detect is the presence of **sniffing software,** which is software that, when left running on a computer, records activities and later reports them to a would-be intruder. An old, well-known example is a program that simulates the operating system's login procedure. Such a program can be used to trick authorized users into thinking they are communicating with the operating system, whereas they are actually supplying their names and passwords to an impostor.

With all the technical complexities associated with computer security, it is surprising to many that one of the major obstacles to the security of computer systems is the carelessness of the users themselves. They select passwords that are relatively easy to guess (such as names and dates), they share their passwords with friends, they fail to change their passwords on a timely basis, they subject off-line mass storage devices to potential degradation by transferring them back and forth between machines, and they import unapproved software into the system that might subvert the system's security. For problems like these, most institutions with large computer installations adopt and enforce policies that catalog the requirements and responsibilities of the users.

Attacks from Within

Once an intruder (or perhaps an authorized user with malicious intent) gains access to a computer system, the next step is usually to explore, looking for information of interest or for places to insert destructive software. This is a straightforward process if the prowler has gained access to the administrator's account, which is why the administrator's password is closely guarded. If, however, access is through a general user's account, it becomes necessary to trick the operating system into allowing the intruder to reach beyond the privileges granted to that user. For example, the intruder may try to trick the memory manager into allowing a process to access main memory cells outside its allotted area, or the prowler may try to trick the file manager into retrieving files whose access should be denied.

Today's CPUs are enhanced with features that are designed to foil such attempts. As an example, consider the need to restrict a process to the area of main memory assigned to it by the memory manager. Without such restrictions, a process could erase the operating system from main memory and take control of the computer itself. To counter such attempts, CPUs designed for multiprogramming systems typically contain special-purpose registers in which the operating system can store the upper and lower limits of a process's allotted memory area. Then, while performing the process, the CPU compares each memory reference to these registers to ensure that the reference is within the designated limits. If the reference is found to be outside the process's designated area, the CPU automatically transfers control back to the operating system (by performing an interrupt sequence) so that the operating system can take appropriate action.

Embedded in this illustration is a subtle but significant problem. Without further security features, a process could still gain access to memory cells outside of its designated area merely by changing the special-purpose registers that contain its memory limits. That is, a process that wanted access to additional memory could merely increase the value in the register containing the upper memory limit and then proceed to use the additional memory space without approval from the operating system.

To protect against such actions, CPUs for multiprogramming systems are designed to operate in one of two **privilege levels;** we will call one "privileged mode," the other we will call "nonprivileged mode." When in privileged mode, the CPU is able to execute all the instructions in its machine language. However, when in nonprivileged mode, the list of acceptable instructions is limited. The instructions that are available only in privileged mode are called **privileged instructions.** (Typical examples of privileged instructions include instructions that change the contents of memory limit registers and instructions that change the current privilege mode of the CPU.) An attempt to execute a privileged instruction when the CPU is in nonprivileged mode causes an interrupt. This interrupt converts the CPU to privileged mode and transfers control to an interrupt handler within the operating system.

When first turned on, the CPU is in privileged mode. Thus, when the operating system starts at the end of the boot process, all instructions are executable. However, each time the operating system allows a process to start a time slice, it switches the CPU to nonprivileged mode by executing a "change privilege mode" instruction. In turn, the operating system will be notified if the process attempts to execute a privileged instruction, and thus the operating system will be in position to maintain the integrity of the computer system.

Privileged instructions and the control of privilege levels is the major tool available to operating systems for maintaining security. However, the use of these tools is a complex component of an operating system's design, and errors continue to be found in current systems. A single flaw in privilege level control can open the door to disaster from malicious programmers or from inadvertent programming errors. If a process is allowed to alter the timer that controls the system's multiprogramming system, that process can extend its time slice and dominate the machine. If a process is allowed to access peripheral devices directly, then it can read files without supervision by the system's file manager. If a process is allowed to access memory cells outside its allotted area, it can read and even alter data being used by other processes. Thus, maintaining security continues to be an important task of an administrator as well as a goal in operating system design.

Questions & Exercises

1. Give some examples of poor choices for passwords and explain why they would be poor choices.
2. Processors in Intel's Pentium series provide for four privilege levels. Why would the designers of CPUs decide to provide four levels rather than three or five?
3. If a process in a multiprogramming system could access memory cells outside its allotted area, how could it gain control of the machine?

Chapter Review Problems

(Asterisked problems are associated with optional sections.)

1. List four activities of a typical operating system.

2. Summarize the distinction between batch processing and interactive processing.

3. Suppose three items R, S, and T are placed in a queue in that order. Then two items are removed from the queue before a fourth item, X, is placed in the queue. Then two items are removed from the queue, the items Y and Z are placed in the queue, and then the queue is emptied by removing one item at a time. List all the items in the order in which they were removed.

4. What is the difference between interactive processing and real-time processing?

5. What is a multitasking operating system?

6. If you have a PC, identify some situations in which you can take advantage of its multitasking capabilities.

7. On the basis of a computer system with which you are familiar, identify two units of application software and two units of utility software. Then explain why you classified them as you did.

8. a. What is the role of the shell of an operating system?
   b. What is the role of the kernel of an operating system?

9. What directory structure is described by the path X/Y/Z?

10. Define the term "process" as it is used in the context of operating systems.

11. What information is contained in a process table within an operating system?

12. What is the difference between a process that is ready and a process that is waiting?

13. What is the difference between virtual memory and main memory?

14. Suppose a computer contained 512MB (MiB) of main memory, and an operating system needed to create a virtual memory of twice that size using pages of 2KB (KiB). How many pages would be required?

15. What complications could arise in a time-sharing/multitasking system if two processes require access to the same file at the same time? Are

there cases in which the file manager should grant such requests? Are there cases in which the file manager should deny such requests?

16. What is the distinction between application software and system software? Give an example of each.

17. Define load balancing and scaling in the context of multiprocessor architectures.

18. Summarize the booting process.

19. Why is the booting process necessary?

20. If you have a PC, record the sequence activities that you can observe when you turn it on. Then determine what messages appear on the computer screen before the booting process actually begins. What software writes these messages?

21. Suppose a multiprogramming operating system allocated time slices of 20 milliseconds and the machine executed an average of 5 instructions per microsecond. How many instructions could be executed in a single time slice?

22. If a typist types 60 words per minute (where a word is considered five characters), how much time would pass between typing each character? If a multiprogramming operating system allocated time slices in 20 millisecond units and we ignore the time required for process switches, how many time-slices could be allocated between characters being typed?

23. Suppose a multiprogramming operating system is allotting time slices of 50 milliseconds. If it normally takes 8 milliseconds to position a disk's read/write head over the desired track and another 17 milliseconds for the desired data to rotate around to the read/write head, how much of a program's time slice can be spent waiting for a read operation from a disk to take place? If the machine is capable of executing ten instructions each microsecond, how many instructions can be executed during this waiting period? (This is why when a process performs an operation with a peripheral device, a multiprogramming system terminates that process's time slice and allows another

process to run while the first process is waiting for the services of the peripheral device.)

24. List five resources to which a multitasking operating system might have to coordinate access.

25. A process is said to be I/O-bound if it requires a lot of I/O operations, whereas a process that consists of mostly computations within the CPU/memory system is said to be compute-bound. If both a compute-bound process and an I/O-bound process are waiting for a time slice, which should be given priority? Why?

26. Would greater throughput be achieved by a system running two processes in a multiprogramming environment if both processes were I/O-bound (refer to Problem 25) or if one was I/O-bound and the other was compute-bound? Why?

27. Write a set of directions that tells an operating system's dispatcher what to do when a process's time slice is over.

28. What information is contained in the state of a process?

29. Identify a situation in a multiprogramming system in which a process does not consume the entire time slice allocated to it.

30. List in chronological order the major events that take place when a process is interrupted.

31. Answer each of the following in terms of an operating system that you use:
    a. How do you ask the operating system to copy a file from one location to another?
    b. How do you ask the operating system to show you the directory on a disk?
    c. How do you ask the operating system to execute a program?

32. Answer each of the following in terms of an operating system that you use:
    a. How does the operating system restrict access to only those who are approved users?
    b. How do you ask the operating system to show you what processes are currently in the process table?

c. How do you tell the operating system that you do not want other users of the machine to have access to your files?

*33. Explain an important use for the test-and-set instruction found in many machine languages. Why is it important for the entire test-and-set process to be implemented as a single instruction?

*34. A banker with only $100,000 loans $50,000 to each of two customers. Later, both customers return with the story that before they can repay their loans they must each borrow another $10,000 to complete the business deals in which their previous loans are involved. The banker resolves this deadlock by borrowing the additional funds from another source and passing on this loan (with an increase in the interest rate) to the two customers. Which of the three conditions for deadlock has the banker removed?

*35. Students who want to enroll in Model Railroading II at the local university are required to obtain permission from the instructor and pay a laboratory fee. The two requirements are fulfilled independently in either order and at different locations on campus. Enrollment is limited to 20 students; this limit is maintained by both the instructor, who will grant permission to only 20 students, and the financial office, which will allow only 20 students to pay the laboratory fee. Suppose that this registration system has resulted in 19 students having successfully registered for the course, but with the final space being claimed by 2 students—one who has only obtained permission from the instructor and another who has only paid the fee. Which requirement for deadlock is removed by each of the following solutions to the problem:
a. Both students are allowed in the course.
b. The class size is reduced to 19, so neither of the two students is allowed to register for the course.
c. The competing students are both denied entry to the class and a third student is given the twentieth space.
d. It is decided that the only requirement for entry into the course is the payment of the fee. Thus the student who has paid the fee gets into the course, and entry is denied to the other student.

*36. Since each area on a computer's monitor screen can be used by only one process at a time (otherwise the image on the screen would be unreadable), these areas are nonshareable resources that are allocated by the window manager. Which of the three conditions necessary for deadlock does the window manager remove in order to avoid deadlock?

*37. Suppose each nonshareable resource in a computer system is classified as a level 1, level 2, or level 3 resource. Moreover, suppose each process in the system is required to request the resources it needs according to this classification. That is, it must request all the required level 1 resources at once before requesting any level 2 resources. Once it receives the level 1 resources, it can request all the required level 2 resources, and so on. Can deadlock occur in such a system? Why or why not?

*38. Each of two robot arms is programmed to lift assemblies from a conveyor belt, test them for tolerances, and place them in one of two bins depending on the results of the test. The assemblies arrive one at a time with a sufficient interval between them. To keep both arms from trying to grab the same assembly, the computers controlling the arms share a common memory cell. If an arm is available as an assembly approaches, its controlling computer reads the value of the common cell. If the value is nonzero, the arm lets the assembly pass. Otherwise, the controlling computer places a nonzero value in the memory cell, directs the arm to pick up the assembly, and places the value 0 back into the memory cell after the action is complete. What sequence of events could lead to a tug-of-war between the two arms?

*39. Identify the use of a queue in the process of spooling output to a printer.

*40. A process that is waiting for a time slice is said to suffer **starvation** if it is never given a time slice.

a. The pavement in the middle of an intersection can be considered as a non-shareable resource for which cars approaching the intersection compete. A traffic light rather than an operating system is used to control the allocation of the resource. If the light is able to sense the amount of traffic arriving from each direction and is programmed to give the green light to the heavier traffic, the lighter traffic might suffer from starvation. How is starvation avoided?

b. In what sense can a process starve if the dispatcher always assigns time slices according to a priority system in which the priority of each process remains fixed? (*Hint:* What is the priority of the process that just completed its time slice in comparison to the processes that are waiting, and consequently which routine gets the next time slice?) How, would you guess, do many operating systems avoid this problem?

*41. What is the similarity between deadlock and starvation? (Refer to Problem 40.) What is the difference between deadlock and starvation?

*42. The following is the "dining philosophers" problem that was originally proposed by E. W. Dijkstra and is now a part of computer science folklore.

Five philosophers are sitting at a round table. In front of each is a plate of spaghetti. There are five forks on the table, one between each plate. Each philosopher wants to alternate between thinking and eating. To eat, a philosopher requires possession of both the forks that are adjacent to the philosopher's plate.

Identify the possibilities of deadlock and starvation (see Problem 40) that are present in the dining philosophers problem.

*43. What problem arises as the lengths of the time slices in a multiprogramming system are made shorter and shorter? What about as they become longer and longer?

*44. As computer science has developed, machine languages have been extended to provide specialized instructions. Three such machine instructions were introduced in Section 4 that are used extensively by operating systems. What are these instructions?

45. Identity two activities that can be performed by an operating system's administrator but not by a typical user.

46. How does an operating system keep a process from accessing another process's memory space?

47. Suppose a password consisted of a string of nine characters from the English alphabet (26 characters). If each possible password could be tested in a millisecond, how long would it take to test all possible passwords?

48. Why are CPUs that are designed for multitasking operating systems capable of operating at different privilege levels?

49. Identify two activities that are typically requested by privileged instructions.

50. Identify three ways in which a process could challenge the security of a computer system if not prevented from doing so by the operating system.

Social Issues

The following questions are intended as a guide to the ethical/social/legal issues associated with the field of computing. The goal is not merely to answer these questions. You should also consider why you answered as you did and whether your justifications are consistent from one question to the next.

1. Suppose you are using a multiuser operating system that allows you to view the names of the files belonging to other users as well as to view the contents of

those files that are not otherwise protected. Would viewing such information without permission be similar to wandering through someone's unlocked home without permission, or would it be more like reading materials placed in a common lounge such as a physician's waiting room?

2. When you have access to a multiuser computer system, what responsibilities do you have when selecting your password?

3. If a flaw in an operating system's security allows a malicious programmer to gain unauthorized access to sensitive data, to what extent should the developer of the operating system be held responsible?

4. Is it your responsibility to lock your house in such a way that intruders cannot get in, or is it the public's responsibility to stay out of your house unless invited? Is it the responsibility of an operating system to guard access to a computer and its contents, or is it the responsibility of hackers to leave the machine alone?

5. In *Walden,* Henry David Thoreau argues that we have become tools of our tools; that is, instead of benefiting from the tools that we have, we spend our time obtaining and maintaining our tools. To what extent is this true with regard to computing? For example, if you own a personal computer, how much time do you spend earning the money to pay for it, learning how to use its operating system, learning how to use its utility and application software, maintaining it, and downloading upgrades to its software in comparison to the amount of time you spend benefiting from it? When you use it, is your time well spent? Are you more socially active with or without a personal computer?

Additional Reading

Bishop, M. *Introduction to Computer Security.* Boston, MA: Addison-Wesley, 2005.

Davis, W. S. and T. M. Rajkumar. *Operating Systems: A Systematic View*, 6th ed. Boston, MA: Addison-Wesley, 2005.

Deitel, P. and D. Deitel. *Operating Systems*, 3rd ed. Upper Saddle River, NJ: Prentice-Hall, 2004.

Nutt, G. *Operating Systems: A Modern Approach*, 3rd ed. Boston, MA: Addison-Wesley, 2004.

Rosenoer, J. *CyberLaw, The Law of the Internet.* New York: Springer, 1997.

Silberschatz, A., P. B. Galvin, and G. Gagne. *Operating System Concepts*, 7th ed. New York: Wiley, 2004.

Stallings, W. *Operating Systems*, 5th ed. Upper Saddle River, NJ: Prentice-Hall, 2006.

Tanenbaum, A. S. *Modern Operating Systems*, 3rd ed. Upper Saddle River, NJ: Prentice-Hall, 2008.

Answers to Questions & Exercises

Section 1

1. A traditional example is the line of people waiting to buy tickets to an event. In this case there might be someone who tries to "break in line," which would violate the FIFO structure.

2. Options (b), (c), and (e).

3. Real-time processing refers to coordinating the execution of a program with activities in the machine's environment. Interactive processing refers to a person's interaction with a program as it executes. Good real-time characteristics are needed for successful interactive processing.

4. Time-sharing refers to more than one user accessing a machine at the same time. Multitasking refers to a user performing more than one task at the same time.

Section 2

1. *Shell:* Communicates with the machine's environment.

   File manager: Coordinates the use of the machine's mass storage.

   Device drivers: Handle communication with the machine's peripheral devices.

   Memory manager: Coordinates the use of the machine's main memory.

   Scheduler: Coordinates the processes in the system.

   Dispatcher: Controls the assignment of processes to CPU time.

2. The line is vague, and the distinction is often in the eye of the beholder. Roughly speaking, utility software performs basic, universal tasks, whereas application software performs tasks unique to the machine's application.

3. Virtual memory is the imaginary memory space whose apparent presence is created by the process of swapping data and programs back and forth between main memory and mass storage.

4. When the machine is turned on, the CPU begins executing the bootstrap, which resides in ROM. This bootstrap directs the CPU through the process of transferring the operating system from mass storage into the volatile area of main memory. When this transfer is complete, the bootstrap directs the CPU to jump to the operating system.

Section 3

1. A program is a set of directions. A process is the action of following those directions.

2. The CPU completes its current machine cycle, saves the state of the current process, and sets its program counter to a predetermined value (which is the location of the interrupt handler). Thus the next instruction executed will be the first instruction within the interrupt handler.

3. They could be given higher priorities so that they would be given preference by the dispatcher. Another option would be to give the higher-priority processes longer time slices.

4. If each process consumed its entire time slice, the machine could provide a complete slice to almost 20 processes in one second. If processes did not consume their entire time slices, this value could be much higher, but then the time required to perform a context switch might become more significant (see Problem 5).

5. A total of $^{5000}/_{5001}$ of the machine's time would be spent actually performing processes. However, when a process requests an I/O activity, its time slice is terminated while the controller performs the request. Thus if each process made such a request after only one microsecond of its time slice, the efficiency of the machine would drop to $\frac{1}{2}$. That is, the machine would spend as much time performing context switches as it would executing processes.

Section 4

1. This system guarantees that the resource is not used by more than one process at a time; however, it dictates that the resource be allocated in a strictly alternating fashion. Once a process has used and relinquished the resource, it must wait for the other process to use the resource before the original process can access it again. This is true even if the first process needs the resource right away and the other process will not need it for some time.

2. If two cars enter opposite ends of the tunnel at the same time, they will not be aware of the other's presence. The process of entering and turning on the lights is another example of a critical region, or in this case we might call it a critical process. In this terminology, we could summarize the flaw by saying that cars at opposite ends of the tunnel could execute the critical process at the same time.

3. a. This guarantees that the nonshareable resource is not required and allocated on a partial basis; that is, a car is given the whole bridge or nothing at all.
   b. This means that the nonshareable resource can be forcibly retrieved.
   c. This makes the nonshareable resource shareable, which removes the competition.

4. A sequence of arrows that forms a closed loop in the directed graph. It is on this observation that techniques have been developed that allow some operating systems to recognize the existence of deadlock and consequently to take appropriate corrective action.

Section 5

1. Names and dates are considered poor candidates because they are common choices and therefore represent easy targets for password guessers. The use of complete words is also considered poor because password guessers can easily write a program to try the words found in a dictionary. Moreover, passwords containing only characters are discouraged because they are formed from a limited character set.

2. Four is the number of different bit patterns that can be formed using two bits. If more privilege levels were required, the designers would need at least three bits to represent the different levels and would therefore probably choose to use a total of eight levels. In the same manner, the natural choice for fewer than four privilege levels would be two, which is the number of patterns that can be represented with one bit.

3. The process could alter the operating system program so that the dispatcher gave every time slice to that process.

3

Networking and the Internet

In this chapter we discuss the area of computer science known as networking, which encompasses the study of how computers can be linked together to share information and resources. Our study will include the construction and operation of networks, applications of networks, and security issues. A prominent topic will be a particular worldwide network of networks known as the Internet.

The need to share information and resources among different computers has led to linked computer systems, called **networks,** in which computers are connected so that data can be transferred from machine to machine. In these networks, computer users can exchange messages and share resources—such as printing capabilities, software packages, and data storage facilities—that are scattered throughout the system. The underlying software required to support such applications has grown from simple utility packages into an expanding system of network software that provides a sophisticated network-wide infrastructure. In a sense, network software is evolving into a network-wide operating system. In this chapter we will explore this expanding field of computer science.

1 Network Fundamentals

We begin our study of networks by introducing a variety of basic networking concepts.

Network Classifications

A computer network is often classified as being either a **local area network (LAN),** a **metropolitan area network (MAN),** or a **wide area network (WAN).** A LAN normally consists of a collection of computers in a single building or building complex. For example, the computers on a university campus or those in a manufacturing plant might be connected by a LAN. A MAN is a network of intermediate size, such as one spanning a local community. A WAN links machines over a greater distance—perhaps in neighboring cities or on opposite sides of the world.

Another means of classifying networks is based on whether the network's internal operation is based on designs that are in the public domain or on innovations owned and controlled by a particular entity such as an individual or a corporation. A network of the former type is called an **open** network; a network of the latter type is called a **closed,** or sometimes a **proprietary,** network. Open network designs are freely circulated and often grow in popularity to the point that they ultimately prevail over proprietary approaches whose applications are restricted by license fees and contract conditions.

The Internet (a popular worldwide network of networks that we will study in this chapter) is an open system. In particular, communication throughout the Internet is governed by an open collection of standards known as the TCP/IP protocol suite, which is the subject of Section 4. Anyone is free to use these standards without paying fees or signing license agreements. In contrast, a company such as Novell Inc. might develop proprietary systems for which it chooses to maintain ownership rights, allowing the company to draw income from selling or leasing these products.

Still another way of classifying networks is based on the topology of the network, which refers to the pattern in which the machines are connected. Two of the more popular topologies are the bus, in which the machines are all connected to a common communication line called a bus (Figure 1a), and the star, in which one machine serves as a central focal point to which all the others are connected (Figure 1b). The bus topology was popularized in the 1990s when it was implemented under a set of standards known as Ethernet, and Ethernet networks remain one of the most popular networking systems in use today. The star topology has roots as far back as the 1970s. It evolved from the paradigm of a large central computer serving many users. As the simple terminals employed by these users grew into small computers themselves, a star network emerged. Today, the star configuration is popular in wireless networks where communication is conducted by means of radio broadcast and the central machine, called the **access point (AP),** serves as a focal point around which all communication is coordinated.

The difference between a bus network and a star network is not always obvious by the physical arrangement of equipment. The distinction is whether the machines in the network envision themselves as communicating directly with each other over a common bus or indirectly through an intermediary central machine. For instance, a bus network might not appear as a long bus from which computers are connected over short links as depicted in Figure 1. Instead, it may have a very short bus with long links to the individual machines, meaning that the network would look more like a star. Indeed, sometimes a bus network is created by running links from each computer to a central location where they are connected to a device called a **hub.** This hub is little more than a very short bus. All it does is relay any signal it receives (with perhaps some amplification) back out to all the machines connected to it. The result is a network that looks like a star network although it operates like a bus network.

Figure 1   Two popular network topologies

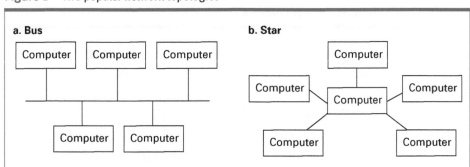

Protocols

For a network to function reliably, it is important to establish rules by which activities are conducted. Such rules are called **protocols.** By developing and adopting protocol standards, vendors are able to build products for network applications that are compatible with products from other vendors. Thus, the development of protocol standards is an indispensable process in the development of networking technologies.

As an introduction to the protocol concept, let us consider the problem of coordinating the transmission of messages among computers in a network. Without rules governing this communication, all the computers might insist on transmitting messages at the same time or fail to assist other machines when that assistance is required.

In a bus network based on the Ethernet standards, the right to transmit messages is controlled by the protocol known as **Carrier Sense, Multiple Access with Collision Detection (CSMA/CD).** This protocol dictates that each message be broadcast to all the machines on the bus (Figure 2). Each machine monitors all the messages but keeps only those addressed to itself. To transmit a message, a machine waits until the bus is silent, and at this time it begins transmitting while continuing to monitor the bus. If another machine also begins transmitting, both machines detect the clash and pause for a brief, independently random period of time before trying to transmit again. The result is a system similar to that used by a small group of people in a conversation. If two people start to talk at once, they both stop. The difference is that people might go through a series such as, "I'm sorry, what were you going to say?", "No, no. You go first," whereas under the CSMA/CD protocol each machine merely tries again later.

Note that CSMA/CD is not compatible with wireless star networks in which all machines communicate through a central AP. This is because a machine may be unabe to detect that its transmissions are colliding with those of another. For example, the machine may not hear the other because its own signal drowns out that of the other machine. Another cause might be that the signals from the

Figure 2   Communication over a bus network

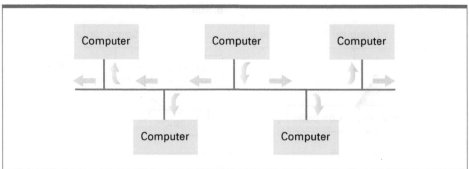

different machines are blocked from each other by objects or distance even though they can all communicate with the central AP (a condition known as the **hidden terminal problem,** Figure 3). The result is that wireless networks adopt the policy of trying to *avoid* collisions rather than trying to *detect* them. Such policies are classified as **Carrier Sense, Multiple Access with Collision Avoidance (CSMA/CA),** many of which are standardized by IEEE within the protocols defined in IEEE 802.11 and commonly referred to as **WiFi.** We emphasize that collision avoidance protocols are designed to avoid collisions and may not eliminate them completely. When collisions do occur, messages must be retransmitted.

The most common approach to collision avoidance is based on giving advantage to machines that have already been waiting for an opportunity to transmit. The protocol used is similar to Ethernet's CSMA/CD. The basic difference is that when a machine first needs to transmit a message and finds the communication channel silent, it does not start transimitting immediately. Instead, it waits for a short period of time and then starts transimitting only if the channel has remained silent throughout that period. If a busy channel is experienced during

Figure 3   The hidden terminal problem

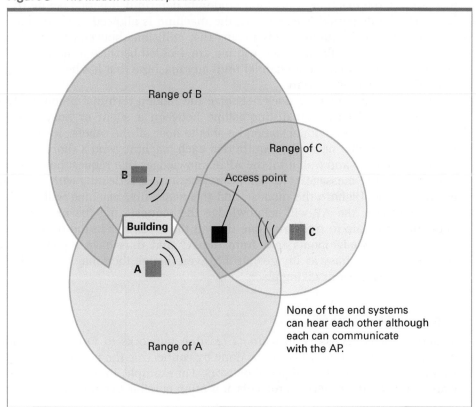

Ethernet

Ethernet is a set of standards for implementing a LAN with a bus topology. Its name is derived from the original Ethernet design in which machines were connected by a coaxial cable called the ether. Originally developed in the 1970s and now standardized by IEEE as a part of the IEEE 802 family of standards, Ethernet is one of the most common methods of networking PCs. Indeed, Ethernet controllers have become a standard component in the PCs available in the current retail market.

Today there are actually several versions of Ethernet, reflecting advances in technology and higher transfer rates. All, however, share common traits that characterize the Ethernet family. Among these are the format in which data are packaged for transmission, the use of Manchester encoding (a method of representing 0s and 1s in which a 0 is represented by a descending signal and a 1 is represented by an ascending signal) for the actual transmission of bits, and the use of CSMA/CD for controlling the right to transmit.

this process, the machine waits for a randomly determined period before trying again. Once this period is exhausted, the machine is allowed to claim a silent channel without hesitation. This means that collisions between "newcomers" and those that have already been waiting are avoided because a "newcomer" is not allowed to claim a silent channel until any machine that has been waiting is given the opportunity to start.

This protocol, however, does not solve the hidden terminal problem. After all, any protocol based on distinquishing between a silent or busy channel requires that each individual station be able to hear all the others. To solve this problem, some WiFi networks require that each machine send a short "request" message to the AP and wait until the AP acknowledges that request before transmitting an entire message. If the AP is busy because it is dealing with a "hidden terminal," it will ignore the request, and the requesting machine will know to wait. Otherwise, the AP will acknowledge the request, and the machine will know that it is safe to transmit. Note that all the machines in the network will hear all acknowledgements sent from the AP and thus have a good idea of whether the AP is busy at any given time, even though they may not be able to hear the transimissions taking place.

Combining Networks

Sometimes it is necessary to connect existing networks to form an extended communication system. This can be done by connecting the networks to form a larger version of the same "type" of network. For example, in the case of bus networks based on the Ethernet protocols, it is often possible to connect the buses to form a single long bus. This is done by means of different devices known as repeaters, bridges, and switches, the distinctions of which are subtle yet informative. The simplest of these is the **repeater,** which is little more than a device that simply passes signals back and forth between the two original buses (usually with some form of amplification) without considering the meaning of the signals (Figure 4a).

A **bridge** is similar to, but more complex than, a repeater. Like a repeater, it connects two buses, but it does not necessarily pass all messages across the connection. Instead, it looks at the destination address that accompanies each message and forwards a message across the connection only when that message is destined for a computer on the other side. Thus, two machines residing on the same side of a bridge can exchange messages without interfering with communication taking place on the other side. A bridge produces a more efficient system than that produced by a repeater.

A **switch** is essentially a bridge with multiple connections, allowing it to connect several buses rather than just two. Thus, a switch produces a network consisting of several buses extending from the switch as spokes on a wheel (Figure 4b). As in the case of a bridge, a switch considers the destination addresses of all messages and forwards only those messages destined for other spokes. Moreover, each message that is forwarded is relayed only into the appropriate spoke, thus minimizing the traffic in each spoke.

It is important to note that when networks are connected via repeaters, bridges, and switches, the result is a single large network. The entire system

Figure 4   Building a large bus network from smaller ones

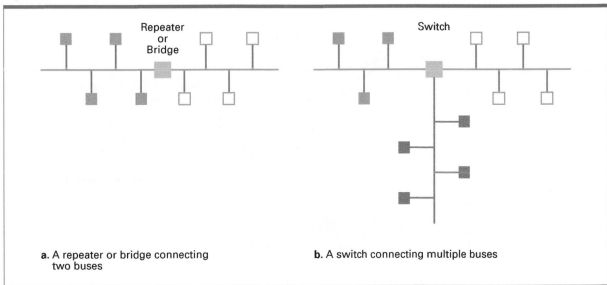

a. A repeater or bridge connecting two buses

b. A switch connecting multiple buses

operates in the same manner (using the same protocols) as each of the original smaller networks.

Sometimes, however, the networks to be connected have incompatible characteristics. For instance, the characteristics of a WiFi network are not readily compatible with an Ethernet network. In these cases the networks must be connected in a manner that builds a network of networks, known as an **internet,** in which the original networks maintain their individuality and continue to function as autonomous networks. (Note that the generic term *internet* is distinct from *the Internet.* The Internet, written with an uppercase *I*, refers to a particular, worldwide internet that we will study in later sections of this chapter. There are many other examples of internets. Indeed, traditional telephone communication was handled by worldwide internet systems well before the Internet was popularized.)

The connection between networks to form an internet is handled by devices known as **routers,** which are special purpose computers used for forwarding messages. Note that the task of a router is different from that of repeaters, bridges, and switches in that routers provide links between networks while allowing each network to maintain its unique internal characteristics. As an example, Figure 5 depicts two WiFi star networks and an Ethernet bus network connected by routers. When a machine in one of the WiFi networks wants to send a message to a machine in the Ethernet network, it first sends the message

Figure 5   Routers connecting two WiFi networks and an Ethernet network to form an internet

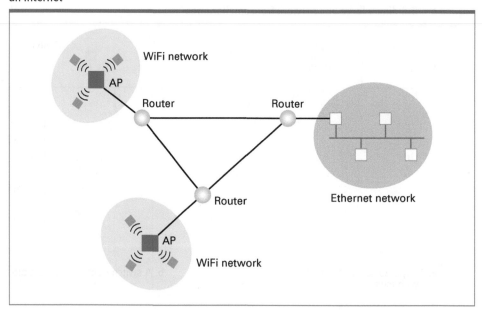

to the AP in its network. From there, the AP sends the message to its associated router, and this router forwards the message to the router at the Ethernet. There the message is given to a machine on the bus, and that machine then forwards the message to its final destination in the Ethernet.

The reason that routers are so named is that their purpose is to forward messages in their proper directions. This forwarding process is based on an internet-wide addressing system in which all the devices in an internet (including the machines in the original networks and the routers) are assigned unique addresses. (Thus, each machine in one of the original networks has two addresses: its original "local" address within its own network and its internet address.) A machine wanting to send a message to a machine in a distant network attaches the internet address of the destination to the message and directs the message to its local router. From there it is forwarded in the proper direction. For this forwarding purpose, each router maintains a **forwarding table** that contains the router's knowledge about the direction in which messages should be sent depending on their destination addresses.

The "point" at which one network is linked to an internet is often called a **gateway** because it serves as a passageway between the network and the outside world. Gateways can be found in a variety of forms, and thus the term is used rather loosely. In many cases a network's gateway is merely the router through which it communicates with the rest of the internet. In other cases the term *gateway* may be used to refer to more than just a router. For example, in most residential WiFi networks that are connected to the Internet, the term *gateway* refers collectively to both the network's AP and the router connected to the AP because these two devices are normally packaged in a single unit.

Methods of Process Communication

The various activities (or processes) executing on the different computers within a network (or even executing on the same machine via time-sharing/multitasking) must often communicate with each other to coordinate their actions and to perform their designated tasks. Such communication between processes is called **interprocess communication.**

A popular convention used for interprocess communication is the **client/server** model. This model defines the basic roles played by the processes as either a **client,** which makes requests of other processes, or a **server,** which satisfies the requests made by clients.

An early application of the client/server model appeared in networks connecting all the computers in a cluster of offices. In this situation, a single, high-quality printer was attached to the network where it was available to all the machines in the network. In this case the printer played the role of a server (often called a **print server**), and the other machines were programmed to play the role of clients that sent print requests to the print server.

Another early application of the client/server model was used to reduce the cost of magnetic disk storage while also removing the need for duplicate copies of records. Here one machine in a network was equipped with a high-capacity mass storage system (usually a magnetic disk) that contained all of an organization's records. Other machines on the network then requested access to the records as they needed them. Thus the machine that actually contained the records played the role of a server (called a **file server**), and the other machines played the role of clients that requested access to the files that were stored at the file server.

Today the client/server model is used extensively in network applications, as we will see later in this chapter. However, the client/server model is not the only means of interprocess communication. Another model is the **peer-to-peer** (often abbreviated **P2P**) model. Whereas the client/server model involves one process (the server) providing a service to numerous others (clients), the peer-to-peer model involves processes that provide service to and receive service from each other (Figure 6). Moreover, whereas a server must execute continuously so that it is prepared to serve its clients at any time, the peer-to-peer model usually involves processes that execute on a temporary basis. For example, applications of the peer-to-peer model include instant messaging in which people carry on a written conversation over the Internet as well as situations in which people play competitive interactive games.

The peer-to-peer model is also a popular means of distributing files such as music recordings and motion pictures via the Internet. In this case, one peer may receive a file from another and then provide that file to other peers. The

Figure 6   The client/server model compared to the peer-to-peer model

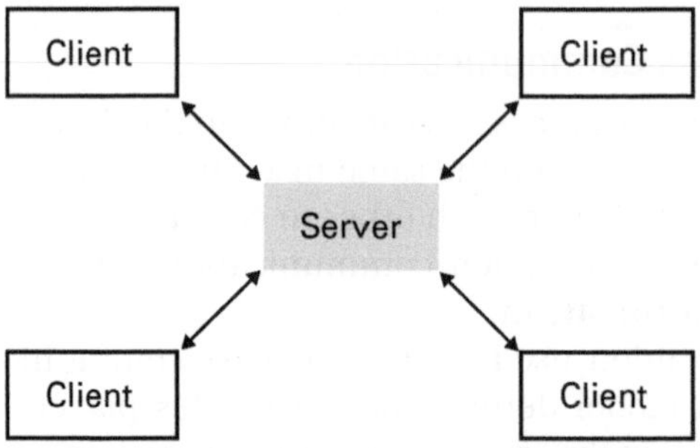

a. Server must be prepared to serve multiple clients at any time.

b. Peers communicate as equals on a one-to-one basis.

collection of peers participating in such a distribution is sometimes called a swarm. The swarm approach to file distribution is in contrast to earlier approaches that applied the client/server model by establishing a central distribution center (the server) from which clients downloaded files (or at least found sources for those files).

One reason that the P2P model is replacing the client/server model for file sharing is that it distributes the service task over many peers rather than concentrating it at one server. This lack of a centralized base of operation leads to a more efficient system. Unfortunately, another reason for the popularity of file distribution systems based on the P2P model is that, in cases of questionable legality, the lack of a central server makes legal efforts to enforce copyright laws more difficult. There are numerous cases, however, in which individuals have discovered that "difficult" does not mean "impossible" and have found themselves faced with significant liabilities due to copyright infringement violations.

You might often read or hear the term *peer-to-peer network*, which is an example of how misuse of terminology can evolve when technical terms are adopted by the nontechnical community. The term *peer-to-peer* refers to a system by which two processes communicate over a network (or internet). It is not a property of the network (or internet). A process might use the peer-to-peer model to communicate with another process and later use the client/server model to communicate with another process over the same network. Thus, it would be more accurate to speak of communicating by means of the peer-to-peer model rather than communicating over a peer-to-peer network.

Distributed Systems

With the success of networking technology, interaction between computers via networks has become common and multifaceted. Many modern software systems, such as global information retrieval systems, company-wide accounting and inventory systems, computer games, and even the software that controls a network's infrastructure itself are designed as **distributed systems,** meaning that they consist of software units that execute as processes on different computers.

Early distributed systems were developed independently from scratch. But today, research is revealing a common infrastructure running throughout these systems, including such things as communication and security systems. In turn, efforts have been made to produce prefabricated systems that provide this basic infrastructure and therefore allow distributed applications to be constructed by merely developing the part of the system that is unique to the application.

One result of such undertakings is the system known as Enterprise JavaBeans (developed by Sun Microsystems), which is a development environment that aids in the construction of new distributed software systems. Using Enterprise JavaBeans, a distributed system is constructed from units called beans that automatically inherit the enterprise infrastructure. Thus, only the unique application-dependent portions of a new system must be developed. Another approach is the software development environment called .NET Framework (developed by Microsoft). In the .NET terminology the components of a distributed system are called assemblies. Again, by developing these units in the .NET environment, only the characteristics that are unique to the particular application need to be constructed—the infrastructure is prefabricated.

Questions & Exercises

1. What is an open network?
2. Summarize the distinction between a repeater and a bridge.
3. What is a router?
4. Identify some relationships in society that conform to the client/server model.
5. Identify some protocols used in society.

2 The Internet

The most notable example of an internet is the **Internet** (note the uppercase *I*), which originated from research projects going back to the early 1960s. The goal was to develop the ability to link a variety of computer networks so that they could function as a connected system that would not be disrupted by local disasters. Much of this work was sponsored by the U.S. government through the Defense Advanced Research Projects Agency (DARPA—pronounced "DAR–pa"). Over the years, the development of the Internet shifted from a government-sponsored project to an academic research project, and today it is largely a commercial undertaking that links a worldwide combination of LANs, MANs, and WANs involving millions of computers.

Internet Architecture

As we have already mentioned, the Internet is a collection of connected networks. In general, these networks are constructed and maintained by organizations called **Internet Service Providers (ISPs).** It is also customary to use the term ISP in reference to the networks themselves. Thus, we will speak of connecting to an ISP, when what we really mean is connecting to the network provided by an ISP.

The system of networks operated by the ISPs can be classified in a hierarchy according to the role they play in the overall Internet structure (Figure 7). At the top of this hierarchy are relatively few **tier-1 ISPs** that consist of very high-speed, high-capacity, international WANs. These networks are thought of as the backbone of the Internet. They are typically operated by large companies that are in the communications business. An example would be a company that originated as a traditional telephone company and has expanded its scope into providing other communication services.

Figure 7   Internet Composition

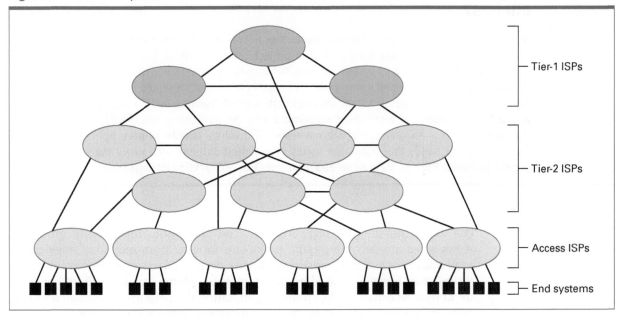

Connecting to the tier-1 ISPs are the **tier-2 ISPs** that tend to be more regional in scope and less potent in their capabilities. (The distinction between the tier-1 and tier-2 ISPs is often a matter of opinion.) Again, these networks tend to be operated by companies in the communications business.

Tier-1 and tier-2 ISPs are essentially networks of routers that collectivly provide the Internet's communication infrastructure. As such, they can be thought of as the core of the Internet. Access to this core is usually provided by an intermediary called an access ISP. An **access ISP** is essentially an independent internet, sometimes called an **intranet,** operated by a single authority that is in the business of supplying Internet access to individual users. Examples include companies such as AOL, Microsoft, and local cable and telephone companies that charge for their service as well as organizations such as universities or corporations that take it upon themselves to provide Internet access to individuals within their organizations.

The devices that individual users connect to the access ISPs are known as **end systems** or **hosts.** These end systems are not necessarily computers in the traditional sense. They range over a multitude of devices including telephones, video cameras, automobiles, and home appliances. After all, the Internet is essentially a communications system, and thus any device that would benefit from communicating with other devices is a potential end system.

The technology by which end systems connect to access ISPs is also varied. Perhaps the fastest growing are wireless connections based on WiFi technology. The strategy is to connect the AP to an access ISP and thus provide Internet access through that ISP to end systems within the AP's broadcast range.

Internet2

Now that the Internet has shifted from a research project to a household commodity, the research community has moved on to a project called Internet2. Internet2 is intended as an academic-only system and involves numerous universities working in partnership with industry and government. The goal is to conduct research in internet applications requiring high bandwidth communication, such as remote access and control of costly state-of-the-art equipment such as telescopes and medical diagnostic devices. An example of current research involves remote surgery performed by robot hands that mimic the hands of a distant surgeon who views the patient by video. You can learn more about Internet2 at http://www.internet2.org.

The area within the AP's range is often called a **hot spot.** Hot spots and groupings of hot spots are becoming quite prevalent, ranging from individual residences, hotel and office buildings, small businesses, parks, and in some cases entire cities. A similar technology is used by the cellular telephone industry where hot spots are known as cells and the "routers" generating the cells are coordinated to provide continuous service as an end system moves from one cell to another.

Other popular techniques for connecting to access ISP's use telephone lines or cable/satellite systems. These technologies may be used to provide direct connection to an end system or to a customer's router to which multiple end systems are connected. This latter tactic is becoming increasingly popular for individual residences where a local hot spot is created by a router/AP connected to an access ISP by means of existing cable or telephone lines.

Existing cable and satellite links are inherently more compatible with high-speed data transfer than traditional telephone lines, which were originally installed with voice communication in mind. However, several clever schemes have been developed to extend these links to accommodate transmission of digital data. These make use of devices called **modems** (short for modulator/demodulator) that convert the digital data to be transferred into a form compatible with the transmission medium being used. An example is **DSL (digital subscriber line)** in which the frequency range below 4 KHz (4,000 kilocycles per second) is reserved for traditional voice communication and the higher frequencies are used for transferring digital data. Another, older approach is to convert the digital data into sound and transmit it in the same manner as voice. This latter practice is called **dial-up** access in reference to the fact that it is used for temporary connections in which the user places a traditional telephone call to an access ISP's router and then connects his or her telephone to the end system to be used. Because dial-up tends to be inexpensive and readily available, it continues to be widely used. However, its relatively slow data transfer rate is increasingly unable to handle today's Internet applications that may require real-time video communication or the transmission of large blocks of data.

Internet Addressing

As we learned in Section 1, an internet needs an internet-wide addressing system that assigns a unique identifying address to each computer in the system. In the Internet these addresses are known as **IP addresses.** (The term *IP* refers to "Internet Protocol," which is a term we will learn more about in Section 4.) Originally, each IP address was a pattern of 32 bits, but to provide a larger set of addresses, the process of converting to 128-bit addresses is currently underway (see the discussion of IPv6 in Section 4). Blocks of consecutively numbered IP addresses are awarded to ISPs by the **Internet Corporation for Assigned Names and Numbers (ICANN),** which is a nonprofit corporation established to coordinate the Internet's operation. The ISPs are then allowed to allocate the addresses within their awarded blocks to machines within their region of authority. Thus, machines throughout the Internet are assigned unique IP addresses.

IP addresses are traditionally written in **dotted decimal notation** in which the bytes of the address are separated by periods and each byte is expressed as an integer represented in traditional base ten notation. For example, using dotted decimal notation, the pattern 5.2 would represent the two-byte bit pattern 0000010100000010, which consists of the byte 00000101 (represented by 5) followed by the byte 00000010 (represented by 2), and the pattern 17.12.25 would represent the three-byte bit pattern consisting of the byte 00010001 (which is 17 written in binary notation), followed by the byte 00001100 (12 written in binary), followed by the byte 00011001 (25 written in binary). In summary, a 32-bit IP address might appear as 192.207.177.133 when expressed in dotted decimal notation.

Addresses in bit-pattern form (even when compressed using dotted decimal notation) are rarely conducive to human consumption. For this reason the Internet has an alternative addressing system in which machines are identified by mnemonic names. This addressing system is based on the concept of a **domain,** which can be thought of as a "region" of the Internet operated by a single authority such as a university, club, company, or government agency. (The word region is in quotations here because, as we will soon see, such a region may not correspond to a physical area of the Internet.) Each domain must be registered with ICANN—a process handled by companies, called **registrars,** that have been assigned this role by ICANN. As a part of this registration process, the domain is assigned a mnemonic **domain name,** which is unique among all the domain names throughout the Internet. Domain names are often descriptive of the organization registering the domain, which enhances their utility for humans.

As an example, the domain name of the Addison-Wesley publishing company is aw.com. Note the suffix following the period. It is used to reflect the domain's classification, which in this case is "commercial" as indicated by the com suffix. These suffixes are called **top-level domains (TLDs).** Other TLDs include edu for educational institutions, gov for U.S. government institutions, org for nonprofit organizations, museum for museums, info for unrestricted use, and net, which was originally intended for ISPs but is now used on a much broader scale. In addition to these general TLDs, there are also two-letter TLDs for specific countries (called **country-code TLDs**) such as au for Australia and ca for Canada.

Once a domain's mnemonic name is registered, the organization that registered the name is free to extend the name to obtain mnemonic identifiers for individual items within the domain. For example, an individual machine within Addison-Wesley may be identified as ssenterprise.aw.com. Note that domain names are extended to the left and separated by a period. In some cases multiple extensions, called **subdomains,** are used as a means of organizing the names within a domain. These subdomains often represent different networks within the domain's jurisdiction. For example, if Nowhere University was assigned the domain name nowhereu.edu, then an individual computer at Nowhere University might have a name such as r2d2.compsc.nowhereu.edu, meaning that the computer r2d2 is in the subdomain compsc within the domain nowhereu within the TLD edu. (We should emphasize that the dotted notation used in mnemonic addresses is not related to the dotted decimal notation used to represent addresses in bit pattern form.)

Although mnemonic addresses are convenient for humans, messages are always transferred over the Internet by means of IP addresses. Thus, if a human wants to send a message to a distant machine and identifies the destination by means of a mnemonic address, the software being used must be able to convert that address into an IP address before transmitting the message. This conversion is performed with the aid of numerous servers, called **name servers,** that are essentially directories that provide address translation services to clients. Collectively, these name servers are used as an Internet-wide directory system known as the **domain name system (DNS).** The process of using the DNS to perform a translation is called a **DNS lookup.**

Thus, for a machine to be accessible by means of a mnemonic domain name, that name must be represented in a name server within the DNS. In those cases in which the entity establishing the domain has the resources, it can establish and maintain its own name server containing all the names within that domain. Indeed, this is the model on which the domain system was originally based. Each registered domain represented a physical region of the Internet that was operated by a local authority such as a company, university, or government agency. This authority was essentially an access ISP that provided Internet access to its members by means of its own intranet that was linked to the Internet. As part of this system, the organization maintained its own name server that provided translation services for all the names used within its domain.

This model is still common today. However, many individuals or small organizations want to establish a domain presence on the Internet without committing the resources necessary to support it. For example, it might be beneficial for a local chess club to have a presence on the Internet as KingsandQueens.org, but the club would likely not have the resources to establish its own network, maintain a link from this network to the Internet, and implement its own name server. In this case, the club can contract with an access ISP to create the appearance of a registered domain using the resources already established by the ISP. Typically, the club, perhaps with the assistance of the ISP, registers the name chosen by the club and contracts with the ISP to have that name included in the ISP's name server. This means that all DNS lookups regarding the new domain name will be directed to the ISP's name server, from which the proper translation will be obtained. In this way, many registered domains can reside within a single ISP, each often occupying only a small portion of a single computer.

Internet Applications

In this subsection we discuss some applications of the Internet, beginning with three *traditional* applications. However, these "conventional" applications fall short of capturing the excitement of today's Internet. Indeed, the distinction between a computer and other electronic devices is becoming blurred. Telephones, televisions, sound systems, burglar alarms, microwave ovens, and video cameras are all potential "Internet devices." In turn, the traditional applications of the Internet are being dwarfed by an expanding flood of new uses including instant messaging, video conferencing, Internet telephony, and Internet radio. After all, the Internet is merely a communication system over which data can be transferred. As technology continues to increase the transfer rates of that system, the content of the data being transferred will be limited only by one's imagination. Thus, we will include two newer Internet applications, telephony and radio broadcast, to demonstrate some of the issues associated with today's emerging Internet, including the need for additional protocol standards, the need to link the Internet to other communication systems, and the need to expand the functionality of the Internet's routers.

Electronic Mail One of the most popular uses of the Internet is **email** (short for electronic mail), a system by which messages are transferred among Internet users. For the purpose of providing email service, a domain's local authority may designate a particular machine within its domain to play the role of a **mail server.** Typically, mail servers are established within domains operated by access ISPs for the purpose of providing mail service to users within its realm. When a user sends email from his or her local machine, it is first transferred to the user's mail server. There it is forwarded to the destination mail server where it is stored until the recipient contacts the mail server and asks to view the accumulated mail.

The protocol used to transfer mail between mail servers as well as to send a new message from its author's local machine to the author's mail server is **SMTP (Simple Mail Transfer Protocol).** Because SMTP was initially designed for transferring text messages encoded with ASCII, additional protocols such as **MIME (Multipurpose Internet Mail Extensions)** have been developed to convert non-ASCII data to SMTP compatible form.

There are two popular protocols that may be used for accessing email that has arrived and accumulated at a user's mail server. These are **POP3 (Post Office Protocol version 3)** and **IMAP (Internet Mail Access Protocol).** POP3 (pronounced "pop-THREE") is the simpler of the two. Using POP3, a user transfers (downloads) messages to his or her local computer where they can be read, stored in various folders, edited, and otherwise manipulated as the user desires. This is done on the user's local machine using the local machine's mass storage. IMAP (pronounced "EYE-map") allows a user to store and manipulate messages and related materials on the same machine as the mail server. In this manner, a user who must access his or her email from different computers can maintain records at the mail server that are then accessible from any remote computer to which the user may have access.

With the role of a mail server in mind, it is easy to understand the structure of an individual's email address. It consists of a symbol string (sometimes called the account name) identifying the individual, followed by the symbol @ (read "at"), followed by the mnemonic string that ultimately identifies the mail server that should receive the mail. (In reality this string often merely identifies the destination domain, and the domain's mail server is ultimately identified by means of a DNS lookup.) Thus the email address of an individual at Addison-Wesley Inc. might appear as shakespeare@aw.com. In other words, a message sent to this address is to go to the mail server in the domain aw.com where it should be held for the person identified by the symbol string shakespeare.

The File Transfer Protocol   One means of transferring files (such as documents, photographs, or other encoded information) is to attach them to email messages. However, a more efficient means is to take advantage of the **File Transfer Protocol (FTP),** which is a client/server protocol for transferring files across the Internet. To transfer a file using FTP, a user at one computer in the Internet uses a software package that implements FTP to establish contact with another computer. (The original computer plays the role of a client. The computer it contacts plays the role of a server, which is usually called an FTP server.) Once this connection is established, files can be transferred between the two computers in either direction.

FTP has become a popular way of providing limited access to data via the Internet. Suppose, for example, that you want to allow certain people to retrieve a file while prohibiting access by anyone else. You need merely place the file in a machine with FTP server facilities and guard access to the file via a password. Then, people who know the password will be able to gain access to the file via FTP, while all others will be blocked. A machine in the Internet used in this manner is sometimes called an FTP site because it constitutes a location in the Internet at which files are available via FTP.

FTP sites are also used to provide unrestricted access to files. To accomplish this, FTP servers use the term *anonymous* as a universal login name. Such sites are often referred to as **anonymous FTP** sites and provide unrestricted access to files under their auspices.

A commonly misunderstood feature of FTP is the distinction it makes between "text files" and "binary files." Newer implementations of FTP tend to shield users from such concerns, but it exemplifies the problems associated with transferring data among computers and thus warrants our consideration. The source of the problem is that when printing a text document with early teletype devices, a new line of text required both a line feed (a vertical movement) and a carriage return (a horizontal movement), each of which is encoded individually in ASCII. (A line feed is indicated by the pattern 00001010, whereas a carriage return is indicated by 00001101.) For the sake of efficiency, many early programmers found it convenient to mark line breaks in a text file with only one of these codes. For example, if everyone agreed to mark line breaks with only a carriage return rather than both a carriage return and a line feed, then eight bits of file space would be saved for each line of text in the file. All one had to do was remember to insert a line feed each time a carriage return was reached when printing the file. These shortcuts have survived in today's systems. In particular, the UNIX operating system assumes that a line break in a text file is indicated by only a line feed, whereas systems developed by Apple use only a carriage return, and Microsoft's software requires both a carriage return and a line feed. The result is that when these files are transferred from one system to another, conversions must be made.

This, then, leads to the distinction between "text files" and "binary files" in FTP. If a file is transferred as a "text file" using FTP, the required conversions will be made as part of the transfer process; if the file is transferred as a "binary file," no conversions will be made. Thus even though you might think of a file produced by a word processor as being text, it should not be transferred as a "text file" because these files use proprietary codes for representing carriage returns and line feeds. If such a "binary file" is accidentally transferred as a "text file," it will be subject to unintentional alterations.

Telnet and Secure Shell One of the early uses of the Internet was to allow computer users to access computers from great distances. **Telnet** is a protocol system that was established for this purpose. Using telnet, a user (running telnet client software) can contact the telnet server at a distant computer and then follow that operating system's login procedure to gain access to the distant machine. Thus, by means of telnet, a distant user has the same access to the applications and utilities on the computer that a local user has.

Having been designed early in the development of the Internet, telnet has several shortcomings. One of the more critical ones is that communication via telnet is not encrypted. This is significant even if the subject of the communication is not sensitive because the user's password is part of the communication during the login process. Thus the use of telnet opens the possibility that an eavesdropper might intercept a password and later misuse this critical information. **Secure Shell (SSH)** is an alternative to telnet that offers a solution to this problem and is rapidly replacing telnet. Among the features of SSH is that it provides for encryption of data being transferred as well as authentication (Section 5), which is the process of making sure that the two parties communicating are, in fact, who they claim to be.

VoIP As an example of a more recent Internet application, consider **VoIP (Voice over Internet Protocol)** in which the Internet infrastructure is used to provide voice communication similar to that of traditional telephone systems. In its simplest form, VoIP consists of two processes on different machines transferring audio data via the P2P model—a process that in itself presents no significant problems. However, tasks such as initiating and receiving calls, linking VoIP with traditional telephone systems, and providing services such as emergency 911 communication are issues that extend beyond traditional Internet applications. Moreover, governments that own their country's traditional telephone companies view VoIP as a threat and have either taxed it heavily or outlawed it completely. Combining these complications with the fact that VoIP is struggling to find universally accepted protocol standards means that the future direction of VoIP remains uncertain.

In the meantime, existing VoIP systems are competing for popularity. An example is Skype, which consists of application software that allows PC users to place calls to, and then communicate with, other Skype users. Skype also provides its clients with links to the traditional telephone communication system. One drawback to Skype is that it is a proprietary system, and thus much of its operational structure is not publicly known. This means that Skype users must trust the integrity of the Skype software without third-party verification. For instance, to receive calls, a Skype user must leave his or her PC connected to the Internet and available to the Skype system, which means that some of the PC's resources may be used to support other Skype communications without the PC owner's awareness—a feature that has generated some resistence.

Internet Radio Another recent Internet application is the transmission of radio station programming—a process called *webcasting* as opposed to *broadcasting* because the signals are transferred via the Internet rather than "over the air." More precisely, Internet radio is a specific example of **streaming audio,** which refers to the transfer of sound data on a real-time basis.

On the surface, Internet radio may not seem to require special consideration. One might guess that a station could merely establish a server that would send program messages to each of the clients who requested them. This technique is known as **N-unicast.** (More precisely, *unicast* refers to one sender sending messages to one receiver, whereas *N-unicast* refers to a single sender involved with multiple unicasts.) The N-unicast approach has been applied but has the drawback of placing a substantial burden on the station's server as well as on the server's immediate Internet neighbors. Indeed, N-unicast forces the server to send individual messages to each of its clients on a real-time basis, and all these messages must be forwarded by the server's neighbors.

Most alternatives to N-unicast represent attempts to alleviate this problem. One applies the P2P model in a manner reminisent of file sharing systems. That is, once a peer has received data, it begins to distribute that data to those peers that are still waiting, meaning that much of the distribution problem is transferred from the data's source to the peers.

Another alternative, called **multicast,** transfers the distribution problem to the Internet routers. Using multicast, a server transmits a message to multiple clients by means of a single address and relies on the routers in the Internet to recognize the significance of that address and to produce and forward copies of the message to the appropriate destinations. The single address used in multicast is called a group address and is identified by a specific initial bit pattern. The remaining bits are used to identify the broadcasting station, which in multicasting terminology is called the group. When a client wants to receive the messages from a particular station (wants to subscribe to a particular group), it notifies its nearest router of its desire. That router essentially forwards that desire back through the Internet so that other routers know to begin forwarding all future messages with that group address in the direction of the client. In short, when using multicast, the server transmits only one copy of the program regardless of how many clients are listening, and it is the responsibility of the routers to make copies of these messages as needed and route them to their appropriate destinations. Note then that applications relying on multicast require that the functionality of the Internet routers be expanded beyond their original duties. This process is currently underway.

We see then that Internet radio, like VoIP, is growing in popularity while it is searching for its foundations. Exactly what the future holds is not certain. However, as the capabilities of the Internet infrastructure continue to expand, applications of webcasting are certain to develop with it. Indeed, Internet television is on the horizon.

Questions & Exercises

1. What is the purpose of tier-1 and tier-2 ISPs? What is the purpose of access ISPs?
2. What is the DNS?
3. What bit pattern is represented by 3.4.5 in dotted decimal notation? Express the bit pattern 0001001100010000 using dotted decimal notation.
4. In what way is the structure of a mnemonic address of a computer on the Internet (such as r2d2.compsc.nowhereu.edu) similar to a traditional postal address? Does this same structure occur in IP addresses?
5. Name three types of servers found on the Internet and tell what each does.
6. Why is SSH considered superior to telnet?
7. In what way do the P2P and multicast approaches to Internet radio broadcast differ from N-unicast?

3 The World Wide Web

In this section we focus on an Internet application by which multimedia information is disseminated over the Internet. It is based on the concept of **hypertext,** a term that originally referred to text documents that contained links, called **hyperlinks,** to other documents. Today, hypertext has been expanded to encompass images, audio, and video, and because of this expanded scope it is sometimes referred to as **hypermedia.**

The World Wide Web Consortium

The World Wide Web Consortium (W3C) was formed in 1994 to promote the World Wide Web by developing protocol standards (known as W3C standards). W3C is headquartered at CERN, the high-energy particle physics laboratory in Geneva, Switzerland. CERN is where the original HTML markup language was developed as well as the HTTP protocol for transferring HTML documents over the Internet. Today W3C is the source of many standards (including standards for XML and numerous multimedia applications) that lead to compatibility over a wide range of Internet products. You can learn more about W3C via its website at http://www.w3c.org.

When using a GUI, the reader of a hypertext document can follow the hyperlinks associated with it by pointing and clicking with the mouse. For example, suppose the sentence "The orchestra's performance of 'Bolero' by Maurice Ravel was outstanding" appeared in a hypertext document and the name *Maurice Ravel* was linked to another document—perhaps giving information about the composer. A reader could choose to view that associated material by pointing to the name *Maurice Ravel* with the mouse and clicking the mouse button. Moreover, if the proper hyperlinks are installed, the reader might listen to an audio recording of the concert by clicking on the name *Bolero*.

In this manner, a reader of hypertext documents can explore related documents or follow a train of thought from document to document. As portions of various documents are linked to other documents, an intertwined web of related information is formed. When implemented on a computer network, the documents within such a web can reside on different machines, forming a network-wide web. The web that has evolved on the Internet spans the entire globe and is known as the **World Wide Web** (also referred to as **WWW, W3,** or the **Web**). A hypertext document on the World Wide Web is often called a **Web page.** A collection of closely related Web pages is called a **website.**

The World Wide Web had its origins in the work of Tim Berners-Lee who realized the potential of combining the linked-document concept with internet technology and produced the first software for implementing the WWW in December of 1990.

Web Implementation

Software packages that allow users to access hypertext on the Internet fall into one of two categories: packages that play the role of clients, and packages that play the role of servers. A client package resides on the user's computer and is charged with the tasks of obtaining materials requested by the user and presenting these materials to the user in an organized manner. It is the client that provides the user interface that allows a user to browse within the Web. Hence the client is often referred to as a **browser,** or sometimes as a Web browser. The server package (often called a **Web server**) resides on a computer containing hypertext documents to be accessed. Its task is to provide access to the documents under its control as requested by clients. In summary, a user gains access to hypertext documents by means of a browser residing on the user's computer. This browser, playing the role of a client, obtains the documents by soliciting the services of the Web servers scattered throughout the Internet. Hypertext documents are normally transferred between browsers and Web servers using a protocol known as the **Hypertext Transfer Protocol (HTTP).**

In order to locate and retrieve documents on the World Wide Web, each document is given a unique address called a **Uniform Resource Locator (URL).** Each URL contains the information needed by a browser to contact the proper server and request the desired document. Thus to view a Web page, a person first provides his or her browser with the URL of the desired document and then instructs the browser to retrieve and display the document.

A typical URL is presented in Figure 8. It consists of four segments: the protocol to use to communicate with the server controlling access to the document, the mnemonic address of the machine containing the server, the directory path needed for the server to find the directory containing the document, and the name of the document itself. In short, the URL in Figure 8 tells a browser to contact the Web server on the computer known as ssenterprise. aw.com using the protocol HTTP and to retrieve the document named Julius_Caesar. html found within the subdirectory Shakespeare within the directory called authors.

Sometimes a URL might not explicitly contain all the segments shown in Figure 8. For example, if the server does not need to follow a directory path to reach the document, no directory path will appear in the URL. Moreover, sometimes a URL will consist of only a protocol and the mnemonic address of a computer. In these cases, the Web server at that computer will return a predetermined document, typically called a home page, that usually describes the information available at that website. Such shortened URLs provide a simple means of contacting organizations. For example, the URL http://www.aw.com

Figure 8   A typical URL

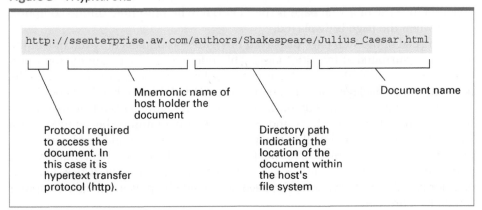

http://ssenterprise.aw.com/authors/Shakespeare/Julius_Caesar.html

Protocol required to access the document. In this case it is hypertext transfer protocol (http).

Mnemonic name of host holder the document

Directory path indicating the location of the document within the host's file system

Document name

will lead to the home page of Addison-Wesley Inc., which contains hyperlinks to numerous other documents relating to the company and its products.

To further simplify locating websites, many browsers assume that the HTTP protocol should be used if no protocol is identified. These browsers correctly retrieve the Addison-Wesley home page when given the "URL" consisting merely of www.aw.com.

HTML

A traditional hypertext document is similar to a text file because its text is encoded character by character using a system such as ASCII or Unicode. The distinction is that a hypertext document also contains special symbols, called **tags,** that describe how the document should appear on a display screen, what multi-media resources (such as images) should accompany the document, and which items within the document are linked to other documents. This system of tags is known as **Hypertext Markup Language (HTML).**

Thus, it is in terms of HTML that an author of a Web page describes the information that a browser needs in order to present the page on the user's screen and to find any related documents referenced by the current page. The process is analogous to adding typesetting directions to a plain typed text (perhaps using a red pen) so that a typesetter will know how the material should appear in its final form. In the case of hypertext, the red markings are replaced by HTML tags, and a browser ultimately plays the role of the typesetter, reading the HTML tags to learn how the text is to be presented on the computer screen.

The HTML encoded version (called the **source** version) of an extremely simple Web page is shown in Figure 9a. Note that the tags are delineated by the symbols < and >. The HTML source document consists of two sections—a head (surrounded by the <head> and </head> tags) and a body (surrounded by the <body> and </body> tags). The distinction between the head and body of a Web page is similar to that of the head and body of an interoffice memo. In both cases, the head contains preliminary information about the document (date, subject, etc. in the case of a memo). The body contains the meat of the document, which in the case of a Web page is the material to be presented on the computer screen when the page is displayed.

The head of the Web page displayed in Figure 9a contains only the title of the document (surrounded by "title" tags). This title is only for documentation purposes; it is not part of the page that is to be displayed on the computer screen. The material that is displayed on the screen is contained in the body of the document.

The first entry in the body of the document in Figure 9a is a level-one heading (surrounded by the <h1> and </h1> tags) containing the text "My Web Page." Being a level-one heading means that the browser should display this text prominently on the screen. The next entry in the body is a paragraph of text (surrounded by the <p> and </p> tags) containing the text "Click here for another page." Figure 9b shows the page as it would be presented on a computer screen by a browser.

Figure 9   A simple Web page

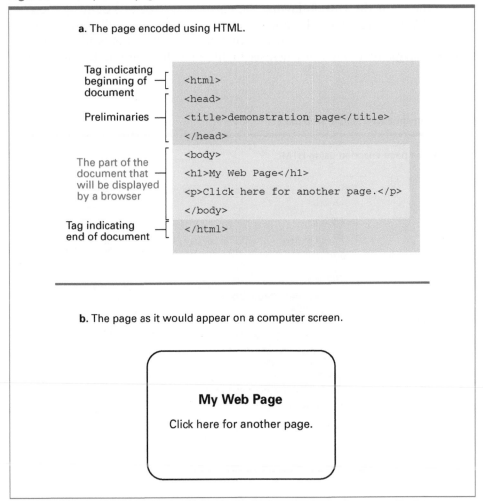

a. The page encoded using HTML.

Tag indicating beginning of document
Preliminaries
The part of the document that will be displayed by a browser
Tag indicating end of document

```
<html>
<head>
<title>demonstration page</title>
</head>
<body>
<h1>My Web Page</h1>
<p>Click here for another page.</p>
</body>
</html>
```

b. The page as it would appear on a computer screen.

My Web Page

Click here for another page.

In its present form, the page in Figure 9 is not fully functional in the sense that nothing will happen when the viewer clicks on the word *here*, even though the page implies that doing so will cause the browser to display another page. To cause the appropriate action, we must link the word *here* to another document.

Let us suppose that, when the word *here* is clicked, we want the browser to retrieve and display the page at the URL http://crafty.com/demo.html. To do so, we must first surround the word *here* in the source version of the page with the tags <a> and </a>, which are called anchor tags. Inside the opening anchor tag we insert the parameter

```
href = http://crafty.com/demo.html
```

(as shown in Figure 10a) indicating that the hypertext reference (`href`) associated with the tag is the URL following the equal sign (`http://crafty.com/demo.html`). Having added the anchor tags, the Web page will now appear on a computer screen as shown in Figure 10b. Note that this is identical to Figure 9b except that the word *here* is highlighted by color indicating that

Figure 10   An enhanced simple Web page

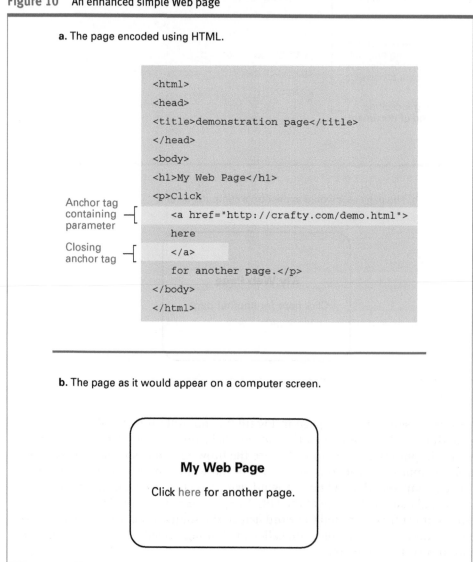

a. The page encoded using HTML.

```
<html>
<head>
<title>demonstration page</title>
</head>
<body>
<h1>My Web Page</h1>
<p>Click
    <a href="http://crafty.com/demo.html">
    here
    </a>
    for another page.</p>
</body>
</html>
```

Anchor tag containing parameter

Closing anchor tag

b. The page as it would appear on a computer screen.

> ## My Web Page
> Click here for another page.

it is a link to another Web document. Clicking on such highlighted terms will cause the browser to retrieve and display the associated Web document. Thus, it is by means of anchor tags that Web documents are linked to each other.

Finally, we should indicate how an image could be included in our simple Web page. For this purpose, let us suppose that a JPEG encoding of the image we want to include is stored as the file named OurPic.jpg in the directory Images at Images.com and is available via the Web server at that location. Under these conditions, we can tell a browser to display the image at the top of the Web page by inserting the image tag <img src = "http://Images.com/Images/OurPic.jpg"> immediately after the <body> tag in the HTML source document. This tells the browser that the image named OurPic.jpg should be displayed at the beginning of the document. (The term src is short for "source," meaning that the information following the equal sign indicates the source of the image to be displayed.) When the browser finds this tag, it will send a message to the HTTP server at Images.com requesting the image called OurPic.jpg and then display the image appropriately.

If we moved the image tag to the end of the document just before the </body> tag, then the browser would display the image at the bottom of the Web page. There are, of course, more sophisticated techniques for positioning an image on a Web page, but these need not concern us now.

XML

HTML is essentially a notational system by which a text document along with the document's appearance can be encoded as a simple text file. In a similar manner we can also encode nontextual material as text files—an example being sheet music. At first glance the pattern of staffs, measure bars, and notes in which music is traditionally represented does not conform to the character-by-character format dictated by text files. However, we can overcome this problem by developing an alternative notation system. More precisely, we could agree to represent the start of a staff by <staff clef = "treble">, the end of the staff by </staff>, a time signature with the form <time> 2/4 </time>, the beginning and ending of a measure by <measure> and </measure>, respectively, a note such as an eighth note on C as <notes> egth C </notes>, and so on. Then the text

```
<staff clef = "treble"> <key>C minor</key>
<time> 2/4 </time>
<measure> <rest> egth </rest> <notes> egth G,
egth G, egth G </notes></measure>
<measure> <notes> hlf E </notes></measure>
</staff>
```

could be used to encode the music shown in Figure 11. Using such notation, sheet music could be encoded, modified, stored, and transferred over the Internet as text files. Moreover, software could be written to present the contents of such files in the form of traditional sheet music or even to play the music on a synthesizer.

Note that our sheet music encoding system encompasses the same style used by HTML. We chose to delineate the tags that identify components by the symbols < and >. We chose to indicate the beginning and end of structures (such as a staff, string of notes, or measure) by tags of the same name—the ending tag being designated by a slash (a <measure> was terminated with the tag </measure>). And we chose to indicate special attributes within tags by expressions such as clef = "treble". This same style could also be used to develop systems for representing other formats such as mathematical expressions and graphics.

The **eXtensible Markup Language (XML)** is a standardized style (similar to that of our music example) for designing notational systems for representing data as text files. (Actually, XML is a simplified derivative of an older set of standards called the Standard Generalized Markup Language, better known as SGML.) Following the XML standard, notational systems called **markup languages** have been developed for representing mathematics, multimedia presentations, and music. In fact, HTML is the markup language based on the XML standard that was developed for representing Web pages. (Actually, the original version of HTML was developed before the XML standard was solidified, and therefore some features of HTML do not strictly conform to XML. That is why you might see references to XHTML, which is the version of HTML that rigorously adheres to XML.)

XML provides a good example of how standards are designed to have wide-ranging applications. Rather than designing individual, unrelated markup languages for encoding various types of documents, the approach represented by XML is to develop a standard for markup languages in general. With this standard, markup languages can be developed for various applications. Markup languages developed in this manner possess a uniformity that allows them to be combined to obtain markup languages for complex applications such as text documents that contain segments of sheet music and mathematical expressions.

Figure 11   The first two bars of Beethoven's Fifth Symphony

Finally we should note that XML allows the development of new markup languages that differ from HTML in that they emphasize semantics rather than appearance. For example, with HTML the ingredients in a recipe can be marked so that they appear as a list in which each ingredient is positioned on a separate line. But if we used semantic-oriented tags, ingredients in a recipe could be marked as ingredients (perhaps using the tags <ingredient> and </ingredient>) rather than merely items in a list. The difference is subtle but important. The semantic approach would allow **search engines** (websites that assist users in locating Web material pertaining to a subject of interest) to identify recipes that contain or do not contain certain ingredients, which would be a substantial improvement over the current state of the art in which only recipes that do or do not contain certain words can be isolated. More precisely, if semantic tags are used, a search engine can identify recipes for lasagna that do not contain spinach, whereas a similar search based merely on word content would skip over a recipe that started with the statement "This lasagna does not contain spinach." In turn, by using an Internet-wide standard for marking documents according to semantics rather than appearance, a World Wide *Semantic* Web, rather than the World Wide *Syntactic* Web we have today, would be created.

Client-Side and Server-Side Activities

Consider now the steps that would be required for a browser to retrieve the simple Web page shown in Figure 10 and display it on the browser's computer screen. First, playing the role of a client, the browser would use the information in a URL (perhaps obtained from the person using the browser) to contact the Web server controlling access to the page and ask that a copy of the page be transferred to it. The server would respond by sending the text document displayed in Figure 10a to the browser. The browser would then interpret the HTML tags in the document to determine how the page should be displayed and present the document on its computer screen accordingly. The user of the browser would see an image like that depicted in Figure 10b. If the user then clicked the mouse over the word *here*, the browser would use the URL in the associated anchor tag to contact the appropriate server to obtain and display another Web page. In summary, the process consists of the browser merely fetching and displaying Web pages as directed by the user.

But what if we wanted a Web page involving animation or one that allows a customer to fill out an order form and submit the order? These needs would require additional activity by either the browser or the Web server. Such activities are called **client-side** activities if they are performed by a client (such as a browser) or **server-side** activities if they are performed by a server (such as a Web server).

As an example, suppose a travel agent wanted customers to be able to identify desired destinations and dates of travel, at which time the agent would present the customer with a customized Web page containing only the information pertinent to that customer's needs. In this case the travel agent's website would first provide a Web page that presented a customer with the available destinations. On the basis of this information, the customer would specify the destinations of interest and desired dates of travel (a client-side activity). This information would then be transferred back to the agent's server where it would be used to construct the appropriate customized Web page (a server-side activity) which would then be sent to the customer's browser.

Another example occurs when using the services of a search engine. In this case a user at the client specifies a topic of interest (a client-side activity) which is then transferred to the search engine where a customized Web page identifying documents of possible interest is constructed (a server-side activity) and sent back to the client. Still another example occurs in the case of **Web mail**—an increasingly popular means by which computer users are able to access their email by means of Web browsers. In this case, the Web server is an intermediary between the client and the client's mail server. Essentially, the Web server builds Web pages that contain information from the mail server (a server-side activity) and sends those pages to the client where the client's browser displays them (a client-side activity). Conversely, the browser allows the user to create messages (a client-side activity) and sends that information to the Web server, which then forwards the messages to the mail server (a server-side activity) for mailing.

There are numerous systems for performing client- and server-side activities, each competing with the others for prominence. An early and still popular means of controlling client-side activities is to include programs written in the language JavaScript (developed by Netscape Communications, Inc.) within the HTML source document for the Web page. From there a browser can extract the programs and follow them as needed. Another approach (developed by Sun Microsystems) is to first transfer a Web page to a browser and then transfer additional program units called applets (written in the language Java) to the browser as requested within the HTML source document. Still another approach is the system Flash (developed by Macromedia) by which extensive multimedia client-side presentations can be implemented.

An early means of controlling server-side activities was to use a set of standards called CGI (Common Gateway Interface) by which clients could request the execution of programs stored at a server. A variation of this approach (developed by Sun Microsystems) is to allow clients to cause program units called servlets to be executed at the server side. A simplified version of the servlet approach is applicable when the requested server-side activity is the construction of a customized Web page, as in our travel agent example. In this case Web page templates called JavaServer Pages (JSP) are stored at the Web server and completed using information received from a client. A similar approach is used by Microsoft, where the templates from which customized Web pages are constructed are called Active Server Pages (ASP). In contrast to these proprietary systems, PHP (originally standing for Personal Home Page but now considered to mean PHP Hypertext Processor) is an open source system for implementing server-side functionality.

Finally, we would be remiss if we did not recognize the security and ethical problems that arise from allowing clients and servers to execute programs on the other's machine. The fact that Web servers routinely transfer programs to clients where they are executed leads to ethical questions on the server side and security questions on the client side. If the client blindly executes any program sent to it by a Web server, it opens itself to malicious activities by the server. Likewise, the fact that clients can cause programs to be executed at the server leads to ethical questions on the client side and security questions on the server side. If the server blindly executes any program sent to it by a client, security breaches and potential damage at the server could result.

Questions & Exercises

1. What is a URL? What is a browser?
2. What is a markup language?
3. What is the difference between HTML and XML?
4. What is the purpose of each of the following HTML tags?

   a. `<html>`

   b. `<head>`

   c. `</body>`

   d. `</a>`

5. To what do the terms *client side* and *server side* refer?

4 Internet Protocols

In this section we investigate how messages are transferred over the Internet. This transfer process requires the cooperation of all the computers in the system, and therefore software for controlling this process resides on every computer in the Internet. We begin by studying the overall structure of this software.

The Layered Approach to Internet Software

A principal task of networking software is to provide the infrastructure required for transferring messages from one machine to another. In the Internet, this message-passing activity is accomplished by means of a hierarchy of software units, which perform tasks analogous to those that would be performed if you were to send a gift in a package from the West Coast of the United States to a friend on the East Coast (Figure 12). You would first wrap the gift as a package and write the appropriate address on the outside of the package. Then, you would take the package to a shipping company such as the U.S. Postal Service. The shipping company might place the package along with others in a large container and deliver the container to an airline, whose services it has contracted. The airline would place the container in an aircraft and transfer it to the destination city, perhaps with intermediate stops along the way. At the final destination, the airline would remove the container from the aircraft and give it to the shipping company's office at the destination. In turn, the shipping company would take your package out of the container and deliver it to the addressee.

In short, the transportation of the gift would be carried out by a three-level hierarchy: (1) the user level (consisting of you and your friend), (2) the shipping company, and (3) the airline. Each level uses the next lower level as an abstract tool. (You are not concerned with the details of the shipping company, and the shipping company is not concerned with the internal operations of the airline.) Each level in the hierarchy has representatives at both the origin and the destination, with the representatives at the destination tending to do the reverse of their counterparts at the origin.

Such is the case with software for controlling communication over the Internet, except that the Internet software has four layers rather than three, each consisting of a collection of software routines rather than people and businesses. The four layers are known as the **application layer,** the **transport layer,** the **network layer,** and the **link layer** (Figure 13). A message typically originates in the application layer. From there it is passed down through the transport and network layers as it is prepared for transmission, and finally it is transmitted by the

Figure 12   Package-shipping example

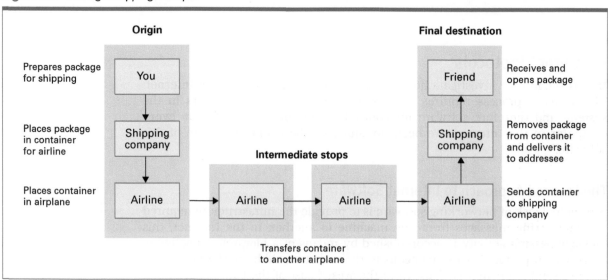

Figure 13   The Internet software layers

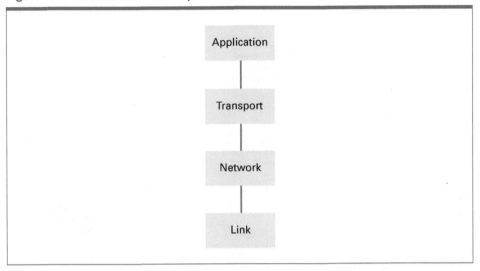

link layer. The message is received by the link layer at the destination and passed back up the hierarchy until it is delivered to the application layer at the message's destination.

Let us investigate this process more thoroughly by tracing a message as it finds its way through the system (Figure 14). We begin our journey with the application layer.

The application layer consists of those software units such as clients and servers that use Internet communication to carry out their tasks. Although the names are similar, this layer is not restricted to software in the application classification but also includes many utility packages. For example, software for transferring files using FTP or for providing remote login capabilities using SSH have become so common that they are normally considered utility software.

The application layer uses the transport layer to send and receive messages over the Internet in much the same way that you would use a shipping company to send and receive packages. Just as it is your responsibility to provide an address compatible with the specifications of the shipping company, it is the application layer's responsibility to provide an address that is compatible with the Internet infrastructure. To fulfill this need, the application layer may use the services of the name servers within the Internet to translate mnemonic addresses used by humans into Internet-compatible IP addresses.

An important task of the transport layer is to accept messages from the application layer and to ensure that the messages are properly formatted for transmission over the Internet. Toward this latter goal, the transport layer divides long messages into small segments, which are transmitted over the Internet as individual units. This division is necessary because a single long message can

Figure 14   Following a message through the Internet

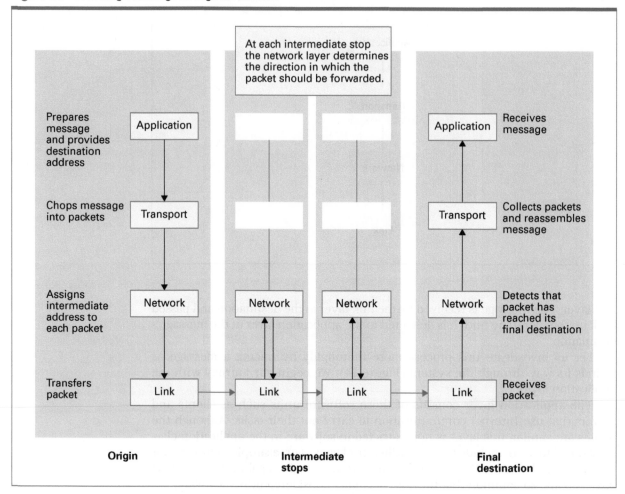

obstruct the flow of other messages at the Internet routers where numerous messages cross paths. Indeed, small segments of messages can interweave at these points, whereas a long message forces others to wait while it passes (much like cars waiting for a long train to pass at a railroad crossing).

The transport layer adds sequence numbers to the small segments it produces so that the segments can be reassembled at the message's destination. Then it hands these segments, known as **packets,** to the network layer. From this point, the packets are treated as individual, unrelated messages until they reach the transport layer at their final destination. It is quite possible for the packets related to a common message to follow different paths through the Internet.

It is the network layer's job to decide which direction a packet should be sent at each step along the packet's path through the Internet. In fact, the combination of the network layer and the link layer below it constitutes the software residing on the Internet routers. The network layer is in charge of maintaining the router's forwarding table and using that table to determine the direction in which to forward packets. The link layer at the router is in charge of receiving and transmitting the packets.

Thus, when the network layer at a packet's origin receives the packet from the transport layer, it uses its forwarding table to determine where the packet should be sent to get it started on its journey. Having determined the proper direction, the network layer hands the packet to the link layer for actual transmission.

The link layer has the responsibility of transferring the packet. Thus the link layer must deal with the communication details particular to the individual network in which the computer resides. For instance, if that network is an Ethernet, the link layer applies CSMA/CD. If the network is a WiFi network, the link layer applies CSMA/CA.

When a packet is transmitted, it is received by the link layer at the other end of the connection. There, the link layer hands the packet up to its network layer where the packet's final destination is compared to the network layer's forwarding table to determine the direction of the packet's next step. With this decision made, the network layer returns the packet to the link layer to be forwarded along its way. In this manner each packet hops from machine to machine on its way to its final destination.

Note that only the link and network layers are involved at the intermediate stops during this journey (see again Figure 14), and thus these are the only layers present on routers, as previously noted. Moreover, to minimize the delay at each of these intermediate "stops," the forwarding role of the network layer within a router is closely integrated with the link layer. In turn, the time required for a modern router to forward a packet is measured in millionths of a second.

At a packet's final destination, it is the network layer that recognizes that the packet's journey is complete. In that case the network layer hands the packet to its transport layer rather than forwarding it. As the transport layer receives packets from the network layer, it extracts the underlying message segments and reconstructs the original message according to the sequence numbers that were provided by the transport layer at the message's origin. Once the message is assembled, the transport layer hands it to the appropriate unit within the application layer—thus completing the message transmission process.

Determining which unit within the application layer should receive an incoming message is an important task of the transport layer. This is handled by assigning unique **port numbers** to the various units and requiring that the appropriate port number be appended to a message's address before starting the message on its journey. Then, once the message is received by the transport layer at the destination, the transport layer merely hands the message to the application layer software at the designated port number.

Users of the Internet rarely need to be concerned with port numbers because the common applications have universally accepted port numbers. For example, if a Web browser is asked to retrieve the document whose URL is http://www.zoo.org/animals/frog.html, the browser assumes that it should contact the HTTP server at www.zoo.org via port number 80. Likewise, when transferring a file, an FTP client assumes that it should communicate with the FTP server through port numbers 20 and 21.

In summary, communication over the Internet involves the interaction of four layers of software. The application layer deals with messages from the application's point of view. The transport layer converts these messages into segments that are compatible with the Internet and reassembles messages that are received before delivering them to the appropriate application. The network layer deals with directing the segments through the Internet. The link layer handles the actual transmission of segments from one machine to another. With all this activity, it is somewhat amazing that the response time of the Internet is measured in milliseconds, so that many transactions appear to take place instantaneously.

The TCP/IP Protocol Suite

The demand for open networks has generated a need for published standards by which manufacturers can supply equipment and software that function properly with products from other vendors. One standard that has resulted is the **Open System Interconnection (OSI)** reference model, produced by the International Organization for Standardization. This standard is based on a seven-level hierarchy as opposed to the four-level hierarchy we have just described. It is an often-quoted model because it carries the authority of an international organization, but it has been slow to replace the four-level point of view, mainly because it was established after the four-level hierarchy had already become the de facto standard for the Internet.

The TCP/IP protocol suite is a collection of protocol standards used by the Internet to implement the four-level communication hierarchy implemented in the Internet. Actually, the **Transmission Control Protocol (TCP)** and the **Internet Protocol (IP)** are the names of only two of the protocols in this vast collection—so the fact that the entire collection is referred to as the TCP/IP protocol suite is rather misleading. More precisely, TCP defines a version of the transport layer. We say a *version* because the TCP/IP protocol suite provides for more than one way of implementing the transport layer; one of the other options is defined by the **User Datagram Protocol (UDP).** This diversity is analogous to the fact that when shipping a package, you have a choice of different shipping companies, each of which offers the same basic service but with its own unique characteristics. Thus, depending on the particular quality of service required, a unit within the application layer might choose to send data via a TCP or UDP version of the transport layer (Figure 15).

There are several differences between TCP and UDP. One is that before sending a message as requested by the application layer, a transport layer based on TCP sends its own message to the transport layer at the destination telling it that a message is about to be sent. It then waits for this message to be acknowledged before starting to send the application layer's message. In this manner, a TCP transport layer is said to establish a connection before sending a message. A transport layer based on UDP does not establish such a connection prior to sending a message. It merely sends the message to the address it was given and forgets

Figure 15   Choosing between TCP and UDP

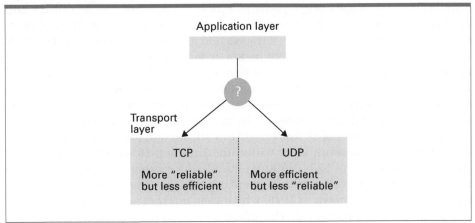

about it. For all it knows, the destination computer might not even be operational. For this reason, UDP is called a connectionless protocol.

Another difference between TCP and UDP is that TCP transport layers at the origin and destination work together by means of acknowledgments and packet retransmissions to assure that all segments of a message are successfully transferred to the destination. For this reason TCP is called a reliable protocol, whereas UDP, which does not offer such retransmission services, is said to be an unreliable protocol.

Still another distinction between TCP and UDP is that TCP provides for both **flow control,** meaning that a TCP transport layer at a message's origin can reduce the rate at which it transmits segments to keep from overwhelming its counterpart at the destination, as well as **congestion control,** meaning that a TCP transport layer at a message's origin can adjust its transmission rate to alleviate congestion between it and the message's destination.

All this does not mean that UDP is a poor choice. After all, a transport layer based on UDP is more streamlined than a layer based on TCP, and thus if an application is prepared to handle the potential consequences of UDP, that option might be the better choice. For example, the efficiency of UDP makes it the protocol of choice for DNS lookups and VoIP. However, because email is less time sensitive, mail servers use TCP to transfer email.

IP is the Internet's standard for implementing the tasks assigned to the network layer. We have already observed that this task consists of **forwarding,** which involves relaying packets through the Internet, and **routing,** which involves updating the layer's forwarding table to reflect changing conditions. For instance, a router may malfunction, meaning that traffic should no longer be forwarded in its direction, or a section of the Internet may become congested, meaning that traffic should be routed around the blockage. Much of the IP standard associated with routing deals with the protocols used for communication among neighboring network layers as they interchange routing information.

An interesting feature associated with forwarding is that each time an IP network layer at a message's origin prepares a packet, it appends a value called a **hop count,** or time to live, to that packet. This value is a limit to the number of times the packet should be forwarded as it tries to find its way through the Internet. Each time an IP network layer forwards a packet, it decrements that packet's hop count by one. With this information, the network layer can protect the Internet from packets circling endlessly within the system. Although the Internet continues to grow on a daily basis, an initial hop count of 64 remains more than sufficient to allow a packet to find its way through the maze of routers within today's ISPs.

For years a version of IP known as IPv4 (IP version four) has been used for implementing the network layer within the Internet. However, the Internet is rapidly outgrowing the 32-bit internet addressing system dictated by IPv4. To solve this problem as well as to implement other improvements such as multicast, a new version of IP known as IPv6, which uses internet addresses consisting of 128 bits, has been established. The process of converting from IPv4 to IPv6 is currently underway. (This is the conversion that was alluded to in our introduction of Internet addresses in Section 2.) and it is expected that the use of 32-bit addresses within the Internet will be extinct by 2025.

Questions & Exercises

1. What layers of the Internet software hierarchy are used at a router?
2. What are some differences between a transport layer based on the TCP protocol and another based on the UDP protocol?
3. How does the Internet software ensure that messages are not relayed within the Internet forever?
4. What keeps a computer on the Internet from recording copies of all the messages passing through it?

5 Security

When a computer is connected to a network, it becomes subject to unauthorized access and vandalism. In this section we address topics associated with these problems.

Forms of Attack

There are numerous ways that a computer system and its contents can be attacked via network connections. Many of these incorporate the use of malicious software (collectively called **malware**). Such software might be transferred to, and executed on, the computer itself, or it might attack the computer from a distance. Examples

The Computer Emergency Response Team

In November 1988 a worm released into the Internet caused significant disruption of service. Consequently, the U.S. Defense Advanced Research Projects Agency (DARPA—pronounced "DAR–pa") formed the Computer Emergency Response Team (CERT—pronounced "SERT"), located at the CERT Coordination Center at Carnegie-Mellon University. The CERT is the Internet's security "watchdog." Among its duties are the investigation of security problems, the issuance of security alerts, and the implementation of public awareness campaigns to improve Internet security. The CERT Coordination Center maintains a Web site at http://www.cert.org where it posts notices of its activities.

of software that is transferred to, and executed on, the computer under attack include viruses, worms, Trojan horses, and spyware, whose names reflect the primary characteristic of the software.

A **virus** is software that infects a computer by inserting itself into programs that already reside in the machine. Then, when the "host" program is executed, the virus is also executed. When executed, many viruses do little more than try to transfer themselves to other programs within the computer. Some viruses, however, perform devastating actions such as degrading portions of the operating system, erasing large blocks of mass storage, or otherwise corrupting data and other programs.

A **worm** is an autonomous program that transfers itself through a network, taking up residence in computers and forwarding copies of itself to other computers. As in the case of a virus, a worm can be designed merely to replicate itself or to perform more extreme vandalism. A characteristic consequence of a worm is an explosion of the worm's replicated copies that degrades the performance of legitimate applications and can ultimately overload an entire network or internet.

A **Trojan horse** is a program that enters a computer system disguised as a desirable program, such as a game or useful utility package, that is willingly imported by the victim. Once in the computer, however, the Trojan horse performs additional activities that might have harmful effects. Sometimes these additional activities start immediately. In other instances, the Trojan horse might lie dormant until triggered by a specific event such as the occurrence of a preselected date. Trojan horses often arrive in the form of attachments to enticing email messages. When the attachment is opened (that is, when the recipient asks to view the attachment), the misdeeds of the Trogan horse are activated. Thus, email attachments from unknown sources should never be opened.

Another form of malicious software is **spyware** (sometimes called **sniffing** software), which is software that collects information about activities at the computer on which it resides and reports that information back to the instigator of the attack. Some companies use spyware as a means of building customer profiles, and in this context, it has questionable ethical merit. In other cases, spyware is used for blatantly malicious purposes such as recording the symbol sequences typed at the computer's keyboard in search of passwords or credit card numbers.

As opposed to obtaining information secretly by sniffing via spyware, **phishing** is a technique of obtaining information explicitly by simply asking for it. The term *phishing* is a play on the word *fishing* because the process involved is to cast numerous "lines" in hopes that someone will "take the bait." Phishing is often carried out via email, and in this form, it is little more than an old telephone con. The perpetrator sends email messages posing as a financial institution, a government bureau, or perhaps a law enforcement agency. The email asks the potential victim for information that is supposedly needed for legitimate purposes. However, the information obtained is used by the perpetrator for hostile purposes.

In contrast to suffering from such internal infections as viruses and spyware, a computer in a network can also be attacked by software being executed on other computers in the system. An example is a **denial of service (DoS)** attack, which is the process of overloading a computer with messages. Denial of service attacks have been launched against large commercial Web servers on the Internet to disrupt the company's business and in some cases have brought the company's commercial activity to a halt.

A denial of service attack requires the generation of a large number of messages over a brief period of time. To accomplish this, an attacker usually plants software on numerous unsuspecting computers that will generate messages when a signal is given. Then, when the signal is given, all of these computers swamp the target with messages. Inherent, then, in denial of service attacks is the availability of unsuspecting computers to use as accomplices. This is why all PC users are discouraged from leaving their computers connected to the Internet when not in use. It has been estimated that once a PC is connected to the Internet, at least one intruder will attempt to exploit its existence within 20 minutes. In turn, an unprotected PC represents a significant threat to the integrity of the Internet.

Another problem associated with an abundance of unwanted messages is the proliferation of unwanted junk email, called **spam.** However, unlike a denial of service attack, the volume of spam is rarely sufficient to overwhelm the computer system. Instead, the effect of spam is to overwhelm the person receiving the spam. This problem is compounded by the fact that, as we have already seen, spam is a widely adopted medium for phishing and instigating Trojan horses that might spread viruses and other detrimental software.

Protection and Cures

The old adage "an ounce of prevention is worth a pound of cure" is certainly true in the context of controlling vandalism over network connections. A primary prevention technique is to filter traffic passing through a point in the network, usually with a program called a **firewall.** For instance, a firewall might be installed at the gateway of an organization's intranet to filter messages passing in and out of the region. Such firewalls might be designed to block outgoing messages with certain destination addresses or to block incoming messages from origins that are known to be sources of trouble. This latter function is a tool for terminating a denial of service attack because it provides a means of blocking traffic from the attacking computers. Another common role of a firewall at a gateway is to block all incoming messages that have origin addresses within the region accessed through the gateway because such a message would indicate that an outsider is pretending to be a member of the inside region. Masquerading as a party other than one's self is known as **spoofing.**

Firewalls are also used to protect individual computers rather than entire networks or domains. For example, if a computer is not being used as a Web server, a name server, or an email server, then a firewall should be installed at that computer to block all incoming traffic addressed to such applications. Indeed, one way an intruder might gain entry to a computer is by establishing contact through a "hole" left by a nonexistent server. In particular, one method for retrieving information gathered by spyware is to establish a clandestine server on the infected computer by which malicious clients can retrieve the spyware's findings. A properly installed firewall could block the messages from these malicious clients.

Some variations of firewalls are designed for specific purposes—an example being **spam filters,** which are firewalls designed to block unwanted email. Many spam filters use rather sophisticated techniques to distinguish between desirable email and spam. Some learn to make this distinction via a training process in which the user identifies items of spam until the filter acquires enough examples to make decisions on its own. These filters are examples of how a variety of subject areas (probability theory, artificial intelligence, etc.) can jointly contribute to developments in other fields.

Another preventative tool that has filtering connotations is the proxy server. A **proxy server** is a software unit that acts as an intermediary between a client and a server with the goal of shielding the client from adverse actions of the server. Without a proxy server, a client communicates directly with a server, meaning that the server has an opportunity to learn a certain amount about the client. Over time, as many clients within an organization's intranet deal with a distant server, that server can collect a multitude of information about the intranet's internal structure—information that can later be used to for malicious activity. To counter this, an organization can establish a proxy server for a particular kind of service (FTP, HTTP, telnet, etc.). Then, each time a client within the intranet tries to contact a server of that type, the client is actually placed in contact with the proxy server. In turn, the proxy server, playing the role of a client, contacts the actual server. From then on the proxy server plays the role of an intermediary between the actual client and the actual server by relaying messages back and forth. The first advantage of this arrangement is that the actual server has no way of knowing that the proxy server is not the true client, and in fact, it is never aware of the actual client's existence. In turn, the actual server has no way of learning about the intranet's internal features. The second advantage is that the proxy server is in position to filter all the messages sent from the server to the client. For example, an FTP proxy server could check all incoming files for the presence of known viruses and block all infected files.

Still another tool for preventing problems in a network environment is auditing software that is similar to the auditing software we learned about in our discussion on operating system security. Using network auditing software, a system administrator can detect a sudden increase in message traffic at various locations within the administrator's realm, monitor the activities of the system's firewalls, and analyze the pattern of requests being made by the individual computers in order to detect irregularities. In effect, auditing software is an administrator's primary tool for identifying problems before they grow out of control.

Another means of defense against invasions via network connections is software called **antivirus software,** which is used to detect and remove the presence of known viruses and other infections. (Actually, antivirus software represents a broad class of software products, each designed to detect and remove a specific type of infection. For example, whereas many products specialize in virus control, others specialize in spyware protection.) It is important for users of these packages to understand that, just as in the case of biological systems, new computer infections are constantly coming on the scene that require updated vaccines. Thus, antivirus software must be routinely maintained by downloading updates from the software's vendor. Even this, however, does not guarantee the safety of a computer. After all, a new virus must first infect some computers before it is discovered and a vaccine is produced. Thus, a wise computer user never opens email attachments from unfamiliar sources, does not download software without first confirming its reliability, does not respond to pop-up adds, and does not leave a PC connected to the Internet when such connection is not necessary.

Encryption

In some cases the purpose of network vandalism is to disrupt the system (as in denial of service attacks), but in other cases the ultimate goal is to gain access to information. The traditional means of protecting information is to control its access through the use of passwords. However, passwords can be compromised and are of little value when data are transferred over networks and internets where messages are relayed by unknown entities. In these cases encryption can be used so that even if the data fall into unscrupulous hands, the encoded information will remain confidential. Today, many traditional Internet applications have been altered to incorporate encryption techniques, producing what are called "secure versions" of the applications. Examples include **FTPS,** which is a secure version of FTP, and SSH, which we introduced in Section 2 as a secure replacement for telnet.

Still another example is the secure version of HTTP, known as **HTTPS,** which is used by most financial institutions to provide customers with secure Internet access to their accounts. The backbone of HTTPS is the protocol system known as **Secure Sockets Layer (SSL),** which was originally developed by Netscape to provide secure communication links between Web clients and servers. Most browsers indicate the use of SSL by displaying a tiny padlock icon on the computer screen. (Some use the presence or absence of the icon to indicate whether SSL is being used; others display the padlock in either the locked or unlocked position.)

One of the more fascinating topics in the field of encryption is **public-key encryption,** which involves techniques by which encryption systems are designed so that having knowledge about how messages are encrypted does not allow one to decrypt messages. This characteristic is somewhat counterintuitive. After all, intuition would suggest that if a person knows how messages are encrypted, then that person should be able to reverse the encryption process and thus decrypt messages. But public-key encryption systems defy this intuitive logic.

A public-key encryption system involves the use of two values called **keys.** One key, known as the **public key,** is used to encrypt messages; the other key, known as the **private key,** is required to decrypt messages. To use the system, the public key is first distributed to those who might need to send messages to a particular destination. The private key is held in confidence at this destination. Then, the originator of a message can encrypt the message using the public key and send the message to its destination with assurance that its contents are safe, even if it is handled by intermediaries who also know the public key. Indeed, the only party that can decrypt the message is the party at the message's destination who holds the private key. Thus if Bob creates a public-key encryption system and gives both Alice and Carol the public key, then both Alice and Carol can encrypt messages to Bob, but they cannot spy on the other's communication. Indeed, if Carol intercepts a message from Alice, she cannot decrypt it even though she knows how Alice encrypted it (Figure 16).

Figure 16   Public key encryption

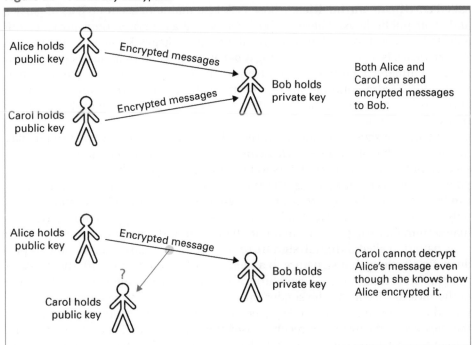

Pretty Good Privacy

Perhaps the most popular public-key encryption systems used within the Internet are based on the RSA algorithm, named after its inventors Ron Rivet, Adi Shamir, and Len Adleman. RSA techniques (among others) are used in a collection of software packages produced by PGP Corporation. PGP stands for Pretty Good Privacy. These packages are compatible with most e-mail software used on PCs and available without charge for personal, noncommercial use at http://www.pgp.com. Using PGP software, an individual can generate public and private keys, encrypt messages with public keys, and decrypt messages with private keys.

There are, of course, subtle problems lurking within public-key systems. One is to ensure that the public key being used is, in fact, the proper key for the destination party. For example, if you are communicating with your bank, you want to be sure that the public key you are using for encryption is the one for the bank and not an impostor. If an impostor presents itself as the bank (an example of spoofing) and gives you its public key, the messages you encrypt and send to the "bank" would be meaningful to the impostor and not your bank. Thus, the task of associating public keys with correct parties is significant.

One approach to resolving this problem is to establish trusted Internet sites, called **certificate authorities,** whose task is to maintain accurate lists of parties and their public keys. These authorities, acting as servers, then provide reliable public-key information to their clients in packages known as certificates. A **certificate** is a package containing a party's name and that party's public key. Many commercial certificate authorities are now available on the Internet, although it is also common for organizations to maintain their own certificate authorities in order to maintain tighter control over the security of the organization's communication.

Finally, we should comment on the role public-key encryption systems play in solving problems of **authentication**—making sure that the author of a message is, in fact, the party it claims to be. The critical point here is that, in some public-key encryption systems, the roles of the encryption and decryption keys can be reversed. That is, text can be encrypted with the private key, and because only one party has access to that key, any text that is so encrypted must have originated from that party. In this manner, the holder of the private key can produce a bit pattern, called a **digital signature,** that only that party knows how to produce. By attaching that signature to a message, the sender can mark the message as being authentic. A digital signature can be as simple as the encrypted version of the message itself. All the sender must do is encrypt the message being transmitted using his or her private key (the key typically used for decrypting). When the message is received, the receiver uses the sender's public key to decrypt the signature. The message that is revealed is guaranteed to be authentic because only the holder of the private key could have produced the encrypted version.

Legal Approaches to Network Security

Another way of enhancing the security of computer networking systems is to apply legal remedies. There are, however, two obstacles to this approach. The first is that making an action illegal does not preclude the action. All it does is provide a legal recourse. The second is that the international nature of networking means that obtaining recourse is often very difficult. What is illegal in one country might be legal in another. Ultimately, enhancing network security by legal means is an international project, and thus must be handled by international legal bodies—a potential player would be the International Court of Justice in The Hague.

Having made these disclaimers, we must admit that, although less than perfect, legal forces still have a tremendous influence, and thus it behooves us to explore some of the legal steps that are being taken to resolve conflicts in the networking arena. For this purpose, we use examples from the federal laws of the United States. Similar examples could be drawn from other government bodies such as the European Union.

We begin with the proliferation of malware. In the United States this problem is addressed by the Computer Fraud and Abuse Act, which was first passed in 1984, although it has been amended several times. It is under this act that most cases involving the introduction of worms and viruses have been prosecuted. In short, the act requires proof that the defendant knowingly caused the transmission of a program or data that intentionally caused damage.

The Computer Fraud and Abuse Act also covers cases involving the theft of information. In particular, the act outlaws obtaining anything of value via the unauthorized access of a computer. Courts have tended to assign a broad interpretation to the phrase "anything of value," and thus the Computer Fraud and Abuse Act has been applied to more than the theft of information. For instance, courts have ruled that the mere use of a computer might constitute "anything of value."

The right of privacy is another, and perhaps the most controversial, networking issue facing the legal community. Questions involving an employer's right to monitor the communications of employees and the extent to which an Internet service provider is authorized to access the information being communicated by its clients have been given considerable thought. In the United States, many of these questions are addressed by the Electronic Communication Privacy Act (ECPA) of 1986, which has its origins in legislation to control wiretapping. Although the act is lengthy, its intent is captured in a few short excerpts. In particular, it states that

> Except as otherwise specifically provided in this chapter any person who intentionally intercepts, endeavors to intercept, or procures any other person to intercept or endeavor to intercept, any wire, oral, or electronic communication . . . shall be punished as provided in subsection (4) or shall be subject to suit as provided in subsection (5).

and

> . . . any person or entity providing an electronic communication service to the public shall not intentionally divulge the contents of any communication . . . on that service to any person or entity other than an addressee or intended recipient of such communication or an agent of such addressee or intended recipient.

In brief, the ECPA confirms an individual's right to private communication—it is illegal for an Internet service provider to release information about the communication of its clients, and it is illegal for unauthorized personnel to eavesdrop on another's communication. But the ECPA leaves room for debate. For example, the question regarding the rights of an employer to monitor the communication of employees becomes a question of authorization, which courts have tended to grant to employers when the communication is carried out using the employer's equipment.

Moreover, the act goes on to give some government agencies authority to monitor electronic communications under certain restrictions. These provisions have been the source of much debate. For example, in 2000 the FBI revealed the existence of its system, called Carnivore, that reports on the communication of all subscribers of an Internet service provider rather than just a court-designated target, and in 2001 in response to the terrorist attack on the World Trade Center, congress passed the controversial USA PATRIOT (Uniting and Strengthening America by Providing Appropriate Tools Required to Intercept and Obstruct Terrorism) Act that modified the restrictions under which government agencies must operate.

In addition to the legal and ethical controversies raised by these developments, providing monitoring rights raises some technical problems that are more pertinent to our study. One is that to provide these capabilities, a communication system must be constructed and programmed so that communications can be monitored. To establish such capabilities was the goal of the Communications Assistance for Law Enforcement Act (CALEA). It requires telecommunication carriers to modify their equipment to accommodate law enforcement taps—a requirement that has been complex and expensive to meet.

Another controversial issue involves the clash between the government's right to monitor communications and the public's right to use encryption. If the messages being monitored are well encrypted, then tapping the communication is of limited value to law enforcement agencies. Governments in the United States, Canada, and Europe are considering systems that would require the registration of ciphering keys, but such demands are being fought by corporations. After all, due to corporate espionage it is understandable that requiring the registration of ciphering keys would make many law-abiding corporations, as well as citizens, uncomfortable. How secure can the registration system be?

Finally, as a means of recognizing the scope of legal issues surrounding the Internet, we cite the Anticybersquatting Consumer Protection Act of 1999 that is designed to protect organizations from impostors who might otherwise establish look-a-like domain names (a practice known as cybersquatting). The act prohibits the use of domain names that are identical or confusingly similar to another's trademark or "common law trademark." One effect is that although the act does not outlaw domain name speculation (the process of registering potentially desirable domain names and later selling the rights to that name), it limits the practice to generic domain names. Thus, a domain name speculator might legally register a generic name such as GreatUsedCars.com but might not be able to claim rights to the name BigAlUsedCars.com if Big Al is already in the used car business. Such distinctions are often the subject of debate in lawsuits based on the Anticybersquatting Consumer Protection Act.

Questions & Exercises

1. What are two common ways that malware gains access to a computer system?
2. What distinction is there between the types of firewalls that can be placed at a domain's gateway as opposed to an individual host within the domain?
3. Technically, the term *data* refers to representations of information, whereas *information* refers to the underlying meaning. Does the use of passwords protect data or information? Does the use of encryption protect data or information?
4. What advantage does public-key encryption have over more traditional encryption techniques?
5. What problems are associated with legal attempts to protect against network security problems?

Chapter Review Problems

(Asterisked problems are associated with optional sections.)

1. What is a protocol? Identify three protocols introduced in this chapter and describe the purpose of each.
2. Describe the client/server model.
3. Describe the peer-to-peer model.
4. Identify two ways of classifying computer networks.
5. What is the difference between an open network and a closed network?
6. Why is the CSMA/CD protocol not applicable in a wireless network?
7. Describe the steps followed by a machine that wants to transmit a message in a network using the CSMA/CD protocol.
8. What is the hidden terminal problem? Describe a technique for solving it.
9. How does a hub differ from a repeater?
10. How does a router differ from such devices as repeaters, bridges, and switches?
11. What is the distinction between a network and an internet?

12. Identify two protocols for controlling the right to transmit a message in a network.

13. Using 32-bit Internet addresses was originally thought to provide ample room for expansion, but that conjecture is not proving to be accurate. IPv6 uses 128-bit addressing. Will that prove to be adequate? Justify your answer. (For example, you might compare the number of possible addresses to the population of the world.)

14. Encode each of the following bit patterns using dotted decimal notation.
    a. 000000010000001000000011
    b. 1000000000000000
    c. 0001100000001100

15. What bit pattern is represented by each of the following dotted decimal patterns?
    a. 0.0
    b. 25.18.1
    c. 5.12.13.10

16. Suppose the address of an end system on the Internet is quoted as 134.48.4.123. What is the 32-bit address in hexadecimal notation?

17. What is a DNS lookup?

18. If a computer's mnemonic Internet address is batman.batcave.metropolis.gov what might you conjecture about the structure of the domain containing the machine?

19. Explain the components of the email address kermit@animals.com

20. In the context of FTP, what is the distinction between a "text file" and a "binary file"?

21. What is the role of a mail server?

22. What is the distinction between N-unicast and multicast?

23. Define each of the following:
    a. Name server
    b. Access ISP
    c. Router
    d. End system

24. Define each of the following:
    a. Hypertext
    b. HTML
    c. Browser

25. Many "lay users" of the Internet interchange the terms *Internet* and *World Wide Web*. To what do each of the terms correctly refer?

26. When viewing a simple Web document, ask your browser to display the source version of the document. Then identify the basic structure of the document. In particular, identify the head and the body of the document and list some of the statements you find in each.

27. List five HTML tags and describe their meaning.

28. Modify the HTML document below so that the word "Rover" is linked to the document whose URL is http://animals.org/pets/dogs.html.
```
<html>
<head>
<title>Example</title>
</head>
<body>
<h1>My Pet Dog</h1>
<p>My dog's name is Rover.</p>
</body>
</html>
```

29. Draw a sketch showing how the following HTML document would appear when displayed on a computer screen.
```
<html>
<head>
<title>Example</title>
</head>
<body>
<h1>My Pet Dog</h1>
<img src = "Rover.jpg">
</body>
</html>
```

30. Using the informal XML style presented in the text, design a markup language for representing simple algebraic expressions as text files.

31. Using the informal XML style presented in the text, design a set of tags that a word processor might use for marking the underlying text. For example, how would a word processor indicate what text should be bold, italic, underlined, and so on?

32. Using the informal XML style presented in the text, design a set of tags that could be used to mark motion picture reviews according to the way the text items should appear on a printed page. Then design a set of tags that could be used to mark the reviews according to the meaning of the items in the text.

33. Using the informal XML style presented in the text, design a set of tags that could be used to mark articles about sporting events according to the way the text items should appear on a printed page. Then design a set of tags that could be used to mark the articles according to the meaning of the items in the text.

34. Identify the components of the following URL and describe the meaning of each.
`http://lifeforms.com/animals/moviestars/kermit.html`

35. Identify the components of each of the following abbreviated URLs.
 a. `http://www.farmtools.org/windmills.html`
 b. `http://castles.org/`
 c. `www.coolstuff.com`

36. How would the action of a browser differ if you asked it to "find the document" at the URL `http://stargazer.universe.org` as opposed to `https://stargazer.universe.org`?

37. Give two examples of client-side activities on the Web. Give two examples of server-side activities on the Web.

*38. What is the OSI reference model?

*39. In a network based on the bus topology, the bus is a nonshareable resource for which the machines must compete in order to transmit messages. How is deadlock controlled in this context?

*40. List the four layers in the Internet software hierarchy and identify a task performed by each layer.

*41. Why does the transport layer chop large messages into small packets?

*42. When an application asks the transport layer to use TCP to transmit a message, what additional messages will be sent by the transport layer in order to fulfill the application layer's request?

*43. In what way could TCP be considered a better protocol for implementing the transport layer than UDP? In what way could UDP be considered better than TCP?

*44. What does it mean to say that UDP is a connectionless protocol?

*45. At what layer in the TCP/IP protocol hierarchy could a firewall be placed to filter incoming traffic by means of
 a. message content
 b. source address
 c. type of application

46. Suppose you wanted to establish a firewall to filter out email messages containing certain terms and phrases. Would this firewall be placed at your domain's gateway or at the domain's mail server? Explain your answer.

47. What is a proxy server and what are its benefits?

48. Summarize the principles of public-key encryption.

49. In what way is an unprotected idle PC a danger to the Internet?

50. In what sense does the global nature of the Internet limit legal solutions to Internet problems?

Social Issues

The following questions are intended as a guide to the ethical/social/legal issues associated with the field of computing. The goal is not merely to answer these questions. You should also consider why you answered as you did and whether your justifications are consistent from one question to the next.

1. The ability to connect computers via networks has popularized the concept of working at home. What are some pros and cons of this movement? Will it affect the consumption of natural resources? Will it strengthen families? Will it reduce "office politics"? Will those who work at home have the same career advancement opportunities as those who work on site? Will community ties be weakened? Will reduced personal contact with peers have a positive or negative effect?

2. Ordering merchandise over the Internet is becoming an alternative to "hands on" shopping. What effect will such a shift in shopping habits have on communities? What about shopping malls? What about small shops, such as bookstores and clothing stores, in which you like to browse without buying? To what extent is buying at the lowest possible price good or bad? Is there any moral obligation to pay more for an item in order to support a local business? Is it ethical to compare products at a local store and then order your selection at a lower price via the Internet? What are the long-term consequences of such behavior?

3. To what extent should a government control its citizens' access to the Internet (or any international network)? What about issues that involve national security? What are some security issues that might occur?

4. Electronic bulletin boards allow users of networks to post messages (often anonymously) and read messages posted by others. Should the manager of such a bulletin board be held responsible for its contents? Should a telephone company be held responsible for the contents of telephone conversations? Should the manager of a grocery store be held responsible for the contents of a community bulletin board located in the store?

5. Should the use of the Internet be monitored? Should it be regulated? If so, by whom and to what extent?

6. How much time do you spend using the Internet? Is that time well spent? Has Internet access altered your social activities? Do you find it easier to talk to people via the Internet than in person?

7. When you buy a software package for a personal computer, the developer usually asks you to register with the developer so that you can be notified of future upgrades. This registration process is increasingly being handled via the Internet. You are usually asked to give such things as your name, address, and perhaps how you learned of the product, and then the developer's software automatically transfers this data to the developer. What ethical issues would be raised if the developer designed the registration software so that it

sent additional information to the developer during the registration process? For example, the software might scan the contents of your system and report the other software packages found.

8. When you visit a website, that site has the capability of recording data, called cookies, on your computer indicating that you have visited that site. These cookies can then be used to identify return visitors and to record their previous activities so that future visits to the site can be handled more efficiently. The cookies on your computer also provide a record of the sites you have visited. Should a website have the capability to record cookies on your computer? Should a website be allowed to record cookies on your computer without your knowledge? What are possible benefits of cookies? What problems could arise from the use of cookies?

9. If corporations are required to register their encryption keys with a government agency, will they be safe?

10. In general, etiquette tells us to avoid calling a friend at his or her place of work for personal or social matters such as making arrangements for a weekend outing. Likewise, most of us would hesitate to call a customer at his or her home to describe a new product. In a similar manner, we mail wedding invitations to the guests' residences, whereas we mail announcements of business conferences to the attendees' work addresses. Is it proper to send personal email to a friend via the mail server at the friend's place of employment?

11. Suppose a PC owner leaves the PC connected to the Internet where it ultimately is used by another party to implement a denial of service attack. To what extent should the PC owner be liable? Does your answer depend on whether the owner installed proper firewalls?

12. Is it ethical for companies that produce candy or toys to provide games on their company websites that entertain children while promoting the company's products? What if the game is designed to collect information from the children? What are the boundaries between entertaining, advertising, and exploitation?

Additional Reading

Antoniou, G. and F. van Harmelem. *A Semantic Web Primer*. Cambridge, MA: MIT Press, 2004.

Bishop, M. *Introduction to Computer Security*. Boston, MA: Addison-Wesley, 2005.

Comer, D. E. and R. Droms. *Computer Networks and Internets,* 4th ed. Upper Saddle River, NJ: Prentice-Hall, 2004.

Comer, D. E. *Internetworking with TCP/IP,* Vol. 1, 5th ed. Upper Saddle River, NJ: Prentice-Hall, 2006.

Goldfarb, C. F. and P. Prescod. *The XML Handbook,* 5th ed. Upper Saddle River, NJ: Prentice-Hall, 2004.

Halsal, F. *Computer Networking and the Internet,* Boston, MA: Addison-Wesley, 2005.

Harrington, J. L. *Network Security: A Practical Appoach.* San Francisco: Morgan Kaufmann, 2005.

Kurose, J. F. and K. W. Ross. *Computer Networking: A Top Down Approach Featuring the Internet,* 4th ed. Boston, MA: Addison-Wesley, 2008.

Peterson, L. L. and B. S. Davie. *Computer Networks: A Systems Approach,* 3rd ed. San Francisco: Morgan Kaufmann, 2003.

Rosenoer, J. *CyberLaw, The Law of the Internet.* New York: Springer, 1997.

Spinello, R. A. and H. T. Tavani. *Readings in CyberEthics.* Sudbury, MA: Jones and Bartlett, 2001.

Stallings, W. *Cryptography and Network Security,* 4th ed. Upper Saddle River, NJ: Prentice-Hall, 2006.

Stevens, W. R. *TCP/IP Illustrated,* Vol. 1. Boston, MA: Addison-Wesley, 1994.

Answers to Questions & Exercises

Section 1

1. An open network is one whose specifications and protocols are public, allowing different vendors to produce compatible products.
2. Both connect two buses to form a larger bus network. However, a repeater forwards all messages whereas a bridge forwards only those messages destined for the other side of the bridge.
3. A router is a device that directs messages between networks in an internet.
4. How about a mail order business and its clients, a bank teller and the bank's customers, or a pharmacist and his or her customers?
5. There are numerous protocols involved in traffic flow, verbal telephone communication, and etiquette.

Section 2

1. Tier-1 and tier-2 ISPs provide the Internet's communication "core," whereas access ISPs provide access to that core to their customers.
2. The DNS (Domain Name System) is the Internet-wide collection of name servers that allow translation from mnemonic addresses to IP addresses (and in the other direction as well).

3. The expression 3.4.5 represents the three-byte pattern 000000110000010000000101. The bit pattern 0001001100010000 would be represented as 19.16 in dotted decimal notation.

4. There could be several answers to this. One is that both progress from the specific to the general. Internet addresses in mnemonic form begin with the name of a particular machine and progress to the name of the TLD. Postal addresses begin with the name of an individual and progress to increasingly larger regions such as city, state, and country. This order is reversed in IP addresses, which start with the bit pattern identifying the domain.

5. Name servers help translate mnemonic addresses into IP addresses. Mail servers send, receive, and store e-mail messages. FTP servers provide file transfer service.

6. SSH provides encryption and authentication.

7. They relieve the initial server from the burden of sending individual messages to each client. The P2P approach shifts this burden to the clients (peers) themselves, whereas multicast shifts this burden to the Internet routers.

Section 3

1. A URL is essentially the address of a document in the World Wide Web. A browser is a program that assists a user in accessing hypertext.

2. A markup language is a system for inserting explanatory information in a document.

3. HTML is a particular markup language. XML is a standard for producing markup languages.

4. a. <html> marks the beginning of an HTML document.
   b. <head> marks the beginning of a document's head.
   c. </body> marks the end of a document's body.
   d. </a> marks the end of an item that is linked to another document.

5. *Client side* and *server side* are terms used to identify whether an activity is performed at the client's computer or the server's computer.

Section 4

1. Only the link layer and the network layer. The link layer receives the message and hands it to the network layer. The network layer determines the direction in which the message should be forwarded and gives the message back to the link layer to be forwarded.

2. Unlike TCP, UDP is a connectionless protocol that does not confirm that the message was received at the destination.

3. Each message is assigned a hop count that determines the maximum number of times the message will be relayed.

4. Nothing really. A programmer at any host could modify the software at that host to keep such records. This is why sensitive data should be encrypted.

Section 5

1. Probably the most common way for malware to enter a computer system is via attachments to email messages or being hidden in software that is downloaded by the victim. However, spyware is often placed on unsuspecting computers by Web servers that are merely visited by the victim.

2. A region's gateway is a router that merely forwards packets (parts of messages) as they pass through. Thus a firewall at the gateway cannot filter traffic by its content but merely by its address information.

3. The use of passwords protects data (and therefore information as well). The use of encryption protects information.

4. In the case of a public-key encryption system, knowing how messages are encrypted does not allow messages to be decrypted.

5. The problems are international in nature and therefore not subject to the laws of a single government. Moreover, legal remedies merely provide recourse to injured parties rather than preventing the injuries.

Marking Up with HTML

A Hypertext Markup Language Primer

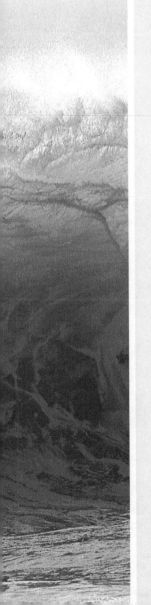

Learning Objectives

> Know the meaning of and use hypertext terms

> Use HTML tags to structure a document

> Use the basics of HTML tag attributes

> Use HTML tags to link to other files

> Explain the differences between absolute and relative pathnames

> Use HTML to encode lists and tables

Most of the fundamental ideas of science are essentially simple and may
as a rule be expressed in a language comprehensible to everyone.

—ALBERT EINSTEIN

WEB PAGES are created, stored, and sent in encoded form; a
browser converts them to the image we see on the screen. The Hypertext
Markup Language (HTML) is the main language used to define how a
Web page should look. Features like background color, font, and layout
are all specified in HTML. Learning to "speak" HTML is easy. So easy, in
fact, that most Web pages are not created by writing HTML directly, but
by using Web authoring software; that is, by using programs that write
the HTML automatically. Learning basic HTML helps you to understand
the World Wide Web, gives you experience directing a computer to do
tasks for you, and prepares you for other Fluency study topics. When
you are finished, you will speak a new "foreign" language!

This chapter begins by reviewing the concept of tags, and we introduce the dozen most basic HTML tags from the xHTML dialect. Next
comes document structuring, including details such as headings and
alignment. After discussing special characters, we create an example of a
text-only Web page. We decide that the page should have an image and
hyperlinks, so we discuss placing images and links and how to connect
them. With this knowledge we improve our sample page. Finally, we
introduce the basics of lists, tables, and colors, which give us more
control over the "look and feel" of our Web pages.

Marking Up with HTML

HTML is straightforward: The words on a Web page are simply structured by hidden formatting tags that describe how they should look.

Formatting with Tags

Tags are words or abbreviations enclosed in angle brackets, `<` and `>`, like `<title>`, and that tags come in pairs, the second with a slash (/), like `</title>` (the same forward slash as used in division). The tag pair surrounds the text to be formatted like parentheses. So a title, which every HTML Web page has, is written as

`<title>Tiger Woods, Masters Champion</title>`

These two tags can be read as "beginning of title text" and "end of title text." The title appears on the title bar of the browser (the very top of the window where the close button is) when the page is displayed. In xHTML, the tags must be lower case, making `<TITLE>`, `<Title>`, and `<tITle>` unacceptable.

Tags for Bold and Italic

HTML has tags for bold text, `<b>` and `</b>`; for italic text, `<i>` and `</i>`; and for paragraphs, `<p>` and `</p>`. You can use more than one kind of formatting at a time, such as bold italic text, by "nesting" the tags, as in

`<p><b><i>Veni, Vidi, Vici!</i></b></p>`

which produces

Veni, Vidi, Vici!

It doesn't matter whether italic follows bold, or vice versa. You get the same result if you put the italic before the bold:

`<p><i><b>Veni, Vidi, Vici!</b></i></p>`

The key is to make sure the tags are nested correctly. All the tags between a starting tag and its ending tag should be matched. So, in the *Veni, Vidi, Vici* example, between the starting `<p>` tag and its ending `</p>` tag, all other starting tags are properly nested with their matching ending tags.

A few tags are not paired and so do not have a matching / tag. In those cases, the closing angle bracket is replaced by `/>`. One example is the horizontal rule `<hr />` tag, which displays a horizontal line. Another example is the break `<br />` tag, which continues the text on the next line and is useful for ending each line of an address. These tags do not apply to text, so they don't surround anything.

An HTML Web page file begins with the `<html>` tag, ends with the `</html>` tag, and has the following structure:

```
<html>
    <head>
        Preliminary material goes here
    </head>
    <body>
        The main content of the page goes here
    </body>
</html>
```

The section surrounded by **<head>** and **</head>** contains the beginning material like the title. The section surrounded by **<body>** and **</body>** contains the content of the page. *This form must always be followed, and all of these tags are required.*

There's not very much to HTML. By the end of the next section, we will have created a respectable Web page—our first!

> **Use Simple Text Editors.** HTML must be written using basic ASCII characters. For now, think of ASCII as the characters from the keyboard. Standard word processors (e.g., WordPerfect, Word, and AppleWorks) produce files with ASCII characters, but they also include special formatting information that browsers do not like. For that reason, you *must* write HTML using a basic text editor such as Notepad or Notepad++ (Windows), TextEdit or TextWrangler (Mac), BBEdit (UNIX), or the like. And always make sure that you save your file using Text format. This way the HTML file will make sense to Web browsers. Also, be sure that your file name ends with the **.html** extension so that the browser knows it is reading an HTML document.

Structuring Documents

The point of a markup language is to describe how a document's parts fit together. Because those parts are mostly paragraphs, headings, and text styles like italic and bold, the tags of this section are the most common and most useful.

Headings in HTML

Because documents have headings, subheadings, and so on, HTML gives us several levels of *heading* tags to choose from, from level one (the highest) headings, **<h1>** and **</h1>**, to level two, **<h2>** and **</h2>**, all the way to level eight, **<h8>** and **</h8>**. The headings display their content in larger letters on a new line. For example,

<h1>Pope</h1> <h2>Cardinal</h2> <h3>Archbishop</h3>

appears as

Pope
Cardinal
Archbishop

You should use the heading levels in numerical order without skipping a level, although you don't have to start at level one. Notice that the headings are bold and get less "strong" (smaller and perhaps less bold) as the level number increases.

HTML Format Versus Display Format

Notice that although the HTML text was run together on one line, it was displayed formatted on separate lines. This illustrates the important point that the HTML source tells the browser how to produce the formatted image based on the *meanings* of the tags, not on how the source instructions look. Though the source's form is unimportant, we usually write HTML in a structured way to make it easier for people to understand. There is no agreed upon form, but the example might have been written with indenting to emphasize the levels:

```
<h1>Pope</h1>
   <h2>Cardinal</h2>
      <h3>Archbishop</h3>
```

White Space

The two HTML forms give us the same result. Computer experts call space that has been inserted for readability **white space**. We create white space with spaces, tabs, and new lines. HTML ignores white space. The browser turns any sequence of white space characters into a single space before it begins processing the HTML. The only exception is **preformatted** information contained within `<pre>` and `</pre>` tags, which is displayed as it appears.

The fact that white space is ignored is important when the browser formats paragraphs. All text within paragraph tags, `<p>` and `</p>`, is treated as a paragraph, and any sequence of white space characters is converted to a single space. So

```
<p> <b>Xeno's Paradox: </b>
Achilles and a turtle were to run a race. Achilles could
run twice as fast as the turtle. The turtle,
being a slower runner,
got a 10 meter head start, whereupon
Achilles started and ran the 10 meter distance. At that
moment the turtle was 5 meters farther. When Achilles had run
that distance the turtle had gone another 2.5 meters,
and so forth. Paradoxically, the turtle always remained
ahead. </p>
```

appears as

Xeno's Paradox: Achilles and a turtle were to run a race. Achilles could run twice as fast as the turtle. The turtle, being a slower runner, got a 10 meter head start, whereupon Achilles started and ran the 10 meter distance. At that moment the turtle was 5 meters farther. When Achilles had run that distance the turtle had gone another 2.5 meters, and so forth. Paradoxically, the turtle always remained ahead.

The width of the line is determined by the width of the browser window. Of course, a narrower or wider browser window makes the lines break in different places, which is why HTML ignores white space and changes the paragraph's formatting to fit the space available. Table 1 summarizes the basic HTML tags.

Table 1 Basic HTML tags

Start Tag	End Tag	Meaning	Required
`<html>`	`</html>`	HTML document; first and last tags in an HTML file	✓
`<title>`	`</title>`	Title bar text; describes page	✓
`<head>`	`</head>`	Preliminary material; e.g., title at start of page	✓
`<body>`	`</body>`	The main part of the page	✓
`<p>`	`</p>`	Paragraph, can use `align` attribute	
`<hr />`		Line (horizontal rule), can use `width` and `size` attributes	
`<h1>...<h8>`	`</h1>...</h8>`	Headings, eight levels, use in order, can use `align` attribute	
`<b />`	`</b>`	Bold	
`<i>`	`</i>`	Italic	
`<a href="`*fn*`">`	`</a>`	Anchor reference, *fn* must be a pathname to an HTML file	
`<img src="`*fn*`" />`		Image source reference, *fn* must be a pathname to `.jpg` or `.gif` file	
` `		Break, continue text on a new line	

Brackets in HTML: The Escape Symbol

Notice that there would be a problem if our Web page had to show a math relationship such as 0<p>r, because the browser might misinterpret <p> as a paragraph tag and not display it. So to show angle brackets, we use an **escape symbol**—the ampersand (`&`)—followed by an abbreviation, followed by a semicolon. For example:

> `&lt;` displays as <
>
> `&gt;` displays as >
>
> `&amp;` displays as &

Notice that the escape symbol, the ampersand, needs an escape, too! So, our math problem would be solved in HTML by

`<i>0&lt;p&gt;r</i>`

Accent Marks in HTML

Letters with accent marks also use the escape symbol. The general form is an ampersand followed by the letter (and whether it is uppercase or lowercase makes a difference) followed by the name of the accent mark followed by a semicolon. So, for example, `&eacute;` displays as é, `&Egrave;` displays as È, `&ntilde;` displays as ñ, and `&ouml;` displays as ö. Table 2 lists a few useful special symbols for some Western European languages. You can find a complete list at `http://www.w3schools.com/tags/ref_entities.asp`

Table 2 Special symbols for Western European Language accent marks

Symbol	HTML	Symbol	HTML	Symbol	HTML	Symbol	HTML
à	`&agrave;`	á	`&aacute;`	â	`&acirc;`	ã	`&atilde;`
ä	`&auml;`	å	`&aring;`	ç	`&ccedil;`	è	`&egrave;`
é	`&eacute;`	ê	`&ecirc;`	ë	`&euml;`	ì	`&igrave;`
í	`&iacute;`	î	`&icirc;`	ï	`&iuml;`	ñ	`&ntilde;`
ò	`&ograve;`	ó	`&oacute;`	ô	`&ocirc;`	õ	`&otilde;`
ö	`&ouml;`	ø	`&oslash;`	ù	`&ugrave;`	ú	`&uacute;`
û	`&ucirc;`	ü	`&uuml;`				

Note: For an accent mark on an uppercase letter, make the letter following the & uppercase.

Attributes in HTML

Though most text properties are a single key term or abbreviation, some properties, such as how to align text, require more information. For example, we can't just say we want text justified; we have to specify that we want it left justified, centered, or right justified. We do this by using the tag's **attributes**. Attributes, which are generally optional, appear inside the angle brackets.

Align, Justify. For example, paragraphs and headings have an align attribute specifying whether the text should be left justified, centered, or right justified. The attribute follows the tag word, separated by a space, and is separated from its value (in double quotes) by an equal sign. So

```
<p align = "center"> <b>Thought for Today:</b> </p>
<p> As I would not be a <i>slave</i>, so I would not be a
<i>master</i>. This expresses my idea of democracy. Whatever
differs from this, to the extent of the difference, is no
democracy.</p>
<p align = "right"> — Abraham Lincoln</p>
```

displays as

> **Thought for Today:**
> As I would not be a *slave*, so I would not be a *master*. This expresses my idea of democracy. Whatever differs from this, to the extent of the difference, is no democracy.
>
> — Abraham Lincoln

Notice that when we don't specify the alignment attribute, as in the second line, the default is left justified.

Horizontal Rule Attribute. The horizontal rule tag `<hr />`, mentioned earlier, also has attributes. One attribute, `width`, specifies how wide the line should be as a percentage of the browser window's width; another attribute, `size`, says how thick the line should be. So `<hr width="50%" size="1" />` displays a horizontal line that takes up half of the horizontal width and is the minimum thickness, as in

---

The default size is 2. Experiment to find the size that works best for your application. Notice that the width, `50%`, is enclosed in quotation marks. All attribute values must be enclosed in quotation marks.

*fit*ALERT

> **Misquotes.** Quotation marks are the cause of many HTML errors. Of course, quotes must match, and it is easy to forget one of the pair. But, there are also different kinds of quotes: Simple quotes (" and ') are the kind HTML likes; the fancy, curved quotes, called "smart quotes" ("" and ") are the kind HTML doesn't like. Check *carefully* for messed-up quotes if your HTML produces an incorrect result.

Though we have introduced only a few HTML tags so far, we can already create Web pages, as shown in Figure 1. Study the HTML and notice the following points:

> ❯ The title is shown on the title bar of the browser window.
>
> ❯ The alignment attribute has been used in the level one heading to center the heading.
>
> ❯ The level two headings are left justified because that is the default.
>
> ❯ The statement of Russell's Paradox is in bold.
>
> ❯ The HTML source paragraphs are indented more than the `<h2>` heading lines to make them more readable.
>
> ❯ The line between the two paragraphs is three quarters the width of the browser window.

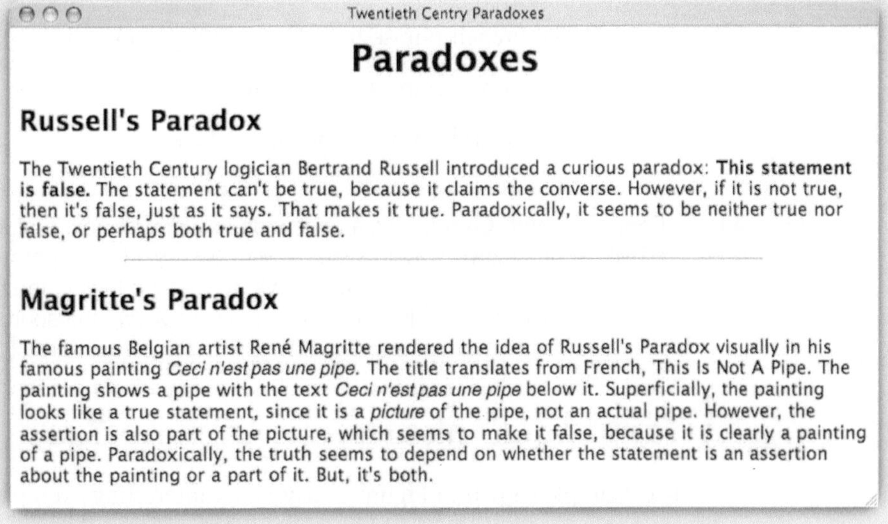

```html
<html>
    <head> <title> Twentieth Century Paradoxes </title>
    </head>
    <body>
        <h1 align="center">Paradoxes</h1>
        <h2>Russell's Paradox</h2>
            <p> The Twentieth Century logician Bertrand Russell
            introduced a curious paradox: <b>This statement is
            false.</b> The statement can't be true, because it
            claims the converse. However, if it is not true, then
            it's false, just as it says. That makes it true.
            Paradoxically, it seems to be neither true nor false,
            or perhaps both true and false.</p>
            <hr width="75%" />
        <h2> Magritte's Paradox</h2>
            <p> The famous Belgian artist Ren&eacute;
            Magritte rendered the idea of Russell's Paradox
            visually in his famous painting <i>Ceci n'est pas une
            pipe</i>. The title translates from French, This Is Not
            A Pipe. The painting shows a pipe with the text
            <i>Ceci n'est pas une pipe</i> below it. Superficially,
            the painting looks like a true statement, since it is a
            <i>picture</i> of the pipe, not an actual pipe. However,
            the assertion is also part of the picture, which seems
            to make it false, because it is clearly a painting of a
            pipe. Paradoxically, the truth seems to depend on
            whether the statement is an assertion about the painting
            or a part of it. But, it's both.</p>
    </body>
</html>
```

Figure 1 HTML source of `paradoxes.html` and the corresponding Web page resulting from its interpretation by a browser.

> Acute accents are used in Magritte's first name.

> The French phrase from the painting is in italics.

> The word *picture* is in italics for emphasis.

It's a simple page and it was simple to produce.

 Compose and Check. It's a good idea to write the text first and then format it in HTML. A productive way to work is with two windows open: your text editor and your browser. After writing a few HTML formatting tags in the editor, *save* your file and then check the result in the browser by *reloading* the source.

 ## Marking Links with Anchor Tags

The example shown in Figure 1 may be an interesting Web page, but it doesn't use hypertext at all. It would be more informative, perhaps, if it linked to biographies of Russell and Magritte. Also, it would be easier to understand if it showed Magritte's painting or linked to it.

Two Sides of a Link

In this section we discuss how to make hyperlinks. When a user clicks on a hyperlink, the browser loads a new Web page. This means there must be two parts to a hyperlink: the text in the current document that is highlighted, called the **anchor text**, and the address of the other Web page, called the **hyperlink reference**.

 Both parts of the hyperlink are specified in the **anchor tag**, which is constructed as follows.

☑ *Begin with* **<a** *making sure there's a space after the* **a**. *The* **a** *is for anchor.*

☑ *Give the hyperlink reference using* **href="***filename***"**, *making sure to include the double quotes.*

☑ *Close the anchor tag with the* **>** *symbol.*

☑ *Specify the anchor text, which will be highlighted when it is displayed by the browser.*

☑ *End the hyperlink with the* **</a>** *tag.*

For example, suppose **http://www.bioz.com/bios/sci/russell.html** were the URL for a Web biography of Bertrand Russell; we would anchor it to his last name on our Web page with the anchor tag

```
Bertrand <a href="http://www.bioz.com/bios/sci/russell.html">Russell</a>
```
    normal text   hyperlink reference   anchor

This hyperlink would be displayed with Russell's last name highlighted as

Bertrand Russell

When the browser displays the page and the user clicks on Russell, the browser downloads the biographical page given in the `href`. As another example, if Magritte's biography were at the same site, the text

`<a href="http://www.bioz.com/bios/art/magritte.html">Magritte</a>`

would give the reference and anchor for his hyperlink.

Absolute Pathnames (URLs)

In these anchor tag examples, the hyperlink reference is an entire URL because the Web browser needs to know how to find the page. Remember that the URL is made from a protocol specification, `http://`, a domain or IP address, `www.bioz.com`, and a path to the file, `/bios/sci/russell.html`. The files are two levels down in the directory (folder) hierarchy of the site.

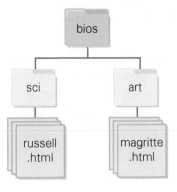

From the Russell and Magritte examples, we guess that at the Bioz Company site, the biographies have been grouped together in a top-level folder called `bios`. Probably the scientists, like Russell, are grouped together in the subfolder called `sci`, and the artists are grouped together under the subfolder called `art`. Within these folders are the individual biography files: `russell.html` and `magritte.html`. The slash (/) separates levels in the directory hierarchy, and "crossing a slash" moves us lower in the hierarchy into a subfolder. Such complete URLs are called **absolute pathnames**; they are the right way to reference pages at other Web sites.

Relative Pathnames

Often a link refers to other Web pages on the same site. Because these pages will all be stored in the same or nearby folders, their anchor tags use **relative pathnames**. A relative pathname describes how to find the referenced file *relative* to the file in which the anchor tag appears. So, for example, if the anchor tag is in an HTML file that is in folder X, and the anchor references another file also in folder X, only the name of the file is given, not its whole absolute path.

Suppose that we have written our own biographies for Russell and Magritte for our `paradoxes.html` page. If the files are named `russellbio.html` and `magrittebio.html`, and they are in the same folder as `paradoxes.html`, the anchor tags of the Paradoxes page can use relative references:

`<a href="russellbio.html">Russell</a>`

and

`<a href="magrittebio.html">Magritte</a>`

This saves us typing the protocol part, the domain part, and the path to the folder part, but that's not why we like relative pathnames. Relative pathnames are more flexible because they let us move Web files around as a group without having to change the references. This flexibility is important as you begin to manage your own Web page.

Going "Deeper" in a Folder.   Relative pathnames are very simple when the file containing the anchor and the referenced file are in the same folder—we just give the file name. When the referenced file is "deeper" in the directory hierarchy, perhaps in a folder or in a folder inside another folder, we simply give the path from the current folder down to the file. For example, in the folder containing `paradoxes.html` we create a subfolder, `biographies`, which contains the two profiles. Then the anchor for the Russell bio becomes

```
<a href="biographies/russellbio.html">Russell</a>
```

because we must say how to navigate to the file from the location of the Paradoxes page. Of course, using relative pathnames means that the files for the pages must be kept together in a fixed structure, but that's the easiest solution anyway.

Going "Higher" in a Hierarchy.   The only problem left is how to refer to folders higher up in the hierarchy. The technique for doing this (which comes from the UNIX operating system) is to refer to the next outer level of the hierarchy—that is, the containing folder—as `..` (pronounced "*dot dot*"). So if we imagine that the directory structure has the form

```
mypages
    biographies
        russellbio.html
        magrittebio.html
    coolstuff
        paradoxes.html
```

then, in `paradoxes.html`, the Russell biography anchor would be

```
<a href="../biographies/russellbio.html">Russell</a>
```

because the biography can't be reached by going down from the folder (`coolstuff`) containing `paradoxes.html`. Instead, we have to go up to the next higher level to `mypages`. From there, we can navigate down to the bios through the `biographies` folder. We can use a sequence of dots and slashes (`../../`), so that each pair of dots moves the reference up one level higher in the hierarchy. For example, another page with the reference

```
<a href="../../humorpages/dumbjokes/knockknock4.html">
```

moves up to the folder containing the folder containing the page, then down through the `humorpages` and `dumbjokes` folders to the actual `knockknock4` HTML page.

Summarizing, hyperlinks are specified using anchor tags. The path to the file is given as the **href** attribute of the anchor tag, and the text to be highlighted (the anchor) is given between the anchor tag and its closing **</a>**. Paths can be absolute paths—that is, standard URLs—for offsite pages. Relative pathnames should be used for all onsite pages. The relative path can be just a name if the referenced file is in the same folder as the page that links to it; it can specify a path deeper, through descendant folders; or it can use the **..** notation to move higher in the directory structure. These path rules apply to images as well as hyperlinks.

Including Pictures with Image Tags

Pictures are worth a thousand words, as the saying goes, so we include them in an HTML document to enhance our page. To link to a picture, that is, to enable the reader to click on a link to see a picture, we use the anchor tags as just explained. To display the picture, that is, to show it on the page, we use an image tag.

Image Tag Format

An image tag, which is analogous to an anchor tag, specifies a file containing an image. The image tag format is

<img src="*filename***" />**

where **src** stands for "source" and the *filename* uses the same rules for absolute and relative pathnames as anchor tags. So, for example, if the image of Magritte's painting is stored in a file **pipe.jpg**, in the same folder as the Paradoxes page, we can include the image with a relative pathname

<img src="pipe.jpg" />

which finds the image and places it in the document.

GIF and JPEG Images

Images can come in several formats, but two of them are important for Web pages: **GIF** (preferred pronunciation is *jif*) and **JPEG** (pronounced *JAY-peg*.) GIFs (Graphics Interchange Format) are best suited for cartoons and simple drawings. JPEGs, named for the Joint Photographic Experts Group, are appropriate for high-resolution photographs and complex artwork. To tell the browser which format the image is in, the file name should have the extension **.gif**, **.jpg**, or **.jpeg**.

Positioning the Image in the Document

Where does the image go on the Web page? To understand how images are placed, notice that HTML lays out text in the browser window from *left to right*, and from *top to bottom*, the same way English is written. If the image is the same size or smaller than the letters, it is placed in line just like a letter at the point where the image tag occurs in the HTML. For example, when we insert a small image ▢ in the text, it is simply drawn in place. This is convenient for icons or smiley faces in the text. If the image is larger than the letters ▢, it appears in the text in the same way, but the line spacing is increased to separate it from the neighboring lines. The HTML default rule is: *Images are inserted in the page at the point where the tag is specified in the HTML, and the text lines up with the bottom of the image.*

We can use the `align` attribute in the image tag to line up the top of the image with the top of the text (`align="top"`) or to center the text on the image (`align="middle"`) in the image. In all cases, the `bottom` (default), `middle`, and `top` alignments apply only to the line of text in which the image has been inserted.

Another common and visually pleasing way to place images in text is to flow the text around them, either by having the image on the left with the text to its right, or vice versa. To make the text flow around the image, we use the `align` attribute in the image tag with the value `"left"` or `"right"`. This forces the image to the left or right of the browser window. The text will continue from left to right, and from top to bottom, in the remaining space, flowing around the image.

Finally, to display an image by itself without any text around it, simply enclose the image tag within paragraph tags. That will separate it from the paragraphs above and below. You can even center the paragraph to center the image:

So how do we put the image of Magritte's painting in the Paradoxes page? Perhaps the most pleasing solution is to right-justify it and let the paragraph flow around it. We can do this by writing

```
<img src="pipe.jpg" align="right" />
```

as long as the picture doesn't take up all or most of the window, which would prevent the text from flowing naturally.

To specify how large the picture should be, use the `height` and `width` attributes in the image tag. Give the size in pixels. Thus,

```
<img src="pipe.jpg" align="right" height="130" width="192" />
```

specifies an image that will be about one eighth of the width of a thousand-pixel screen. If the natural size of the image is different from the `height/width` specifications, the browser shrinks or stretches it to fit in the allotted space. (The natural size of an image is the best size to use, if possible. However, in our example the natural size is too large, so we divide the dimensions by 3 and round to the nearest whole number.)

 Image Size. You can determine the size of an image in Windows by hovering over its icon or in the Mac OS X by opening it in Preview and choosing *Get Info* from the *Tools* menu.

We can also use images to fill in a background by **tiling**, which is copying a small image over and over to make a background pattern. Use bland, low-contrast, evenly colored images for background tiling, so they are not distracting. Collections of pictures and graphics to use as backgrounds are widely available, including ones that make your pages look like fine textured linen paper. The image is specified as the background attribute of the body tag, as in

```
<body background="filename">
```

where the *filename* has the same path properties as hyperlink references for anchor tags.

 ## Handling Color

Color can improve a Web page dramatically and can be used for both the background and text. The **bgcolor** attribute of the body tag gives you a solid color for the background. You can specify the color either by number, as explained later, or by using a small set of predefined color terms, as in

```
<body bgcolor="silver">
```

The color choices are shown in Table 3. The body tag attribute **text** is used to give the entire document's text a specific color. The example

```
<body text="aqua" link="fuchsia">
```

illustrates how to control the link colors, too. You can change the text in specific places by using the font tag with the color attribute. So, to make Russell's Paradox red, write

```
<b><font color="red">This statement is false.</font></b>
```

The predefined colors are handy, but you may want to access more than 16 colors; that's where the numeric colors come in.

Table 3 Predefined HTML colors

black	silver	white	gray
red	fuchsia	maroon	purple
blue	navy	aqua	teal
lime	green	yellow	olive

Color by Number

Computer colors are usually described by their amounts of red, green, and blue light. The intensity of each color is specified by a number from 0 through 255. So, for example, a zero amount of all three colors (0,0,0) produces the color black. If all three colors are at full intensity (255, 255, 255), the color is white because white is a mix of the three colors of light. Though it makes no difference for black and white, the order is always red, green, blue—so we call it **RGB** color specification. Thus, if there is full intensity of one color and none of the other two, as in

> **(255, 0, 0)** Intense Red
>
> **(0, 255, 0)** Intense Green
>
> **(0, 0, 255)** Intense Blue

we get the three pure colors.

*fit*BYTE

> **Eye Color.** The original choice of red, green, and blue comes from the color receptors in the human eye.

You can select custom colors for backgrounds and fonts in HTML by giving the three RGB intensity values. The only catch is that you do not specify them as whole numbers between 0 and 255, but as pairs of hex digits between 00 and FF. A hexadeximal (hex) digit is one of the symbols {0, 1, 2, 3, 4, 5, 6, 7, 8, 9, A, B, C, D, E, F} from the base-16 or **hexadecimal** numbering system. We can use them now without understanding hex. Because the smallest value is 00, which is the same as a normal 0, and the largest value is FF, which is the same as a normal 255, the three pure colors are expressed in HTML as

> **#FF0000** Intense Red
>
> **#00FF00** Intense Green
>
> **#0000FF** Intense Blue

The number sign (#) means that what follows is a hexadecimal number. The easiest way to find the values for a custom color, say (255, 142, 42), which is the color of a carrot, is to look up the numbers in Table 4 to find their two hex digits. First find the intensity for each color in the table, and then read the first hex digit from the left end of the row and the second hex digit from the top of the column. Thus the carrot color is

> **#FF8E2A** Carrot Orange

because 255 is **FF**, 142 is **8E**, and 42 is **2A**.

Even though numeric colors need two levels of translation—first the translation of the color into the three RGB intensities, and then the translation of those values into hex digit pairs—they give us much more flexibility in Web page design, so most HTML programmers prefer them.

Table 4 Hexadecimal Digit Equivalents

Hex	0	1	2	3	4	5	6	7	8	9	A	B	C	D	E	F
0	0	1	2	3	4	5	6	7	8	9	10	11	12	13	14	15
1	16	17	18	19	20	21	22	23	24	25	26	27	28	29	30	31
2	32	33	34	35	36	37	38	39	40	41	42	43	44	45	46	47
3	48	49	50	51	52	53	54	55	56	57	58	59	60	61	62	63
4	64	65	66	67	68	69	70	71	72	73	74	75	76	77	78	79
5	80	81	82	83	84	85	86	87	88	89	90	91	92	93	94	95
6	96	97	98	99	100	101	102	103	104	105	106	107	108	109	110	111
7	112	113	114	115	116	117	118	119	120	121	122	123	124	125	126	127
8	128	129	130	131	132	133	134	135	136	137	138	139	140	141	142	143
9	144	145	146	147	148	149	150	151	152	153	154	155	156	157	158	159
A	160	161	162	163	164	165	166	167	168	169	170	171	172	173	174	175
B	176	177	178	179	180	181	182	183	184	185	186	187	188	189	190	191
C	192	193	194	195	196	197	198	199	200	201	202	203	204	205	206	207
D	208	209	210	211	212	213	214	215	216	217	218	219	220	221	222	223
E	224	225	226	227	228	229	230	231	232	233	234	235	236	237	238	239
F	240	241	242	243	244	245	246	247	248	249	250	251	252	253	254	255

Note: Find the decimal number in the table and then combine the entries in the left column and the top row symbols to form the hexadecimal equivalent. Thus decimal 180 is hexadecimal B4.

There is another way to find the numeric specification for a color, and it is the easiest. In the appendix HTML Reference, Table 1 shows a standard set of HTML colors and their hex specification. (These colors give best results on most monitors.) Find the color in the table and read the hex digits.

With the information you have learned in the last three sections, it's possible to enhance the Web page shown in Figure 1. The result is shown in Figure 2. Notice the local pathnames to our own biographical profiles of Russell and Magritte, the background and text colors, the change of color for the font and for the headings, and, of course, the added image.

 ## Handling Lists

There are many kinds of lists in HTML, the easiest being an unnumbered list. The unnumbered list tags `<ul>` and `</ul>` surround the items of the list, which are themselves enclosed in list item tags, `<li>` and `</li>`. The browser formats the list with each item bulleted, indented, and starting on its own line. As usual, though the form of the HTML doesn't matter to the browser, we write the HTML list instructions in list form. So, for example, the HTML for a movie list is

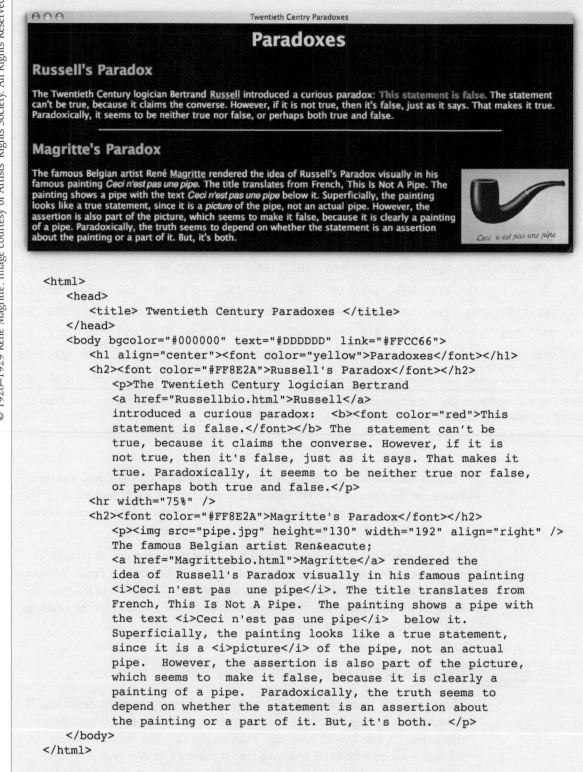

Figure 2 Completed Web page and the HTML source.

```
<ul>
   <li>Luxo Jr.</li>
   <li>Toy Story</li>
   <li>Monsters, Inc.</li>
</ul>
```

which looks like

- Luxo Jr.
- Toy Story
- Monsters, Inc.

Another kind of list is an ordered list, which uses the tags `<ol>` and `</ol>` and replaces the bullets with numbers. Otherwise, the ordered list behaves just like an unnumbered list. Thus, the HTML for the start of the list of chemical elements is

```
<ol>
   <li> Hydrogen, H, 1.008, 1 </li>
   <li> Helium, He, 4.003, 2</li>
   <li> Lithium, Li, 6.941, 2 1 </li>
   <li> Beryllium, Be, 9.012, 2 2 </li>
</ol>
```

which looks like

1. Hydrogen, H, 1.008, 1
2. Helium, He, 4.003, 2
3. Lithium, Li, 6.941, 2 1
4. Beryllium, Be, 9.012, 2 2

We can also have a list within a list, simply by making the sublists items of the main list. Applying this idea in HTML

```
<ul>
   <li>Pear</li>
   <li>Apple</li>
      <ul>
         <li>Granny Smith</li>
         <li>Fuji </li>
      </ul>
   <li>Cherry</li>
</ul>
```

looks like

> - Pear
> - Apple
>   - Granny Smith
>   - Fuji
> - Cherry

Finally, there is a handy list form called the **definitional list**, indicated by the tags `<dl>` and `</dl>`. A definitional list is usually made up of a sequence of definitional terms, surrounded by the tags `<dt>` and `</dt>`, and definitional data, surrounded by the tags `<dd>` and `</dd>`. So, for example, a definitional list is expressed in HTML as

```
<dl>
   <dt> Man </dt>
   <dd> <i>Homo sapiens</i>, the greatest achievement
      of evolution. </dd>
   <dt> Woman </dt>
   <dd> <i>Homo sapiens</i>, a greater achievement of
      evolution, and clever enough not to mention it to man.
   </dd>
</dl>
```

and would be formatted by browsers as

> Man
> > *Homo sapiens*, the greatest achievement of evolution.
>
> Woman
> > *Homo sapiens*, a greater achievement of evolution, and clever enough
> > not to mention it to man.

Of course, other formatting commands such as italics and bold can be used within any line items.

 ## Handling Tables

A table is a good way to present certain types of information. Creating a table in HTML is straightforward. It is like defining a list of lists, where each of the main list items, called *rows*, has one or more items, called *cells*. The browser aligns cells to form columns.

Table Tags

The table is enclosed in table tags, `<table>` and `</table>`. If you want the table to have a border around it, use the attribute `border` inside the table tag. Each row is enclosed in table row tags, `<tr>` and `</tr>`. The cells of each row are surrounded by table data tags, `<td>` and `</td>`. So a table with two rows, each with three cells of the form

Canada	Ottawa	English/French
Iceland	Reykjavik	Icelandic

is defined by

```
<table border>
    <tr>
        <td>Canada</td>
        <td>Ottawa</td>
        <td>English/French</td>
    </tr>
    <tr>
        <td>Iceland</td>
        <td>Reykjavik</td>
        <td>Icelandic</td>
    </tr>
</table>
```

You can give tables captions and column headings. The caption tags are `<caption>` and `</caption>`. You place them within the table tags around the table's caption. The caption is shown centered at the top of the table in bold. You place the column headings as the first row of the table. In the heading row, you replace the table data tags with table heading tags, `<th>` and `</th>`, which also display in bold. The table row tags are `<tr>` and `</tr>` as usual. Thus we can change our sample table to give it a caption and column headings:

```
<table border>
    <caption>Country Data</caption>
    <tr>
        <th>Country</th>
        <th>Capital</th>
        <th>Language(s)</th>
    </tr>
    <tr>
        <td>Canada</td>
        <td>Ottawa</td>
        <td>English/French</td>
    </tr>
```

```
    <tr>
        <td>Iceland</td>
        <td>Reykjavik</td>
        <td>Icelandic</td>
    </tr>
    <tr>
        <td>Norway</td>
        <td>Oslo</td>
        <td>Norwegian</td>
    </tr>
</table>
```

which will look like this:

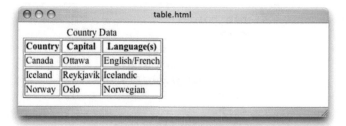

Notice that the first row uses the **<th>** tag rather than the **<td>** tag to specify the headings.

Controlling Text with Tables

Tables are a handy way to control the arrangement of information on the page. An example where this control might be desirable is when we have a series of links listed across the top of a page. The links only form a one-row table, but the table helps keep the links together. Figures 3 and 4 show two different HTML sources, one simply listing the links in sequence and the other placing the links into a table. When there is enough window space, the two solutions look the same.

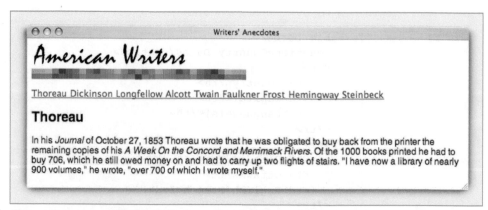

Figure 3 A page and its HTML for a simple listing of links (*continues next page*).

```
<html>
   <head> <title>Writers' Anecdotes</title>
   </head>
   <body bgcolor="white" text="black">
      <img src="AWA.gif" />
         <p>
            <a href="hdt.html"> Thoreau      </a>
            <a href="ed.html">  Dickinson    </a>
            <a href="hwl.html"> Longfellow    </a>
            <a href="lma.html"> Alcott        </a>
            <a href="sc.html">  Twain         </a>
            <a href="wf.html">  Faulkner      </a>
            <a href="rf.html">  Frost         </a>
            <a href="eh.html">  Hemingway     </a>
            <a href="js.html">  Steinbeck     </a>
         </p>
      <h2><font face="helvetica">Thoreau</h2>
         <p><font face="helvetica">
         In his <i>Journal</i> of October 27, 1853 Thoreau
         wrote that he was obligated to buy back from the
         printer the remaining copies of his <i>A Week On the
         Concord and Merrimack Rivers</i>. Of the 1000 books
         printed he had to buy 706, which he still owed money
         on and had to carry up two flights  of stairs. "I
         have now a library of nearly 900 volumes," he wrote,
         "over 700 of which I wrote myself."</font></p>
   </body>
</html>
```

Figure 3 (*continued*) A page and its HTML for a simple listing of links.

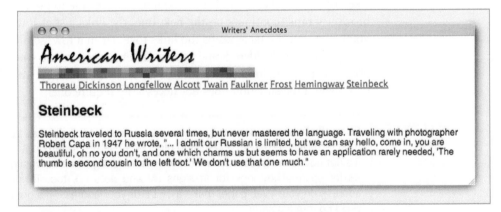

Figure 4 A page and its HTML for listing links in a table (*continues next page*).

```
<html>
    <head><title>Writers' Anecdotes</title></head>
    <body bgcolor="white" text="black">
        <img src="AWA.gif" />
        <table>
            <tr>
                <td> <a href="hdt.html">Thoreau</a>      </td>
                <td> <a href="ed.html">Dickinson</a>     </td>
                <td> <a href="hwl.html">Longfellow</a>   </td>
                <td> <a href="lma.html">Alcott</a>       </td>
                <td> <a href="sc.html">Twain</a>         </td>
                <td> <a href="wf.html">Faulkner</a>      </td>
                <td> <a href="rf.html">Frost</a>         </td>
                <td> <a href="eh.html">Hemingway</a>     </td>
                <td> <a href="js.html">Steinbeck</a>     </td>
            </tr>
        </table>
        <h2><font face="helvetica">Steinbeck</font></h2>
            <p><font face="helvetica">
            Steinbeck traveled to Russia several times, but never
            mastered the language. Traveling with photographer Robert
            Capa in 1947 he wrote, "... I admit our Russian is
            limited, but we can say hello, come in, you are beautiful, oh
            no you don't, and one which charms us but seems to have an
            application rarely needed, 'The thumb is second cousin to
            the left foot.' We don't use that one much."</font></p>
    </body>
</html>
```

Figure 4 (*continued*) A page and its HTML for listing links in a table.

The difference is apparent when there is only a small amount of window space (see Figure 5). When there is not enough space for the full sequence of links, the browser **wraps** (continues on the next line) the links just as it wraps normal paragraph text. But the table keeps the links together in a row; scroll bars are added and the links are hidden. Some people prefer the row to the wrap. Some people don't. Keeping the links in a row is an example of when you would use an HTML table even if the situation does not necessarily require one.

*fit*BYTE

Spam Buster. Analogous to `<a href ...>`, HTML has `<mailto: ...>` to link to an emailer, so users can easily reply to Web content. Although originally popular, it's not now used because crawlers look for this tag when harvesting email addresses for spam. They look for at signs (`@`) and dots (`.`), too. To include your email address on your Web page, make a `.gif` of your address. It's not as convenient as `mailto`, but it's safer.

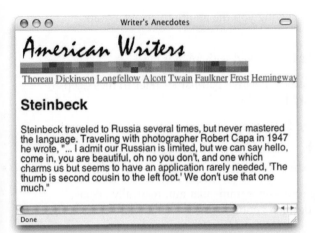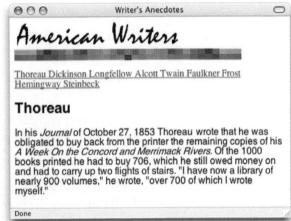

Figure 5 The display of the two pages from Figures 3 and 4 in a small window showing that the table keeps the links in a single row (left) rather than wrapping them (right).

 ## HTML Wrap-Up

In learning HTML, you have seen how a Web page is encoded. Though HTML has a few more exotic features beyond those presented here, and the other Web languages have even more powerful features, they are all variations on the same theme: Tags surround all objects that appear on the page, the context is set by specifying global properties of the page (e.g., `<body bgcolor="white">`), and each feature of the format is specified in detail, `<i>isn't it?!</i>`. It's so easy, even a computer can do it!

Indeed, that's what happens most of the time. Web authors usually don't write HTML directly; they use Web authoring tools, such as Macromedia Dreamweaver, or standard text editors like Microsoft Word. They build the page as it should look on the screen using a WYSIWYG Web authoring program, and then the computer generates the HTML to implement it.

*fit*BYTE **Uploading.** Pages are created and tested on a personal computer. To be accessed from other computers on the Internet, the HTML files, the image files, and the directory structure created for them must be uploaded (transmitted) to a Web server, a process known as **publishing**.

 ## SUMMARY

You learned that Web pages are stored and transmitted in an encoded form before a browser turns them into images, and that HTML is the most widely used encoding form. The chapter opened by recalling the idea of using tags for formatting and went on to introduce you to:

> A working set of HTML tags, giving you the ability to create a Web page.

> An explanation of how links are marked with anchor tags.

> Absolute and relative pathnames. Relative pathnames refer to files deeper and higher in the directory hierarchy.

> The two most popular image formatting schemes—GIF and JPEG—and how to place them in a page.

> Numeric colors, lists, and tables.

> WYSIWYG Web authoring tools—programs that automatically create the HTML when the page design is complete.

 Review Questions

Multiple Choice

1. HTML commands are called
   a. hops
   b. brackets
   c. tags
   d. tokens

2. HTML tags are words enclosed in
   a. ( )
   b. // \\
   c. { }
   d. < >

3. Which of the following would put "Kelly Clarkson — In Concert" in the title bar of a Web page?
   a. `<title> Kelly Clarkson — In Concert</title>`
   b. `</title> Kelly Clarkson — In Concert<title>`
   c. `<title> Kelly Clarkson — In Concert<title/>`
   d. `<TITLE/> Kelly Clarkson — In Concert</TITLE>`

4. Which of the following tags is not paired?
   a. `<hr />`
   b. `<i>`
   c. `<p>`
   d. `<html>`

5. The `<p>  </p>` tags indicate the beginning and end of a
   a. table
   b. picture
   c. paragraph
   d. preformatted text section

6. The `<a...>` tag is called an
   a. anchor
   b. address
   c. add
   d. append

7. The attribute specifying a blue background is
   a. `bgcolor = #000000`
   b. `background = "blue"`
   c. `<color = blue>`
   d. `bgcolor = blue`

8. The `..` notation in a relative path of hypertext reference means to
   a. open a folder and go down a folder
   b. close a folder and open the parent folder
   c. search a folder
   d. create a folder

9. To get an image to sit on the right side of the window with the text filling the area to the left of the image, your tag would need to look like
   a. `<img src = "mountains.jpg" align = "right" />`
   b. `<img src align = "mountains.jpg" "right" />`
   c. `<img = "mountains.jpg" src align = "right" />`
   d. `<img "mountains.jpg" align src = "right" />`

10. The dimensions for an image on a Web page
    a. are set using the `x` and `y` attributes
    b. are set using the `width` and `height` attributes
    c. must be set to the actual size of the image
    d. are automatically adjusted by the browser to fit in the space allotted

Short Answer

1. Today most Web pages are created using _____.

2. To improve readability of HTML text, the computer experts suggest adding _____ to the source instructions.

3. The _____ tag is a way to get more than one consecutive space in a line of a Web page.

4. _____ tags are tags between other tags.

5. Special commands inside a tag are called _____.

6. _____ are usually used to link to pages on the same site.

7. A `..` in a hypertext reference indicates a _____ path.

8. The `src` in an image tag stands for _____.

9. GIF stands for _____.

10. JPEG stands for _____.

11. To get the RGB color black using hexadecimal numbers, you would write _____.

12. To put the ten greatest inventions of all time, in order, on a Web page, you should use a(n) _____.

Exercises

1. Why learn HTML at all if authoring tools will do the work for you? Give other examples of where you are expected to learn something when there are tools available that will do the work.

2. Use HTML to properly display the following.

General
Colonel
Major
Captain
Lieutenant
Sergeant

Corporal

Private

3. Explain why a page needs to be reloaded in a browser to see the results of editing changes made in the text editor of an HTML document.

4. Indicate the hyperlink reference and the anchor text in this anchor tag. Then break down the hyperlink reference into the protocol, domain, path, and file name.

```
<a href="http://www.nasm.si.edu/nasm/museum/museum.htm">
National Air and Space Museum</a>
```

5. Treat your birthday (mm/dd/yy) as hexadecimal and then determine what color it is.

6. Experiment with hexadecimal colors until you find the seven combinations that will give you the colors of the rainbow.

7. Create a calendar for the current month using a table. Put the name of the month in a caption at the top. Change the color of the text for Sunday and holidays. Make note of any special days during the month. Add an appropriate graphic to one of the blank cells at the end of the calendar.

8. Create a page with links to your favorite friends. Use one column for their names, another for their homepages, and a third column for their email addresses. Link to their homepages.

9. View and then print the source for the author's homepage. It's at

www.cs.washington.edu/homes/snyder/index.html

What is the title of the page? Indicate the heading and the body for the page. Find the table. Find the list. Find the email links. Find the absolute hyperlinks and the relative hyperlinks. How many graphics are on this page?

Answers to Selected Questions

Multiple Choice

1. C. The commands used in HTML are called tags. They are enclosed in < >.

3. A. The first one has the tags properly paired.

5. C. These are paragraph tags and put a double space around the text to set it off from the rest of the page.

7. D.

9. A. `img src = "filename.ext"` will get the image. Then use `align` = and enclose the proper alignment in quotes.

Short Answer

1. Web authoring software

3. `<br>` *or* `<pre>`

5. attributes

7. relative

9. Graphics Interchange Format

11. `#000000`

5

Data Storage

In this chapter, we consider topics associated with data representation and the storage of data within a computer. The types of data we will consider include text, numeric values, images, audio, and video. Much of the information in this chapter is also relevant to fields other than traditional computing, such as digital photography, audio/video recording and reproduction, and long-distance communication.

We begin our study of computer science by considering how information is encoded and stored inside computers. Our first step is to discuss the basics of a computer's data storage devices and then to consider how information is encoded for storage in these systems. We will explore the ramifications of today's data storage systems and how such techniques as data compression and error handling are used to overcome their shortfalls.

1 Bits and Their Storage

Inside today's computers information is encoded as patterns of 0s and 1s. These digits are called **bits** (short for *binary digits*). Although you may be inclined to associate bits with numeric values, they are really only symbols whose meaning depends on the application at hand. Sometimes patterns of bits are used to represent numeric values; sometimes they represent characters in an alphabet and punctuation marks; sometimes they represent images; and sometimes they represent sounds.

Boolean Operations

To understand how individual bits are stored and manipulated inside a computer, it is convenient to imagine that the bit 0 represents the value *false* and the bit 1 represents the value *true* because that allows us to think of manipulating bits as manipulating true/false values. Operations that manipulate true/false values are called **Boolean operations,** in honor of the mathematician George Boole (1815–1864), who was a pioneer in the field of mathematics called logic. Three of the basic Boolean operations are AND, OR, and XOR (exclusive or) as summarized in Figure 1. These operations are similar to the arithmetic operations TIMES and PLUS because they combine a pair of values (the operation's input) to produce a third value (the output). In contrast to arithmetic operations, however, Boolean operations combine true/false values rather than numeric values.

The Boolean operation AND is designed to reflect the truth or falseness of a statement formed by combining two smaller, or simpler, statements with the conjunction *and.* Such statements have the generic form

   P AND *Q*

where *P* represents one statement and *Q* represents another—for example,

   Kermit is a frog AND Miss Piggy is an actress.

The inputs to the AND operation represent the truth or falseness of the compound statement's components; the output represents the truth or falseness of the compound statement itself. Since a statement of the form *P* AND *Q* is true only when both of its components are true, we conclude that 1 AND 1 should be 1, whereas all other cases should produce an output of 0, in agreement with Figure 1.

In a similar manner, the OR operation is based on compound statements of the form

   P OR *Q*

where, again, P represents one statement and Q represents another. Such statements are true when at least one of their components is true, which agrees with the OR operation depicted in Figure 1.

There is not a single conjunction in the English language that captures the meaning of the XOR operation. XOR produces an output of 1 (true) when one of its inputs is 1 (true) and the other is 0 (false). For example, a statement of the form P XOR Q means "either P or Q but not both." (In short, the XOR operation produces an output of 1 when its inputs are different.)

The operation NOT is another Boolean operation. It differs from AND, OR, and XOR because it has only one input. Its output is the opposite of that input; if the input of the operation NOT is true, then the output is false, and vice versa. Thus, if the input of the NOT operation is the truth or falseness of the statement

> Fozzie is a bear.

then the output would represent the truth or falseness of the statement

> Fozzie is not a bear.

Gates and Flip-Flops

A device that produces the output of a Boolean operation when given the operation's input values is called a **gate.** Gates can be constructed from a variety of technologies such as gears, relays, and optic devices. Inside today's computers, gates are usually implemented as small electronic circuits in which the digits 0 and 1 are represented as voltage levels. We need not concern ourselves with such details, however. For our purposes, it suffices to represent gates in their

Figure 1   The Boolean operations AND, OR, and XOR (exclusive or)

The AND operation

0	0	1	1
AND 0	AND 1	AND 0	AND 1
0	0	0	1

The OR operation

0	0	1	1
OR 0	OR 1	OR 0	OR 1
0	1	1	1

The XOR operation

0	0	1	1
XOR 0	XOR 1	XOR 0	XOR 1
0	1	1	0

symbolic form, as shown in Figure 2. Note that the AND, OR, XOR, and NOT gates are represented by distinctively shaped symbols, with the input values entering on one side and the output exiting on the other.

Gates provide the building blocks from which computers are constructed. One important step in this direction is depicted in the circuit in Figure 3. This is a particular example from a collection of circuits known as flip-flops. A **flip-flop** is a circuit that produces an output value of 0 or 1, which remains constant until a temporary pulse from another circuit causes it to shift to the other value. In other words, the output will flip or flop between two values under control of external stimuli. As long as both inputs in the circuit in Figure 3 remain 0, the output (whether 0 or 1) will not change. However, temporarily placing a 1 on the upper input will force the output to be 1, whereas temporarily placing a 1 on the lower input will force the output to be 0.

Figure 2 A pictorial representation of AND, OR, XOR, and NOT gates as well as their input and output values

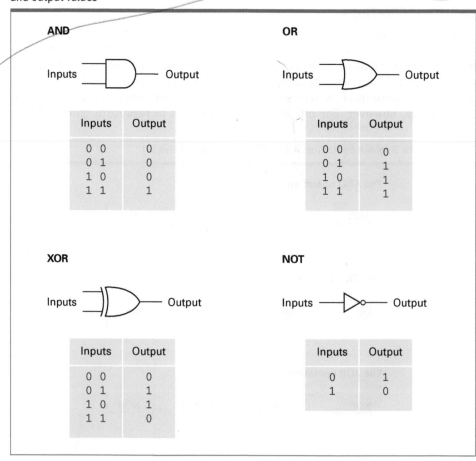

AND

Inputs ──⊐D── Output

Inputs	Output
0 0	0
0 1	0
1 0	0
1 1	1

OR

Inputs ──⊃D── Output

Inputs	Output
0 0	0
0 1	1
1 0	1
1 1	1

XOR

Inputs ──⊃D── Output

Inputs	Output
0 0	0
0 1	1
1 0	1
1 1	0

NOT

Inputs ──▷o── Output

Inputs	Output
0	1
1	0

Figure 3   A simple flip-flop circuit

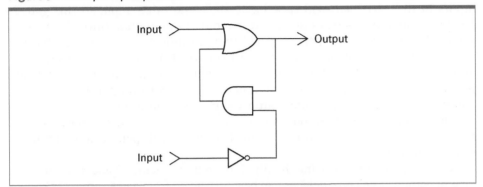

Let us consider this claim in more detail. Without knowing the current output of the circuit in Figure 3, suppose that the upper input is changed to 1 while the lower input remains 0 (Figure 4a). This will cause the output

Figure 4   Setting the output of a flip-flop to 1

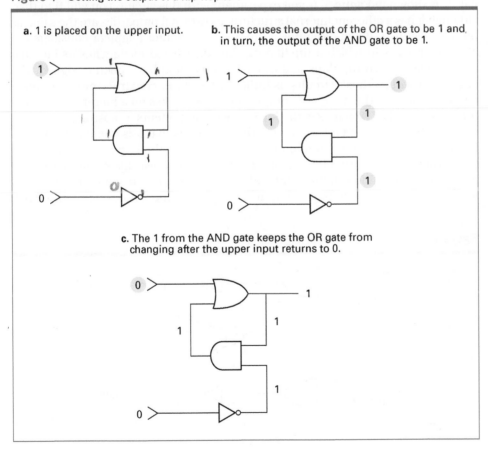

a. 1 is placed on the upper input.

b. This causes the output of the OR gate to be 1 and, in turn, the output of the AND gate to be 1.

c. The 1 from the AND gate keeps the OR gate from changing after the upper input returns to 0.

of the OR gate to be 1, regardless of the other input to this gate. In turn, both inputs to the AND gate will now be 1, since the other input to this gate is already 1 (obtained by passing the lower input of the flip-flop through the NOT gate). The output of the AND gate will then become 1, which means that the second input to the OR gate will now be 1 (Figure 4b). This guarantees that the output of the OR gate will remain 1, even when the upper input to the flip-flop is changed back to 0 (Figure 4c). In summary, the flip-flop's output has become 1, and this output value will remain after the upper input returns to 0.

In a similar manner, temporarily placing the value 1 on the lower input will force the flip-flop's output to be 0, and this output will persist after the input value returns to 0.

Our purpose in introducing the flip-flop circuit in Figures 3 and 4 is threefold. First, it demonstrates how devices can be constructed from gates, a process known as digital circuit design, which is an important topic in computer engineering. Indeed, the flip-flop is only one of many circuits that are basic tools in computer engineering.

Second, the concept of a flip-flop provides an example of abstraction and the use of abstract tools. Actually, there are other ways to build a flip-flop. One alternative is shown in Figure 5. If you experiment with this circuit, you will find that, although it has a different internal structure, its external properties are the same as those of Figure 3. When designing a flip-flop, a computer engineer considers the alternative ways in which a flip-flop can be constructed using gates as building blocks. Then, once flip-flops and other basic circuits have been designed, the engineer can use those circuits as building blocks to construct more complex circuitry. In turn, the design of computer circuitry takes on a hierarchical structure, each level of which uses the lower level components as abstract tools.

The third purpose for introducing the flip-flop is that it is one means of storing a bit within a modern computer. More precisely, a flip-flop can be set to have the output value of either 0 or 1. Other circuits can adjust this value by sending pulses to the flip-flop's inputs, and still other circuits can respond to the stored value by using the flip-flop's output as their inputs. Thus, many flip-flops,

Figure 5   Another way of constructing a flip-flop

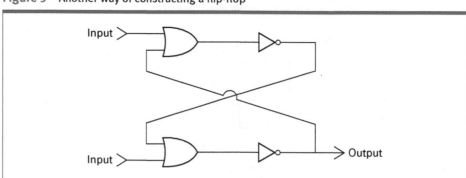

constructed as very small electrical circuits, can be used inside a computer as a means of recording information that is encoded as patterns of 0s and 1s. Indeed, technology known as **very large-scale integration (VLSI),** which allows millions of electrical components to be constructed on a wafer (called a **chip**), is used to create miniature devices containing millions of flip-flops along with their controlling circuitry. In turn, these chips are used as abstract tools in the construction of computer systems. In fact, in some cases VLSI is used to create an entire computer system on a single chip.

Hexadecimal Notation

When considering the internal activities of a computer, we must deal with strings of bits, some of which can be quite long. A long string of bits is often called a **stream.** Unfortunately, streams are difficult for the human mind to comprehend. Merely transcribing the pattern 101101010011 is tedious and error prone. To simplify the representation of such bit patterns, therefore, we usually use a shorthand notation called **hexadecimal notation,** which takes advantage of the fact that bit patterns within a machine tend to have lengths in multiples of four. In particular, hexadecimal notation uses a single symbol to represent a pattern of four bits, meaning that a string of twelve bits can be represented by only three symbols.

Figure 6 presents the hexadecimal encoding system. The left column displays all possible bit patterns of length four; the right column shows the symbol

Figure 6   The hexadecimal encoding system

Bit pattern	Hexadecimal representation
0000	0
0001	1
0010	2
0011	3
0100	4
0101	5
0110	6
0111	7
1000	8
1001	9
1010	A
1011	B
1100	C
1101	D
1110	E
1111	F

used in hexadecimal notation to represent the bit pattern to its left. Using this system, the bit pattern 10110101 is represented as B5. This is obtained by dividing the bit pattern into substrings of length four and then representing each substring by its hexadecimal equivalent—1011 is represented by B, and 0101 is represented by 5. In this manner, the 16-bit pattern 1010010011001000 can be reduced to the more palatable form A4C8.

We will use hexadecimal notation extensively in the next chapter. There you will come to appreciate its efficiency.

Questions & Exercises

1. What input bit patterns will cause the following circuit to produce an output of 1?

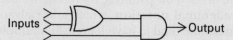

2. In the text, we claimed that placing a 1 on the lower input of the flip-flop in Figure 3 (while holding the upper input at 0) will force the flip-flop's output to be 0. Describe the sequence of events that occurs within the flip-flop in this case.

3. Assuming that both inputs to the flip-flop in Figure 5 are 0, describe the sequence of events that occurs when the upper input is temporarily set to 1.

4. It is often necessary to coordinate the activities of various components within a computer. This is accomplished by connecting a pulsating signal (called a *clock*) to those circuits that require coordination. As the clock alternates between the values 0 and 1, it activates the various circuit components. Below is an example of one part of such a circuit that involves the flip-flop shown in Figure 3. For what clock values will the flip-flop be shielded from the effects of the circuit's input values? For what clock values will the flip-flop respond to the circuit's input values?

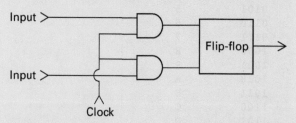

5. a. If the output of an OR gate is passed through a NOT gate, the combination computes the Boolean operation called NOR that has an output

of 1 only when both its inputs are 0. The symbol for a NOR gate is the same as an OR gate except that it has a circle at its output. Below is a circuit containing an AND gate and two NOR gates. What Boolean operation does the circuit compute?

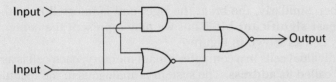

b. If the output of an AND gate is passed through a NOT gate, the combination computes the Boolean operation called NAND, which has an output of 0 only when both its inputs are 1. The symbol for a NAND gate is the same as an AND gate except that it has a circle at its output. Below is a circuit containing NAND gates. What Boolean operation does the circuit compute?

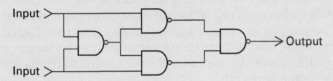

6. Use hexadecimal notation to represent the following bit patterns:

   a. 0110101011110010   b. 111010000101010100010111
   c. 01001000

7. What bit patterns are represented by the following hexadecimal patterns?

   a. 5FD97   b. 610A   c. ABCD   d. 0100

2 Main Memory

For the purpose of storing data, a computer contains a large collection of circuits (such as flip-flops), each capable of storing a single bit. This bit reservoir is known as the machine's **main memory.**

Memory Organization

A computer's main memory is organized in manageable units called **cells,** with a typical cell size being eight bits. (A string of eight bits is called a **byte.** Thus, a typical memory cell has a capacity of one byte.) Small computers used in such household devices as microwave ovens may have main memories consisting of only a few hundred cells, whereas large computers may have billions of cells in their main memories.

Although there is no left or right within a computer, we normally envision the bits within a memory cell as being arranged in a row. The left end of this row is called the **high-order end,** and the right end is called the **low-order end.** The last bit at the high-order end is called either the high-order bit or the **most significant bit** in reference to the fact that if the contents of the cell were interpreted as representing a numeric value, this bit would be the most significant digit in the number. Similarly, the bit at the right end is referred to as the low-order bit or the **least significant bit.** Thus we may represent the contents of a byte-size memory cell as shown in Figure 7.

To identify individual cells in a computer's main memory, each cell is assigned a unique "name," called its **address.** The system is analogous to the technique of identifying houses in a city by addresses. In the case of memory cells, however, the addresses used are entirely numeric. To be more precise, we envision all the cells being placed in a single row and numbered in this order starting with the value zero. Such an addressing system not only gives us a way of uniquely identifying each cell but also associates an order to the cells (Figure 8), giving us phrases such as "the next cell" or "the previous cell."

An important consequence of assigning an order to both the cells in main memory and the bits within each cell is that the entire collection of bits within a computer's main memory is essentially ordered in one long row. Pieces of this long row can therefore be used to store bit patterns that may be longer than the length of a single cell. In particular, we can still store a string of 16 bits merely by using two consecutive memory cells.

To complete the main memory of a computer, the circuitry that actually holds the bits is combined with the circuitry required to allow other circuits to store and retrieve data from the memory cells. In this way, other circuits can get data from the memory by electronically asking for the contents of a certain address (called a read operation), or they can record information in the memory by requesting that a certain bit pattern be placed in the cell at a particular address (called a write operation).

Because a computer's main memory is organized as individual, addressable cells, the cells can be accessed independently as required. To reflect the ability to access cells in any order, a computer's main memory is often called **random access memory (RAM).** This random access feature of main memory is in stark contrast to the mass storage systems that we will discuss in the next section, in which long strings of bits are manipulated as amalgamated blocks.

Figure 7 The organization of a byte-size memory cell

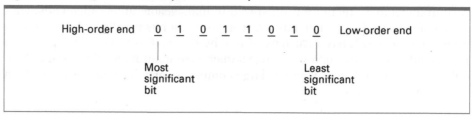

Figure 8 Memory cells arranged by address

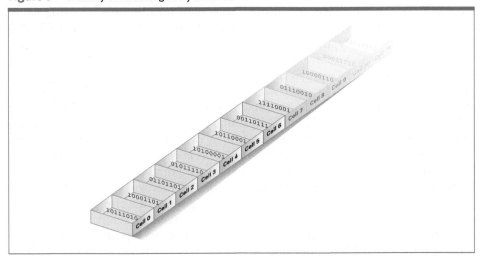

Although we have introduced flip-flops as a means of storing bits, the RAM in most modern computers is constructed using other technologies that provide greater miniaturization and faster response time. Many of these technologies store bits as tiny electric charges that dissipate quickly. Thus these devices require additional circuitry, known as a refresh circuit, that repeatedly replenishes the charges many times a second. In recognition of this volatility, computer memory constructed from such technology is often called **dynamic memory,** leading to the term **DRAM** (pronounced "DEE–ram") meaning Dynamic RAM. Or, at times the term **SDRAM** (pronounced "ES-DEE-ram") meaning Synchronous DRAM is used in reference to DRAM that applies additional techniques to decrease the time needed to retrieve the contents from its memory cells.

Measuring Memory Capacity

As we will learn in the next chapter, it is convenient to design main memory systems in which the total number of cells is a power of two. In turn, the size of the memories in early computers were often measured in 1024 (which is 2^{10}) cell units. Since 1024 is close to the value 1000, many in the computing community adopted the prefix *kilo* in reference to this unit. That is, the term *kilobyte* (abbreviated KB) was used to refer to 1024 bytes. Thus, a machine with 4096 memory cells was said to have a 4KB memory ($4096 = 4 \times 1024$). As memories became larger, this terminology grew to include the prefixes *mega* for 1,048,576 (which is 2^{20}) and *giga* for 1,073,741,824 (which is 2^{30}), and units such as MB (megabyte) and GB (gigabyte) became popular.

Unfortunately, this application of prefixes represents a misuse of terminology because these prefixes are already used in other fields in reference to units that are powers of ten. For example, when measuring distance, *kilometer* refers to 1000 meters, and when measuring radio frequencies, *megahertz* refers to 1,000,000 hertz. To make matters even worse, some manufacturers of computer equipment have mixed the two sets of terminology by using KB to refer to 1024 bytes but using MB to mean an even 1000KB (which is 1,024,000 bytes). Needless to say, these discrepancies have led to confusion and misunderstandings over the years.

To clarify matters, a proposal has been made to reserve the prefixes *kilo, mega,* and *giga* for units that are powers of ten, and to introduce the new prefixes *kibi* (short for kilobinary and abbreviated Ki), *mebi* (short for megabinary and abbreviated Mi), and *gibi* (short for gigabinary and abbreviated Gi) in reference to the corresponding units that are powers of two. Under this system, the term *kibibyte* (KiB) would refer to 1024 bytes, whereas *kilobyte* (KB) would refer to 1000 bytes. Whether these prefixes become a part of the popular vernacular remains to be seen. For now, the traditional "misuse" of the prefixes *kilo, mega,* and *giga* remains ingrained in the computing community when referring to main memory, and thus we will follow this tradition in our study when referring to data storage. However, the proposed prefixes *kibi, megi,* and *gibi* do represent an attempt to solve a growing problem, and one would be wise to interpret terms such as *kilobyte* and *megabyte* with caution in the future.

Questions & Exercises

1. If the memory cell whose address is 5 contains the value 8, what is the difference between writing the value 5 into cell number 6 and moving the contents of cell number 5 into cell number 6?

2. Suppose you want to interchange the values stored in memory cells 2 and 3. What is wrong with the following sequence of steps:

   Step 1. Move the contents of cell number 2 to cell number 3.
   Step 2. Move the contents of cell number 3 to cell number 2.

   Design a sequence of steps that correctly interchanges the contents of these cells.

3. How many bits would be in the memory of a computer with 4KB (more precisely KiB) memory?

3 Mass Storage

Due to the volatility and limited size of a computer's main memory, most computers have additional memory devices called **mass storage** (or secondary storage) systems, including magnetic disks, CDs, DVDs, magnetic tapes, and flash drives (all of which we will discuss shortly). The advantages of mass storage systems over main memory include less volatility, large storage capacities, low cost, and in many cases, the ability to remove the storage medium from the machine for archival purposes.

The terms *on-line* and *off-line* are often used to describe devices that can be either attached to or detached from a machine. **On-line** means that the device or information is connected and readily available to the machine without human intervention. **Off-line** means that human intervention is required before the device or information can be accessed by the machine—perhaps because the device must be turned on, or the medium holding the information must be inserted into some mechanism.

A major disadvantage of mass storage systems is that they typically require mechanical motion and therefore require significantly more time to store and retrieve data than a machine's main memory, where all activities are performed electronically.

Magnetic Systems

For years, magnetic technology has dominated the mass storage arena. The most common example in use today is the **magnetic disk,** in which a thin spinning disk with magnetic coating is used to hold data (Figure 9). Read/write heads are placed above and/or below the disk so that as the disk spins, each head traverses a circle, called a **track,** around the disk's upper or lower surface. By repositioning the read/write heads, different concentric tracks can be accessed. In many cases, a disk storage system consists of several disks mounted on a common spindle, one on top of the other, with enough space for the read/write heads to slip between the platters. In such cases, the read/write heads move in unison. Each time the read/write heads are repositioned, a new set of tracks—which is called a **cylinder**—becomes accessible.

Figure 9   A disk storage system

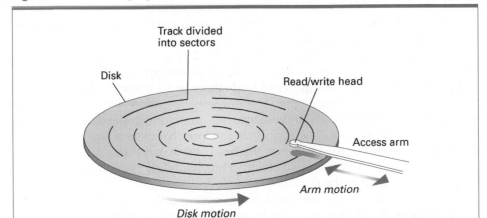

Since a track can contain more information than we would normally want to manipulate at any one time, each track is divided into small arcs called **sectors** on which information is recorded as a continuous string of bits. All sectors on a disk contain the same number of bits (typical capacities are in the range of 512 bytes to a few KB), and in the simplest disk storage systems each track contains the same number of sectors. Thus, the bits within a sector on a track near the outer edge of the disk are less compactly stored than those on the tracks near the center, since the outer tracks are longer than the inner ones. In fact, in high capacity disk storage systems, the tracks near the outer edge are capable of containing significantly more sectors than those near the center, and this capability is often utilized by applying a technique called **zoned-bit recording.** Using zoned-bit recording, several adjacent tracks are collectively known as zones, with a typical disk containing approximately ten zones. All tracks within a zone have the same number of sectors, but each zone has more sectors per track than the zone inside of it. In this manner, the storage space near the outer edge of the disk is used more efficiently than in a traditional disk system. Regardless of the details, a disk storage system consists of many individual sectors, each of which can be accessed as an independent string of bits.

The location of tracks and sectors is not a permanent part of a disk's physical structure. Instead, they are marked magnetically through a process called **formatting** (or initializing) the disk. This process is usually performed by the disk's manufacturer, resulting in what are known as formatted disks. Most computer systems can also perform this task. Thus, if the format information on a disk is damaged, the disk can be reformatted, although this process destroys all the information that was previously recorded on the disk.

The capacity of a disk storage system depends on the number of disks used and the density in which the tracks and sectors are placed. Lower-capacity systems consist of a single plastic disk known as a **diskette** or, in those cases in which the disk is flexible, by the less prestigious title of **floppy disk.** Diskettes are easily inserted and removed from their corresponding read/write units and are easily stored. As a consequence, diskettes have been popular for off-line storage of information. However, since the generic 3½-inch diskettes have a capacity of only 1.44MB, their use has largely been replaced by other technologies.

High-capacity disk systems, capable of holding many gigabytes, consist of perhaps five to ten rigid disks mounted on a common spindle. The fact that the disks used in these systems are rigid leads them to be known as hard-disk systems, in contrast to their floppy counterparts. To allow for faster rotation speeds, the read/write heads in these systems do not touch the disk but instead "float" just off the surface. The spacing is so close that even a single particle of dust could become jammed between the head and disk surface, destroying both (a phenomenon known as a head crash). Thus hard-disk systems are housed in cases that are sealed at the factory.

Several measurements are used to evaluate a disk system's performance: (1) **seek time** (the time required to move the read/write heads from one track to another); (2) **rotation delay** or **latency time** (half the time required for the disk to make a complete rotation, which is the average amount of time required for the desired data to rotate around to the read/write head once the head has been positioned over the desired track); (3) **access time** (the sum of seek time and rotation delay); and (4) **transfer rate** (the rate at which data can be transferred to or from the disk). (Note that in the case of zone-bit recording, the amount of data passing a read/write head in a single disk rotation is greater for tracks in an outer zone than for an inner zone, and therefore the data transfer rate varies depending on the portion of the disk being used.)

Hard-disk systems generally have significantly better characteristics than floppy systems. Since the read/write heads do not touch the disk surface in a hard-disk system, one finds rotation speeds of several thousand revolutions per minute, whereas disks in floppy-disk systems rotate on the order of 300 revolutions-per-minute. Consequently, transfer rates for hard-disk systems, usually measured in MB per second, are much greater than those associated with floppy-disk systems, which tend to be measured in KB per second.

Since disk systems require physical motion for their operation, both hard and floppy systems suffer when compared to speeds within electronic circuitry. Delay times within an electronic circuit are measured in units of nanoseconds (billionths of a second) or less, whereas seek times, latency times, and access times of disk systems are measured in milliseconds (thousandths of a second). Thus the time required to retrieve information from a disk system can seem like an eternity to an electronic circuit awaiting a result.

Disk storage systems are not the only mass storage devices that apply magnetic technology. An older form of mass storage using magnetic technology is **magnetic tape** (Figure 10). In these systems, information is recorded on the magnetic coating of a thin plastic tape that is wound on a reel for storage. To access the data, the tape is mounted in a device called a tape drive that typically can read, write, and rewind the tape under control of the computer. Tape drives range in size from small

Figure 10   A magnetic tape storage mechanism

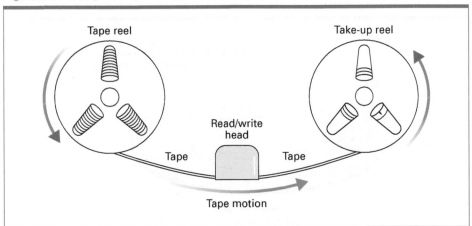

cartridge units, called streaming tape units, which use tape similar in appearance to that in stereo systems to older, large reel-to-reel units. Although the capacity of these devices depends on the format used, most can hold many GB.

A major disadvantage of magnetic tape is that moving between different positions on a tape can be very time-consuming owing to the significant amount of tape that must be moved between the reels. Thus tape systems have much longer data access times than magnetic disk systems in which different sectors can be accessed by short movements of the read/write head. In turn, tape systems are not popular for on-line data storage. Instead, magnetic tape technology is reserved for off-line archival data storage applications where its high capacity, reliability, and cost efficiency are beneficial, although advances in alternatives, such as DVDs and flash drives, are rapidly challenging this last vestige of magnetic tape.

Optical Systems

Another class of mass storage systems applies optical technology. An example is the **compact disk (CD).** These disks are 12 centimeters (approximately 5 inches) in diameter and consist of reflective material covered with a clear protective coating. Information is recorded on them by creating variations in their reflective surfaces. This information can then be retrieved by means of a laser beam that monitors irregularities on the reflective surface of the CD as it spins.

CD technology was originally applied to audio recordings using a recording format known as **CD-DA (compact disk-digital audio),** and the CDs used today for computer data storage use essentially the same format. In particular, information on these CDs is stored on a single track that spirals around the CD like a groove in an old-fashioned record, however, unlike old-fashioned records, the track on a CD spirals from the inside out (Figure 11). This track is divided into units called sectors, each with its own identifying markings and a capacity of 2KB of data, which equates to $\frac{1}{75}$ of a second of music in the case of audio recordings.

Figure 11   CD storage format

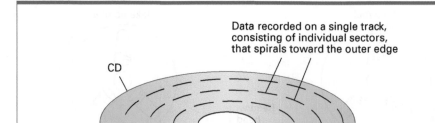

Note that the distance around the spiraled track is greater toward the outer edge of the disk than at the inner portion. To maximize the capacity of a CD, information is stored at a uniform linear density over the entire spiraled track, which means that more information is stored in a loop around the outer portion of the spiral than in a loop around the inner portion. In turn, more sectors will be read in a single revolution of the disk when the laser beam is scanning the outer portion of the spiraled track than when the beam is scanning the inner portion of the track. Thus, to obtain a uniform rate of data transfer, CD-DA players are designed to vary the rotation speed depending on the location of the laser beam. However, most CD systems used for computer data storage spin at a faster, constant speed and thus must accommodate variations in data transfer rates.

As a consequence of such design decisions, CD storage systems perform best when dealing with long, continuous strings of data, as when reproducing music. In contrast, when an application requires access to items of data in a random manner, the approach used in magnetic disk storage (individual, concentric tracks divided into individually accessible sectors) outperforms the spiral approach used in CDs.

Traditional CDs have capacities in the range of 600 to 700MB. However, newer **DVDs (Digital Versatile Disks),** which are constructed from multiple, semitransparent layers that serve as distinct surfaces when viewed by a precisely focused laser, provide storage capacities of several GB. Such disks are capable of storing lengthy multimedia presentations, including entire motion pictures.

Flash Drives

A common property of mass storage systems based on magnetic or optic technology is that physical motion, such as spinning disks, moving read/write heads, and aiming laser beams, is required to store and retrieve data. This means that data storage and retrieval is slow compared to the speed of electronic circuitry. **Flash memory** technology has the potential of alleviating this drawback. In a flash memory system, bits are stored by sending electronic signals directly to the storage medium where they cause electrons to be trapped in tiny chambers of silicon dioxide, thus altering the characteristics of small electronic circuits. Since these chambers are able to hold their captive electrons for many years, this technology is suitable for off-line storage of data.

Although data stored in flash memory systems can be accessed in small byte-size units as in RAM applications, current technology dictates that stored data be erased in large blocks. Moreover, repeated erasing slowly damages the silicon dioxide chambers, meaning that current flash memory technology is not suitable for general main memory applications where its contents might be altered many times a second. However, in those applications in which alterations can be controlled to a reasonable level, such as in digital cameras, cellular telephones, and hand-held PDAs, flash memory has become the mass storage technology of choice. Indeed, since flash memory is not sensitive to physical shock (in contrast to magnetic and optic systems) its potential in portable applications is enticing.

Flash memory devices called **flash drives,** with capacities of up to a few GB, are available for general mass storage applications. These units are packaged in small plastic cases approximately three inches long with a removable cap on one end to protect the unit's electrical connector when the drive is off-line. The high capacity of these portable units as well as the fact that they are easily connected to and disconnected from a computer make them ideal for off-line data storage. However, the vulnerability of their tiny storage chambers dictates that they are not as reliable as optical disks for truly long term applications.

File Storage and Retrieval

Information stored in a mass storage system is conceptually grouped into large units called **files.** A typical file may consist of a complete text document, a photograph, a program, a music recording, or a collection of data about the employees in a company. We have seen that mass storage devices dictate that these files be stored and retrieved in smaller, multiple byte units. For example, a file stored on a magnetic disk must be manipulated by sectors, each of which is a fixed predetermined size. A block of data conforming to the specific characteristics of a storage device is called a **physical record.** Thus, a large file stored in mass storage will typically consist of many physical records.

In contrast to this division into physical records, a file often has natural divisions determined by the information represented. For example, a file containing information regarding a company's employees would consist of multiple units, each consisting of the information about one employee. Or, a file containing a text document would consist of paragraphs or pages. These naturally occurring blocks of data are called **logical records.**

Logical records often consist of smaller units called **fields.** For example, a logical record containing information about an employee would probably consist of fields such as name, address, employee identification number, etc. Sometimes each logical record within a file is uniquely identified by means of a particular field within the record (perhaps an employee's identification number, a part number, or a catalogue item number). Such an identifying field is called a **key field.** The value held in a key field is called a **key.**

Logical record sizes rarely match the physical record size dictated by a mass storage device. In turn, one may find several logical records residing within a single physical record or perhaps a logical record split between two or more physical records (Figure 12). The result is that a certain amount of unscrambling is associated with retrieving data from mass storage systems. A common solution to this problem is to set aside an area of main memory that is large enough to hold several physical records and to use this memory space as a regrouping area. That is, blocks of data compatible with physical records can be transferred between this main memory area and the mass storage system, while the data residing in the main memory area can be referenced in terms of logical records.

An area of memory used in this manner is called a **buffer.** In general, a buffer is a storage area used to hold data on a temporary basis, usually during

Figure 12   Logical records versus physical records on a disk

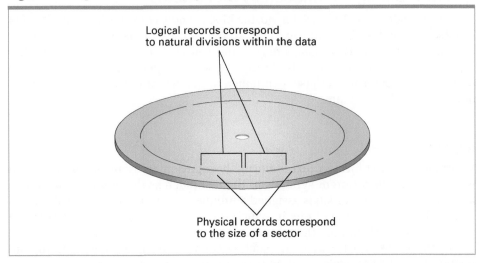

Logical records correspond
to natural divisions within the data

Physical records correspond
to the size of a sector

the process of being transferred from one device to another. For example, modern printers contain memory circuitry of their own, a large part of which is used as a buffer for holding portions of a document that have been received by the printer but not yet printed.

Questions & Exercises

1. What advantage does a hard-disk system gain from the fact that its disks spin faster than disks in a floppy-disk system?

2. When recording data on a multiple-disk storage system, should we fill a complete disk surface before starting on another surface, or should we first fill an entire cylinder before starting on another cylinder?

3. Why should the data in a reservation system that is constantly being updated be stored on a magnetic disk instead of a CD or DVD?

4. Sometimes, when modifying a document with a word processor, adding text does not increase the apparent size of the file in mass storage, but at other times the addition of a single symbol can increase the apparent size of the file by several hundred bytes. Why?

5. What advantage do flash drives have over the other mass storage systems introduced in this section?

6. What is a buffer?

4 Representing Information as Bit Patterns

Having considered techniques for storing bits, we now consider how information can be encoded as bit patterns. Our study focuses on popular methods for encoding text, numerical data, images, and sound. Each of these systems has repercussions that are often visible to a typical computer user. Our goal is to understand enough about these techniques so that we can recognize their consequences for what they are.

Representing Text

Information in the form of text is normally represented by means of a code in which each of the different symbols in the text (such as the letters of the alphabet and punctuation marks) is assigned a unique bit pattern. The text is then represented as a long string of bits in which the successive patterns represent the successive symbols in the original text.

In the 1940s and 1950s, many such codes were designed and used in connection with different pieces of equipment, producing a corresponding proliferation of communication problems. To alleviate this situation, the **American National Standards Institute (ANSI,** pronounced "AN–see") adopted the **American Standard Code for Information Interchange (ASCII,** pronounced "AS–kee"). This code uses bit patterns of length seven to represent the upper- and lowercase letters of the English alphabet, punctuation symbols, the digits 0 through 9, and certain control information such as line feeds, carriage returns, and tabs. Today, ASCII is often extended to an eight-bit-per-symbol format by adding a 0 at the most significant end of each of the seven-bit patterns. This technique not only produces a code in which each pattern fits conveniently into a typical byte-size memory cell but also provides 128 additional bit patterns (those obtained by assigning the extra bit the value 1) that can represent symbols excluded in the original ASCII. Unfortunately, because vendors tend to use their own interpretations for these extra patterns, data in which these patterns appear often are not easily transported from one vendor's application to another.

A portion of ASCII in its eight-bit-per-symbol format is shown in appendix. By referring to this appendix, we can decode the bit pattern

```
01001000   01100101   01101100   01101100   01101111
00101110
```

as the message "Hello." as demonstrated in Figure 13.

Although ACSII has been the dominant code for many years, other more extensive codes, capable of representing documents in a variety of languages, are now competing for popularity. One of these, **Unicode,** was developed through the cooperation of several of the leading manufacturers of hardware and software and is rapidly gaining support in the computing community. This code uses a unique pattern of 16 bits to represent each symbol. As a result, Unicode

Figure 13   The message "Hello." in ASCII

01001000	01100101	01101100	01101100	01101111	00101110
H	e	l	l	o	.

consists of 65,536 different bit patterns—enough to allow text written in such languages as Chinese, Japanese, and Hebrew to be represented.

Standards for a code that could compete with Unicode have been developed by the **International Organization for Standardization** (also known as **ISO,** in reference to the Greek word *isos,* meaning equal). Using patterns of 32 bits, this encoding system has the potential of representing billions of different symbols.

A file consisting of a long sequence of symbols encoded using ASCII or Unicode is often called a **text file.** It is important to distinguish between simple text files that are manipulated by utility programs called **text editors** (or often simply editors) and the more elaborate files produced by **word processors** such as Microsoft's Word. Both consist of textual material. However, a text file contains only a character-by-character encoding of the text, whereas a file produced by a word processor contains numerous proprietary codes representing changes in fonts, alignment information, etc. Moreover, word processors may even use proprietary codes rather than a standard such as ASCII or Unicode for representing the text itself.

Representing Numeric Values

Storing information in terms of encoded characters is inefficient when the information being recorded is purely numeric. To see why, consider the problem of storing the value 25. If we insist on storing it as encoded symbols in ASCII using one byte per symbol, we need a total of 16 bits. Moreover, the largest number we could store using 16 bits is 99. However, as we will shortly see, by using **binary notation** we can store any integer in the range from 0 to 65535 in these 16 bits. Thus, binary notation (or variations of it) is used extensively for encoded numeric data for computer storage.

Binary notation is a way of representing numeric values using only the digits 0 and 1 rather than the digits 0, 1, 2, 3, 4, 5, 6, 7, 8, and 9 as in the traditional decimal, or base ten, system. We will study the binary system more thoroughly in Section 5. For now, all we need is an elementary understanding of the system. For this purpose consider an old-fashioned car odometer whose display wheels contain only the digits 0 and 1 rather than the traditional digits 0 through 9. The odometer starts with a reading of all 0s, and as the car is driven for the first few miles, the rightmost wheel rotates from a 0 to a 1. Then, as that 1 rotates back to a 0, it causes a 1 to appear to its left, producing the pattern 10. The 0 on the right then rotates to a 1, producing 11. Now the rightmost wheel rotates from 1 back to

The American National Standards Institute

The American National Standards Institute (ANSI) was founded in 1918 by a small consortium of engineering societies and government agencies as a nonprofit federation to coordinate the development of voluntary standards in the private sector. Today, ANSI membership includes more than 1300 businesses, professional organizations, trade associations, and government agencies. ANSI is headquartered in New York and represents the United States as a member body in the ISO. The website for the American National Standards Institute is at http://www.ansi.org.

Similar organizations in other countries include Standards Australia (Australia), Standards Council of Canada (Canada), China State Bureau of Quality and Technical Supervision (China), Deutsches Institut für Normung (Germany), Japanese Industrial Standards Committee (Japan), Dirección General de Normas (Mexico), State Committee of the Russian Federation for Standardization and Metrology (Russia), Swiss Association for Standardization (Switzerland), and British Standards Institution (United Kingdom).

0, causing the 1 to its left to rotate to a 0 as well. This in turn causes another 1 to appear in the third column, producing the pattern 100. In short, as we drive the car we see the following sequence of odometer readings:

```
0000
0001
0010
0011
0100
0101
0110
0111
1000
```

This sequence consists of the binary representations of the integers zero through eight. Although tedious, we could extend this counting technique to discover that the bit pattern consisting of sixteen 1s represents the value 65535, which confirms our claim that any integer in the range from 0 to 65535 can be encoded using 16 bits.

Due to this efficiency, it is common to store numeric information in a form of binary notation rather than in encoded symbols. We say "a form of binary notation" because the straightforward binary system just described is only the basis for several numeric storage techniques used within machines. Some of these variations of the binary system are discussed later in this chapter. For now, we merely note that a system called **two's complement** notation (see Section 6) is common for storing whole numbers because it provides a convenient method for representing negative numbers as well as positive. For representing numbers with fractional parts such as $4\frac{1}{2}$ or $\frac{3}{4}$, another technique, called **floating-point** notation (see Section 7), is used.

Representing Images

One means of representing an image is to interpret the image as a collection of dots, each of which is called a **pixel,** short for "picture element." The appearance of each pixel is then encoded and the entire image is represented as a collection of these encoded pixels. Such a collection is called a **bit map.** This approach is popular because many display devices, such as printers and computer monitors, operate on the pixel concept. In turn, images in bit map form are easily formatted for display.

The method of encoding the pixels in a bit map varies among applications. In the case of a simple black and white image, each pixel can be represented by a single bit whose value depends on whether the corresponding pixel is black or white. This is the approach used by most facsimile machines. For more elaborate back and white photographs, each pixel can be represented by a collection of bits (usually eight), which allows a variety of shades of grayness to be represented.

In the case of color images, each pixel is encoded by more complex system. Two approaches are common. In one, which we will call RGB encoding, each pixel is represented as three color components—a red component, a green component, and a blue component—corresponding to the three primary colors of light. One byte is normally used to represent the intensity of each color component. In turn, three bytes of storage are required to represent a single pixel in the original image.

An alternative to simple RGB encoding is to use a "brightness" component and two color components. In this case the "brightness" component, which is called the pixel's luminance, is essentially the sum of the red, green, and blue components. (Actually, it is considered to be the amount of white light in the pixel, but these details need not concern us here.) The other two components, called the blue chrominance and the red chrominance, are determined by computing the difference between the pixel's luminance and the amount of blue or red light, respectively, in the pixel. Together these three components contain the information required to reproduce the pixel.

The popularity of encoding images using luminance and chrominance components originated in the field of color television broadcast because this approach provided a means of encoding color images that was also compatible with older black-and-white television receivers. Indeed, a gray-scale version of an image can be produced by using only the luminance components of the encoded color image.

A disadvantage of representing images as bit maps is that an image cannot be rescaled easily to any arbitrary size. Essentially, the only way to enlarge the image is to make the pixels bigger, which leads to a grainy appearance. (This is the technique called "digital zoom" used in digital cameras as opposed to "optical zoom" that is obtained by adjusting the camera lens.)

An alternate way of representing images that avoids this scaling problem is to describe the image as a collection of geometric structures, such as lines and curves, that can be encoded using techniques of analytic geometry. Such

ISO—The International Organization for Standardization

The International Organization for Standardization (more commonly called ISO) was established in 1947 as a worldwide federation of standardization bodies, one from each country. Today, it is headquartered in Geneva, Switzerland and has more than 100 member bodies as well as numerous correspondent members. (A correspondent member is usually a standardization body from a country that does not have a nationally recognized standardization body. Such members cannot participate directly in the development of standards but are kept informed of ISO activities.) ISO maintains a website at http://www.iso.ch.

a description allows the device that ultimately displays the image to decide how the geometric structures should be displayed rather than insisting that the device reproduce a particular pixel pattern. This is the approach used to produce the scalable fonts that are available via today's word processing systems. For example, TrueType (developed by Microsoft and Apple) is a system for geometrically describing text symbols. Likewise, PostScript (developed by Adobe Systems) provides a means of describing characters as well as more general pictorial data. This geometric means of representing images is also popular in **computer-aided design (CAD)** systems in which drawings of three-dimensional objects are displayed and manipulated on computer screens.

The distinction between representing an image in the form of geometric structures as opposed to bit maps is evident to users of many drawing software systems (such as Microsoft's Paint utility) that allow the user to draw pictures consisting of pre-established shapes such as rectangles, ovals, and elementary curves. The user simply selects the desired geometric shape from a menu and then directs the drawing of that shape via a mouse. During the drawing process, the software maintains a geometric description of the shape being drawn. As directions are given by the mouse, the internal geometric representation is modified, reconverted to bit map form, and displayed. This allows for easy scaling and shaping of the image. Once the drawing process is complete, however, the underlying geometric description is discarded and only the bit map is preserved, meaning that additional alterations (other than repositioning or rotating around specific axes, which are easily performed on bit maps) require a tedious pixel-by-pixel modification process.

Representing Sound

The most generic method of encoding audio information for computer storage and manipulation is to sample the amplitude of the sound wave at regular intervals and record the series of values obtained. For instance, the series 0, 1.5, 2.0, 1.5, 2.0, 3.0, 4.0, 3.0, 0 would represent a sound wave that rises in amplitude, falls briefly, rises to a higher level, and then drops back to 0 (Figure 14). This technique,

Figure 14   The sound wave represented by the sequence 0, 1.5, 2.0, 1.5, 2.0, 3.0, 4.0, 3.0, 0

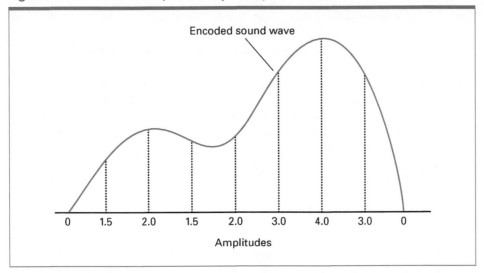

using a sample rate of 8000 samples per second, has been used for years in long-distance voice telephone communication. The voice at one end of the communication is encoded as numeric values representing the amplitude of the voice every eight-thousandth of a second. These numeric values are then transmitted over the communication line to the receiving end, where they are used to reproduce the sound of the voice.

Although 8000 samples per second may seem to be a rapid rate, it is not sufficient for high-fidelity music recordings. To obtain the quality sound reproduction obtained by today's musical CDs, a sample rate of 44,100 samples per second is used. The data obtained from each sample are represented in 16 bits (32 bits for stereo recordings). Consequently, each second of music recorded in stereo requires more than a million bits.

An alternative encoding system known as Musical Instrument Digital Interface (MIDI, pronounced "MID–ee") is widely used in the music synthesizers found in electronic keyboards, for video game sound, and for sound effects accompanying websites. By encoding directions for producing music on a synthesizer rather than encoding the sound itself, MIDI avoids the large storage requirements of the sampling technique. More precisely, MIDI encodes what instrument is to play which note for what duration of time, which means that a clarinet playing the note D for two seconds can be encoding in three bytes rather than more than two million bits when sampled at a rate of 44,100 samples per second.

In short, MIDI can be thought of as a way of encoding the sheet music read by a performer rather than the performance itself, and in turn, a MIDI "recording" can sound significantly different when performed on different synthesizers.

Questions & Exercises

1. Here is a message encoded in ASCII using eight bits per symbol. What does it say?

   01000011 01101111 01101101 01110000 01110101 01110100
   01100101 01110010 00100000 01010011 01100011 01101001
   01100101 01101110 01100011 01100101

2. In the ASCII code, what is the relationship between the codes for an uppercase letter and the same letter in lowercase?

3. Encode these sentences in ASCII:

   a. Where are you?

   b. "How?" Cheryl asked.

   c. 2 + 3 = 5.

4. Describe a device from everyday life that can be in either of two states, such as a flag on a flagpole that is either up or down. Assign the symbol 1 to one of the states and 0 to the other, and show how the ASCII representation for the letter *b* would appear when stored with such bits.

5. Convert each of the following binary representations to its equivalent base ten form:

   a. 0101   b. 1001   c. 1011
   d. 0110   e. 10000   f. 10010

6. Convert each of the following base ten representations to its equivalent binary form:

   a. 6   b. 13   c. 11
   d. 18   e. 27   f. 4

7. What is the largest numeric value that could be represented with three bytes if each digit were encoded using one ASCII pattern per byte? What if binary notation were used?

8. An alternative to hexadecimal notation for representing bit patterns is **dotted decimal notation** in which each byte in the pattern is represented by its base ten equivalent. In turn, these byte representations are separated by periods. For example, 12.5 represents the pattern 0000110000000101 (the byte 00001100 is represented by 12, and 00000101 is represented by 5), and the pattern 1000100000001000000000111 is represented by 136.16.7. Represent each of the following bit patterns in dotted decimal notation.

   a. 0000111100001111   b. 001100110000000010000000
   c. 0000101010100000

9. What is an advantage of representing images via geometric structures as opposed to bit maps? What about bit map techniques as opposed to geometric structures?

10. Suppose a stereo recording of one hour of music is encoded using a sample rate of 44,100 samples per second as discussed in the text. How does the size of the encoded version compare to the storage capacity of a CD?

5 The Binary System

In Section 4 we saw that binary notation is a means of representing numeric values using only the digits 0 and 1 rather than the ten digits 0 through 9 that are used in the more common base ten notational system. It is time now to look at binary notation more thoroughly.

Binary Notation

Recall that in the base ten system, each position in a representation is associated with a quantity. In the representation 375, the 5 is in the position associated with the quantity one, the 7 is in the position associated with ten, and the 3 is in the position associated with the quantity one hundred (Figure 15a). Each quantity is ten times that of the quantity to its right. The value represented by the entire expression is obtained by multiplying the value of each digit by the quantity associated with that digit's position and then adding those products. To illustrate, the pattern 375 represents $(3 \times \text{hundred}) + (7 \times \text{ten}) + (5 \times \text{one})$, which, in more technical notation, is $(3 \times 10^2) + (7 \times 10^1) + (5 \times 10^0)$.

The position of each digit in binary notation is also associated with a quantity, except that the quantity associated with each position is twice the quantity associated with the position to its right. More precisely, the rightmost digit in a binary representation is associated with the quantity one (2^0), the next position to the left is associated with two (2^1), the next is associated with four (2^2), the next with eight (2^3), and so on. For example, in the binary representation 1011, the

Figure 15 The base ten and binary systems

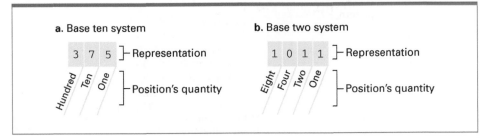

a. Base ten system

```
3  7  5  ]─ Representation

Hundred  Ten  One  ]─ Position's quantity
```

b. Base two system

```
1  0  1  1  ]─ Representation

Eight  Four  Two  One  ]─ Position's quantity
```

rightmost 1 is in the position associated with the quantity one, the 1 next to it is in the position associated with two, the 0 is in the position associated with four, and the leftmost 1 is in the position associated with eight (Figure 15b).

To extract the value represented by a binary representation, we follow the same procedure as in base ten—we multiply the value of each digit by the quantity associated with its position and add the results. For example, the value represented by 100101 is 37, as shown in Figure 16. Note that since binary notation uses only the digits 0 and 1, this multiply-and-add process reduces merely to adding the quantities associated with the positions occupied by 1s. Thus the binary pattern 1011 represents the value eleven, because the 1s are found in the positions associated with the quantities one, two, and eight.

In Section 4 we learned how to count in binary notation, which allowed us to encode small integers. For finding binary representations of large values, you may prefer the approach described by the algorithm in Figure 17. Let us apply this algorithm to the value thirteen (Figure 18). We first divide thirteen by two, obtaining a quotient of six and a remainder of one. Since the quotient was not zero, Step 2 tells us to divide the quotient (six) by two, obtaining a new quotient of three and a remainder of zero. The newest quotient is still not zero, so we divide it by two, obtaining a quotient of one and a remainder of one. Once again, we divide the newest quotient (one) by two, this time obtaining a quotient of zero and a remainder of one. Since we have now acquired a quotient of zero, we move on to Step 3, where we learn that the binary representation of the original value (thirteen) is 1101, obtained from the list of remainders.

Binary Addition

To understand the process of adding two integers that are represented in binary, let us first recall the process of adding values that are represented in traditional base ten notation. Consider, for example, the following problem:

$$
\begin{array}{r}
58 \\
+\ 27 \\
\end{array}
$$

Figure 16   Decoding the binary representation 100101

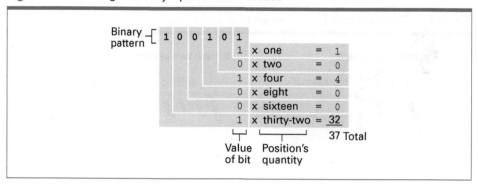

Figure 17   An algorithm for finding the binary representation of a positive integer

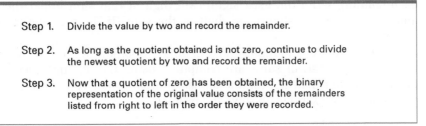

Step 1.	Divide the value by two and record the remainder.
Step 2.	As long as the quotient obtained is not zero, continue to divide the newest quotient by two and record the remainder.
Step 3.	Now that a quotient of zero has been obtained, the binary representation of the original value consists of the remainders listed from right to left in the order they were recorded.

We begin by adding the 8 and the 7 in the rightmost column to obtain the sum 15. We record the 5 at the bottom of that column and carry the 1 to the next column, producing:

```
  1
 58
+ 27
  5
```

We now add the 5 and 2 in the next column along with the 1 that was carried to obtain the sum 8, which we record at the bottom of the column. The result is:

```
 58
+ 27
 85
```

Figure 18   Applying the algorithm in Figure 17 to obtain the binary representation of thirteen

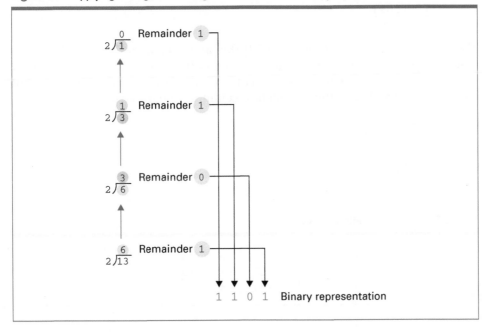

In short, the procedure is to progress from right to left as we add the digits in each column, write the least significant digit of that sum under the column, and carry the more significant digit of the sum (if there is one) to the next column.

To add two integers represented in binary notation, we follow the same procedure except that all sums are computed using the addition facts shown in Figure 19 rather than the traditional base ten facts that you learned in elementary school. For example, to solve the problem

```
  111010
+  11011
```

we begin by adding the rightmost 0 and 1; we obtain 1, which we write below the column. Now we add the 1 and 1 from the next column, obtaining 10. We write the 0 from this 10 under the column and carry the 1 to the top of the next column. At this point, our solution looks like this:

```
       1
  111010
+  11011
      01
```

We add the 1, 0, and 0 in the next column, obtain 1, and write the 1 under this column. The 1 and 1 from the next column total 10; we write the 0 under the column and carry the 1 to the next column. Now our solution looks like this:

```
      1
  111010
+  11011
    0101
```

The 1, 1, and 1 in the next column total 11 (binary notation for the value three); we write the low-order 1 under the column and carry the other 1 to the top of the next column. We add that 1 to the 1 already in that column to obtain 10. Again, we record the low-order 0 and carry the 1 to the next column. We now have

```
     1
   111010
+   11011
   010101
```

Figure 19   The binary addition facts

```
  0     1     0     1
+ 0   + 0   + 1   + 1
───   ───   ───   ───
  0     1     1    10
```

The only entry in the next column is the 1 that we carried from the previous column so we record it in the answer. Our final solution is this:

```
  111010
+  11011
 1010101
```

Fractions in Binary

To extend binary notation to accommodate fractional values, we use a **radix point** in the same role as the decimal point in decimal notation. That is, the digits to the left of the point represent the integer part (whole part) of the value and are interpreted as in the binary system discussed previously. The digits to its right represent the fractional part of the value and are interpreted in a manner similar to the other bits, except their positions are assigned fractional quantities. That is, the first position to the right of the radix is assigned the quantity $\frac{1}{2}$ (which is 2^{-1}), the next position the quantity $\frac{1}{4}$ (which is 2^{-2}), the next $\frac{1}{8}$ (which is 2^{-3}), and so on. Note that this is merely a continuation of the rule stated previously: Each position is assigned a quantity twice the size of the one to its right. With these quantities assigned to the bit positions, decoding a binary representation containing a radix point requires the same procedure as used without a radix point. More precisely, we multiply each bit value by the quantity assigned to that bit's position in the representation. To illustrate, the binary representation 101.101 decodes to $5\frac{5}{8}$, as shown in Figure 20.

For addition, the techniques applied in the base ten system are also applicable in binary. That is, to add two binary representations having radix points, we merely align the radix points and apply the same addition process as before. For example, 10.011 added to 100.11 produces 111.001, as shown here:

```
   10.011
+ 100.110
  111.001
```

Figure 20   Decoding the binary representation 101.101

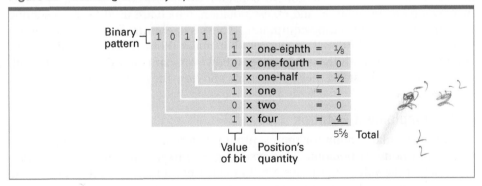

Questions & Exercises

1. Convert each of the following binary representations to its equivalent base ten form:

   a. 101010   b. 100001   c. 10111   d. 0110
   e. 11111

2. Convert each of the following base ten representations to its equivalent binary form:

   a. 32   b. 64   c. 96   d. 15
   e. 27

3. Convert each of the following binary representations to its equivalent base ten form:

   a. 11.01   b. 101.111   c. 10.1   d. 110.011
   e. 0.101

4. Express the following values in binary notation:

   a. $4\frac{1}{2}$ b. 2   c. $1\frac{1}{8}$ d. $5\frac{1}{16}$
   e. $5\frac{5}{8}$

5. Perform the following additions in binary notation:

   a. 11011   b. 1010.001   c. 11111   d. 111.11
      + 1100   +   1.101   + 0001   + 00.01

6 Storing Integers

Mathematicians have long been interested in numeric notational systems, and many of their ideas have turned out to be very compatible with the design of digital circuitry. In this section we consider two of these notational systems, two's complement notation and excess notation, which are used for representing integer values in computing equipment. These systems are based on the binary system but have additional properties that make them more compatible with computer design. With these advantages, however, come disadvantages as well. Our goal is to understand these properties and how they affect computer usage.

Two's Complement Notation

The most popular system for representing integers within today's computers is **two's complement** notation. This system uses a fixed number of bits to represent each of the values in the system. In today's equipment, it is common to use a two's complement system in which each value is represented by a pattern of

32 bits. Such a large system allows a wide range of numbers to be represented but is awkward for demonstration purposes. Thus, to study the properties of two's complement systems, we will concentrate on smaller systems.

Figure 21 shows two complete two's complement systems—one based on bit patterns of length three, the other based on bit patterns of length four. Such a system is constructed by starting with a string of 0s of the appropriate length and then counting in binary until the pattern consisting of a single 0 followed by 1s is reached. These patterns represent the values 0, 1, 2, 3, ... The patterns representing negative values are obtained by starting with a string of 1s of the appropriate length and then counting backward in binary until the pattern consisting of a single 1 followed by 0s is reached. These patterns represent the values -1, -2, -3, ... (If counting backward in binary is difficult for you, merely start at the very bottom of the table with the pattern consisting of a single 1 followed by 0s, and count up to the pattern consisting of all 1s.)

Note that in a two's complement system, the leftmost bit of a bit pattern indicates the sign of the value represented. Thus, the leftmost bit is often called the **sign bit.** In a two's complement system, negative values are represented by the patterns whose sign bits are 1; nonnegative values are represented by patterns whose sign bits are 0.

In a two's complement system, there is a convenient relationship between the patterns representing positive and negative values of the same magnitude. They are identical when read from right to left, up to and including the first 1. From there on, the patterns are complements of one another. (The **complement** of a pattern is

Figure 21   Two's complement notation systems

a. Using patterns of length three		b. Using patterns of length four	
Bit pattern	Value represented	Bit pattern	Value represented
011	3	0111	7
010	2	0110	6
001	1	0101	5
000	0	0100	4
111	-1	0011	3
110	-2	0010	2
101	-3	0001	1
100	-4	0000	0
		1111	-1
		1110	-2
		1101	-3
		1100	-4
		1011	-5
		1010	-6
		1001	-7
		1000	-8

the pattern obtained by changing all the 0s to 1s and all the 1s to 0s; 0110 and 1001 are complements.) For example, in the four-bit system in Figure 21 the patterns representing 2 and −2 both end with 10, but the pattern representing 2 begins with 00, whereas the pattern representing −2 begins with 11. This observation leads to an algorithm for converting back and forth between bit patterns representing positive and negative values of the same magnitude. We merely copy the original pattern from right to left until a 1 has been copied, then we complement the remaining bits as they are transferred to the final bit pattern (Figure 22).

Understanding these basic properties of two's complement systems also leads to an algorithm for decoding two's complement representations. If the pattern to be decoded has a sign bit of 0, we need merely read the value as though the pattern were a binary representation. For example, 0110 represents the value 6, because 110 is binary for 6. If the pattern to be decoded has a sign bit of 1, we know the value represented is negative, and all that remains is to find the magnitude of the value. We do this by applying the "copy and complement" procedure in Figure 22 and then decoding the pattern obtained as though it were a straightforward binary representation. For example, to decode the pattern 1010, we first recognize that since the sign bit is 1, the value represented is negative. Hence, we apply the "copy and complement" procedure to obtain the pattern to 0110, recognize that this is the binary representation for 6, and conclude that the original pattern represents −6.

Addition in Two's Complement Notation   To add values represented in two's complement notation, we apply the same algorithm that we used for binary addition, except that all bit patterns, including the answer, are the same length. This means that when adding in a two's complement system, any extra bit generated on the left of the answer by a final carry must be truncated. Thus "adding" 0101 and 0010 produces 0111, and "adding" 0111 and 1011 results in 0010 (0111 + 1011 = 10010, which is truncated to 0010).

With this understanding, consider the three addition problems in Figure 23. In each case, we have translated the problem into two's complement notation

Figure 22   Encoding the value −6 in two's complement notation using four bits

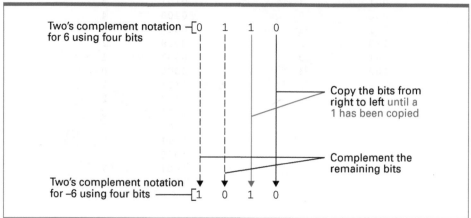

(using bit patterns of length four), performed the addition process previously described, and decoded the result back into our usual base ten notation.

Observe that the third problem in Figure 23 involves the addition of a positive number to a negative number, which demonstrates a major benefit of two's complement notation: Addition of any combination of signed numbers can be accomplished using the same algorithm and thus the same circuitry. This is in stark contrast to how humans traditionally perform arithmetic computations. Whereas elementary schoolchildren are first taught to add and later taught to subtract, a machine using two's complement notation needs to know only how to add.

For example, the subtraction problem $7 - 5$ is the same as the addition problem $7 + (-5)$. Consequently, if a machine were asked to subtract 5 (stored as 0101) from 7 (stored as 0111), it would first change the 5 to -5 (represented as 1011) and then perform the addition process of $0111 + 1011$ to obtain 0010, which represents 2, as follows:

$$
\begin{array}{ccccc}
7 & & 0111 & & 0111 \\
\underline{-5} & \rightarrow & \underline{-\ 0101} & \rightarrow & \underline{+\ 1011} \\
& & & & 0010 \quad \rightarrow \quad 2
\end{array}
$$

We see, then, that when two's complement notation is used to represent numeric values, a circuit for addition combined with a circuit for negating a value is sufficient for solving both addition and subtraction problems.

The Problem of Overflow   One problem we have avoided in the preceding examples is that in any two's complement system there is a limit to the size of the values that can be represented. When using two's complement with patterns of four bits, the largest positive integer that can be represented is 7, and the most negative integer is -8. In particular, the value 9 can not be represented, which means that we cannot hope to obtain the correct answer to the problem $5 + 4$. In fact, the result would appear as -7. This phenomenon is called **overflow.** That is,

Figure 23   Addition problems converted to two's complement notation

Problem in base ten		Problem in two's complement	Answer in base ten
$\begin{array}{r} 3 \\ +\ 2 \\ \hline \end{array}$	→	$\begin{array}{r} 0011 \\ +\ 0010 \\ \hline 0101 \end{array}$	→ 5
$\begin{array}{r} -3 \\ +\ -2 \\ \hline \end{array}$	→	$\begin{array}{r} 1101 \\ +\ 1110 \\ \hline 1011 \end{array}$	→ -5
$\begin{array}{r} 7 \\ +\ -5 \\ \hline \end{array}$	→	$\begin{array}{r} 0111 \\ +\ 1011 \\ \hline 0010 \end{array}$	→ 2

overflow is the problem that occurs when a computation produces a value that falls outside the range of values that can be represented. When using two's complement notation, this might occur when adding two positive values or when adding two negative values. In either case, the condition can be detected by checking the sign bit of the answer. An overflow is indicated if the addition of two positive values results in the pattern for a negative value or if the sum of two negative values appears to be positive.

Of course, because most computers use two's complement systems with longer bit patterns than we have used in our examples, larger values can be manipulated without causing an overflow. Today, it is common to use patterns of 32 bits for storing values in two's complement notation, allowing for positive values as large as 2,147,483,647 to accumulate before overflow occurs. If still larger values are needed, longer bit patterns can be used or perhaps the units of measure can be changed. For instance, finding a solution in terms of miles instead of inches results in smaller numbers being used and might still provide the accuracy required.

The point is that computers can make mistakes. So, the person using the machine must be aware of the dangers involved. One problem is that computer programmers and users become complacent and ignore the fact that small values can accumulate to produce large numbers. For example, in the past it was common to use patterns of 16 bits for representing values in two's complement notation, which meant that overflow would occur when values of $2^{15} = 32,768$ or larger were reached. On September 19, 1989, a hospital computer system malfunctioned after years of reliable service. Close inspection revealed that this date was 32,768 days after January 1, 1900, and the machine was programmed to compute dates based on that starting date. Thus, because of overflow, September 19, 1989 produced a negative value—a phenomenon for which the computer's program was not designed to handle.

Excess Notation

Another method of representing integer values is **excess notation.** As is the case with two's complement notation, each of the values in an excess notation system is represented by a bit pattern of the same length. To establish an excess system, we first select the pattern length to be used, then write down all the different bit patterns of that length in the order they would appear if we were counting in binary. Next, we observe that the first pattern with a 1 as its most significant bit appears approximately halfway through the list. We pick this pattern to represent zero; the patterns following this are used to represent 1, 2, 3, . . .; and the patterns preceding it are used for −1, −2, −3, ... The resulting code, when using patterns of length four, is shown in Figure 24. There we see that the value 5 is represented by the pattern 1101 and −5 is represented by 0011. (Note that the difference between an excess system and a two's complement system is that the sign bits are reversed.)

The system represented in Figure 24 is known as excess eight notation. To understand why, first interpret each of the patterns in the code using the traditional binary system and then compare these results to the values represented in the excess notation. In each case, you will find that the binary interpretation

Figure 24   An excess eight conversion table

Bit pattern	Value represented
1111	7
1110	6
1101	5
1100	4
1011	3
1010	2
1001	1
1000	0
0111	−1
0110	−2
0101	−3
0100	−4
0011	−5
0010	−6
0001	−7
0000	−8

exceeds the excess notation interpretation by the value 8. For example, the pattern 1100 in binary notation represents the value 12, but in our excess system it represents 4; 0000 in binary notation represents 0, but in the excess system it represents negative 8. In a similar manner, an excess system based on patterns of length five would be called excess 16 notation, because the pattern 10000, for instance, would be used to represent zero rather than representing its usual value of 16. Likewise, you may want to confirm that the three-bit excess system would be known as excess four notation (Figure 25).

Figure 25   An excess notation system using bit patterns of length three

Bit pattern	Value represented
111	3
110	2
101	1
100	0
011	−1
010	−2
001	−3
000	−4

Analog Versus Digital

Prior to the 21st century, many researchers debated the pros and cons of digital versus analog technology. In a digital system, a value is encoded as a series of digits and then stored using several devices, each representing one of the digits. In an analog system, each value is stored in a single device that can represent any value within a continuous range.

Let us compare the two approaches using buckets of water as the storage devices. To simulate a digital system, we could agree to let an empty bucket represent the digit 0 and a full bucket represent the digit 1. Then we could store a numeric value in a row of buckets using floating-point notation (see Section 7). In contrast, we could simulate an analog system by partially filling a single bucket to the point at which the water level represented the numeric value being represented. At first glance, the analog system may appear to be more accurate since it would not suffer from the truncation errors inherent in the digital system (again see Section 7). However, any movement of the bucket in the analog system could cause errors in detecting the water level, whereas a significant amount of sloshing would have to occur in the digital system before the distinction between a full bucket and an empty bucket would be blurred. Thus the digital system would be less sensitive to error than the analog system. This robustness is a major reason why many applications that were originally based on analog technology (such as telephone communication, audio recordings, and television) are shifting to digital technology.

Questions & Exercises

1. Convert each of the following two's complement representations to its equivalent base ten form:

   a. 00011   b. 01111   c. 11100

   d. 11010   e. 00000   f. 10000

2. Convert each of the following base ten representations to its equivalent two's complement form using patterns of eight bits:

   a. 6   b. −6   c. −17

   d. 13   e. −1   f. 0

3. Suppose the following bit patterns represent values stored in two's complement notation. Find the two's complement representation of the negative of each value:

a. 00000001   b. 01010101   c. 11111100
d. 11111110   e. 00000000   f. 01111111

4. Suppose a machine stores numbers in two's complement notation. What are the largest and smallest numbers that can be stored if the machine uses bit patterns of the following lengths?

   a. four   b. six   c. eight

5. In the following problems, each bit pattern represents a value stored in two's complement notation. Find the answer to each problem in two's complement notation by performing the addition process described in the text. Then check your work by translating the problem and your answer into base ten notation.

   a.   0101   b.   0011   c.   0101   d.   1110   e.   1010
       + 0010   + 0001   + 1010   + 0011   + 1110

6. Solve each of the following problems in two's complement notation, but this time watch for overflow and indicate which answers are incorrect because of this phenomenon.

   a.   0100   b.   0101   c.   1010   d.   1010   e.   0111
       + 0011   + 0110   + 1010   + 0111   + 0001

7. Translate each of the following problems from base ten notation into two's complement notation using bit patterns of length four, then convert each problem to an equivalent addition problem (as a machine might do), and perform the addition. Check your answers by converting them back to base ten notation.

   a.   6   b.   3   c.   4   d.   2   e.   1
       − (−1)   − 2   − 6   − (−4)   − 5

8. Can overflow ever occur when values are added in two's complement notation with one value positive and the other negative? Explain your answer.

9. Convert each of the following excess eight representations to its equivalent base ten form without referring to the table in the text:

   a. 1110   b. 0111   c. 1000
   d. 0010   e. 0000   f. 1001

10. Convert each of the following base ten representations to its equivalent excess eight form without referring to the table in the text:

    a. 5   b. −5   c. 3
    d. 0   e. 7   f. −8

11. Can the value 9 be represented in excess eight notation? What about representing 6 in excess four notation? Explain your answer.

7 Storing Fractions

In contrast to the storage of integers, the storage of a value with a fractional part requires that we store not only the pattern of 0s and 1s representing its binary representation but also the position of the radix point. A popular way of doing this is based on scientific notation and is called **floating-point** notation.

Floating-Point Notation

Let us explain floating-point notation with an example using only one byte of storage. Although machines normally use much longer patterns, this eight-bit format is representative of actual systems and serves to demonstrate the important concepts without the clutter of long bit patterns.

We first designate the high-order bit of the byte as the sign bit. Once again, a 0 in the sign bit will mean that the value stored is nonnegative, and a 1 will mean that the value is negative. Next, we divide the remaining seven bits of the byte into two groups, or fields, the **exponent field** and the **mantissa field.** Let us designate the three bits following the sign bit as the exponent field and the remaining four bits as the mantissa field. Figure 26 illustrates how the byte is divided.

We can explain the meaning of the fields by considering the following example. Suppose a byte consists of the bit pattern 01101011. Analyzing this pattern with the preceding format, we see that the sign bit is 0, the exponent is 110, and the mantissa is 1011. To decode the byte, we first extract the mantissa and place a radix point on its left side, obtaining

    .1011

Next, we extract the contents of the exponent field (110) and interpret it as an integer stored using the three-bit excess method (see again Figure 25). Thus the pattern in the exponent field in our example represents a positive 2. This tells us to move the radix in our solution to the right by two bits. (A negative exponent would mean to move the radix to the left.) Consequently, we obtain

    10.11

Figure 26   Floating-point notation components

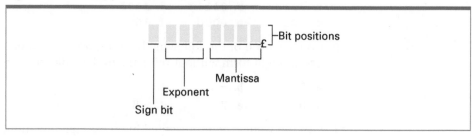

10.11

0 1 ᴨ0ᴵ0

2–+   + 1·0ᴵ0

which is the binary representation for $2\frac{3}{4}$. Next, we note that the sign bit in our example is 0; the value represented is thus nonnegative. We conclude that the byte 01101011 represents $2\frac{3}{4}$. Had the pattern been 11101011 (which is the same as before except for the sign bit), the value represented would have been $-2\frac{3}{4}$.

As another example, consider the byte 00111100. We extract the mantissa to obtain

    .1100

and move the radix one bit to the left, since the exponent field (011) represents the value -1. We therefore have

    .01100

which represents $\frac{3}{8}$. Since the sign bit in the original pattern is 0, the value stored is nonnegative. We conclude that the pattern 00111100 represents $\frac{3}{8}$.

To store a value using floating-point notation, we reverse the preceding process. For example, to encode $1\frac{1}{8}$, first we express it in binary notation and obtain 1.001. Next, we copy the bit pattern into the mantissa field from left to right, starting with the leftmost 1 in the binary representation. At this point, the byte looks like this:

    _ _ _ _ 1 0 0 1

We must now fill in the exponent field. To this end, we imagine the contents of the mantissa field with a radix point at its left and determine the number of bits and the direction the radix must be moved to obtain the original binary number. In our example, we see that the radix in .1001 must be moved one bit to the right to obtain 1.001. The exponent should therefore be a positive one, so we place 101 (which is positive one in excess four notation as shown in Figure 25) in the exponent field. Finally, we fill the sign bit with 0 because the value being stored is nonnegative. The finished byte looks like this:

    0 1 0 1 1 0 0 1

There is a subtle point you may have missed when filling in the mantissa field. The rule is to copy the bit pattern appearing in the binary representation from left to right, starting with the leftmost 1. To clarify, consider the process of storing the value $\frac{3}{8}$, which is .011 in binary notation. In this case the mantissa will be

    _ _ _ _ 1 1 0 0

It will not be

    _ _ _ _ 0 1 1 0

This is because we fill in the mantissa field *starting with the leftmost 1* that appears in the binary representation. Representations that conform to this rule are said to be in **normalized form.**

Using normalized form eliminates the possibility of multiple representations for the same value. For example, both 00111100 and 01000110 would decode to the value $\frac{3}{8}$, but only the first pattern is in normalized form. Complying with normalized form also means that the representation for all nonzero values will have a mantissa that starts with 1. The value zero, however, is a special case; its floating-point representation is a bit pattern of all 0s.

Truncation Errors

Let us consider the annoying problem that occurs if we try to store the value $2\frac{5}{8}$ with our one-byte floating-point system. We first write $2\frac{5}{8}$ in binary, which gives us 10.101. But when we copy this into the mantissa field, we run out of room, and the rightmost 1 (which represents the last $\frac{1}{8}$) is lost (Figure 27). If we ignore this problem for now and continue by filling in the exponent field and the sign bit, we end up with the bit pattern 01101010, which represents $2\frac{1}{2}$ instead of $2\frac{5}{8}$. What has occurred is called a **truncation error,** or **round-off error**—meaning that part of the value being stored is lost because the mantissa field is not large enough.

The significance of such errors can be reduced by using a longer mantissa field. In fact, most computers manufactured today use at least 32 bits for storing values in floating-point notation instead of the 8 bits we have used here. This also allows for a longer exponent field at the same time. Even with these longer formats, however, there are still times when more accuracy is required.

Another source of truncation errors is a phenomenon that you are already accustomed to in base ten notation: the problem of nonterminating expansions, such as those found when trying to express $\frac{1}{3}$ in decimal form. Some values cannot be accurately expressed regardless of how many digits we use. The difference between our traditional base ten notation and binary notation is that more values have nonterminating representations in binary than in decimal notation. For example, the value one-tenth is nonterminating when expressed in binary. Imagine the problems this might cause the unwaryperson using

Figure 27   Encoding the value $2\frac{5}{8}$

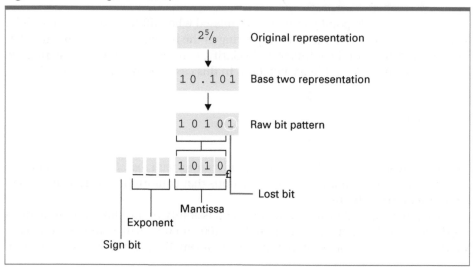

floating-point notation to store and manipulate dollars and cents. In particular, if the dollar is used as the unit of measure, the value of a dime could not be stored accurately. A solution in this case is to manipulate the data in units of pennies so that all values are integers that can be accurately stored using a method such as two's complement.

Truncation errors and their related problems are an everyday concern for people working in the area of numerical analysis. This branch of mathematics deals with the problems involved when doing actual computations that are often massive and require significant accuracy.

The following is an example that would warm the heart of any numerical analyst. Suppose we are asked to add the following three values using our one-byte floating-point notation defined previously:

$$2\tfrac{1}{4} + \tfrac{1}{8} + \tfrac{1}{8}$$

If we add the values in the order listed, we first add $2\tfrac{1}{2}$ to $\tfrac{1}{8}$ and obtain $2\tfrac{5}{8}$, which in binary is 10.101. Unfortunately, because this value cannot be stored accurately (as seen previously), the result of our first step ends up being stored as $2\tfrac{1}{2}$ (which is the same as one of the values we were adding). The next step is to add this result to the last $\tfrac{1}{8}$. Here again a truncation error occurs, and our final result turns out to be the incorrect answer $2\tfrac{1}{2}$.

Now let us add the values in the opposite order. We first add $\tfrac{1}{8}$ to $\tfrac{1}{8}$ to obtain $\tfrac{1}{4}$. In binary this is .01; so the result of our first step is stored in a byte as 00111000, which is accurate. We now add this $\tfrac{1}{4}$ to the next value in the list, $2\tfrac{1}{2}$, and obtain $2\tfrac{3}{4}$, which we can accurately store in a byte as 01101011. The result this time is the correct answer.

To summarize, in adding numeric values represented in floating-point notation, the order in which they are added can be important. The problem is that if a very large number is added to a very small number, the small number may be truncated. Thus, the general rule for adding multiple values is to add the smaller values together first, in hopes that they will accumulate to a value that is significant when added to the larger values. This was the phenomenon experienced in the preceding example.

Designers of today's commercial software packages do a good job of shielding the uneducated user from problems such as this. In a typical spreadsheet system, correct answers will be obtained unless the values being added differ in size by a factor of 10^{16} or more. Thus, if you found it necessary to add one to the value

    10,000,000,000,000,000

you might get the answer

    10,000,000,000,000,000

rather than

    10,000,000,000,000,001

Such problems are significant in applications (such as navigational systems) in which minor errors can be compounded in additional computations and ultimately produce significant consequences, but for the typical PC user the degree of accuracy offered by most commercial software is sufficient.

Questions & Exercises

1. Decode the following bit patterns using the floating-point format discussed in the text:

   a. 01001010 **b.** 01101101 **c.** 00111001 **d.** 11011100   **e.** 10101011

2. Encode the following values into the floating-point format discussed in the text. Indicate the occurrence of truncation errors.

   a. $2\frac{3}{4}$ **b.** $5\frac{1}{4}$ **c.** $\frac{3}{4}$ **d.** $-3\frac{1}{2}$ **e.** $-4\frac{3}{8}$

3. In terms of the floating-point format discussed in the text, which of the patterns 01001001 and 00111101 represents the larger value? Describe a simple procedure for determining which of two patterns represents the larger value.

4. When using the floating-point format discussed in the text, what is the largest value that can be represented? What is the smallest positive value that can be represented?

8 Data Compression

For the purpose of storing or transferring data, it is often helpful (and sometimes mandatory) to reduce the size of the data involved while retaining the underlying information. The technique for accomplishing this is called **data compression.** We begin this section by considering some generic data compression methods and then look at some approaches designed for specific applications.

Generic Data Compression Techniques

Data compression schemes fall into two categories. Some are **lossless,** others are **lossy.** Lossless schemes are those that do not lose information in the compression process. Lossy schemes are those that may lead to the loss of information. Lossy techniques often provide more compression than lossless ones and are therefore popular in settings in which minor errors can be tolerated, as in the case of images and audio.

In cases where the data being compressed consist of long sequences of the same value, the compression technique called **run-length encoding,** which is a lossless method, is popular. It is the process of replacing sequences of identical data elements with a code indicating the element that is repeated and the number of times it occurs in the sequence. For example, less space is required to indicate that a bit pattern consists of 253 ones, followed by 118 zeros, followed by 87 ones than to actually list all 458 bits.

Another lossless data compression technique is **frequency-dependent encoding,** a system in which the length of the bit pattern used to represent a data item is inversely related to the frequency of the item's use. Such codes are examples of variable-length codes, meaning that items are represented by patterns of different lengths as opposed to codes such as Unicode, in which all symbols are represented by 16 bits. David Huffman is credited with discovering an algorithm that is commonly used for developing frequency-dependent codes, and it is common practice to refer to codes developed in this manner as **Huffman codes.** In turn, most frequency-dependent codes in use today are Huffman codes.

As an example of frequency-dependent encoding, consider the task of encoded English language text. In the English language the letters *e, t, a,* and *i* are used more frequently than the letters *z, q,* and *x*. So, when constructing a code for text in the English language, space can be saved by using short bit patterns to represent the former letters and longer bit patterns to represent the latter ones. The result would be a code in which English text would have shorter representations than would be obtained with uniform-length codes.

In some cases, the stream of data to be compressed consists of units, each of which differs only slightly from the preceding one. An example would be consecutive frames of a motion picture. In these cases, techniques using **relative encoding,** also known as **differential encoding,** are helpful. These techniques record the differences between consecutive data units rather than entire units; that is, each unit is encoded in terms of its relationship to the previous unit. Relative encoding can be implemented in either lossless or lossy form depending on whether the differences between consecutive data units are encoded precisely or approximated.

Still other popular compression systems are based on **dictionary encoding** techniques. Here the term *dictionary* refers to a collection of building blocks from which the message being compressed is constructed, and the message itself is encoded as a sequence of references to the dictionary. We normally think of dictionary encoding systems as lossless systems, but as we will see in our discussion of image compression, there are times when the entries in the dictionary are only approximations of the correct data elements, resulting in a lossy compression system.

Dictionary encoding can be used by word processors to compress text documents because the dictionaries already contained in these processors for the purpose of spell checking make excellent compression dictionaries. In particular, an entire word can be encoded as a single reference to this dictionary rather than as a sequence of individual characters encoded using a system such as ASCII or Unicode. A typical dictionary in a word processor contains approximately 25,000 entries, which means an individual entry can be identified by an integer in the range of 0 to 24,999. This means that a particular entry in the dictionary can be identified by a pattern of only 15 bits. In contrast, if the word being referenced consisted of six letters, its character-by-character encoding would require 42 bits using seven-bit ASCII or 96 bits using Unicode.

A variation of dictionary encoding is **adaptive dictionary encoding** (also known as dynamic dictionary encoding). In an adaptive dictionary encoding system, the dictionary is allowed to change during the encoding process. A popular example is **Lempel-Ziv-Welsh (LZW) encoding** (named after its creators, Abraham Lempel, Jacob Ziv, and Terry Welsh). To encode a message using LZW, one starts with a dictionary containing the basic building blocks from which the message is constructed, but as larger units are found in the message, they are added to the dictionary—meaning that future occurrences of those units can be encoded as single, rather than multiple, dictionary references. For example, when encoding English text, one could start with a dictionary containing individual characters, digits, and punctuation marks. But as words in the message are identified, they could be added to the dictionary. Thus, the dictionary would grow as the message is encoded, and as the dictionary grows, more words (or recurring patterns of words) in the message could be encoded as single references to the dictionary.

The result would be a message encoded in terms of a rather large dictionary that is unique to that particular message. But this large dictionary would not have to be present to decode the message. Only the original small dictionary would be needed. Indeed, the decoding process could begin with the same small dictionary with which the encoding process started. Then, as the decoding process continues, it would encounter the same units found during the encoding process, and thus be able to add them to the dictionary for future reference just as in the encoding process.

To clarify, consider applying LZW encoding to the message

    xyx xyx xyx xyx

starting with a dictionary with three entries, the first being *x*, the second being *y*, and the third being a space. We would begin by encoding *xyx* as 121, meaning that the message starts with the pattern consisting of the first dictionary entry, followed by the second, followed by the first. Then the space is encoded to produce 1213. But, having reached a space, we know that the preceding string of characters forms a word, and so we add the pattern *xyx* to the dictionary as the fourth entry. Continuing in this manner, the entire message would be encoded as 121343434.

If we were now asked to decode this message, starting with the original three-entry dictionary, we would begin by decoding the initial string 1213 as *xyx* followed by a space. At this point we would recognize that the string *xyx* forms a word and add it to the dictionary as the fourth entry, just as we did during the encoding process. We would then continue decoding the message by recognizing that the 4 in the message refers to this new fourth entry and decode it as the word *xyx*, producing the pattern

    xyx xyx

Continuing in this manner we would ultimately decode the string 121343434 as

    xyx xyx xyx xyx

which is the original message.

Compressing Images

In Section 4, we saw how images are encoded using bit map techniques. Unfortunately, the bit maps produced are often very large. In turn, numerous compression schemes have been developed specifically for image representations.

One system known as **GIF** (short for Graphic Interchange Format and pronounced "Giff" by some and "Jiff" by others) is a dictionary encoding system that was developed by CompuServe. It approaches the compression problem by reducing the number of colors that can be assigned to a pixel to only 256. The red-green-blue combination for each of these colors is encoded using three bytes, and these 256 encodings are stored in a table (a dictionary) called the palette. Each pixel in an image can then be represented by a single byte whose value indicates which of the 256 palette entries represents the pixel's color. (Recall that a single byte can contain any one of 256 different bit patterns.) Note that GIF is a lossy compression system when applied to arbitrary images because the colors in the palette may not be identical to the colors in the original image.

GIF can obtain additional compression by extending this simple dictionary system to an adaptive dictionary system using LZW techniques. In particular, as patterns of pixels are encountered during the encoding process, they are added to the dictionary so that future occurrences of these patterns can be encoded more efficiently. Thus, the final dictionary consists of the original palette and a collection of pixel patterns.

One of the colors in a GIF palette is normally assigned the value "transparent," which means that the background is allowed to show through each region assigned that "color." This option, combined with the relative simplicity of the GIF system, makes GIF a logical choice in simple animation applications in which multiple images must move around on a computer screen. On the other hand, its ability to encode only 256 colors renders it unsuitable for applications in which higher precision is required, as in the field of photography.

Another popular compression system for images is **JPEG** (pronounced "JAY-peg"). It is a standard developed by the **Joint Photographic Experts Group** (hence the standard's name) within ISO. JPEG has proved to be an effective standard for compressing color photographs and is widely used in the photography industry, as witnessed by the fact that most digital cameras use JPEG as their default compression technique.

The JPEG standard actually encompasses several methods of image compression, each with its own goals. In those situations that require the utmost in precision, JPEG provides a lossless mode. However, JPEG's lossless mode does not produce high levels of compression when compared to other JPEG options. Moreover, other JPEG options have proven very successful, meaning that JPEG's lossless mode is rarely used. Instead, the option known as JPEG's baseline standard (also known as JPEG's lossy sequential mode) has become the standard of choice in many applications.

Image compression using the JPEG baseline standard requires a sequence of steps, some of which are designed to take advantage of a human eye's limitations. In particular, the human eye is more sensitive to changes in brightness than to changes in color. So, starting from an image that is encoded in terms of luminance and chrominance components, the first step is to average the chrominance values over two-by-two pixel squares. This reduces the size of the chrominance information by a factor of four while preserving all the original brightness information. The result is a significant degree of compression without a noticeable loss of image quality.

The next step is to divide the image into eight-by-eight pixel blocks and to compress the information in each block as a unit. This is done by applying a mathematical technique known as the discrete cosine transform, whose details need not concern us here. The important point is that this transformation converts the original eight-by-eight block into another block whose entries reflect how the pixels in the original block relate to each other rather than the actual pixel values. Within this new block, values below a predetermined threshold are then replaced by zeros, reflecting the fact that the changes represented by these values are too subtle to be detected by the human eye. For example, if the original block contained a checker board pattern, the new block might reflect a uniform average color. (A typical eight-by-eight pixel block would represent a very small square within the image so the human eye would not identify the checker board appearance anyway.)

At this point, more traditional run-length encoding, relative encoding, and variable-length encoding techniques are applied to obtain additional compression. All together, JPEG's baseline standard normally compresses color images by a factor of at least 10, and often by as much as 30, without noticeable loss of quality.

Still another data compression system associated with images is **TIFF** (short for Tagged Image File Format). However, the most popular use of TIFF is not as a means of data compression but instead as a standardized format for storing photographs along with related information such as date, time, and camera settings. In this context, the image itself is normally stored as red, green, and blue pixel components without compression.

The TIFF collection of standards does include data compression techniques, most of which are designed for compressing images of text documents in facsimile applications. These use variations of run-length encoding to take advantage of the fact that text documents consist of long strings of white pixels. The color image compression option included in the TIFF standards is based on techniques similar to those used by GIF, and are therefore not widely used in the photography community.

Compressing Audio and Video

The most commonly used standards for encoding and compressing audio and video were developed by the **Motion Picture Experts Group (MPEG)** under the leadership of ISO. In turn, these standards themselves are called MPEG.

MPEG encompasses a variety of standards for different applications. For example, the demands for high definition television (HDTV) broadcast are distinct from those for video conferencing in which the broadcast signal must find its way over a variety of communication paths that may have limited capabilities. And, both of these applications differ from that of storing video in such a manner that sections can be replayed or skipped over.

The techniques employed by MPEG are well beyond the scope of this text, but in general, video compression techniques are based on video being constructed as a sequence of pictures in much the same way that motion pictures are recorded on film. To compress such sequences, only some of the pictures, called I-frames, are encoded in their entirety. The pictures between the I-frames are encoded using relative encoding techniques. That is, rather than encode the entire picture, only its distinctions from the prior image are recorded. The I-frames themselves are usually compressed with techniques similar to JPEG.

The best known system for compressing audio is **MP3,** which was developed within the MPEG standards. In fact, the acronym *MP3* is short for *MPEG layer 3*. Among other compression techniques, MP3 takes advantage of the properties of the human ear, removing those details that the human ear cannot perceive. One such property, called **temporal masking,** is that for a short period after a loud sound, the human ear cannot detect softer sounds that would otherwise be audible. Another, called **frequency masking,** is that a sound at one frequency tends to mask softer sounds at nearby frequencies. By taking advantage of such characteristics, MP3 can be used to obtain significant compression of audio while maintaining near CD quality sound.

Using MPEG and MP3 compression techniques, video cameras are able to record as much as an hour's worth of video within 128MB of storage and portable music players can store as many as 400 popular songs in a single GB. But, in contrast to the goals of compression in other settings, the goal of compressing audio and video is not necessarily to save storage space. Just as important is the goal of obtaining encodings that allow information to be transmitted over today's communication systems fast enough to provide timely presentation. If each video frame required a MB of storage and the frames had to be transmitted over a communication path that could relay only one KB per second, there would be no hope of successful video conferencing. Thus, in addition to the quality of reproduction allowed, audio and video compression systems are often judged by the transmission speeds required for timely data communication. These speeds are normally measured in **bits per second (bps).** Common units include **Kbps** (kilo-bps, equal to 1000 bps), **Mbps** (mega-bps, equal to 1 million bps), and **Gbps** (giga-bps, equal to 1 billion bps). Using MPEG techniques, video presentations can be successfully relayed over communication paths that provide transfer rates of 40 Mbps. MP3 recordings generally require transfer rates of no more than 64 Kbps.

Questions & Exercises

1. List four generic compression techniques.
2. What would be the encoded version of the message

   xyx yxxxy xyx yxxxy yxxxy

   if LZW compression, starting with the dictionary containing x, y, and a space (as described in the text), were used?
3. Why would GIF be better than JPEG when encoding color cartoons?
4. Suppose you were part of a team designing a spacecraft that will travel to other planets and send back photographs. Would it be a good idea to compress the photographs using GIF or JPEG's baseline standard to reduce the resources required to store and transmit the images?
5. What characteristic of the human eye does JPEG's baseline standard exploit?
6. What characteristic of the human ear does MP3 exploit?
7. Identify a troubling phenomenon that is common when encoding numeric information, images, and sound as bit patterns.

9 Communication Errors

When information is transferred back and forth among the various parts of a computer, or transmitted from the earth to the moon and back, or, for that matter, merely left in storage, a chance exists that the bit pattern ultimately retrieved may not be identical to the original one. Particles of dirt or grease on a magnetic recording surface or a malfunctioning circuit may cause data to be incorrectly recorded or read. Static on a transmission path may corrupt portions of the data. And, in the case of some technologies, normal background radiation can alter patterns stored in a machine's main memory.

To resolve such problems, a variety of encoding techniques have been developed to allow the detection and even the correction of errors. Today, because these techniques are largely built into the internal components of a computer system, they are not apparent to the personnel using the machine. Nonetheless, their presence is important and represents a significant contribution to scientific research. It is fitting, therefore, that we investigate some of these techniques that lie behind the reliability of today's equipment.

Parity Bits

A simple method of detecting errors is based on the principle that if each bit pattern being manipulated has an odd number of 1s and a pattern with an even number of 1s is encountered, an error must have occurred. To use this principle, we need an encoding system in which each pattern contains an odd number of 1s. This is easily obtained by first adding an additional bit, called a **parity bit,** to each pattern in an encoding system already available (perhaps at the high-order end). In each case, we assign the value 1 or 0 to this new bit so that the entire resulting pattern has an odd number of 1s. Once our encoding system has been modified in this way, a pattern with an even number of 1s indicates that an error has occurred and that the pattern being manipulated is incorrect.

Figure 28 demonstrates how parity bits could be added to the ASCII codes for the letters A and F. Note that the code for A becomes 101000001 (parity bit 1) and the ASCII for F becomes 001000110 (parity bit 0). Although the original eight-bit pattern for A has an even number of 1s and the original eight-bit pattern for F has an odd number of 1s, both the nine-bit patterns have an odd number of 1s. If this technique were applied to all the eight-bit ASCII patterns, we would obtain a nine-bit encoding system in which an error would be indicated by any nine-bit pattern with an even number of 1s.

The parity system just described is called **odd parity,** because we designed our system so that each correct pattern contains an odd number of 1s. Another technique is called **even parity.** In an even parity system, each pattern is designed to contain an even number of 1s, and thus an error is signaled by the occurrence of a pattern with an odd number of 1s.

Figure 28   The ASCII codes for the letters A and F adjusted for odd parity

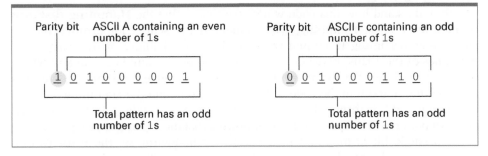

Today it is not unusual to find parity bits being used in a computer's main memory. Although we envision these machines as having memory cells of eight-bit capacity, in reality each has a capacity of nine bits, one bit of which is used as a parity bit. Each time an eight-bit pattern is given to the memory circuitry for storage, the circuitry adds a parity bit and stores the resulting nine-bit pattern. When the pattern is later retrieved, the circuitry checks the parity of the nine-bit pattern. If this does not indicate an error, then the memory removes the parity bit and confidently returns the remaining eight-bit pattern. Otherwise, the memory returns the eight data bits with a warning that the pattern being returned may not be the same pattern that was originally entrusted to memory.

The straightforward use of parity bits is simple but it has its limitations. If a pattern originally has an odd number of 1s and suffers two errors, it will still have an odd number of 1s, and thus the parity system will not detect the errors. In fact, straightforward applications of parity bits fail to detect any even number of errors within a pattern.

One means of minimizing this problem is sometimes applied to long bit patterns, such as the string of bits recorded in a sector on a magnetic disk. In this case the pattern is accompanied by a collection of parity bits making up a **checkbyte.** Each bit within the checkbyte is a parity bit associated with a particular collection of bits scattered throughout the pattern. For instance, one parity bit may be associated with every eighth bit in the pattern starting with the first bit, while another may be associated with every eighth bit starting with the second bit. In this manner, a collection of errors concentrated in one area of the original pattern is more likely to be detected, since it will be in the scope of several parity bits. Variations of this checkbyte concept lead to error detection schemes known as checksums and cyclic redundancy checks (CRC).

Error-Correcting Codes

Although the use of a parity bit allows the detection of an error, it does not provide the information needed to correct the error. Many people are surprised that **error-correcting codes** can be designed so that errors can be not only detected but also corrected. After all, intuition says that we cannot correct errors in a received message unless we already know the information in the message. However, a simple code with such a corrective property is presented in Figure 29.

To understand how this code works, we first define the **Hamming distance** (named after R. W. Hamming, who pioneered the search for error-correcting codes after becoming frustrated with the lack of reliability of the early relay machines of the 1940s) between two patterns to be the number of bits in which the patterns differ. For example, the Hamming distance between the patterns representing A and B in the code in Figure 29 is four, and the Hamming distance between B and C is three. The important feature of the code in Figure 29 is that any two patterns are separated by a Hamming distance of at least three.

If a single bit is modified in a pattern from Figure 29, the error can be detected since the result will not be a legal pattern. (We must change at least

Figure 29 An error-correcting code

Symbol	Code
A	000000
B	001111
C	010011
D	011100
E	100110
F	101001
G	110101
H	111010

three bits in any pattern before it will look like another legal pattern.) Moreover, we can also figure out what the original pattern was. After all, the modified pattern will be a Hamming distance of only one from its original form but at least two from any of the other legal patterns.

Thus, to decode a message that was originally encoded using Figure 29, we simply compare each received pattern with the patterns in the code until we find one that is within a distance of one from the received pattern. We consider this to be the correct symbol for decoding. For example, if we received the bit pattern 010100 and compared this pattern to the patterns in the code, we would obtain the table in Figure 30. Thus, we would conclude that the character transmitted must have been a D because this is the closest match.

You will observe that using this technique with the code in Figure 29 actually allows us to detect up to two errors per pattern and to correct one error. If we designed the code so that each pattern was a Hamming distance of at least five from each of the others, we would be able to detect up to four errors per pattern and correct up to two. Of course, the design of efficient codes associated with

Figure 30 Decoding the pattern 010100 using the code in Figure 29

Character	Code	Pattern received	Distance between received pattern and code
A	0 0 0 0 0 0	0 1 0 1 0 0	2
B	0 0 1 1 1 1	0 1 0 1 0 0	4
C	0 1 0 0 1 1	0 1 0 1 0 0	3
D	0 1 1 1 0 0	0 1 0 1 0 0	1 — Smallest distance
E	1 0 0 1 1 0	0 1 0 1 0 0	3
F	1 0 1 0 0 1	0 1 0 1 0 0	5
G	1 1 0 1 0 1	0 1 0 1 0 0	2
H	1 1 1 0 1 0	0 1 0 1 0 0	4

large Hamming distances is not a straightforward task. In fact, it constitutes a part of the branch of mathematics called algebraic coding theory, which is a subject within the fields of linear algebra and matrix theory.

Error-correcting techniques are used extensively to increase the reliability of computing equipment. For example, they are often used in high-capacity magnetic disk drives to reduce the possibility that flaws in the magnetic surface will corrupt data. Moreover, a major distinction between the original CD format used for audio disks and the later format used for computer data storage is in the degree of error correction involved. CD-DA format incorporates error-correcting features that reduce the error rate to only one error for two CDs. This is quite adequate for audio recordings, but a company using CDs to supply software to customers would find that flaws in 50 percent of the disks would be intolerable. Thus, additional error-correcting features are employed in CDs used for data storage, reducing the probability of error to one in 20,000 disks.

Questions & Exercises

1. The following bytes were originally encoded using odd parity. In which of them do you know that an error has occurred?

   a. 10101101 b. 10000001 c. 00000000 d. 11100000 e. 11111111

2. Could errors have occurred in a byte from Question 1 without your knowing it? Explain your answer.

3. How would your answers to Questions 1 and 2 change if you were told that even parity had been used instead of odd?

4. Encode these sentences in ASCII using odd parity by adding a parity bit at the high-order end of each character code:

   a. Where are you?
   b. "How?" Cheryl asked.
   c. 2 + 3 = 5.

5. Using the error-correcting code presented in Figure 29, decode the following messages:

   a. 001111 100100 001100
   b. 010001 000000 001011
   c. 011010 110110 100000 011100

6. Construct a code for the characters A, B, C, and D using bit patterns of length five so that the Hamming distance between any two patterns is at least three.

(handwritten margin notes, top right):
true and false
XOR
one true
of
both true
AND
①

Chapter Review Problems

(Asterisked problems are associated with optional sections.)

1. Determine the output of each of the following circuits, assuming that the upper input is 1 and the lower input is 0.

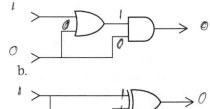

a.

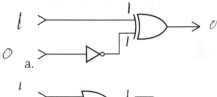

b.

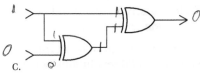

c.

2. For each of the following circuits, identify the input combinations that produce an output of 1.

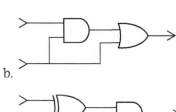

a.

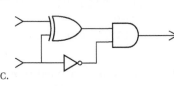

b.

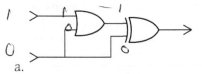

c.

3. In each circuit below, the rectangles represent the same type of gate. Based on the input and output information given, identify

whether the gate involved is an AND, OR, or XOR.

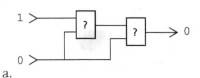

a.

b.

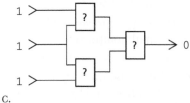

c.

4. Assume that both of the inputs in the circuit below are 1. Describe what would happen if the upper input were temporarily changed to 0. Describe what would happen if the lower input were temporarily changed to 0. Redraw the circuit using NAND gates.

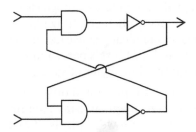

5. The following table represents the addresses and contents (using hexadecimal notation) of some cells in a machine's main memory.

Starting with this memory arrangement, follow the sequence of instructions and record the final contents of each of these memory cells:

Address	Contents
00	AB 02
01	53
02	D6 01
03	02 53

Step 1. Move the contents of the cell whose address is 03 to the cell at address 00.

Step 2. Move the value 01 into the cell at address 02.

Step 3. Move the value stored at address 01 into the cell at address 03.

6. How many cells can be in a computer's main memory if each cell's address can be represented by two hexadecimal digits? What if four hexadecimal digits are used?

7. What bit patterns are represented by the following hexadecimal notations?
   a. CB   b. 67   c. A9   d. 10   e. FF

8. What is the value of the most significant bit in the bit patterns represented by the following hexadecimal notations?
   a. 7F   b. FF   c. 8F   d. 1F

9. Express the following bit patterns in hexadecimal notation:

   a. 101010101010
   b. 110010110111
   c. 000011101011

10. Suppose a digital camera has a storage capacity of 256MB. How many photographs could be stored in the camera if each consisted of 1024 pixels per row and 1024 pixels per column if each pixel required three bytes of storage?

11. Suppose a picture is represented on a computer screen by a rectangular array containing 1024 columns and 768 rows of pixels. If eight bits are required to encode the color and intensity of each pixel, how many byte-size memory cells are required to hold the entire picture?

12. a. Identify two advantages that main memory has over magnetic disk storage.
    b. Identify two advantages that magnetic disk storage has over main memory.

13. Suppose that only 50GB of your personal computer's 120GB hard-disk drive is empty. Would it be reasonable to use CDs to store all the material you have on the drive as a backup? What about DVDs?

14. If each sector on a magnetic disk contains 1024 bytes, how many sectors are required to store a single page of text (perhaps 50 lines of 100 characters) if each character is represented in Unicode?

15. How many bytes of storage space would be required to store a 400-page novel in which each page contains 3500 characters if ASCII were used? How many bytes would be required if Unicode were used?

16. How long is the latency time of a typical hard-disk drive spinning at 60 revolutions per second?

17. What is the average access time for a hard disk spinning at 60 revolutions per second with a seek time of 10 milliseconds?

18. Suppose a typist could type 60 words per minute continuously day after day. How long would it take the typist to fill a CD whose capacity is 640MB? Assume one word is five characters and each character requires one byte of storage.

19. Here is a message in ASCII. What does it say?
    01010111 01101000 01100001 01110100
    00100000 01100100
    01101111 01100101 01110011 00100000
    01101001 01110100
    00100000 01110011 01100001 01111001
    00111111

20. The following is a message encoded in ASCII using one byte per character and then represented in hexadecimal notation. What is the message?
    68657861646563696D616C

21. Encode the following sentences in ASCII using one byte per character.
    a. 100/5 = 20
    b. To be or not to be?
    c. The total cost is $7.25.

22. Express your answers to the previous problem in hexadecimal notation.

23. List the binary representations of the integers from 6 to 16.

24. a. Write the number 26 by representing the 2 and 6 in ASCII.
    b. Write the number 26 in binary representation.

25. What values have binary representations in which only one of the bits is 1? List the binary representations for the smallest six values with this property.

*26. Convert each of the following binary representations to its equivalent base ten representation:
    a. 111   b. 0001   c. 10101
    d. 10001   e. 10011   f. 000000
    g. 100   h. 1000   i. 10000
    j. 11001   k. 11010   l. 11011

*27. Convert each of the following base ten representations to its equivalent binary representation:
    a. 7   b. 11   c. 16
    d. 15   e. 33

*28. Convert each of the following excess 16 representations to its equivalent base ten representation:
    a. 10000   b. 10011   c. 01101
    d. 01111   e. 10111

*29. Convert each of the following base ten representations to its equivalent excess four representation:
    a. 0   b. 3   c. −3
    d. −1   e. 1

*30. Convert each of the following two's complement representations to its equivalent base ten representation:
    a. 01111   b. 10011   c. 01101
    d. 10000   e. 10111

*31. Convert each of the following base ten representations to its equivalent two's complement representation in which each value is represented in seven bits:
    a. 12   b. −12   c. −1
    d. 0   e. 8

*32. Perform each of the following additions assuming the bit strings represent values in two's complement notation. Identify each case in which the answer is incorrect because of overflow.

    a.   00101   b.   11111   c.   01111
        +01000   +00001   +00001

    d.   10111   e.   00111   f.   00111
        +11010   +00111   +01100

    g.   11111   h.   01010   i.   01000
        +11111   +00011   +01000

    j.   01010
        +10101

*33.   Solve each of the following problems by translating the values into two's complement notation (using patterns of five bits), converting any subtraction problem to an equivalent addition problem, and performing that addition. Check your work by converting your answer to base ten notation. (Watch out for overflow.)

    a.   7   b.   7   c.   12
         +1   −1   −4

    d.   8   e.   12   f.   5
         −7   −4   −11

*34. Convert each of the following binary representations into its equivalent base ten representation:
    a. 11.01   b. 100.0101   c. 0.1101
    d. 1.0   e. 10.001

*35. Express each of the following values in binary notation:
    a. 5$\frac{1}{4}$ b. $\frac{1}{16}$ c. 7$\frac{7}{8}$
    d. 1$\frac{3}{4}$ e. 6$\frac{5}{8}$

*36. Decode the following bit patterns using the floating-point format described in Figure 26:
    a. 01011010   b. 11001000
    c. 00101100   d. 10111001

*37. Encode the following values using the eight-bit floating-point format described in Figure 26. Indicate each case in which a truncation error occurs.
a. ½   b. 7½   c. –3¾
d. ⁵/₃₂   e. ³¹/₃₂

*38. Assuming you are not restricted to using normalized form, list all the bit patterns that could be used to represent the value ³/₈ using the floating-point format described in Figure 26.

*39. What is the best approximation to the square root of 2 that can be expressed in the eight-bit floating-point format described in Figure 26? What value is actually obtained if this approximation is squared by a machine using this floating-point format?

*40. What is the best approximation to the value one-tenth that can be represented using the eight-bit floating-point format described in Figure 26?

*41. Explain how errors can occur when measurements using the metric system are recorded in floating-point notation. For example, what if 110 cm was recorded in units of meters?

*42. Using the eight-bit floating-point format described in Figure 26, what would be the result of computing the sum ⅛ + ⅛ + ⅛ + 2½ from left to right? How about from right to left?

*43. What answer would be given to each of the following problems by a machine using the eight-bit floating-point format described in Figure 26?
a. 1½ + ³/₁₆ =
b. 3¼ + 1⅛ =
c. 2¼ + 1⅛ =

44. In each of the following addition problems, interpret the bit patterns using the eight-bit floating-point format presented in Figure 26, add the values represented, and encode the

answer in the same floating-point format. Identify those cases in which truncation errors occur.
a.   01011100   b.   01011000
    +01101000   −01011000

c.   01111000   d.   01101010
    +00011000   −00111000

*45. One of the bit patterns 01011 and 11011 represents a value stored in excess 16 notation and the other represents the same value stored in two's complement notation.
a. What can be determined about this common value?
b. What is the relationship between a pattern representing a value stored in two's complement notation and the pattern representing the same value stored in excess notation when both systems use the same bit pattern length?

*46. The three bit patterns 01101000, 10000010, and 00000010 are representations of the same value in two's complement, excess, and the eight-bit floating-point format presented in Figure 26, but not necessarily in that order. What is the common value, and which pattern is in which notation?

*47. In each of the following cases, the different bit strings represent the same value but in different numeric encoding systems that we have discussed. Identify each value and the encoding systems used to represent it.
a. 11111010 0011 1011
b. 11111101 01111101 11101100
c. 1010 0010 01101000

*48. Which of the following bit patterns are not valid representations in an excess 16 notation system?
a. 01001   b. 101   c. 010101
d. 00000   e. 1000   f. 000000
g. 1111

*49. Which of the following values cannot be represented accurately in the floating-point format introduced in Figure 26?
   a. $6\frac{1}{2}$ b. 9   c. $\frac{13}{16}$
   d. $\frac{17}{32}$ e. $\frac{15}{16}$

*50. If you doubled the length of the bit strings being used to represent integers in binary from four bits to eight bits, what change would be made in the value of the largest integer you could represent? What if you were using two's complement notation?

*51. What would be the hexadecimal representation of the largest memory address in a memory consisting of 4MB if each cell had a one-byte capacity?

*52. Using gates, design a circuit with four inputs and one output such that the output is 1 or 0 depending on whether the four-bit input pattern has odd or even parity, respectively.

*53. What would be the encoded version of the message
   xxy yyx xxy xxy yyx
   if LZW compression, starting with the dictionary containing x, y, and a space (as described in Section 8), were used?

*54. The following message was compressed using LZW compression with a dictionary whose first, second, and third entries are x, y, and space, respectively. What is the decompressed message?
   22123113431213536

*55. If the message
   xxy yyx xxy xxyy
   were compressed using LZW with a starting dictionary whose first, second, and third entries were x, y, and space, respectively, what would be the entries in the final dictionary?

*56. As we will learn one means of transmitting bits over traditional telephone systems is to convert the bit patterns into sound, transfer the sound over the telephone lines, and then convert the sound back into bit patterns. Such techniques are limited to transfer rates of 57.6 Kbps. Is this sufficient for teleconferencing if the video is compressed using MPEG?

*57. Encode the following sentences in ASCII using one byte per character. Use the most significant bit of each byte as an (odd) parity bit.
   a. $100/5 = 20$
   b. To be or not to be?
   c. The total cost is $7.25.

*58. The following message was originally transmitted with odd parity in each short bit string. In which strings have errors definitely occurred?
   11001 11011 10110 00000 11111
   10001 10101 00100 01110

*59. Suppose a 24-bit code is generated by representing each symbol by three consecutive copies of its ASCII representation (for example, the symbol A is represented by the bit string 010000010100000101000001). What error-correcting properties does this new code have?

*60. Using the error-correcting code described in Figure 30, decode the following words:
   a. 111010   110110
   b. 101000   100110   001100
   c. 011101   000110   000000   010100
   d. 010010   001000   001110   101111
      000000   110111   100110
   e. 010011   000000   101001   100110

Social Issues

The following questions are intended as a guide to the ethical/social/legal issues associated with the field of computing. The goal is not merely to answer these questions. You should also consider why you answered as you did and whether your justifications are consistent from one question to the next.

1. A truncation error has occurred in a critical situation, causing extensive damage and loss of life. Who is liable, if anyone? The designer of the hardware? The designer of the software? The programmer who actually wrote that part of the program? The person who decided to use the software in that particular application? What if the software had been corrected by the company that originally developed it, but that update had not been purchased and applied in the critical application? What if the software had been pirated?

2. Is it acceptable for an individual to ignore the possibility of truncation errors and their consequences when developing his or her own applications?

3. Was it ethical to develop software in the 1970s using only two digits to represent the year (such as using 76 to represent the year 1976), ignoring the fact that the software would be flawed as the turn of the century approached? Is it ethical today to use only three digits to represent the year (such as 982 for 1982 and 015 for 2015)? What about using only four digits?

4. Many argue that encoding information often dilutes or otherwise distorts the information, since it essentially forces the information to be quantified. They argue that a questionnaire in which subjects are required to record their opinions by responding within a scale from one to five is inherently flawed. To what extent is information quantifiable? Can the pros and cons of different locations for a waste disposal plant be quantified? Is the debate over nuclear power and nuclear waste quantifiable? Is it dangerous to base decisions on averages and other statistical analysis? Is it ethical for news agencies to report polling results without including the exact wording of the questions? Is it possible to quantify the value of a human life? Is it acceptable for a company to stop investing in the improvement of a product, even though additional investment could lower the possibility of a fatality relating to the product's use?

5. Should there be a distinction in the rights to collect and disseminate data depending on the form of the data? That is, should the right to collect and disseminate photographs, audio, or video be the same as the right to collect and disseminate text?

6. Whether intentional or not, a report submitted by a journalist usually reflects that journalist's bias. Often by changing only a few words, a story can be given either a positive or negative connotation. (Compare, "The majority of those surveyed opposed the referendum." to "A significant portion of those surveyed supported the referendum.") Is there a difference between altering

a story (by leaving out certain points or carefully selecting words) and altering a photograph?

7. Suppose that the use of a data compression system results in the loss of subtle but significant items of information. What liability issues might be raised? How should they be resolved?

Additional Reading

Drew, M. and Z. Li. *Fundamentals of Multimedia*. Upper Saddle River, NJ: Prentice-Hall, 2004.

Halsall, F. *Multimedia Communications*. Boston, MA: Addison-Wesley, 2001.

Hamacher, V. C., Z. G. Vranesic, and S. G. Zaky. *Computer Organization*, 5th ed. New York: McGraw-Hill, 2002.

Knuth, D. E. *The Art of Computer Programming*, Vol. 2, 3rd ed. Boston, MA: Addison-Wesley, 1998.

Long, B. *Complete Digital Photography*, 3rd ed. Hingham, MA: Charles River Media, 2005.

Miano, J. *Compressed Image File Formats*. New York: ACM Press, 1999.

Salomon, D. *Data Compression: The Complete Reference*, 4th ed. New York: Springer, 2007.

Sayood, K. *Introduction to Data Compression*, 3rd ed. San Francisco: Morgan Kaufmann, 2005.

Answers to Questions & Exercises

Section 1

1. One and only one of the upper two inputs must be 1, and the lowest input must be 1.

2. The 1 on the lower input is negated to 0 by the NOT gate, causing the output of the AND gate to become 0. Thus both inputs to the OR gate are 0 (remember that the upper input to the flip-flop is held at 0) so the output of the OR gate becomes 0. This means that the output of the AND gate will remain 0 after the lower input to the flip-flop returns to 0.

3. The output of the upper OR gate will become 1, causing the upper NOT gate to produce an output of 0. This will cause the lower OR gate to produce

a 0, causing the lower NOT gate to produce a 1. This 1 is seen as the output of the flip-flop as well as being fed back to the upper OR gate, where it holds the output of that gate at 1, even after the flip-flop's input has returned to 0.

4. The flip-flop will be shielded from the circuit's input values when the clock is 0. The flip-flop will respond to the circuit's input values when the clock is 1.

5. a. The entire circuit is equivalent to a single XOR gate.
   b. This entire circuit is also equivalent to a single XOR gate.

6. a. 6AF2   b. E85517   c. 48

7. a. 01011111110110010111
   b. 0110000100001010
   c. 1010101111001101
   d. 0000000100000000

Section 2

1. In the first case, memory cell number 6 ends up containing the value 5. In the second case, it ends up with the value 8.

2. Step 1 erases the original value in cell number 3 when the new value is written there. Consequently, Step 2 does not place the original value from cell number 3 in cell number 2. The result is that both cells end up with the value that was originally in cell number 2. A correct procedure is the following:

   Step 1. Move the contents of cell number 2 to cell number 1.

   Step 2. Move the contents of cell number 3 to cell number 2.

   Step 3. Move the contents of cell number 1 to cell number 3.

3. 32768 bits.

Section 3

1. Faster retrieval of data and higher transfer rates.

2. The point to remember here is that the slowness of mechanical motion compared with the speed of the internal functioning of the computer dictates that we minimize the number of times we must move the read/write heads. If we fill a complete surface before starting the next, we must move the read/write head each time we finish with a track. The number of moves therefore is approximately the same as the total number of tracks on the two surfaces. If, however, we alternate between surfaces by electronically switching between the read/write heads, we must move the read/write heads only after each cylinder has been filled.

3. In this application, information must be retrieved from mass storage in a random manner, which would be time consuming in the context of the spiral system used on CDs and DVDs. (Moreover, current technology does not allow individual portions of data to be updated on a CD or DVD.)

4. Storage space is allocated in units of physical sectors (actually in units of groups of sectors in most cases). If the last physical sector is not full, additional text can be added without increasing the storage space allocated to the file. If the last physical sector is full, any addition to the document will require additional physical sectors to be allocated.

5. Flash drives do not require physical motion so they have shorter response times and do not suffer from physical wear.

6. A buffer is a data storage area used to hold data on a temporary basis, usually as a means of absorbing inconsistencies between the data's source and ultimate destination.

Section 4

1. Computer Science.

2. The two patterns are the same, except that the sixth bit from the low-order end is always 0 for uppercase and 1 for lowercase.

3. a.
01010111	01101000	01100101	01110010
01100101	00100000	01100001	01110010
01100101	00100000	01111001	01101111
01110101	00111111		

   b.
00100010	01001000	01101111	01110111
00111111	00100010	00100000	01000011
01101000	01100101	01110010	01111001
01101100	00100000	01100001	01110011
01101011	01100101	01100100	00101110

   c.
00110010	00101011	00110011	00111101
00110101	00101110		

4.

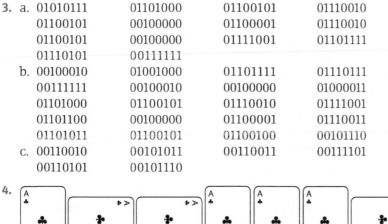

5. a. 5   b. 9   c. 11   d. 6   e. 16   f. 18

6. a. 110   b. 1101   c. 1011   d. 10010   e. 11011   f. 100

7. In 24 bits, we can store three symbols using ASCII. Thus we can store values as large as 999. However, if we use the bits as binary digits, we can store values up to 16,777,215.

8. a. 15.15   b. 51.0.128   c. 10.160

9. Geometric representations are more conducive to changes in scale than images encoded as bit maps. However, geometric representations do not typically provide the same photographic quality that bit maps produce. Indeed, as discussed in Section 8, JPEG representations of bit maps are very popular in photography.

10. With a sample rate of 44,100 samples per second, one hour of stereo music would require 635,040,000 bytes of storage. Thus, it would just about fill a CD whose capacity is slightly more than 600MB.

Section 5

1. a. 42   b. 33   c. 23   d. 6   e. 31

2. a. 100000   b. 1000000   c. 1100000   d. 1111   e. 11011

3. a. $3\frac{1}{4}$ b. $5\frac{7}{8}$ c. $2\frac{1}{2}$ d. $6\frac{3}{8}$ e. $\frac{5}{8}$

4. a. 100.1   b. 10.11   c. 1.001   d. 0.0101   e. 101.101

5. a. 100111   b. 1011.110   c. 100000   d. 1000.00

Section 6

1. a. 3   b. 15   c. −4   d. −6   e. 0   f. −16

2. a. 00000110   b. 11111010   c. 11101111
d. 00001101   e. 11111111   f. 00000000

3. a. 11111111   b. 10101011   c. 00000100
d. 00000010   e. 00000000   f. 10000001

4. a. With 4 bits the largest value is 7 and the smallest is −8.
b. With 6 bits the largest value is 31 and the smallest is −32.
c. With 8 bits the largest value is 127 and the smallest is −128.

5. a. 0111 (5 + 2 = 7)   b. 0100 (3 + 1 = 4)   c. 1111 (5 + (−6) = −1)
d. 0001 (−2 + 3 = 1)   e. 1000 (−6 + (−2) = −8)

6. a. 0111   b. 1011 (overflow)   c. 0100 (overflow)
d. 0001   e. 1000 (overflow)

7.

a.	0110	b.	0011	c.	0100	d.	0010	e.	0001
	+ 0001		+ 1110		+ 1010		+ 0100		+ 1011
	0111		0001		1110		0110		1100

8. No. Overflow occurs when an attempt is made to store a number that is too large for the system being used. When adding a positive value to a negative value, the result must be between the values being added. Thus, if the original values are small enough to be stored, the result is also.

9. a. 6 because 1110 → 14 − 8
    b. −1 because 0111 → 7 − 8
    c. 0 because 1000 → 8 − 8
    d. −6 because 0010 → 2 − 8
    e. −8 because 0000 → 0 − 8
    f. 1 because 1001 → 9 − 8

10. a. 1101 because 5 + 8 = 13 → 1101
    b. 0011 because −5 + 8 = 3 → 0011
    c. 1011 because 3 + 8 = 11 → 1011
    d. 1000 because 0 + 8 = 8 → 1000
    e. 1111 because 7 + 8 = 15 → 1111
    f. 0000 because −8 + 8 = 0 → 0000

11. No. The largest value that can be stored in excess eight notation is 7, repre-
    sented by 1111. To represent a larger value, at least excess 16 (which uses pat-
    terns of 5 bits) must be used. Similarly, 6 cannot be represented in excess four
    notation. (The largest value that can be represented in excess four notation is 3.)

Section 7

1. a. $\frac{5}{8}$ b. $3\frac{1}{4}$ c. $\frac{9}{32}$ d. $-1\frac{1}{2}$ e. $-\left(\frac{11}{64}\right)$

2. a. 01101011   b. 01111010 (truncation error)
    c. 01001100   d. 11101110   e. 11111000 (truncation error)

3. 01001001 ($\frac{9}{16}$) is larger than 00111101 ($\frac{13}{32}$). The following is a simple way of
    determining which of two patterns represents the larger value:

    Case 1. If the sign bits are different, the larger is the one with 0 sign bit.

    Case 2. If the sign bits are both 0, scan the remaining portions of the patterns
             from left to right until a bit position is found where the two patterns
             differ. The pattern containing the 1 in this position represents the
             larger value.

    Case 3. If the sign bits are both 1, scan the remaining portions of the pat-
             terns from left to right until a bit position is found where the two
             patterns differ. The pattern containing the 0 in this position repre-
             sents the larger value.

    The simplicity of this comparison process is one of the reasons for repre-
    senting the exponent in floating-point systems with an excess notation rather
    than with two's complement.

4. The largest value would be $7\frac{1}{2}$, which is represented by the pattern
    01111111. As for the smallest positive value, you could argue that there are
    two "correct" answers. First, if you stick to the coding process described in
    the text, which requires the most significant bit of the mantissa to be 1
    (called normalized form), the answer is $\frac{1}{32}$, which is represented by the

pattern 00001000. However, most machines do not impose this restriction for values close to 0. For such a machine, the correct answer is $^1/_{256}$ represented by 00000001.

Section 8

1. Run-length encoding, frequency-dependent encoding, relative encoding, and dictionary encoding.
2. 121321112343535
3. Color cartoons consist of blocks of solid color with sharp edges. Moreover, the number of colors involved is limited.
4. No. Both GIF and JPEG are lossy compression systems, meaning that details in the image will be lost.
5. JPEG's baseline standard takes advantage of the fact that the human eye is not as sensitive to changes in color as it is to changes in brightness. Thus it reduces the number of bits used to represent color information without noticeable loss in image quality.
6. Temporal masking and frequency masking.
7. When encoding information, approximations are made. In the case of numeric data, these approximations are compounded when computations are performed, which can lead to erroneous results. Approximations are not as critical in the cases of images and sound because the encoded data are normally only stored, transferred, and reproduced. If, however, images or sound were repeatedly reproduced, rerecorded, and then reencoded, these approximations could compound and ultimately lead to worthless data.

Section 9

1. b, c, and e.
2. Yes. If an even number of errors occurs in one byte, the parity technique does not detect them.
3. In this case, errors occur in bytes a and d of Question 1. The answer to Question 2 remains the same.
4. a.

001010111	001101000	101100101
101110010	101100101	000100000
001100001	101110010	101100101
000100000	001111001	101101111
001110101	100111111	

   b.

100100010	101001000	101101111
101110111	100111111	100100010
000100000	001000011	001101000
101100101	101110010	001111001
101101100	000100000	001100001
001110011	001101011	101100101
001100100	100101110	

   c. 000110010   100101011   100110011
      000111101   100110101   100101110

5. a. BED   b. CAB   c. HEAD

6. One solution is the following:
A 0 0 0 0 0
B 1 1 1 0 0
C 0 1 1 1 1
D 1 0 0 1 1

6

Data Manipulation

In this chapter we will learn how a computer manipulates data and communicates with peripheral
devices such as printers and keyboards. In
doing so, we will explore the basics of computer architecture and learn how computers
are programmed by means of encoded
instructions, called machine language
instructions.

We have studied topics relating to the storage of data inside a computer. In this chapter we will see how a computer manipulates that data. This manipulation consists of moving data from one location to another as well as performing operations such as arithmetic calculations, text editing, and image manipulation. We begin by extending our understanding of computer architecture beyond that of data storage systems.

1 Computer Architecture

The circuitry in a computer that controls the manipulation of data is called the **central processing unit,** or **CPU** (often referred to as merely the processor). In the machines of the mid-twentieth century, CPUs were large units comprised of perhaps several racks of electronic circuitry that reflected the significance of the unit. However, technology has shrunk these devices drastically. The CPUs found in today's PCs (such as the Pentium and Celeron processors made by Intel or the Athlon and Sempron processors made by AMD) are packaged as small flat squares (approximately two inches by two inches) whose connecting pins plug into a socket mounted on the machine's main circuit board (called the **motherboard**). Due to their small size, these processors are called **microprocessors.**

CPU Basics

A CPU consists of three parts (Figure 1): the **arithmetic/logic unit,** which contains the circuitry that performs operations on data (such as addition and subtraction); the **control unit,** which contains the circuitry for coordinating the machine's activities; and the **register unit,** which contains data storage cells (similar to main memory cells), called **registers,** that are used for temporary storage of information within the CPU.

Some of the registers within the register unit are considered **general-purpose registers** whereas others are **special-purpose registers.** We will discuss some of the special-purpose registers in Section 3. For now, we are concerned only with the general-purpose registers.

General-purpose registers serve as temporary holding places for data being manipulated by the CPU. These registers hold the inputs to the arithmetic/logic unit's circuitry and provide storage space for results produced by that unit. To perform an operation on data stored in main memory, the control unit transfers the data from memory into the general-purpose registers, informs the arithmetic/logic unit which registers hold the data, activates the appropriate circuitry within the arithmetic/logic unit, and tells the arithmetic/logic unit which register should receive the result.

For the purpose of transferring bit patterns, a machine's CPU and main memory are connected by a collection of wires called a **bus** (see again Figure 1). Through this bus, the CPU extracts (reads) data from main memory by supplying the address of the pertinent memory cell along with an electronic signal telling the memory circuitry that it is supposed to retrieve the data in the indicated cell. In a similar

Figure 1 CPU and main memory connected via a bus

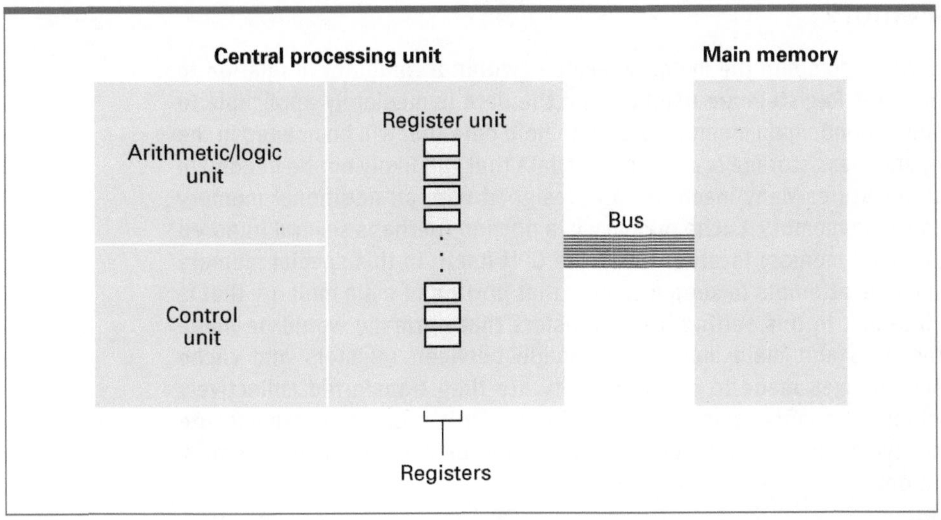

manner, the CPU places (writes) data in memory by providing the address of the destination cell and the data to be stored together with the appropriate electronic signal telling main memory that it is supposed to store the data being sent to it.

Based on this design, the task of adding two values stored in main memory involves more than the mere execution of the addition operation. The data must be transferred from main memory to registers within the CPU, the values must be added with the result being placed in a register, and the result must then be stored in a memory cell. The entire process is summarized by the five steps listed in Figure 2.

Figure 2 Adding values stored in memory

Step 1. Get one of the values to be added from memory and place it in a register.

Step 2. Get the other value to be added from memory and place it in another register.

Step 3. Activate the addition circuitry with the registers used in Steps 1 and 2 as inputs and another register designated to hold the result.

Step 4. Store the result in memory.

Step 5. Stop.

Cache Memory

It is instructive to compare the memory facilities within a computer in relation to their functionality. Registers are used to hold the data immediately applicable to the operation at hand; main memory is used to hold data that will be needed in the near future; and mass storage is used to hold data that will likely not be needed in the immediate future. Many machines are designed with an additional memory level, called cache memory. **Cache memory** is a portion (perhaps several hundred KB) of high-speed memory located within the CPU itself. In this special memory area, the machine attempts to keep a copy of that portion of main memory that is of current interest. In this setting, data transfers that normally would be made between registers and main memory are made between registers and cache memory. Any changes made to cache memory are then transferred collectively to main memory at a more opportune time. The result is a CPU that can execute its machine cycle more rapidly because it is not delayed by main memory communication.

The Stored-Program Concept

Early computers were not known for their flexibility—the steps that each device executed were built into the control unit as a part of the machine. To gain more flexibility, some of the early electronic computers were designed so that the CPU could be conveniently rewired. This flexibility was accomplished by means of a pegboard arrangement similar to old telephone switchboards in which the ends of jumper wires were plugged into holes.

A breakthrough (credited, apparently incorrectly, to John von Neumann) came with the realization that a program, just like data, can be encoded and stored in main memory. If the control unit is designed to extract the program from memory, decode the instructions, and execute them, the program that the machine follows can be changed merely by changing the contents of the computer's memory instead of rewiring the CPU.

The idea of storing a computer's program in its main memory is called the **stored-program concept** and has become the standard approach used today—so standard, in fact, that it seems obvious. What made it difficult originally was that everyone thought of programs and data as different entities: Data were stored in memory; programs were part of the CPU. The result was a prime example of not seeing the forest for the trees. It is easy to be caught in such ruts, and the development of computer science might still be in many of them today without our knowing it. Indeed, part of the excitement of the science is that new insights are constantly opening doors to new theories and applications.

Questions & Exercises

1. What sequence of events do you think would be required to move the contents of one memory cell in a computer to another memory cell?
2. What information must the CPU supply to the main memory circuitry to write a value into a memory cell?
3. Mass storage, main memory, and general-purpose registers are all storage systems. What is the difference in their use?

2 Machine Language

To apply the stored-program concept, CPUs are designed to recognize instructions encoded as bit patterns. This collection of instructions along with the encoding system is called the **machine language.** An instruction expressed in this language is called a machine-level instruction or, more commonly, a **machine instruction.**

The Instruction Repertoire

The list of machine instructions that a typical CPU must be able to decode and execute is quite short. In fact, once a machine can perform certain elementary but well-chosen tasks, adding more features does not increase the machine's theoretical capabilities. In other words, beyond a certain point, additional features may increase such things as convenience but add nothing to the machine's fundamental capabilities.

The degree to which machine designs should take advantage of this fact has lead to two philosophies of CPU architecture. One is that a CPU should be designed to execute a minimal set of machine instructions. This approach leads to what is called a **reduced instruction set computer (RISC).** The argument in favor of RISC architecture is that such a machine is efficient and fast. On the other hand, others argue in favor of CPUs with the ability to execute a large number of complex instructions, even though many of them are technically redundant. The result of this approach is known as a **complex instruction set computer (CISC).** The argument in favor of CISC architecture is that the more complex CPU is easier to program because a single instruction can be used to accomplish a task that would require a multi-instruction sequence in a RISC design.

Both CISC and RISC processors are commercially available. The Pentium series of processors, developed by Intel, are examples of CISC architecture; the PowerPC series of processors (including those that Apple calls G4 and G5), developed by Apple, IBM, and Motorola are examples of RISC architecture. (Apple is now building computers based on Intel products. The shift, however, was for commercial reasons rather than distinctions between RISC and CISC philosophies.) Other popular examples of RISC processors include the SPARC (Scalable Processor ARChitecture) series, which is a product of Sun Microsystems.

Regardless of the choice between RISC and CISC, a machine's instructions can be categorized into three groupings: (1) the data transfer group, (2) the arithmetic/logic group, and (3) the control group.

Data Transfer　The data transfer group consists of instructions that request the movement of data from one location to another. Steps 1, 2, and 4 in Figure 2 fall into this category. We should note that using terms such as *transfer* or *move* to identify this group of instructions is actually a misnomer. It is rare that the data being transferred is erased from its original location. The process involved in a transfer instruction is more like copying the data rather than moving it. Thus terms such as *copy* or *clone* better describe the actions of this group of instructions.

While on the subject of terminology, we should mention that special terms are used when referring to the transfer of data between the CPU and main memory. A request to fill a general-purpose register with the contents of a memory cell is commonly referred to as a LOAD instruction; conversely, a request to transfer the contents of a register to a memory cell is called a STORE instruction. In Figure 2, Steps 1 and 2 are LOAD instructions, and Step 4 is a STORE instruction.

An important group of instructions within the data transfer category consists of the commands for communicating with devices outside the CPU-main memory context (printers, keyboards, monitors, disk drives, etc.). Since these instructions handle the input/output (I/O) activities of the machine, they are called **I/O instructions** and are sometimes considered as a category in their own right. On the other hand, Section 5 describes how these I/O activities can be handled by the same instructions that request data transfers between the CPU and main memory. Thus, we shall consider the I/O instructions to be a part of the data transfer group.

Arithmetic/Logic　The arithmetic/logic group consists of the instructions that tell the control unit to request an activity within the arithmetic/logic unit. Step 3 in Figure 2 falls into this group. As its name suggests, the arithmetic/logic unit is capable of performing operations other than the basic arithmetic operations. Some of these additional operations are the Boolean operations AND, OR, and XOR, which we will discuss in more detail later in this chapter.

Another collection of operations available within most arithmetic/logic units allows the contents of registers to be moved to the right or the left within the register. These operations are known as either SHIFT or ROTATE operations, depending on whether the bits that "fall off the end" of the register are merely discarded (SHIFT) or are used to fill the holes left at the other end (ROTATE).

Control　The control group consists of those instructions that direct the execution of the program rather than the manipulation of data. Step 5 in Figure 2 falls

Figure 3   Dividing values stored in memory

Step 1. LOAD a register with a value
from memory.

Step 2. LOAD another register with
another value from memory.

Step 3. If this second value is zero,
JUMP to Step 6.

Step 4. Divide the contents of the
first register by the second
register and leave the result
in a third register.

Step 5. STORE the contents of the
third register in memory.

Step 6. STOP.

into this category, although it is an extremely elementary example. This group contains many of the more interesting instructions in a machine's repertoire, such as the family of JUMP (or BRANCH) instructions used to direct the CPU to execute an instruction other than the next one in the list. These JUMP instructions appear in two varieties: **unconditional jumps** and **conditional jumps.** An example of the former would be the instruction "Skip to Step 5"; an example of the latter would be, "If the value obtained is 0, then skip to Step 5." The distinction is that a conditional jump results in a "change of venue" only if a certain condition is satisfied. As an example, the sequence of instructions in Figure 3 represents an algorithm for dividing two values where Step 3 is a conditional jump that protects against the possibility of division by zero.

Variable-Length Instructions

To simplify explanations in the text, the machine language used for examples in this chapter uses a fixed size (two bytes) for all instructions. Thus, to fetch an instruction, the CPU always retrieves the contents of two consecutive memory cells and increments its program counter by two. This consistency streamlines the task of fetching instructions and is characteristic of RISC machines. CISC machines, however, have machine languages whose instructions vary in length. The Pentium series, for example, has instructions that range from single-byte instructions to multiple-byte instructions whose length depends on the exact use of the instruction. CPUs with such machine languages determine the length of the incoming instruction by the instruction's op-code. That is, the CPU first fetches the op-code of the instruction and then, based on the bit pattern received, knows how many more bytes to fetch from memory to obtain the rest of the instruction.

An Illustrative Machine Language

Let us now consider how the instructions of a typical computer are encoded. The machine that we will use for our discussion is described and summarized in Figure 4. It has 16 general-purpose registers and 256 main memory cells, each with a capacity of eight bits. For referencing purposes, we label the registers with the values 0 through 15 and address the memory cells with the values 0 through 255. For convenience we think of these labels and addresses as values represented in base two and compress the resulting bit patterns using hexadecimal notation. Thus, the registers are labeled 0 through F, and the memory cells are addressed 00 through FF.

The encoded version of a machine instruction consists of two parts: the **op-code** (short for operation code) field and the **operand** field. The bit pattern appearing in the op-code field indicates which of the elementary operations, such as STORE, SHIFT, XOR, and JUMP, is requested by the instruction. The bit patterns found in the operand field provide more detailed information about the operation specified by the op-code. For example, in the case of a STORE operation, the information in the operand field indicates which register contains the data to be stored and which memory cell is to receive the data.

The entire machine language of our illustrative machine consists of only 12 basic instructions. Each of these instructions is encoded using a total of 16 bits, represented by four hexadecimal digits (Figure 5). The op-code for each instruction consists of the first four bits or, equivalently, the first hexadecimal digit. Note that these op-codes are represented by the hexadecimal digits 1 through C. In particular, an instruction beginning with the hexadecimal digit 3 refers to a STORE

Figure 4   The architecture of the machine

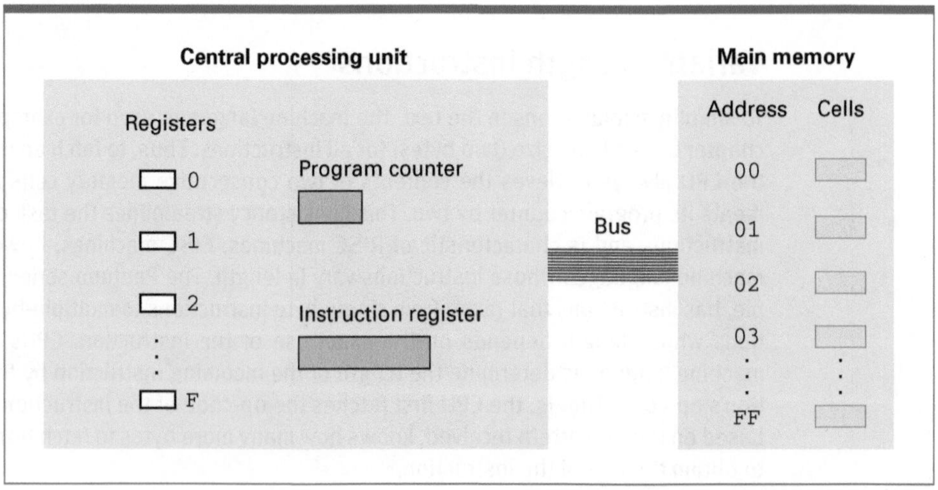

Figure 5   The composition of an instruction for the machine

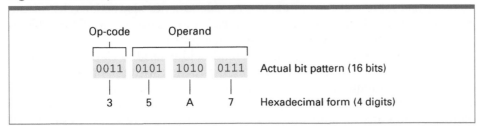

instruction, and an instruction beginning with hexadecimal A refers to a ROTATE instruction.

The operand field of each instruction in our illustrative machine consists of three hexadecimal digits (12 bits), and in each case (except for the HALT instruction, which needs no further refinement) clarifies the general instruction given by the op-code. For example (Figure 6), if the first hexadecimal digit of an instruction were 3 (the op-code for storing the contents of a register), the next hexadecimal digit of the instruction would indicate which register is to be stored, and the last two hexadecimal digits would indicate which memory cell is to receive the data. Thus the instruction 35A7 (hexadecimal) translates to the statement "STORE the bit pattern found in register 5 in the memory cell whose address is A7." (Note how the use of hexadecimal notation simplifies our discussion. In reality, the instruction 35A7 is the bit pattern 0011010110100111.)

(The instruction 35A7 also provides an explicit example of why main memory capacities are measured in powers of two. Because eight bits in the instruction are reserved for specifying the memory cell utilized by this instruction, it is possible to reference exactly 2^8 different memory cells. It behooves us therefore

Figure 6   Decoding the instruction 35A7

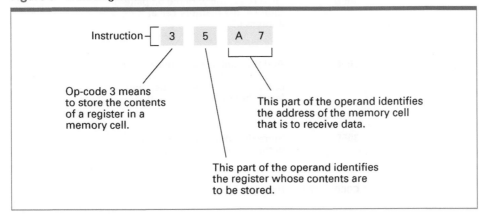

to build main memory with this many cells—addressed from 0 to 255. If main memory had more cells, we would not be able to write instructions that distinguished between them; if main memory had fewer cells, we would be able to write instructions that referenced non-existing cells.)

As another example of how the operand field is used to clarify the general instruction given by op-code, consider an instruction with the op-code 7 (hexadecimal), which requests that the contents of two registers be ORed. (We will see what it means to OR two registers in Section 4. For now we are interested merely in how instructions are encoded.) In this case, the next hexadecimal digit indicates the register in which the result should be placed, while the last two hexadecimal digits indicate which two registers are to be ORed. Thus the instruction 70C5 translates to the statement "OR the contents of register C with the contents of register 5 and leave the result in register 0."

A subtle distinction exists between our machine's two LOAD instructions. Here we see that the op-code 1 (hexadecimal) identifies an instruction that loads a register with the contents of a memory cell, whereas the op-code 2 (hexadecimal) identifies an instruction that loads a register with a particular value. The difference is that the operand field in an instruction of the first type contains an address, whereas in the second type the operand field contains the actual bit pattern to be loaded.

Figure 7   An encoded version of the instructions in Figure 2

Encoded instructions	Translation
156C	Load register 5 with the bit pattern found in the memory cell at address 6C.
166D	Load register 6 with the bit pattern found in the memory cell at address 6D.
5056	Add the contents of register 5 and 6 as though they were two's complement representation and leave the result in register 0.
306E	Store the contents of register 0 in the memory cell at address 6E.
C000	Halt.

Note that the machine has two ADD instructions: one for adding two's complement representations and one for adding floating-point representations. This distinction is a consequence of the fact that adding bit patterns that represent values encoded in two's complement notation requires different activities within the arithmetic/logic unit from adding values encoded in floating-point notation.

We close this section with Figure 7, which contains an encoded version of the instructions in Figure 2. We have assumed that the values to be added are stored in two's complement notation at memory addresses 6C and 6D and the sum is to be placed in the memory cell at address 6E.

Questions & Exercises

1. Why might the term *move* be considered an incorrect name for the operation of moving data from one location in a machine to another?

2. In the text, JUMP instructions were expressed by identifying the destination explicitly by stating the name (or step number) of the destination within the JUMP instruction (for example, "Jump to Step 6"). A drawback of this technique is that if an instruction name (number) is later changed, we must be sure to find all jumps to that instruction and change that name also. Describe another way of expressing a JUMP instruction so that the name of the destination is not explicitly stated.

3. Is the instruction "If 0 equals 0, then jump to Step 7" a conditional or unconditional jump? Explain your answer.

4. Write the example program in Figure 7 in actual bit patterns.

5. The following are instructions written in the machine language. Rewrite them in English.

   a. 368A   b. BADE   c. 803C   d. 40F4

6. What is the difference between the instructions 15AB and 25AB in the machine language?

7. Here are some instructions in English. Translate each of them into machine language.

   a. LOAD register number 3 with the hexadecimal value 56.
   b. ROTATE register number 5 three bits to the right.
   c. AND the contents of register A with the contents of register 5 and leave the result in register 0.

3 Program Execution

A computer follows a program stored in its memory by copying the instructions from memory into the CPU as needed. Once in the CPU, each instruction is decoded and obeyed. The order in which the instructions are fetched from memory corresponds to the order in which the instructions are stored in memory unless otherwise altered by a JUMP instruction.

To understand how the overall execution process takes place, it is necessary to consider two of the special purpose registers within the CPU: the **instruction register** and the **program counter** (see again Figure 4). The instruction register is used to hold the instruction being executed. The program counter contains the address of the next instruction to be executed, thereby serving as the machine's way of keeping track of where it is in the program.

The CPU performs its job by continually repeating an algorithm that guides it through a three-step process known as the **machine cycle.** The steps in the machine cycle are fetch, decode, and execute (Figure 8). During the fetch step, the CPU requests that main memory provide it with the instruction that is stored at the address indicated by the program counter. Since each instruction in our machine is two bytes long, this fetch process involves retrieving the contents of two memory cells from main memory. The CPU places the instruction received from memory in its instruction register and then increments the program counter by two so that the counter contains the address of the next instruction stored in memory. Thus the program counter will be ready for the next fetch.

Figure 8   The machine cycle

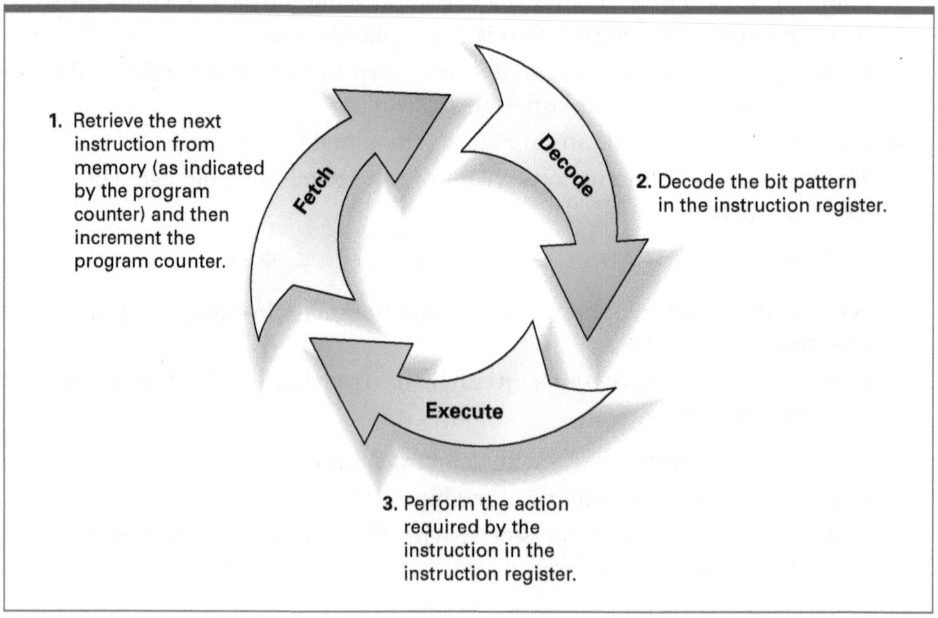

1. Retrieve the next instruction from memory (as indicated by the program counter) and then increment the program counter.

Fetch

Decode

2. Decode the bit pattern in the instruction register.

Execute

3. Perform the action required by the instruction in the instruction register.

With the instruction now in the instruction register, the CPU decodes the instruction, which involves breaking the operand field into its proper components based on the instruction's op-code.

The CPU then executes the instruction by activating the appropriate circuitry to perform the requested task. For example, if the instruction is a load from memory, the CPU sends the appropriate signals to main memory, waits for main memory to send the data, and then places the data in the requested register; if the instruction is for an arithmetic operation, the CPU activates the appropriate circuitry in the arithmetic/logic unit with the correct registers as inputs and waits for the arithmetic/logic unit to compute the answer and place it in the appropriate register.

Once the instruction in the instruction register has been executed, the CPU again begins the machine cycle with the fetch step. Observe that since the program counter was incremented at the end of the previous fetch, it again provides the CPU with the correct address.

A somewhat special case is the execution of a JUMP instruction. Consider, for example, the instruction B258 (Figure 9), which means "JUMP to the instruction at address 58 (hexadecimal) if the contents of register 2 is the same as that of register 0." In this case, the execute step of the machine cycle begins with the comparison of registers 2 and 0. If they contain different bit patterns, the execute step terminates and the next machine cycle begins. If, however, the contents of these registers are equal, the machine places the value 58 (hexadecimal) in its program counter during the execute step. In this case, then, the next fetch step finds 58 in the program counter, so the instruction at that address will be the next instruction to be fetched and executed.

Note that if the instruction had been B058, then the decision of whether the program counter should be changed would depend on whether the contents of register 0 was equal to that of register 0. But these are the same registers and

Figure 9 Decoding the instruction B258

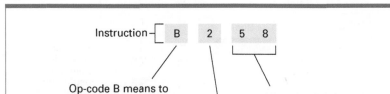

Instruction — B 2 5 8

Op-code B means to change the value of the program counter if the contents of the indicated register is the same as that in register 0.

This part of the operand is the address to be placed in the program counter.

This part of the operand identifies the register to be compared to register 0.

thus must have equal content. In turn, any instruction of the form B0XY will cause a jump to be executed to the memory location XY regardless of the contents of register 0.

An Example of Program Execution

Let us follow the machine cycle applied to the program presented in Figure 7 which retrieves two values from main memory, computes their sum, and stores that total in a main memory cell. We first need to put the program somewhere in memory. For our example, suppose the program is stored in consecutive addresses, starting at address A0 (hexadecimal). With the program stored in this manner, we can cause the machine to execute it by placing the address (A0) of the first instruction in the program counter and starting the machine (Figure 10).

The CPU begins the fetch step of the machine cycle by extracting the instruction stored in main memory at location A0 and placing this instruction (156C) in its instruction register (Figure 11a). Notice that, in our machine, instructions are 16 bits (two bytes) long. Thus the entire instruction to be fetched occupies the memory cells at both address A0 and A1. The CPU is designed to take this into account so it retrieves the contents of both cells and places the bit patterns received in the instruction register, which is 16 bits long. The CPU then

Figure 10 The program from Figure 7 stored in main memory ready for execution

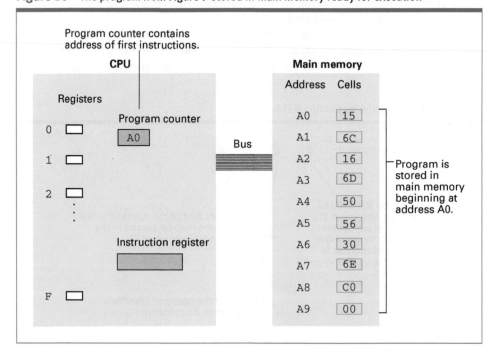

00   02   04   1004
1004   1004   3045   3045
                              C000

06

C000

Figure 11   Performing the fetch step of the machine cycle

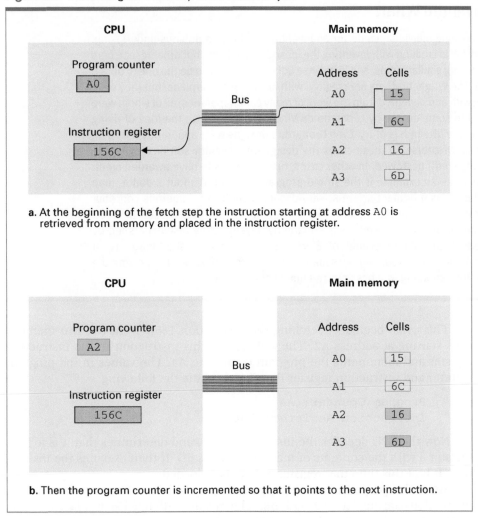

a. At the beginning of the fetch step the instruction starting at address A0 is retrieved from memory and placed in the instruction register.

b. Then the program counter is incremented so that it points to the next instruction.

adds two to the program counter so that this register contains the address of the next instruction (Figure 11b). At the end of the fetch step of the first machine cycle, the program counter and instruction register contain the following data:

```
Program Counter: A2
Instruction Register: 156C
```

Next, the CPU analyzes the instruction in its instruction register and concludes that it is to load register 5 with the contents of the memory cell at address 6C. This load activity is performed during the execution step of the machine cycle, and the CPU then begins the next cycle.

Who Invented What?

Awarding a single individual credit for an invention is always a dubious undertaking. Thomas Edison is credited with inventing the incandescent lamp, but other researchers were developing similar lamps, and in a sense Edison was lucky to be the one to obtain the patent. The Wright brothers are credited with inventing the airplane, but they were competing with and benefited from the work of many contemporaries, all of whom were pre-empted to some degree by Leonardo da Vinci, who toyed with the idea of flying machines in the fifteenth century. Even Leonardo's designs were apparently based on earlier ideas. Of course, in these cases the designated inventor still has legitimate claims to the credit bestowed. In other cases, history seems to have awarded credit inappropriately—an example is the stored-program concept. Without a doubt, John von Neumann was a brilliant scientist who deserves credit for numerous contributions. But one of the contributions for which popular history has chosen to credit him, the stored-program concept, was apparently developed by researchers led by J. P. Eckert at the Moore School of Electrical Engineering at the University of Pennsylvania. John von Neumann was merely the first to publish work reporting the idea and thus computing lore has selected him as the inventor.

This cycle begins by fetching the instruction 166D from the two memory cells starting at address A2. The CPU places this instruction in the instruction register and increments the program counter to A4. The values in the program counter and instruction register therefore become the following:

```
Program Counter: A4
Instruction Register: 166D
```

Now the CPU decodes the instruction 166D and determines that it is to load register 6 with the contents of memory address 6D. It then executes the instruction. It is at this time that register 6 is actually loaded.

Since the program counter now contains A4, the CPU extracts the next instruction starting at this address. The result is that 5056 is placed in the instruction register, and the program counter is incremented to A6. The CPU now decodes the contents of its instruction register and executes it by activating the two's complement addition circuitry with inputs being registers 5 and 6.

During this execution step, the arithmetic/logic unit performs the requested addition, leaves the result in register 0 (as requested by the control unit), and reports to the control unit that it has finished. The CPU then begins another machine cycle. Once again, with the aid of the program counter, it fetches the next instruction (306E) from the two memory cells starting at memory location A6 and increments the program counter to A8. This instruction is then decoded and executed. At this point, the sum is placed in memory location 6E.

The next instruction is fetched starting from memory location A8, and the program counter is incremented to AA. The contents of the instruction register

(C000) are now decoded as the halt instruction. Consequently, the machine stops during the execute step of the machine cycle, and the program is completed.

In summary, we see that the execution of a program stored in memory involves the same process you and I might use if we needed to follow a detailed list of instructions. Whereas we might keep our place by marking the instructions as we perform them, the CPU keeps its place by using the program counter. After determining which instruction to execute next, we would read the instruction and extract its meaning. Then, we would perform the task requested and return to the list for the next instruction in the same manner that the CPU executes the instruction in its instruction register and then continues with another fetch.

Programs Versus Data

Many programs can be stored simultaneously in a computer's main memory, as long as they occupy different locations. Which program will be run when the machine is started can then be determined merely by setting the program counter appropriately.

One must keep in mind, however, that because data are also contained in main memory and encoded in terms of 0s and 1s, the machine alone has no way of knowing what is data and what is program. If the program counter were assigned the address of data instead of the address of the desired program, the CPU, not knowing any better, would extract the data bit patterns as though they were instructions and execute them. The final result would depend on the data involved.

Comparing Computer Power

When shopping for a personal computer, you will find that clock speeds are often used to compare machines. A computer's **clock** is a circuit, called an oscillator, which generates pulses that are used to coordinate the machine's activities—the faster this oscillating circuit generates pulses, the faster the machine performs its machine cycle. Clock speeds are measured in hertz (abbreviated as Hz) with one Hz equal to one cycle (or pulse) per second. Typical clock speeds in desktop computers are in the range of a few hundred MHz (older models) to several GHz. (MHz is short for megahertz, which is a million Hz. GHz is short for gigahertz, which is 1000 MHz.)

Unfortunately, different CPU designs might perform different amounts of work in one clock cycle, and thus clock speed alone fails to be relevant in comparing machines with different CPUs. If you are comparing a machine based on a PowerPC to one based on a Pentium, it would be more meaningful to compare performance by means of **benchmarking,** which is the process of comparing the performance of different machines when executing the same program, known as a benchmark. By selecting benchmarks representing different types of applications, you get meaningful comparisons for various market segments.

We should not conclude, however, that providing programs and data with a common appearance in a machine's memory is bad. In fact, it has proved a useful attribute because it allows one program to manipulate other programs (or even itself) the same as it would data. Imagine, for example, a program that modifies itself in response to its interaction with its environment and thus exhibits the ability to learn, or perhaps a program that writes and executes other programs in order to solve problems presented to it.

Questions & Exercises

1. Suppose the memory cells from addresses 00 to 05 in the machine contain the (hexadecimal) bit patterns given in the following table:

Address	Contents
00	14
01	02
02	34
03	17
04	C0
05	00

   If we start the machine with its program counter containing 00, what bit pattern is in the memory cell whose address is hexadecimal 17 when the machine halts?

2. Suppose the memory cells at addresses B0 to B8 in the machine contain the (hexadecimal) bit patterns given in the following table:

Address	Contents
B0	13
B1	B8
B2	A3
B3	02
B4	33
B5	B8
B6	C0
B7	00
B8	0F

   a. If the program counter starts at B0, what bit pattern is in register number 3 after the first instruction has been executed?

   b. What bit pattern is in memory cell B8 when the halt instruction is executed?

3. Suppose the memory cells at addresses A4 to B1 in the machine contain the (hexadecimal) bit patterns given in the following table:

Address	Contents
A4	20
A5	00
A6	21
A7	03
A8	22
A9	01
AA	B1
AB	B0
AC	50
AD	02
AE	B0
AF	AA
B0	C0
B1	00

When answering the following questions, assume that the machine is started with its program counter containing A4.

a. What is in register 0 the first time the instruction at address AA is executed?

b. What is in register 0 the second time the instruction at address AA is executed?

c. How many times is the instruction at address AA executed before the machine halts?

4. Suppose the memory cells at addresses F0 to F9 in the machine contain the (hexadecimal) bit patterns described in the following table:

Address	Contents
F0	20
F1	C0
F2	30
F3	F8
F4	20
F5	00
F6	30
F7	F9
F8	FF
F9	FF

If we start the machine with its program counter containing F0, what does the machine do when it reaches the instruction at address F8?

4 Arithmetic/Logic Instructions

As indicated earlier, the arithmetic/logic group of instructions consists of instructions requesting arithmetic, logic, and shift operations. In this section, we look at these operations more closely.

Logic Operations

We introduced the logic operations AND, OR, and XOR (exclusive or) as operations that combine two input bits to produce a single output bit. These operations can be extended to operations that combine two strings of bits to produce a single output string by applying the basic operation to individual columns. For example, the result of ANDing the patterns 10011010 and 11001001 results in

```
        10011010
AND  11001001
        10001000
```

where we have merely written the result of ANDing the two bits in each column at the bottom of the column. Likewise, ORing and XORing these patterns would produce

```
        10011010                    10011010
OR  11001001            XOR  11001001
        11011011                    01010011
```

One of the major uses of the AND operation is for placing 0s in one part of a bit pattern while not disturbing the other part. Consider, for example, what happens if the byte 00001111 is the first operand of an AND operation. Without knowing the contents of the second operand, we still can conclude that the four most significant bits of the result will be 0s. Moreover, the four least significant bits of the result will be a copy of that part of the second operand, as shown in the following example:

```
        00001111
AND  10101010
        00001010
```

This use of the AND operation is an example of the process called **masking.** Here one operand, called a **mask,** determines which part of the other operand will affect the result. In the case of the AND operation, masking produces a result that is a partial replica of one of the operands, with 0s occupying the nonduplicated positions.

Such an operation is useful when manipulating a **bit map,** a string of bits in which each bit represents the presence or absence of a particular object. We have already encountered bit maps in the context of representing images, where each bit is associated with a pixel. As another example, a string of 52 bits, in which each bit is associated with a particular playing card, can be used to represent a poker hand by assigning 1s to those 5 bits associated with the cards in the hand and 0s to all the others. Likewise, a bit map of 52 bits, of which 13 are

1s, can be used to represent a hand of bridge, or a bit map of 32 bits can be used to represent which of 32 ice cream flavors are available.

Suppose, then, that the eight-bits in a memory cell are being used as a bit map, and we want to find out whether the object associated with the third bit from the high-order end is present. We merely need to AND the entire byte with the mask 00100000, which produces a byte of all 0s if and only if the third bit from the high-order end of the bit map is itself 0. A program can then act accordingly by following the AND operation with a conditional branch instruction. Moreover, if the third bit from the high-order end of the bit map is a 1, and we want to change it to a 0 without disturbing the other bits, we can AND the bit map with the mask 11011111 and then store the result in place of the original bit map.

Where the AND operation can be used to duplicate a part of a bit string while placing 0s in the nonduplicated part, the OR operation can be used to duplicate a part of a string while putting 1s in the nonduplicated part. For this we again use a mask, but this time we indicate the bit positions to be duplicated with 0s and use 1s to indicate the nonduplicated positions. For example, ORing any byte with 11110000 produces a result with 1s in its most significant four bits while its remaining bits are a copy of the least significant four bits of the other operand, as demonstrated by the following example:

```
     11110000
OR   10101010
     11111010
```

Consequently, whereas the mask 11011111 can be used with the AND operation to force a 0 in the third bit from the high-order end of a byte, the mask 00100000 can be used with the OR operation to force a 1 in that position.

A major use of the XOR operation is in forming the complement of a bit string. XORing any byte with a mask of all 1s produces the complement of the byte. For example, note the relationship between the second operand and the result in the following example:

```
     11111111
XOR  10101010
     01010101
```

In the machine language, op-codes 7, 8, and 9 are used for the logic operations OR, AND, and XOR, respectively. Each requests that the corresponding logic operation be performed between the contents of two designated registers and that the result be placed in another designated register. For example, the instruction 7ABC requests that the result of ORing the contents of registers B and C be placed in register A.

Rotation and Shift Operations

The operations in the class of rotation and shift operations provide a means for moving bits within a register and are often used in solving alignment problems.

These operations are classified by the direction of motion (right or left) and whether the process is circular. Within these classification guidelines are numerous variations with mixed terminology. Let us take a quick look at the ideas involved.

Consider a register containing a byte of bits. If we shift its contents one bit to the right, we imagine the rightmost bit falling off the edge and a hole appearing at the leftmost end. What happens with this extra bit and the hole is the distinguishing feature among the various shift operations. One technique is to place the bit that fell off the right end in the hole at the left end. The result is a **circular shift,** also called a **rotation.** Thus, if we perform a right circular shift on a byte-size bit pattern eight times, we obtain the same bit pattern we started with.

Another technique is to discard the bit that falls off the edge and always fill the hole with a 0. The term **logical shift** is often used to refer to these operations. Such shifts to the left can be used for multiplying two's complement representations by two. After all, shifting binary digits to the left corresponds to multiplication by two, just as a similar shift of decimal digits corresponds to multiplication by ten. Moreover, division by two can be accomplished by shifting the binary string to the right. In either shift, care must be taken to preserve the sign bit when using certain notational systems. Thus, we often find right shifts that always fill the hole (which occurs at the sign bit position) with its original value. Shifts that leave the sign bit unchanged are sometimes called **arithmetic shifts.**

Among the variety of shift and rotate instructions possible, the machine language contains only a right circular shift, designated by op-code A. In this case the first hexadecimal digit in the operand specifies the register to be rotated, and the rest of the operand specifies the number of bits to be rotated. Thus the instruction A501 means "Rotate the contents of register 5 to the right by 1 bit." In particular, if register 5 originally contained the bit pattern 65 (hexadecimal), then it would contain B2 after this instruction is executed (Figure 12). (You may wish to experiment with how other shift and rotate instructions can be produced with combinations of the instructions provided in the machine language. For example, since a register is eight bits long, a right circular shift of three bits produces the same result as a left circular shift of five bits.)

Arithmetic Operations

Although we have already mentioned the arithmetic operations of add, subtract, multiply, and divide, a few loose ends should still be connected. First, we have already seen that subtraction can be simulated by means of addition and negation. Moreover, multiplication is merely repeated addition and division is repeated subtraction. (Six divided by two is three because three two's can be subtracted from six.) For this reason, some small CPUs are designed with only the add or perhaps only the add and subtract instructions.

We should also mention that numerous variations exist for each arithmetic operation. We have already alluded to this in relation to the add operations available

Figure 12   Rotating the bit pattern 65 (hexadecimal) one bit to the right

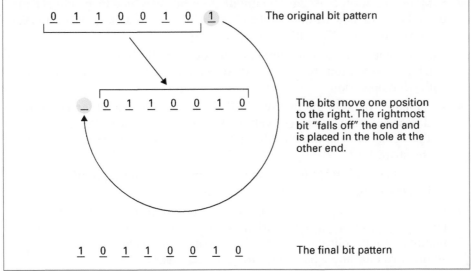

on our machine. In the case of addition, for example, if the values to be added are stored in two's complement notation, the addition process must be performed as a straightforward column by column addition. However, if the operands are stored as floating-point values, the addition process must extract the mantissa of each, shift them right or left according to the exponent fields, check the sign bits, perform the addition, and translate the result into floating-point notation. Thus, although both operations are considered addition, the action of the machine is not the same.

Questions & Exercises

1. Perform the indicated operations.

   a.   01001011   b.   10000011   c.   11111111
      AND 10101011   AND 11101100   AND 00101101

   d.   01001011   e.   10000011   f.   11111111
      OR 10101011   OR 11101100   OR 00101101

   g.   01001011   h.   10000011   i.   11111111
      XOR 10101011   XOR 11101100   XOR 00101101

2. Suppose you want to isolate the middle four bits of a byte by placing 0s in the other four bits without disturbing the middle four bits. What mask must you use together with what operation?

3. Suppose you want to complement the four middle bits of a byte while leaving the other four bits undisturbed. What mask must you use together with what operation?

4. a. Suppose you XOR the first two bits of a string of bits and then continue down the string by successively XORing each result with the next bit in the string. How is your result related to the number of 1s appearing in the string?

   b. How does this problem relate to determining what the appropriate parity bit should be when encoding a message?

5. It is often convenient to use a logical operation in place of a numeric one. For example, the logical operation AND combines two bits in the same manner as multiplication. Which logical operation is almost the same as adding two bits, and what goes wrong in this case?

6. What logical operation together with what mask can you use to change ASCII codes of lowercase letters to uppercase? What about uppercase to lowercase?

7. What is the result of performing a three-bit right circular shift on the following bit strings:

   a. 01101010   b. 00001111   c. 01111111

8. What is the result of performing a one-bit left circular shift on the following bytes represented in hexadecimal notation? Give your answer in hexadecimal form.

   a. AB   b. 5C   c. B7   d. 35

9. A right circular shift of three bits on a string of eight bits is equivalent to a left circular shift of how many bits?

10. What bit pattern represents the sum of 01101010 and 11001100 if the patterns represent values stored in two's complement notation? What if the patterns represent values stored in the floating-point format?

11. Using the machine language, write a program that places a 1 in the most significant bit of the memory cell whose address is A7 without modifying the remaining bits in the cell.

12. Using the machine language, write a program that copies the middle four bits from memory cell E0 into the least significant four bits of memory cell E1, while placing 0s in the most significant four bits of the cell at location E1.

5 Communicating with Other Devices

Main memory and the CPU form the core of a computer. In this section, we investigate how this core, which we will refer to as the computer, communicates with peripheral devices such as mass storage systems, printers, keyboards, mice, monitors, digital cameras, and even other computers.

The Role of Controllers

Communication between a computer and other devices is normally handled through an intermediary apparatus known as a **controller.** In the case of a personal computer, a controller may consist of circuitry permanently mounted on the computer's motherboard or, for flexibility, it may take the form of a circuit board that plugs into a slot on the motherboard. In either case, the controller connects via cables to peripheral devices within the computer case or perhaps to a connector, called a **port,** on the back of the computer where external devices can be attached. These controllers are sometimes small computers themselves, each with its own memory circuitry and simple CPU that performs a program directing the activities of the controller.

A controller translates messages and data back and forth between forms compatible with the internal characteristics of the computer and those of the peripheral device to which it is attached. Originally, each controller was designed for a

USB and FireWire

The universal serial bus (USB) and FireWire are standardized serial communication systems that simplify the process of adding new peripheral devices to a personal computer. USB was developed under the lead of Intel. The development of FireWire was led by Apple. In both cases the underlying theme is for a single controller to provide external ports at which a variety of peripheral devices can be attached. In this setting, the controller translates the internal signal characteristics of the computer to the appropriate USB or FireWire standard signals. In turn, each device connected to the controller converts its internal idiosyncrasies to the same USB or FireWire standard, allowing communication with the controller. The result is that attaching a new device to a PC does not require the insertion of a new controller. Instead, one merely plugs any USB compatible device into a USB port or a FireWire compatible device into a FireWire port.

Of the two, FireWire provides a faster transfer rate, but the lower cost of USB technology has made it the leader in the lower-cost mass market arena. USB compatible devices on the market today include mice, keyboards, printers, scanners, digital cameras, and mass storage systems designed for backup applications. FireWire applications tend to focus on devices that require higher transfer rates such as video recorders and online mass storage systems.

particular type of device; thus, purchasing a new peripheral device often required the purchase of a new controller as well.

Recently, steps have been taken within the personal computer arena to develop standards, such as the **universal serial bus (USB)** and **FireWire,** by which a single controller is able to handle a variety of devices. For example, a single USB controller can be used as the interface between a computer and any collection of USB-compatible devices. The list of devices on the market today that can communicate with a USB controller includes mice, printers, scanners, mass storage devices, and digital cameras.

Each controller communicates with the computer itself by means of connections to the same bus that connects the computer's CPU and main memory (Figure 13). From this position it is able to monitor the signals being sent between the CPU and main memory as well as to inject its own signals onto the bus.

With this arrangement, the CPU is able to communicate with the controllers attached to the bus in the same manner that it communicates with main memory. To send a bit pattern to a controller, the bit pattern is first constructed in one of the CPU's general-purpose registers. Then an instruction similar to a STORE instruction is executed by the CPU to "store" the bit pattern in the controller. Likewise, to receive a bit pattern from a controller, an instruction similar to a LOAD instruction is used.

In some computer designs the transfer of data to and from controllers is directed by the same LOAD and STORE op-codes that are already provided for communication with main memory. In these cases, each controller is designed to respond to references to a unique set of addresses while main memory is designed to ignore references to these locations. Thus when the CPU sends a message on the bus to store a bit pattern at a memory location that is assigned to a controller, the bit pattern is actually "stored" in the controller rather than main

Figure 13   Controllers attached to a machine's bus

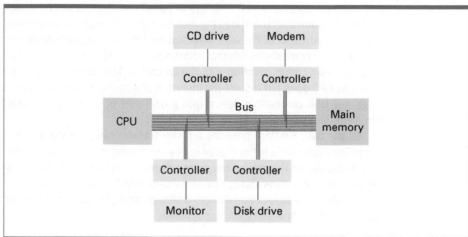

memory. Likewise, if the CPU tries to read data from such a memory location, as in a LOAD instruction, it will receive a bit pattern from the controller rather than from memory. Such a communication system is called **memory-mapped I/O** because the computer's input/output devices appear to be in various memory locations (Figure 14).

An alternative to memory-mapped I/O is to provide special op-codes in the machine language to direct transfers to and from controllers. Instructions with these op-codes are called I/O instructions. As an example, if the language followed this approach, it might include an instruction such as F5A3 to mean "STORE the contents of register 5 in the controller identified by the bit pattern A3."

Direct Memory Access

Since a controller is attached to a computer's bus, it can carry on its own communication with main memory during those nanoseconds in which the CPU is not using the bus. This ability of a controller to access main memory is known as **direct memory access (DMA),** and it is a significant asset to a computer's performance. For instance, to retrieve data from a sector of a disk, the CPU can send requests encoded as bit patterns to the controller attached to the disk asking the controller to read the sector and place the data in a specified area of main memory. The CPU can then continue with other tasks while the controller performs the read operation and deposits the data in main memory via DMA. Thus two activities will be performed at the same time. The CPU will be executing a program and the controller will be overseeing the transfer of data between the disk and main memory. In this manner, the computing resources of the CPU are not wasted during the relatively slow data transfer.

The use of DMA also has the detrimental effect of complicating the communication taking place over a computer's bus. Bit patterns must move between the CPU and main memory, between the CPU and each controller, and between each controller and main memory. Coordination of all this activity on the bus is a major design issue. Even with excellent designs, the central bus can become an impediment as the CPU and the controllers compete for bus access. This impediment is known as the **von Neumann bottleneck** because it is a consequence of the underlying **von Neumann architecture** in which a CPU fetches its instructions from memory over a central bus.

Figure 14   A conceptual representation of memory-mapped I/O

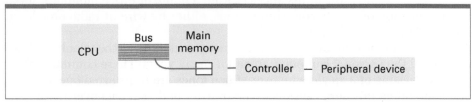

Handshaking

The transfer of data between two computer components is rarely a one-way affair. Even though we may think of a printer as a device that receives data, the truth is that a printer also sends data back to the computer. After all, a computer can produce and send characters to a printer much faster than the printer can print them. If a computer blindly sent data to a printer, the printer would quickly fall behind, resulting in lost data. Thus a process such as printing a document involves a constant two-way dialogue, known as **handshaking,** in which the computer and the peripheral device exchange information about the device's status and coordinate their activities.

Handshaking often involves a **status word,** which is a bit pattern that is generated by the peripheral device and sent to the controller. The status word is a bit map in which the bits reflect the conditions of the device. For example, in the case of a printer, the value of the least significant bit of the status word may indicate whether the printer is out of paper, while the next bit may indicate whether the printer is ready for additional data. Still another bit may be used to indicate the presence of a paper jam. Depending on the system, the controller may respond to this status information itself or make it available to the CPU. In either case, the status word provides the mechanism by which communication with a peripheral device can be coordinated.

Popular Communication Media

Communication between computing devices is handled over two types of paths: parallel and serial. These terms refer to the manner in which signals are transferred with respect to each other. In the case of **parallel communication,** several signals are transferred at the same time, each on a separate "line." Such a technique is capable of transferring data rapidly but requires a relatively complex communication path. Examples include a computer's internal bus where multiple wires are used to allow large blocks of data and other signals to be transferred simultaneously. Moreover, most PCs are equipped with at least one "parallel port" through which data can be transferred to and from the machine eight bits at a time.

In contrast, **serial communication** is based on transferring signals one after the other over a single line. Thus serial communication requires a simpler data path than parallel communication, which is the reason for its popularity. USB and FireWire, which offer relatively high speed data transfer over short distances of only a few meters, are examples of serial communication systems. For slightly longer distances (within a home or office building), serial communication over Ethernet connections, either by wire or radio broadcast, are popular.

For communication over greater distances, traditional voice telephone lines dominated the personal computer arena for many years. These communication paths, consisting of a single wire over which tones are transferred one after the other, are inherently serial systems. The transfer of digital data over these lines is accomplished by first converting bit patterns into audible tones by means of a **modem** (short for *modulator-demodulator*), transferring these tones serially over the telephone system, and then converting the tones back into bits by another modem at the destination.

For faster long-distance communication over traditional telephone lines, telephone companies offer a service known as **DSL (Digital Subscriber Line),** which takes advantage of the fact that existing telephone lines are capable of handling a wider frequency range than that used by traditional voice communication. More precisely, DSL uses frequencies above the audible range to transfer digital data while leaving the lower frequency spectrum for voice communication. Other technologies that compete with DSL and offer higher transfer rates include cable, as used in cable television systems, and satellite links via high frequency radio broadcast.

Communication Rates

The rate at which bits are transferred from one computing component to another is measured in **bits per second (bps).** Common units include **Kbps** (kilo-bps, equal to 1000 bps), **Mbps** (mega-bps, equal to 1 million bps), and **Gbps** (giga-bps, equal to 1 billion bps). (Note the distinction between bits and bytes—that is, 8 Kbps is equal to 1 KB per second. In abbreviations, a lowercase b usually means *bit* whereas an uppercase B means *byte*.)

For short distance communication, USB and FireWire provide transfer rates of several hundred Mbps, which is sufficient for most multimedia applications. This, combined with their convenience and relatively low cost, is why they are popular for communication between home computers and local peripherals such as printers, external disk drives, and cameras.

By combining **multiplexing** (the encoding or interweaving of data so that a single communication path serves the purpose of multiple paths) and data compression techniques, traditional voice telephone systems are able to support transfer rates of 57.6 Kbps, which falls short of the needs of today's multimedia applications. To play MP3 music recordings requires a transfer rate of about 64 Kbps, and to play better quality video recordings requires transfer rates measured in units of Mbps. This is why alternatives such as DSL, cable, and satellite links, which provide transfer rates well into the Mbps range, are rapidly replacing traditional audio telephone systems for long range data transfer. (For example, DSL offers transfer rates on the order of 54 Mbps.)

The maximum rate available in a particular setting depends on the type of the communication path and the technology used in its implementation. This maximum rate is often loosely equated to the communication path's **bandwidth,** although the term *bandwidth* also has connotations of capacity rather than transfer rate. That is, to say that a communication path has a high bandwidth (or provides **broadband** service) means that the communication path has the ability to transfer bits at a high rate as well as the capacity to carry large amounts of information simultaneously.

Questions & Exercises

1. Assume that the machine uses memory-mapped I/O and that the address B5 is the location within the printer port to which data to be printed should be sent.

   a. If register 7 contains the ASCII code for the letter A, what machine language instruction should be used to cause that letter to be printed at the printer?

   b. If the machine executes a million instructions per second, how many times can this character be sent to the printer in one second?

   c. If the printer is capable of printing five traditional pages of text per minute, will it be able to keep up with the characters being sent to it in (b)?

2. Suppose that the hard disk on your personal computer rotates at 3000 revolutions a minute, that each track contains 16 sectors, and that each sector contains 1024 bytes. Approximately what communication rate is required between the disk drive and the disk controller if the controller is going to receive bits from the disk drive as they are read from the spinning disk?

3. Estimate how long would it take to transfer a 300-page novel encoded in Unicode at a transfer rate of 54 Mbps.

6 Other Architectures

To broaden our perspective, let us consider some alternatives to the traditional machine architecture we have discussed so far.

Pipelining

Electric pulses travel through a wire no faster than the speed of light. Since light travels approximately 1 foot in a nanosecond (one billionth of a second), it requires at least 2 nanoseconds for the CPU to fetch an instruction from a memory cell that is 1 foot away. (The read request must be sent to memory, requiring at least 1 nanosecond, and the instruction must be sent back to the CPU, requiring at least another nanosecond.) Consequently, to fetch and execute an instruction in such a machine requires several nanoseconds—which means that increasing the execution speed of a machine ultimately becomes a miniaturization problem.

However, increasing execution speed is not the only way to improve a computer's performance. The real goal is to improve the machine's **throughput,** which refers to the total amount of work the machine can accomplish in a given amount of time.

An example of how a computer's throughput can be increased without requiring an increase in execution speed involves **pipelining,** which is the technique of allowing the steps in the machine cycle to overlap. In particular, while one instruction is being executed, the next instruction can be fetched, which means that more than one instruction can be in "the pipe" at any one time, each at a different stage of being processed. In turn, the total throughput of the machine is increased even though the time required to fetch and execute each individual instruction remains the same. (Of course, when a JUMP instruction is reached, any gain that would have been obtained by prefetching is not realized because the instructions in "the pipe" are not the ones needed after all.)

Modern machine designs push the pipelining concept beyond our simple example. They are often capable of fetching several instructions at the same time and actually executing more than one instruction at a time when those instructions do not rely on each other.

Multiprocessor Machines

Pipelining can be viewed as a first step toward **parallel processing,** which is the performance of several activities at the same time. However, true parallel processing requires more than one processing unit, resulting in computers known as multiprocessor machines.

A variety of computers today are designed with this idea in mind. One strategy is to attach several processing units, each resembling the CPU in a single-processor machine, to the same main memory. In this configuration, the processors can proceed independently yet coordinate their efforts by leaving messages to one another in the common memory cells. For instance, when one processor is faced with a large task, it can store a program for part of that task in the common memory and then request another processor to execute it. The result is a machine in which different instruction sequences are performed on different sets of data, which is called a **MIMD** (multiple-instruction stream, multiple-data stream) architecture, as opposed to the more traditional **SISD** (single-instruction stream, single-data stream) architecture.

A variation of multiple-processor architecture is to link the processors together so that they execute the same sequence of instructions in unison, each with its own set of data. This leads to a **SIMD** (single-instruction stream, multiple-data stream) architecture. Such machines are useful in applications in which the same task must be applied to each set of similar items within a large block of data.

Another approach to parallel processing is to construct large computers as conglomerates of smaller machines, each with its own memory and CPU. Within such an architecture, each of the small machines is coupled to its neighbors so that tasks assigned to the whole system can be divided among the individual machines. Thus if a task assigned to one of the internal machines can be broken into independent subtasks, that machine can ask its neighbors to perform these

The Multi-Core CPU

As technology provides ways of placing more and more circuitry on a silicon chip, the physical distinction between a computer's components diminishes. For instance, a single chip might contain a CPU and main memory. This is an example of the "system-on-a-chip" approach in which the goal is to provide a complete apparatus in a single device that can be used as an abstract tool in higher level designs. In other cases multiple copies of the same circuit are provided within a single device. This latter tatic originally appeared in the form of chips containing several independent gates or perhaps multiple flip-flops. Today's state of the art allows for more than one entire CPU to be placed on a single chip. This is the underlying architecture of devices known as multi-core CPUs, which consist of two or more CPUs residing on the same chip along with shared cache memory. (Multi-core CPUs containing two processing units are typically called dual-core CPUs.) Such devices simplify the construction of MIMD systems and are readily available for use in home computers.

subtasks concurrently. The original task can then be completed in much less time than would be required by a single-processor machine.

We will study yet another multiprocessor architecture, artificial neural networks, whose design is based on theories of biological neural systems. These machines consist of many elementary processors, or processing units, each of whose output is merely a simple reaction to its combined inputs. These simple processors are linked to form a network in which the outputs of some processors are used as inputs to others. Such a machine is programmed by adjusting the extent to which each processor's output is allowed to influence the reaction of those processors to which it is connected. This is based on the theory that biological neural networks learn to produce a particular reaction to a given stimulus by adjusting the chemical composition of the junctions (synapses) between neurons, which in turn adjusts the ability of one neuron to affect the actions of others.

Proponents of artificial neural networks argue that, although technology is approaching the ability to construct electronic circuitry with roughly as many switching circuits as there are neurons in the human brain (neurons are believed to be nature's switching circuits), the capabilities of today's machines still fall far short of those of the human mind. This, they argue, is a result of the inefficient use of a traditional computer's components as dictated by the von Neumann architecture. After all, if a machine is constructed with a lot of memory circuitry supporting a few processors, then most of its circuitry is destined to be idle most of the time. In contrast, much of the human mind can be active at any given moment.

Thus, research in computer design is expanding the basic CPU-main memory model and in some cases breaking away from it altogether in order to develop more useful machines.

Questions & Exercises

1. Referring back to Question 3 of Section 3, if the machine used the pipeline technique discussed in the text, what will be in "the pipe" when the instruction at address AA is executed? Under what conditions would pipelining not prove beneficial at this point in the program?

2. What conflicts must be resolved in running the program in Question 4 of Section 3 on a pipeline machine?

3. Suppose there were two "central" processing units attached to the same memory and executing different programs. Furthermore, suppose that one of these processors needs to add one to the contents of a memory cell at roughly the same time that the other needs to subtract one from the same cell. (The net effect should be that the cell ends up with the same value with which it started.)

   a. Describe a sequence in which these activities would result in the cell ending up with a value one less than its starting value.

   b. Describe a sequence in which these activities would result in the cell ending up with a value one greater than its starting value.

Chapter Review Problems

(Asterisked problems are associated with optional sections.)

1. a. In what way are general-purpose registers and main memory cells similar?
   b. In what way do general-purpose registers and main memory cells differ?

2. Answer the following questions in terms of the machine language.
   a. Write the instruction 2105 (hexadecimal) as a string of 16 bits.
   b. Write the op-code of the instruction A324 (hexadecimal) as a string of four bits.
   c. Write the operand field of the instruction A324 (hexadecimal) as a string of 12 bits.

3. Suppose a block of data is stored in the memory cells of the machine from address B9 to C1, inclusive. How many memory cells are in this block? List their addresses.

4. What is the value of the program counter in the machine immediately after executing the instruction B0BA?

5. Suppose the memory cells at addresses 00 through 05 in the machine contain the following bit patterns:

Address	Contents
00	21
01	04
02	31
03	00
04	C0
05	00

Assuming that the program counter initially contained 00, record the contents of the program counter, instruction register, and memory cell at address 00 at the end of each fetch phase of the machine cycle until the machine halts.

6. Suppose three values x, y, and z are stored in a machine's memory. Describe the sequence of events (loading registers from memory, saving values in memory, and so on) that leads to the computation of $x + y + z$. How about $(2x) + y$?

7. The following are instructions written in the machine language. Translate them into English.
   a. 407E   b. 8008   c. A403
   d. 2835   e. B3AD

8. Suppose a machine language is designed with an op-code field of four bits. How many different instruction types can the language contain? What if the op-code field is increased to eight bits?

9. Translate the following instructions from English into the machine language.
   a. LOAD register 7 with the hexadecimal value 66.
   b. LOAD register 7 with the contents of memory cell 66.
   c. AND the contents of registers F and 2 leaving the result in register 0.
   d. ROTATE register 4 three bits to the right.
   e. JUMP to the instruction at memory location 31 if the contents of register 0 equals the value in register B.

10. Rewrite the program in Figure 7 assuming that the values to be added are encoded using floating-point notation rather than two's complement notation.

11. Classify each of the following instructions in terms of whether its execution changes the contents of the memory cell at location 3B, retrieves the contents of the memory cell at location 3B, or is independent of the contents of the memory cell at location 3B.

   a. 153B   b. 253B   c. 353B
   d. 3B3B   e. 403B

12. Suppose the memory cells at addresses 00 through 03 in the machine contain the following bit patterns:

Address	Contents
00	24
01	05
02	C0
03	00

   a. Translate the first instruction into English.
   b. If the machine is started with its program counter containing 00, what bit pattern is in register 4 when the machine halts?

13. Suppose the memory cells at addresses 00 through 02 in the machine contain the following bit patterns:

Address	Contents
00	24
01	1B
02	34

   a. What would be the first instruction executed if we started the machine with its program counter containing 00?
   b. What would be the first instruction executed if we started the machine with its program counter containing 01?

14. Suppose the memory cells at addresses 00 through 05 in the machine contain the following bit patterns:

Address	Contents
00	10
01	04
02	30
03	45
04	C0
05	00

   When answering the following questions, assume that the machine starts with its program counter equal to 00.

a. Translate the instructions that are executed into English.

b. What bit pattern is in the memory cell at address 45 when the machine halts?

c. What bit pattern is in the program counter when the machine halts?

15. Suppose the memory cells at addresses 00 through 09 in the machine contain the following bit patterns:

Address	Contents
00	1A
01	02
02	2B
03	02
04	9C
05	AB
06	3C
07	00
08	C0
09	00

Assume that the machine starts with its program counter containing 00.

a. What will be in the memory cell at address 00 when the machine halts?

b. What bit pattern will be in the program counter when the machine halts?

16. Suppose the memory cells at addresses 00 through 07 in the machine contain the following bit patterns:

Address	Contents
00	1A
01	06
02	3A
03	07
04	C0
05	00
06	23
07	00

a. List the addresses of the memory cells that contain the program that will be executed if we start the machine with its program counter containing 00.

b. List the addresses of the memory cells that are used to hold data.

17. Suppose the memory cells at addresses 00 through 0D in the machine contain the following bit patterns:

Address	Contents
00	20
01	03
02	21
03	01
04	40
05	12
06	51
07	12
08	B1
09	0C
0A	B0
0B	06
0C	C0
0D	00

Assume that the machine starts with its program counter containing 00.

a. What bit pattern will be in register 1 when the machine halts?

b. What bit pattern will be in register 0 when the machine halts?

c. What bit pattern is in the program counter when the machine halts?

18. Suppose the memory cells at addresses F0 through FD in the machine contain the following (hexadecimal) bit patterns:

Address	Contents
F0	20
F1	00
F2	21
F3	01
F4	23
F5	05
F6	B3
F7	FC
F8	50
F9	01
FA	B0
FB	F6
FC	C0
FD	00

If we start the machine with its program counter containing F0, what is the value in register 0 when the machine finally executes the halt instruction at location FC?

19. If the machine executes an instruction every microsecond (a millionth of a second), how long does it take to complete the program in Problem 18?

20. Suppose the memory cells at addresses 20 through 28 in the machine contain the following bit patterns:

Address	Contents
20	12
21	20
22	32
23	30
24	B0
25	21
26	20
27	C0
28	00

Assume that the machine starts with its program counter containing 20.
a. What bit patterns will be in registers 0, 1, and 2 when the machine halts?
b. What bit pattern will be in the memory cell at address 30 when the machine halts?
c. What bit pattern will be in the memory cell at address B0 when the machine halts?

21. Suppose the memory cells at addresses AF through B1 in the machine contain the following bit patterns:

Address	Contents
AF	B0
B0	B0
B1	AF

What would happen if we started the machine with its program counter containing AF?

22. Suppose the memory cells at addresses 00 through 05 in the machine contain the following (hexadecimal) bit patterns:

Address	Contents
00	25
01	B0
02	35
03	04
04	C0
05	00

If we start the machine with its program counter containing 00, when does the machine halt?

23. In each of the following cases, write a short program in the machine language to perform the requested activities. Assume that each of your programs is placed in memory starting at address 00.
a. Move the value at memory location 8D to memory location B3.
b. Interchange the values stored at memory locations 8D and B3.
c. If the value stored in memory location 45 is 00, then place the value CC in memory location 88; otherwise, put the value DD in memory location 88.

24. A game that used to be popular among computer hobbyists is core wars—a variation of battleship. (The term *core* originates from an early memory technology in which 0s and 1s were represented as magnetic fields in little rings of magnetic material. The rings were called cores.) The game is played between two opposing programs, each stored in different locations of the same computer's memory. The computer is assumed to alternate between the two programs, executing an instruction from one followed by an instruction from the other. The goal of each program is to cause the other to malfunction by writing extraneous data on top of it; however, neither program knows the location of the other.
a. Write a program in the machine language that approaches the game in a defensive manner by being as small as possible.

b. Write a program that tries to avoid any attacks from the opposing program by moving to different locations. More precisely, write your program to start at location 00, copy itself to location 70, and then jump to this new copy.

c. Extend the program in (b) to continue relocating to new memory locations. In particular, make your program move to location 70, then to E0 (= 70 + 70), then to 60 (= 70 + 70 + 70), etc.

25. Write a program in the machine language to compute the sum of the two's complement values stored at memory locations A1, A2, A3, and A4. Your program should store the total at memory location A5.

26. Suppose the memory cells at addresses 00 through 05 in the machine contain the following (hexadecimal) bit patterns:

Address	Contents
00	20
01	C0
02	30
03	04
04	00
05	00

What happens if we start the machine with its program counter containing 00?

27. What happens if the memory cells at addresses 06 and 07 of the machine contain the bit patterns B0 and 06, respectively, and the machine is started with its program counter containing the value 06?

28. Suppose the following program, written in the machine language, is stored in main memory beginning at address 30 (hexadecimal). What task will the program perform when executed?

```
2003
2101
2200
2310
```

```
1400
3410
5221
5331
3239
333B
B248
B038
C000
```

29. Summarize the steps involved when the machine performs an instruction with op-code B. Express your answer as a set of directions as though you were telling the CPU what to do.

*30. Summarize the steps involved when the machine performs an instruction with op-code 5. Express your answer as a set of directions as though you were telling the CPU what to do.

*31. Summarize the steps involved when the machine performs an instruction with op-code 6. Express your answer as a set of directions as though you were telling the CPU what to do.

*32. Suppose the registers 4 and 5 in the machine contain the bit patterns 3C and C8, respectively. What bit pattern is left in register 0 after executing each of the following instructions:

a. 5045   b. 6045   c. 7045
d. 8045   e. 9045

*33. Using the machine language write programs to perform each of the following tasks:
a. Copy the bit pattern stored in memory location 66 into memory location BB.
b. Change the least significant four bits in the memory cell at location 34 to 0s while leaving the other bits unchanged.
c. Copy the least significant four bits from memory location A5 into the least significant four bits of location A6 while leaving the other bits at location A6 unchanged.

d. Copy the least significant four bits from memory location A5 into the most significant four bits of A5. (Thus, the first four bits in A5 will be the same as the last four bits.)

*34. Perform the indicated operations:

a.
```
    111000
AND 101001
```

b.
```
    000100
AND 101010
```

c.
```
    000100
AND 010101
```

d.
```
    111011
AND 110101
```

e.
```
   111000
OR 101001
```

f.
```
   000100
OR 101010
```

g.
```
   000100
OR 010101
```

h.
```
   111011
OR 110101
```

i.
```
    111000
XOR 101001
```

j.
```
    000100
XOR 101010
```

k.
```
    000100
XOR 010101
```

l.
```
    111011
XOR 110101
```

*35. Identify both the mask and the logical operation needed to accomplish each of the following objectives:
a. Put 0s in the middle four bits of an eight-bit pattern without disturbing the other bits.
b. Complement a pattern of eight bits.
c. Complement the most significant bit of an eight-bit pattern without changing the other bits.
d. Put a 1 in the most significant bit of an eight-bit pattern without disturbing the other bits.
e. Put 1s in all but the most significant bit of an eight-bit pattern without disturbing the most significant bit.

*36. Identify a logical operation (along with a corresponding mask) that, when applied to an input string of eight bits, produces an output string of all 0s if and only if the input string is 10000001.

*37. Describe a sequence of logical operations (along with their corresponding masks) that, when applied to an input string of eight bits, produces an output byte of all 0s if the input string both begins and ends with 1s. Otherwise, the output should contain at least one 1.

*38. What would be the result of performing a four-bit left circular shift on the following bit patterns?
a. 10101   b. 11110000   c. 001
d. 101000   e. 00001

*39. What would be the result of performing a one-bit right circular shift on the following bytes represented in hexadecimal notation (give your answers in hexadecimal notation)?
a. 3F   b. 0D   c. FF   d. 77

*40. a. What single instruction in the machine language could be used to accomplish a three-bit right circular shift of register B?
b. What single instruction in the machine language could be used to accomplish a three-bit left circular shift of register B?

*41. Write a program in the machine language that reverses the contents of the memory cell at address 8C. (That is, the final bit pattern at address 8C when read from left to right should agree with the original pattern when read from right to left.)

*42. Write a program in the machine language that subtracts the value stored at A1 from the value stored at address A0 and places the result at address A2. Assume that the values are encoded in two's complement notation.

*43. Can a printer, printing 40 characters per second, keep up with a string of ASCII characters (one byte per symbol) arriving serially at the rate of 300 bps? What about 1200 bps?

*44. Suppose a person is typing 30 words per minute at a keyboard. (A word is considered to be five characters.) If a machine executes 50 instructions every microsecond (millionth of a second), how many instructions does the machine execute during the time between the typing of two consecutive characters?

*45. How many bits per second must a keyboard transmit to keep up with a typist typing 30 words per minute? (Assume each character is encoded in ASCII along with a parity bit and each word consists of five characters.)

*46. Suppose the machine communicates with a printer using the technique of memory-mapped I/O. Suppose also that address FF is used to send characters to the printer, and address FE is used to receive information about the printer's status. In particular, suppose the least significant bit at the address FE indicates whether the printer is ready to receive another character (with a 0 indicating "not ready" and a 1 indicating "ready"). Starting at address 00, write a machine language routine that waits until the printer is ready for another character and then sends the character represented by the bit pattern in register 5 to the printer.

*47. Write a program in the machine language that places 0s in all the memory cells from address A0 through C0 but is small enough to fit in the memory cells from address 00 through 13 (hexadecimal).

*48. Suppose a machine has 20GB of storage space available on a hard disk and receives data over a telephone connection at the rate of 14,400 bps. At this rate, how long will it take to fill the available storage space?

*49. Suppose a communication line is being used to transmit data serially at 14,400 bps. If a burst of interference lasts .01 second, how many data bits will be affected?

*50. Suppose you are given 32 processors, each capable of finding the sum of two multidigit numbers in a millionth of a second. Describe how parallel processing techniques can be applied to find the sum of 64 numbers in only six-millionths of a second. How much time does a single processor require to find this same sum?

*51. Summarize the difference between a CISC architecture and a RISC architecture.

*52. Identify two approaches to increasing throughput.

*53. Describe how the average of a collection of numbers can be computed more rapidly with a multiprocessor machine than a single-processor machine.

Social Issues

The following questions are intended as a guide to the ethical/social/legal issues associated with the field of computing. The goal is not merely to answer these questions. You should also consider why you answered as you did and whether your justifications are consistent from one question to the next.

1. Suppose a computer manufacturer develops a new machine architecture. To what extent should the company be allowed to own that architecture? What policy would be best for society?

2. In a sense, the year 1923 marked the birth of what many now call *planned obsolescence*. This was the year that General Motors, led by Alfred Sloan, introduced the automobile industry to the concept of model years. The idea was to increase sales by changing styling rather than necessarily introducing a better automobile. Sloan is quoted as saying, "We want to make you dissatisfied with your current car so you will buy a new one." To what extent is this marketing ploy used today in the computer industry?

3. We often think in terms of how computer technology has changed our society. Many argue, however, that this technology has often kept changes from

occurring by allowing old systems to survive and, in some cases, become more entrenched. For example, would a central government's role in society have survived without computer technology? To what extent would centralized authority be present today had computer technology not been available? To what extent would we be better or worse off without computer technology?

4. Is it ethical for an individual to take the attitude that he or she does not need to know anything about the internal details of a machine because someone else will build it, maintain it, and fix any problems that arise? Does your answer depend on whether the machine is a computer, automobile, nuclear power plant, or toaster?

5. Suppose a manufacturer produces a computer chip and later discovers a flaw in its design. Suppose further that the manufacturer corrects the flaw in future production but decides to keep the original flaw a secret and does not recall the chips already shipped, reasoning that none of the chips already in use are being used in an application in which the flaw will have consequences. Is anyone hurt by the manufacturer's decision? Is the manufacturer's decision justified if no one is hurt and the decision keeps the manufacturer from loosing money and possibly having to layoff employees?

6. Does advancing technology provide cures for heart disease or is it a source of a sedentary life style that contributes to heart disease?

7. It is easy to imagine financial or navigational disasters that may occur as the result of arithmetic errors due to overflow and truncation problems. What consequences could result from errors in image storage systems due to loss of image details (perhaps in fields such as reconnaissance or medical diagnosis)?

Additional Reading

Carpinelli, J. D. *Computer Systems Organization and Architecture*. Boston, MA: Addison-Wesley, 2001.

Comer, D. E. *Essentials of Computer Architecture*. Upper Saddle River, NJ: Prentice-Hall, 2005.

Hamacher, V. C., Z. G. Vranesic, and S. G. Zaky. *Computer Organization*, 5th ed. New York: McGraw-Hill, 2002.

Knuth, D. E. *The Art of Computer Programming*, Vol. 1, 3rd ed. Boston, MA: Addison-Wesley, 1998.

Murdocca, M. J. and V. P. Heuring. *Computer Architecture and Organization: An Integrated Approach*, New York: Wiley, 2007.

Stallings, W. *Computer Organization and Architecture*, 7th ed. Upper Saddle River, NJ: Prentice-Hall, 2006.

Tanenbaum, A. S. *Structured Computer Organization*, 5th ed. Upper Saddle River, NJ: Prentice-Hall, 2006.

Answers to Questions & Exercises

Section 1

1. On some machines this is a two-step process consisting of first reading the contents from the first cell into a register and then writing it from the register into the destination cell. On most machines, this is accomplished as one activity without using an intermediate register.

2. The value to be written, the address of the cell in which to write, and the command to write.

3. General-purpose registers are used to hold the data immediately applicable to the operation at hand; main memory is used to hold data that will be needed in the near future; and mass storage is used to hold data that will likely not be needed in the near future.

Section 2

1. The term *move* often carries the connotation of removing from one location and placing in another, thus leaving a hole behind. In most cases within a machine, this removal does not take place. Rather, the object being moved is most often copied (or cloned) into the new location.

2. A common technique, called relative addressing, is to state how far rather than where to jump. For example, an instruction might be to jump forward three instructions or jump backward two instructions. You should note, however, that such statements must be altered if additional instructions are later inserted between the origin and the destination of the jump.

3. This could be argued either way. The instruction is stated in the form of a conditional jump. However, because the condition that 0 be equal to 0 is always satisfied, the jump will always be made as if there were no condition stated at all. You will often find machines with such instructions in their repertoires because they provide an efficient design. For example, if a machine is designed to execute an instruction with a structure such as "If ... jump to..." this instruction form can be used to express both conditional and unconditional jumps.

4. 156C = 0001010101101100
   166D = 0001011001101101
   5056 = 0101000001010110
   306E = 0011000001101110
   C000 = 1100000000000000

5. a. STORE the contents of register 6 in memory cell number 8A.
   b. JUMP to location DE if the contents of register A equals that of register 0.
   c. AND the contents of registers 3 and C, leaving the result in register 0.
   d. MOVE the contents of register F to register 4.

6. The instruction 15AB requires that the CPU query the memory circuitry for the contents of the memory cell at address AB. This value, when obtained from memory, is then placed in register 5. The instruction 25AB does not require such a request of memory. Rather, the value AB is placed in register 5.

7. a. 2356   b. A503   c. 80A5

Section 3

1. Hexadecimal 34

2. a. 0F   b. C3

3. a. 00   b. 01   c. four times

4. It halts. This is an example of what is often called self-modifying code. That is, the program modifies itself. Note that the first two instructions place hexadecimal C0 at memory location F8, and the next two instructions place 00 at location F9. Thus, by the time the machine reaches the instruction at F8, the halt instruction (C000) has been placed there.

Section 4

1. a. 00001011   b. 10000000   c. 00101101
   d. 11101011   e. 11101111   f. 11111111
   g. 11100000   h. 01101111   i. 11010010

2. 00111100 with the AND operation

3. 00111100 with the XOR operation

4. a. The final result is 0 if the string contained an even number of 1s. Otherwise it is 1.
   b. The result is the value of the parity bit for even parity.

5. The logical XOR operation mirrors addition except for the case where both operands are 1, in which case the XOR produces a 0, whereas the sum is 10. (Thus the XOR operation can be considered an addition operation with no carry.)

6. Use AND with the mask 11011111 to change lowercase to uppercase. Use OR with 00100000 to change uppercase to lowercase.

7. a. 01001101   b. 11100001   c. 11101111

8. a. 57   b. B8   c. 6F   d. 6A

9. 5

10. 00110110 in two's complement; 01011110 in floating-point. The point here is that the procedure used to add the values is different depending on the interpretation given the bit patterns.

11. One solution is as follows:

   12A7 (LOAD register 2 with the contents of memory cell A7.)
   2380 (LOAD register 3 with the value 80.)
   7023 (OR registers 2 and 3 leaving the result in register 0.)
   30A7 (STORE contents of register 0 in memory cell A7.)
   C000 (HALT.)

12. One solution is as follows:

   15E0 (LOAD register 5 with the contents of memory cell E0.)
   A502 (ROTATE 2 bits to the right the contents of register 5.)
   260F (LOAD register 6 with the value 0F.)
   8056 (AND registers 5 and 6, leaving the result in register 0.)
   30E1 (STORE the contents of register 0 in memory cell E1.)
   C000 (HALT.)

Section 5

1. a. 37B5
   b. One million times
   c. No. A typical page of text contains less than 4000 characters. Thus the ability to print five pages in a minute indicates a printing rate of no more than 20,000 characters per minute, which is much less than one million characters per second. (The point is that a computer can send characters to a printer much faster than the printer can print them; thus the printer needs a way of telling the computer to wait.)

2. The disk will make 50 revolutions in one second, meaning that 800 sectors will pass under the read/write head in a second. Because each sector contains 1024 bytes, bits will pass under the read/write head at approximately 6.5 Mbps. Thus communication between the controller and the disk drive will have to be at least this fast if the controller is going to keep up with the data being read from the disk.

3. A 300-page novel represented in Unicode consists of about 2MB or 16,000,000 bits. Thus approximately 0.3 seconds would be required to transfer the entire novel at 54 Mbps.

Section 6

1. The pipe would contain the instructions B1B0 (being executed), 5002, and perhaps even B0AA. If the value in register 1 is equal to the value in register 0, the jump to location B0 is executed, and the effort already expended on the instructions in the pipe is wasted. On the other hand, no time is wasted because the effort expended on these instructions did not require extra time.

2. If no precautions are taken, the information at memory locations F8 and F9 is fetched as an instruction before the previous part of the program has had a chance to modify these cells.

3. a. The CPU that is trying to add 1 to the cell can first read the value in the cell. Following this the other CPU reads the cell's value. (Note that at this point both CPUs have retrieved the same value.) If the first CPU now finishes its addition and writes its result back in the cell before the second finishes its subtraction and writes its result, the final value in the cell reflects only the activity of the second CPU.

   b. The CPUs might read the data from the cell as before, but this time the second CPU might write its result before the first. Thus only the activity of the first CPU is reflected in the cell's final value.

7

Fill-in-the-Blank Computing

The Basics of Spreadsheets

Learning Objectives

> Explain how data is organized in spreadsheet software

> Describe how to refer to spreadsheet rows, columns, and cell ranges

> Explain relative and absolute references

> Apply concepts of relative and absolute references when filling a formula

> Explain the concept of tab-delimited input and output

There are 10 kinds of people in the world: Those who know binary and those who don't.

—ANONYMOUS

FROM THE VERY BEGINNING of mankind's use of symbols and writing, we have arranged information to make it more useful. Organized information is easier to understand, easier to remember, and easier to navigate. With the invention of information technology, there is a further reason to organize information: Computers can process it for us. This is a bonus we gain for very little effort, especially when we use spreadsheets.

In this chapter we introduce the basic ideas of spreadsheets. Because they make computer users so effective, especially in business, spreadsheets have become very sophisticated. This chapter introduces you to the basic ideas, making them personally useful. If you need more power, you'll have a great foundation for learning more; if not, you'll be acquainted with a very versatile tool.

We begin by introducing the basics of spreadsheet use, including constructing lists, sorting them, naming cells, and controlling the format of the entries. Next we add numeric information to the spreadsheet and learn how to manipulate it, which teaches you about formulas, relative and absolute references, and functions. Computing new numbers from numbers already in the table is what spreadsheets do best and, happily, they are extremely easy to learn and use. After learning these basic concepts, we practice them on "everyday" problems; that is, tasks of personal interest: We build a 1-minute calendar for our weekly schedule, set up a transportation schedule so we don't miss the bus so often, make a "cheat sheet" for computing discounts at the music store, and develop data for helping decide how much to borrow for a "big ticket" purchase like a car or stereo. None of these tasks is so difficult as to require a computer, but since we're using a computer anyway, we can solve them quickly to our personal satisfaction. Finally, we use the Best Movie list to practice manipulating data in a spreadsheet.

Arranging Information

Commonly, textual information is organized into lists, as we know from making shopping lists, invitation lists, "to do" lists, class lists, and many others. As a running example, we'll use a list of migratory birds:

```
Short-tailed shearwater
Swainson's hawk
Wheatear
Arctic tern
Willow warbler
Long-tailed skua
```

Looking at the list, you see that it contains six bird names even though you may not be too familiar with birds. You probably figured it out because you know that hawks and warblers are birds and the items appear on separate lines. The names themselves are quite diverse as text: single word names, double word names, hyphenated names, and even a possessive. Since the computer doesn't have your knowledge, it needs to be told the extent of each entry, that is, how much text there is in each entry. The separate line cue helps, but if the entries were very long, they would spill to another line, and that cue wouldn't work.

*fit*TIP   **Kinda the Same.** Spreadsheet software is available from many sources. The content of this chapter applies generally to Microsoft Excel, OpenOffice, AppleWorks, Lotus 1-2-3, and others. Every system is different, however, because menus and defaults are particular to each system. With a moment's exploration, you should be able to perform the operation on your system.

An Array of Cells

To help us create a list, spreadsheets give us an array of **cells** that we fill in to set up our list.

Microsoft Excel - birds.xls	

	A	B	C	D	
1					
2		Short-tailed shearwater			
3		Swainson's hawk			
4		Wheatear			
5		Arctic tern			
6		Willow warbler			
7		Long-tailed skua			
8					

Sheet1 / Sheet2
Ready

The lines are part of the graphic user interface; they help us and the computer agree on what an item is and how the positions of items are related to each other.

Notice that four of the six items in the list do not fit within the lines provided. Even though it takes more space to display the entry than the computer provides, entries do not straddle cells. Each occupies only the cell into which it is typed, as is shown when we enter test data in the cells to their right.

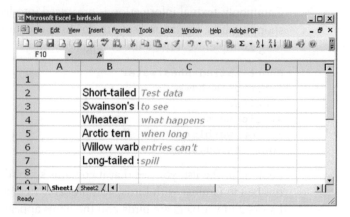

The test data, which blocks the long entries from spilling to the empty cells on the right, indicates that entries that are too long are clipped. (Items only spill when the cells to their right are unused.) We can either let the entries be clipped, or make the cells wider, as explained later in Table 1. We choose the latter.

Sorting the Data

A common operation on any list, especially when it gets long, is to alphabetize or sort it. Spreadsheet software makes sorting easy. We must specify which items to sort, so naturally, we must select the list. We select the list by dragging the cursor across the cells; the resulting selection is indicated with highlighting.

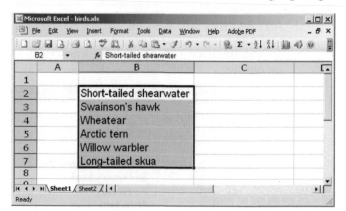

All of the items inside the blue box are selected, including the white item, which is a different color only because it was the first cell selected, that is, it's the place where the dragging began. The *Sort. . .* operation is found among the menu items. It allows us to choose ascending or descending order. The software uses an algorithm to sort audio CDs. Sorting our list of birds in ascending order produces the following result.

Notice that the sorting software orders the list alphabetically on the first letter of the entry, not on the type of bird, for example, "hawk." This is consistent with the spreadsheet view that the cell entries are "atomic" or "monolithic" from the computer's point of view, meaning that the computer does not consider any of their constituent parts. If the list contained both Swainson's hawk and Swainson's warbler, they would appear together in sorted order. But if we wanted those birds to be grouped with the hawks and the warblers respectively, then it would be necessary to sort on the second part of the name. That would require the type of the bird (e.g., "hawk" or "warbler") to be in a separate cell—in its own column.

Adding More Data to the List

Our list is not so complete. We will leave the common names in a single column, but we'll add the scientific names using two columns, one for genus and one for species.

As you know, scientific names are usually written in italics. Spreadsheets give us the ability to format cell entries with the kinds of formatting facilities found in word processors, such as italics, bold, font styles, font sizes, justification, colored text and backgrounds, and so on. Naturally, the formatting facilities are found under the *Format* menu. We italicize the scientific names and right justify the genus name so it looks like it is paired with the species name.

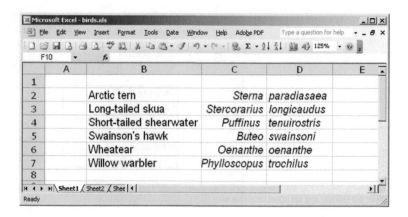

Naming Rows and Columns. Now suppose we want to alphabetize on the second column, the genus. We begin by selecting the whole list because that is the information we want to reorder. With three columns selected, how do we specify that the second column is the one to sort on rather than the first column?

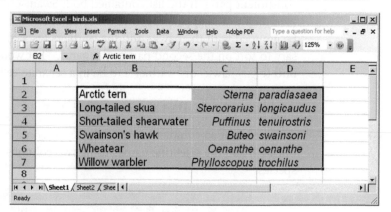

Spreadsheet programs automatically provide a naming scheme for referring to specific cells. The columns are labeled with letters and the rows are labeled with numbers. This allows us to refer to a whole column, as in column C, or to a whole row, as in row 4, or to a single cell by specifying both the column letter and the row number, as in B2. Thus, when we request to sort the entries, the sorting software displays this *Sort* GUI.

We choose to sort the selected rows based on entries in column **c** (which contains our *genus* entries) by clicking on the directional arrows. This produces the following result.

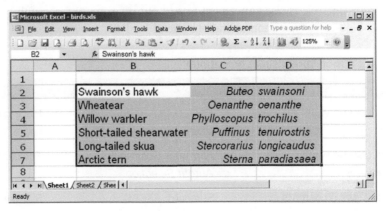

Notice that the naming scheme allows us to refer to a group of cells, by naming the first cell and the last cell and placing a colon (:) in between, as in "the cells **B2:D7** are highlighted in the figure." This kind of reference is called a **cell range**.

> try it   What is the cell range for the scientific names of the birds whose common name includes "-tailed"?
>
> *Answer:* **C5:D6** because the two birds with "-tailed" in their names are in rows **5** and **6**, and the scientific names span columns **C** and **D**.

Headings. Though the software provides names for referring to cells, it is convenient for us to name the rows and columns with more meaningful names. For example, we can label the columns with the type of information entered.

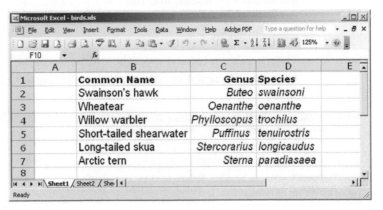

Summarizing, spreadsheets are made up of cells that are displayed to the user as rectangles in a grid. Information is entered in a cell and treated as an elemental piece of data no matter how long it is or if it contains spaces or other punctuation symbols. Generally, we build a list of items that can be sorted simply by selecting them and requesting the sorting operation. If multiple columns must be sorted, we select all of the information to be reordered, request *Sort*, and specify the column to sort on when the GUI asks for it. Spreadsheets automatically provide a labeling for specifying the column/row position of any element in the grid, but it is also convenient to add our own, more meaningful names. Table 1 gives other common operations useful for lists.

Table 1 Common spreadsheet operations

Operation	Using Excel...	Using Open Office...
Change column width manually	Place cursor at right side of column name, then drag	Place cursor at right side of column name, then drag
Change column width automatically	*Format > Column > Autofit Selection*	*Format > Column > Optimal Width...*
Cut, copy, paste contents	Standard: ^X, ^C, ^V	Standard: ^X, ^C, ^V
Fancy formatting	*Format > Cells...*	*Format > Cells...*
Clear cells	*Edit > Clear > All*	*Edit > Delete Contents...*
Delete columns, rows	*Edit > Delete*	*Edit > Delete Cells...*
Hide a column or row	*Format > Column > Hide*	*Format > Column > Hide*

Note: All spreadsheet applications provide these common operations; explore your system.

 ## Computing with Spreadsheets

Though spreadsheets don't have to contain a single number to be useful, their most common application is to process numerical data. Numerical data is usually associated with textual information, too, so most spreadsheets have both. For example, suppose our migratory bird spreadsheet has been further filled out, as shown in Figure 1.

The `Migration` column gives the end points of the bird's semiannual migration route, the `Distance` column gives the approximate length of that flight in kilome-

	B	C	D	E	F	G
1	Common Name	Genus	Species	Migration	Distance (km)	Body Len (m)
2	Swainson's hawk	*Buteo*	*swainsoni*	USA-Argentina	13500	0.52
3	Wheatear	*Oenanthe*	*oenanthe*	Alaska-E Africa	13500	0.16
4	Willow warbler	*Phylloscopus*	*trochilus*	Chukotka-S Africa	15500	0.11
5	Short-tailed shearwater	*Puffinus*	*tenuirostris*	Tasmania-Bering Strait	12500	0.43
6	Long-tailed skua	*Stercorarius*	*longicaudus*	N Greenland-Southern Ocean	16000	0.51
7	Arctic tern	*Sterna*	*paradiasaea*	Greenland-Antarctic	19000	0.35
8						

Figure 1 Bird migration spreadsheet.

ters, and **Body Len** gives the size of the bird (length) in meters. In the following discussion the **Genus**, **Species**, and **Migration** columns will be hidden.

Writing a Formula

Suppose we want to find out how far the Swainson's hawk flies in miles rather than kilometers. Because one kilometer is 0.621 miles, we must multiply the value in cell **F2** by 0.621 to find out. We can perform this specific computation with a calculator, but we will probably want to know the distances in miles for all of the migration flights. So, we decide to create a new column for the distance in miles and instruct the spreadsheet how to compute it.

What entry do we want in position **H2**? We'd like it to be equal to **F2** × 0.621, so we type

```
=F2*0.621
```

which appears in the **H2** window and the *Edit Formula* window on the edit bar above.

Notice that we use an asterisk (*) for the multiplication symbol rather than a cross or dot. When we type return, the value in **H2** is the result of the computation, that is, 8,383.5 miles.

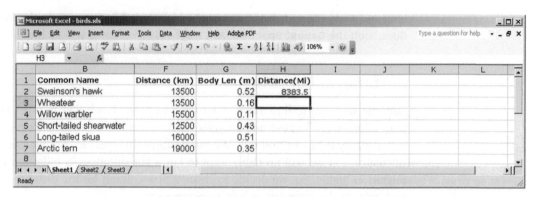

We have just instructed the spreadsheet software to compute the value in cell **H2** by telling it what the cell should equal. We did this by typing a formula into the cell. Formulas, which begin with an equal sign (=), define the value for the entry based on the values of other entries. We used numbers (0.621), cell references (**F2**), and standard arithmetic operations (*) as found on a calculator. If we ever change our estimate of the distance Swainson's hawks migrate, that is, change the value in **F2**, then the spreadsheet software will *automatically change* the value in **H2** to reflect the revision.

Equal Opportunity. When we type characters into a cell, the spreadsheet software needs to know if we are giving it data that should be stored, or if we are giving it a formula saying how to compute information for that cell. The equal sign (=) is the indicator: It's a formula if it starts with =; otherwise it's data.

Consider the formula a bit more. We entered the formula =**F2*0.621** into cell **H2**. The cell contains this formula, not 8383.5. We can prove this by temporarily changing the value in **F2** from 13,500 to, say, 14,000, and noting that **H2** automatically increases to 8,694.

By specifying this formula, we have defined an equation

H2 = **F2** × 0.621

just as we would in algebra. Recall that such an equation means that both sides of the equal sign refer to the same value. So, entering the formula into **H2** means that we want the cell to have the value of **F2** * **0.621** now and forever. Because **F2** presently contains the data 13,500, cell **H2** displays as 8383.5. When we change the value of **F2**, the value of **H2** must change, because the equality must be preserved. Thus, when we put a formula into a cell (the right side of the equation), the computer does the math and displays its value (the left side of the equation).

Repeating a Formula

We can specify a similar computation for cell **H3** and the other cells in that column by entering them in the same way.

Copy/Paste. Thinking about it, however, we might guess that *Copy/Paste* will work to replicate the equation to other cells. So, we select cell H2, which, in Excel, is indicated by an animated highlight (the dashes revolve around the box). Other spreadsheet software simply shows a solid box around the item.

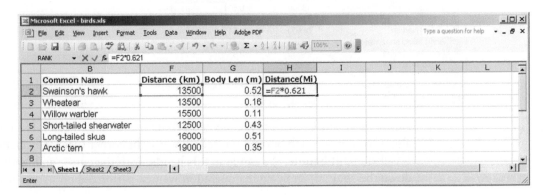

The cell's contents are shown in the *Edit Formula* window. We *Copy* this cell (^c), select the remaining cells in the column by dragging the mouse across them, and *Paste* (^v). The result shows all of the distance values computed. This is quite a bit of computation for very little effort on our part.

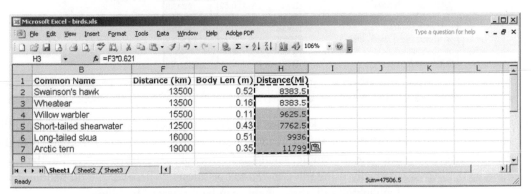

Notice that in the *Edit Formula* window the equation shows as F3*0.621. This corresponds to the computation for the cell H3, the first of the highlighted cells (white) into which we pasted the formula. And we notice a curious thing: Whereas the formula we pasted was F2*0.621, the formula was transformed into F3*0.621 when it was pasted into H3; it was transformed into F4*0.621 for H4, and so on. This is exactly what we want for this column, namely that the value in column H is based on the corresponding values in column F. The software makes this transformation for us automatically. (This is explained later in the *Transforming Formulas* section.)

Filling. It's possible for these computations to be performed even more easily! Let's go back and redo them from the point where we had just entered the formula for the Swainson's hawk,

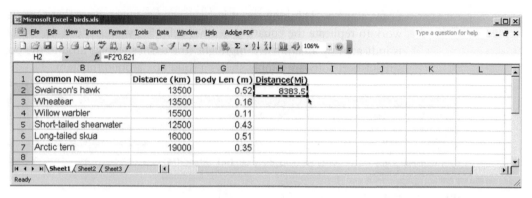

Notice in the image that the highlighted cell **H2** is outlined in color, but there is also a small box or tab beyond the cell's lower right corner (near the cursor). This is called its **fill handle**. We can grab this handle with the cursor and "pull" it down the column, applying the operation we just performed on **H2** to those cells.

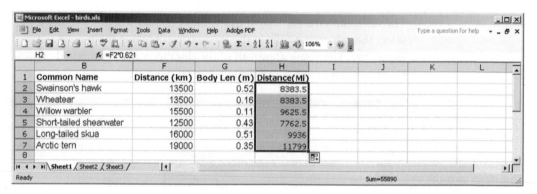

This process is known as **filling**. It's automated copying and pasting! Filling is a shortcut that allows us to replicate, that is, *Copy/Paste*, the contents of the cell with the fill handle, saving us from explicitly setting each cell in the column or manually using the *Copy/Paste* operations. Whenever the fill handle is visible on a highlighted cell, the contents can be replicated by filling.

---

try it   Suppose we would also like to see the birds' body lengths measured in inches. Using the fact that a meter is 39.37 inches, what steps do we perform to add this information to the spreadsheet?

Answer:

Step 1. The recommended first step is to label the next column, **I**, with an appropriate heading, though it is not actually required.

Step 2. Enter the formula **=G2*39.37** in cell **I2**, which computes the length of Swainson's hawks in inches; it's 20.28 inches.

Step 3. Click once on cell **I2** to select it, and drag the fill handle down the column to fill in the lengths of the other birds.

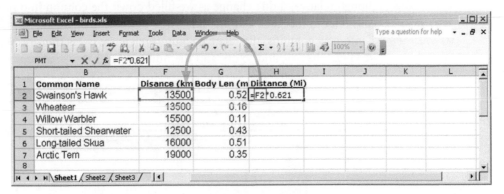

Transforming Formulas: Relative Versus Absolute

The software automatically transforms the formulas as it pastes them or fills them into a cell because we used a **relative cell reference** when we wrote F2 and G2. Spreadsheets allow two kinds of cell references—relative and absolute—and we must be careful which we use. The **absolute cell references** to these cells are $F$2 and $G$2; they tell the software never to change the reference when filling or pasting. Here's what's happening.

Relative means "relative position from a cell." When we pasted the formula =F2*0.621 into H2, the software noticed that cell F2 is two cells to the left of H2. That is, the formula refers to a cell in the same row, but two cells to the left.

Since this is a relative reference, the software preserves the relationship of "two cells to the left in the same row" between the position of the referenced cell and the cell where the formula is pasted. So, when we *Paste* or fill this same formula into H3, the software transforms the formula so it still refers to the cell two cells to the left in the same row; that is, the formula is changed to =F3*0.621. Similarly, this occurs whenever a relative formula is pasted or filled.

An absolute reference always refers to the fixed position—the software never adjusts it.

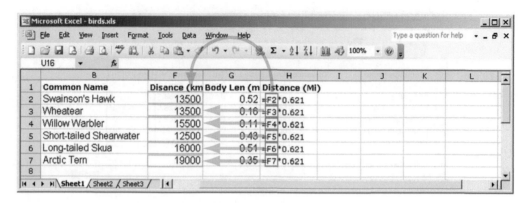

Because there are two dimensions in spreadsheets—columns and rows—there are actually two ways a formula can be relative. This makes four cases:

F2—column and row are both relative

$F2—absolute column, but relative row

F$2—relative column, but absolute row

$F$2—column and row are both absolute

For example, assume cell A1 contains 1. When the formula =A$1+1 is filled from A2 down column A into new rows, the formula is untransformed and 2's are computed, because the cell's row reference ($1) is absolute and the column reference, though relative, didn't change as we filled down the column into new rows. All cells refer to the same cell, A1. But when that formula is filled from B1 across row 1 into new columns, the relative column reference (A) is transformed, =B$1+1, =C$1+1, =D$1+1, and so on, and the numbers 2, 3, 4, . . . are computed.

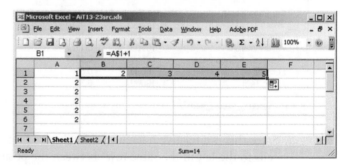

The spreadsheet software preserves the relative position in whichever dimension(s) you specify, and leaves absolute references unchanged.

---

*fit*TIP

Use Squiggle   In Microsoft Excel, a handy way to prove that cells actually contain formulas—and are not the result of computing the formula—is to type Ctrl-~. This displays all of the contents of the spreadsheet's cells, including the formulas.

Cell Formats

Although it is amazing that the migratory birds fly so far twice a year, it is perhaps even more impressive that the smaller birds do it. One analysis that a biologist might make to take both distance and size into consideration is to divide the bird's size into the distance flown. This *flying score* measures each bird in a way that allows a more equal comparison.

We will use the distance in kilometers (column F) and length in meters (column G) so that the "meters" cancel out giving a "unitless" score. As before, we define a new column and enter the equation into the first cell. After finding the hawk's score, we fill the column with the formula and compute the results.

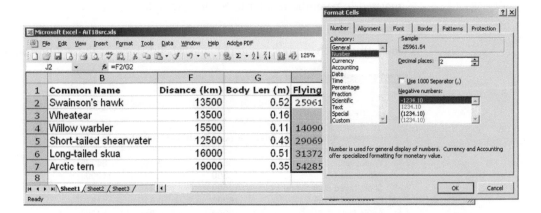

The scores are somewhat difficult to read because they have too many digits, or as a mathematician might say, more digits than are significant. For the numbers to be useful, we need to format them, say, by making them whole numbers.

All spreadsheet software provides control over the format of the information displayed. For example, Excel displays this GUI for formatting cells.

This GUI gives us control over the types of information in the fields (*Category*); control over the number of decimal digits for the *Number* category chosen; control over setting the "1000s" separators (commas for North America); and control over the display of negative numbers.

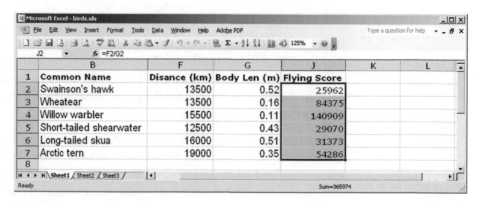

When we reduce the number of decimal digits to 0, that is, specify whole numbers only, we get this result.

This confirms our intuition that smaller birds score higher even if their distances flown are not the largest.

 ## Functions

Picking the Willow warbler as the most amazing flier is based on its being the maximum value in the **Flying Score** column. Visually finding the maximum for this column is easy to do, but it's somewhat harder to do for the other columns because the entries have the same number of digits; also, the list could be much longer. So we set up the spreadsheet to compute the maximum.

Finding the Maximum

Spreadsheet software provides **functions** for computing common summary operations such as totals (**sum**), averages, maximums (**max**), and many others. To use these functions, we give the function name and specify the cell range to be summarized in parentheses after it. So, for example, we write

`=max(J2:J7)`

in a cell at the bottom of column **J**, and label that row with the "**Maximum:**" caption.

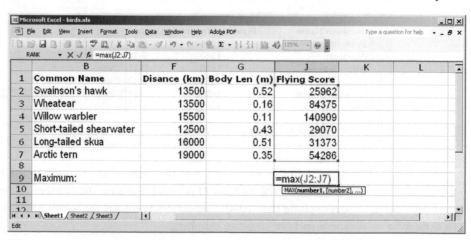

The formula directs the software to find the largest value in the cell range **J2:J7**, that is, the **Flying Score** column. Notice that there is a triangle pointer by the function **MAX** in the upper left corner of the image. We'll find a list of the available functions here. If you don't remember the function names, you can check this list or check the list under *Edit > Insert Function . . . .*

*fit*TIP

> **The Easy Case.** Functions and column letters are not case sensitive in spread-sheets, so we can type them however we wish. The software stores the result as uppercase, which is how it's displayed after its initial entry.

Having computed the maximum for **Flying Score**, we can figure the maximum of the other columns as before, by filling. That is, we grab the **J9** cell by its fill handle and pull it left to column **F**. The result is curious.

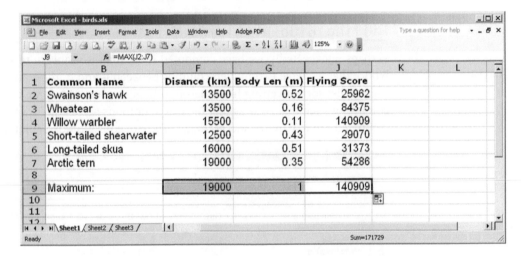

The "1" in the **Body Len** column is a whole number rather than 0.52, the largest of the two-decimal-digit fractions in column **G**. Why? Because the maximum value computation in the **Flying Score** column inherits the whole number setting from before. When we drag it across to the other columns, it brings its formatting with it. So, the software looks for the largest value in **Body Len**, finds that it is 0.52, and then rounds it to a whole number, that is, 1. Formatting this cell so that it displays numbers with two decimal digits fixes the problem.

For completeness, let's also compute the average for each column using the average function. The result requires some additional formatting in the last two columns.

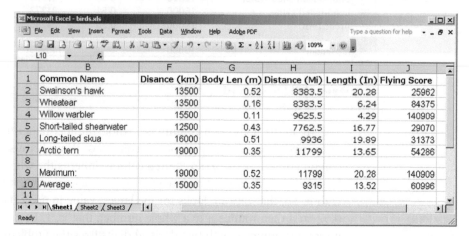

Filling Hidden Columns

Perhaps unexpectedly, we have computed more than is visible in this image. Notice that we have two hidden columns between G and J, the columns that we used earlier for converting from metric to English units. When we "unhide" these columns we see that by dragging the cell definitions across the rows, we have computed the maximum and average of the previously hidden columns, too.

This makes sense because these columns are part of our spreadsheet; they just were not displayed previously. Of course, if we no longer wanted the English conversion columns, we could delete them. The final spreadsheet, slightly adjusted in formatting, is shown in Figure 2.

	B	C	D	E	F	G	H	I	J
1	Common Name	Genus	Species	Migration	Disance (km)	Body Len (m)	Distance (Mi)	Length (In)	Flying Score
2	Swainson's hawk	Buteo	swainsoni	USA-Argentina	13500	0.52	8383.5	20.28	25962
3	Wheatear	Oenanthe	oenanthe	Alaska-E Africa	13500	0.16	8383.5	6.24	84375
4	Willow warbler	Phylloscopus	trochilus	Chukotka-S Africa	15500	0.11	9625.5	4.29	140909
5	Short-tailed shearwat	Puffinus	tenuirostris	Tasmania-Bering Strait	12500	0.43	7762.5	16.77	29070
6	Long-tailed skua	Stercorarius	longicaudus	N Greenland-Southern Oce	16000	0.51	9936	19.89	31373
7	Arctic tern	Sterna	paradiasaea	Greenland-Antarctic	19000	0.35	11799	13.65	54286
8									
9				Maximum:	19000	0.52	11799	20	140909
10				Average:	15000	0.35	9315	13.52	60996

Figure 2 Final spreadsheet for the migratory birds.

Charts

The spreadsheet organizes our data and computes new values, but it is often helpful to see the results graphically when comparing values. Spreadsheet software makes creating charts remarkably easy.

The process is to select the values to be plotted and then click on *Chart…* under the *Insert* menu. A wizard walks us through the graphing process. To see what happens, imagine we have selected the items in the Flying Score column. When we click on *Chart…*, the wizard gives us a choice of graph styles, as shown in Figure 3(a). To get an idea of what the graph will look like with our data, we can see a preview, shown in Figure 3(b). For this data, the horizontal bar graph looks good.

The remaining steps of the wizard are largely self-explanatory. Most of this entails defining the labels. This requires a little care, because the wizard uses terms like

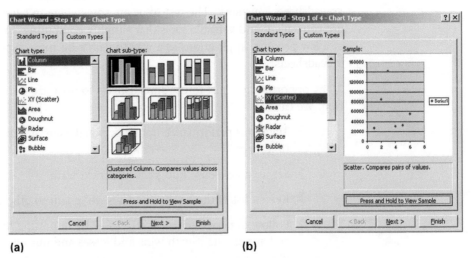

(a)   **(b)**

Figure 3 GUI from the Excel charting wizard: (a) initial display; (b) the preview of a scatter plot graph.

the "X-axis," and it's not always easy to decide which one is meant. But, make a guess; if it's wrong, you can edit it later. On completion, we are presented with the final result. Clicking on any part of the graph displays a pop-up window that offers us editing options. Figure 4 shows our final result.

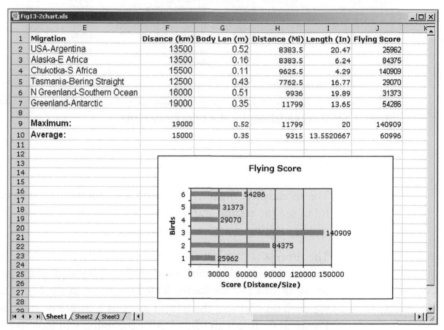

Figure 4 The horizontal bar chart displaying the Flying Score.

Daily Spreadsheets

Some people use computers all day and never use a spreadsheet; others use spreadsheets constantly. The rest of us are somewhere in between: Spreadsheets are convenient and versatile tools that simplify computing. In this section we look at a few personal applications as a way to gain a bit more experience with using spreadsheets.

Many opportunities exist to use spreadsheets to organize our personal information. We can

> Track our performance in our personal exercise program—distances, time, reps

> Set up an expense budget for the next term

> Keep a list of the books and CDs we've lent to others

> Follow our favorite team's successes by importing the season schedule and annotating it with wins and losses and our own comments about the games

> Record flight hours or dives after each flying or scuba lesson

> Document expenses such as travel, or income such as tips for income tax purposes

> Save records generated while online banking

Spreadsheets can even serve as an address book or recipe file.

Here are more ways to apply spreadsheets in personally relevant ways.

Calendar

Calendars are everywhere, and computers come with calendar software, so making a calendar with a spreadsheet hardly seems like an important application. But you would be surprised. Some people find calendar software clumsy; some people want to restructure their week, beginning, say on Wednesday; some people want a mix of larger/smaller appointment timeslots; workers with "2-on-1-off" jobs want double week calendars; and so on. At a meeting, you might set up a schedule for room or equipment usage or for a team's practices; it's often convenient to present information as a calendar, such as espresso sales by hour and day. Making a custom calendar solves these problems, and it only takes a minute. Really!

To begin we enter a day of the week into a cell in the spreadsheet, say `Sunday`, and format it as we like it, perhaps with bold letters and a background color. Depending on which software we are using, we either drag the fill handle across the next six columns to fill in the successive days of the week, or we request such a fill operation using the menus.

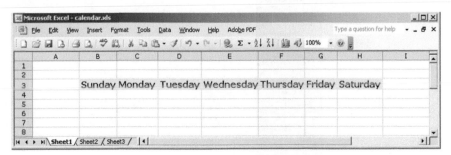

The result should be enhanced by the day of the month. So, we enter a date, say `January 2`, in the row below, format it, and fill it across.

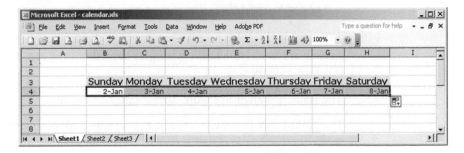

That result is ready for the times of day. We enter **8:00 AM** into cell **A5**, format it to taste, including bold and color. We want half hour appointment slots, but normally the time fill increments by hours rather than half hours. We could figure out how to change the increment, but instead we enter **8:30 AM** in cell **A6**.

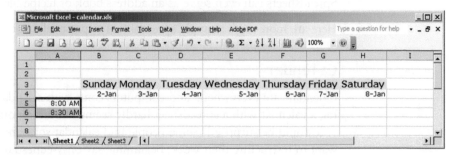

Using this pair of cells we fill down the column to **8:00 PM**. This achieves the desired half hour appointment times.

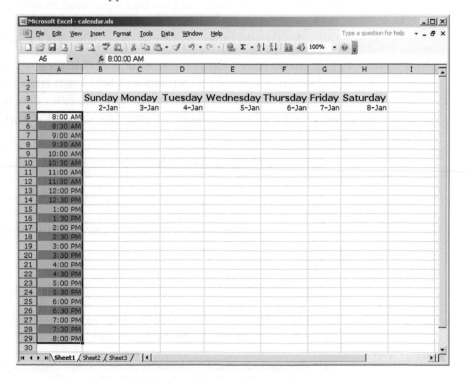

This double-cell fill is an easy way to cause the spreadsheet software to count by a specific amount. Note that entering **8:00** without the "**AM**" results in an international or military time fill.

The result is shown in Figure 5 with sample contents.

The point is not that we've created a spectacular appointment calendar, but that the spreadsheet software makes it easy to create one. We did almost no typing: We entered **Sunday** and filled; we entered **January 2** and filled; we entered **8:00 AM**

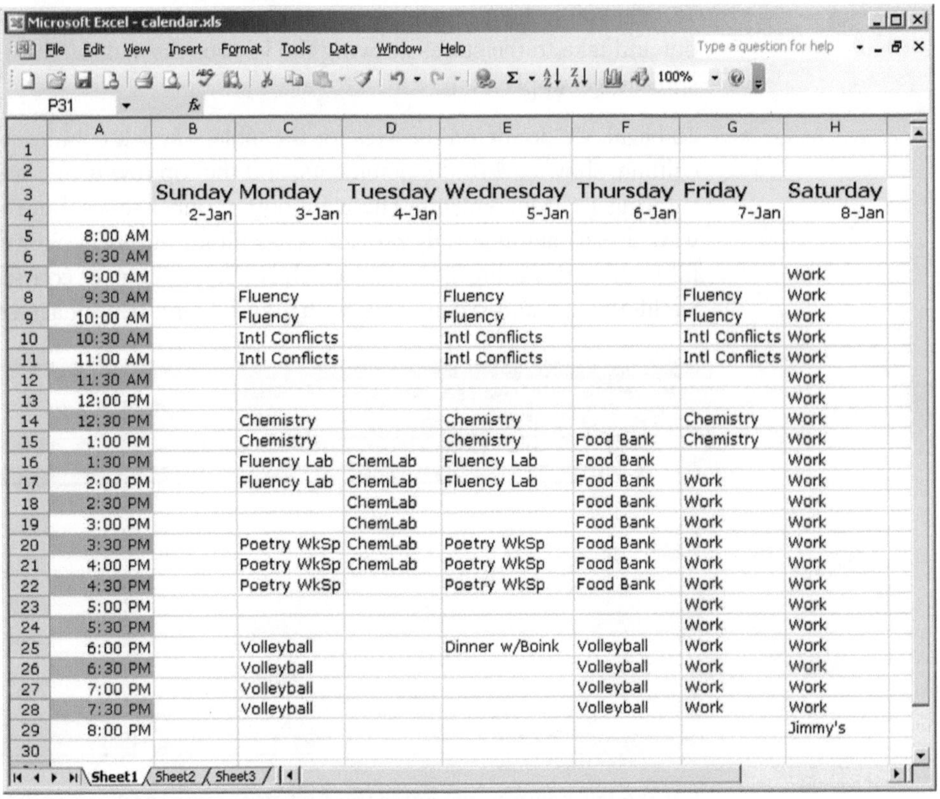

	A	B	C	D	E	F	G	H
1								
2								
3		Sunday	Monday	Tuesday	Wednesday	Thursday	Friday	Saturday
4		2-Jan	3-Jan	4-Jan	5-Jan	6-Jan	7-Jan	8-Jan
5	8:00 AM							
6	8:30 AM							
7	9:00 AM							Work
8	9:30 AM		Fluency		Fluency		Fluency	Work
9	10:00 AM		Fluency		Fluency		Fluency	Work
10	10:30 AM		Intl Conflicts		Intl Conflicts		Intl Conflicts	Work
11	11:00 AM		Intl Conflicts		Intl Conflicts		Intl Conflicts	Work
12	11:30 AM							Work
13	12:00 PM							Work
14	12:30 PM		Chemistry		Chemistry		Chemistry	Work
15	1:00 PM		Chemistry		Chemistry	Food Bank	Chemistry	Work
16	1:30 PM		Fluency Lab	ChemLab	Fluency Lab	Food Bank		Work
17	2:00 PM		Fluency Lab	ChemLab	Fluency Lab	Food Bank	Work	Work
18	2:30 PM			ChemLab		Food Bank	Work	Work
19	3:00 PM			ChemLab		Food Bank	Work	Work
20	3:30 PM		Poetry WkSp	ChemLab	Poetry WkSp	Food Bank	Work	Work
21	4:00 PM		Poetry WkSp	ChemLab	Poetry WkSp	Food Bank	Work	Work
22	4:30 PM		Poetry WkSp		Poetry WkSp	Food Bank	Work	Work
23	5:00 PM						Work	Work
24	5:30 PM						Work	Work
25	6:00 PM		Volleyball		Dinner w/Boink	Volleyball	Work	Work
26	6:30 PM		Volleyball			Volleyball	Work	Work
27	7:00 PM		Volleyball			Volleyball	Work	Work
28	7:30 PM		Volleyball			Volleyball	Work	Work
29	8:00 PM							Jimmy's
30								

Figure 5 **Calendar spreadsheet with entries added.**

and `8:30 AM` and filled the pair. We were done! It's possible to do this in under a minute. We have a custom calendar exactly matching our needs.

The calendar was so easy because spreadsheet software, when it fills certain types of data such as days, dates, times, and such, automatically increments, that is, automatically adds 1 as it fills each cell forming a **series**. The software knows that "adding 1" to Sunday results in Monday, and "adding 1" to January 31 results in February 1. It assumes, when it sees values like Sunday, that it's not ASCII data, but rather one of these special data types. If you type in **`Sunday`** and you want to copy the word *Sunday*, that is, you don't want to treat it as a special type of data, then don't use series fill. Simply *Copy/Paste*. Finally, double-cell fill also indicates a series, where the amount of increment between successive items is the difference between the pair.

Discount Table

Because downloading music for MP3 players is so popular, music stores that sell CDs try to compete by offering "store credit" discounts, that is, discounts on future purchases at the store. One store offers

- $1.00 store credit for each $10.00 spent plus
- $3.00 store credit for every two CDs purchased (one CD earns only $1.00 credit)

To help you to figure your credits, you can construct a table, which you can print out and take to the store, showing the various discounts. This is another very easy spreadsheet application.

To begin, we decide on the axes for the table: The left column is the "dollars spent" column, showing $10.00 increments, and the top row is the "CDs purchased" row, showing 1 CD increments. These are both number series, but the spreadsheet software doesn't automatically provide series fill for numbers. So we must choose it, or fill in the series using formulas, which is also possible, of course. For the top row, we fill the first and second cells with 1 and 2 and then fill across.

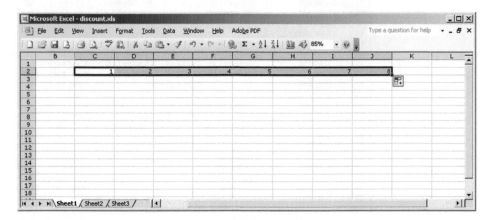

For the left column, we enter the first two items, $10.00 and $20.00, select the pair, and fill down.

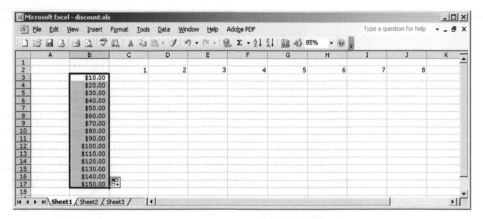

The software figures out that we want to increment by $10.00. All that remains is to specify the table entries. For that, we write a formula.

For each $10.00 spent the store gives a $1.00 credit. So, part of the formula is to divide the item in column B by 10. For example

`=$B3/10`

To ensure that the number we are dividing is always in column B, we make the column reference absolute. The row reference should be relative because we want the calculation to apply to whatever row the formula is in.

The store also gives $3.00 credit for every two CDs purchased. The easiest way to apply this rule is to multiply the CD axis entry (in row 2) by 3/2.

```
=(3/2)*C$2
```

which is the right answer when the number of CDs is even, but for an odd number of CDs it is too much by half. For example, `1*3/2` is 1.5, that is, $1.50, but the store only gives $1.00 credit. The solution is to throw away any fractional digits, that is, to truncate the number. Spreadsheets have a function, `trunc`, for this purpose,

```
=trunc((3/2)*C$2)
```

As with the first rule, we use an absolute reference and a relative reference. Row 2 is absolute so that all entries refer to it, but the column should be relative, so that the computation applies to the column that the formula is in.

The combined formula for both discount rules is

```
=$B3/10 + trunc((3/2)*C$2)
```

which we enter into cell `C3`. This yields the right answer: $2.00 ($1.00 for the amount paid plus $1.00 for the single CD).

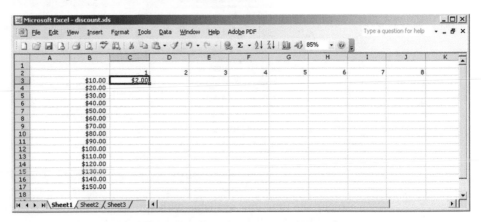

Filling the formula down the column and then across the rows produces the final table.

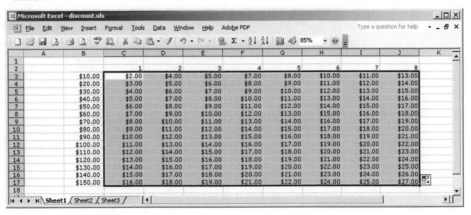

We can print out the table and take it with us to the store to help strategize our purchases to get the biggest discount. For example, we might trade CD purchases with a friend to get a larger combined discount, which we then share.

The table was easy to construct. We used two series, one for the dollars and one for the CDs, to create the axes. The table entries used a single formula that referenced the axis entries with one absolute and one relative coordinate so that the entry for the column/row position was computed correctly. This technique works whenever we have two axes.

Paying Off a Loan

Suppose you are considering a large purchase, which may or may not have woofers. Your uncle has agreed to lend you the money, but ever the businessman, he's charging you 5 percent interest. To decide how much to spend, you want to create a table of the monthly payments required for different amounts borrowed for different times. The table setup follows the strategy of the last section: Fill a row across the top with different numbers of payments, and fill a column with different amounts.

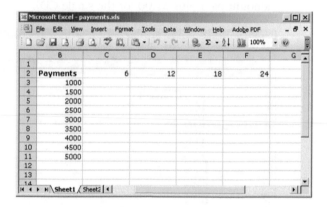

Among the functions available with spreadsheets is the "payment" computation, PMT. When we click on it under the *Insert > Functions. . .* menu, a GUI is displayed for PMT.

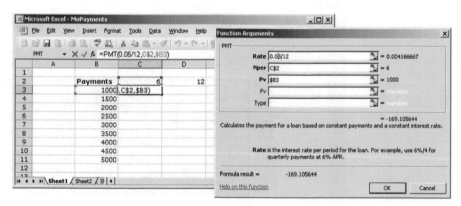

The inputs to the function are the monthly interest **Rate**, which is $1/12^{th}$ of the annual rate your uncle is charging, the number of payments (**Nper**), and the present value, or the amount of the loan (**Pv**). As with the discount table in the previous section, the inputs mix absolute and relative references to refer to the row and column entries. The formula result, shown at the bottom of the GUI, is the amount required to repay $1,000 in six payments. Notice that the result is negative, because the payment is a cost to you.

Filling the formula down the column and across the rows results in a table with red, parenthesized values, which is the default display form for negative numbers.

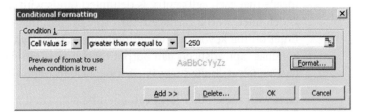

If we don't like the parentheses, we can reformat the entries, say leaving them red.

Perhaps, because the table is intended to help us decide how much to borrow, the best way to display the entries is to display them in two colors: Green for those within our budget and red for those over our budget. Deciding that a payment of $250 per month is a comfortable limit, we click on *Format > Conditional Formatting* . . . and get this GUI.

We specify that cells greater than or equal to –250 should be formatted green. (Remember, the numbers tell how much we *pay*, so a number closer to 0 means less.) The green font is specified by clicking on the *Format* . . . button in the Conditional Formatting dialog and picking a color. The final result makes it visually easy to decide how much to borrow.

	B	C	D	E	F	G
1						
2	Payments	6	12	18	24	
3	1000	($169.11)	($85.61)	($57.78)	($43.87)	
4	1500	($253.66)	($128.41)	($86.67)	($65.81)	
5	2000	($338.21)	($171.21)	($115.56)	($87.74)	
6	2500	($422.76)	($214.02)	($144.45)	($109.68)	
7	3000	($507.32)	($256.82)	($173.34)	($131.61)	
8	3500	($591.87)	($299.63)	($202.23)	($153.55)	
9	4000	($676.42)	($342.43)	($231.12)	($175.49)	
10	4500	($760.98)	($385.23)	($260.01)	($197.42)	
11	5000	($845.53)	($428.04)	($288.90)	($219.36)	
12						

Importing Data

Much of the data we are interested in comes from some other source, that is, we didn't produce it. This probably means it has already been organized, and so may already exist in a spreadsheet or in a table in another application. Call this **foreign data**—data from another application that we want to import into a spreadsheet. Though importing previously formatted data into a spreadsheet can be tricky, there are some guidelines to make it easier.

Tab-Delimited Data

As a rule, spreadsheets prefer to import foreign data as **tab-delimited text**. "Text" means ASCII text, that is, files with **.txt** extensions. Because they are text files, numbers like *100* are represented as three numeral characters rather than as a single binary number. This allows the spreadsheet software to convert the ASCII form into whatever internal number representation it prefers. "Tab-delimited" means that each cell's entry is delimited (ends with) a tab in the file, and each row is delimited with a carriage return (the symbol that results from pressing [Return] or Enter on the keyboard). Other delimiters are recognized, too, such as spaces and commas. Spreadsheets can output their lists as tab-delimited text. Copying and pasting tab-delimited text is a simple way to import foreign data.

Lists with some other form can often be converted into the preferred tab-delimited form by copying the foreign data into a text editor or word processor and editing it using *Search/Replace*, possibly using the placeholder technique. The goal is to substitute a tab or other preferred delimiter for a delimiter in the file that the spreadsheet software doesn't understand. Writing the result to a text file eliminates any formatting characters from the word processor.

Another important source of data is the World Wide Web. The information is already in text form, and often is formatted with HTML table tags. It seems it should be possible to *Copy* a table from HTML and *Paste* it into a spreadsheet. For some browser-spreadsheet combinations it works, but for others it doesn't. It all depends on how the browser delimits "copies" taken from the screen. If you try to *Copy/Paste* table data from the Web and it doesn't work, try another browser before beginning the tedious task of reformatting the foreign data by other means. You'll probably get lucky.

✓ check LIST   **Guidelines for importing foreign data:**

☑ *When possible, save foreign data as tab-delimited ASCII text in a file with a* `.txt` *extension.*

☑ *When foreign data comes from the Web, select a browser that supports Copy/Paste of tagged tables.*

☑ *When the foreign data format is messed up, use a text editor with Search/Replace, apply the placeholder technique, and write the revised data with a* `.txt` *extension. Import the resulting file.*

For example, suppose you want to print out a custom bus schedule. Transportation schedules often include more data than we need, so if we grab a copy of the whole schedule from the Web, we can trim and edit it to match our needs in a spreadsheet. Visiting the city's Web page, we locate the bus schedule and *Copy* it, as shown in Figure 6, and then *Paste* it into the spreadsheet.

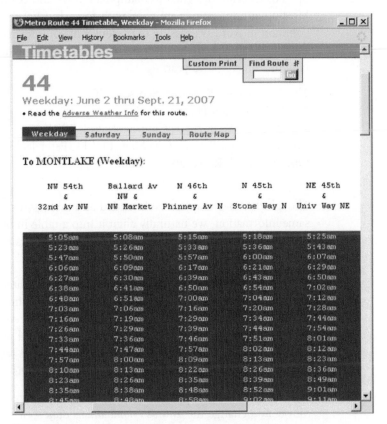

Figure 6 Bus schedule from the Web selected for copying.

We only want the departure time from our stop and the arrival time at campus. By deleting columns we can create a simple two-column schedule. Adding the two columns for the return trip produces a custom schedule, as shown in Figure 7, that can be printed and kept in a wallet or purse.

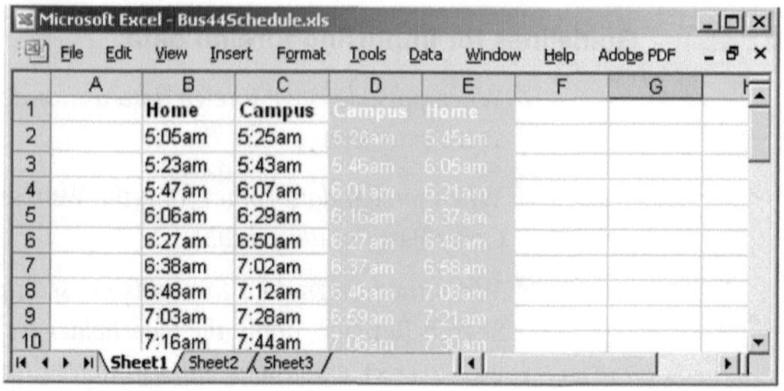

Figure 7 Customized schedule with "to campus" in white, "from campus" in purple.

Arranging Columns

Spreadsheets are designed to manipulate rows and columns of information easily. Most other applications are good with rows, but not columns. For example, it is common in word processing to present a list of information, one item per line, as in this 79-item list of Best Picture winners, which includes Oscar awards / nominations, director, and year.

The Departed, 4 / 5, Martin Scorsese, 2006
Crash, 3 / 6, Paul Haggis, 2005
Million Dollar Baby, 4 / 7, Clint Eastwood, 2004
Lord of the Rings: Return of the King, 11 / 11, Peter Jackson, 2003
Chicago, 6 / 13, Rob Marshall, 2002
. . .

Though the lines may not be intended as a table, when each one contains the same information, we naturally align it into a table in our minds. Adding new rows is easy. Inserting or rearranging the columns is a headache. Spreadsheets can help.

To manipulate columns in an application not well suited to the task, we must create a consistently delimited text file of the data, and import it into a spreadsheet, as described earlier. (Most entries are delimited with commas, so only the slash (/) presents a problem.) We then manipulate the list and write out the file as text. After being revised in the spreadsheet, the file can be returned to the application. We will illustrate this idea by rearranging the columns of the movie list.

For example, suppose we want to reorder the columns so the year follows the movie, and change the *awards / nominations* data so it reads, for *The Departed*, "4 of 5 Oscars."

To begin:

> Make a file containing only the list

> Use *Search/Replace* to replace every space-slash-space (" / ") with a comma (","), so that the numbers get separate columns.

> Import the file into the spreadsheet

The result is shown in Figure 8.

	A	B	C	D	E	F	G	H
1								
2								
3		The Departed	4	5	Martin Sccorcese	2006		
4		Crash	3	6	Paul Haggis	2005		
5		Million Dollar Baby	4	7	Clint Eastwood	2004		
6		Lord of the Rings: Return of the Ki	11	11	Peter Jackson	2003		
7		Chicago	6	13	Rob Marshall	2002		
8		A Beautiful Mind	4	8	Ron Howard	2001		

Figure 8 The movie list imported into a spreadsheet.

Using *Cut* and *Paste* we move the last column to become the second column. We also create a new column that allows us to combine the awards and nominations into one phrase. The formula uses an operation called **concatenate**, which means to join pieces of text together, one after the other. We will join four pieces of text together: the number of awards, the text " of " (ƀofƀ), the number of nominations, and the text " Oscars" (ƀOscars); where ƀ is our symbol for a space.

awards " of " *nominations* " Oscars"

This is expressed by the formula

```
=concatenate(c3," of ",d3," Oscars")
```

	B	C	D	E	F	G
2						
3	The Departed	4	5	Martin Sccorcese	2006	=CONCATENATE(C3," of ",D3," Oscars "
4	Crash	3	6	Paul Haggis	2005	
5	Million Dollar Baby	4	7	Clint Eastwood	2004	
6	Lord of the Rings: Return of the King	11	11	Peter Jackson	2003	
7	Chicago	6	13	Rob Marshall	2002	
8	A Beautiful Mind	4	8	Ron Howard	2001	

For the movie *The Departed*, the formula produces the phrase: **4 of 5 Oscars**. The function **concatenate** can join any number of text pieces, and is a handy tool for combining words and numbers.

The result, after filling into column **G**, is shown in Figure 9(a). This revised column converts two columns of data to a phrase that can replace them. We move the two numerical columns to the end of the table (we need to keep them or the **concatenate** formula won't work) and reorder the columns as we intend (see Figure 9b).

To complete the table, we want to *Cut* and *Paste* the Oscars column into column **E** and throw away the last two data columns. But if we do that, the data that the Oscars column depends on will be gone. What we must do is *Paste* the Oscars as *values*, that is as text, into column **E**. So, we use *Edit > Paste Special . . .* and select "values". This converts the Oscars column from formulas to text; it no longer depends on the data columns (see Figure 9c).

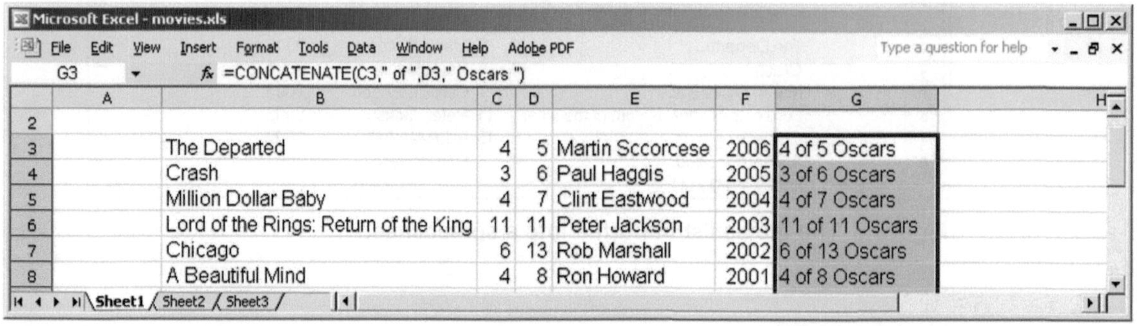

(a)

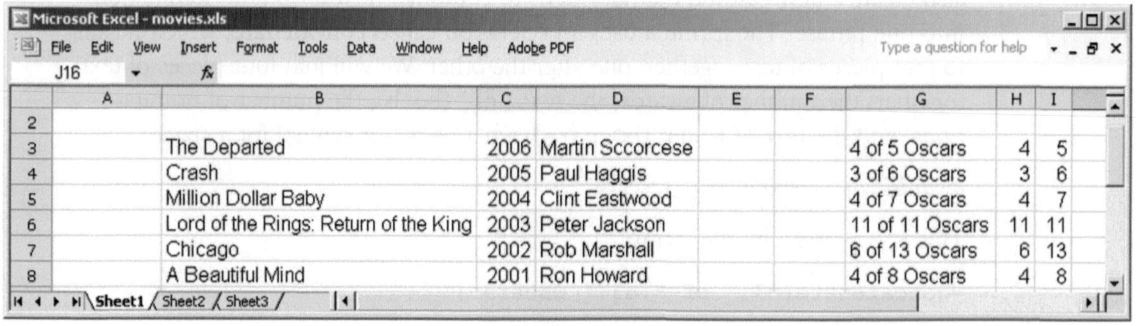

(b)

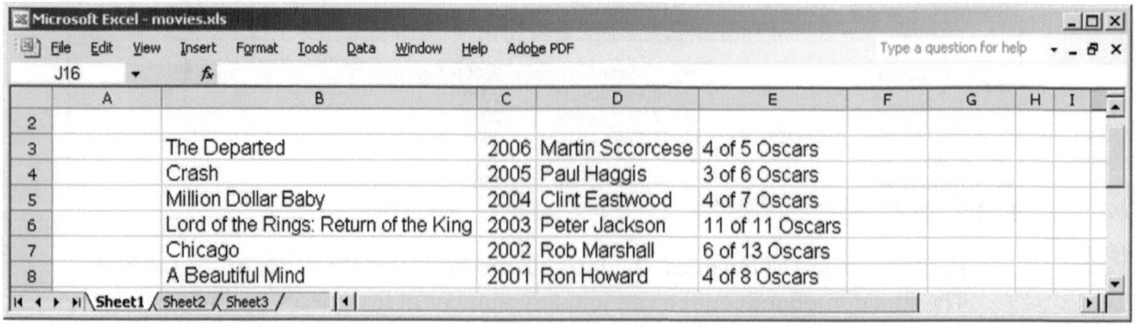

(c)

Figure 9 Revising the movie list. (a) Constructing the phrase, (b) reordering the main columns, (c) the completed table.

This completes our revisions, and we return the final spreadsheet to our document.

The Departed, 2006, Martin Scorsese, 4 of 5 Oscars
Crash, 2005, Paul Haggis, 3 of 6 Oscars
Million Dollar Baby, 2004, Clint Eastwood, 4 of 7 Oscars
Lord of the Rings: Return of the King, 2003, Peter Jackson, 11 of 11 Oscars
Chicago, 2002, Rob Marshall, 6 of 13 Oscars
. . .

The result achieves our intended columnar modifications.

 ## SUMMARY

In this chapter we explored the basic ideas of spreadsheets. We found that:

> Spreadsheets present an array of cells each of which is capable of storing one data item, a number, a letter sequence, or a formula.

> Numbers and text can be formatted so that they display as we prefer— proper font, correct number of digits, and so on.

> The power of spreadsheets comes from entering formulas that calculate new values based on the values in other cells.

> The formula is one side of an equation, which the computer solves for us, preserving the equality whenever the numbers that the formula depends on are changed and displaying the new value in the cell.

> In addition to performing arithmetic on the cells, we can apply functions to individual items or to whole cell ranges.

> Both relative and absolute references to cells are needed depending on the circumstances.

> In addition to sorting, there are functions for finding totals, averages, the maximum or minimum, and others.

> Spreadsheets are a practical tool for routine computing.

> It's easy to teach ourselves more about spreadsheets simply by trying them with courage.

> Spreadsheets may be the most useful software for personal computing.

Review Questions

True/False

1. Text too wide to fit into a cell is truncated.
2. Cells in a spreadsheet are 10 characters wide.
3. Spreadsheets are most commonly used to process numerical data.
4. *Copy/Paste* will duplicate a formula, but it won't utilize relative and absolute cell references.
5. The small box or tab in a selected cell's lower right corner is used to move the contents of a cell.
6. A cell reference cannot contain relative and absolute references at the same time.
7. To change a relative cell reference to an absolute reference, you should use the ampersand (&).
8. Spreadsheet columns can be hidden but rows cannot.
9. Text files are generally stored in ASCII format.
10. A spreadsheet can import any kind of data.

Multiple Choice

1. A series of cells is called a(n)
   a. tuple
   b. group
   c. array
   d. sheet

2. Respectively, rows and columns are designated with
   a. numbers, letters
   b. letters, numbers
   c. numbers, numbers
   d. names, numbers

3. Which of the following is a valid range of cells?
   a. D1:D4
   b. C3:D5
   c. A1:E1
   d. all of the above

4. Which of the following is not a valid range of cells?
   a. A1>A5
   b. C3-C8
   c. 3B:6B
   d. all of the above

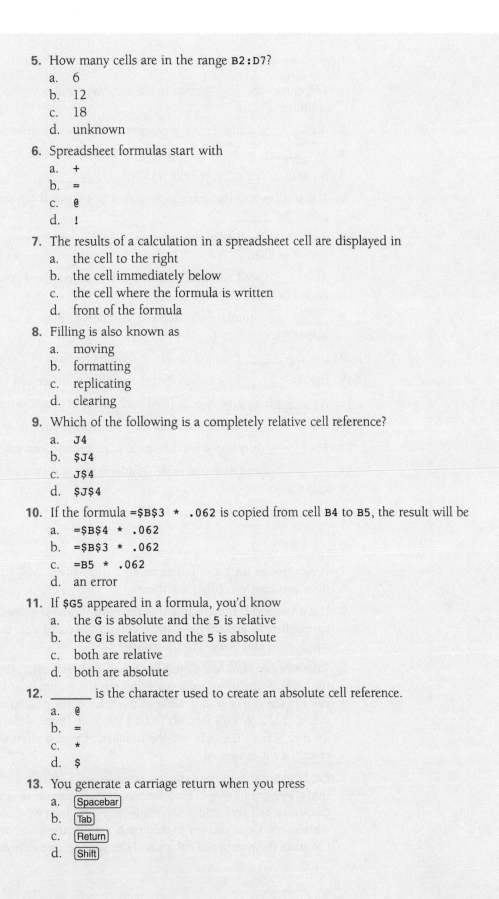

5. How many cells are in the range `B2:D7`?
   a. 6
   b. 12
   c. 18
   d. unknown

6. Spreadsheet formulas start with
   a. +
   b. =
   c. @
   d. !

7. The results of a calculation in a spreadsheet cell are displayed in
   a. the cell to the right
   b. the cell immediately below
   c. the cell where the formula is written
   d. front of the formula

8. Filling is also known as
   a. moving
   b. formatting
   c. replicating
   d. clearing

9. Which of the following is a completely relative cell reference?
   a. `J4`
   b. `$J4`
   c. `J$4`
   d. `$J$4`

10. If the formula `=$B$3 * .062` is copied from cell `B4` to `B5`, the result will be
    a. `=$B$4 * .062`
    b. `=$B$3 * .062`
    c. `=B5 * .062`
    d. an error

11. If `$G5` appeared in a formula, you'd know
    a. the `G` is absolute and the `5` is relative
    b. the `G` is relative and the `5` is absolute
    c. both are relative
    d. both are absolute

12. _____ is the character used to create an absolute cell reference.
    a. @
    b. =
    c. *
    d. $

13. You generate a carriage return when you press
    a. [Spacebar]
    b. [Tab]
    c. [Return]
    d. [Shift]

Short Answer

1. Cell entries are _____, that is, the computer will not consider any of their constituent parts.

2. A(n) _____ is the vertical arrangement of cells in a spreadsheet.

3. A(n) _____ is the horizontal arrangement of cells in a spreadsheet.

4. A group of one or more cells is called a(n) _____.

5. The small box in the lower right corner of a selected cell (or range of cells) is called the _____.

6. A(n) _____ cell reference automatically transforms a formula when it is pasted or filled.

7. A(n) _____ cell reference retains a reference to a fixed position when it is pasted or filled.

8. _____ are formulas built into a spreadsheet to make it easier to create calculations.

9. Use the _____ function to find the largest number in a range of cells.

10. Use the _____ function to find the smallest number in a range of cells.

11. A _____ is a range of cells filled with increments of a certain type of data.

12. Use the _____ function to find only the integer portion of a number.

13. The _____ function should be used to determine loan payments.

14. _____ is useful data that exists in a form that was created by a different application.

15. _____ means "to join together."

Exercises

1. Look through the list of functions for a spreadsheet. Make a list of 10 functions and how you could use them.

2. Use a spreadsheet to create a checkerboard. Resize the rows and columns of a spreadsheet to make 8 rows and 8 columns of equal size. Color alternate squares red and black. Print it in color.

3. Take a bag of M & M's. Count the number of each color. Create a spreadsheet from this. Write down each color and put the number of M & M's of that color in the cell next to it. Change the color of the cells to match the color of the M & M's. Write a formula to find the total. If you want, create a pie chart for this. Select the colors and the numbers. Create a chart and select pie chart. Edit it as needed.

4. Find the number of rows in your spreadsheet. Click on a cell and hold down the ⬇ key until it stops. Find the number of columns in your spreadsheet. Click on a cell and hold down the ➡ key until it stops. Columns are labeled with letters. Once you get to column z, numbering starts over with AA. Calculate the number of columns. Then use the spreadsheet to calculate the

number of cells in the spreadsheet. Use one cell for the number of rows. Use another for the number of columns. Write the formula to display the answer in another cell.

5. Create a spreadsheet to display the classes in your plan of study. Use a column for each semester and enter the classes below it.

6. Modify the spreadsheet for Paying Off a Loan. Change it so you can enter the interest in a cell and have the cell in your formula. Test it to see how changes in the interest rate affect your ability to repay the loan.

7. Go to www.tides.info/. Select a location and get the tide charts for that month. Copy the data and Paste it into a spreadsheet. Change the formatting of it to suit your tastes.

8. Create a spreadsheet to calculate the future value of an investment. Use the FV function for this. Future value is the value of a monthly investment at a certain rate over a period of time. You could use it for calculating your retirement nest egg. Enter the number of years in a row near the top. Start with 5 and go to 40 by fives. On the side enter the amount you're willing to invest each month. Start with $100 and fill it to $2,000.

In the cell above the $100, enter the interest rate you expect to earn on the investment. In the first cell of the table (where the 5 and $100 intersect), enter your formula. Use FV. The first one is the interest rate. Enter that cell. The second one is the years. Enter that cell. The last one is the amount. Enter that cell. When you fill using this cell, the formulas won't work—you'll need to modify them to always stay in the interest rate cell.

You'll need a $ in front of the row and column. For the years, you'll need the $ in front of the column. For the amount, you'll need the $ in front of the row. You'll then be able to copy it. The numbers will be negative. To make them positive (after all, it's money you're saving), use the absolute value function (ABS).

9. Create a personal budget. Put income in its own column. Total it. Put expenses in another column. Total it. The more accurate you are, the closer your budget will be. There should be at least a little money left over at the end of the month!

10. Create a GPA calculator. Enter your classes in one column. Next to it enter the number of credits. Next to that enter the grade points earned for that class. (Usually it's one point per credit for a D, two per credit for a C, three per credit for a B, and four per credit for an A.) Total the credits and the grade points. The GPA is grade points divided by credits.

11. Create a spreadsheet of your expected annual income. Put the year into a column and fill it up until the year you expect to retire. Next to the first year, enter your expected annual income. In the next cell, enter a formula to add three percent to the first year's income. Fill this formula for the rest of the years. If you put the percentage increase in a cell of its own and then use that in the formula, you'll be able to change the annual salary increase to see how that affects your pay.

Answers to Selected Questions

True/False

1. F. It will spill over into the cell to the right if that cell is empty. If text is in the cell, it will display as much as possible. If a number is in the cell, it will display crosshatches (#).
3. T.
5. F. It is used to fill other cells with the contents of the selected cell.
7. F. You should use the dollar sign ($).
9. T.

Multiple Choice

1. C. It is sometimes called a range as well.
3. D. All of the above are valid ranges.
5. C. There are six rows and three columns for a total of 18 cells.
7. C. The results are displayed in the cell. Look at the formula line at the top of the spreadsheet to see the formula.
9. A. When the dollar sign is used in a cell reference it makes that part of the reference absolute.
11. A. The dollar sign in front of the G makes it absolute. Without the dollar sign, the 5 is relative.
13. C. The [Return] and [Enter] keys will both create a carriage return.

Short Answer

1. atomic or monolithic
3. row
5. fill handle
7. absolute
9. max or maximum
11. series
13. Pmt or payment
15. Concatenate

8

"What If" Thinking Helps

Advanced Spreadsheets for Planning

Learning Objectives

> State the two basic design criteria for creating effective spreadsheets

> Explain how conditional formatting of spreadsheet entries applies an interpretation to spreadsheet information

> Explain conditional formulas, and their components and behavior

> Perform "what if" analysis with a spreadsheet

> Use AutoFiltering and advanced filtering to customize spreadsheet lists

> Explain the importance of symbolic naming of spreadsheet cells

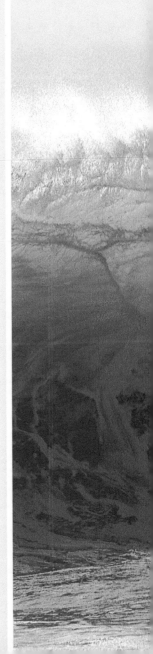

One man's constant is another man's variable.

—ALAN PERLIS, 1968

THE INTRODUCTION to spreadsheets in the last chapter taught only the most basic operations. Based on that explanation you could be excused for wondering how it is that spreadsheets are the "most useful general-purpose computer application." They seem so limited. But you'll soon see that's not the case; in this chapter we introduce advanced spreadsheet techniques. This chapter's study shows that spreadsheets not only help us organize our data and analyze it, but they also allow us to explore possibilities that might arise and to work out strategies for reacting to those changes. These advanced spreadsheet concepts are just as easy to learn as the basic topics of the last chapter were, and they allow us to look into the future.

Spreadsheets are often taught using business applications, but we use a "running example" with more personal interest: a spreadsheet to plan a driving holiday. Perhaps you are the sort of person who likes spontaneous travel and thinks a detailed plan spoils the fun. Or maybe you like to have a carefully plotted itinerary. Either way, the plan helps us to understand important constraints on our travel, such as time and money. Once we know those limits, the trip can be either spontaneous or scheduled.

So far the spreadsheets we have created have been used only once, rather than being saved and used again and again. When a spreadsheet becomes a basic tool of our everyday work or recreation, it must be as useful and convenient as possible. That means good design, and we will present a short list of design guidelines in this chapter.

The advanced features we discuss concern using spreadsheets conditionally. These include adjusting the formats or values of cells based on various circumstances; for example, we may wish to flag values that are "out of bounds." We will also *filter* our spreadsheets, including or excluding data as our analysis requires. Another analytical tool supports "what if" experimentation; that is, the spreadsheet helps us examine alternatives and see the consequences of various decisions.

Designing a Spreadsheet

When we make a spreadsheet to find an answer and then delete it, it hardly matters what form it has as long as the computation is right. When a spreadsheet is used repeatedly, it doesn't only give answers, it becomes a tool of planning, analysis, and decision-making. To be effective, the spreadsheet must be well designed, being as informative and flexible as possible. We give design guidelines that further these goals after we describe what data we will use in our sample spreadsheet.

The Trip

The data we use in our example is about two friends, Pat and Alex, who know that it's not possible to drive to the North Pole, but wonder if it's possible to drive to the Arctic Circle. Turning to the Web, they find the following.

> There is an Arctic Circle Street in Rockford, Illinois (a false start).

> A highway crosses the Arctic Circle in the Yukon Territory of Canada, between Dawson and the Northwest Territories settlement of Inuvik.

> The trip to Inuvik is 3,631 miles from their home in Chicago, and takes 3 days and 14 hours of driving time (see Figure 1).

> The highway is unpaved over several hundred miles of the distance.

Obviously, the given driving time is continuous, which they do not plan to do. So they decide to make a spreadsheet to figure out how long it will take and how much it will cost. We use their spreadsheet as our example in this chapter.

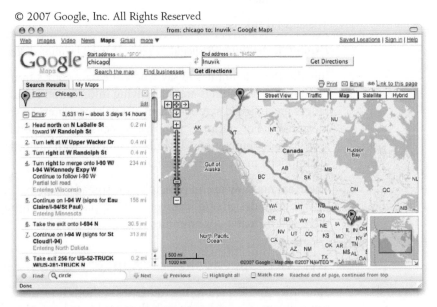

Figure 1 Google map directions for a trip from Chicago, Illinois (green pin), to Inuvik, Northwest Territories (red pin).

*fit*TIP   **Traveling Companion.** Read the following sections at a computer and build the spreadsheets along with the text; it is an extremely effective way to learn these concepts. Moreover, when finished, you will have a spreadsheet to use to plan your travels. Find all the necessary files at **www.aw.com/snyder/**.

Design Guidelines

We adopt two basic principles for setting up effective spreadsheets. The first rule is:

Focus on Form: *Make the form logical, the layout clean, and the entries clear and understandable.*

Because the spreadsheet is not for the computer but for people to use in solving problems, it must be easy to understand and easy to work with. This makes the form of the presentation of data key. Arrange the data logically, which for English speakers generally means that

> ❯ descriptive information should be on the top and left sides, and

> ❯ summary information should be on the bottom and right sides.

Fonts should be clear, possibly different for headings and data. Colors—for both font and fill—should be used in moderation, so that they attract attention to the important aspects of the sheet and aren't a distraction. Use a separate sheet for each table—multiple sheets don't cost more to use and individual sheets make working with mutiple tables more manageable. Hiding information that isn't needed in the current context is also a key way to make a spreadsheet clear and understandable.

The second rule is:

Explain Everything: *It should be possible to know immediately what every cell means.*

Initially, the rule implies to say where the data comes from, and to include meaningful column headings and identifying information about the rows. Cells and ranges are assigned symbolic names (explained later) so the content becomes meaningful. For summary information cells, choose modifiers like *total* and *largest*. For computations, include comments with the cells explaining the assumptions made when creating the formulas.

These are not only useful principles for spreadsheets, but they also apply generally to Web page design and many other IT applications. Throughout this chapter, there will be many opportunities to apply these rules.

Initial Spreadsheet: Applying the Rules

Since Alex and Pat are trying to figure out both how much time and money the trip will cost, it seems as though they could click together a spreadsheet to compute the answer and throw it away. But, because it turns out that the trip will be too expensive for just the two friends, they will need to find others to join them. Thus, they will keep revising the spreadsheet and showing it to others as part of the effort to encourage participation. Accordingly, they should concentrate on applying the design rules to make the spreadsheet flexible, credible, and self-explanatory.

Applying the rules is straightforward. The data they have is for a five-day trek from Chicago to Dawson, Yukon Territory. From there, they will drive up to the Arctic Circle and back to Dawson that night, where they expect to celebrate in the town's renovated 1890s saloons left over from the Gold Rush. Using online mapping software, they formulate the following segments.

Chicago to Carrington, ND:	778 miles,	12 hrs, 2 minutes
Carrington to Battleford, SK:	620 miles,	11 hrs, 6 minutes
Battleford to Fort St. John, BC:	648 miles,	11 hrs, 26 minutes
Fort St. John to Watson Lake, BC:	555 miles,	10 hrs, 17 minutes
Watson Lake to Dawson, YK:	601 miles,	11 hrs, 55 minutes
Round-trip Dawson to Arctic Circle:	484 miles,	14 hours

The friends are interested in how much the trip will cost, so they add a column for fuel costs, which they find on the Web (www.gasbuddy.com). Part of the trip is through the U.S., of course, where gas is priced by the gallon in U.S. dollars, and part of the trip is through Canada, where petrol (gas) is priced by the liter in Canadian dollars, so the spreadsheet lists where the price estimate comes from, as shown in Figure 2.

The principle of "focus on form" is evident in a variety of places. The spreadsheet in Figure 2 has a title listing the authors and stating the completion date. Columns are assigned clear headings. The heading row is filled with a soft color that separates it from the content, which is preferable to intense colors that can distract. A clean, sans serif font presents the data justified in the cells, so the columns align and give a clean, neat appearance.

The principle of "explain everything" is illustrated by three comments, which explain the data sources. Comments are like sticky notes that can be added to cells. Their presence is denoted by the red triangle in the cell's upper right corner, see headings in Figure 2. Hovering the cursor over the cell displays the comment.

Trip to the Arctic Circle
by Pat and Alex; completed 23.June.07

Segment	Time Est.	Miles	Fuel Price Report	Fuel Price
Chicago to Carrington ND	12:02	778	US Chicago	$3.59
Carrington to Battleford SK	11:06	620	US Moorehead MN	$2.96
Battleford to Fort St. John	11:26	648	CA Moose Jaw SK	$1.09
Fort St. John to Waston Lake YK	10:17	555	CA Medicine Hat AB	$1.01
Watson Lake to Dawson YK	11:55	601	CA Mi 54 AK Hiway BC	$1.21
Dawson to Dawson via AC	14:00	484	CA Mi 54 AK Hiway BC	$1.21

Figure 2 Initial spreadsheet for the Arctic Circle road trip.

To insert a comment in Excel, select the cell and then navigate *Insert > Comment*. The author's name is automatically placed at the beginning of the comment. To edit it, select the cell and navigate *Insert > Edit Comment*. To remove a comment, find it as option for *Clear*, that is, navigate *Edit > Clear > Comments*.

These two design principles will be exhibited throughout the remainder of the spreadsheet development.

Conditional Formatting

Another technique to make a spreadsheet more effective is to conditionally format the cells. You saw conditional formatting for calculating loan payments, where monthly payments within the budget were displayed in green and payments exceeding the budget were displayed in red. Conditional formatting allows us to *apply an interpretation to the data*—payments within budget, payments over budget—and express that interpretation in an easy to perceive manner.

Cell Value Is Specifications

The Arctic Circle road trip spreadsheet has a variety of opportunities to use conditional formatting to help the friends understand the data. One thing they notice about the trip is that there is considerable variance in how long they must travel on each segment; some days are much longer than others. To emphasize the long days, they decide to apply conditional formatting to the `Time Estimate` column: Any segment over 12:00 hours of driving is interpreted as "long" and will be displayed in bold. They select the `Time Estimate` entries, and choose *Format > Conditional Formatting...* to arrive at the following dialog window.

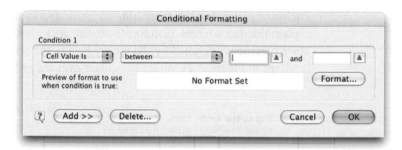

This window lets users specify one or more conditions. If the program finds that these conditions apply to the cell, it formats the entry in the manner specified under *Format*. Users specify the condition by picking one of a set of relationships and filling in the limits. The default condition, *between*, is shown, but the travelers want the *greater than* condition. So, clicking the triangle menu button to the right of *between*, they select *greater than*.

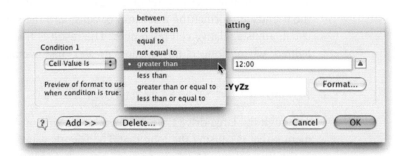

After entering the 12:00 hour time threshold and selecting bold formatting, they click *OK*, creating the result shown in Figure 3.

Trip to the Arctic Circle
by Pat and Alex; completed 23.June.07

Segment	Time Est.	Miles	Fuel Price Report	Fuel Price
Chicago to Carrington ND	**12:02**	778	US Chicago	$3.59
Carrington to Battleford SK	11:06	620	US Moorehead MN	$2.96
Battleford to Fort St. John	11:26	648	CA Moose Jaw SK	$1.09
Fort St. John to Waston Lake YK	10:17	555	CA Medicine Hat AB	$1.01
Watson Lake to Dawson YK	11:55	601	CA Mi 54 AK Hiway BC	$1.21
Dawson to Dawson via AC	**14:00**	484	CA Mi 54 AK Hiway BC	$1.21

Figure 3 The Arctic Circle road trip spreadsheet with conditional formatting for "long days."

Studying the result, the friends notice that the formatting has had the effect of marking the Chicago to Carrington segment as long, but not marking the Watson Lake to Dawson segment, which is only seven minutes shorter. Perhaps rather than having the long day defined by some absolute bound like 12:00 hours, they should define "long day" as "any day that is longer than the average." Conditional formatting allows formulas to be used rather than absolute limits like 12:00 hours. Revising the conditional formatting specification to compare to the formula

=average(b$2:b$7)

results in

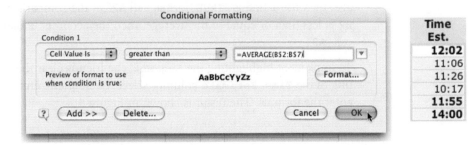

which achieves their goal.

294 What If Thinking Helps - Advanced Spreadsheets for Planning

The absolute references in the range specification (B$2:B$7) are essential, because the friends are formatting a column of cells, and the spreadsheet software, as usual, adjusts relative cell references. The result is that the longer days are highlighted, where "longer" now means "greater than average."

Formula Is Specifications

Although the large drive time *defines* a long segment, it is the travel—the segment—that is causing the long day. The friends want to highlight the information in the first column (A), Segment. It's possible to format those items based on the AVERAGE(B$2,B$7), but there is a problem: The value that must be compared to the average is B2, not A2. That is, making a comparison with some cell other than the one being formatted is not possible using the *Cell Value Is* facility in the Conditional Formatting window. The alternative to *Cell Value Is* is *Formula Is*, and that is the facility the friends want.

Selecting the *Formula Is* option causes the window to be redisplayed as

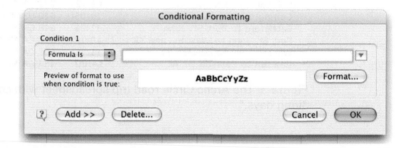

The friends need a formula that is true when the entry is to be formatted and false otherwise. The function they use to decide this condition is the IF() function, which has this general specification:

```
IF(condition, action_on_true_outcome, action_on_false_outcome)
```

They need to specify the format of the IF() function for the A2 cell, so they place

```
IF(B2>AVERAGE(B$2:B$7), TRUE, FALSE)
```

in the A2 cell. This function compares the B2 cell to the average of the Time Estimate values; if the comparison is true, that is, if B2 is greater than the average, then the action is "TRUE, format cell A2"; if the comparison is false, that is, if B2 is less than or equal to the average, then the action is "FALSE, do not format cell A2."

To implement highlighting the Segment, the friends clear the conditional formatting of the Time Estimate column, select the Segment entries of column A, and enter the formula. The result is shown in Figure 4.

Trip to the Arctic Circle
by Pat and Alex; completed 23.June.07

Segment	Time Est.	Miles	Fuel Price Report	Fuel Price
Chicago to Carrington ND	12:02	778	US Chicago	$3.59
Carrington to Battleford SK	11:06	620	US Moorehead MN	$2.96
Battleford to Fort St. John	11:26	648	CA Moose Jaw SK	*$1.09*
Fort St. John to Waston Lake YK	10:17	555	CA Medicine Hat AB	*$1.01*
Watson Lake to Dawson YK	11:55	601	CA Mi 54 AK Hiway BC	*$1.21*
Dawson to Dawson via AC	14:00	484	CA Mi 54 AK Hiway BC	*$1.21*

Figure 4 Conditional formatting to highlight trip `Segments`, whose `Time Estimate` is greater than average.

Distinguish Between the U.S. and Canada

Figure 4 illustrates one more instance of conditional formatting: The prices in the `Fuel Price` column given in Canadian dollars are italicized. Like the `Segment` formatting just considered, the `Fuel Price` formatting requires an `IF()` function in a formula. The complication, however, is determining when a price is in Canadian dollars, because it's not possible to determine that from the amount in the cell. However, the `Fuel Price Report` column has the property that it lists the source of the price quote in the first two letters of the cell, so whenever the country is `CA`, the price should be italicized.

To access letters of a cell value for such comparisons, the function `Left()` is provided, which has the specification

`Left(text_value, num_chars)`

This function "removes" from the left end of the letter sequence (`text_value`) the number of characters (`num_chars`) specified; of course, there is also a similar function `Right()`. For the `text_value` the friends use `D2`, the `Fuel Price Report`; for the second parameter, they use 2. So, to do the match requires the formula

`Left(D2, 2)="CA"`

as the condition for the `IF()` function. Note that quotes are required around `CA` because it must be treated as a letter string. In words, the expression says, "Take the first two characters from the left end of the text in cell `D2` and compare them to the letters `"CA"`." Placing the expression in an `IF()` function as the condition

`IF(Left(D2, 2)="CA", TRUE, FALSE)`

produces the formatting decision: If the text and the string are equal, then format the cell—because the fuel price estimate is in Canadian dollars; if they are not equal (false), do not format the cell. So, to italicize the entries, the friends select the `Fuel Price` entries, request *Format > Conditional Formatting...*,

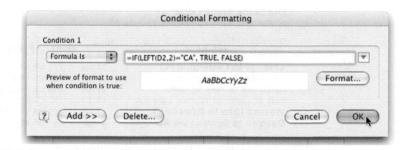

enter the `IF()` function into the formula window, and click *OK*, which yields the result shown in Figure 4. Notice that there was no change in formatting of the first two entries of **Fuel Price** because the first two letters in column **D** were not **"CA"** and so their formatting wasn't changed.

Finally, they add a comment to **Segment** explaining that highlighting means the estimated driving time is above average, and a comment to **Fuel Price** explaining that italic means the price is given in Canadian dollars for a liter of petrol.

 ## Conditional Formulas

In the same way that the friends used an `IF()` function to change the formatting in response to certain conditions, they can make the entire computation of a cell contingent on the outcome of a condition. This is essential for Pat and Alex, because they are using fuel measured in gallons and liters, and money measured in U.S. dollars and Canadian dollars. Figuring how much a tank of fuel costs requires precision. In this section we explain how spreadsheets can compute conditional factors and show how to use this capability to figure out the cost of each segment of the trip. The new column will be called **Amount Paid**. Before considering how to compute it, let's figure out exactly what they need to do.

Figuring the Amount Paid

First, we need to know how far the car typically goes on a unit of fuel, that is, its average mileage. Most drivers have some idea what their mileage is, and Alex's old Subaru averages 22 miles per gallon (mpg) of gas. So, they figure the cost of the fuel as

cost = price * distance/mpg

and add a comment to the **Amount Paid** column stating that the assumed mpg is 22.

The distances listed in the spreadsheet are all in miles because they were reported that way by the mapping software (used from the U.S.). If some distances were in miles and others in kilometers, the friends would have convert one format to the other. Happily, that's not necessary.

Conversion to Miles Per Liter. The friends do have to convert between liters and gallons. Because there are 1.056 quarts per liter, and four quarts in a gallon, they know they can go only 1/4 as far on a quart of fuel as on a gallon of fuel, meaning the Subaru's 22 mpg is really 22/4 = 5.5 mpq (miles per quart). But a liter is a little bit more than a quart, so a liter of fuel should carry them a little bit farther, by that amount. That is, 5.5 mpq is really 5.5*1.056 miles per liter (mpl), which is 5.8 mpl.

We can check this: If we buy 4 liters, we can go 23.2 miles based on the 5.8 mpl. How much more is that than if we bought 4 quarts? Four quarts gets us 22 miles, so it's 23.3/22, or a factor of 1.056 more, when we account for round-off errors. So, we know the mpl. If this sort of thinking gives you brain-fry, simply look up the conversion on the Web (mpl = mpg/3.788).

Applying Two Cases, Conditionally. So, for cases where the two travelers know the price in gallons, they multiply it times distance/mpg; when they know the price in liters, they multiply it times distance/mpl. Obviously, this is a job for the IF() function. Like the previous conditional formatting example, the friends will test on the first two letters of the **Fuel Price Report** field. If the data is from the U.S., they use the first computation, otherwise they use the second. The appropriate equation is

`=IF(LEFT(D2,2)="US", E2*C2/22, E2*C2/5.8)`

Notice that unlike before, this formula compares to "**US**". The result is an estimate of the total of the amounts paid for the fuel purchased for each segment, assuming the price of fuel is the average price of the location listed and the vehicle's mileage is 22 mpg. These assumptions are recorded in a comment. The entry is U.S. dollars in the U.S. and Canadian dollars in Canada, so the friends format **Amount Paid** with italics, as before. These results are shown in Figure 5.

Cost in One Currency

We give one more illustration of conditional formulas. For the friends to know the total cost estimate for their trip, it is essential to know the expenditures in one

Trip to the Arctic Circle
by Pat and Alex; completed 23.June.07

Segment	Miles	Fuel Price Report	Fuel Price	Amount Paid
Chicago to Carrington ND	778	US Chicago	$3.59	$126.96
Carrington to Battleford SK	620	US Moorehead MN	$2.96	$83.42
Battleford to Fort St. John	648	CA Moose Jaw SK	$1.09	$122.23
Fort St. John to Waston Lake YK	555	CA Medicine Hat AB	$1.01	$96.55
Watson Lake to Dawson YK	601	CA Mi 54 AK Hiway BC	$1.21	$125.28
Dawson to Dawson via AC	484	CA Mi 54 AK Hiway BC	$1.21	$100.89

Figure 5 Arctic Circle spreadsheet with Amount Paid column added. Notice that Time Estimate has been hidden, and that a comment noting the assumption of 22 mpg has been added to Amount Paid heading.

currency. Being Americans, they choose U.S. dollars. Therefore, they add a column, Cost. It will contain a copy of the Amount Paid cell when that's reported in U.S. dollars, and it will contain the U.S. dollar equivalent when the Amount Paid is reported in Canadian dollars. The computation uses the same ideas described earlier and will again use the IF() function.

Checking on the Web, Pat finds the exchange rate for Canadian currency to U.S.; it states that a Canadian dollar is worth $0.948 in U.S. dollars. Therefore, for each spreadsheet price given in Canadian dollars, they simply multiply the price times $0.948 to get the price in U.S. dollars.

Developing the IF() function needed for the Cost column (column G), they test column D as usual to determine if the price is in U.S. or Canadian dollars. The test for G2 is Left(D2,2)="CA". If it is Canadian, then they want F2*0.948, and if it is not, then they simply want F2, because it is already in U.S. dollars. The whole expression,

=IF(Left(D2,2)="CA", F2*0.93, F2)

results in an amount expressed in U.S. dollars. They fill the computation down the column and inspect to see that italicized amounts become slightly smaller in the Cost column.

Finally, the friends enter the data for the return trip by the same route—not their first choice, but maybe the quickest and cheapest way home. After doing so, they add a SUM() function to compute the total cost of the trip. The result is shown in Figure 6.

The friends are surprised that it's so expensive—and they have only accounted for the fuel cost. They still need to eat, they need to sleep somewhere besides the Subaru, and they need to buy treats and souvenirs. They need a couple of friends to help share the costs!

Trip to the Arctic Circle
by Pat and Alex; completed 23.June.07

Segment	Miles	Fuel Price Report	Fuel Price	Amount Paid	Cost
Chicago to Carrington ND	778	US Chicago	$3.59	$126.96	$126.96
Carrington to Battleford SK	620	US Moorehead MN	$2.96	$83.42	$83.42
Battleford to Fort St. John BC	648	CA Moose Jaw SK	*$1.09*	*$122.06*	$115.71
Fort St. John to Waston Lake YK	555	CA Medicine Hat AB	*$1.01*	*$96.42*	$91.41
Watson Lake to Dawson YK	601	CA Mi 54 AK Hiway BC	*$1.21*	*$125.11*	$118.60
Dawson to Dawson via Aritic Cir	484	CA Mi 54 AK Hiway BC	*$1.21*	*$100.75*	$95.51
Dawson to Watson Lake YK	601	CA Mi 54 AK Hiway BC	*$1.21*	*$125.11*	$118.60
Waston Lake to Fort St. John BC	555	CA Medicine Hat AB	*$1.01*	*$96.42*	$91.41
Fort St. John to Battleford SK	648	CA Moose Jaw SK	*$1.09*	*$122.06*	$115.71
Battleford to Carrington ND	620	US Moorehead MN	$2.96	$83.42	$83.42
Carrington to Chicago IL	778	US Chicago	$3.59	$126.96	$126.96
				Total:	$1,167.71

Figure 6 Arctic Circle spreadsheet completed to the point of producing an estimate for fuel costs.

Naming: Symbolic Reference

In their development of conditional formatting and conditional formulas, the friends have referred, as usual, to **B2**, **D2**, **E2**, and so on. But this could lead to problems later on. Suppose they insert a column in the spreadsheet. Will the references adjust? Certainly, the earlier comment referring to column **D** will not adjust, thwarting their effort to make the spreadsheet clear. Additionally, they have embedded several assumptions—gas mileage, currency exchange rate—into the formulas. These quantities can change: Exchange rates change by the minute, and they might find another car with better gas mileage to drive. The spreadsheet has become too dependent on the specific positions and data used at the moment. If the goal is to repeatedly use the spreadsheet, they must be more insulated from such changes.

Defining Names

A helpful design methodology is to give names to the components of our spreadsheets. Computer scientists say it is better to refer to cells *symbolically*—that is, by name—than to refer to them *literally*—that is, by their explicit column/row position. A **name** is a word or phrase assigned to a cell or range of cells. Once the name has been assigned, it can be used wherever cell references would normally be used, such as formulas. Using names reduces the chance of messing up range specifications, and minimizes the likelihood errors will creep in when columns and rows are added later.

We illustrate this idea by revising the friends' spreadsheet to use names. After choosing *Insert > Name > Define...*, we are presented with the Define Name window, shown in Figure 7(a). The range is automatically filled in for us based on our selection prior to choosing the command. Enter a name—it generally cannot contain spaces—and the software assigns that range of cells that name. But this action

(a)

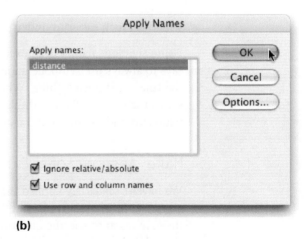

(b)

Figure 7 Name windows: (a) the *Define Name* window and (b) the *Apply Names* window.

has only *defined* a name; it is so far unused. Now, choosing *Insert > Name > Apply* allows us to use the name, as shown in Figure 7(b). Clicking *OK* tells the software to look through the formulas, and wherever it finds a reference for the cells bound to a selected name—that is, in the range `B2:B12` in this example—the symbolic name replaces the literal position in the formula.

Notice that we have chosen to name the column headed `Miles` with the range name of `distance`, because that is a somewhat better description. The point is that names are separate from the labels that we assign, though often we use the same word.

Applying Names

After clicking *OK* in the *Apply Names* dialog, the name `distance` is applied to the spreadsheet formulas. We can look at cells, for example `F2`, in which we have used the `distance` value, `C2`. We see the entry

```
=IF(LEFT(D2,2)="US", E2*distance/22,E2*distance/5.8)
```

in the *Formula Bar*, indicating that the name has been applied to this formula. In addition to being safer, it is easier to read and understand the formula when symbolic names are used.

To see how we could apply this idea to other parts of spreadsheet, let's define some more symbolic names. We choose

```
priceSrc    D2:D12
fuelPrice   E2:E12
amtPaid     F2:F12
cost        G2:G12
```

Then we apply the names to the formulas. When the process is complete, the formula in `F2` has the form

```
=IF(LEFT(priceSrc,2)="US", fuelPrice*distance/22,
                    fuelPrice*distance/5.8)
```

which is much easier to understand.

Using symbolic names is an excellent idea, and we could adopt a design rule that says to always use symbolic names, but we do not have to. It is already implied by the rule Explain Everything. When users select cell `F2`, for example, they should see in the *Formula Bar* a formula that makes sense. Symbolic names are easier for people to understand (and the computer doesn't care).

Make Assumptions Explicit

We haven't *completely* applied the idea of naming all of the quantities of the spreadsheet. The 22 (mpg) and 5.8 (mpl) are not constants of the universe like π; they are instance-specific quantities that our computation depends upon. We should make them symbolic, too.

The difference between the ranges we have named so far and these parameters to the formulas is the latter do not correspond to cells. But, by assigning their values to cells and giving them names, they can be used to explore travel alternatives, as you will see in the next section.

Alex and Pat have established an area below the `Segments` entries where they listed their assumptions. They identified the three parameters used so far: mileage in gallons, mileage in liters, and exchange rate. An additional assumption, the number of travelers, doesn't show up in any formula, but they are pretty sure that the number of travelers will change, so they decided to add a cell for that number, too. Their assumptions area has the form

Assumptions:	
Miles per gallon:	22
Miles per liter:	5.81
US-Canadian Exchange Rate:	0.948
Travlers:	2

The friends assign names to the values to make it easier to replace in the formulas. The names are `mpg`, `mpl`, `xchRate`, and `buddies`. The `mpl` value is computed using the formula

`=mpg/3.788`

implying that it is not independent of `mpg`.

Finally, the constants used in the `Amount Paid` formula must be changed manually. We cannot use the *Insert > Name > Apply* command, because the reference in the formula is to 22, not to a cell containing 22. So, we manually replace 22 by `mpg` in the *Formula Bar*, and fill the new formula into the other cells of the column. Of course, `mpl` and `xchRate` must also be changed manually as well. The modifications are visible in `F2`, which completes the naming.

```
=IF(LEFT(priceSrc,2)="US", fuelPrice*distance/mpg,
                           fuelPrice*distance/mpl)
```

We have revised the spreadsheet to name the relevant cells and ranges, an improvement that has taken a few minutes. Had the names been introduced as the entries were being developed, the cost of using them would have been unnoticed.

 ## "What If" Analysis

Pat and Alex are a little surprised that driving to the Arctic Circle and back is going to cost them roughly $1,200 for gas alone. They will need to find some friends to travel with them to help defray the cost, but before doing that, they need a better idea of what the whole trip will cost them, and whether there are ways to control costs. Because spreadsheets recalculate everything whenever a number is changed, they are ideal for speculating on the consequences of change. Make a change, and notice what happens to the "bottom line."

Direct Experimentation

With their present spreadsheet, Alex and Pat can do some of this speculative analysis directly. It involves changing cells, looking to see what happens, and then undoing the change. It's cumbersome, but it's quick.

For example, they wonder if

> ❯ The Subaru could be tuned up to get 25 mpg, how would that affect fuel costs?
> ❯ With more people and therefore more weight in the vehicle, maybe 22 mpg is too high. What is the effect of 20 mpg?
> ❯ A friend with a 30 mpg vehicle offered to drive, how would that change fuel costs?

By changing mpg, the friends discover that these assumptions change fuel costs to be $1,028, $1,284 and $856, respectively. Obviously, the cost of the trip is very sensitive to the efficiency of the vehicle. Using the same technique, they also discover that the trip is not very sensitive to the currency exchange rate, at least not within the range in which it is likely to fluctuate. So, waiting for the U.S. dollar to strengthen against the Canadian dollar won't help much.

The problem with experimenting directly with the spreadsheet is that it risks making permanent changes to the data and formulas that have been so carefully entered. Fortunately, there is a better way to experiment with a spreadsheet.

Scenarios

The speculative or "what if" analysis that the friends just performed is nicely supported in spreadsheet software by a tool called Scenarios. A **scenario** is a named alternative to a spreadsheet based on different inputs. A scenario is an aid to understanding changes in plans, like changes in gas mileage. Let's see how the friends can use a scenario.

Tune-up Scenario. Selecting the mpg cell, because we are exploring alternatives to the current mileage of 22, we navigate *Tools > Scenarios . . .* and arrive at the Scenario Manager window, as shown in Figure 8(a). This window is the principal interface to the Scenario facility: It is the place to define new scenarios, edit them, and request summaries. Initially, there are no scenarios defined, of course, so we click on *Add . . ..*

The Edit Scenario window (Figure 8(b)) is the place to name a scenario. In addition, the software fills in the cell(s) that will change, and a comment as to who created it and when the scenario was defined. Clicking *OK* takes us to the Scenario Values window (Figure 8(c)), where we enter the alternative value for mpg. Notice that the symbolic name is used for the field, now that we have named the cells. Clicking *OK* takes us back to the Scenario Manager window (Figure 8(d)), where the newly added scenario can be seen in the list. We have created a scenario and archived it.

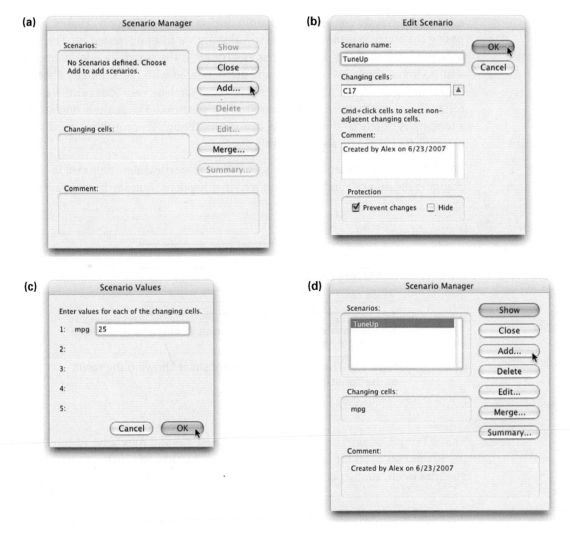

Figure 8 Dialog box sequence for adding a scenario to the Arctic Circle spreadsheet.

Having taken some effort to define the scenario, we can run it. Notice at the bottom of the Scenario Manager window (Figure 8(d)), there is a *Summary* . . . button. When we click it, a dialog box appears asking what cell we consider the "bottom line" of the computation. That is, supposing the scenario came to pass, what value are we most interested in? The software predicted that G15, which is our FuelCost, is the summary information we want to know about. We click *OK*, and are presented with the Summary Sheet shown in Figure 9. The sheet nicely summarizes the base case (Current Values column) and the "bottom line" of our TuneUp scenario. (The analysis implies that a tune-up is beneficial if it costs less than $140, though it's probably a good idea to tune up a car before any long trip!)

The TuneUp scenario setup doesn't seem like it is worthwhile, compared to changing the mpg cell and looking to see what happens. But, the benefits are coming.

Scenario Summary		
	Current Values:	TuneUp
Changing Cells:		
mpg	22	25
Result Cells:		
FuelCost	$1,167.71	$1,027.59

Notes: Current Values column represents values of changing cells at time Scenario Summary Report was created. Changing cells for each scenario are highlighted in gray.

Figure 9 The Scenario Summary sheet showing the result of the TuneUp scenario.

Traveling Companions Scenario. Because Pat and Alex want to consider the advantages of taking along one or more friends, they add, below their FuelCost cell, another cell with the cost per person, as in

Total:	$1,167.71
Cost Each	$583.86

which is implemented by the formula =FuelCost/buddies. They name the per person fuel cost cell ppFuel. Then, they construct another pair of scenarios.

The extra passenger scenario follows the same protocol used for the TuneUp scenario. Figure 10 shows the key steps. Notice first that in the Edit Scenario window, Figure 10(a), two fields are specified by name as varying, mpg and buddies. Having two fields changing means that in the Scenario Values window, Figure 10(b), both values are listed with value fields. They set buddies to 3 and drop mpg to 21 because of the extra weight. Then, in the Scenario Summary window, Figure 10(c), they specify G16, the ppFuel cell, as the one they are most interested in. Finally, in the Scenario Summary sheet, Figure 10(d), the new scenario is presented with the earlier scenario and the base case. As expected, having another person along helps with costs, even if it harms mileage.

Obviously, the "high mileage" scenario develops in the same way.

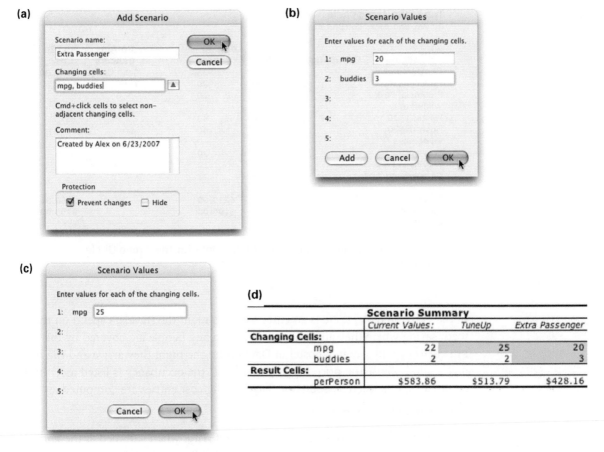

Figure 10 The Extra Passenger scenarios and their effect on `ppFuel`.

Analyzing a Model

The travelers have a good estimate of the fuel costs for their trip and the cost benefits of taking others along. But how much will the trip actually cost them? To answer the question, they build a model that accounts for all of the foreseeable costs of the trip, and how this combines with fuel costs to produce the bottom line expense for going to the Arctic Circle. Here's what they do.

Formulating a Model. To start, they think a little harder about the costs. To save lodging expenses, they decide to camp, which is sensible because they are headed into the wilderness and they own camping equipment. A few moments on the Web reveals that they can camp at public campgrounds, provincial parks, and, once they are in the wilderness, the wilderness itself. On the next page of their spreadsheet, they click together another table, shown in Figure 11.

Trip to the Arctic Circle
by Pat and Alex; completed 23.June.07

Lodging	Occupancy	Price	Lodging Expense		Contingencies	Just In Case
Campground	2	25	25		Base Cost	$100.00
Provincial Park	2	20	20		Tires	$160.00
Provincial Park	2	20	20			
Wilderness	2	0	0			
Hostel@$20	1	20	40			
Hostel@$20	1	20	40			
Wilderness	2	0	0			
Provincial Park	2	20	20			
Provincial Park	2	20	20			
Campground	2	25	25			
Total			$210.00			$260.00
Total Per Person			$105.00			$130.00
Camping	Yes					

Figure 11 The lodging and contingency data for the Arctic Circle road trip.

In the Lodging table, there is an entry for each night the travelers spend on the road, saying where they are staying and how many people are covered by the `Price`. They will stay in a hostel in Dawson on the night they arrive and the next night, and because the price is given "per bed," the occupancy is listed as 1. In the other cases, it is listed as `buddies`. The lodging cost entries are computed as

`=price*buddies/occupancy`

which yields the total lodging expense, `ppLodging`, when summed at the end of the column. Each person's share is found by dividing by `buddies`.

Regarding contingencies, there are tolls and probably an oil change at some point, but they decide that although "stuff happens," it will only total about $100. There is concern about the tread on the rear tires of the Subaru, and they decide to budget some new tires if needed. They compute the total of the entries and divide by `buddies`.

The Model. Finally, with more complete data available, the friends make one more table.

Trip to the Arctic Circle
by Pat and Alex; completed 23.June.07

Costs	Amount Per Person
Fuel	$583.86
Lodging	$105.00
Contingency	$130.00
Total	$818.86

This table summarizes the per person expenses of the spreadsheet. This is their model: It shows `ppFuel`, `ppLodging`, and `ppContin` subcomputations, and computes the grand total, called `estTotal`. It doesn't contain a food charge, because the friends decide that they would eat even if they stayed at home, so food isn't a direct cost of the trip.

Reusing Scenarios. Having set up the scenarios earlier, it is possible to rerun them again to see how the total cost changes as the number of travelers increases. They navigate to the Scenario Manager and click on *Summary...* again. When the Scenario Summary window appears, they change the "bottom line" to the estTotal cell, which is the one that matters now.

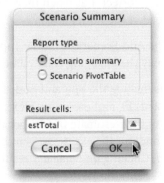

After clicking *OK*, they get the report summarizing the model.

	Scenario Summary		
	Current Values:	1 Extra Traveler	2 Extra Travelers
Changing Cells:			
mpg	22	21	20
buddies	2	3	4
Result Cells:			
estTotal	$818.86	$599.44	$491.12

The model predicts the expenses to the extent that the estimates are correct. It is very convenient.

A Change in Plans. Pat and Alex quickly find the first friend interested in the Arctic Circle trip, provided they get the tires before they go. The next person they speak to is concerned about camping in country famous for bears, and prefers instead to stay at hostels. It seemed silly to stop at a hostel each night, drop off the friend, and the other three continue on to the campground. So they decide to run another scenario to see how staying in hostels would change the cost of the trip.

The Hostel Upgrade scenario requires a new field, camping.

Total		$210.00
Total Per Person		$105.00
Camping	Yes	

This Yes/No field controls the occupancy of the lodging table. That is, the occupancy data, which was previously defined to be the number of people who would stay in the campsite (**buddies**), becomes

```
=IF(camping="Yes", buddies, 1)
```

This formula specifies that everyone either stays in the campsite (**Yes**) or has a bed at the hostel (**No**). They add a comment describing the field's meaning.

Alex and Pat click to the Scenario Manager and request *Add . . .* to define a new scenario. This time the scenario must consider the effect of changing a whole range of values, the **Price** values; when the travelers are camping (**Yes**), the original data is correct, but when they are not camping (**No**), the entries must show what a bed at the hostel costs.

When the Add Scenario window appears, they enter a name, **Hostel Upgrade**, and specify the changing cells' names.

The cells include the **mpg** and **buddies** as usual, the **Price** field of the lodging table (**J2:J11**), and **camping**. Next, the Scenario Values window appears, and they enter their estimate of $18 per night for the hostels—they didn't take the time to find out the exact cost—and the other values, the last of which is **No** to camping. Clicking on *Summary* results in the Scenario Summary table shown in Figure 12.

Notice the form of Figure 12. The changing values are shown with gray fill, and are presented for each of the scenarios without regard to whether they are part of the scenario. That is, even though the lodging prices didn't change in the extra travelers scenarios, they are displayed, because they changed in some scenario (**Hostel Upgrade**).

This model could be used to explore other alternative scenarios.

Scenario Summary				
	Current Values:	1 Extra Traveler	2 Extra Travelers	Hostel Upgrade
Changing Cells:				
mpg	22	21	20	20
buddies	2	3	4	4
$J$2	25	25	25	18
$J$3	20	20	20	18
$J$4	20	20	20	18
$J$5	0	0	0	18
$J$6	20	20	20	18
$J$7	20	20	20	18
$J$8	0	0	0	18
$J$9	20	20	20	18
$J$10	20	20	20	18
$J$11	25	25	25	18
camping	Yes	Yes	Yes	No
Result Cells:				
estTotal	$818.86	$577.77	$458.62	$566.12

Figure 12 Scenario Summary table for the Arctic Circle road trip.

Analyzing Data Using Filtering

Alex and Pat, joined by friends Ali and Chi, left on their epic road trip to the Arctic Circle. With long hours to pass while driving across the Great Plains of central North America, Pat extends the spreadsheet to a second sheet to record entries for their travels; see Figure 13. They called the page the Travel Log.

The Travel Log is an example of a long list of entries that are interesting as a group—that's why they are in the list—and also as subgroups. Filtering is the tool that gives access to subsets of this information. For example, from time to time the friends are interested in seeing only certain entries of their Travel Log record, such as when have they purchased gas.

Auto Filtering Technique

Filtering, as its name implies, selects only certain rows from a list. It applies only to spreadsheet tables that have column headings, as the Travel Log does. Filtering lets users create a customized version of a spreadsheet list that is limited to the rows meeting some criterion. For example, to find out how many times they've stopped for gas so far, the travelers could look through the record in Figure 13 to find all those times and places where they filled up. Or they could filter the list, which is much easier.

Road To Arctic Circle and Back: Stops
Pat, Alex, Chi, Ali

When	Seg. No	Where	Reason	Buy	$	Amt	Mi	Remark
8/4/07 5:45	1	Ali's house IL	Last pick-up			0.00		We're Off!
8/4/07 6:40	1	Toll Booth IL	Alex Fumbles	All tolls	X	2.85		
8/4/07 8:05	1	DriveThru Joe IL	Espresso					Only driver
8/4/07 9:00	1	Beloit WI	Gas & Go	Gas	A	34.50	241	
8/4/07 9:55	1	Madison WI	Snacks					
8/4/07 12:05	1	St. Paul MN	Gas & Go, Eat	Gas	P	28.95	191	Subway
8/4/07 14:45	1	St. Cloud MN	Stretch/Photo					Pretty Here
8/4/07 15:30	1	Sauk Center MN	Snacks					
8/4/07 16:55	1	Fergus Falls MN	Gas & Go	Gas	P	29.22	205	
8/4/07 19:45	1	Fargo ND	Photo in ND					Pat's First
8/4/07 20:25	1	Valley City ND	Supper					Junk Food
8/4/07 22:00	1	Carrington ND	Stay Night	Camp	C	21.45		Great Start
8/5/07 7:25	2	Carrington ND	Gas	Gas	A	37.42	252	
8/5/07 7:55	2	Sykeston ND	Photo					Its flat
8/5/07 10:05	2	Minot ND	Gas & Go,Snx	Gas	X	19.64	135	Ice Cream
8/5/07 11:50	2	Portal ND	Photo in CA					Ali, Pat, 1st
8/5/07 12:25	2	Estevan SK	Lunch					
8/5/07 13:55	2	Weyburn SK	Gas & Go, Eat	Gas	A	33.82	151	
8/5/07 15:45	2	Moose Jaw SK	Snacks					I Scream!

Figure 13 Start of the Travel Log of the Arctic Circle road trip. Seg. No corresponds to a segment of the original plan (Sheet 1), $ refers to who paid a shared expense, Mi is distance traveled since last fuel.

The easiest form of filtering, called *AutoFilter*, is trivial to apply. Select any cell in the list, then choose *Data > Filter > AutoFilter*. The result will be a redrawn spreadsheet list with triangle menu buttons by each column heading.

When ⇕	Seg. Nc ⇕	Where ⇕	Reason ⇕	Buy ⇕	$⇕	Amt ⇕	M ⇕	Remark ⇕
8/4/07 5:45	1	Ali's house IL	Last pick-up			0.00		We're Off!
8/4/07 6:40	1	Toll Booth IL	Alex Fumbles	All tolls	X	2.85		

The menu buttons give you options for filtering the list based on data in that column. Clicking on a button opens the menu and presents the options, which include sorting rows, displaying rows containing a limited number of values, or displaying only those rows matching a specific value in the column. For example, clicking on the **Buy** menu button presents the travelers with these options:

Reason ⇕	Buy ⇕	$⇕	Amt ⇕
Last pick-up		Sort Ascending	).00
Alex Fumbles		Sort Descending	?.85
Espresso		✓ (Show All)	
Gas & Go		(Show Top 10...)	!.50
Snacks		(Custom Filter...)	
Gas & Go, Eat		All tolls	3.95
Stretch/Photo		Camp	
Snacks		Gas	
Gas & Go		(Show Blanks)	
Photo in ND		(Show NonBlanks)	).22

Notice that the three values occurring in the column are listed near the bottom. Choosing one of them, such as **Gas**, causes the list to be filtered, leaving only those rows that match the selected item.

Road To Arctic Circle and Back: Stops
Pat, Alex, Chi, Ali

When ⇕	Seg. Nc ⇕	Where ⇕	Reason ⇕	Buy ⇕	$⇕	Amt ⇕	M ⇕	Remark ⇕
8/4/07 9:00	1	Beloit WI	Gas & Go	Gas	A	34.50	241	
8/4/07 12:05	1	St. Paul MN	Gas & Go, Eat	Gas	P	28.95	191	Subway
8/4/07 16:55	1	Fergus Falls MN	Gas & Go	Gas	P	29.22	205	
8/5/07 7:25	2	Carrington ND	Gas	Gas	A	37.42	252	
8/5/07 10:05	2	Minot ND	Gas & Go,Snx	Gas	X	19.64	135	Ice Cream
8/5/07 13:55	2	Weyburn SK	Gas & Go, Eat	Gas	A	33.82	151	

So, at this point in the trip, the friends have purchased fuel six times. These rows can be further filtered. For example, by clicking on the **$** menu selector and selecting **X**,

Alex is shown a personalized version of the Travel Log **Gas** purchases.

When	Seg. No	Where	Reason	Buy	$	Amt	M	Remark
8/5/07 10:05	2	Minot ND	Gas & Go,Snx	Gas	X	19.64	135	Ice Cream

Notice that in Figure 13 Alex also paid tolls, but that is not reflected in this version of the table, because the first filter was **Buy** column matches **Gas**, and the second was **$** column matches **X**. Of course, the same result would have been found by executing the two filters in the opposite order.

These changes to the list are only logical, that is, the actual list has not been modified. We turn off the AutoFilter simply by selecting it again, that is, it is a toggle, and the original list will be redrawn.

Advanced Filtering Technique

AutoFiltering is easy because the software gives us access to a variety of standard filtering criteria. But most lists contain data that requires more refined analysis. Advanced Filtering is the tool to use to develop precise filtering criteria.

Advanced Filtering Setup. To apply advanced filtering, we give a column name and a filtering criterion. These are presented to the spreadsheet software in a curious way: by adding a new column. The new column will have the *same heading* as the column containing the data to be filtered. Then, in the cell below the heading, users enter a criterion like >175 to indicate that values in the other column by the same name should be filtered to be greater than 175. Once the setup is complete, we can run the filtering operation.

For example, the travelers decide to analyze their gas purchases. So, they add a new column, which must be labeled exactly like the column to be filtered, that is, **Mi**. To filter out the smaller gas purchases, they set the criterion to be >175. The result is

When	Seg. No	Where	Reason	Buy	$	Amt	Mi	Mi
8/4/07 5:45	1	Ali's house IL	Last pick-up			0.00		>175
8/4/07 6:40	1	Toll Booth IL	Alex Fumbles	All tolls	X	2.85		

This two-step process completes the setup for the Advanced Search facility.

Executing an Advanced Filter. To run the actual filtering operation, select a cell in the column to be filtered—not the setup column. This tells the Advanced Filter software which list is to be filtered and which column is considered the source of the filter. Forgetting to select a cell in the filtered column is a common mistake. Next, choose *Data > Filtering > Advanced Search . . .*, which displays the Advanced Filter window.

The *List range* specification simply gives the dimensions of the list that is going to be filtered; the software generally figures it out on its own and preloads it. The *Criteria range* is where users specify the setup column. Enter the range covering the heading and the criterion. (The *Copy to* option is explained momentarily.) Clicking *OK* produces a filtered table.

When	Seg. No	Where	Reason	Buy	$	Amt	Mi	Mi
8/4/07 9:00	1	Beloit WI	Gas & Go	Gas	A	34.50	241	
8/4/07 12:05	1	St. Paul MN	Gas & Go, Eat	Gas	P	28.95	191	
8/4/07 16:55	1	Fergus Falls MN	Gas & Go	Gas	P	29.22	205	
8/5/07 7:25	2	Carrington ND	Gas	Gas	A	37.42	252	

The table appears on the spreadsheet in the position of the original table. To restore the original table, choose *Data > Filtering > Show All*. (Notice that the criterion (**>175**) is not visible because the first row of the original table isn't in the filtered result.)

The *Copy to* option in the *Advanced Filter* window specifies a new place on the spreadsheet to place the filtered result. It is often handy to have both the original and filtered result to compare. Also, once created, the copy can be treated like any other list and analyzed separately. In the *Advanced Filter* window, specify the range in which to place the filtered result. The specification should be as wide as the original list including the setup, but it can be only one row high, because the size of the result is unknown prior to filtering.

Filtering on Multiple Criteria

The Advanced Filtering facility allows multiple criteria. They are specified during setup by defining multiple columns; then, during execution, the *Criteria range* is enlarged to cover all criteria.

For example, having filtered out the smaller gas purchases, the travelers decide to filter out the large purchases. They define another **Mi** column and enter the criterion **<225**. The result

When	Seg. No	Where	Reason	Buy	$	Amt	Mi	Mi	Mi
8/4/07 5:45	1	Ali's house IL	Last pick-up			0.00		>175	<225

is ready to execute. They select a cell in the original **Mi** column, navigate to the *Advanced Filter* command, enter the *Criteria range* as **$J$1:$K$2** (that is, a 2 × 2 range), and click *OK*. The result is

When	Seg. No	Where	Reason	Buy	$	Amt	Mi	Mi	Mi
8/4/07 12:05	1	St. Paul MN	Gas & Go, Eat	Gas	P	28.95	191		
8/4/07 16:55	1	Fergus Falls MN	Gas & Go	Gas	P	29.22	205		

which has eliminated the larger and smaller gas purchases, revealing the curious fact that Pat pays for the fuel when the purchase is in the midrange.

Filtering is extremely useful. For example, when the trip is over and the friends are settling up their accounts, a list of each traveler's payments can be created, processed, and analyzed. In fact, when the trip is over, Pat and Alex can determine how accurate their original predictions about the trip's cost were.

SUMMARY

This chapter has taught several advanced spreadsheet techniques. You learned that:

> Two basic principles underline the design of effective spreadsheets.

> Conditional formatting can apply an interpretation to the data in a spreadsheet in a manner that is easy to perceive.

> Conditional formulas using the **IF()** function allow complex, case-specific data definition and analysis.

> Naming the cells and regions of a spreadsheet allows the parts of a spreadsheet to be referenced in a convenient and less error-prone way.

> "What if" analysis is a particularly powerful application of spreadsheets in which the consequences of alternative information can be assessed.

> Filtering effectively customizes spreadsheet data to particular cases.

> There are other handy spreadsheet operations that have not been covered, and for each of the techniques we have discussed, there are other applications. When you start using spreadsheets as a daily computing tool, you will undoubtedly migrate toward these more powerful facilities.

Review Questions

Multiple Choice

1. The most useful general purpose computer application is
   a. email
   b. Windows
   c. a spreadsheet
   d. a browser

2. All of the following are basic spreadsheet principles except
   a. logical form
   b. clean layout
   c. no text
   d. clear and understandable entries

3. "Explain everything" in a spreadsheet means:
   a. you should easily be able to tell what every cell means
   b. each cell should be labeled
   c. each formula should be explained with a label
   d. all of the above

4. Conditional formatting
   a. allows you to display information in more than one way
   b. allows you to write more than one formula for a cell
   c. automatically finds and flags errors in formulas and formatting
   d. all of the above

5. To get the first characters in a cell you should use the
   a. Begin function
   b. Start function
   c. Left function
   d. Get function

6. Conditional formatting can change the
   a. text color
   b. text format
   c. cell color
   d. more than one of the above

7. Defining names for a spreadsheet allows you to refer to cells
   a. by location
   b. symbolically
   c. conditionally
   d. alphabetically

8. If you found regHours in a spreadsheet formula you'd know it's a
   a. mistake
   b. named reference
   c. constant
   d. function

9. Spreadsheets recalculate
    a. whenever a number is changed
    b. only when saved
    c. only when opened
    d. once a minute

10. Autofiltering can only be used on
    a. named ranges
    b. tables that have column headings
    c. cells containing formulas
    d. rows with unique entries

11. Autofiltering allows
    a. sorting rows
    b. displaying rows with a limited number of values
    c. displaying rows that match specific criteria
    d. all of the above

12. Conditional formatting allows
    a. customized colors for cells in a spreadsheet
    b. cells to be automatically updated from the Internet
    c. for the interpretation of the data in a spreadsheet
    d. none of the above

Short Answer

1. Spreadsheets are great for playing _____, that is, they are useful for putting together various possible scenarios.

2. _____ are a good way to explain a spreadsheet formula.

3. "Post-it-notes" for a spreadsheet are called _____.

4. _____ allows for the application of interpretation to the data in a spreadsheet.

5. Individual pages in a spreadsheet are called _____.

6. When you _____ for a spreadsheet, you create a symbolic reference for a range of cells.

7. A single cell or a related group of cells is called a(n) _____.

8. A(n) _____ is a named alternative to a spreadsheet based on different inputs.

9. The _____ is the interface for managing scenarios.

10. _____ allows the selection of certain spreadsheet rows based on a specified criteria.

Exercises

1. Create a spreadsheet to plan your own trip.

2. Plan a trip using airlines, car rentals and hotel stays. Don't forget to budget for sightseeing. Play "What If" with various scenarios for your trip.

3. Create a table to calculate free throw percentages. Use `IF()` functions to prevent an error when no free throws are shot. Format the results using bold for percentages greater than or equal to 75%.

4. Create a spreadsheet for apartment costs based on the number of bedrooms, the number of roommates and typical living expenses. Plot various scenarios depending on the price, number of roommates, and monthly expenses.

5. Create a spreadsheet to track your monthly expenses. Create categories for the expenses and filter them. Include columns for the day and date and track expenses by the day of the week.

6. Create a spreadsheet to track you computer usage. Create categories as needed and filter activities such as email, browsing, downloading, entertainment, word processing, spreadsheets, etc.

7. Organize your CD or DVD collection. Create categories as needed and filter by genre, year, stars, producers, directors, etc.

8. Create a spreadsheet to track the stats for your favorite basketball team. Create formulas as needed to calculate shooting percentages. Total the columns as needed.

9. Create a spreadsheet of multiple choice questions. Use a column for the question, a column for each possible answer, a column for the correct answer, and a column for the topic. Set up filtering for it based on topic and correct answer.

10. Create a spreadsheet to track your eating habits. Use columns for food types, calories, time of day, and nutritional value. Set up filtering to see how much junk food is eaten and when it's eaten.

11. Set up a spreadsheet to do stock analysis. Track a stock's open, close, high, low, change, and volume. Track it for 30 days and see how many days are up and how many are down. Use conditional formatting with green for up days and red for down days.

12. Create a monthly budget for yourself. Track the actual expenses to see how close you are. Use green for items that are under budget and red for those that are over budget.

13. Create a spreadsheet for your college classes. List each in its own row. Track whether a class is required or an elective. Include the semester it was (will be) taken. Include the prerequisites, delivery method, instructor, and grade. Filter them as needed to analyze your curriculum.

14. Create a spreadsheet to balance your checkbook. Set up a column for the date, check number, payee, amount, and comment. Create a column to track deposits and another to track the balance. Write formulas as needed to keep the running balance. Set up conditional formatting to let you know when the balance falls below a certain level. Filter it as needed to see your spending habits.

15. Do an analysis of various real estate investments. Compare the price, the mortgage amount, interest rate, and term. Create various scenarios to see which investments are best.

16. Do an analysis of various cars purchases. Compare the price, the loan amount, payments, maintenance, insurance, and driving costs. Create various scenarios to see which is the best buy.

 Answers to Selected Questions

Multiple Choice

1. C. Spreadsheets are flexible and powerful.

3. A. To avoid confusion, comments and labels should be used to clarify a spreadsheet.

5. C. The Left function looks at a specified number of characters at the beginning of a cell.

7. B. By defining names, you can refer to a cell or range of cells by name instead of cell reference.

9. A. A spreadsheet recalculates automatically whenever a number in a cell is changed.

11. D. All of the above can be done with autofiltering

Short Answer

1. "what if"

3. comments

5. worksheets

7. range

9. Scenario manager

9

A Table with a View

Introduction to Database Concepts

Learning Objectives

> Use XML to describe the metadata for a table of information, and classify the uses of the tags as identification, affinity, or collection

> Explain the differences between everyday tables and database tables

> Explain how the concepts of entities and attributes are used to design a database table

> Use the six database operations: `Select`, `Project`, `Union`, `Difference`, `Product`, and `Join`

> Describe the differences between physical and logical databases

> Express a query using Query By Example

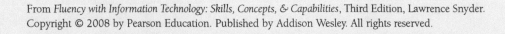

Computers are useless. They only give answers.

—PABLO PICASSO

Now that we have all this useful information, it would be nice to do something with it. (Actually, it can be emotionally fulfilling just to get the information. This is usually only true, however, if you have the social life of a kumquat.)

—UNIX PROGRAMMER'S MANUAL

WE HAVE seen the benefits of using spreadsheets to organize lists of information. By arranging similar information into columns and using a separate row for each new list item, we can easily sort data, use formulas to summarize and compute values, get help from the computer to set up series, and so forth. Spreadsheets are very powerful, but with databases it's possible to apply even greater degrees of organization and receive even more help from the computer.

The key idea is to supply metadata describing the properties of the collected information. Recall that metadata is simply information describing (the properties of) other information. We applied the idea of specifying metadata when we used tags—the metadata—to describe the content of the *Oxford English Dictionary*, enabling the computer to help us search for words and definitions. Some databases use tags for metadata, others use different kinds of metadata, but the same principles apply: Knowing the structure and properties of the data, the computer can help us retrieve, organize, and manage it.

In this chapter we distinguish between the everyday concept of a table and a relational database table. Next, we explain how to set up the metadata for collections of information to create a database. The principles are straightforward and intuitive. We will make the metadata tangible by using a notation called XML. After introducing basic table concepts, we present the five fundamental operations on tables and the `Join` operation. The concepts of physical database and logical database are connected by the concept of queries, and we illustrate how to build a user's logical view from physical tables. Finally, the convenience of Query By Example is illustrated using simple examples.

Differences Between Tables and Databases

When we think of databases, we often think of tables of information. For example, your iTunes or similar application records the title, artist, running time, and so on in addition to the actual MP3 data (the music). Your favorite song is a row in that table. Another example is your state's database of automobile registrations recording the owner's name and address, the vehicle identification number (VIN), the license plate number, and such. Your car is a row in the registration database table. And as a last example, the U.S. Central Intelligence Agency (CIA) keeps an interesting database called the World Factbook; see `https://www.cia.gov/library/publications/the-world-factbook/index.html`. The demographic table records the country name, population, life expectancy, and so on. The U.S. is a row in the demography table.

Comparing Tables

To see the difference between these database tables and other forms of tables, such as spreadsheets and HTML tables, consider the row for Canada in the CIA's demographic database. This row is displayed as

Canada		32805041	1.61	5	80.1

in a table with column headings such as Country, Population, and Birthrate. In the file it is represented as

```
<demogData>
    <country>Canada</country>
    <population>32805041</population>
    <fertility>1.61</fertility>
    <infant>5</infant>
    <lifeExpct>80.1</lifeExpct>
</demogData>
```

where the tags identify the population, fertility or birthrate, infant mortality (per 1,000 live births), and life expectancy. That is, we are shown a row of data as it appears in any other table, but inside the computer it has a tag identifying each of the data fields.

How does this data appear in other table forms? In a spreadsheet, the following is the row for Canada.

36	Cameroon	16988132	4.47	65	50.89	
37	Canada	32805041	1.61	5	80.1	
38	Cape Verde	418224	3.48	48	70.45	

The entries for Canada are the same, but the software knows the values only by position, not by their meaning. So, if a cell is inserted at the beginning, causing all of the data to shift right one position,

36	Cameroon	16988132	4.47	65	50.89	
37		Canada	32805041	1.61	5	80.1
38	Cape Verde	418224	3.48	48	70.45	

the identity of the information is lost. Spreadsheets rely on position to keep the integrity of their data; the information is not known by its `<country>` tag, but rather as `A37`.

HTML tables are possibly even worse. The usual Web page presentation of the data for Canada is represented in HTML as

```
<tr>
   <td>Canada</td>
   <td>32805041</td>
   <td>1.61</td>
   <td>5</td>
   <td>80.1</td>
</tr>
```

where we recall that `<tr>` is a table row tag and `<td>` is a table data tag. These tags simply identify Canada's data as table entries with no unique identity at all; that is, the same kind of `<td>` tags surround all of the different forms of data. HTML is concerned only with how to display the data, not with its meaning.

The Database's Advantage

The metadata is the key advantage of databases over other systems recording data as tables. Here's why. Suppose we want to know the life expectancy of Canadians. Database software can search for the `<country>` tag surrounding Canada. When it's found, the `<country>` tag will be one of several tags surrounded by `<demogData>` tags. These constitute the entry for Canada in the database. The software can then look for the `<lifeExpct>` tag among those tags and report the data that they surround as the data for Canada. The computer knew which data to return based on the availability of the metadata.

The tags for the CIA database just discussed fulfill two of the most important roles in defining metadata.

> **Identify the type of data:** Each different type of value is given a unique tag.

> **Define the affinity of the data:** Tags enclose all data that is logically related.

The `<country>`, `<population>`, and similar tags have the role of identification because they label the content. The `<demogData>` tag has the role of implementing affinity because it keeps an entry's data together. There are other properties of data that metadata must record, as you will see throughout this chapter, but these are perhaps the most fundamental.

 ## XML: A Language for Metadata Tags

To emphasize the importance of metadata and to prepare for our own applications of database technology, let's take a moment to discuss the basics of XML. XML stands for the Extensible Markup Language, and like the Hypertext Markup

Language (HTML), it is basically a tagging scheme, making it rather intuitive. The tagging scheme used for the *Oxford English Dictionary (OED)* was a precursor to XML, and the demographic data of the last section was written in XML.

What makes XML easy and intuitive is that there are no standard tags to learn. *We think up the tags we need!* Computer scientists call this a *self-describing language*, because whatever we create becomes the language (tags) to structure the data. There are a couple of rules—for example, always match tags—but basically anything goes. Perhaps XML is the world's easiest-to-learn "foreign" language.

The same people who coordinate the Web—the World Wide Web Consortium (W3C)—developed XML. As a result, it works very well with browsers and other Web-based applications. So, it comes as no surprise that just as HTML must be written with a text editor rather than a word processor to avoid unintentionally including the word processor's tags, we must also write XML in a simple text editor for the same reason. Use the same editor that you used to practice writing Web pages: for Mac users that might be TextEdit or TextWrangler; for Windows users it might be Notepad or Notepad++.

*fit*TIP | **Use A Text Editor for XML.** Like HTML, XML should be written using a text editor like Notepad++ or TextWrangler rather than a word processor like Word or Word Perfect. Text editors give you only the text you see, but word processors include their own tags and other information that could confuse XML.

An Example from Tahiti

Let's use XML to define tags to specify the metadata for a small data collection. Given the following size data (area in km^2) for Tahiti and its neighboring islands in the Windward Islands archipelago of the South Pacific,

Tahiti	1048
Moorea	130
Maiao	9.5
Mehetia	2.3
Tetiaroa	12.8

we want to add the metadata, that is, identify which data is an island name and which is the area. As usual, the tag and its companion closing tag surround the data. We choose `<iName>` and `<area>` as the tags and write:

```
<iName>Tahiti</iName>      <area>1048</area>
<iName>Moorea</iName>      <area>130</area>
<iName>Maiao</iName>       <area>9.5</area>
<iName>Mehetia</iName>     <area>2.3</area>
<iName>Tetiaroa</iName>    <area>12.8</area>
```

These tags are used in the identification role. Notice that we chose `<iName>` rather than, say, `<island name>`. This is because XML tag names cannot contain spaces. But because both uppercase and lowercase are allowed—XML is case sensitive—

we capitalize the "N" to make the tag more readable. All XML rules are shown later in this section in Table 1.

Though we have labeled each item with a tag describing what it is, we're not done describing the data. We need tags describing what sort of thing the name specifies and the area measures. That's an island, of course. So we enclose each entry with an `<island>` tag, as in

```
<island><iName>Tahiti</iName>    <area>1048</area></island>
<island><iName>Moorea</iName>    <area>130</area></island>
<island><iName>Maiao</iName>     <area>9.5</area></island>
<island><iName>Mehetia</iName>   <area>2.3</area></island>
<island><iName>Tetiaroa</iName>  <area>12.8</area></island>
```

The `<island>` tag serves in the affinity role to keep the two facts together; that is, Tahiti is grouped with its area and it is separated from Moorea and its area.

We're nearly done. The islands are not just randomly dispersed around the ocean. They are part of an archipelago, the proper name for a group of islands. So, we naturally invent one more tag, `<archipelago>`, and surround all of the islands with it. The result is shown in Figure 1.

```
<?xml version = "1.0" encoding="ISO-8859-1" ?>
<archipelago>
<island><iName>Tahiti</iName>    <area>1048</area></island>
<island><iName>Moorea</iName>    <area>130</area></island>
<island><iName>Maiao</iName>     <area>9.5</area></island>
<island><iName>Mehetia</iName>   <area>2.3</area></island>
<island><iName>Tetiaroa</iName>  <area>12.8</area></island>
</archipelago>
```

Figure 1 XML file encoding data for the Windward Islands database. The first line states that the file contains XML tags.

Notice that in Figure 1 an additional line has been added at the beginning of the file. This line, which uses the unusual form of associating question marks (?) within the brackets, identifies the file as containing XML data representations. (It also states that the file's characters are the standard ASCII set used in the U.S.) This first line is required and must be the first line of any XML file. By identifying the file as XML, hundreds of software applications can understand what it contains. In this way the effort to tag all of the information can be repaid by using the data with those applications.

*fit*TIP   **Start Off Right with XML.** XML files must be identified as such, and so they are required to begin with the text

```
<?xml version = "1.0" encoding="ISO-8859-1" ?>
```

(or other encoding) as their first line and without leading spaces. The file should be ASCII text, and the file extension should be `.xml`.

try it   Write an XML metadata coding for the following collection of data from the Galápagos archipelago.

Island	Area	Elevation
Isabela	4588	1707
Fernandina	642	1494
Tower	14	76
Santa Cruz	986	846

For the items of the same type as the data from the Windward archipelago, use the same tags; for the elevation, the highest point on the island, think up a new tag.

Answer: Using a tag name different from `<elev>` for the elevation is possible, but otherwise this is the one solution apart from spacing

```
<archipelago>
   <island> <iName>Isabela</iName>
      <area>4588</area><elev>1707</elev> </island>
   <island> <iName>Fernandina</iName>
      <area>642</area> <elev>1494</elev> </island>
   <island> <iName>Tower</iName>
      <area>14</area>   <elev>76</elev>   </island>
   <island> <iName>Santa Cruz</iName>
      <area>986</area> <elev>846</elev>  </island>
</archipelago>
```

Expanding the Use of XML

Given the XML encoding of two archipelagos—the Windward Islands and the Galápagos Islands—it seems reasonable to combine the encodings.

To create a database of the two archipelagos, we place them in a file, one after the other. This might seem odd because the Windward Islands have only two data values—name and area—while the Galápagos Islands have three—name, area, and elevation. But this is okay. Both archipelago encodings use the same tags for the common information, which is the key issue to consider when combining them. Extra data is allowed and, in fact, we might want to gather the elevation data for the Windward Islands.

With the two archipelagos combined into one database, we want to include the name of each to tell them apart easily. Of course, this means adding another tag for the name. We could use `<name>`, which is different from the `<iName>` tag used before. But in the same way that we added "`i`" to remind ourselves that it is an island name, it is probably wise to use the same idea to create a more specific tag name. Let's adopt the tag `<a_name>`. Notice the use of underscore, which is an allowed punctuation symbol for XML. We will place the name inside the `<archipelago>` tag, since it is data about the archipelago.

Finally, we have two archipelagos and we need to group them together by surrounding them with tags; these tags will serve as the root element of our XML database. A **root element** is the tag that encloses all of the content of the XML file. In Figure 1 the `<archipelago>` tag was the root element, but now with two archipelagos in the file, we need a new tag to enclose them. They are both geographic features of our planet, so we will use `<geo_feature>` as the tag that surrounds both archipelagos. The final result of our revisions is shown in Figure 2.

Notice that the text in the file has been indented to make it more readable. Like HTML, XML doesn't care about white space—spaces, tabs, and new lines—when they are between tags. This allows us to format XML files to simplify working with them, but the indenting is only for our use.

Attributes in XML

Recall that HTML tags can have attributes to give additional information, such as `bgcolor` in `<body bgcolor="blue">`. Our invented tags of XML can also have

```
<?xml version = "1.0"                          <archipelago>
      encoding="ISO-8859-1" ?>                     <a_name>Galapagos Islands
<geo_feature>                                      </a_name>
   <archipelago>  Day                             <island>
      <a_name>Windward Islands                        <iName>Isabella</iName>
      </a_name>                                       <area>4588</area>
      <island>  class                               <elevation>1707</elevation>
         <iName>Tahiti</iName>                     </island>
         <area>1048</area>                        <island>
      </island>                                       <iName>Fernandina</iName>
      <island>                                        <area>642</area>
         <iName>Moorea</iName>                        <elevation>1494</elevation>
         <area>130</area>                         </island>
      </island>                                   <island>
      <island>                                        <iName>Tower</iName>
         <iName>Maiao</iName>                         <area>14</area>
         <area>9.5</area>                            <elevation>76</elevation>
      </island>                                   </island>
      <island>                                    <island>
         <iName>Mehetia</iName>                       <iName>Santa Cruz</iName>
         <area>2.3</area>                            <area>986</area>
      </island>                                       <elevation>846</elevation>
      <island>                                    </island>
         <iName>Tetiaroa</iName>                </archipelago>
         <area>12.8</area>                     </geo_feature>
      </island>
   </archipelago>
```

Figure 2 XML file for the Geographic Features database. XML ignores white space, so the text in the file has been indented for easier reading.

attributes. They have a similar form, and must always be set inside the simple quotation marks—that is, the straight quotes, not the curly "smart" quotes. Tag attribute values can be enclosed either in paired single or double quotes. If the content of the tag attribute requires quotes or an apostrophe (the single quote), then enclose the attribute value in the other form of quotes. So, we might have

```
<entry warnIfNone="Ain't there!">The user entered this
data.</entry>
```

for one instance, and

```
<entry warnIfNone='I say, "Please Enter"'>The data is
from a user.</entry>
```

for another.

Understanding how to write tag attributes is easy enough. Even the rules for using quotes are straightforward. But, we want to use them wisely, which requires some thought.

The best advice about attributes is to use them for additional metadata, not for actual content. So, although we could have written

```
<archipelago name="Galapagos">
```

we chose not to because the name of an archipelago is content. A better use is to give an alternate form of the data, as in

```
<a_name accents="Gal&aacute;pagos">Galapagos</a_name>
```

which records that the second "a" in Galápagos is accented. The name of the islands is still given using a normal tag, but specifying accent marks separately simplifies searching and display options.

Effective Design with XML Tags

XML is a very flexible way to encode metadata. As we have described the archipelagos, we have used a few basic guidelines to decide how to use the tags. To emphasize these rules, let's review our thinking in creating metadata tags for the archipelago data, encapsulating it into three encoding rules.

Identification Rule: Label Data with Tags Consistently. *You can choose whatever tag names you wish to name data, but once you've decided on a tag for a particular kind of data, you must always surround it with that tag.*

Notice that one of the advantages of enclosing data with tags is that it keeps the data together. For example, the island of Santa Cruz in the Galápagos is a two-word name, but we don't have to treat it any differently than the one-word island names since the tags keep the two words together.

You may think that because we can choose our own tag names, it might be difficult to combine databases written by two different people—without planning ahead, they will probably choose different tags. Luckily, such differences are easily resolved: Because the tags are used consistently, it is possible to edit a file using *Find/Replace* to change the tag names. (There are other, more sophisticated ways to make them consistent, too.) For example, if your friend, who gathered the archipelago data for the Northern Hemisphere, used `<Name>` for the archipelago name rather than `<a_name>`, use *Find* to locate `<Name>` and *Replace* to substitute `<a_name>`. Of course, searching for `Name` alone and replacing it with `a_name` does not work since it would match and ruin the `<iName>` tags. (If such cases do get in the way, use the Placeholder Technique.)

Affinity Rule: Group Related Data. *Enclose in a pair of tags all tagged data referring to the same entity. Grouping it keeps it all together, but the idea is much more fundamental: Grouping makes an association of the tagged data items as being related to each other, properties of the same thing.*

We applied this rule when we grouped the island name and area data inside `<island>` tags. We did this because both items referred to the same thing, the island. This is an important association, because the area data is not just area data about some random place on the earth; it is the area data for a specific place that is named Tahiti. This is an extremely important result from the simple act of enclosing data in tags.

When we added elevation data as an additional feature of islands, we included it inside the `<island>` tags for the same reason. As the elevation data shows, it is not necessary for every instance of an object to have data for the same set of characteristics.

Collection Rule: Group Related Instances. *When you have several instances of the same kind of data, enclose them in tags; again, it keeps them together and implies that they are related by being instances of the same type.*

When we had a group of five islands from the same area of the ocean, we grouped them inside an `<archipelago>` tag, and when we had a group of two archipelagos, we grouped them inside a `<geo_feature>` tag. We also added the names to the archipelagos using `<a_name>`, because as a collection they also have this additional property that we want to record.

Notice that the Affinity Rule and Collection Rule are different. The Affinity Rule groups together the data for a single thing—an island. Typically, in this case the tags of the data values will all be different reflecting the different properties of the thing. The Collection Rule groups together the data of several instances of the same thing. Typically, in this case the tags—in our case `<islands>`—will be the same. The first association is among properties of an object, the second is among the objects themselves, which we also call *entities*. Notice that being grouped by the Collection Rule doesn't preclude being an object; the islands grouped together form a larger object, the archipelago, and so it has properties, too, such as a name.

The XML Tree

The rules for producing XML encodings of information produce hierarchical descriptions that can be thought of as trees. See Figure 3 for the tree structure of the encoding of Figure 2. The hierarchy is a consequence of how the tags enclose one another and the data.

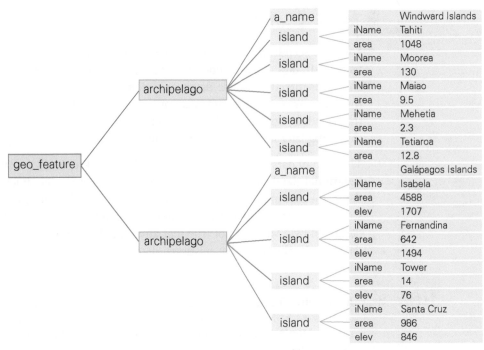

Figure 3 The XML displayed as a tree. The encoding from Figure 2 is shown with the root element (`geo_feature`) to the left and the leaves (content) shown to the right.

Table 1 Rules for writing XML.

Required first line	`<?xml version="1.0" encoding="ISO-8859-1"?>` must appear on the first line, starting in the first position.
First tag	The first tag encountered is the *root* element, and it must enclose all of the file's content; it appears on the second or possibly third line.
Closing tags	All tags must be closed.
Element naming	Observe these rules: • Names can contain letters, numbers, and underscore characters. • Names must not start with a number or punctuation character. • Names must not start with the letters xml (or XML, or Xml, etc.). • Names cannot contain spaces.
Case sensitivity	Tags and attributes are case sensitive.
Proper nesting	All tags must be well-nested.
Attribute quoting	All attribute values must be quoted; paired single quotes (apostrophes) or paired double quotes are okay; use "dumb" quotes only; choose 'opposite' quotes to enclose quoted values.
White space	White space is preserved and converted to a single space.
Comments	XML comments have the form `<!-- This is a comment. -->`.

Tables and Entities

You have seen how you can record metadata about a collection of data values using XML tags. For the moment, let's set aside the topics of tagging and XML, and focus directly on table database systems generally. We want you to understand the concepts of database organization and the desirable properties embodied in the metadata, not simply the way to encode that structure with tags. We'll return to tagging later in the next chapter, but for now, think of tables pure and simple.

The kind of database approach we will discuss is known as a relational database. **Relational databases** describe the relationships among the different kinds of data—the sort of ideas embodied in Affinity and Collection Rules—allowing the software to answer queries about them. Although every relational database can be described by XML, it is not true that anything described by XML is a relational database. It may seem that relational databases are limited, but their power is enormous.

*fit*BYTE   A **Bright Idea.** Though many people contributed to the creation of relational databases, E. F. Codd of IBM is widely credited with the original concept. He received the Association of Computing Machinery's Turing Award, the field's Nobel Prize, for the idea.

Entities

What *do* we want in database tables? Entities. "Entity" is about as vague as "thing" and "stuff," but the inventors of databases didn't want to limit the kinds of information that can be stored. An **entity** is anything that can be identified by a fixed number of its characteristics, called **attributes**; the attributes have names and values, and the values are the data that is stored in the table. (Unfortunately, *attributes* is an overused word in computing; in relational databases, think of an attribute as a "column of a table," where the "attribute names" are the column headings and the "attribute values" are the entries. We use the term *tag attributes* when we mean the attributes of XML.)

To relate entities and attributes to the metadata discussion earlier in this chapter, think of the attribute's name as the tag used in the Identity role, and the attribute values as the content enclosed in the tags. An entity is a group of attributes collected together by a tag used in the Affinity role. When describing affinity, we noted that the tagged data that we were grouping together all applied to one object, which was why it made sense to enclose it in tags. That object is the entity—the thing that the data applies to. Think of the tag used in affinity as the entity's name, and the tags that we allow within it as its attributes. So, an "island" is an entity, and its attributes include "name," "area," and "elevation"; see Figure 4. An "archipelago" is also an entity.

Island		
Name	*Area*	*Elevation*
Isabela	4588	1707
Fernandina	642	1494
Tower	14	76
Santa Cruz	986	846

Figure 4 **A table instance for the island entity.**

So, an entity defines a table. The name of the entity is the name of the table, and each of its possible attributes is assigned a column with the column heading being the attribute name. The values in the columns are the attributes' values, and the rows are the entity instances. We say **entity instances** for a row because a specific set of values for the attributes of an entity—that is, the content of the row—define one particular object, an instance of the entity. So, "name" and "area" are attributes of "island" generally, but "Tahiti" and "1048" define a specific island; a row with those values is an instance of the "island" entity. Any table containing specific rows is said to be a **table instance**.

In addition to having a name, attributes also have a **data type**, such as number, text, image, and so on. (We haven't been concerned about data types so far.) The data type defines the form of the information that can be stored in a field. By specifying the data type, database software can prevent us from accidentally storing bad information in a table. To connect the data type to the tagging discussed earlier, think of the type as a tag attribute, as in `<name type="text">` or `<area type="number">`, though database software uses other forms of metadata to record the data type.

*fit*BYTE

For the Record. Because databases are so important and long-studied, the concepts are known by several terms. The technical term for a row is a **tuple** (short u) from words like quintuple, sextuple, and septuple. Rows are often called **records**, a holdover from computing's punch-card days. Attributes are also known as **fields** and **columns**; an attribute's data type is sometimes referred to as its **format**. Tables are technically known as **relations**.

Properties of Entities

One curious property of a relational database table is that it can be empty. That is, the table has no rows. (Visualize the idea by deleting the last four rows of the table in Figure 4.) It seems odd, but it makes sense. Once we agree that an entity is anything defined by a specific set of attributes, then in principle a table exists with a name and column headings. When we specify entity instances, we'll have rows. So, among the instances of any table is the "empty instance."

Instances Are Unordered. Each distinct table is a different table instance. Two table instances will have a different set of rows. And, tables with the same rows, but reordered—that is, the same rows are listed in different sequence, say one sorted and the other unsorted—are the same table instance. Thus, the order of the rows doesn't matter in databases. We need to list them in some order, of course, but any order will do.

The attributes (columns) are also considered to be unordered, though we must list them in some order. Since the attributes have a name—think of the column heading or the tag—they do not have to be tracked by position.

Notice that the columns are unordered and the rows are unordered, but that doesn't mean that data in the table can go anywhere. Columns stay as columns, because they embody a kind of data being stored, and the items in a row stay as a row, because they are descriptive of an individual entity. The freedom to move the data is limited to exchanging entire rows or exchanging entire columns.

Uniqueness. There are few limits on what an entity can be. Things that can be identified or distinguished from each other based on a fixed set of attributes qualify as entities, which covers almost everything. Amoebas are not entities, because they have no characteristics that allow us to tell them apart. (Perhaps amoebas can tell each other apart, and if we could figure out how, then the characteristics on which they differ could be their attributes, allowing them to become entities.) Of course, one-celled animals are entities.

Because entities can be distinguished by their attributes, they are unique. Accordingly, in a database table no two rows can be the same. Unique instances is usually what we intend when we set up a database. For example, the database containing information about registered students at a college intends for each row—corresponding to a student—to be unique since the students are. When we set up the database, we ensure that we store information that uniquely identifies each student—such as name, birth date, parents' names, and permanent address.

In cases where the entities are unique but it is difficult to process the information, we might select an alternate encoding. For example, killer whales can be distinguished by the arrangement of their black-and-white markings. Even though images can be stored in a database, it is difficult to compare two images to determine if they show the same whale. So, we assign names to the killer whales, which are easy to manipulate, letting a human do the recognition and assign the name.

Notice that the two rows can have the same value for some attributes, just not all attributes.

Keys. The fact that no two rows in a database table are identical motivates us to ask which attributes distinguish them. In most cases, there will be several possibilities. Single attributes might be sufficient, like island name, or pairs of attributes like island name and archipelago name may be needed if certain island names, like Santa Maria, are common. Or we may have to consider three or more attributes taken together to ensure uniqueness. Any set of attributes for which all entities are different is called a **candidate key**. Because database tables usually have several candidate keys, we choose one and call it the primary key. The **primary key** is the one that the database system will use to decide uniqueness.

Notice that candidate keys qualify only if they distinguish among all entities forever, not just those that are in the table at the moment, that is, the given instance. For example, all currently registered college students might have different names (first, middle, and last taken together), making the name attribute unique for the current class. But, as we know, there are many people with identical names, and so that triple is not an actual candidate key.

If no combination of attributes qualifies as a candidate key, then a unique ID must be assigned to each entity. That's why your school issues students IDs: Some other student might match you on all of the attributes that the school records in its database, but because the school doesn't want to worry about the possibility of two distinct students matching on its key, it issues an ID number to guarantee that one attribute distinguishes each student.

Atomic Data. In addition to requiring a description of each attribute's type of data—for example, number, text, or date—databases also treat the information as **atomic**, that is, not decomposable into any smaller parts. So, for example, an address value

`1234 Sesame Street`

is treated in a database table as a single sequence of ASCII characters; the street number and the street name cannot be separated. This is why forms—both paper and Web—have separate fields for street, city, state, and postal code: Most uses of address information must manipulate the city, state, and postal code information independently, which means the data must be assigned to separate fields.

The "only atomic data" rule is usually relaxed for certain types of data, such as dates, time, and currency. Strictly speaking, a date value `01/01/1970` must be treated as a single unity; any use of the date that refers to the month alone has to store the date as three attributes: day, month, and year. But database software usually bends the rules, allowing us to specify the format of the data attribute, say `dd/mm/yyyy`, which allows the program to understand how the field decomposes. This format saves us the trouble of manipulating three attributes.

Database Schemes

Though tags may be a precise way to specify the structure of a table, it is a cumbersome way to define a table. Accordingly, database systems specify a table as a **database scheme** or **database schema**. The scheme is a collection of table definitions that gives the name of the table, lists the attributes and their data types, and identifies the primary key. Each database system has specific requirements for how a scheme is presented, so there are no universal rules. We use an informal approach in which the attributes are given by their name, a data type, and a comment describing the meaning of the field. Figure 5 shows a database scheme for the `Island` table.

```
Island

   iName            Text         Island Name
   area             Number       Area in square kilometers
   elevation        Number       Highest point on the island

Primary Key: iName
```

Figure 5 Database table definition for an `Island` table.

XML Trees and Entities

As mentioned earlier, relational database tables and XML trees are not the same. A full explanation of the differences is for database experts, but basically relational databases are more restrictive than XML trees; the limits make them more powerful and allow them to do more for us, as you'll soon see. For us, the main difference concerns the Collection Rule: When entity instances are grouped, all entities within the tag must have the same structure, because that structure defines the attributes that make up a row.

For example, the `Island` table for the Galápagos in Figure 4, which is a legal relational database table, can be encoded in XML as shown in the answer to the *Try It!*. So, the relational formulation and the XML formulation are the same. But, when we added the `<a_name>` tags inside of the `<archipelago>` tags, we violated the relational requirement that all entities have the same structure: The `<a_name>` was not an `<island>` entity. Including the `<a_name>` tag made sense for XML, but not for the relational model. So, they are related but not identical.

Database Tables Recap

Summarizing the important points of the last few sections, tables in databases are not simply an arrangement of text, but rather they have a structure that is specified by metadata. The structure of a database table is separate from its content. A table structures a set of entities—things that we can tell apart by their attributes—by naming the attributes and giving their data types. The entities of the table are represented as rows. We understand that rows and columns are unordered in databases, though when they are listed they have to be listed in some order. Tables and fields should have names that describe their contents, the fields must be atomic (i.e., indivisible), and one or more attributes define the primary key (i.e., field(s) with the property of having a different value for every row in any table instance ever).

Operations on Tables

A database is a collection of database tables. The main use of a database is to look up information. Users specify what they want to know and the database software finds it. For example, imagine a database containing Olympic records. There might be a table of participants for each Olympics, including attributes of name, country, and event; there might be a table of the medal winners for each Olympics, including attributes for the medal, the winner's name, the winner's country, and perhaps the score, distance, time, or other measure of the achievement. The database has many tables, but if we want to know how many marathon medalists have come from African countries, there is no table to look in—the table of medalists probably includes all winners in all sports, not just marathon winners from African countries. The data is in the database, but it's not stored in a single table where we, or the computer, can look it up. What we need to do is describe the information we want in such a way that the computer can figure out how to find it for us.

Database operations allow us to ask questions of a database in a way that lets the software find the answer for us. For example, we will ask for the number of African marathon winners by asking:

Put together the medalists for all of the Olympic Games (the operation will be called union), find the rows of medalists who won in the marathon (the operation will be called select), and pick out those who come from African countries (the operation will be called join). Count the resulting rows, which is the answer we want.

This example illustrates two important points. First, we can perform operations on tables to produce tables. It's analogous to familiar operations on numbers: Operations like addition combine two numbers and produce another number; operations like union combine two tables and produce another table. Second, the questions we ask of a database are answered with a whole table. If the question has a single answer—who won the marathon in 2000?—then the table instance answering the question will have only a single row. Generally there will be several answers forming the table. Of course, if there is no answer, the table will be empty.

In this section we illustrate the idea of combining tables to produce new tables. For this example, we imagine a table of the countries of the world as might be used by a travel agency. Its structure and sample entries are shown in Figure 6. Using that table, **Nations**, we'll investigate the five fundamental operations that can be performed on tables: **Select**, **Project**, **Union**, **Difference**, and **Product**.

Select Operation

The **Select** operation takes rows from one table to create a new table. Generally we specify the **Select** operation by giving the (single) table from which rows are to be selected and the test for selection. We use the syntax:

Select *Test* **From** *Table*

```
Nations
   Name         text        Common rather than official name
   Domain       text        Internet top-level domain name
   Capital      text        Nation's capital
   Latitude     number      Approx. latitude of capital
   N_S          Boolean     Latitude is N(orth) or S(outh)
   Longitude    number      Approx. longitude of capital
   E_W          Boolean     Longitude is E(ast) or W(est)
   Interest     text        A short description of the country

Primary Key: Name
```

Name	Dom	Capital	Lat	NS	Lon	EW	Interest
Ireland	IE	Dublin	52	N	7	W	History
Israel	IR	Jerusalem	32	N	35	E	History
Italy	IT	Rome	42	N	12	E	Art
Jamaica	JM	Kingston	18	N	77	W	Beach
Japan	JP	Tokyo	35	N	143	E	Kabuki

Figure 6 The Nations table definition and sample entries.

The *Test* is to be applied to each row of the given table to decide if it should be included in the new result table. The *Test* is a short formula that tests attribute values. It is written using attribute names, constants like numbers or letter strings, and the relational operators $<, \leq, \neq, =, \geq, >$. The **relational operators** test whether the attribute value has a particular relationship, for example, Interest = 'Beach' or Latitude < 45. If the *Test* is true, the row is included in the new table; otherwise, it is ignored. Notice that the information used to create the new table is a copy, so the original table is not changed by Select (or any of the other table-building operations discussed here).

To use the Nations table to create a table of countries with beaches, we write a Select command to remove all rows for countries that have Beach as their Interest attribute. The operation is

Select Interest = 'Beach' **From** Nations

This gives us a new table, shown in part in Figure 7. Notice that the information in the last column is constant because the *Test* required the word "Beach" for that field for all selected rows.

The *Test* can be more than a test of a single value. For example, we can use the logical operations AND and OR to search. So, for example, to find countries whose capitals are at least 60° north latitude, we write

Select Latitude $\geq$ 60 AND N_S = 'N' **From** Nations

which should produce a four-row table created from the Nations table's rows for Greenland, Iceland, Norway, and Finland.

Name	Dom	Capital	Lat	NS	Lon	EW	Interest
Australia	AU	Canberra	37	S	148	E	Beach
Bahamas	BS	Nassau	25	N	78	W	Beach
Barbados	BB	Bridgetown	13	N	59	W	Beach
Belize	BZ	Belmopan	17	N	89	W	Beach
Bermuda	BM	Hamilton	32	N	64	W	Beach

Figure 7 Part of the table created by selecting countries with a Test for Interest equal to Beach.

Project Operation

If we can pick out rows of a table (using **Select**), we should be able to pick out columns too. **Project** (pronounced *pro·JECT*) is the operation that builds a new table from the columns of an existing table. We only need to specify the name of a table and the columns (field names) from it to be included in the new table. The syntax is

Project *Field_List* **From** *Table*

For example, to create a new table from the **Nations** table without the **capital** and position information—that is, to keep the other three columns—write

Project Name, Domain, Interest **From** Nations

The new table will have as many rows as the **Nation** table, but just three columns. Figure 8 shows part of that table.

Name	Dom	Word
Nauru	NR	Beach
Nepal	NP	Mountains
Netherlands	NL	Canals
New Caledonia	NC	Beach
New Zealand	NZ	Adventure

Figure 8 Sample entries for a **Project** operation on **Nations**.

Project does not *always* result in a table with the same number of rows as the original table. When the new table includes a key from the old table (e.g., **Name**), the key makes each row distinct, so the new table will include fields from all rows of the original table. But if some of the new table's rows are the same—which can't happen if key columns are included, but can if there is no key among the chosen columns—they will be merged together into a single row. The rows have to be merged because of the rule that the rows of any table must always be distinct. If rows in one table are merged, the two tables will, of course, have different numbers of rows. So, for example, to list the **Interest** descriptions that travel agents use to summarize countries, we create a new table of only the last column of `Nations`.

Project Interest **From** Nations

This produces a one-column table with a row for each descriptive word: `Beach` appears once, `Mountains` appears once, and so on. Thus the table has as many rows as unique words, and because of merging, it does not have as many rows as `Nations`.

We often use `Select` and `Project` operations together to "trim" base tables to keep only some of the rows and some of the columns. To illustrate, we define a table of the countries with northern capitals, called `Northern`, and define it with the command

At60OrAbove = (**Select** Latitude ≥ 60 AND N_S = 'N' **From** Nations)

which is the table we created earlier. To throw away everything except the name, domain, and latitude to produce `Northern`, we write

Northern = (**Project** Name, Domain, Latitude **From** At60OrAbove)

as shown in Figure 9.

Name	Dom	Lat
Finland	FI	61
Greenland	GL	72
Iceland	IS	65
Norway	NO	60

Figure 9 `Northern`, the table of countries with northern capitals.

Another way to achieve the same result is to combine the two operations:

Project Name, Domain, Latitude **From**
    (**Select** Latitude ≥ 60 AND N_S = 'N' **From** Nations)

First a temporary table is created with the four countries, just as before. Then the desired columns are selected. It might be a slightly more efficient solution if we don't need the `At60OrAbove` table for any other purpose, but generally either solution is fine.

Union Operation

Besides picking out rows and columns of a table, another operation on tables is to combine two tables. This only makes sense if they have the same set of attributes, of course. The operation is known as `Union`, and is written as though it were addition:

Table1 + Table2

The plus sign (+) can be read "combined with." So, if the table of countries with capitals at least 45° south latitude are named `At45OrBelow` with the command

`At45OrBelow = (`**`Select`**` Latitude ≥ 45 AND N_S = 'S' `**`From`**` Nations)`

then we can define places with their capitals closest to the poles using the union operation. Call the result `ExtremeGovt` and define it by

`ExtremeGovt = At60OrAbove + At45OrBelow`

The result is shown in Figure 10. This table could also have been created with a complex `Select` command.

Name	Dom	Capital	Lat	NS	Lon	EW	Interest
Falkland Is	FK	Stanley	51	S	58	W	Nature
Finland	FI	Helsinki	61	N	26	E	Nature
Greenland	GL	Nuuk	72	N	40	W	Nature
Iceland	IS	Reykjavik	65	N	18	W	Geysers
Norway	NO	Oslo	60	N	10	E	Vikings

Figure 10 The `ExtremeGovt` table created with `Union`.

`Union` can be used to combine separate tables, say, `Nations` with `Canada_Provinces`. (`Canada_Provinces` gives the same data about the provinces as `Nations` does about countries, except the `Domain` field is `CA` for all rows.) For example, had the `At60OrAbove` table been defined by

`Select`` Latitude ≥ 60 AND N_S = 'N'`
`    `**`From`**` (Nations + Canada_Provinces)`

then the Yukon would be included because its capital, Whitehorse, is north of 60°.

Difference Operation

The opposite of combining two tables with `Union` is to remove from one table the rows also listed in a second table. The operation is known as `Difference` and it is written with the syntax

Table1 – Table2

The operation can be read, "remove from *Table1* any rows also in *Table2*." Like `Union`, `Difference` only makes sense when the table's fields are the same. For example,

`Nations — At60OrAbove`

produces a table without those countries with northern capitals—that is, without Finland, Greenland, Iceland, and Norway. Interestingly, this command works just as well if `At60OrAbove` had included Canadian provinces like the Yukon. That is, in a **Difference** command, the items "subtracted away" do not have to exist in the original table.

Product Operation

Adding and subtracting tables is easy. What is multiplying tables like? The **Product** operation on tables, which is written as

Table1 × *Table2*

creates a supertable. The table has the columns from *both* tables. So, if the first table has five attributes and the second table has six attributes, the **Product** table has eleven attributes. The rows of the new table are created by *appending* or concatenating each row of the second table to each row of the first table—that is, putting the rows together. The result is the "product" of the rows of each table.

For example, if the first table is **Nations** with 230 rows, and the second table has 4 rows, there will be 230 × 4 = 920 rows, because each row of the **Nations** table is appended with each row of the second table to produce a row of the result.

To illustrate, suppose you have a table of your traveling companions, as described in Figure 11(a), containing the information shown in Figure 11(b).

Travelers				Friend	Homeland
Friend	Text	A Traveling Companion		Isabela	Argentina
Homeland	Text	Friend's Home Country		Brian	South Africa
				Wen	China
Primary Key: Friend				Clare	Canada
(a)				**(b)**	

Figure 11 (a) The definition of the `Travelers` table, and (b) its values.

Then the **Product** operation

```
Super = Nations × Travelers
```

creates a new table with ten fields—eight fields from **Nations** and two fields from **Travelers**—a total of 920 rows. Some of the rows of the new table are shown in Figure 12. For each country, there is a row for each of your friends.

The **Product** operation may seem a little odd at first because its all-combinations approach merges information that may not "belong together." And it's true. But most often, **Product** is used to create a supertable that contains both useful and useless rows, and then it is "trimmed down" using **Select**, **Project**, and **Difference** to contain only the intended information. This is a powerful approach that we will use repeatedly in later sections.

To illustrate, suppose your traveling companions volunteer to tutor students preparing for the National Geographic Society's Geography Bee. Each friend agrees

Name	Dom	Capital	Lat	NS	Log	EW	Interest	Friend	Homeland
Cyprus	CY	Nicosia	35	N	32	E	History	Clare	Canada
Czech Rep.	CZ	Prague	51	N	15	E	Pilsner	Isabella	Argentina
Czech Rep.	CZ	Prague	51	N	15	E	Pilsner	Brian	South Africa
Czech Rep.	CZ	Prague	51	N	15	E	Pilsner	Wen	China
Czech Rep.	CZ	Prague	51	N	15	E	Pilsner	Clare	Canada
Denmark	DK	Copenhagen	55	N	12	E	History	Isabella	Argentina

Figure 12 Some rows from the supertable that is the product of Nations and Travelers. For each row in Nations and each row in Travelers, there is a row in the product table that combines them.

to tutor students "on their part of the world," that is, in the quarter of the planet from which they come. So, Isabella, who comes from Argentina in the southern and western hemispheres, agrees to tutor students on the geography of that part of the world, and so on. Then you can produce a master list of who's responsible for each country. We'll call it the **Master** table. It is produced by these commands:

```
Super  = Nations × Travelers
Assign = (Select N_S = 'S' AND E_W = 'W'
              AND Friend = 'Isabella' From Super)
       + (Select N_S = 'S' AND E_W = 'E'
              AND Friend = 'Brian' From Super)
       + (Select N_S = 'N' AND E_W = 'E'
              AND Friend = 'Wen' From Super)
       + (Select N_S = 'N' AND E_W = 'W'
              AND Friend = 'Clare' From Super)
Master = Project Name, Friend From Assign
```

Notice that we have used **Product** (×), **Union** (+), **Select**, and **Project**.

How do these commands work? The **Super** table is the product table discussed earlier with a row for each nation paired with each friend (see Figure 12). Then the **Assign** table is created by the **Union** operation (+) that combines four tables, each created by a **Select** operation from **Super**. The first **Select** keeps only those countries from **Super** with Isabella's name that are also in the southern and western hemispheres. The second **Select** keeps only those countries from **Super** with Brian's name that are in the southern and eastern hemispheres. The same kind of operations are used for Wen and Clare. The resulting **Assign** table has 230 rows—the same as the original **Nations** table—with one of your friends' names assigned to each country.

We know that all of the countries are in the **Assign** table because every country is in one of the four hemisphere pairs, and in **Super** there is a row for each country for each friend. When the right combination "comes up," the country will be chosen by one of the four **Selects**. In addition, **Assign** has the property that each person is given countries in "their" part of the world. (Wen has been assigned the greatest amount of work!) Finally, we throw away all of the location information to create our **Master** list, keeping only the names of the countries and the friends responsible for tutoring students about that geography. Part of the result is shown in Figure 13.

Name	Friend
Chad	Wen
Chile	Isabella
China	Wen
Christmas Is.	Clare
Cocos Is.	Brian

Figure 13 A portion of the `Master` table of your friends' assignments.

We have introduced five basic operations on tables. They are straightforward and simple. It is surprising, therefore, that these five are the only operations needed to create any table in a relational database. In practice, we will rarely use the operations directly, because they are incorporated into database software. When we want to create tables from other tables—an idea that is now quite natural—we will hardly be aware that we're using these operations.

Quotient Intelligence. There is a `Divide` operation on tables, but it's complicated and rather bizarre. Because it doesn't give us any new capabilities, we will leave it to the experts.

 ## Join Operation

Another powerful and useful operation for creating database tables is `Join`. Indeed, it is so useful that although `Join` can be defined from the five primitive database operations of the last section, it is usually provided as a separate operator.

Join Defined

`Join` combines two tables, like the `Product` operation does, but it doesn't necessarily produce all pairings. If the two tables each have fields with a common data type, the new table produced by `Join` combines only the rows from the given tables that match on the fields, not all pairings of rows, as does `Product`. We write the `Join` operation as follows:

Table1 ⋈ *Table2* **On** *Match*

The unusual "bow tie" symbol suggests a special form of `Product` in which the two tables "match up." *Match* is a comparison test involving fields from each table, which when true for a row from each table produces a result row that is their concatenation. To refer to attributes in each table, we use the notation *Table.Field*, as in `Master.Name`.

Join Applied

To show how `Join` works, recall the `Northern` table (Figure 9) and the `Master` table of your friends' assignments (Figure 13). The `Join`

`Master` $\bowtie$ `Northern On Master.Name = Northern.Name`

pairs all rows where the country name matches the home country of a friend. Which rows are those? This is how to find out. Beginning with the first row of the `Master` table (shown here):

Name	Friend
Afghanistan	Wen
Albania	Wen
. . .	. . .

the Afghanistan row does not have the same `Name` field as any of the four countries of `Northern`, so it is not part of the result. Nor does the `Name` in the second row of `Master` (Albania) appear as a `Name` field in `Northern`. Indeed, only four rows of `Master` have the same `Name` field as rows in `Northern`: Finland, Greenland, Iceland, and Norway. We combine those four rows with their corresponding rows in `Northern` to produce the four-row result shown in Figure 14. As you see, `Join` associates the information from the rows of two tables in a sensible way. Thus, `Join` is used to create new associations of information in the database.

There are at least two ways to think about the `Join` operation. One way is to see it as a "lookup" operation on tables. That is, for each row in one table, locate a row (or rows) in the other table with the same value in the common field; if found, combine the two; if not, look up the next row. That's how we explained it in the last paragraph. Another way is to see it as a `Product` operation forming all pairs of the two tables, and then eliminating all rows that don't match in the common fields. Both ideas accurately describe the result, and the computer probably uses still another approach to produce the `Join` table.

`Join`, as described, is called a natural join because the natural meaning of "to match" is for the fields to be equal. But as is typical of IT, it is also possible to join using any relational operator ($<, \leq, \neq, =, \geq, >$), not just = to compare fields. Unnatural or not, a `Join` where `T1.fieldID < T2.fieldID` can be handy.

African Marathon Runners

To complete the task we discussed earlier of finding out how many African marathon winners there have been in the history of the Olympics, we assume there are tables `Medalists1896`, `Medalists1900`, . . ., `Medalists2004`, and that there is a table, `Africa`, of African nation names, which includes colonial names like Rhodesia and modern names like Zimbabwe.

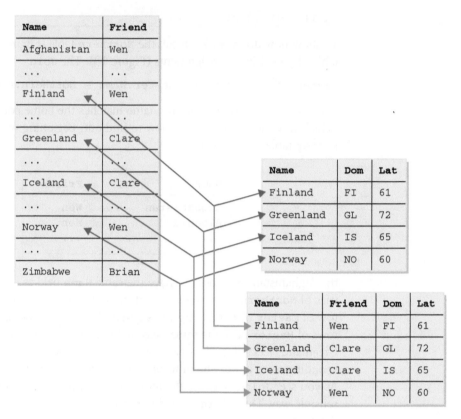

Figure 14 The Join operation: Master ⋈ Northern.

Assuming these tables, we write

```
All_Medalists = Medalists1896 + Medalists1900 +
                ... + Medalists2004
```

which is a lot of typing. The `All_Medalists` table contains the names, medal, event, and country of everyone who won in the Olympics. Next, we pick out the marathon winners with

```
Distance26 = Select medal='gold' AND event='marathon'
             From All_Medalists
```

The `Distance26` table contains all runners who received a gold medal in the Olympic marathon event. Next, eliminate everyone but the African winners with

```
Africa_marathon = Distance26 ⋈ Africa
                  On Distance26.country = Africa.name
```

producing a table of African winners. Counting the rows produces the result. Database software provides a function for counting the number of rows in a table, which is applied in the present case as

```
count(Africa_marathon)
```

Using the operators, we specified a set of tables that allowed us to find our solution. We will refine this skill after the next section.

 You Can Look It Up. Database systems such as Microsoft's Access, MySQL (pronounced my S-Q-L), and commercial database systems such as Oracle give users the ability to answer database queries using the five primitive operations and `Join`.

Structure of a Database

You have learned that by using the five primitive operations and `Join` we can create tables from tables to answer questions from a database. But usually these operations are used in a slightly different way. We don't usually ask a single question and quit. Rather, we want to arrange the information of a database in a way that users see a relevant-to-their-needs view of the data that they will use continually. Figure 15 shows a schematic of this idea.

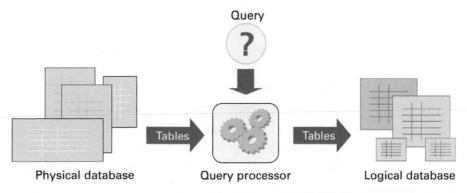

Figure 15 Structure of a database system. The physical database is the permanent repository of the data; the logical database, or view of the database, is the form of the database the users see. The transformation is implemented by the query processor, and is based on queries that define the logical database tables from the physical database tables.

In Figure 15 you see that there are two forms of tables. The physical database, stored on the disk drives of the computer system, is the permanent repository of the database. The logical database, also known as the *view of the database*, is created for users on-the-fly and is customized for their needs. Why do we use this two-level solution? The answer requires that we look a little closer at the two groups of tables.

Physical and Logical Databases

The point of the two-level system is to separate the management of the data, which is typically done at the physical database level, from the presentation of the data, which typically involves many different versions for many different users.

Physical Database. The physical database is designed by database administrators so that the data is fast to access. More importantly, the physical database is set up to avoid redundancy, that is, duplicating information. It seems obvious that data should not be stored repeatedly because it will waste space, but disk space is *extremely* cheap, implying that that isn't the reason to avoid redundancy. Rather, if data is stored in multiple places in the physical database, there is a chance—possibly, a good chance—that when it's changed in one place, it will not be changed in every other place where it is stored. This causes the data to be *inconsistent*.

For example, if your school stores your home address, and your major department also stores a separate copy of your address, then when you notify the school of your new residence, both addresses should be changed. But, with multiple copies, that might not occur. If the database contains two different addresses for you, then the school has no idea which address is correct; perfectly good information gets turned into garbage because it is inconsistent. For this reason, database administrators make sure that there is only one copy of each piece of data. That is, data is not stored redundantly.

It might seem risky to keep only one copy of the data: What happens if it accidentally gets deleted or the disk crashes? Database administrators worry about this problem all the time, and have a process of making backup copies of the database, which they store in a safe place, *never to be used*. That is, until the data is accidentally deleted or the disk crashes—in other words—when the other copy is gone. There is still only one copy.

Avoiding redundancy is obviously good, but keeping one copy seems to ignore the fact that multiple users need the information. The administration needs to send tuition bills, the dean needs to send notification that you "made the list," and the Sports Center needs to send you the picture of your photo finish; they all need your address. Where do they get their copy? That's where the logical database comes in.

Logical Database. The logical database shows users the view of the information that they need and want. It doesn't exist permanently, but is created for them fresh every time they look at it. This solves the problem of getting everyone a copy of the address. It's retrieved from the one copy stored in the physical database, and provided to the users as needed, fresh every time. Creating a new copy each time is essential, because if it were to be created once and then stored on the user's computer, then there would be two copies of the information again—the copy in the physical database and the one in the logical database—making the data redundantly stored. So, it never stays on the user's computer; it's always recreated. As a result, when you notify the administration that you moved in the morning, the dean can send you a congratulatory letter in the afternoon and have your correct address.

The other advantage of creating specialized versions of the database for each user is that different users want to see different information. For example, the Sports Center needs to record a student's locker number, but no other unit on campus cares. Similarly, the fact that a student is on academic probation is information that most users of the school's database don't need to know, and it should not be included in their view. In principle, each user wants a different view of the database.

Queries. Queries are the key to making this two-level organization work. Each user group, say the Dean's Office, needs a version of the database created for them. For each user table a query is formulated. A **query** is a specification using the five operations and `Join` that define a table from other tables. Think of the query as being written as described in the previous sections, but it is actually written in the standard database language SQL, short for Structured Query Language. Then, when the dean clicks on the table of Spring Term Grades, the database system runs the query that defines that table, creating it and displaying it to the dean. It probably doesn't exist in that form in the physical database, but `Select`, `Project`, and the other operations can define how to create it from the data that is physically stored. On the next day, when the dean opens the table of Spring Term Grades again, a new copy will be created, which means that the grade change made the previous afternoon by some physics professor (and stored in the physical database) will be visible to the dean.

It all seems pretty complicated, but it is not. Indeed, in the next section you will see that it is all rather straightforward.

Defining Physical Tables

In this section we define two tables to be used for illustration purposes, focusing on the roles of keys and relationships.

Database Schemes. Recall that the metadata specification of a database's tables is given by a database schema, or database scheme. Interactive software can help us define a database schema, but, as we saw earlier, declaring an entity's structure is easy enough to do without software. The database schema is important because it describes the database design. When we want to analyze a database design, we look at its schema.

To illustrate the basics of the two-level approach, imagine a college having a set of tables in its database schema, two of which are `Student` and `Home_Base`.

Student

Student_ID	Number	*Eight digits*
First_Name	Text	*Single name, capitalized*
Middle_Name	Text	*All other names, but family*
Last_Name	Text	*Family name*
Birthdate	Date	
Grade_Point	Number	*0 <= GPA <= 4*
Major	Text	*None, or degree granting unit*
On_Probation	Boolean	*0 is 'no'; 1 is 'yes'*

Primary Key: Student_ID

```
Home_Base
Student_ID       Number      Eight digits
Street           Text        All address info before city
City             Text        No abbreviations like NYC
State            Text        Or province, canton, prefecture ...
Country          Text        Standard postal abbreviations OK
Postal_Code      Text        Full postal code

Primary Key: Student_ID
```

Figure 16 shows the preceding table definitions as they appear in the Microsoft Access database system. Notice that they are different forms of the same thing.

Connecting Database Tables by Relationships

The **Student** entity records the information basic to the person's identity and associates a student with his or her **Student_ID**. This is the college's master record of each student. Part of each student's information is where he or she lives.

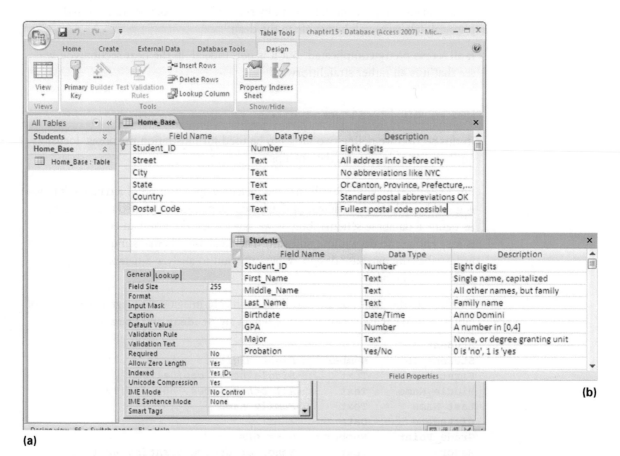

(a)

(b)

Figure 16 Table declarations from Microsoft Access 2007: (a) Home_Base table declaration shown in the design view; and (b) students table declaration. Notice that the key is specified by the tiny key next to Student_ID in the first column.

Though we could put addresses in the `Student` table, we decide not to. This is because other campus units will want to access the address information, but they shouldn't have access to all of the information (especially the sensitive information) about each student. The addresses are stored in a different table, the `Home_Base` table, which can have a lower security rating. Though these two tables are separate, they are not independent. The `Student_ID` connects each row in `Student` with his or her address in `Home_Base`. We say that there is a relationship between the two entities.

The Idea of Relationships. A **relationship** is a correspondence between rows of one table and the rows of another table. Relationships are part of the metadata of a database, and because they are critical to building the logical database from the physical database, we give them names and characterize their properties.

The relationship between `Student` and `Home_Base`—that is, for each row in `Student` there is a single row in `Home_Base` (found by the `Student_ID`)—will be called *Lives_At*. Setting up the tables in this way is largely equivalent to storing the address in `Student`, but not all relationships are so close. This one is especially close because it is based on the `Student_ID`, which is the key for both tables. (Recall that keys are unique, meaning no two rows can have the same value.) The *Lives_At* relationship is said to be one-to-one.

Because we used the key `Student_ID` in both tables, we not only can find the address for each student, but we can also find the student for each address. That is, there is a second relationship in the opposite direction, which we can call *Home_Of*, meaning that the home base entry is the address of the student who has that ID. Like *Lives_At*, *Home_Of* is a one-to-one relationship, because each row in `Home_Base` corresponds to a single row in `Student`.

Relationship Examples. Familiar relationships that we encounter every day illustrate that their description often ends with a preposition.

> *Father_Of*, the relationship between a man and his child

> *Daughter_Of*, the relationship between a girl and her parent

> *Employed_By*, the relationships between people and companies

> *Stars_In*, the relationships between actors and movies

Names of database relationships should be meaningful to help people working with the database, but like all names in computing, the computer doesn't know whether the name makes sense or not.

Relationships in Practice. Database software systems need to know what relationships exist among the tables if they are to help us create the logical databases. The systems allow us to define relationships among tables. The details are specific to each system, of course, but the example of *Lives_At* and *Home_Of* are shown in Figure 17 as they would appear in Microsoft Access.

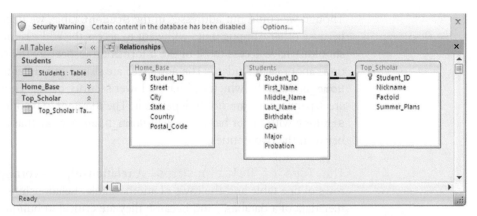

Figure 17 The *Relationships* window from the Microsoft Access database system; the 1-to-1 *Lives_At* and *Home_Of* relationships are shown between `Home_Base` and `Students`.

Defining Logical Tables

The school's administration probably thinks there is a single master list recording all of the data for each student. Because that's what they want to see, it's part of the administration's logical view of the database. So, we create it for them from the physical database.

Construction Using Join. The relationships between the `Student` and `Home_Base` tables allow us to construct a single table, `Master_List`, which contains the combined information from both tables. How? Using the natural `Join` operation, described earlier in this chapter. Recall that the natural `Join` creates a table out of two other tables by joining rows that match—it's an equality test—on specified fields. Thus, we write

```
Master_List = Student ⋈ Home_Base
              On Student.Student_ID = Home_Base.Student_ID
```

where the match is on the common field of `Student_ID`. Fields of the resulting table are shown in Figure 18. We don't lose anything by storing the basic student information in one table and the addresses in another, because with this simple command, we can create a table that recombines the information just as if it were stored in a single table.

The important idea here is that although we chose to store the information in two tables, we never lost the association of the information because we kept the `Student_ID` with the addresses. The relationship *Lives_At* lets us connect each student with his or her address by the `Student_ID`. The approach gives us the flexibility to arrange tables so as to avoid problems of redundancy—though we haven't demonstrated that benefit yet—while keeping track of important information, like where a person lives.

```
Student_ID
First_Name
Middle_Name
Last_Name
Birthdate
On_Probation
Street_Address
City
State
Country
Postal_Code
```

Figure 18 Attributes of the `Master_List` table. Being created from `Student` and `Home_Base` allows `Master_List` to inherit its data types and key (`Student_ID`) from the component tables.

Practical Construction Using QBE. Though it wasn't difficult to write the natural `Join` query in the last section to create the `Master_List` table, database systems can make it even easier for us. A technique developed at IBM in the 1970s, called **Query By Example (QBE)**, is available to us in the Microsoft Access system. Basically, the software gives us a template of a table, and we fill in what we want in the fields. That is, we give an example of what we want in the table, referencing fields from other tables that have already been defined. The software then figures out a query that creates the table from the sample table. It couldn't be easier! Figure 19 shows the QBE query window that will create `Master_List`.

The database software automatically creates the query needed for `Master_List`. What query did it create? We can ask and find out what it generated; see Figure 20. The query is expressed in SQL, the standard database query language. If we could read SQL—it's actually not too hard—we'd see that this query is the query we created for `Master_List`.

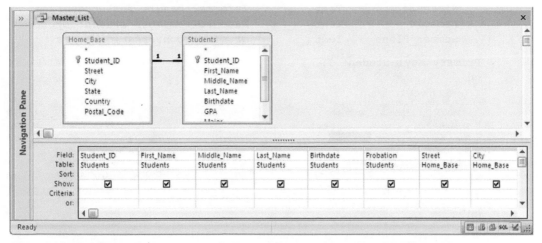

Figure 19 The Query By Example definition of the `Master_List` table from MS Access.

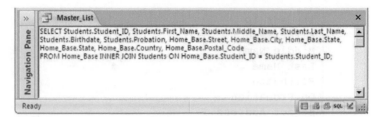

Figure 20 SQL query created from the Query By Example data in Figure 19.

The Dean's View

Because the school administrators probably want to see the entire student record, there isn't much advantage to breaking the files into smaller tables in the physical design, but it does make sense for others who only need to see parts of the database in their view. To illustrate one more logical database, we create a view for the dean.

Storing the Dean's Data. We imagine that the database administrators have set up a special table with the dean's record of the students in the college. The table definition is shown in Figure 21. The **Top_Scholar** is basically information of interest only to the dean.

The table has a one-to-one relationship with the **Home_Base** table, based on the **Student_ID** attribute, just as **Student** does: For each scholar, there is an address in **Home_Base**. Therefore, there is a relationship between the **Top_Scholar** and the **Home_Base** tables, which we'll call *Resides_At*. The relationship gives the dean access to the student's hometown, which is something the dean wants to be

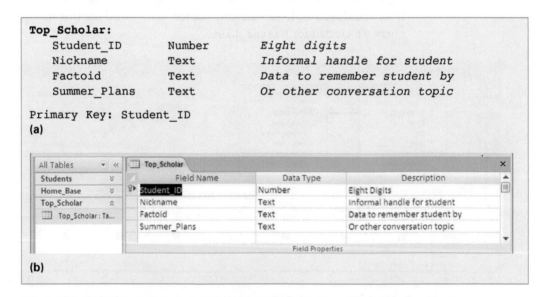

Figure 21 The **Top_Scholar** definition: (a) informal form, (b) in MS Access.

reminded of. Of course, there is a relationship in the opposite direction, too, from `Home_Base` to `Top_Scholar`.

`Student_ID` also connects `Top_Scholar` to `Student`. This is lucky, because otherwise the dean doesn't know a student's legal name, only the nickname. All of this data can be combined in tables for the dean's office using natural `Join` operations like we did in the last section, but the dean doesn't want to see all that information.

Creating a Dean's View. Imagine a table, known as the Dean's View, containing information specific to the dean's unique needs. For example, because the dean is not the person who sends letters to top students telling them they made the "Dean's List," the Dean's View doesn't need the students' full home addresses. (Someone else in the dean's office will need them.) The students' hometowns are enough information for the dean to make small talk at parties in honor of the good students. So the Dean's View will include information selected from the physical tables, as shown in Figure 22.

Deans_View		
Name	**Source Table**	
Nickname	Top_Scholar	Used by the dean to seem "chummy"
First_Name	Student	Name information required because
Last_Name	Student	the dean forgets the person's actual name, being so chummy
Birthdate	Student	Is student of "drinking age"?
City	Home_Base	Hometown (given by city, state) is
State	Home_Base	important for small talk, but full address not needed by dean
Major	Student	Indicates what the student's doing in college besides hanging out
GPA	Student	How's student doing grade-wise
Factoid	Top_Scholar	Data to remember student by
Summer_Plans	Top_Scholar	Or other conversation topic

Figure 22 The Dean's View fields showing their source in physical database tables.

Notice that the dean doesn't even want to see the student ID. We use it to create the Dean's View, but it doesn't have to be part of what the dean looks at in the database view.

Join Three Tables into One. The first step in creating a query for the Dean's View is to note that it contains information from three tables: `Top_Scholar`, the table actually storing the data the dean wants kept; `Student`, the college's permanent record of the student; and `Home_Base`, the college's current address list. The information for each student must be associated to create the `Deans_View` table, and the `Join` operation is the key to doing it. The expression

```
Dean_Data_Collect = ((Top_Scholar ⋈ (Student ⋈ Home_Base
                    On Student.Student_ID=Home_Base.Student_ID)
                    On Student.Student_ID=Top_Scholar.Student_ID)
```

makes a table that has a row for each student in the dean's `Top_Scholar` table, but it also has all of the information from all three tables for that student. The association of each student's row in each table is accomplished by matching on the `Student_ID` attribute.

Trim the Table. The resulting table contains too much information, of course, because it has all the columns from the three tables. The dean doesn't want to see so much information. So, the second step is to retrieve only the columns the dean wants to see.

The `Project` operation retrieves columns:

```
Deans_View =
    Project Nickname, First_Name, Last_Name, Birthdate,
            City, State, Major, GPA, Factoid, Summer_Plans
    From Dean_Data_Collect
```

In English, the query says, "Save the `Nickname` column, `First_Name` column, and so forth, from the table, `Dean_Data_Collect`, that is formed by joining—that is, associating on `Student_ID`—the three tables `Top_Scholar`, `Student`, and `Home_Base`." This is precisely what the dean wants. The query defines the `Deans_View` table. Although the dean probably thinks the table exists physically, it is created fresh every time it's needed.

The join-then-trim strategy used to create the Dean's View is a standard approach to creating logical tables: a supertable is formed by joining several physical tables. These are then trimmed down to keep only the information of interest to the user. The `Deans_View` query used `Project`, but `Select` and `Difference` are also frequently used.

Software Creates Dean's View. If we add `Top_Scholar` to the Access database schema given in Figure 16, and include the one-to-one relationship between it and the other tables based on the `Student_ID`, as shown in Figure 17, then we can use Query By Example again to define the Dean's View, saving ourselves the effort of working out our own query, though writing SQL directly wouldn't be that difficult. Figure 23 shows the QBE window from Microsoft Access that defines the Dean's View from the three tables.

For the record, the SQL query that Access produced for us based on our example from Figure 23 is shown in Figure 24. It is the identical query we developed ourselves, expressed in SQL syntax. (Notice that SQL uses the word "Select" where we used "Project"; the concepts are the same, but the term is different between the theory of relational databases and the SQL language. This naming inconsistency is an annoying feature of the study of databases.)

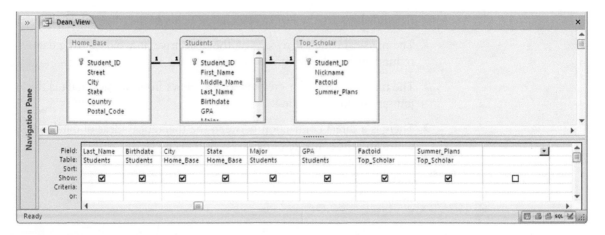

Figure 23 The Query By Example definition of the Dean's View table as expressed in Microsoft Access 2007.

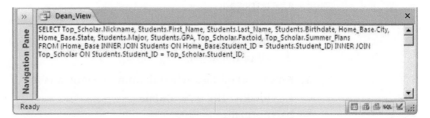

Figure 24 SQL query created for the Dean's View by the Query By Example data in Figure 22.

SUMMARY

In this chapter we followed a path from XML tagging through to the construction of logical views using QBE. You learned a lot, including:

> XML tags are an effective way to record metadata in a file.

> Metadata is used to identify values, can capture the affinity among values of the same entity, and can collect together a group of entity instances.

> Database tables have names and fields that describe the attributes of the entity contained in the table.

> The data that quantitatively records each property has a specific data type and is atomic.

> There are five fundamental operations on tables: **Select**, **Project**, **Union**, **Difference**, and **Product**. These operations are the only ones you need to create new tables from other database tables.

> **Join** is an especially useful operation that associates information from separate tables in new ways, based on matching fields.

> Relationships are the key to associating fields of the physical database.

> The physical database resides on the disk drive; it avoids storing data redundantly and is optimized for speed.

> The main approach for creating logical views from physical data is the join-and-trim technique.

> There is a direct connection between the theoretical ideas of database tables and the software of database systems.

 Review Questions

Multiple Choice

1. If you know the structure and properties of data you can
   a. retrieve it
   b. organize it
   c. manage it
   d. all of the above

2. An important task when defining metadata is to
   a. identify the type of data
   b. normalize the data
   c. define the affinity of the data
   d. more than one of the above

3. Which of the following is an invalid XML tag?
   a. `<address>`
   b. `<stud ID>`
   c. `<cellPhone>`
   d. `<SSN>`

4. Which of the following is a valid XML tag?
   a. `<active?>`
   b. `<grad-date>`
   c. `<zip code>`
   d. `<DOB>`

5. The first tag in an XML document is known as a(n)
   a. metatag
   b. tree
   c. root element
   d. entity

6. An XML comment looks like
   a. `<!--Updated 09-26-07-->`
   b. `<! Updated 09-26-07 !>`
   c. `<" Updated 09-26-07 ">`
   d. `</ Updated 09-26-07>`

7. In database terminology, a set of entities refers to
   a. field
   b. column
   c. table
   d. information

8. The kind of information stored in a field in a database is described by the
   a. tuple
   b. field name
   c. data type
   d. record

9. A `Project` operation will
   a. return a table with as many rows as the original tables
   b. return only unique rows and merge duplicate rows
   c. automatically sort the list in alphabetical order by the first field
   d. all of the above

10. The *Test* in a `Select` command is used to
    a. add rows to an existing table
    b. remove rows from an existing table
    c. include rows in a new table
    d. describe rows in any table

11. Databases store data just once
    a. in order to avoid data redundancy
    b. because data storage is expensive
    c. because data access is slow
    d. all of the above

Short Answer

1. _____ is information describing other information.

2. XML is _____, that is, the tags create the structure of the data.

3. XML should be edited with a _____.

4. XML attributes must be enclosed in _____.

5. A(n) _____ is a group of related items in an XML document.

6. The rules for XML encodings are a hierarchical description called _____.

7. _____ describe the relationships among the different kinds of data.

8. A(n) _____ is used to ensure that all entities in a database are unique.

9. Data that cannot be decomposed into smaller parts is considered _____.

10. A(n) _____ is a collection of table definitions that give the name of the table, list of the attributes and their data types, and identifies the primary key.

11. A(n) _____ is a specification using the five operations and `join` that define a table from other tables.

12. A(n) _____ between two tables means that there is a corresponding row in one table for every row in the other table.

Exercises

1. Use XML to define your class schedule.

2. Create a list of IDs you have that could be considered primary keys in a database.

3. For the following, either indicate that the field is atomic or divide the field to make the result atomic.

Field	Contents
Phone	(212) 555-1212
Name	Maria Murray
Class	CSE 100
City	Seattle, WA
DOB	September 26, 1948

4. Take your class schedule from Exercise 1 and define it as a database table.

5. Define the attribute names, data types, and optional comments needed to create a table that could be used as a datebook.

6. Write an operation to display the Name and Interest from the `Nations` table for those countries with Beach, and store it in a table called `Vacation`.

7. Create tables that might exist with your student information on campus. Include such areas as Registrar, Bursar, Library, Financial Aid, Food Service, Residence Halls, Parking, and so forth.

8. Take a look at one of your monthly bills, such as the cable bill, phone bill or utility bill. What fields are used and what is their structure?

9. Using a text editor, create your own XML file containing CD or DVD information. Open the file in a browser.

10. Create a table with information from your driver's license.

Answers to Selected Questions

Multiple Choice

1. D. Relational database are used for this.
3. B. XML tags cannot have a space in them.
5. C. The first tag encountered is the root element and must enclose all of the file content.
7. C. When entities are grouped, they become a table.
9. B. Duplicate records are combined.
11. A. Data redundancy is a major concern for databases.

Short Answer

1. Metadata
3. self-describing
5. quotes
7. trees
9. primary key
11. database
13. one-to-one relationship

10

The iDiary Database

A Case Study in Database Organization

Learning Objectives

> Explain the relationship between XML and XSL

> Describe how to express metadata using XML

> Demonstrate the incremental creation of a database

> Explain the relationship between tags and templates

> Show how to use tag attributes to display images

> State how information is hidden in XML databases

Software is like Entropy; it's hard to grasp, weighs nothing, and obeys the Second Law of Thermodynamics, i.e., it is always increasing.

—NORMAN AUGUSTINE

MANY PEOPLE keep a diary, and in the Information Age it is natural to keep it in digital form. It's not a blog—that's for information to be shared with others. A diary is for one's own personal use, and it is not for public entertainment. Traditionally, diaries have been text only, handwritten, and organized linearly. But in the world of online information, a digital diary can contain a wide variety of electronic information, including links to Web sites, photos, animations, as well as the daily record of one's private thoughts. In this new form, a diary is not a linear chain of text, but a personal database. And that fact makes it an ideal topic for a case study in creating databases, an opportunity to learn database principles in a personally useful way.

In this chapter we build a diary database by applying the XML approach to structure our data. That's our physical database. To display the iDiary, we convert the XML to HTML so it can be viewed with a browser. The conversion uses a language based on XML, called the Extensible Stylesheet Language, or XSL. Since the idea is that each of us will personalize a diary to our own needs, the database of this chapter only illustrates the *principles*. We create a fictional diary built around someone's record of the most interesting thing learned each day.

After illustrating an example of the database we will be creating, we review XML by constructing a small database recording the foreign countries we have visited. We then introduce XSL to display the Travels database. Prepared with the right knowledge, we incrementally build the iDiary database with its companion display information. We include text, titles, captions, images, videos, and poetry to illustrate how irregular data can be organized in a coherent, rational way. Finally, we consider how our database facilities will be used each day.

Thinking About a Personal Database

To start, we analyze the problem of making a personal database that can store any information that catches our interest. Though we will be thinking about how to solve the technical problems of database design, the discussion will guide us in the organization of the chapter as well.

Regular Versus Irregular Data

Relational databases, as discussed in the last chapter, can be expressed in neat tables with regular rows, attributes, keys, relationships, and so on. This regularity and the science of databases enable us to create queries in which computers do all of the difficult work of organizing and displaying the information we want to see. The key is the regularity of the data and the rigid structure imposed on it. Relational databases may be powerful, but very often the information we want to record isn't so homogenous. We need a more flexible approach. The iDiary database is an example of an irregular data collection.

We record things in the iDiary that we find interesting in our daily lives, which can be almost anything: text, photos, URLs to interesting sites, animations, poems, videos, and so forth. Because we don't want to limit the kinds of information we can store, we will use XML to specify the metadata, implying the database will be an XML tree. In tagging the items stored in the database, we will use the Identity, Affinity, and Collection rules. In this way the computer can know what kinds of data it is storing.

Collecting information into a heap, however, is not enough organization. We need to impose some structure on the data. Organizing it helps us keep track of what we have, and it also helps the computer to display it. Since it is natural to think of the iDiary being added to each day, we will organize the database in time sequence, that is, by date. That's not much structure compared to a relational database, but it will be enough to make our irregular data orderly enough to be useful.

Physical Versus Logical

The XML tree will be our physical database. It is the structure into which we store the data. Because our database is mostly an archive rather than a "working database," we do not expect continuous revisions and updates, but only additions. That means we do not worry about the sorts of things that concern database administrators, like redundancy and access speed. All we want is convenience, which will still take some preparation.

The logical database is, of course, our view of the iDiary. If it were a relational database, we could specify queries to show the information of interest to us, merging tables to have just the information of importance. But the XML tree is not a relational database. Instead of using queries, we create a short description using

XSL that picks out of the XML tree the data we want to display. The XSL description converts the data into HTML so that it can be displayed on the screen using a browser. As with all database views, the XSL approach gives us flexibility. We can decide to display everything in the XML tree, or we can choose instead only to display part of it—for example, the movie reviews—and leave everything else hidden. Therefore, the XSL description will be like our queries, plucking data from the physical database and showing us exactly what we want to see.

The iDiary

Our strategy will be to build the iDiary database and its stylesheet display together and incrementally. By beginning small and adding as we go, we will not be intimidated by a huge task. Also, if our small database is working and we then add some new feature to it, causing it not to work, we know that the error is in the part that was just added. This is a reliable way to limit the problems of debugging a complicated system. Finally, the step-by-step approach mirrors the way in which databases and other systems are enhanced over time. The plan will ensure success and be a good example for independent database projects.

Figure 1 shows a sample from the database we are creating. To familiarize yourself with the database, notice that the image of the database is a long list of daily entries. The entries are quite diverse—science news, poetry, book reviews, and other topics. Not only are these few entries interesting, but we expect that over time this will be a rich archive of factoids that we want to remember.

We build the iDiary after the next section. First, we need to explore the ideas with a practice database.

 ## A Preliminary Exercise

To become familiar with the techniques of creating and displaying XML databases, let's take a moment to construct a separate application, which is a database of countries visited. This database will have a similar organization to the iDiary, but is much simpler, allowing us to focus on how it's done.

Travels Database

Imagine that in our travels we have visited Italy, Switzerland, France, and Japan. Our database will list the countries, and for each country list a few places—usually cities—that we visited. We will use nontextual data by displaying the country's flag.

The XML Definition. Our entries in the database will be a list of countries, and each will have a name and a tour that contains a list of sights. The name of the file containing the country's flag will be given as a tag attribute for the `<name>`

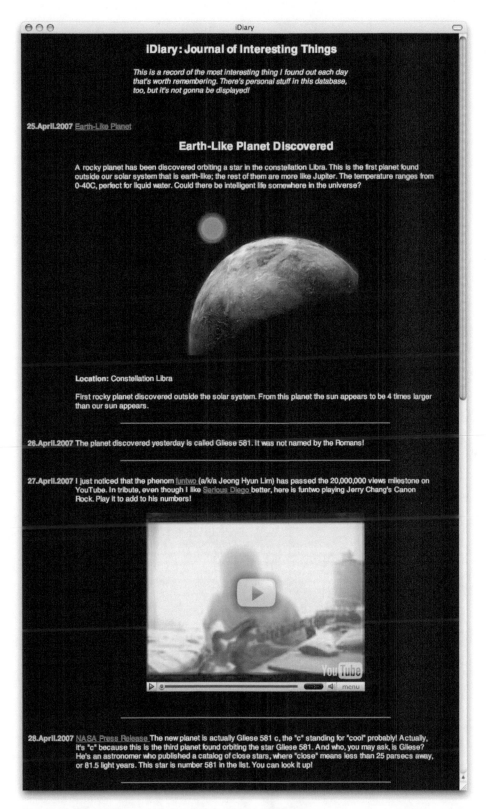

Figure 1 Part 1: An example of the planned iDiary.

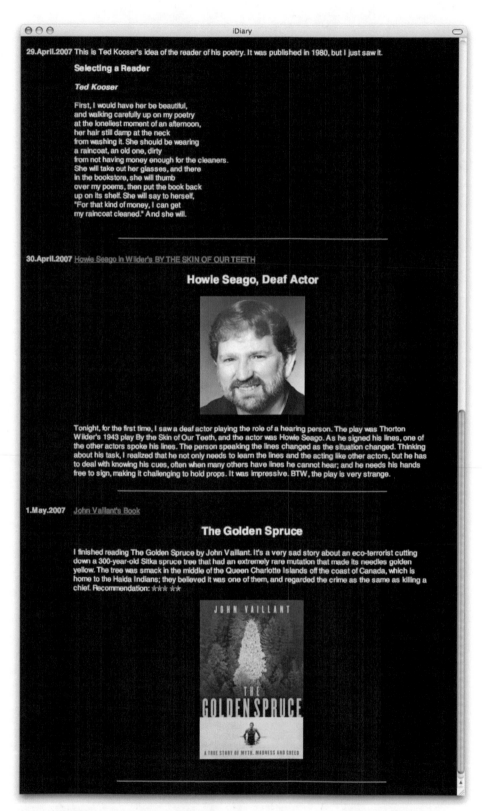

29.April.2007 This is Ted Kooser's idea of the reader of his poetry. It was published in 1980, but I just saw it.

Selecting a Reader

Ted Kooser

First, I would have her be beautiful,
and walking carefully up on my poetry
at the loneliest moment of an afternoon,
her hair still damp at the neck
from washing it. She should be wearing
a raincoat, an old one, dirty
from not having money enough for the cleaners.
She will take out her glasses, and there
in the bookstore, she will thumb
over my poems, then put the book back
up on its shelf. She will say to herself,
"For that kind of money, I can get
my raincoat cleaned." And she will.

30.April.2007 Howie Seago In Wilder's BY THE SKIN OF OUR TEETH

Howie Seago, Deaf Actor

Tonight, for the first time, I saw a deaf actor playing the role of a hearing person. The play was Thorton Wilder's 1943 play By the Skin of Our Teeth, and the actor was Howie Seago. As he signed his lines, one of the other actors spoke his lines. The person speaking the lines changed as the situation changed. Thinking about his task, I realized that he not only needs to learn the lines and the acting like other actors, but he has to deal with knowing his cues, often when many others have lines he cannot hear; and he needs his hands free to sign, making it challenging to hold props. It was impressive. BTW, the play is very strange.

1.May.2007 John Vaillant's Book

The Golden Spruce

I finished reading The Golden Spruce by John Vaillant. It's a very sad story about an eco-terrorist cutting down a 300-year-old Sitka spruce tree that had an extremely rare mutation that made its needles golden yellow. The tree was smack in the middle of the Queen Charlotte Islands off the coast of Canada, which is home to the Haida Indians; they believed it was one of them, and regarded the crime as the same as killing a chief. Recommendation: ★★★ ★★

Figure 1 Part 2: An example of the planned iDiary.

tag. Therefore, the database will be a sequence of country instances with the structure

```
<country>
    <name flag=file.gif> Country name </name>
    <tour>
        <sight> Sight name </sight>
        ...
        <sight> Sight name </sight>
    </tour>
</country>
```

We use a standard text editor to enter the data into a file, tagging as we go. Recall that to identify the file as XML, we must give it the `.xml` file extension and include as the first line of the file this exact text:

```
<?xml version = "1.0" encoding = "ISO-8859-1" ?>
```

However, if we use a computer configured for another language, the `"ISO-8859-1"` part may have to be changed to identify a different character encoding. Recalling that the root element is the Collective tag enclosing all items in an XML file, we make `<travels>` the root element of our tree, and within that we list countries using the structure just shown. Finally, we save the file as `Travels.xml`.

Direct Check of XML. We can have a browser display our XML as written by just opening the file with a browser, as shown in Figure 2. The browser looks for stylesheet information—we explain that momentarily—but finding none, it shows the XML tree. The color coding helps us to check that we have the structure right, and we verify that our intended organization is what the file contains. Notice that the display is active in that we can close and open tags used in the Affinity or Collective manner. For example, the inset in Figure 2 shows the result of closing the `<tour>` tags by clicking on the minus (–) signs. Closing parts of the database allows us to see the `<country>` tags without the clutter of the `<tour>` tags.

Displaying the Travels with XSL

The message from the browser in Figure 2 said that no style information was found. Style information tells the browser how to display a markup language like XML. Using the style information, the tags are eliminated and the information is displayed according to the style description. For example, the `Travels.xml` file can be displayed as shown in Figure 3 using XSL, which is designed to provide the style information. In this section we discuss how to do this.

*fit*TIP   **Use a Text Editor for XSL.** Like HTML and XML, XSL should be written using a text editor like Notepad++ or TextWrangler rather than a word processor like Word or Word Perfect. Text editors give you only the text you see, but word processors include their own tags that can confuse stylesheet processing.

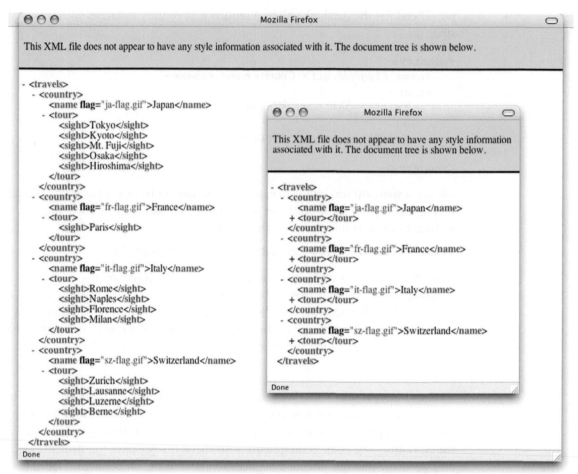

Figure 2 The display of the `Travels.xml` file using the Firefox browser. The inset shows the result of clicking on the minus signs (–) in front of the <tour> tags.

Connecting XML with Style. The XSL style information needed to display an XML file comes from a companion file, which has the file extension `.xsl`. So, we will put our style information in a file named `TravelsSS.xsl`. These two files get associated because we put in the XML file, as the second line, the text

```
<?xml-stylesheet type="text/xsl" href="TravelsSS.xsl"?>
```

which tells the browser, when it starts to process the XML file, where to find the style information. This is the line the browser didn't find in Figure 2. The line must be exactly as shown, except, of course, for the file name.

The Idea of XSL. Here's how XSL formats XML. The `.xsl` file contains a series of rules on how to format the information enclosed in XML tags. Expect one rule per tag. The rules are called **templates** in XSL, because they describe how the information is to look without actually having the information. (The information, of course, is in the XML file.) How does the template describe how the informa-

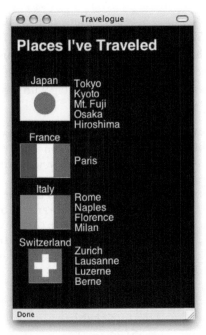

Figure 3 The display of the
`Travels.xml` file using the
`TravelsSS.xsl` style information.

tion is to be displayed? It uses HTML. And this is what makes XSL easy to learn:
It is basically describing a page with the familiar HTML.

Figure 4 shows this approach schematically. The database (DB) and stylesheet (SS)
are input to a transformer—which is part of the browser software—that "walks"
the XML tree, converting all of the tags to HTML according to the template's specification. When an XML tag is found, the transformer looks up the template for
that tag in the stylesheet file, and does what the template says, producing HTML
which is accumulated to be displayed at the end. Usually, each
template gives a bit of HTML and the transformer "stuffs in" the data from the
XML file in the right places. Finally, when the "walk" of the XML tree is over, the
HTML page is displayed.

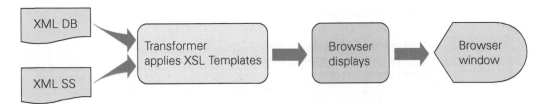

Figure 4 Schematic diagram showing how the XML database tree and the XSL style
information are merged to produce HTML; the final HTML result is displayed by the browser.

XSL Templates. It's time to look at some XSL templates. Figure 5 shows the XSL file used to display the image in Figure 3. Notice that there are tags everywhere. This is because XSL is really just XML! You will recognize the first line as the required first line of any XML file. The second line, also required, is a `<xsl:stylesheet ...>` tag with tag attributes specifying the details of the

```
<?xml version="1.0" encoding="ISO-8859-1" ?>
<xsl:stylesheet version="1.0"
    xmlns:xsl="http://www.w3.org/1999/XSL/Transform">

<xsl:template match="travels">
    <html><head><title>Travelogue</title></head>
        <body bgcolor="black" text="white">
            <font face="helvetica">
            <h2>Places I've Traveled</h2>
            <p>
                <table>
                    <xsl:apply-templates/>
                </table>
            </p>
            </font>
        </body>
    </html>
</xsl:template>

<xsl:template match="country">
    <tr>
        <xsl:apply-templates/>
    </tr>
</xsl:template>

<xsl:template match="name">
    <td align="center">
        <xsl:apply-templates/><br />
            <img src="{@flag}"/>
    </td>
</xsl:template>

<xsl:template match="tour">
    <td>
        <xsl:apply-templates/>
    </td>
</xsl:template>

<xsl:template match="sight">
    <br /><xsl:apply-templates/>
</xsl:template>

</xsl:stylesheet>
```

Figure 5 The contents of the `TravelsSS.xsl` file that produced Figure 3.

stylesheet; these make it an XSL file. After that come the templates, one for each tag. Notice that because the **<xsl:stylesheet ...>** tag is the root element of this XML file, it must be closed with **</xsl:stylesheet>** at the end.

There are five different tags used in the XML tree, and five templates in the XSL file, one for each. Notice that the templates have a standard form, which specifies how to display the tags in HTML.

```
<xsl:template match="tag name">
    ...
</xsl:template>
```

This **match** tag attribute tells which XML tag the template is for. Between the start and end tags is the specification in HTML (and possibly other XSL tags) for how to display the XML.

---

fit TIP   **Use the Right Style for XSL.** XSL files must be identified as such, and so they are required to begin with the standard XML tag on the first line

```
<?xml version = "1.0" encoding="ISO-8859-1" ?>
```

followed by the required XSL tag

```
<xsl:stylesheet version="1.0"
    xmlns:xsl="http://www.w3.org/1999/XSL/Transform">
```

on the second line. The file should be ASCII text, and the extension should be **.xsl**.

Because there are tags everywhere, it is important to understand how the computer tells them all apart—it's a good way for us to tell them apart! The tag at the start **<?xml...?>** is the standard XML tag. The tags beginning with **<xsl:...>** are XSL tags. The rest of the tags are HTML tags. So, when the transformer is using this file to look up how to display the XML, it can keep everything straight.

Next, we explain how each of the templates works.

Creating the Travelogue Display. Consider the templates of **TravelsSS.xsl**. The first template, which matches the **<travels>** XML tag, has the form

```
<xsl:template match="travels">
    <html><head><title>Travelogue</title></head>
        <body bgcolor="black" text="white">
            <h2><font face="helvetica">
                Places I've Traveled</font></h2>        Start of the
            <p>                                          HTML page
                <table>
                    <xsl:apply-templates/>
                </table>
            </p>                                         End of the
        </body>                                          HTML page
    </html>
</xsl:template>
```

Notice that between the `<xsl:template...>` tags are HTML tags, which you might recognize as the start of a Web page and the end of that same Web page. (We explain the `<xsl:apply...>` momentarily.) This template says that whenever the transformer encounters a `<travels>` tag in the XML file, it should include this HTML text as a description of how to display the `<travels>` tag. Of course, there is only one `<travels>` tag in the XML file, because it is the root element tag of the XML tree. So, the way to display this one tag is to set up the Web page for the display. Then, as the other tags are processed, they will fill in other parts of the page.

You can see that the template includes the necessary heading and body tags to make the image shown in Figure 3. At the "deepest point" in these tags are `<table>` tags, because the content of the `Travels.xml` file is going to be displayed as a table. Each `<country>` will be a row in this table, with the general structure

Info for `<name>` tag Flag display here	`<sight>` entry . . . `<sight>` entry

This structure calls for two items in the first cell of the table—the name and the flag image—and a list of items in the second cell, depending on how many sights there are in a tour.

We know that a row of the table will correspond to each `<country>` tag, because the template matching `"country"` places the `<tr>` tags for the table rows. Also, the `<name>` tag and the `<tour>` tags place the table data tags `<td>`. The following table summarizes the style roles of the XML tags we have.

XML Tag	XSL Template Task for Displaying the Tag's Data
`<travels>`	Set up the page, start and finish, including the tags for a table.
`<country>`	Set up a table row.
`<name>`	Set up the table data tags for the first cell of a row, place the name, skip to the next line, and place the image of the flag.
`<tour>`	Set up the table data tags for the second cell.
`<sight>`	Break to a new line and display the sight.

Each XML tag has a stylistic role to play in the overall creation of the Web page.

How does the data get inside the table data tags? As the transformer is processing the XML file, it is always looking for tags and trying to match them to the templates of the XSL file. Anything it finds that is not a tag—that is, the actual data—it puts directly into the HTML definition. So, to get the content of the file displayed requires no effort at all.

The Apply Operation. A curious aspect of the XSL specification in Figure 5 is the

```
<xsl:apply-templates/>
```

tag. We know from the `/>` that this is a stand-alone tag, like `<br />`, with no mate. Also, notice that the tag is included once in each of the templates. The `<xsl:apply-templates />` tag means, "now process whatever is inside this tag." So, for example, the template matching `<tour>`:

```
<xsl:template match="tour">
    <td>
        <xsl:apply-templates/>
    </td>
</xsl:template>
```

can be expressed in English as: "When encountering a `<tour>` tag, place a `<td>` tag in the accumulating HTML definition; then process the items found within the `<tour>` tag, which as we know will be a bunch of `<sight>` tags; finally, when that processing is over, place the `</td>` tag to complete the table data specification."

Notice that although the tag is called **apply-templates**, it really means, "now process whatever is inside this tag," even though it may not have any more tagged items, but only data. As you now know, when actual data is encountered, the transformer simply puts the data into the accumulating HTML definition, which is what we want.

Tag Attributes. Of special interest is the template matching the `<name>` tag, whose definition is

```
<xsl:template match="name">
    <td align="center">
        <xsl:apply-templates/><br />
            <img src="{@flag}"/>
    </td>
</xsl:template>
```

The template obviously places `<td>` tags for the left cell of the table row, but it is also responsible for including in its cell the image of the flag. To display an image requires the `<img src.../>` tag, of course, as can be seen on the fourth line. It has the usual form except for `{@flag}`. The `@flag` refers to the value of the tag attribute of the `<name>` tag, which gives the file name of the *flag*.`gif`; see the XML in Figure 5. By placing a tag attribute reference in braces, we cause the tag attribute's value to be placed inside the quotes specifying the file source name, as shown next.

```
<name flag="fr-flag.gif">
    France      <img src="{@flag}"/> ⟶ <img src="fr-flag.gif"/>
</name>
```

This is a standard technique for placing information in matched quotes, and we will have several opportunities to use it.

Summary of XSL. When we open our `Travels.xml` file with a browser, it looks to see what style information is provided. It finds that we specifed the `TravelsSS.xsl` file. After opening the style file, the browser's transformer begins to process the XML tree. Finding the `<travels>` tag first, it checks for a template in the `.xsl` file. Finding one, it does what the template says: Place the starting HTML commands in the HTML definition up to a `<table>` tag, then process the other information within the `<travels>` tag. When that's done, append the remaining HTML tags to the HTML definition, and, when finished, display the resulting Web page.

While processing "the other information within the `<travels>` tag," the transformer encounters more tags, which it matches with templates and follows their style specifications. Somewhere within each of those templates, there is a `<xsl:apply-templates />` tag, which requests processing of the information that the tag encloses. The process continues: match a template, do what needs to be done before processing the enclosed information, process the enclosed information, do what needs to be done after processing the enclosed information, and consider that tag processed. It's a very elegant scheme.

That's all you need to know about XSL, although it is a rich, complex language that gives much more power than we need to manage our iDiary.

 ## The iDiary Database

We are now ready to create the iDiary displayed in Figure 1. As explained earlier, we solve the problem incrementally, beginning small and adding more information and greater ability to process it as a Web page. It's a good strategy when creating anything significant.

 Computer Tutor. Read the following sections at a computer, and build the database along with the text; this is an extremely effective way to learn these concepts. Moreover, when finished you will have a database into which you can place your own curious information. Find all the necessary files at **www.aw.com/snyder/**.

The incremental approach will naturally lead us to follow these steps:

1. Getting started
2. Creating the first entry (April 26)
3. Thinking about the nature of things
4. Developing tags and templates
5. Critiquing and evaluating the results

These five steps will be the section headings for the following explanations.

Getting Started

Our first concern is building the XML database that will be the physical repository of our iDiary. Because XML allows us to think up the tags, and therefore lets us have any structure we want, we have a design task: We must figure out our needs and design a structure that meets those needs. In the present case, we need an XML tree in which we can store information about the interesting and curious things that we encounter in our daily lives. This naturally suggests a *sequence* of entries, perhaps one per day, which have a date entry and then the information that we are storing.

Creating the XML Database. With only this small amount of thinking, we can make two decisions about our XML database: First, we can decide on **<entry>** tags as the Affinity tags to enclose the information we add each day, and second, because we need a root element to enclose the **<entry>** tags, we can choose **<idiary>** as our Collection tag. So, with these two tags decided upon, we can already create a database that contains no data. We create a file with our text editor called **iDiary.xml** and enter into it

```
<?xml version = "1.0"
    encoding="ISO-8859-1"?>
<!-- <?xml-stylesheet
    type="text/xsl"
    href="iDiarySS.xsl"?> -->

<idiary>
  <entry> This is the first entry  </entry>
  <entry> This is the second entry </entry>
</idiary>
```

which has the form displayed at left. Notice that the stylesheet specification has been commented out (see the green text in the browser window), because we do not have a style file defined. We know we will need it, and have decided to call it **iDiarySS.xsl**. We can begin building it, now, too.

Creating the XSL Stylesheet. The XSL stylesheet will need to recognize the two kinds of tags. Using our earlier Travels database as a guideline, we decide to set up the page with the root element **<idiary>**, and have the **<entry>** tags produce successive rows of a table. (Of course, the table has only one column at the moment.) Using a text editor we enter the following lines in the **iDiarySS.xsl** file.

```
<?xml version="1.0" encoding="ISO-8859-1"?>
<xsl:stylesheet version="1.0"
    xmlns:xsl="http://www.w3.org/1999/XSL/Transform">

<xsl:template match="idiary">
```

```
<html><head><title>iDiary</title></head>
    <body bgcolor="black" text="white">
        <h2 align="center"><font face="helvetica">
            iDiary: Journal of Interesting Stuff</font></h2>
        <p align = "center">
            <table width="425">
                <tr><td><font face="helvetica"><i>
                    This is a record of the most interesting
                    thing I found out each day that's worth
                    remembering. There's personal stuff in this
                    database, too, but it's not gonna be dis-
                    played! </i></font></td>
                </tr>
            </table>
        </p><br />
        <p><table>
            <xsl:apply-templates/>
        </table></p>
    </body>
</html>
</xsl:template>

<xsl:template match="entry">
    <tr><td>
        <xsl:apply-templates/>
    </td></tr>
</xsl:template>

</xsl:stylesheet>
```

This contains the setup for the Web page, with the title, heading, and italicized comment at the start of the page. (A separate table was used for the italicized comment to keep it compact and narrower than the main table of entries.) The table containing the entries is also specified as part of the **<idiary>** template. The template for **<entry>** tags places the **<tr>** and **<td>** tags, and then processes the entry itself. This stylesheet produces

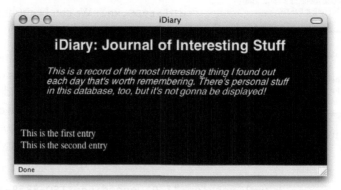

when we uncomment the stylesheet tag (the second line) of the XML file and open the XML file with a browser.

With the XML and the XSL files started, the iDiary project is well underway.

Creating the First Entry (April 26)

Continuing our design planning, we consider what goes inside of each `<entry>` tag. Since the entry is the entity that we're putting in the database, the items enclosed are the attributes (using the terminology introduced in the previous chapter). Obviously, the date is one attribute and, of course, there must be some actual content. This motivates two more tags, `<date>` and `<mit>`, which is an abbreviation for "most interesting thing." (Tags don't have to make sense to anyone but you, though it is often helpful to put in a comment saying what the tag means since you will almost certainly forget.)

Date Tagging. This sounds like a party game, but it refers to the decisions surrounding the metadata for calendar dates. Data in databases is atomic. If we write

```
<date>April 26, 2007</date>
```

we cannot refer to the day, month, and year separately, though, as we mentioned, some commercial database systems let us cheat. In the XML-XSL approach, if we want to control the formatting specially for dates, we need tags surrounding each of the components.

That might motivate us to put tags around the parts now, even if we don't have immediate plans to do something fancy, because we could add fancy formatting in the future.

On the other hand,

```
<date><month>April</month><day>26></day><year>2007</year></date>
```

is a lot to type just to enter the date, and there are many ways to change the date structure later if we decide we need the whole date tagged. So, being lazy, we decide to let it be atomic, and pick a date format we like and simply surround it with tags.

Revising an `<entry>`. With the two new tags decided upon, we can revise the two temporary `<entry>` tags used earlier and replace them in the `iDiary.xml` file with this single structure:

```
<entry>
    <date>26.April.2007</date>
    <mit> The planet discovered yesterday is called Gliese 581.
        It was not named by the Romans!
    </mit>
</entry>
```

Having added tags, we need to add templates to the `iDiary.xsl` file. The `<entry>` tag places the `<tr>` tags as before, but no longer places `<td>` tags. Its structure is

```
<xsl:template match="entry">
    <tr>
        <xsl:apply-templates/>
    </tr>
</xsl:template>
```

To handle the two new tags, we make a two-column table. The first column is assigned to the date, and the second column is assigned to the most interesting thing. The appropriate templates are

```
<xsl:template match="date">
    <td>
        <xsl:apply-templates/>
    </td>
</xsl:template>

<xsl:template match="mit"> <!-- Most Interesting Thing -->
    <td>
        <xsl:apply-templates/>
    </td>
</xsl:template>
```

which results in the following page, which displays the data for the April 26th entry in two columns.

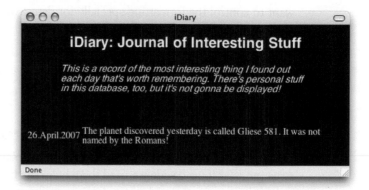

Critiquing the Design. In any design, it is wise to critique the result to determine if it meets our needs. The new page has two columns—one for the date and one for the entry—which is a rational way to present the information. The style could use some work, however.

One aspect that could be improved is the position of the date. The table row is two lines wide, causing the date to be centered vertically in its cell. We prefer to have the date at the top of the cell, so we revise its table data tag to include a vertical alignment tag attribute: `valign="top"`. Another feature we'd like to modify is the color and face of the date font. We prefer a sans sarif font like Helvetica, and think a red color might enhance the page. So, we revise the template to

```
<xsl:template match="date">
    <td valign="top">
        <font face="helvetica" color="red">
            <xsl:apply-templates/>
        </font>
    </td>
</xsl:template>
```

which produces the right result.

Thinking About the Nature of Things

The second column is for the "most interesting thing" we learn each day, but as Figure 1 shows, this entity can take many forms. The different kinds of data—the most interesting thing's attributes—affect both the XML and the XSL definitions.

Recognizing the Need for Specific Tags. When considering the design of the XML, notice that we must specify different data for each type of content that we attribute to an entity. The following list includes some examples.

Type	Specification
Link	URL
Image	Source file, and possibly width and height
Text	Written directly into the file, possibly with a special font
Video	URL, player dimensions, other parameters

Each of these requires that we specify different information. They also require different formatting. Additionally, the text can take several different forms, including:

Type	Style
Titles	Centered with enlarged sized
Captions	Labeled caption, left justified
Poems	Title, author, and line breaks at specific points

We cannot use a single type of tag if we intend to recognize these differences.

Choosing Specific Tags. Knowing that different kinds of data need different tags—or, stating it in database terms, each attribute requires its own tag—we assign a new tag to each kind of data we store in the iDiary database. Accordingly, we propose to use the following tags for the iDiary.

Tag	Encloses
`<fact>`	Normal text—the most interesting thing
`<title>`	Text to be centered; font is enlarged
`<link>`	Anchor text; the URL is a tag attribute
`<pic>`	Stand-alone tag with file name, width, and height as tag attributes
`<remark>`	Text to be left justified; for caption, include the word Caption, etc.
`<poem>`	Groups `<p_title>`, `<poet>`, and `<lines>` tags
`<ytvideo>`	URL of video

The **<poem>** tag is an Affinity tag grouping three other tags that give the title of the poem, the author, and the lines. Notice that in addition to **<title>** we include a **<p-title>** for the poems. The difference is that **<title>** will be centered and larger than the normal text, abstracting the idea of a heading; the **<p-title>** captures the idea of the title for a literary work, which will be italicized and not centered. Such distinctions are small, but if we recognize differences among the properties of an object or we are fussy about how we want our iDiary to look, we add tags to recognize such differences. And why not? Tags are free, and templates take half a minute to write.

The tags just enumerated are sufficient to handle the kinds of data displayed in Figure 1, but as new kinds of information present themselves, we can introduce more tags. Our database system can evolve to meet our needs.

Notice that because we recognized the need for different tags for different kinds of information that describe the most interesting thing, the role of the **<mit>** tag changes slightly. Previously it was an Identification tag, and it enclosed the most interesting thing, as if it were just a single thing, such as text. But because we now understand that the most interesting things can have many properties as identified by the foregoing tags, the role of the **<mit>** tag becomes that of an Affinity tag. It groups together all of the different forms of information that we associate with the most interesting thing for one day.

The change in the way we think of the **<mit>** tag is only a change in our thinking: The **<mit>** tag is still a sister to the **<date>** tag in the XML tree, it still identifies the most interesting thing, and its style role continues to be to place **<td>** tags.

Developing Tags and Templates

Having worked out that we need several new tags, we take a moment to think about each of them, because some have characteristics that need discussing. With each, we give its companion stylesheet template.

The Fact Tag. The simplest is the **<fact>** tag. It encloses text

```
<fact>The planet discovered yesterday is called
      Gliese 581. It was not named by the Romans!
</fact>
```

that is displayed in Helvetica font, with a line break at the end, as in

```
<xsl:template match="fact">
   <font face="Helvetica">
      <xsl:apply-templates/>
      <br />
   </font>
</xsl:template>
```

Keep in mind that the **<fact>** is enclosed by the **<mit>** tag.

The Title Tag. The `<title>` tag announces the most interesting thing entry, when appropriate.

```
<title>Earth-Like Planet Discovered</title>
```

The text should be centered and can use the HTML heading tags to enlarge the font.

```
<xsl:template match="title">
    <h2 align="center"><font face="Helvetica">
       <xsl:apply-templates/>
    </font>
    </h2>
</xsl:template>
```

We can also choose to use the same typeface as `<fact>` uses.

The Link Tag. The `<link>` tag specifies a Web link. As usual, the Web link has two parts: The tag encloses the anchor text—the highlighted text of the link—and the URL is specified using the tag attribute of that name. For example,

```
<link
url="http://www.npr.org/templates/story/story.php?storyId=9796321">
    Earth-Like Planet
</link>
```

illustrates the structure. The stylesheet must place an `<a href...>` tag and enclose the tag attribute value in quotes. A template to do that is

```
<xsl:template match="link">
    <a href="{@url}">
       <xsl:apply-templates/>
    </a>
</xsl:template>
```

As explained earlier in this chapter, the @ symbol is the XSL reference to the tag attribute of the XML tag. By enclosing the reference in curly braces, we can place the tag attribute's value in the HTML text.

The Picture Tag. The `<pic>` tag is a stand-alone tag because all of its information is expressed as tag attributes. The tag encodes the file name of the image and its desired display width and display height, as shown in this next example.

```
<pic file="planet.jpg" width="500" height="360"/>
```

Note that as a stand-alone tag, `<pic.../>` is terminated by the `/>`.

```
<xsl:template match="pic">
    <p align="center">
       <img src="{@file}" width="{@width}" height="{@height}"/>
    </p>
</xsl:template>
```

Of course, being a stand-alone tag, it does not enclose anything. Accordingly, there is no need for the `<xsl:apply-templates/>` tag that would normally request continued processing of the enclosed tags or content. This makes the `<pic>` tag slightly different from those we've seen.

The Remark Tag. Content such as captions and other small pieces of text that serve in a labeling role will use the `<remark>` tag. In addition to having a different role than the title, they differ in style: The text is the same size as the `<fact>` text and it is left justified rather than centered. For example:

`<remark>Location: Constellation Libra</remark>`

Because `<remark>` text may follow facts, pictures, and other items, it is necessary to include a break to ensure that they appear on their own line. Thus, the template is

```
<xsl:template match="remark">
   <br /><font face="helvetica">
      <xsl:apply-templates/>
      </font>
   <br />
</xsl:template>
```

As usual, we keep the font consistent.

The Poetry Tags. We identify several attributes of poetry—title, author, and lines—and assign tags to each. These will all be enclosed in the Affinity tag `<poem>`. As noted earlier, we do not use the `<title>` tag to title a poem. Rather, we invent another, `<p_title>` tag, which will also allow for different formatting. So, an example is

```
<poem>
   <p_title>Trees, Excerpt</p_title>
   <poet>Joyce Kilmer</poet>
      <line> . . . </line>
      <line>Poems are made by fools like me,</line>
      <line>But only God can make a tree.</line>
</poem>
```

The templates for these new tags are, by now, straightforward. They are

```
<xsl:template match="poem">
   <p><font face="helvetica">
      <xsl:apply-templates/>
   </font></p>
</xsl:template>

<xsl:template match="p_title">
   <h3><font face="helvetica">
      <xsl:apply-templates/>
   </font></h3>
</xsl:template>
```

```
<xsl:template match="poet">
    <h4><font face="helvetica"><i>
        <xsl:apply-templates/>
    </i></font></h4>
</xsl:template>

<xsl:template match="line">
        <xsl:apply-templates/>
    <br />
</xsl:template>
```

The poetry formatting will not be sufficient for poets like e. e. cummings, but we put that problem off for another day.

The Video Tag. The best way to include videos in the iDiary is to display a player as an embedded object. The `<object>` tag is part of HTML for incorporating multimedia, and the YouTube site, expecting us to use the `<object>` tag to run their videos, provides all the necessary HTML in a window pane labeled *Embed*, shown just below the URL in Figure 6.

The embedding information, which we can copy and paste, has the following form.

```
<object width="425" height="350">
    <param name="movie"
        value="http://www.youtube.com/v/QjA5faZF1A8"></param>
    <param name="wmode" value="transparent"></param>
    <embed src="http://www.youtube.com/v/QjA5faZF1A8"
        type="application/x-shockwave-flash" wmode="transparent"
        width="425" height="350">
    </embed>
</object>
```

This is obviously HTML, but mysterious HTML to us. However, we can avoid learning all of the details of this HTML by recognizing that the only part that changes from video to video is the URL; all of the rest of it is the same each time we want to embed a YouTube video. So, our new XML video tag needs only to capture the URL in a tag attribute; the rest of the `<object>` information can go into the template. Using the tag attribute for the URL makes it very similar to the `<pic .../>` tag Thus, our stand-alone video tag has this form:

```
<ytvideo utube="http://www.youtube.com/v/QjA5faZF1A8"/>
```

Notice that we name the tag `<ytvideo.../>` rather than, say, `<video...>`, because we are placing all of the display information in the template, which is special to YouTube. Other video sources might use different embedding tags with different values; if so, we can make a tag for videos from those sources. Also, unlike the `<pic.../>` tag, we do not specify the width and height for each video, because the player is the same dimensions every time.

Figure 6 YouTube display marking the embedding information.

The `<ytvideo...>` template contains all of the information from the YouTube *Embed* pane, except for the two URLs. We notice that they are the same, so we simply reference them, using the familiar `{@...}` structure to reference the tag attribute. The template is

```
<xsl:template match="ytvideo">
   <p align="center">
      <object width="425" height="350">
         <param name="movie" value="{@utube}"></param>
         <param name="wmode" value="transparent"></param>
         <embed src="{@utube}"
            type="application/x-shockwave-flash"
            wmode="transparent" width="425" height="350">
         </embed>
      </object>
   </p>
</xsl:template>
```

Notice that because `<ytvideo...>` is a stand-alone tag like `<pic.../>`, we do not need to process any enclosed information, so we do not need a `<xsl:apply-templates/>` tag.

A Check of the Design. We have added a variety of tags and templates. Normally, we check each new tag and each associated template as we create them. To summarize what we have done, we created the small page shown in Figure 7, and display it using a browser in Figure 8.

```
<?xml version = "1.0" encoding="ISO-8859-1" ?>
<?xml-stylesheet type="text/xsl" href="iDiarySS.xsl"?>

<idiary>
    <entry>
        <date>25.April.2007</date>
        <mit>
            <link url="http://www.npr.org/ ">Earth-like Planet</link>
            <title>Earth-like Planet Discovered</title>
            <fact>A rocky planet has been discovered orbiting a star in the
                constellation Libra. This is the first planet found outside our
                solar system that is earth-like; the rest of them are more like
                Jupiter. Is there intelligent life somewhere in the universe?
            </fact>
            <pic file="planet.jpg" width="125" height="90"/>
            <remark>Location: Constellation Libra</remark>
        </mit>
    </entry>
    <entry>
        <date>27.April.2007</date>
        <mit>
            <fact>These are Kilmer's most famous lines. </fact>
            <poem>
                <p_title>Trees, Excerpt</p_title>
                <poet>Joyce Kilmer</poet>
                <line> . . . </line>
                <line>Poems are made by fools like me,</line>
                <line>But only God can make a tree.</line>
            </poem>
            <ytvideo utube="http://www.youtube.com/v/QjA5faZF1A8"/>
        </mit>
    </entry>
</idiary>
```

Figure 7 Sample database entries for checking the iDiary tags and templates.

Critiquing and Evaluating the Results

As always, once a design is finished, it must be evaluated to see that it meets our needs. In Figure 8, we see several features worth reconsidering.

Form of Entries. The two sample entries seem to run together. Because this is a digital diary, we are not wasting paper if we space out the entries. So, we decide to add some breaks and a horizontal line at the end of the **<mit>** template to separate it from the entry that follows. This change is straightforward.

Also, we notice that the entry tends to spread out horizontally, as the browser expands the table to fill the available screen real estate. (The image has been purposely shown tiny to emphasize this point.) It might be more attractive if the

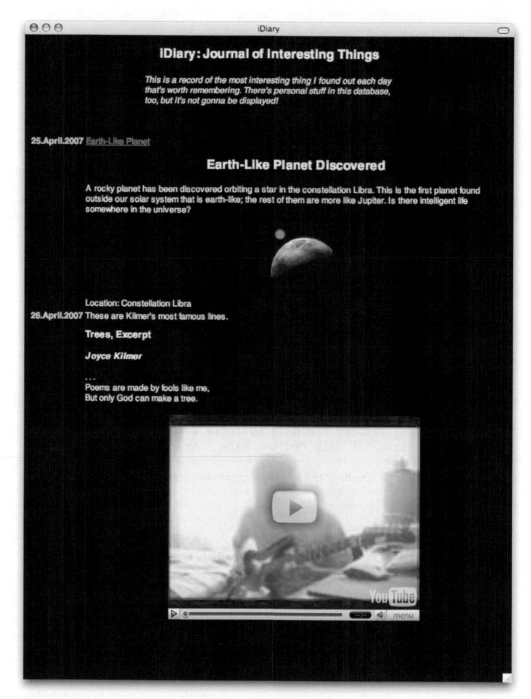

Figure 8 Firefox display of the sample diary in Figure 7.

entries are more compact, so that the text and pictures are more in scale. How do we make the entry compact? We limit the size of the table data by adding a width specification to the `<td>` tag in the `<mit>` template. Adopt a size of, say, 700 pixels.

These two changes, which affect only the template for `<mit>`, result in a new version as follows.

```
<xsl:template match="mit"> <!-- Most Interesting Thing -->
   <td width="700">
      <xsl:apply-templates/>
         <br /><hr width="75%" /><br />
   </td>
</xsl:template>
```

Our `<pic.../>` tag gives the ability to control the size of the images using the width and height tag attributes. Having adopted 700 pixels as the width of our `<mit>` entry, we should scale our images so their width is no more than 700.

 Scaling Images. Recall that images have a width and height given in pixels. This can be adjusted using graphics software, but it is not necessary. Simply scale (divide) both sizes by the same amount (rounding down to give a whole number), and use those values as the `width` and `height`.

Remarks On `<remark>`. The `<remark>` tag—the tag used for the Location information in Figure 8—should have the word Location emphasized in bold. This change has nothing to do with the type of data; we just prefer a different style. If we place `<b>` and `</b>` tags in the XML entry, they are treated as (meaningless) XML tags. Rather, we need to add a new tag, say, `<label>`, that labels the kind of remark we have in the database. For example, we could write

```
<remark><label>Location :</label>Constellation Libra</remark>
```

The `<label>` tag will have a template that simply places `<b>` and `</b>` tags around the information that it encloses.

Those are the only changes that we want now. The XML and XSL files are "living documents" in that we will be adding to the XML file daily, and if we add a new kind of content that we've never seen before—say audio—then we will make changes to the XSL templates.

Using the iDiary Daily

The database we created has the flexibility to record any digital data and to display it in an attractive way. We do not have to be constrained when we consider what was the most interesting thing that we learned. So we assume that adding to the iDiary is an activity that we will perform frequently.

Archiving Photos

As we've built the page, the `iDiary.xml` and `iDiarySS.xsl` files and the photos have all been on the desktop. They need to be placed in a permanent location. Because the page will likely include many photos, we should store them in a separate folder within the folder containing the two database files. Call the folder

imFiles, and notice that we have two choices for specifying the path to these pictures. We can put the path in the XML file as part of the **<pic.../>** tag, as in

```
<pic file="imFiles/planet.jpg" width="500" height="360"/>
```

or we could put it in the XSL file as part of the **<pic.../>** tag template, as in

```
<img src="imFiles/{@file}" width="{@width}" height="{@height}">
```

Though both solutions work, the first solution is the more flexible. By placing the full path in the XML file, image references can be in different places; if the path is specified by the template in the XSL file, then all files referenced by the **<pic.../>** tag must be in the same place. In fact, putting the path in the XML file allows us to make references to images stored elsewhere on the Internet.

Hiding Information

So far, we have displayed all of the information in the database, but we don't have to. We *do* have to tag everything, and we *must* provide a template to process each tag. But, we don't have to display it.

Suppose we have a tag, **<personal>**, that encloses our personal thoughts. Though the information can go anywhere in the database, we should consider where we want it placed when we do display it. Assume the **<personal>** tag is included inside of the **<mit>** tag, as part of the most interesting thing. Then, the template to display the **<personal>** content is

```
<xsl:template match="personal">
    <xsl:apply-templates/> <!-- Display personal information-->
</xsl:template>
```

as we expect; it's wise to include a comment to remind ourselves that we're displaying personal information.

Because the **<xsl:apply-templates/>** tag tells the transformer to "process the information enclosed in the matched tag," all we need to do is leave that tag out of the template. That is, we write

```
<xsl:template match="personal">
    <!--Don't display personal information-->
</xsl:template>
```

When the transformer gets to a **<personal>** tag, it will check to see what to do, and with no instructions to apply templates to the enclosed information, it will just skip the information inside the tags, as if it were not there. The result is that our personal content is not displayed, though it is part of the database.

Note that including personal information in the file without enclosing it in tags, or tagging it but not providing a template for the tag, both result in the information being displayed. In both cases the transformer doesn't know what to do with the information, so the transformer just adds the information to the HTML file, causing it to display on the page. Hiding information requires that we treat it properly, including saying how to display it. Not.

Entering Data into the Database

Because we have built our own database system without using commercial database software, we will be adding in new data using our trusty text editor, and we'll be tagging everything ourselves. But we can simplify the task so that it is not an annoyance by setting up our own template in the comments.

In the XML database we include a comment in the form

```
<!-- The following tags are available for adding a new entry.
   Change the places containing x's

<entry>
   <date>xxx.xxmonthxx.20xx</date>
   <mit>
      <link url="http://www.xxx/xxx"> xx anchor of link xx
      </link>
      <title>xx title of entryxx</title>
      <fact>xx facts are entered here xxx </fact>
      <pic file="xxx.jpg" width="xxx" height="xx"/>
      <remark><label>xxLabelxx</label> xx remark text xx
      </remark>
      <poem>
         <p_title>xx Poem title xx</p_title>
         <poet>xx author xx</poet>
         <line>xx line of poem xx</line>
      </poem>
      <ytvideo utube="xx YouTube URL xx"/>
   </mit>
</entry>


Edit all places with xx   -->
```

Then, by copying and pasting the interior portion of the comment—the `<entry>` tags and the lines they contain—we have all of the tags we need. We delete tags we don't need and edit those we do. This ensures that we match tags and don't make typing errors in the tags.

 SUMMARY

In this chapter we have applied the database ideas to a personally relevant task of making a digital diary capable of recording and displaying the many types of media we encounter online. From this case study you now understand:

> XML databases can record irregular data that relational databases cannot.

> An XML database can be directly displayed by opening it in a browser.

> Adding a stylesheet line to XML and building templates in XSL allows the XML file to be displayed using a browser.

> A complex database can be set up incrementally, adding tags and templates one at a time, and checking that they work as planned.

> An XML database can optionally hide some of its information, allowing for the selective display of its contents.

 Review Questions

Multiple Choice

1. The `<idiary>` tag is a
   a. Collection tag
   b. Affinity tag
   c. Identification tag
   d. none of the above

2. The `<country>` tag is a
   a. Collection tag
   b. Affinity tag
   c. Identification tag
   d. None of the above

3. The root element `<xsl:stylesheet...>` tag is a
   a. Collection tag
   b. Affinity tag
   c. Identification tag
   d. none of the above

4. XML files are viewable in a browser using:
   a. HTML
   b. XSL
   c. SQL
   d. none of the above

5. An incremental approach to development has the advantage of
   a. shortening development time
   b. making the final product smaller
   c. limiting errors to recently developed materials
   d. all of the above

6. When you open an XML file without a stylesheet in a browser, it
   a. won't display and returns an error
   b. displays the text of the file
   c. displays a tree showing the structure of your file
   d. brings up a dialog box to find the stylesheet

7. XSL tag rules are called
   a. licenses
   b. structures
   c. policies
   d. templates

8. The second line of an XML file that uses an XSL template begins with
   a. `<xml:stylesheet`
   b. `<html>`
   c. `<!--xsl`
   d. `<xsl:stylesheet`

9. iDiary is ordered by
   a. event
   b. date
   c. friend
   d. class

10. Each attribute in an XSL file requires its own
    a. file
    b. tag
    c. table
    d. link

11. To add entries to iDiary you would
    a. modify the XML file
    b. modify the XSL file
    c. make changes to both files
    d. once created the file cannot be changed

Short Answer

1. XSL stands for _____.

2. XSL templates describe how the information should be displayed by using _____.

3. XML and XSL files are combined in a(n) _____ where they're converted to HTML for display in a browser.

4. A(n) _____ tag is the top-most tag in an XSL stylesheet.

5. The root element tag of a stylesheet is a _____ tag.

6. A(n) _____ tag is used to produce successive entries on a page.

7. Items enclosed in an entity are called _____.

8. Each attribute in an XSL file requires its own _____.

9. A description of how a page should be displayed is called a(n) _____.

10. Use the _____ tag to embed multimedia in a page.

Exercises

1. Use XML to define your class schedule.

2. Create a list of other content that could be added to the iDiary database.

3. Design a database similar to iDiary with details for a vacation.

4. Create an online resume using XML and XSL.

5. Create a family history using XML and XSL.

6. Create an iStore database to display items you have for sale.

7. Use XML and XSL to create a testbank of true/false, multiple choice, and short answer questions. Build into it the ability to display pictures.

8. A used car dealer wants you to develop a Web site to display their vehicles. Their inventory changes daily. Explain what you would include on the site and how you would update on a daily basis.

Alan Kay is one of the earliest pioneers of personal computing, and his research continues today. In 1967–1969 Alan co-invented the FLEX Machine, one of the earliest modern desktops, and designed the "Dynabook," considered by many to be the prototype for the notebook computer. At Xerox PARC in the early 1970s Alan invented Smalltalk, the first complete dynamic object-oriented language, development, and operating system. There, he also invented the now ubiquitous overlapping window interface. Most of his contributions have been the result of trying to create better learning environments, mainly for children.

Alan has been a Xerox Fellow, Chief Scientist of Atari, Apple Fellow, Disney Fellow and a Senior Fellow at Hewlett-Packard. In 2001 he founded Viewpoints Research Institute, a nonprofit organization dedicated to improving education through new computing technologies where he continues to serve as President.

Alan has his BA in Mathematics and Molecular Biology with minor concentrations in English and Anthropology from the University of Colorado, 1966, and his MS and PhD in Computer Science from the University of Utah, 1968 and 1969. He is the recipient of numerous awards including the ACM Turing Award, the NAE Draper Prize, and the Inamori Foundation Kyoto Prize.

You started out in show business. What led you to become a computer scientist?

I was a professional jazz musician of modest abilities for about 10 years and did some teaching of guitar in that period. My general background included an artistic and musical mother, a scientific and mathematical father, and a grandfather who wrote and illustrated many books. So I grew up interested in many things and didn't make much distinction between what are called the Arts and the Sciences. I came across a number of books about computers and how to build them as a teenager in the 1950s, and when taking a computer aptitude test in the Air Force was an option, I took it, got a good score on it, and starting programming in the early 1960s.

In college I carried full majors in mathematics and biology and supported this by being a programmer at the National Center for Atmospheric Research in Boulder. I was also still playing jazz in clubs at this time.

I wound up at the University of Utah ARPA (Advanced Research Projects Agency) project for grad school in 1966 as a complete fluke without any planning or knowledge about ARPA. From the moment I got there and met (Professor) Dave Evans (later, my advisor) I "got" what ARPA was trying to do and it was a huge stroke of "romance" that I responded to.

How does the musician in you continue to influence the computer scientist?

Analogies can often be misleading, but there are some interesting ones to be made between music and computing (and mathematics and biology). The big ones for me have been the large aesthetic content of music and math and a wish for computing to always be that beautiful, the textures of different kinds of things interacting over time, the incredible ratio of parsimony to effect, etc.

You often talk about education and the art of teaching. Did someone in particular inspire your concept of the ideal teacher?

The initial ideas about "teaching people to think better—even qualitatively better" came from a number of science fiction novels, one of which led me to the General Semantics movement started by Alfred Korzybski. I also had one truly fantastic teacher in the fourth grade. She knew how to reach and realize the potential in the many different kinds of children in her classroom "without teaching," and she has been one of the main models for me for how to go about helping people learn.

You have said that "literacy is not just about being able to read street signs or medicine labels. It means being able to deal in the world of ideas." What does it mean to you for someone to be computer literate?

I like Frank Smith's general definition of literacy as something that starts with important ideas, finds ways to write them down in some kind of language, and helps develop more "readers and writers." The computer has ways of "writing" down representation systems of all kinds—it is a simulator and a metamedium. By metamedium, I mean that it is a holder of all the media you can think of, as well as ones you haven't thought of yet. Computer literacy is all about important ideas written and read as simulations. And the writing and reading are actually some kind of programming, where the programs—like mathematics or a musical score or an essay—are a means for expressing a powerful idea.

What many consider to be the prototype for the laptop computer is a machine you designed about 35 years ago, the Dynabook, yet, you often contend that the Dynabook is still a dream . . .

It is indeed now possible to not just make a physical Dynabook, but one with many more capabilities than my original conception. However, the physical part of the Dynabook is about 5 percent of the dream. In musical terms, we can now make the body of the violin but we are still struggling with the strings, fingerboard, and bow (the user interface that includes authoring) and we still only have a few instances of what the musical expression will be like (the content of the Dynabook). The other difficult part of the design is that we somehow want the early parts of the Dynabook experience to be a lot more value-laden and fun than learning to play the violin usually is. More importantly, we want users to keep experimenting, move on, and not get complacent as many do, for example, after learning to play three chords on the guitar.

What is Squeak?

Squeak is free and open source software, orignally created by my research team, for getting to better places in all the areas we've been discussing. It is derived from one of the last Xerox PARC Smalltalks and has been brought forward to twenty-first-century graphics, etc. It contains models of itself, which make it easy to port, and now exists on more than 25 platforms running "bit-identically" (exactly the same). From the computer science standpoint it is a little more interesting than most of the other stuff that is around, but pretty much all of its ideas date from the 1970s, so its interesting features are more of a commentary on what didn't happen in computer science in the last 20 years.

We have now done and tested a child's environment that is working out pretty well, and contains a number of new language and structuring ideas. This has been used to implement a much more comprehensive adult/media authoring environment (a kind of super-duper Hypercard) that contains the child's environment as a subset. This is essentially what we think the Dynabook should be like, plus, you can now download it and use it for free.

You have said, "The best way to predict the future is to invent it." What advice do you have for students who are planning a career in the field of technology?

Gain wide perspective by majoring in something else while an undergraduate. Try to find partial answers to Jerome Bruner's questions: What makes humans human? How did we get that way? How can we become more so? In other words, try to understand human beings and the role that representation systems for ideas have played in this journey called "civilization."

 ## Answers to Selected Questions

Multiple Choice

1. A. Collection tag
3. A. Collection tag
5. C. Debugging is easier because the errors are usually limited to newly developed materials.
7. D. The rules are called templates in XSL.
9. B. iDiary is organized by date. Each new date brings a new entry to it.
11. A. To add entries, simply add the changes to the XML file.

Short Answer

1. Extensible Stylesheet Language
3. Transformer
5. Collective
7. attributes
9. stylesheet

11

Algorithms

The central theme of computer science is the study
of algorithms. It is time now for us to focus on
this core topic. Our goal is to explore enough
of this foundational material so that we can
truly understand and appreciate the
science of computing.

Before a computer can perform a task, it must be given an algorithm telling it precisely what to do; consequently, the study of algorithms is the cornerstone of computer science. In this chapter we introduce many of the fundamental concepts of this study, including the issues of algorithm discovery and representation as well as the major control concepts of iteration and recursion. In so doing we also present a few well-known algorithms for searching and sorting. We begin by reviewing the concept of an algorithm.

1 The Concept of an Algorithm

Informally defined, an algorithm as a set of steps that define how a task is performed. In this section we look more closely at this fundamental concept.

An Informal Review

We have encountered a multitude of algorithms in our study. We have found algorithms for converting numeric representations from one form to another, detecting and correcting errors in data, compressing and decompressing data files, controlling multiprogramming in a multitasking environment, and many more. Moreover, we have seen that the machine cycle that is followed by a CPU is nothing more than the simple algorithm

```
As long as the halt instruction has not been executed
continue to execute the following steps:
    a. Fetch an instruction.
    b. Decode the instruction.
    c. Execute the instruction.
```

Algorithms are not restricted to technical activities. Indeed, they underlie even such mundane activities as shelling peas:

```
Obtain a basket of unshelled peas and an empty bowl.
As long as there are unshelled peas in the basket continue
to execute the following steps:
    a. Take a pea from the basket.
    b. Break open the pea pod.
    c. Dump the peas from the pod into the bowl.
    d. Discard the pod.
```

In fact, many researchers believe that every activity of the human mind, including imagination, creativity, and decision making, is actually the result of algorithm execution—a conjecture we will revisit in our study of artificial intelligence.

But before we proceed further, let us consider the formal definition of an algorithm.

The Formal Definition of an Algorithm

Informal, loosely defined concepts are acceptable and common in everyday life, but a science must be based on well-defined terminology. Consider, then, the formal definition of an algorithm stated in Figure 1.

Note that the definition requires that the set of steps in an algorithm be ordered. This means that the steps in an algorithm must have a well-established structure in terms of the order of their execution. This does not mean, however, that the steps must be executed in a sequence consisting of a first step, followed by a second, and so on. Some algorithms, known as parallel algorithms, contain more than one sequence of steps, each designed to be executed by different processors in a multiprocessor machine. In such cases the overall algorithm does not possess a single thread of steps that conforms to the first-step, second-step scenario. Instead, the algorithm's structure is that of multiple threads that branch and reconnect as different processors perform different parts of the overall task. Other examples include algorithms executed by circuits such as the flip-flop in which each gate performs a single step of the overall algorithm. Here the steps are ordered by cause and effect, as the action of each gate propagates throughout the circuit.

Next, consider the requirement that an algorithm must consist of executable steps. To appreciate this condition, consider the instruction

    Make a list of all the positive integers

which would be impossible to perform because there are infinitely many positive integers. Thus any set of instructions involving this instruction would not be an algorithm. Computer scientists use the term *effective* to capture the concept of being executable. That is, to say that a step is effective means that it is doable.

Another requirement imposed by the definition in Figure 1 is that the steps in an algorithm be unambiguous. This means that during execution of an algorithm, the information in the state of the process must be sufficient to determine uniquely and completely the actions required by each step. In other words, the execution of each step in an algorithm does not require creative skills. Rather, it requires only the ability to follow directions. (We will learn that "algorithms," called nondeterministic algorithms, that do not conform to this restriction are an important topic of research.)

Figure 1   The definition of an algorithm

An algorithm is an ordered set
of unambiguous, executable steps
that defines a terminating process.

The definition in Figure 1 also requires that an algorithm define a terminating process, which means that the execution of an algorithm must lead to an end. The origin of this requirement is in theoretical computer science, where the goal is to answer such questions as "What are the ultimate limitations of algorithms and machines?" Here computer science seeks to distinguish between problems whose answers can be obtained algorithmically and problems whose answers lie beyond the capabilities of algorithmic systems. In this context, a line is drawn between processes that culminate with an answer and those that merely proceed forever without producing a result.

There are, however, meaningful applications for nonterminating processes, including monitoring the vital signs of a hospital patient and maintaining an aircraft's altitude in flight. Some would argue that these applications involve merely the repetition of algorithms, each of which reaches an end and then automatically repeats. Others would counter that such arguments are simply attempts to cling to an overly restrictive formal definition. In any case, the result is that the term *algorithm* is often used in applied, or informal settings in reference to sets of steps that do not necessarily define terminating processes. An example is the long-division "algorithm" that does not define a terminating process for dividing 1 by 3. Technically, such instances represent misuses of the term.

The Abstract Nature of Algorithms

It is important to emphasize the distinction between an algorithm and its representation—a distinction that is analogous to that between a story and a book. A story is abstract, or conceptual, in nature; a book is a physical representation of a story. If a book is translated into another language or republished in a different format, it is merely the representation of the story that changes—the story itself remains the same.

In the same manner, an algorithm is abstract and distinct from its representation. A single algorithm can be represented in many ways. As an example, the algorithm for converting temperature readings from Celsius to Fahrenheit is traditionally represented as the algebraic formula

$$F = (9/5)C + 32$$

But it could be represented by the instruction

Multiply the temperature reading in Celsius by $9/5$
and then add 32 to the product

or even in the form of an electronic circuit. In each case the underlying algorithm is the same; only the representations differ.

The distinction between an algorithm and its representation presents a problem when we try to communicate algorithms. A common example involves the level of detail at which an algorithm must be described. Among meteorologists, the instruction "Convert the Celsius reading to its Fahrenheit equivalent" suffices, but a layperson, requiring a more detailed description, might argue that the instruction is ambiguous. The problem, however, is not with the underlying algorithm but that the algorithm is not represented in enough detail for the layperson. In the next section we will see how the concept of primitives can be used to eliminate such ambiguity problems in an algorithm's representation.

Finally, while on the subject of algorithms and their representations, we should clarify the distinction between two other related concepts—programs and processes. A program is a representation of an algorithm. (Here we are using the term *algorithm* in its less formal sense in that many programs are representations of nonterminating "algorithms.") In fact, within the computing community the term *program* usually refers to a formal representation of an algorithm designed for computer application. We defined a *process* to be the activity of executing a program. Note, however, that to execute a program is to execute the algorithm represented by the program, so a process could equivalently be defined as the activity of executing an algorithm. We conclude that programs, algorithms, and processes are distinct, yet related, entities. A program is the representation of an algorithm, whereas a process is the activity of executing an algorithm.

Questions & Exercises

1. Summarize the distinctions between a process, an algorithm, and a program.
2. Give some examples of algorithms with which you are familiar. Are they really algorithms in the precise sense?
3. Identify some points of vagueness in our informal definition of an algorithm introduced in Section 1 of the introductory chapter.
4. In what sense do the steps described by the following list of instructions fail to constitute an algorithm?

   Step 1. Take a coin out of your pocket and put it on the table.

   Step 2. Return to Step 1.

2 Algorithm Representation

In this section we consider issues relating to an algorithm's representation. Our goal is to introduce the basic concepts of primitives and pseudocode as well as to establish a representation system for our own use.

Primitives

The representation of an algorithm requires some form of language. In the case of humans this might be a traditional natural language (English, Spanish, Russian,

Japanese) or perhaps the language of pictures, as demonstrated in Figure 2, which describes an algorithm for folding a bird from a square piece of paper. Often, however, such natural channels of communication lead to misunderstandings, sometimes because the terminology used has more than one meaning. (The sentence, "Visiting grandchildren can be nerve-racking," could mean either that the grandchildren cause problems when they come to visit or that going to see them is problematic.) Problems also arise over misunderstandings regarding the level of detail required. Few readers could successfully fold a bird from the directions given in Figure 2, yet a student of origami would probably have little difficulty. In short, communication problems arise when the language used for an algorithm's representation is not precisely defined or when information is not given in adequate detail.

Figure 2   Folding a bird from a square piece of paper

Computer science approaches these problems by establishing a well-defined set of building blocks from which algorithm representations can be constructed. Such a building block is called a **primitive.** Assigning precise definitions to these primitives removes many problems of ambiguity, and requiring algorithms to be described in terms of these primitives establishes a uniform level of detail. A collection of primitives along with a collection of rules stating how the primitives can be combined to represent more complex ideas constitutes a **programming language.**

Each primitive has its own syntax and semantics. Syntax refers to the primitive's symbolic representation; semantics refers to the meaning of the primitive. The syntax of *air* consists of three symbols, whereas the semantics is a gaseous substance that surrounds the world. As an example, Figure 3 presents some of the primitives used in origami.

Figure 3   Origami primitives

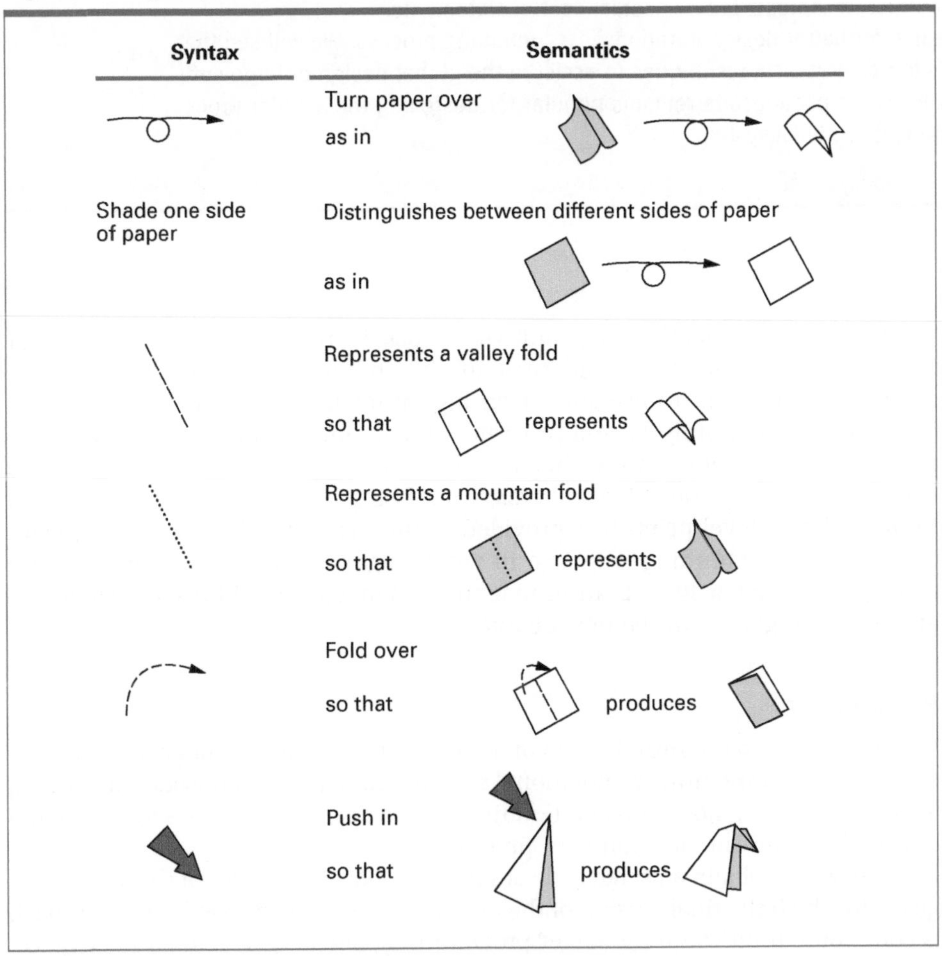

Algorithm Representation During Algorithm Design

The task of designing a complex algorithm requires that the designer keep track of numerous interrelated concepts—a requirement that can exceed the capabilities of the human mind. Thus the designer of complex algorithms needs a way to record and recall portions of an evolving algorithm as his or her concentration requires.

During the 1950s and 1960s, flowcharts (by which algorithms are represented by geometric shapes connected by arrows) were the state-of-the-art design tool. However, flowcharts often became tangled webs of crisscrossing arrows that made understanding the structure of the underlying algorithm difficult. Thus the use of flowcharts as design tools has given way to other representation techniques. An example is the pseudocode used in this text, by which algorithms are represented with well-defined textual structures. Flowcharts are still beneficial when the goal is presentation rather than design. For example, Figures 8 and 9 apply flowchart notation to demonstrate the algorithmic structure represented by popular control statements.

The search for better design notations is a continuing process. We will see that the trend is to use graphical techniques to assist in the global design of large software systems, while pseudocode remains popular for designing the smaller procedural components within a system.

To obtain a collection of primitives to use in representing algorithms for computer execution, we could turn to the individual instructions that the machine is designed to execute. If an algorithm is expressed at this level of detail, we will certainly have a program suitable for machine execution. However, expressing algorithms at this level is tedious, and so one normally uses a collection of "higher-level" primitives, each being an abstract tool constructed from the lower-level primitives provided in the machine's language. The result is a formal programming language in which algorithms can be expressed at a conceptually higher level than in machine language. We will discuss such programming languages in the next chapter.

Pseudocode

For now, we forgo the introduction of a formal programming language in favor of a less formal, more intuitive notational system known as pseudocode. In general, a **pseudocode** is a notational system in which ideas can be expressed informally during the algorithm development process.

One way to obtain a pseudocode is simply to loosen the rules of the formal language in which the final version of the algorithm is to be expressed. This approach is commonly used when the target programming language is known in advance.

There the pseudocode used during the early stages of program development consists of syntax-semantic structures similar to, but less formal than, those used in the target programming language.

Our goal, however, is to consider the issues of algorithm development and representation without confining our discussion to a particular programming language. Thus our approach to pseudocode is to develop a consistent, concise notation for representing recurring semantic structures. In turn, these structures will become the primitives in which we attempt to express future ideas.

One such recurring semantic structure is the saving of a computed value. For example, if we have computed the sum of our checking and savings account balances, we may want to save the result so we can refer to it later. In such cases, we will use the form

```
name ← expression
```

where *name* is the name by which we will refer to the result and *expression* describes the computation whose result is to be saved. We will read these statements as "assign *name* the value of *expression*," and we will refer to such statements as **assignment statements.** For example, the statement

```
RemainingFunds ← CheckingBalance + SavingsBalance
```

is an assignment statement that assigns the sum of CheckingBalance and SavingsBalance to the name RemainingFunds. Thus, the term RemainingFunds can be used in future statements to refer to that sum.

Another recurring semantic structure is the selection of one of two possible activities depending on the truth or falseness of some condition. Examples include:

> If the gross domestic product has increased, buy common stock; otherwise, sell common stock.
>
> Buy common stock if the gross domestic product has increased and sell it otherwise.
>
> Buy or sell common stock depending on whether the gross domestic product has increased or decreased, respectively.

Each of these statements could be rewritten to conform to the structure

```
if (condition) then (activity)
             else (activity)
```

where we have used the key words if, then, and else to announce the different substructures within the main structure and have used parentheses to delineate the boundaries of these substructures. By adopting this syntactic structure for our pseudocode, we acquire a uniform way in which to express this common semantic structure. Thus, whereas the statement

> Depending on whether or not the year is a leap year, divide the total by 366 or 365, respectively.

might possess a more creative literary style, we will consistently opt for the straightforward

```
if (year is leap year)
    then (daily total ← total divided by 366)
    else (daily total ← total divided by 365)
```

We also adopt the shorter syntax

```
if (condition) then (activity)
```

for those cases not involving an else activity. Using this notation, the statement

Should it be the case that sales have decreased, lower the price by 5%.

will be reduced to

```
if (sales have decreased) then (lower the price by 5%)
```

Still another common semantic structure is the repeated execution of a statement or sequence of statements as long as some condition remains true. Informal examples include

As long as there are tickets to sell, continue selling tickets.

and

While there are tickets to sell, keep selling tickets.

For such cases, we adopt the uniform pattern

```
while (condition) do (activity)
```

for our pseudocode. In short, such a statement means to check the *condition* and, if it is true, perform the *activity* and return to check the *condition* again. If, however, the *condition* is found to be false, move on to the next instruction following the `while` structure. Thus both of the preceding statements are reduced to

```
while (tickets remain to be sold) do (sell a ticket)
```

Indentation often enhances the readability of a program. For example, the statement

```
if (not raining)
    then (if (temperature = hot)
            then (go swimming)
            else (play golf)
        )
    else (watch television)
```

is easier to comprehend than the otherwise equivalent

```
if (not raining) then (if (temperature = hot) then (go
swimming) else (play golf)) else (watch television)
```

Thus we will adopt the use of indentation in our pseudocode. (Note that we can even use indentation to align a closing parenthesis directly below its partner to simplify the process of identifying the scope of statements or phrases.)

We want to use our pseudocode to describe activities that can be used as abstract tools in other applications. Computer science has a variety of terms for such program units, including subprogram, subroutine, procedure, module, and function, each with its own variation of meaning. We will adopt the term **procedure** for our pseudocode and use this term to announce the title by which the pseudocode unit will be known. More precisely, we will begin a pseudocode unit with a statement of the form

> **procedure** *name*

where *name* is the particular name of the unit. We will then follow this introductory statement with the statements that define the unit's action. For example, Figure 4 is a pseudocode representation of a procedure called Greetings that prints the message "Hello" three times.

When the task performed by a procedure is required elsewhere in our pseudocode, we will merely request it by name. For example, if two procedures were named `ProcessLoan` and `RejectApplication`, then we could request their services within an `if-then-else` structure by writing

> **if** (. . .) **then** (Execute the procedure ProcessLoan)
>   **else** (Execute the procedure RejectApplication)

which would result in the execution of the procedure `ProcessLoan` if the tested condition were true or in the execution of `RejectApplication` if the condition were false.

If procedures are to be used in different situations, they should be designed to be as generic as possible. A procedure for sorting lists of names should be designed to sort any list—not a particular list—so it should be written in such a way that the list to be sorted is not specified in the procedure itself. Instead, the list should be referred to by a generic name within the procedure's representation.

In our pseudocode, we will adopt the convention of listing these generic names (which are called **parameters**) in parentheses on the same line on which we identify the procedure's name. In particular, a procedure named `Sort`, which is designed to sort any list of names, would begin with the statement

> **procedure** Sort (List)

Figure 4   The procedure Greetings in pseudocode

```
            procedure Greetings
            Count ← 3;
            while (Count > 0) do
                (print the message "Hello" and
                Count ← Count −1)
```

Naming Items in Programs

In a natural language, items often have multiword names such as "cost of producing a widget" or "estimated arrival time." Experience has shown that use of such multiword names in the representation of an algorithm can complicate the algorithm's description. It is better to have each item identified by a single contiguous block of text. Over the years many techniques have been used to compress multiple words into a single lexical unit to obtain descriptive names for items in programs. One is to use underlines to connect words, producing names such as `estimated_arrival_time`. Another is to use uppercase letters to help a reader comprehend a compressed multiword name. For example, one could start each word with an uppercase letter to obtain names such as `EstimatedArrivalTime`. This technique is called **Pascal casing,** because it was popularized by users of the Pascal programming language. A variation of Pascal casing is called **camel casing,** which is identical to Pascal casing except that the first letter remains in lowercase as in `estimatedArrivalTime`. In this text we lean toward Pascal casing, but the choice is largely a matter of taste.

Later in the representation where a reference to the list being sorted is required, the generic name `List` would be used. In turn, when the services of `Sort` are required, we will identify which list is to be substituted for `List` in the procedure `Sort`. Thus we will write something such as

```
Apply the procedure Sort to the organization's membership list
```
and
```
Apply the procedure Sort to the wedding guest list
```
depending on our needs.

Keep in mind that the purpose of our pseudocode is to provide a means of representing algorithms in a readable, informal manner. We want a notational system that will assist us in expressing our ideas—not enslave us to rigorous, formal rules. Thus we will feel free to expand or modify our pseudocode when needed. In particular, if the statements within a set of parentheses involve parenthetical statements themselves, it can become difficult to pair opening and closing parenthesis visually. In these cases, many people find it helpful to follow a closing parenthesis with a short comment explaining which statement or phrase is being terminated. In particular, one might follow the final parenthesis in a `while` statement with the words `end while`, producing a statement such as

```
while (...) do
 (.
  .
  .
 )end while
```

or perhaps

```
while (...) do
  (if (...)
     then (.
            .
            .
          )end if
  )end while
```

where we have indicated the end of both the **if** and **while** statements.

The point is that we are trying to express an algorithm in a readable form, and thus we introduce visual aids (indentation, comments, etc.) at times to achieve this goal. Moreover, if we encounter a recurring theme that is not yet incorporated in our pseudocode, we might choose to extend our pseudocode by adopting a consistent syntax for representing the new concept.

Questions & Exercises

1. A primitive in one context might turn out to be a composite of primitives in another. For instance, our **while** statement is a primitive in our pseudocode, yet it is ultimately implemented as a composite of machine-language instructions. Give two examples of this phenomenon in a non-computer setting.

2. In what sense is the construction of procedures the construction of primitives?

3. The Euclidean algorithm finds the greatest common divisor of two positive integers X and Y by the following process:

   As long as the value of neither X nor Y is zero, continue dividing the larger of the values by the smaller and assigning X and Y the values of the divisor and remainder, respectively. (The final value of X is the greatest common divisor.)

   Express this algorithm in our pseudocode.

4. Describe a collection of primitives that are used in a subject other than computer programming.

3 Algorithm Discovery

The development of a program consists of two activities—discovering the underlying algorithm and representing that algorithm as a program. Up to this point we have been concerned with the issues of algorithm representation without considering the question of how algorithms are discovered in the first place. Yet algorithm discovery is usually the more challenging step in the software development process. After all, discovering an algorithm to solve a problem requires finding a method of solving that problem. Thus, to understand how algorithms are discovered is to understand the problem-solving process.

The Art of Problem Solving

The techniques of problem solving and the need to learn more about them are not unique to computer science but rather are topics pertinent to almost any field. The close association between the process of algorithm discovery and that of general problem solving has caused computer scientists to join with those of other disciplines in the search for better problem-solving techniques. Ultimately, one would like to reduce the process of problem solving to an algorithm in itself, but this has been shown to be impossible. Thus the ability to solve problems remains more of an artistic skill to be developed than a precise science to be learned.

As evidence of the elusive, artistic nature of problem solving, the following loosely defined problem-solving phases presented by the mathematician G. Polya in 1945 remain the basic principles on which many attempts to teach problem-solving skills are based today.

Phase 1. Understand the problem.

Phase 2. Devise a plan for solving the problem.

Phase 3. Carry out the plan.

Phase 4. Evaluate the solution for accuracy and for its potential as a tool for solving other problems.

Translated into the context of program development, these phases become

Phase 1. Understand the problem.

Phase 2. Get an idea of how an algorithmic procedure might solve the problem.

Phase 3. Formulate the algorithm and represent it as a program.

Phase 4. Evaluate the program for accuracy and for its potential as a tool for solving other problems.

Having presented Polya's list, we should emphasize that these phases are not steps to be followed when trying to solve a problem but rather phases that will be completed sometime during the solution process. The key word here is *followed*. You do not solve problems by following. Rather, to solve a problem, you must take the initiative and lead. If you approach the task of solving a problem in the frame of mind depicted by "Now I've finished Phase 1, it's time to move on to Phase 2," you are not likely to be successful. However, if you become involved with the problem and ultimately solve it, you most likely can look back at what you did and realize that you performed Polya's phases.

Another important observation is that Polya's phases are not necessarily completed in sequence. Successful problem solvers often start formulating strategies for solving a problem (Phase 2) before the problem itself is entirely understood (Phase 1). Then, if these strategies fail (during Phases 3 or 4), the potential problem solver gains a deeper understanding of the intricacies of the problem and, with this deeper understanding, can return to form other and hopefully more successful strategies.

Keep in mind that we are discussing how problems are solved—not how we would like them to be solved. Ideally, we would like to eliminate the waste inherent in the trial-and-error process just described. In the case of developing large software systems, discovering a misunderstanding as late as Phase 4 can represent a tremendous loss in resources. Avoiding such catastrophes is a major goal of software engineers, who have traditionally insisted on a thorough understanding of a problem before proceeding with a solution. One could argue, however, that a true understanding of a problem is not obtained until a solution has been found. The mere fact that a problem is unsolved implies a lack of understanding. To insist on a complete understanding of the problem before proposing any solutions is therefore somewhat idealistic.

As an example, consider the following problem:

> Person A is charged with the task of determining the ages of person B's three children. B tells A that the product of the children's ages is 36. After considering this clue, A replies that another clue is required, so B tells A the sum of the children's ages. Again, A replies that another clue is needed, so B tells A that the oldest child plays the piano. After hearing this clue, A tells B the ages of the three children.
>
> How old are the three children?

At first glance the last clue seems to be totally unrelated to the problem, yet it is apparently this clue that allows A to finally determine the ages of the children. How can this be? Let us proceed by formulating a plan of attack and following this plan, even though we still have many questions about the problem. Our plan will be to trace the steps described by the problem statement while keeping track of the information available to person A as the story progresses.

The first clue given A is that the product of the children's ages is 36. This means that the triple representing the three ages is one of those listed in Figure 5(a). The

Figure 5

a. Triples whose product is 36		b. Sums of triples from part (a)	
(1,1,36)	(1,6,6)	$1 + 1 + 36 = 38$	$1 + 6 + 6 = 13$
(1,2,18)	(2,2,9)	$1 + 2 + 18 = 21$	$2 + 2 + 9 = 13$
(1,3,12)	(2,3,6)	$1 + 3 + 12 = 16$	$2 + 3 + 6 = 11$
(1,4,9)	(3,3,4)	$1 + 4 + 9 = 14$	$3 + 3 + 4 = 10$

next clue is the sum of the desired triple. We are not told what this sum is, but we are told that this information is not enough for A to isolate the correct triple; therefore the desired triple must be one whose sum appears at least twice in the table of Figure 5(b). But the only triples appearing in Figure 5(b) with identical sums are (1,6,6) and (2,2,9), both of which produce the sum 13. This is the information available to A at the time the last clue is given. It is at this point that we finally understand the significance of the last clue. It has nothing to do with playing the piano; rather it is the fact that there is an oldest child. This rules out the triple (1,6,6) and thus allows us to conclude that the children's ages are 2, 2, and 9.

In this case, then, it is not until we attempt to implement our plan for solving the problem (Phase 3) that we gain a complete understanding of the problem (Phase 1). Had we insisted on completing Phase 1 before proceeding, we would probably never have found the children's ages. Such irregularities in the problem-solving process are fundamental to the difficulties in developing systematic approaches to problem solving.

Another irregularity is the mysterious inspiration that might come to a potential problem solver who, having worked on a problem without apparent success, at a later time suddenly sees the solution while doing another task. This phenomenon was identified by H. von Helmholtz as early as 1896 and was discussed by the mathematician Henri Poincaré in a lecture before the Psychological Society in Paris. There, Poincaré described his experiences of realizing the solution to a problem he had worked on after he had set it aside and begun other projects. The phenomenon reflects a process in which a subconscious part of the mind appears to continue working and, if successful, forces the solution into the conscious mind. Today, the period between conscious work on a problem and the sudden inspiration is known as an incubation period, and its understanding remains a goal of current research.

Getting a Foot in the Door

We have been discussing problem solving from a somewhat philosophical point of view while avoiding a direct confrontation with the question of how we should go about trying to solve a problem. There are, of course, numerous problem-solving approaches, each of which can be successful in certain settings. We will identify some of them shortly. For now, we note that there seems to be a common thread running through these techniques, which simply stated is "get your foot in the door." As an example, let us consider the following simple problem:

Before A, B, C, and D ran a race they made the following predictions:

    A predicted that B would win.
    B predicted that D would be last.
    C predicted that A would be third.
    D predicted that A's prediction would be correct.

Only one of these predictions was true, and this was the prediction made by the winner. In what order did A, B, C, and D finish the race?

After reading the problem and analyzing the data, it should not take long to realize that since the predictions of A and D were equivalent and only one prediction was true, the predictions of both A and D must be false. Thus neither A nor D were winners. At this point we have our foot in the door, and obtaining the complete solution to our problem is merely a matter of extending our knowledge from here. If A's prediction was false, then B did not win either. The only remaining choice for the winner is C. Thus, C won the race, and C's prediction was true. Consequently, we know that A came in third. That means that the finishing order was either CBAD or CDAB. But the former is ruled out because B's prediction must be false. Therefore the finishing order was CDAB.

Of course, being told to get our foot in the door is not the same as being told how to do it. Obtaining this toehold, as well as realizing how to expand this initial thrust into a complete solution to the problem, requires creative input from the would-be problem solver. There are, however, several general approaches that have been proposed by Polya and others for how one might go about getting a foot in the door. One is to try working the problem backward. For instance, if the problem is to find a way of producing a particular output from a given input, one might start with that output and attempt to back up to the given input. This approach is typical of people trying to discover the bird-folding algorithm in the previous section. They tend to unfold a completed bird in an attempt to see how it is constructed.

Another general problem-solving approach is to look for a related problem that is either easier to solve or has been solved before and then try to apply its solution to the current problem. This technique is of particular value in the context of program development. Generally, program development is not the process of solving a particular instance of a problem but rather of finding a general algorithm that can be used to solve all instances of the problem. More precisely, if we were faced with the task of developing a program for alphabetizing lists of names, our task would not be to sort a particular list but to find a general algorithm that could be used to sort any list of names. Thus, although the instructions

```
Interchange the names David and Alice.
Move the name Carol to the position between Alice and David.
Move the name Bob to the position between Alice and Carol.
```

correctly sort the list David, Alice, Carol, and Bob, they do not constitute the general-purpose algorithm we desire. What we need is an algorithm that can sort this list as well as other lists we might encounter. This is not to say that our solution for sorting a particular list is totally worthless in our search for a general-purpose algorithm. We might, for instance, get our foot in the door by considering such special cases in an attempt to find general principles that can in turn be used to develop the desired general-purpose algorithm. In this case, then, our solution is obtained by the technique of solving a collection of related problems.

Still another approach to getting a foot in the door is to apply **stepwise refinement,** which is essentially the technique of not trying to conquer an entire task (in all its detail) at once. Rather, stepwise refinement proposes that one first view the problem at hand in terms of several subproblems. The idea is that by breaking the original problem into subproblems, one is able to approach the overall solution in terms of steps, each of which is easier to solve than the entire original problem. In turn, stepwise refinement proposes that these steps be decomposed into smaller steps and these smaller steps be broken into still smaller ones until the entire problem has been reduced to a collection of easily solved subproblems.

In this light, stepwise refinement is a **top-down methodology** in that it progresses from the general to the specific. In contrast, a **bottom-up methodology** progresses from the specific to the general. Although contrasting in theory, the two approaches often complement each other in creative problem solving. The decomposition of a problem proposed by the top-down methodology of stepwise refinement is often guided by the problem solver's intuition, which might be working in a bottom-up mode.

The top-down methodology of stepwise refinement is essentially an organizational tool whose problem-solving attributes are consequences of this organization. It has long been an important design methodology in the data processing community, where the development of large software systems encompasses a significant organizational component. But large software systems are increasingly being constructed by combining prefabricated components—an approach that is inherently bottom-up. Thus, both top-down and bottom-up methodologies remain important tools in computer science.

The importance of maintaining such a broad perspective is exemplified by the fact that bringing preconceived notions and preselected tools to the problem-solving task can sometimes mask a problem's simplicity. The ages-of-the-children problem discussed earlier in this section is an excellent example of this phenomenon. Students of algebra invariably approach the problem as a system of simultaneous equations, an approach that leads to a dead end and often traps the would-be problem solver into believing that the information given is not sufficient to solve the problem.

Another example is the following:

> As you step from a pier into a boat, your hat falls into the water, unbeknownst to you. The river is flowing at 2.5 miles per hour so your hat begins to float downstream. In the meantime, you begin traveling upstream in the boat at a speed of 4.75 miles per hour relative to the water. After 10 minutes you realize that your hat is missing, turn the boat around, and begin to chase your hat down the river. How long will it take to catch up with your hat?

Most algebra students as well as calculator enthusiasts approach this problem by first determining how far upstream the boat will have traveled in 10 minutes as well as how far downstream the hat will have traveled during that same time.

Then, they determine how long it will take for the boat to travel downstream to this position. But, when the boat reaches this position, the hat will have floated farther downstream. Thus, the problem solver either begins to apply techniques of the calculus or becomes trapped in a cycle of computing where the hat will be each time the boat goes to where the hat was.

The problem is much simpler than this, however. The trick is to resist the urge to begin writing formulas and making calculations. Instead, we need to put these skills aside and adjust our perspective. The entire problem takes place in the river. The fact that the water is moving in relation to the shore is irrelevant. Think of the same problem posed on a large conveyer belt instead of a river. First, solve the problem with the conveyer belt at rest. If you place your hat at your feet while standing on the belt and then walk away from your hat for 10 minutes, it will take 10 minutes to return to your hat. Now turn on the conveyer belt. This means that the scenery will begin to move past the belt, but, because you are on the belt, this does not change your relationship to the belt or your hat. It will still take 10 minutes to return to your hat.

We conclude that algorithm discovery remains a challenging art that must be developed over a period of time rather than taught as a subject consisting of well-defined methodologies. Indeed, to train a potential problem solver to follow certain methodologies is to quash those creative skills that should instead be nurtured.

Questions & Exercises

1. a. Find an algorithm for solving the following problem: Given a positive integer n, find the list of positive integers whose product is the largest among all the lists of positive integers whose sum is n. For example, if n is 4, the desired list is 2, 2 because 2×2 is larger than $1 \times 1 \times 1 \times 1$, $2 \times 1 \times 1$, and 3×1. If n is 5, the desired list is 2, 3.
   b. What is the desired list if $n = 2001$?
   c. Explain how you got your foot in the door.

2. a. Suppose we are given a checkerboard consisting of 2^n rows and 2^n columns of squares, for some positive integer n, and a box of L-shaped tiles, each of which can cover exactly three squares on the board. If any single square is cut out of the board, can we cover the remaining board with tiles such that tiles do not overlap or hang off the edge of the board?
   b. Explain how your solution to (a) can be used to show that $2^{2n} - 1$ is divisible by 3 for all positive integers n.
   c. How are (a) and (b) related to Polya's phases of problem solving?

3. Decode the following message, then explain how you got your foot in the door. *Pdeo eo pda yknnayp wjosan.*

4. Would you be following a top-down methodology if you attempted to solve a picture puzzle merely by pouring the pieces out on a table and trying to piece them together? Would your answer change if you looked at the puzzle box to see what the entire picture was supposed to look like?

4 Iterative Structures

Our goal now is to study some of the repetitive structures used in describing algorithmic processes. In this section we discuss **iterative structures** in which a collection of instructions is repeated in a looping manner. In the next section we will introduce the technique of recursion. As a side effect, we will introduce some popular algorithms—the sequential search, the binary search, and the insertion sort. We begin by introducing the sequential search algorithm.

The Sequential Search Algorithm

Consider the problem of searching within a list for the occurrence of a particular target value. We want to develop an algorithm that determines whether that value is in the list. If the value is in the list, we consider the search a success; otherwise we consider it a failure. We assume that the list is sorted according to some rule for ordering its entries. For example, if the list is a list of names, we assume the names appear in alphabetical order, or if the list consists of numeric values, we assume its entries appear in order of increasing magnitude.

To get our foot in the door, we imagine how we might search a guest list of perhaps 20 entries for a particular name. In this setting we might scan the list from its beginning, comparing each entry with the target name. If we find the target name, the search terminates as a success. However, if we reach the end of the list without finding the target value, our search terminates as a failure. In fact, if we reach a name greater than (alphabetically) the target name without finding the target, our search terminates as a failure. (Remember, the list is arranged in alphabetical order, so reaching a name greater than the target name indicates that the target does not appear in the list.) In summary, our rough idea is to continue searching down the list as long as there are more names to be investigated and the target name is greater than the name currently being considered.

In our pseudocode, this process can be represented as

```
Select the first entry in the list as TestEntry.
while (TargetValue > TestEntry and
        there remain entries to be considered)
    do (Select the next entry in the list as TestEntry)
```

Upon terminating this `while` structure, one of two conditions will be true: either the target value has been found or the target value is not in the list. In either case we can detect a successful search by comparing the test entry to the target value. If they are equal, the search has been successful. Thus we add the statement

```
if (TargetValue = TestEntry)
   then (Declare the search a success.)
   else (Declare the search a failure.)
```

to the end of our pseudocode routine.

Finally, we observe that the first statement in our routine, which selects the first entry in the list as the test entry, is based on the assumption that the list in question contains at least one entry. We might reason that this is a safe guess, but just to be sure, we can position our routine as the else option of the statement

```
if (List empty)
   then (Declare search a failure.)
   else (. . .)
```

This produces the procedure shown in Figure 6. Note that this procedure can be used from within other procedures by using statements such as

```
Apply the procedure Search to the passenger list
using Darrel Baker as the target value.
```

to find out if Darrel Baker is a passenger and

```
Apply the procedure Search to the list of ingredients
using nutmeg as the target value.
```

to find out if nutmeg appears in the list of ingredients.

In summary, the algorithm represented by Figure 6 considers the entries in the sequential order in which they occur in the list. For this reason, the

Figure 6   The sequential search algorithm in pseudocode

```
procedure Search (List, TargetValue)
if (List empty)
   then
      (Declare search a failure)
   else
      (Select the first entry in List to be TestEntry;
      while (TargetValue > TestEntry and
              there remain entries to be considered)
         do (Select the next entry in List as TestEntry.);
      if (TargetValue = TestEntry)
         then (Declare search a success.)
         else (Declare search a failure.)
      ) end if
```

algorithm is called the **sequential search** algorithm. Because of its simplicity, it is often used for short lists or when other concerns dictate its use. However, in the case of long lists, sequential searches are not as efficient as other techniques (as we shall soon see).

Loop Control

The repetitive use of an instruction or sequence of instructions is an important algorithmic concept. One method of implementing such repetition is the iterative structure known as the **loop,** in which a collection of instructions, called the body of the loop, is executed in a repetitive fashion under the direction of some control process. A typical example is found in the sequential search algorithm represented in Figure 6. Here we use a `while` statement to control the repetition of the single statement `Select the next entry in List as the TestEntry`. Indeed, the `while` statement

      `while` (*condition*) `do` (*body*)

exemplifies the concept of a loop structure in that its execution traces the cyclic pattern

```
check the condition.
execute the body.
check the condition.
execute the body.
      .
      .
      .
check the condition.
```

until the condition fails.

As a general rule, the use of a loop structure produces a higher degree of flexibility than would be obtained merely by explicitly writing the body several times. For example, to execute the statement

```
Add a drop of sulfuric acid.
```

three times, we could write:

```
Add a drop of sulfuric acid.
Add a drop of sulfuric acid.
Add a drop of sulfuric acid.
```

But we cannot produce a similar sequence that is equivalent to the loop structure

      `while` (the pH level is greater than 4) `do`
        (add a drop of sulfuric acid)

because we do not know in advance how many drops of acid will be required.

Let us now take a closer look at the composition of loop control. You might be tempted to view this part of a loop structure as having minor importance. After all, it is typically the body of the loop that actually performs the task at hand (for example, adding drops of acid)—the control activities appear merely as the overhead involved because we chose to execute the body in a repetitive fashion. However, experience has shown that the control of a loop is the more error-prone part of the structure and therefore deserves our attention.

The control of a loop consists of the three activities initialize, test, and modify (Figure 7), with the presence of each being required for successful loop control. The test activity has the obligation of causing the termination of the looping process by watching for a condition that indicates termination should take place. This condition is known as the **termination condition.** It is for the purpose of this test activity that we provide a condition within each while statement of our pseudocode. In the case of the while statement, however, the condition stated is the condition under which the body of the loop should be executed—the termination condition is the negation of the condition appearing in the while structure. Thus, in the statement

```
while (the pH level is greater than 4) do
    (add a drop of sulfuric acid)
```

the termination condition is "the pH level is *not* greater than 4," and in the while statement of Figure 6, the termination condition could be stated as

(TargetValue ≤ TestEntry) or (there are no more entries to be considered)

The other two activities in the loop control ensure that the termination condition will ultimately occur. The initialization step establishes a starting condition, and the modification step moves this condition toward the termination condition. For instance, in Figure 6, initialization takes place in the statement preceding the while statement, where the current test entry is established as the first list entry. The modification step in this case is actually accomplished within the loop body, where our position of interest (identified by the test entry) is moved toward the end of the list. Thus, having executed the initialization step, repeated application of the modification step results in

Figure 7 Components of repetitive control

Initialize:	Establish an initial state that will be modified toward the termination condition
Test:	Compare the current state to the termination condition and terminate the repetition if equal
Modify:	Change the state in such a way that it moves toward the termination condition

the termination condition being reached. (Either we will reach a test entry that is greater than or equal to the target value or we ultimately reach the end of the list.)

We should emphasize that the initialization and modification steps must lead to the appropriate termination condition. This characteristic is critical for proper loop control, and thus one should always double-check for its presence when designing a loop structure. Failure to make such an evaluation can lead to errors even in the simplest cases. A typical example is found in the statements

```
Number ← 1;
while (Number ≠ 6) do
  (Number ← Number + 2)
```

Here the termination condition is "Number = 6." But the value of Number is initialized at 1 and then incremented by 2 in the modification step. Thus, as the loop cycles, the values assigned to Number will be 1, 3, 5, 7, 9, and so on, but never the value 6. In turn, the loop will never terminate.

The order in which the components of loop control are executed can have subtle consequences. In fact, there are two common loop structures that differ merely in this regard. The first is exemplified by our pseudocode statement

```
while (condition) do (activity)
```

whose semantics are represented in Figure 8 in the form of a **flowchart.** (Such charts use various shapes to represent individual steps and use arrows to indicate the order of the steps. The distinction between the shapes indicates the type of action involved in the associated step. A diamond indicates a decision and a rectangle indicates an arbitrary statement or sequence of state-

Figure 8   The while loop structure

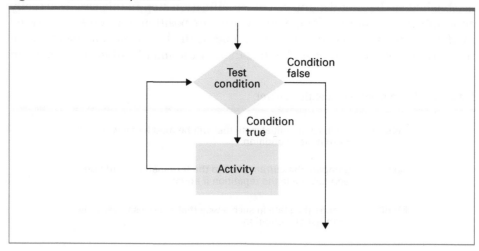

ments.) Note that the test for termination in the **while** structure occurs before the loop's body is executed.

In contrast, the structure in Figure 9 requests that the body of the loop be executed before the test for termination is performed. In this case, the loop's body is always performed at least once, whereas in the while structure, the body is never executed if the termination condition is satisfied the first time it is tested.

We will use the syntactic form

> **repeat** (*activity*) **until** (*condition*)

in our pseudocode to represent the structure shown in Figure 9. Thus, the statement

> **repeat** (take a coin from your pocket)
> **until** (there are no coins in your pocket)

assumes there is a coin in your pocket at the beginning, but

> **while** (there is a coin in your pocket) **do**
> (take a coin from your pocket)

does not.

Following the terminology of our pseudocode, we will usually refer to these structures as the **while** loop structure or the **repeat** loop structure. In a more generic context you might hear the **while** loop structure referred to as a **pretest loop** (since the test for termination is performed before the body is executed) and the **repeat** loop structure referred to as a **posttest loop** (since the test for termination is performed after the body is executed).

Figure 9 The repeat loop structure

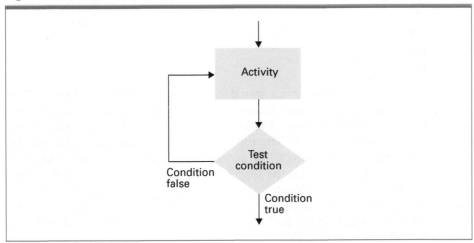

The Insertion Sort Algorithm

As an additional example of using iterative structures, let us consider the problem of sorting a list of names into alphabetical order. But before proceeding, we should identify the constraints under which we will work. Simply stated, our goal is to sort the list "within itself." In other words, we want to sort the list by shuffling its entries as opposed to moving the list to another location. Our situation is analogous to the problem of sorting a list whose entries are recorded on separate index cards spread out on a crowded desktop. We have cleared off enough space for the cards but are not allowed to push additional materials back to make more room. This restriction is typical in computer applications, not because the workspace within the machine is necessarily crowded like our desktop, but simply because we want to use the storage space available in an efficient manner.

Let us get a foot in the door by considering how we might sort the names on the desktop. Consider the list of names

> Fred
>
> Alex
>
> Diana
>
> Byron
>
> Carol

One approach to sorting this list is to note that the sublist consisting of only the top name, Fred, is sorted but the sublist consisting of the top two names, Fred and Alex, is not. Thus we might pick up the card containing the name Alex, slide the name Fred down into the space where Alex was, and then place the name Alex in the hole at the top of the list, as represented by the first row in Figure 10. At this point our list would be

> Alex
>
> Fred
>
> Diana
>
> Byron
>
> Carol

Now the top two names form a sorted sublist, but the top three do not. Thus we might pick up the third name, Diana, slide the name Fred down into the hole where Diana was, and then insert Diana in the hole left by Fred, as summarized in the second row of Figure 10. The top three entries in the list would now be sorted. Continuing in this fashion, we could obtain a list in which the top four entries are sorted by picking up the fourth name, Byron, sliding the names Fred and Diana down, and then inserting Byron in the hole (see the third row of Figure 10). Finally, we can complete the sorting process by picking up Carol, sliding Fred and Diana down, and then inserting Carol in the remaining hole (see the fourth row of Figure 10).

Figure 10   Sorting the list Fred, Alex, Diana, Byron, and Carol alphabetically

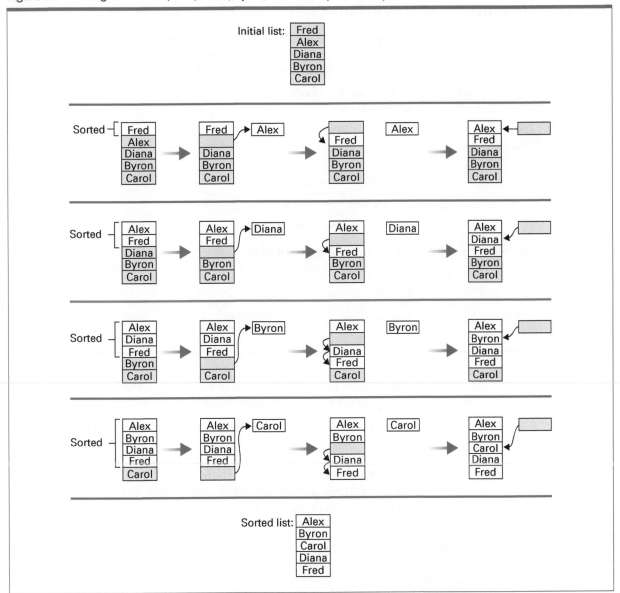

Having analyzed the process of sorting a particular list, our task now is to generalize this process to obtain an algorithm for sorting general lists. To this end, we observe that each row of Figure 10 represents the same general process: Pick up the first name in the unsorted portion of the list, slide the names greater than the extracted name down, and insert the extracted name

Iterative Structures in Music

Musicians were using and programming iterative structures centuries before computer scientists. Indeed, the structure of a song (being composed of multiple verses, each followed by the chorus) is exemplified by the while statement

```
while (there is a verse remaining) do
    (sing the next verse;
    sing the chorus)
```

Moreover, the notation

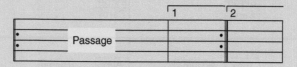

is merely a composer's way of expressing the structure

```
N ← 1;
while (N < 3) do
  (play the passage;
  play the Nth ending;
  N ← N + 1)
```

back in the list where the hole appears. If we identify the extracted name as the pivot entry, this process can be expressed in our pseudocode as

```
Move the pivot entry to a temporary location leaving a hole
in List;
while (there is a name above the hole and
        that name is greater than the pivot) do
  (move the name above the hole down into the hole
    leaving a hole above the name)
Move the pivot entry into the hole in List.
```

Next, we observe that this process should be executed repeatedly. To begin the sorting process, the pivot should be the second entry in the list and then, before each additional execution, the pivot selection should be one more entry down the list until the last entry has been positioned. That is, as the preceding routine is repeated, the initial position of the pivot entry should advance from the second entry to the third, then to the fourth, etc., until the routine has positioned the last entry in the list. Following this lead we can control the required repetition with the statements

```
N ← 2;
while (the value of N does not exceed the length of List) do
  (Select the Nth entry in List as the pivot entry;
```

$$\vdots$$

$$N \leftarrow N + 1)$$

where N represents the position to use for the pivot entry, the length of List refers to the number of entries in the list, and the dots indicate the location where the previous routine should be placed.

Our complete pseudocode program is shown in Figure 11. In short, the program sorts a list by repeatedly removing an entry and inserting it into its proper place. It is because of this repeated insertion process that the underlying algorithm is called the **insertion sort.**

Note that the structure of Figure 11 is that of a loop within a loop, the outer loop being expressed by the first while statement and the inner loop represented by the second while statement. Each execution of the body of the outer loop results in the inner loop being initialized and executed until its termination condition is obtained. Thus, a single execution of the outer loop's body will result in several executions of the inner loop's body.

The initialization component of the outer loop's control consists of establishing the initial value of N with the statement

$$N \leftarrow 2;$$

The modification component is handled by incrementing the value of N at the end of the loop's body with the statement

$$N \leftarrow N + 1$$

The termination condition occurs when the value of N exceeds the length of the list.

The inner loop's control is initialized by removing the pivot entry from the list and thus creating a hole. The loop's modification step is accomplished by moving entries down into the hole, thus causing the hole to move up. The termination condition consists of the hole being immediately below a name that is not greater than the pivot or of the hole reaching the top of the list.

Figure 11   The insertion sort algorithm expressed in pseudocode

```
procedure Sort (List)
N ← 2;
while (the value of N does not exceed the length of List) do
    (Select the Nth entry in List as the pivot entry;
    Move the pivot entry to a temporary location leaving a hole in List;
    while (there is a name above the hole and that name is greater than the pivot)
        do (move the name above the hole down into the hole
            leaving a hole above the name)
    Move the pivot entry into the hole in List;
    N ← N + 1
    )
```

Questions & Exercises

1. Modify the sequential search procedure in Figure 6 to allow for lists that are not sorted.

2. Convert the pseudocode routine

```
Z ← 0;
X ← 1;
while (X < 6) do
  (Z ← Z + X;
   X ← X + 1)
```

to an equivalent routine using a **repeat** statement.

3. Some of the popular programming languages today use the syntax

```
while (. . .) do (. . .)
```

to represent a pretest loop and the syntax

```
do (. . .) while (. . .)
```

to represent a posttest loop. Although elegant in design, what problems could result from such similarities?

4. Suppose the insertion sort as presented in Figure 11 was applied to the list Gene, Cheryl, Alice, and Brenda. Describe the organization of the list at the end of each execution of the body of the outer **while** structure.

5. Why would we not want to change the phrase "greater than" in the **while** statement in Figure 11 to "greater than or equal to"?

6. A variation of the insertion sort algorithm is the **selection sort.** It begins by selecting the smallest entry in the list and moving it to the front. It then selects the smallest entry from the remaining entries in the list and moves it to the second position in the list. By repeatedly selecting the smallest entry from the remaining portion of the list and moving that entry forward, the sorted version of the list grows from the front of the list, while the back portion of the list consisting of the remaining unsorted entries shrinks. Use our pseudocode to express a procedure simzilar to that in Figure 11 for sorting a list using the selection sort algorithm.

7. Another well-known sorting algorithm is the **bubble sort.** It is based on the process of repeatedly comparing two adjacent names and interchanging them if they are not in the correct order relative to each other. Let us suppose that the list in question has n entries. The bubble sort would begin by comparing (and possibly interchanging) the entries in positions n and $n - 1$. Then, it would consider the entries in positions $n - 1$ and $n - 2$, and continue moving forward in the list until the first and

second entries in the list had been compared (and possibly inter-changed). Observe that this pass through the list will pull the smallest entry to the front of the list. Likewise, another such pass will ensure that the next to the smallest entry will be pulled to the second position in the list. Thus, by making a total of $n - 1$ passes through the list, the entire list will be sorted. (If one watches the algorithm at work, one sees the small entries bubble to the top of the list—an observation from which the algorithm gets its name.) Use our pseudocode to express a procedure similar to that in Figure 11 for sorting a list using the bubble sort algorithm.

5 Recursive Structures

Recursive structures provide an alternative to the loop paradigm for implementing the repetition of activities. Whereas a loop involves repeating a set of instructions in a manner in which the set is completed and then repeated, recursion involves repeating the set of instructions as a subtask of itself. As an analogy, consider the process of conducting telephone conversations with the call waiting feature. There, an incomplete telephone conversation is set aside while another incoming call is processed. The result is that two conversations take place. However, they are not performed one-after-the-other as in a loop structure, but instead one is performed within the other.

The Binary Search Algorithm

As a way of introducing recursion, let us again tackle the problem of searching to see whether a particular entry is in a sorted list, but this time we get our foot in the door by considering the procedure we follow when searching a dictionary. In this case we do not perform a sequential entry-by-entry or even a page-by-page procedure. Rather, we begin by opening the directory to a page in the area where we believe the target entry is located. If we are lucky, we will find the target value there; otherwise, we must continue searching. But at this point we will have narrowed our search considerably.

Of course, in the case of searching a dictionary, we have prior knowledge of where words are likely to be found. If we are looking for the word *somnambulism,* we would start by opening to the latter portion of the dictionary. In the case of generic lists, however, we do not have this advantage, so let us agree to always start our search with the "middle" entry in the list. Here we write the word *middle* in quotation marks because the list might have an even number of entries and thus no middle entry in the exact sense. In this case, let us agree that the "middle" entry refers to the first entry in the second half of the list.

If the middle entry in the list is the target value, we can declare the search a success. Otherwise, we can at least restrict the search process to the first or last

Searching and Sorting

The sequential and binary search algorithms are only two of many algorithms for performing the search process. Likewise, the insertion sort is only one of many sorting algorithms. Other classic algorithms for sorting include the merge sort the selection sort (Question/Exercise 6 in Section 4), the bubble sort (Question/Exercise 7 in Section 4), the quick sort (which applies a divide-and-conquer approach to the sorting process), and the heap sort (which uses a clever technique for finding the entries that should be moved forward in the list). You will find discussions of these algorithms in the books listed under Additional Reading at the end of this chapter.

half of the list depending on whether the target value is less than or greater than the entry we have considered. (Remember that the list is sorted.)

To search the remaining portion of the list, we could apply the sequential search, but instead let us apply the same approach to this portion of the list that we used for the whole list. That is, we select the middle entry in the remaining portion of the list as the next entry to consider. As before, if that entry is the target value, we are finished. Otherwise we can restrict our search to an even smaller portion of the list.

This approach to the searching process is summarized in Figure 12, where we consider the task of searching the list on the left of the figure for the entry

Figure 12   Applying our strategy to search a list for the entry John

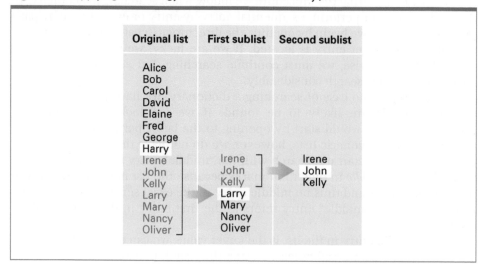

John. We first consider the middle entry Harry. Since our target belongs after this entry, the search continues by considering the lower half of the original list. The middle of this sublist is found to be Larry. Since our target should precede Larry, we turn our attention to the first half of the current sublist. When we interrogate the middle of that secondary sublist, we find our target John and declare the search a success. In short, our strategy is to successively divide the list in question into smaller segments until the target is found or the search is narrowed to an empty segment.

We need to emphasize this last point. If the target value is not in the original list, our approach to searching the list will proceed by dividing the list into smaller segments until the segment under consideration is empty. At this point our algorithm should recognize that the search is a failure.

Figure 13 is a first draft of our thoughts using our pseudocode. It directs us to begin a search by testing to see if the list is empty. If so, we are told to report that the search is a failure. Otherwise, we are told to consider the middle entry in the list. If this entry is not the target value, we are told to search either the front half or the back half of the list. Both of these possibilities require a secondary search. It would be nice to perform these searches by calling on the services of an abstract tool. In particular, our approach is to apply a procedure named **Search** to carry out these secondary searches. To complete our program, therefore, we must provide such a procedure.

But this procedure should perform the same task that is expressed by the pseudocode we have already written. It should first check to see if the list it is given is empty, and if it is not, it should proceed by considering the middle entry of that list. Thus we can supply the procedure we need merely by identifying the current routine as being the procedure named **Search** and inserting references

Figure 13   A first draft of the binary search technique

```
    if (List empty)
    then
     (Report that the search failed.)
    else
     [Select the "middle" entry in the List to be the TestEntry;
      Execute the block of instructions below that is
        associated with the appropriate case.
          case 1: TargetValue = TestEntry
               (Report that the search succeeded.)
          case 2: TargetValue < TestEntry
               (Search the portion of List preceding TestEntry for
                   TargetValue, and report the result of that search.)
          case 3: TargetValue > TestEntry
               (Search the portion of List following TestEntry for
                   TargetValue, and report the result of that search.)
     ] end if
```

to that procedure where the secondary searches are required. The result is shown in Figure 14.

Note that this procedure contains a reference to itself. If we were following this procedure and came to the instruction

```
Apply the procedure Search . . .
```

we would apply the same procedure to the smaller list that we were applying to the original one. If that search succeeded, we would return to declare our original search successful; if this secondary search failed, we would declare our original search a failure.

To see how the procedure in Figure 14 performs its task, let us follow it as it searches the list Alice, Bill, Carol, David, Evelyn, Fred, and George, for the target value Bill. Our search begins by selecting David (the middle entry) as the test entry under consideration. Since the target value (Bill) is less than this test entry, we are instructed to apply the procedure `Search` to the list of entries preceding David—that is, the list Alice, Bill, and Carol. In so doing, we create a second copy of the search procedure and assign it to this secondary task.

We now have two copies of our search procedure being executed, as summarized in Figure 15. Progress in the original copy is temporarily suspended at the instruction

```
Apply the procedure Search to see if TargetValue is
    in the portion of List preceding the TestEntry
```

Figure 14   The binary search algorithm in pseudocode

```
        procedure Search (List, TargetValue)
        if (List empty)
          then
            (Report that the search failed.)
          else
            [Select the "middle" entry in List to be the TestEntry;
             Execute the block of instructions below that is
                associated with the appropriate case.
                   case 1: TargetValue = TestEntry
                       (Report that the search succeeded.)
                   case 2: TargetValue < TestEntry
                       (Apply the procedure Search to see if TargetValue
                            is in the portion of the List preceding TestEntry,
                            and report the result of that search.)
                   case 3: TargetValue > TestEntry
                       (Apply the procedure Search to see if TargetValue
                            is in the portion of List following TestEntry,
                            and report the result of that search.)
            ] end if
```

Figure 15

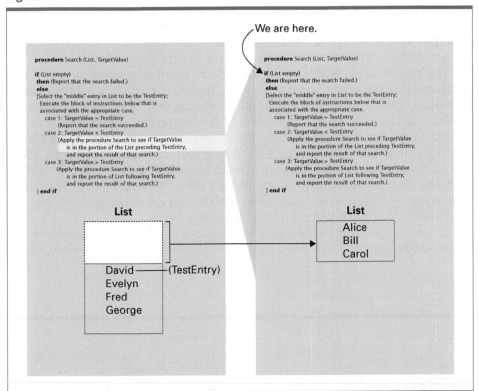

while we apply the second copy to the task of searching the list Alice, Bill, and Carol. When we complete this secondary search, we will discard the second copy of the procedure, report its findings to the original copy, and continue progress in the original. In this way, the second copy of the procedure executes as a subordinate to the original, performing the task requested by the original module and then disappearing.

The secondary search selects Bill as its test entry because that is the middle entry in the list Alice, Bill, and Carol. Since this is the same as the target value, it declares its search to be a success and terminates.

At this point, we have completed the secondary search as requested by the original copy of the procedure, so we are able to continue the execution of that original copy. Here we are told that the result of the secondary search should be reported as the result of the original search. Thus we report that the original search has succeeded. Our process has correctly determined that Bill is a member of the list Alice, Bill, Carol, David, Evelyn, Fred, and George.

Let us now consider what happens if we ask the procedure in Figure 14 to search the list Alice, Carol, Evelyn, Fred, and George for the entry David.

This time the original copy of the procedure selects Evelyn as its test entry and concludes that the target value must reside in the preceding portion of the list. It therefore requests another copy of the procedure to search the list of entries appearing in front of Evelyn—that is, the two-entry list consisting of Alice and Carol. At this stage our situation is as represented in Figure 16.

The second copy of the procedure selects Carol as its current entry and concludes that the target value must lie in the latter portion of its list. It then requests a third copy of the procedure to search the list of names following Carol in the list Alice and Carol. This sublist is empty, so the third copy of the procedure has the task of searching the empty list for the target value David. Our situation at this point is represented by Figure 17. The original copy of the procedure is charged with the task of searching the list Alice, Carol, Evelyn, Fred, and George, with the test entry being Evelyn; the second copy is charged with searching the list Alice and Carol, with its test entry being Carol; and the third copy is about to begin searching the empty list.

Of course, the third copy of the procedure quickly declares its search to be a failure and terminates. The completion of the third copy's task allows the second

Figure 16

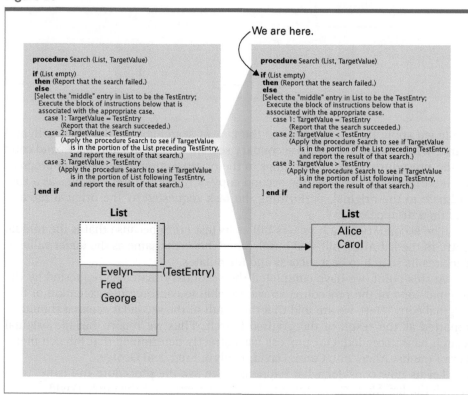

Figure 17

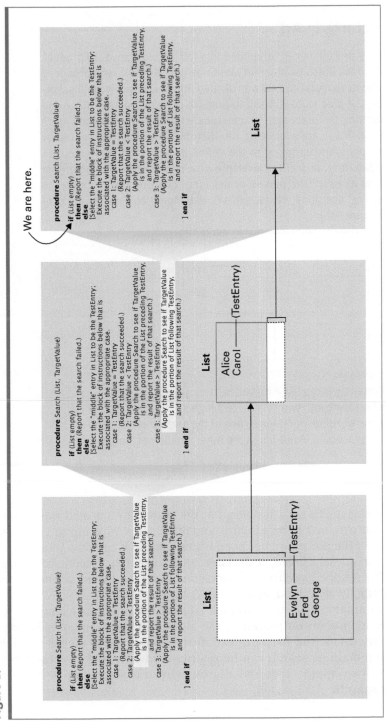

procedure Search (List, TargetValue)

if (List empty)
   then (Report that the search failed.)
else
   [Select the "middle" entry in List to be the TestEntry;
   Execute the block of instructions below that is
   associated with the appropriate case.
      case 1: TargetValue = TestEntry
         (Report that the search succeeded.)
      case 2: TargetValue < TestEntry
         (Apply the procedure Search to see if TargetValue
         is in the portion of the List preceding TestEntry,
         and report the result of that search.)
      case 3: TargetValue > TestEntry
         (Apply the procedure Search to see if TargetValue
         is in the portion of List following TestEntry,
         and report the result of that search.)
   ] **end if**

List

Evelyn
Fred   (TestEntry)
George

procedure Search (List, TargetValue)

if (List empty)
   then (Report that the search failed.)
else
   [Select the "middle" entry in List to be the TestEntry;
   Execute the block of instructions below that is
   associated with the appropriate case.
      case 1: TargetValue = TestEntry
         (Report that the search succeeded.)
      case 2: TargetValue < TestEntry
         (Apply the procedure Search to see if TargetValue
         is in the portion of the List preceding TestEntry,
         and report the result of that search.)
      case 3: TargetValue > TestEntry
         (Apply the procedure Search to see if TargetValue
         is in the portion of List following TestEntry,
         and report the result of that search.)
   ] **end if**

List

Alice
Carol   (TestEntry)

We are here.

procedure Search (List, TargetValue)

if (List empty)
   then (Report that the search failed.)
else
   [Select the "middle" entry in List to be the TestEntry;
   Execute the block of instructions below that is
   associated with the appropriate case.
      case 1: TargetValue = TestEntry
         (Report that the search succeeded.)
      case 2: TargetValue < TestEntry
         (Apply the procedure Search to see if TargetValue
         is in the portion of the List preceding TestEntry,
         and report the result of that search.)
      case 3: TargetValue > TestEntry
         (Apply the procedure Search to see if TargetValue
         is in the portion of List following TestEntry,
         and report the result of that search.)
   ] **end if**

List

Recursive Structures in Art

The following recursive procedure can be applied to a rectangular canvas to produce drawings of the style of the Dutch painter Piet Mondrian (1872–1944), who produced paintings in which the rectangular canvas was divided into successively smaller rectangles. Try following the procedure yourself to produce drawings similar to the one shown. Begin by applying the procedure to a rectangle representing the canvas on which you are working. (If you are wondering whether the algorithm represented by this procedure is an algorithm according to the definition in Section 1, your suspicions are well-founded. It is, in fact, an example of a nondeterministic algorithm since there are places at which the person or machine following the procedure is asked to make "creative" decisions. Perhaps this is why Mondrian's results are considered art while ours are not.)

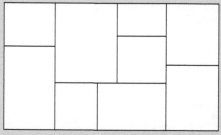

procedure Mondrian (Rectangle)
if (the size of Rectangle is too large for your artistic taste)
  then (divide Rectangle into two smaller rectangles;
       apply the procedure Mondrian to one of the smaller rectangles;
       apply the procedure Mondrian to the other smaller rectangle)

copy to continue its task. It notes that the search it requested was unsuccessful, declares its own task to be a failure, and terminates. This report is what the original copy of the procedure has been waiting for, so it can now proceed. Since the search it requested failed, it declares its own search to have failed and terminates. Our routine has correctly concluded that David is not contained in the list Alice, Carol, Evelyn, Fred, and George.

In summary, if we were to look back at the previous examples, we could see that the process employed by the algorithm represented in Figure 14 is to repeatedly divide the list in question into two smaller pieces in such a way that the remaining search can be restricted to only one of these pieces. This divide-by-two approach is the reason why the algorithm is known as the **binary search.**

Recursive Control

The binary search algorithm is similar to the sequential search in that each algorithm requests the execution of a repetitive process. However, the implementation of this repetition is significantly different. Whereas the sequential search involves a circular form of repetition, the binary search executes each stage of the repetition as a subtask of the previous stage. This technique is known as **recursion.**

As we have seen, the illusion created by the execution of a recursive procedure is the existence of multiple copies of the procedure, each of which is called an activation of the procedure. These activations are created dynamically in a telescoping manner and ultimately disappear as the algorithm advances. Of those activations existing at any given time, only one is actively progressing. The others are effectively in limbo, each waiting for another activation to terminate before it can continue.

Being a repetitive process, recursive systems are just as dependent on proper control as are loop structures. Just as in loop control, recursive systems are dependent on testing for a termination condition and on a design that ensures this condition will be reached. In fact, proper recursive control involves the same three ingredients—initialization, modification, and test for termination—that are required in loop control.

In general, a recursive procedure is designed to test for the termination condition (often called the **base case** or **degenerative case**) before requesting further activations. If the termination condition is not met, the routine creates another activation of the procedure and assigns it the task of solving a revised problem that is closer to the termination condition than that assigned to the current activation. However, if the termination condition is met, a path is taken that causes the current activation to terminate without creating additional activations.

Let us see how the initialization and modification phases of repetitive control are implemented in our binary search procedure of Figure 14. In this case, the creation of additional activations is terminated once the target value is found or the task is reduced to that of searching an empty list. The process is initialized implicitly by being given an initial list and a target value. From this initial configuration the procedure modifies its assigned task to that of searching a smaller list. Since the original list is of finite length and each modification step reduces the length of the list in question, we are assured that the target value ultimately is found or the task is reduced to that of searching the empty list. We can therefore conclude that the repetitive process is guaranteed to cease.

Finally, since both loop and recursive control structures are ways to cause the repetition of a set of instructions, we might ask whether they are equivalent in power. That is, if an algorithm were designed using a loop structure, could another algorithm using only recursive techniques be designed that would solve the same problem and vice versa? Such questions are important in computer science because their answers ultimately tell us what features should be provided in a programming language in order to obtain the most powerful programming system possible. We will return to these ideas when we consider some of the more theoretical aspects of computer science and its mathematical foundations. With this background, we will then be able to prove the equivalence of iterative and recursive structures.

Questions & Exercises

1. What names are interrogated by the binary search (Figure 14) when searching for the name Joe in the list Alice, Brenda, Carol, Duane, Evelyn, Fred, George, Henry, Irene, Joe, Karl, Larry, Mary, Nancy, and Oliver?

2. What is the maximum number of entries that must be interrogated when applying the binary search to a list of 200 entries? What about a list of 100,000 entries?

3. What sequence of numbers would be printed by the following recursive procedure if we started it with N assigned the value 1?

```
procedure Exercise (N)
print the value of N;
if (N < 3) then (apply the procedure Exercise to the
                 value N + 1);
print the value of N.
```

4. What is the termination condition in the recursive procedure of Question/Exercise 3?

6 Efficiency and Correctness

In this section we introduce two topics that constitute important research areas within computer science. The first of these is algorithm efficiency, and the second is algorithm correctness.

Algorithm Efficiency

Even though today's machines are capable of executing millions of instructions each second, efficiency remains a major concern in algorithm design. Often the choice between efficient and inefficient algorithms can make the difference between a practical solution to a problem and an impractical one.

Let us consider the problem of a university registrar faced with the task of retrieving and updating student records. Although the university has an actual enrollment of approximately 10,000 students during any one semester, its "current student" file contains the records of more than 30,000 students who are considered current in the sense that they have registered for at least one course in the past few years but have not completed a degree. For now, let us assume that these records are stored in the registrar's computer as a list ordered by student identification numbers. To find any student record, the registrar would therefore search this list for a particular identification number.

We have presented two algorithms for searching such a list: the sequential search and the binary search. Our question now is whether the choice between these two algorithms makes any difference in the case of the registrar. We consider the sequential search first.

Given a student identification number, the sequential search algorithm starts at the beginning of the list and compares the entries found to the identification number desired. Not knowing anything about the source of the target value, we cannot conclude how far into the list this search must go. We can say, though, that after many searches we expect the average depth of the searches to be halfway through the list; some will be shorter, but others will be longer. Thus, we estimate that over a period of time, the sequential search will investigate roughly 15,000 records per search. If retrieving and checking each record for its identification number requires 10 milliseconds (10 one-thousandths of a second), such a search would require an average of 150 seconds or 2.5 minutes—an unbearably long time for the registrar to wait for a student's record to appear on a computer screen. Even if the time required to retrieve and check each record were reduced to only 1 millisecond, the search would still require an average of 15 seconds, which is still a long time to wait.

In contrast, the binary search proceeds by comparing the target value to the middle entry in the list. If this is not the desired entry, then at least the remaining search is restricted to only half of the original list. Thus, after interrogating the middle entry in the list of 30,000 student records, the binary search has at most 15,000 records still to consider. After the second inquiry, at most 7,500 remain, and after the third retrieval, the list in question has dropped to no more than 3,750 entries. Continuing in this fashion, we see that the target record will be found after retrieving at most 15 entries from the list of 30,000 records. Thus, if each of these retrievals can be performed in 10 milliseconds, the process of searching for a particular record requires only 0.15 of a second—meaning that access to any particular student record will appear to be instantaneous from the registrar's point of view. We conclude that the choice between the sequential search algorithm and the binary search algorithm would have a significant impact in this application.

This example indicates the importance of the area of computer science known as algorithm analysis that encompasses the study of the resources, such as time or storage space, that algorithms require. A major application of such studies is the evaluation of the relative merits of alternative algorithms.

Algorithm analysis often involves best-case, worst-case, and average-case scenarios. In our example, we performed an average-case analysis of the sequential search algorithm and a worst-case analysis of the binary search algorithm in order to estimate the time required to search through a list of 30,000 entries.

In general such analysis is performed in a more generic context. That is, when considering algorithms for searching lists, we do not focus on a list of a particular length, but instead try to identify a formula that would indicate the algorithm's performance for lists of arbitrary lengths. It is not difficult to generalize our previous reasoning to lists of arbitrary lengths. In particular, when applied to a list with n entries, the sequential search algorithm will interrogate an average of $n/2$ entries, whereas the binary search algorithm will interrogate at most $\lg n$ entries in its worst-case scenario. ($\lg n$ represents the base two logarithm of n.)

Let us analyze the insertion sort algorithm (summarized in Figure 11) in a similar manner. Recall that this algorithm involves selecting a list entry, called the pivot entry, comparing this entry to those preceding it until the proper place for the pivot is found, and then inserting the pivot entry in this place. Since the activity of comparing two entries dominates the algorithm, our approach will be to count the number of such comparisons that are performed when sorting a list whose length is n.

The algorithm begins by selecting the second list entry to be the pivot. It then progresses by picking successive entries as the pivot until it has reached the end of the list. In the best possible case, each pivot is already in its proper place, and thus it needs to be compared to only a single entry before this is discovered. Thus, in the best case, applying the insertion sort to a list with n entries requires $n - 1$ comparisons. (The second entry is compared to one entry, the third entry to one entry, and so on.)

In contrast, the worst-case scenario is that each pivot must be compared to all the preceding entries before its proper location can be found. This occurs if the original list is in reverse order. In this case the first pivot (the second list entry) is compared to one entry, the second pivot (the third list entry) is compared to two entries, and so on (Figure 18). Thus the total number of comparisons when sorting a list of n entries is $1 + 2 + 3 + \ldots + (n - 1)$, which is equivalent to $(\tfrac{1}{2})(n^2 - n)$. In particular, if the list contained

Figure 18   Applying the insertion sort in a worst-case situation

Initial list	Comparisons made for each pivot				Sorted list
	1st pivot	2nd pivot	3rd pivot	4th pivot	
Elaine	1 ↗ Elaine	3 ↗ David	6 ↗ Carol	10 ↗ Barbara	Alfred
David	David	2 Elaine	5 David	9 Carol	Barbara
Carol	Carol	Carol	Elaine	8 David	Carol
Barbara	Barbara	Barbara	4 Barbara	Elaine	David
Alfred	Alfred	Alfred	Alfred	7 Alfred	Elaine

10 entries, the worst-case scenario of the insertion sort algorithm would require 45 comparisons.

In the average case of the insertion sort, we would expect each pivot to be compared to half of the entries preceding it. This results in half as many comparisons as were performed in the worst case, or a total of $(\frac{1}{4})(n^2 - n)$ comparisons to sort a list of n entries. If, for example, we use the insertion sort to sort a variety of lists of length 10, we expect the average number of comparisons per sort to be 22.5.

The significance of these results is that the number of comparisons made during the execution of the insertion sort algorithm gives an approximation of the amount of time required to execute the algorithm. Using this approximation, Figure 19 shows a graph indicating how the time required to execute the insertion sort algorithm increases as the length of the list increases. This graph is based on our worst-case analysis of the algorithm, where we concluded that sorting a list of length n would require at most $(\frac{1}{2})(n^2 - n)$ comparisons between list entries. On the graph, we have marked several list lengths and indicated the time required in each case. Notice that as the list lengths increase by uniform increments, the time required to sort the list increases by increasingly greater amounts. Thus the algorithm becomes less efficient as the size of the list increases.

Figure 19 Graph of the worst-case analysis of the insertion sort algorithm

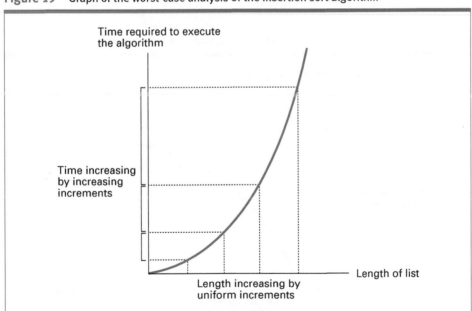

Let us apply a similar analysis to the binary search algorithm. Recall that we concluded that searching a list with n entries using this algorithm would require interrogating at most $\lg n$ entries, which again gives an approximation to the amount of time required to execute the algorithm for various list sizes. Figure 20 shows a graph based on this analysis on which we have again marked several list lengths of uniformly increasing size and identified the time required by the algorithm in each case. Note that the time required by the algorithm increases by decreasing increments. That is, the binary search algorithm becomes more efficient as the size of the list increases.

The distinguishing factor between Figures 19 and 20 is the general shape of the graphs involved. This general shape reveals how well an algorithm should be expected to perform for larger and larger inputs. Moreover, the general shape of a graph is determined by the type of the expression being represented rather than the specifics of the expression—all linear expressions produce a straight line; all quadratic expressions produce a parabolic curve; all logarithmic expressions produce the logarithmic shape shown in Figure 20. It is customary to identify a shape with the simplest expression that produces that shape. In particular, we identify the parabolic shape with the expression n^2 and the logarithmic shape with the expression $\lg n$.

Since the shape of the graph obtained by comparing the time required for an algorithm to perform its task to the size of the input data reflects the efficiency characteristics of the algorithm, it is common to classify algorithms according to the shapes of these graphs—normally based on the algorithm's worst-case analysis.

Figure 20   Graph of the worst-case analysis of the binary search algorithm

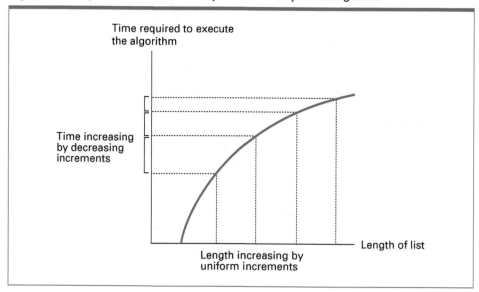

The notation used to identify these classes is sometimes called **big-theta notation.** All algorithms whose graphs have the shape of a parabola, such as the insertion sort, are put in the class represented by $\Theta(n^2)$ (read "big theta of n squared"); all algorithms whose graphs have the shape of a logarithmic expression, such as the binary search, fall in the class represented by $\Theta(lg\ n)$ (read "big theta of *log n*"). Knowing the class in which a particular algorithm falls allows us to predict its performance and to compare it against other algorithms that solve the same problem. Two algorithms in $\Theta(n^2)$ will exhibit similar changes in time requirements as the size of the inputs increases. Moreover, the time requirements of an algorithm in $\Theta(lg\ n)$ will not expand as rapidly as that of an algorithm in $\Theta(n^2)$.

Software Verification

Recall that the fourth phase in Polya's analysis of problem solving (Section 3) is to evaluate the solution for accuracy and for its potential as a tool for solving other problems. The significance of the first part of this phase is exemplified by the following example:

> A traveler with a gold chain of seven links must stay in an isolated hotel for seven nights. The rent each night consists of one link from the chain. What is the fewest number of links that must be cut so that the traveler can pay the hotel one link of the chain each morning without paying for lodging in advance?

To solve this problem we first realize that not every link in the chain must be cut. If we cut only the second link, we could free both the first and second links from the other five. Following this insight, we are led to the solution of cutting only the second, fourth, and sixth links in the chain, a process that releases each link while cutting only three (Figure 21). Furthermore, any fewer cuts leaves two links connected, so we might conclude that the correct answer to our problem is three.

Upon reconsidering the problem, however, we might make the observation that when only the third link in the chain is cut, we obtain three pieces of chain

Figure 21   Separating the chain using only three cuts

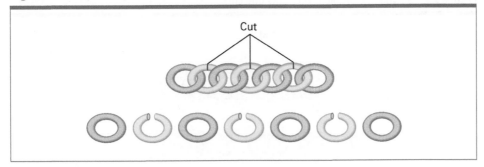

of lengths one, two, and four (Figure 22). With these pieces we can proceed as follows:

First morning: Give the hotel the single link.

Second morning: Retrieve the single link and give the hotel the two-link piece.

Third morning: Give the hotel the single link.

Fourth morning: Retrieve the three links held by the hotel and give the hotel the four-link piece.

Fifth morning: Give the hotel the single link.

Sixth morning: Retrieve the single link and give the hotel the double-link piece.

Seventh morning: Give the hotel the single link.

Consequently, our first answer, which we thought was correct, is incorrect. How, then, can we be sure that our new solution is correct? We might argue as follows: Since a single link must be given to the hotel on the first morning, at least one link of the chain must be cut, and since our new solution requires only one cut, it must be optimal.

Translated into the programming environment, this example emphasizes the distinction between a program that is believed to be correct and a program that is correct. The two are not necessarily the same. The data processing community is rich in horror stories involving software that although "known" to be correct still failed at a critical moment because of some unforeseen situation. Verification of software is therefore an important undertaking, and the search for efficient verification techniques constitutes an active field of research in computer science.

A major line of research in this area attempts to apply the techniques of formal logic to prove the correctness of a program. That is, the goal is to apply formal logic to prove that the algorithm represented by a program does what it is intended to do. The underlying thesis is that by reducing the verification process to a formal procedure, one is protected from the inaccurate conclusions that might be associated with intuitive arguments, as was the case in the gold chain problem. Let us consider this approach to program verification in more detail.

Just as a formal mathematical proof is based on axioms (geometric proofs are often founded on the axioms of Euclidean geometry, whereas other proofs

Figure 22   Solving the problem with only one cut

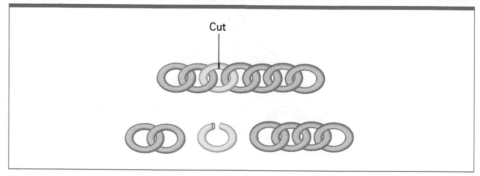

Beyond Verification of Software

Verification problems, as discussed in the text, are not unique to software. Equally important is the problem of confirming that the hardware that executes a program is free of flaws. This involves the verification of circuit designs as well as machine construction. Again, the state of the art relies heavily on testing, which, as in the case of software, means that subtle errors can find their way into finished products. Records indicate that the Mark I, constructed at Harvard University in the 1940s, contained wiring errors that were not detected for many years. A more recent example is a flaw in the floating-point portion of the early Pentium microprocessors. In both of these cases, the error was detected before serious consequences developed.

are based on the axioms of set theory), a formal proof of a program's correctness is based on the specifications under which the program was designed. To prove that a program correctly sorts lists of names, we are allowed to begin with the assumption that the program's input is a list of names, or if the program is designed to compute the average of one or more positive numbers, we assume that the input does, in fact, consist of one or more positive numbers. In short, a proof of correctness begins with the assumption that certain conditions, called **preconditions,** are satisfied at the beginning of the program's execution.

The next step in a proof of correctness is to consider how the consequences of these preconditions propagate through the program. For this purpose, researchers have analyzed various program structures to determine how a statement, known to be true before the structure is executed, is affected by executing the structure. As a simple example, if a certain statement about the value of Y is known to hold prior to executing the instruction

       X ← Y

then that same statement can be made about X after the instruction has been executed. More precisely, if the value of Y is not 0 before the instruction is executed, then we can conclude that the value of X will not be 0 after the instruction is executed.

A slightly more involved example occurs in the case of an `if-then-else` structure such as

         if (*condition*) **then** (*instruction A*)
                       else (*instruction B*)

Here, if some statement is known to hold before execution of the structure, then immediately before executing *instruction A*, we know that both that statement and the condition tested are true, whereas if *instruction B* is to be executed, we know the statement and the negation of the condition tested must hold.

Following rules such as these, a proof of correctness proceeds by identifying statements, called **assertions,** that can be established at various points in the program. The result is a collection of assertions, each being a consequence of the program's preconditions and the sequence of instructions that lead to the point in the program at which the assertion is established. If the assertion so established at the end of the program corresponds to the desired output specifications (which are called **postconditions**), we conclude that the program is correct.

As an example, consider the typical `while` loop structure represented in Figure 23. Suppose, as a consequence of the preconditions given at point A, we can establish that a particular assertion is true each time the test for termination is performed (point B) during the repetitive process. (An assertion at a point in a loop that is true every time that point in the loop is reached is known as a **loop invariant.**) Then, if the repetition ever terminates, execution moves to point C, where we can conclude that both the loop invariant and the termination condition hold. (The loop invariant still holds because the test for termination does not alter any values in the program, and the termination condition holds because otherwise the loop does not terminate.) If these combined statements imply the desired postconditions, our proof of correctness can be completed merely by showing that the initialization and modification components of the loop ultimately lead to the termination condition.

You should compare this analysis to our example of the insertion sort shown in Figure 11. The outer loop in that program is based on the loop invariant

> Each time the test for termination is performed, the entries in the list from position 1 through position $N - 1$ are sorted

Figure 23 The assertions associated with a typical while structure

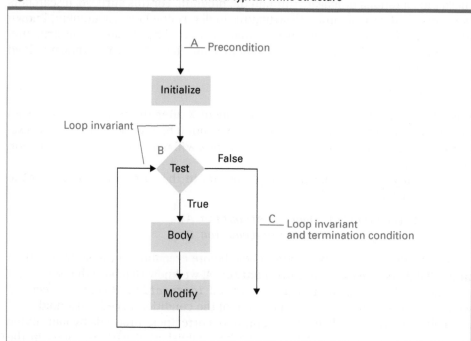

and the termination condition is

The value of N is greater than the length of the list.

Thus, if the loop ever terminates, we know that both conditions must be satisfied, which implies that the entire list would be sorted.

Progress in the development of program verification techniques continues to be challenging. However, advancements are being made. One of the more significant is found in the programming language SPARK, which is closely related to the more popular language Ada. (Ada is one of the languages from which we will draw examples in the next chapter.) In addition to allowing programs to be expressed in a high-level form such as our pseudocode, SPARK gives programmers a means of including assertions such as preconditions, postconditions, and loop invariants within the program. Thus, a program written in SPARK contains not only the algorithm to be applied but also the information required for the application of formal proof-of-correctness techniques. To date, SPARK has been used successfully in numerous software development projects involving critical software applications, including secure software for the U.S. National Security Agency, internal control software used in Lockheed Martin's C130J Hercules aircraft, and critical rail transportation control systems.

In spite of successes such as SPARK, formal program verification techniques have not yet found widespread usage, and thus most of today's software is "verified" by testing—a process that is shaky at best. After all, verification by testing proves nothing more than that the program performs correctly for the cases under which it was tested. Any additional conclusions are merely projections. The errors contained in a program are often consequences of subtle oversights that are easily overlooked during testing as well as development. Consequently errors in a program, just as our error in the gold chain problem, can, and often do, go undetected, even though significant effort may be exerted to avoid it. A dramatic example occurred at AT&T: An error in the software controlling 114 switching stations went undetected from the software's installation in December 1989 until January 15, 1990, at which time a unique set of circumstances caused approximately five million calls to be unnecessarily blocked over a nine-hour period.

Questions & Exercises

1. Suppose we find that a machine programmed with our insertion sort algorithm requires an average of one second to sort a list of 100 names. How long do you estimate it takes to sort a list of 1000 names? How about 10,000 names?
2. Give an example of an algorithm in each of the following classes: $\Theta(lg\ n)$, $\Theta(n)$, and $\Theta(n^2)$.

3. List the classes $\Theta(n^2)$, $\Theta(lg\ n)$, $\Theta(n)$, and $\Theta(n^3)$ in decreasing order of efficiency.

4. Consider the following problem and a proposed answer. Is the proposed answer correct? Why or why not?

Problem: Suppose a box contains three cards. One of three cards is painted black on both sides, one is painted red on both sides, and the third is painted red on one side and black on the other. One of the cards is drawn from the box, and you are allowed to see one side of it. What is the probability that the other side of the card is the same color as the side you see?
Proposed answer: One-half. Suppose the side of the card you can see is red. (The argument would be symmetric with this one if the side were black.) Only two cards among the three have a red side. Thus the card you see must be one of these two. One of these two cards is red on the other side, while the other is black. Thus the card you can see is just as likely to be red on the other side as it is to be black.

5. The following program segment is an attempt to compute the quotient (forgetting any remainder) of two positive integers (a dividend and a divisor) by counting the number of times the divisor can be subtracted from the dividend before what is left becomes less than the divisor. For instance, 7/3 should produce 2 because 3 can be subtracted from 7 twice. Is the program correct? Justify your answer.

```
Count ← 0;
Remainder ← Dividend;
repeat (Remainder ← Remainder − Divisor;
         Count ← Count + 1)
until (Remainder < Divisor)
Quotient ← Count.
```

6. The following program segment is designed to compute the product of two nonnegative integers X and Y by accumulating the sum of X copies of Y— that is, 3 times 4 is computed by accumulating the sum of three 4s. Is the program correct? Justify your answer.

```
Product ← Y;
Count ← 1;
while (Count < X) do
  (Product ← Product + Y;
   Count ← Count + 1)
```

7. Assuming the precondition that the value associated with N is a positive integer, establish a loop invariant that leads to the conclusion that if the following routine terminates, then Sum is assigned the value $0 + 1 + \ldots + N$.

```
    Sum ← 0;
    K ← 0;
    while (K < N) do
      (K ← K + 1;
       Sum ← Sum + K)
```

Provide an argument to the effect that the routine does in fact terminate.

8. Suppose that both a program and the hardware that executes it have been formally verified to be accurate. Does this ensure accuracy?

Chapter Review Problems

(Asterisked problems are associated with optional sections.)

1. Give an example of a set of steps that conforms to the informal definition of an algorithm given in the opening paragraph of Section 1 but does not conform to the formal definition given in Figure 1.

2. Explain the distinction between an ambiguity in a proposed algorithm and an ambiguity in the representation of an algorithm.

3. Describe how the use of primitives helps remove ambiguities in an algorithm's representation.

4. Select a subject with which you are familiar and design a pseudocode for giving directions in that subject. In particular, describe the primitives you would use and the syntax you would use to represent them. (If you are having trouble thinking of a subject, try sports, arts, or crafts.)

5. Does the following program represent an algorithm in the strict sense? Why or why not?

```
Count ← 0;
while (Count not 5) do
  (Count ← Count + 2)
```

6. In what sense do the following three steps not constitute an algorithm?

Step 1: Draw a straight line segment between the points with rectangular coordinates (2,5) and (6,11).

Step 2: Draw a straight line segment between the points with rectangular coordinates (1,3) and (3,6).

Step 3: Draw a circle whose center is at the intersection of the previous line segments and whose radius is two.

7. Rewrite the following program segment using a repeat structure rather than a while structure. Be sure the new version prints the same values as the original.

```
Count ← 2;
while (Count < 7) do
  (print the value assigned to Count and
   Count ← Count + 1)
```

8. Rewrite the following program segment using a while structure rather than a repeat structure. Be sure the new version prints the same values as the original.

```
Count ← 1;
repeat
   (print the value assigned to Count and
    Count ← Count + 1)
until (Count = 5)
```

9. What must be done to translate a posttest loop expressed in the form

repeat (. . .) until (. . .)

into an equivalent posttest loop expressed in the form

do (. . .) while (. . .)

10. Design an algorithm that, when given an arrangement of the digits 0, 1, 2, 3, 4, 5, 6, 7, 8, 9, rearranges the digits so that the new arrangement represents the next larger value that can be represented by these digits (or reports that no such rearrangement exists if no rearrangement produces a larger value). Thus 5647382901 would produce 5647382910.

11. Design an algorithm for finding all the factors of a positive integer. For example, in the case of the integer 12, your algorithm should report the values 1, 2, 3, 4, 6, and 12.

12. Design an algorithm for determining the day of the week of any date since January 1, 1700. For example, August 17, 2001 was a Friday.

13. What is the difference between a formal programming language and a pseudocode?

14. What is the difference between syntax and semantics?

15. The following is an addition problem in traditional base ten notation. Each letter represents a different digit. What digit does each letter represent? How did you get your foot in the door?

$$\begin{array}{r} XYZ \\ + \ YWY \\ \hline ZYZW \end{array}$$

16. The following is a multiplication problem in traditional base ten notation. Each letter represents a different digit. What digit does each letter represent? How did you get your foot in the door?

$$\begin{array}{r} XY \\ \times \ YX \\ \hline XY \\ YZ \\ \hline WVY \end{array}$$

17. The following is an addition problem in binary notation. Each letter represents a unique binary digit. Which letter represents 1 and which represents 0? Design an algorithm for solving problems like this.

$$\begin{array}{r} YXX \\ + \ XYX \\ \hline XYYY \end{array}$$

18. Four prospectors with only one lantern must walk through a mine shaft. At most, two prospectors can travel together and any prospector in the shaft must be with the lantern. The prospectors, named Andrews, Blake, Johnson, and Kelly, can walk through the shaft in one minute, two minutes, four minutes, and eight minutes, respectively. When two walk together they travel at the speed of the slower prospector. How can all four prospectors get through the mine shaft in only 15 minutes? After you have solved this problem, explain how you got your foot in the door.

19. Starting with a large wine glass and a small wine glass, fill the small glass with wine and then pour that wine into the large glass. Next, fill the small glass with water and pour some of that water into the large glass. Mix the contents of the large glass, and then pour the mixture back into the small glass until the small glass is full. Will there be more water in the large glass than there is wine in the small glass? After you have solved this problem, explain how you got your foot in the door.

20. Two bees, named Romeo and Juliet, live in different hives but have met and fallen in love. On a windless spring morning, they simultaneously leave their respective hives to visit each other. Their routes meet at a point 50 meters from the closest hive, but they fail to see each other and continue on to their destinations. At their destinations, they spend the same amount of time to discover that the other is not home and begin their return trips. On their return trips, they meet at a point that is 20 meters from the closest hive. This time they see each other and have a picnic lunch before returning home. How far apart are the

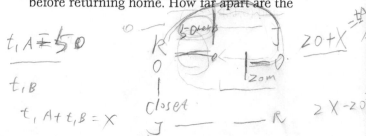

two hives? After you have solved this problem, explain how you got your foot in the door.

21. Design an algorithm that, given two strings of characters, tests whether the first string appears as a substring somewhere in the second.

22. The following algorithm is designed to print the beginning of what is known as the Fibonacci sequence. Identify the body of the loop. Where is the initialization step for the loop control? The modification step? The test step? What list of numbers is produced?

```
Last ← 0;
Current ← 1;
while (Current < 100) do
  (print the value assigned to Current;
   Temp ← Last;
   Last ← Current; and
   Current ← Last + Temp)
```

23. What sequence of numbers is printed by the following algorithm if it is started with input values 0 and 1?

```
procedure MysteryWrite (Last, Current)
if (Current < 100) then
(print the value assigned to Current;
 Temp ← Current + Last;
 apply MysteryWrite to the values Cur-
    rent and Temp)
```

24. Modify the procedure MysteryWrite in the preceding problem so that the values are printed in reverse order.

25. What letters are interrogated by the binary search (Figure 14) if it is applied to the list A, B, C, D, E, F, G, H, I, J, K, L, M, N, O when searching for the value J? What about searching for the value Z?

26. After performing many sequential searches on a list of 6,000 entries, what would you expect to be the average number of times that the target value would have been compared to a list entry? What if the search algorithm was the binary search?

27. Identify the termination condition in each of the following iterative statements.
    a. while (Count < 5) do (   )
    b. repeat (   )
       until (Count = 1)
    c. while ((Count < 5) and (Total < 56))
       do (   )

28. Identify the body of the following loop structure and count the number of times it will be executed. What happens if the test is changed to read while (Count not 6)?

```
Count ← 1;
while (Count not 7) do
  (print the value assigned to Count and
   Count ← Count + 3)
```

29. What problems do you expect to arise if the following program is implemented on a computer? (Hint: Remember the problem of round-off errors associated with floating-point arithmetic.)

```
Count ← one-tenth;
repeat
  (print the value assigned to Count and
   Count ← Count + one-tenth)
until (Count equals 1)
```

30. Design a recursive version of the Euclidean algorithm (Question 3 of Section 2).

31. Suppose we apply both Test1 and Test2 (defined below) to the input value 1. What is the difference in the printed output of the two routines?

```
procedure Test1 (Count)
if (Count not 5)
  then (print the value assigned to Count;
        apply Test1 to the value
            Count + 1)

procedure Test2 (Count)
if (Count not 5)
  then (apply Test2 to the value
            Count + 1;
        print the value assigned to
            Count)
```

32. Identify the important constituents of the control mechanism in the routines of the previous problem. In particular, what condition causes the process to terminate? Where is the state of the process modified toward this termination condition? Where is the state of the control process initialized?

33. Identify the termination condition in the following recursive procedure.

```
procedure XXX (N)
if (N = 5) then (apply the procedure XXX
                 to the value N + 1)
```

34. Apply the procedure MysteryPrint (defined below) to the value 3 and record the values that are printed.

```
procedure MysteryPrint (N)
if (N > 0) then (print the value of N and
                 apply the procedure
                 MysteryPrint to the
                 value N − 2)
Print the value of N + 1.
```

35. Apply the procedure MysteryPrint (defined below) to the value 2 and record the values that are printed.

```
procedure MysteryPrint (N)
if (N > 0)
    then (print the value of N and
          apply the procedure MysteryPrint
            to the value N − 2)
    else (print the value of N and
          if (N > −1)
              then (apply the procedure
                    MysteryPrint
                    to the value N + 1))
```

36. Design an algorithm to generate the sequence of positive integers (in increasing order) whose only prime divisors are 2 and 3; that is, your program should produce the sequence 2, 3, 4, 6, 8, 9, 12, 16, 18, 24, 27, ... Does your program represent an algorithm in the strict sense?

37. Answer the following questions in terms of the list: Alice, Byron, Carol, Duane, Elaine, Floyd, Gene, Henry, Iris.

a. Which search algorithm (sequential or binary) will find the name Gene more quickly?

b. Which search algorithm (sequential or binary) will find the name Alice more quickly?

c. Which search algorithm (sequential or binary) will detect the absence of the name Bruce more quickly?

d. Which search algorithm (sequential or binary) will detect the absence of the name Sue more quickly?

e. How many entries will be interrogated when searching for the name Elaine when using the sequential search? How many will be interrogated when using the binary search?

38. The factorial of 0 is defined to be 1. The factorial of a positive integer is defined to be the product of that integer times the factorial of the next smaller nonnegative integer. We use the notation n! to express the factorial of the integer n. Thus the factorial of 3 (written 3!) is $3 \times (2!) = 3 \times (2 \times (1!)) = 3 \times (2 \times (1 \times (0!))) = 3 \times (2 \times (1 \times (1))) = 6$. Design a recursive algorithm that computes the factorial of a given value.

39. a. Suppose you must sort a list of five names, and you have already designed an algorithm that sorts a list of four names. Design an algorithm to sort the list of five names by taking advantage of the previously designed algorithm.

b. Design a recursive algorithm to sort arbitrary lists of names based on the technique used in (a).

40. The puzzle called the Towers of Hanoi consists of three pegs, one of which contains several rings stacked in order of descending diameter from bottom to top. The problem is to move the stack of rings to another peg. You are allowed to move only one ring at a time, and at no time is a ring to be placed on top of a smaller one. Observe that if the puzzle involved only one

ring, it would be extremely easy. Moreover, when faced with the problem of moving several rings, if you could move all but the largest ring to another peg, the largest ring could then be

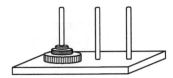

placed on the third peg, and then the problem would be to move the remaining rings on top of it. Using this observation, develop a recursive algorithm for solving the Towers of Hanoi puzzle for an arbitrary number of rings.

41. Another approach to solving the Towers of Hanoi puzzle (Problem 40) is to imagine the pegs arranged on a circular stand with a peg mounted at each of the positions of 4, 8, and 12 o'clock. The rings, which begin on one of the pegs, are numbered 1, 2, 3, and so on, starting with the smallest ring being 1. Odd-numbered rings, when on top of a stack, are allowed to move clockwise to the next peg; likewise, even-numbered rings are allowed to move counterclockwise (as long as that move does not place a ring on a smaller one). Under

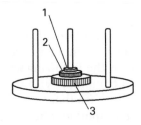

this restriction, always move the largest-numbered ring that can be moved. Based on this observation, develop a nonrecursive algorithm for solving the Towers of Hanoi puzzle.

42. Develop two algorithms, one based on a loop structure and the other on a recursive struc-

ture, to print the daily salary of a worker who each day is paid twice the previous day's salary (starting with one penny for the first day's work) for a 30-day period. What problems relating to number storage are you likely to encounter if you implement your solutions on an actual machine?

43. Design an algorithm to find the square root of a positive number by starting with the number itself as the first guess and repeatedly producing a new guess from the previous one by averaging the previous guess with the result of dividing the original number by the previous guess. Analyze the control of this repetitive process. In particular, what condition should terminate the repetition?

44. Design an algorithm that lists all possible rearrangements of the symbols in a string of five distinct characters.

45. Design an algorithm that, given a list of names, finds the longest name in the list. Determine what your solution does if there are several "longest" names in the list. In particular, what would your algorithm do if all the names had the same length?

46. Design an algorithm that, given a list of five or more numbers, finds the five smallest and five largest numbers in the list without sorting the entire list.

47. Arrange the names Brenda, Doris, Raymond, Steve, Timothy, and William in an order that requires the least number of comparisons when sorted by the insertion sort algorithm (Figure 11).

48. What is the largest number of entries that are interrogated if the binary search algorithm (Figure 14) is applied to a list of 4000 names? How does this compare to the sequential search (Figure 6)?

49. Use big-theta notation to classify the traditional grade school algorithms for addition and multiplication. That is, if asked to add two numbers each having n digits, how

many individual additions must be performed. If requested to multiply two *n*-digit numbers, how many individual multiplications are required?

50. Sometimes a slight change in a problem can significantly alter the form of its solution. For example, find a simple algorithm for solving the following problem and classify it using big-theta notation:

Divide a group of people into two disjoint subgroups (of arbitrary size) such that the difference in the total ages of the members of the two subgroups is as large as possible.

Now change the problem so that the desired difference is as small as possible and classify your approach to the problem.

51. From the following list, extract a collection of numbers whose sum is 3165. How efficient is your approach to the problem?

26, 39, 104, 195, 403, 504, 793, 995, 1156, 1677

52. Does the loop in the following routine terminate? Explain your answer. Explain what might happen if this routine is actually executed by a computer.

```
X ← 1;
Y ← 1/2;
while (X not equal 0) do
   (X ← X − Y;
    Y ← Y ÷ 2)
```

53. The following program segment is designed to compute the product of two nonnegative integers X and Y by accumulating the sum of X copies of Y; that is, 3 times 4 is computed by accumulating the sum of three 4s. Is the program segment correct? Explain your answer.

```
Product ← 0;
Count ← 0;
repeat (Product ← Product + Y,
        Count ← Count + 1)
until (Count = X)
```

54. The following program segment is designed to report which of the positive integers X and Y is larger. Is the program segment correct? Explain your answer.

```
Difference ← X − Y;
if (Difference is positive)
   then (print "X is bigger than Y")
   else (print "Y is bigger than X")
```

55. The following program segment is designed to find the largest entry in a nonempty list of integers. Is it correct? Explain your answer.

```
TestValue ← first list entry;
CurrentEntry ← first list entry;
while (CurrentEntry is not the last
       entry) do
   (if (CurrentEntry > TestValue)
        then (TestValue ← CurrentEntry)
    CurrentEntry ← the next list entry)
```

56. a. Identify the preconditions for the sequential search as represented in Figure 6. Establish a loop invariant for the **while** structure in that program that, when combined with the termination condition, implies that upon termination of the loop, the algorithm will report success or failure correctly.

b. Give an argument showing that the **while** loop in Figure 6 does in fact terminate.

57. Based on the preconditions that X and Y are assigned nonnegative integers, identify a loop invariant for the following **while** structure that, when combined with the termination condition, implies that the value associated with Z upon loop termination must be X − Y.

```
Z ← X;
J ← 0;
while (J < Y) do
   (Z ← Z − 1;
    J ← J + 1)
```

Social Issues

The following questions are intended as a guide to the ethical/social/legal issues associated with the field of computing. The goal is not merely to answer these questions. You should also consider why you answered as you did and whether your justifications are consistent from one question to the next.

1. As it is currently impossible to verify completely the accuracy of complex programs, under what circumstances, if any, should the creator of a program be liable for errors?

2. Suppose you have an idea and develop it into a product that many people can use. Moreover, it has required a year of work and an investment of $50,000 to develop your idea into a form that is useful to the general public. In its final form, however, the product can be used by most people without buying anything from you. What right do you have for compensation? Is it ethical to pirate computer software? What about music and motion pictures?

3. Suppose a software package is so expensive that it is totally out of your price range. Is it ethical to copy it for your own use? (After all, you are not cheating the supplier out of a sale because you would not have bought the package anyway.)

4. Ownership of rivers, forests, oceans, etc. has long been an issue of debate. In what sense should someone or some institution be given ownership of an algorithm?

5. Some people feel that new algorithms are discovered, whereas others feel that new algorithms are created. To which philosophy do you subscribe? Would the different points of view lead to different conclusions regarding ownership of algorithms and ownership rights?

6. Is it ethical to design an algorithm for performing an illegal act? Does it matter whether the algorithm is ever executed? Should the person who creates such an algorithm have ownership rights to that algorithm? If so, what should those rights be? Should algorithm ownership rights be dependent on the purpose of the algorithm? Is it ethical to advertise and circulate techniques for breaking security? Does it matter what is being broken into?

7. An author is paid for the motion picture rights to a novel even though the story is often altered in the film version. How much of a story has to change before it becomes a different story? What alterations must be made to an algorithm for it to become a different algorithm?

8. Educational software is now being marketed for children in the 18 months or younger age group. Proponents argue that such software provides sights and sounds that would otherwise not be available to many children. Opponents argue that it is a poor substitute for personal parent/child interaction. What is your opinion? Should you take any action based on your opinion without knowing more about the software? If so, what action?

Additional Reading

Aho, A. V., J. E. Hopcroft, and J. D. Ullman. *The Design and Analysis of Computer Algorithms.* Boston, MA: Addison-Wesley, 1974.

Baase, S. *Computer Algorithms: Introduction to Design and Analysis,* 3rd ed. Boston, MA: Addison-Wesley, 2000.

Barnes, J. *High Integrity Software: The SPARK Approach to Safety and Security.* Boston, MA: Addison-Wesley, 2003.

Gries, D. *The Science of Programming.* New York: Springer-Verlag, 1998.

Harbin, R. *Origami—the Art of Paper Folding.* London: Hodder Paperbacks, 1973.

Johnsonbaugh, R. and M. Schaefer. *Algorithms.* Upper Saddle River, NJ: Prentice-Hall, 2004.

Kleinberg, J. and E. Tardos. *Algorithm Design.* Boston, MA: Addision-Wesley, 2006.

Knuth, D. E. *The Art of Computer Programming,* Vol. 3, 3rd ed. Boston, MA: Addison-Wesley, 1998.

Levitin, A. V. *Introduction to the Design and Analysis of Algorithms,* 2nd ed. Boston, MA: Addison-Wesley, 2007.

Polya, G. *How to Solve It.* Princeton, NJ: Princeton University Press, 1973.

Roberts, E. S. *Thinking Recursively.* New York: Wiley, 1986.

Answers to Questions & Exercises

Section 1

1. A process is the activity of executing an algorithm. A program is a representation of an algorithm.

2. In the introductory chapter we cited algorithms for playing music, operating washing machines, constructing models, and performing magic tricks, as well as the Euclidean algorithm. Many of the "algorithms" you meet in everyday life fail to be algorithms according to our formal definition. The example of the long-division algorithm was cited in the text. Another is the algorithm executed by a clock that continues to advance its hands and ring its chimes day after day.

3. The informal definition fails to require that the steps be ordered and unambiguous. It merely hints at the requirements that the steps be executable and lead to an end.

4. There are two points here. The first is that the instructions define a nonterminating process. In reality, however, the process will ultimately reach the state in which there are no coins in your pocket. In fact, this might be the starting state. At this point the problem is that of ambiguity. The algorithm, as represented, does not tell us what to do in this situation.

Section 2

1. One example is found in the composition of matter. At one level, the primitives are considered molecules, yet these particles are actually composites made up of atoms, which in turn are composed of electrons, protons, and neutrons. Today, we know that even these "primitives" are composites.

2. Once a procedure is correctly constructed, it can be used as a building block for larger program structures without reconsidering the procedure's internal composition.

3.
```
X ← the larger input;
Y ← the smaller input;
while (Y not zero) do
  (Remainder ← remainder after dividing X by Y;
   X ← Y;
   Y ← Remainder);
GCD ← X
```

4. All other colors of light can be produced by combining red, blue, and green. Thus a television picture tube is designed to produce these three basic colors.

Section 3

1. a.
```
if (n = 1 or n = 2)
     then (the answer is the list containing the single value n)
     else (Divide n by 3, obtaining a quotient q and a remainder r.
              if (r = 0)
                   then (the answer is the list containing q 3s)
              if (r = 1)
                   then (the answer is the list containing (q - 1) 3s
                            and two 2s;)
              if (r = 2)
                   then (the answer is the list containing q 3s and one 2)
         )
```
   b. The result would be the list containing 667 threes.

c. You probably experimented with small input values until you began to see a pattern.

2. a. Yes. *Hint:* Place the first tile in the center so that it avoids the quadrant containing the hole while covering one square from each of the other quadrants. Each quadrant then represents a smaller version of the original problem.

b. The board with a single hole contains $2^{2n} - 1$ squares, and each tile covers exactly three squares.

c. Parts (a) and (b) of this question provide an excellent example of how knowing a solution to one problem helps solve another. See Polya's fourth phase.

3. It says, "This is the correct answer."

4. Simply trying to assemble the pieces would be a bottom-up approach. However, by looking at the puzzle box to see what the picture is supposed to look like adds a top-down component to your approach.

Section 4

1. Change the test in the `while` statement to read "target value not equal to current entry and there remain entries to be considered."

2. ```
Z ← 0;
X ← 1;
repeat (Z ← Z + X;
        X ← X + 1)
until (X = 6)
```

3. This has proven to be a problem with the C language. When the *do* and *while* key words are separated by several lines, readers of a program often stumble over the proper interpretation of a *while* clause. In particular, the *while* at the end of a *do* statement is often interpreted as the beginning of a *while* statement. Thus experience would say that it is better to use different key words to represent pretest and posttest loop stuctures.

4.
| Cheryl | Alice | Alice |
|--------|--------|--------|
| Gene | Cheryl | Brenda |
| Alice | Gene | Cheryl |
| Brenda | Brenda | Gene |

5. It is a waste of time to insist on placing the pivot above an identical entry in the list. For instance, make the proposed change and then try the new program on a list in which all entries are the same.

6. ```
procedure sort (List)
  N ← 1;
  while (N is less than the length of List) do
    (J ← N + 1;
```

```
while (J is not greater than length of List) do
   (if (the entry in position J is less than the entry in
       position N)
       then (interchange the two entries);
    J ← J + 1)
N ← N + 1)
```

7. The following is an inefficient solution. Can you make it more efficient?
```
procedure sort (List)
N ← the length of List;
while (N is greater than 1) do
   (J ← the length of List;
    while (J is greater than 1) do
       (if (the entry in position J is less than the entry in
           position J − 1)
           then (interchange the two entries);
        J ← J − 1)
    N ← N − 1)
```

Section 5

1. The first name considered would be Henry, the next would be Larry, and the last would be Joe.

2. 8, 17

3. 1, 2, 3, 3, 2, 1

4. The termination condition is "N is bigger than or equal to 3" (or "N is not less than 3"). This is the condition under which no additional activations are created.

Section 6

1. If the machine can sort 100 names in one second, it can perform $\frac{1}{4}$ (10,000 − 100) comparisons in one second. This means that each comparison takes approximately 0.0004 second. Consequently, sorting 1000 names [which requires an average of $\frac{1}{4}$ (1,000,000 − 1000) comparisons] requires roughly 100 seconds or $1\frac{2}{3}$ minutes.

2. The binary search belongs to $\Theta(\lg n)$ the sequential search belongs to $\Theta(n)$ and the insertion sort belongs to $\Theta(n^2)$.

3. The class $\Theta(\lg n)$ is most efficient, followed by $\Theta(n)$, $\Theta(n^2)$, and $\Theta(n^3)$.

4. No. The answer is not correct, although it might sound right. The truth is that two of the three cards are the same on both sides. Thus the probability of picking such a card is two-thirds.

5. No. If the dividend is less than the divisor, such as in $\frac{3}{7}$, the answer given is 1, although it should be 0.

6. No. If the value of X is zero and the value of Y is nonzero, the answer given will not be correct.

7. Each time the test for termination is conducted, the statement "Sum = 1 + 2 + ... + K and K less than or equal to N" is true. Combining this with the termination condition "K greater than or equal to N" produces the desired conclusion "Sum = 1 + 2 + ... + N." Because K is initialized at zero and incremented by one each time through the loop, its value must ultimately reach that of N.

8. Unfortunately, no. Problems beyond the control of hardware and software design, such as mechanical malfunctions and electrical problems, can affect computations.

12

Introduction to Computers and Programming

1 Introduction

Think about some of the different ways that people use computers. In school, students use computers for tasks such as writing papers, searching for articles, sending email, and participating in online classes. At work, people use computers to analyze data, make presentations, conduct business transactions, communicate with customers and coworkers, control machines in manufacturing facilities, and do many other things. At home, people use computers for tasks such as paying bills, shopping online, communicating with friends and family, and playing computer games. And don't forget that cell phones, iPods®, BlackBerries®, car navigation systems, and many other devices are computers too. The uses of computers are almost limitless in our everyday lives.

Computers can do such a wide variety of things because they can be programmed. This means that computers are not designed to do just one job, but to do any job that their programs tell them to do. A *program* is a set of instructions that a computer follows to perform a task. For example, Figure 1 shows screens from two commonly used programs, Microsoft Word and Adobe Photoshop. Microsoft Word is a word processing program that allows you to create, edit, and print documents with your computer. Adobe Photoshop is an image editing program that allows you to work with graphic images, such as photos taken with your digital camera.

Programs are commonly referred to as *software*. Software is essential to a computer because it controls everything the computer does. All of the software that we use to make our computers useful is created by individuals working as programmers or software developers. A *programmer*, or *software developer*, is a person with the training and skills necessary to design, create, and test computer programs. Computer programming is an exciting and rewarding career. Today, you will find programmers' work used in business, medicine, government, law enforcement, agriculture, academics, entertainment, and many other fields.

Figure 1   A word processing program and an image editing program

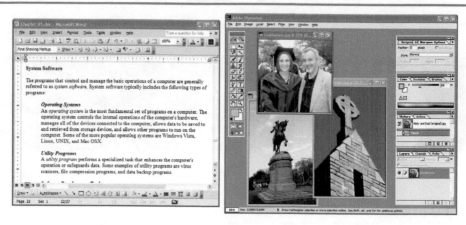

This book introduces you to the fundamental concepts of computer programming using the Python language. Before we begin exploring those concepts, you need to understand a few basic things about computers and how they work. This chapter will build a solid foundation of knowledge that you will continually rely on as you study computer science. First, we will discuss the physical components that computers are commonly made of. Next, we will look at how computers store data and execute programs. Finally, we will get a quick introduction to the software that you will use to write Python programs.

Hardware and Software

CONCEPT: The physical devices that a computer is made of are referred to as the computer's hardware. The programs that run on a computer are referred to as software.

Hardware

The term *hardware* refers to all of the physical devices, or *components,* that a computer is made of. A computer is not one single device, but a system of devices that all work together. Like the different instruments in a symphony orchestra, each device in a computer plays its own part.

If you have ever shopped for a computer, you've probably seen sales literature listing components such as microprocessors, memory, disk drives, video displays, graphics cards, and so on. Unless you already know a lot about computers, or at least have a friend that does, understanding what these different components do might be challenging. As shown in Figure 2, a typical computer system consists of the following major components:

- The central processing unit (CPU)
- Main memory
- Secondary storage devices
- Input devices
- Output devices

Figure 2   Typical components of a computer system

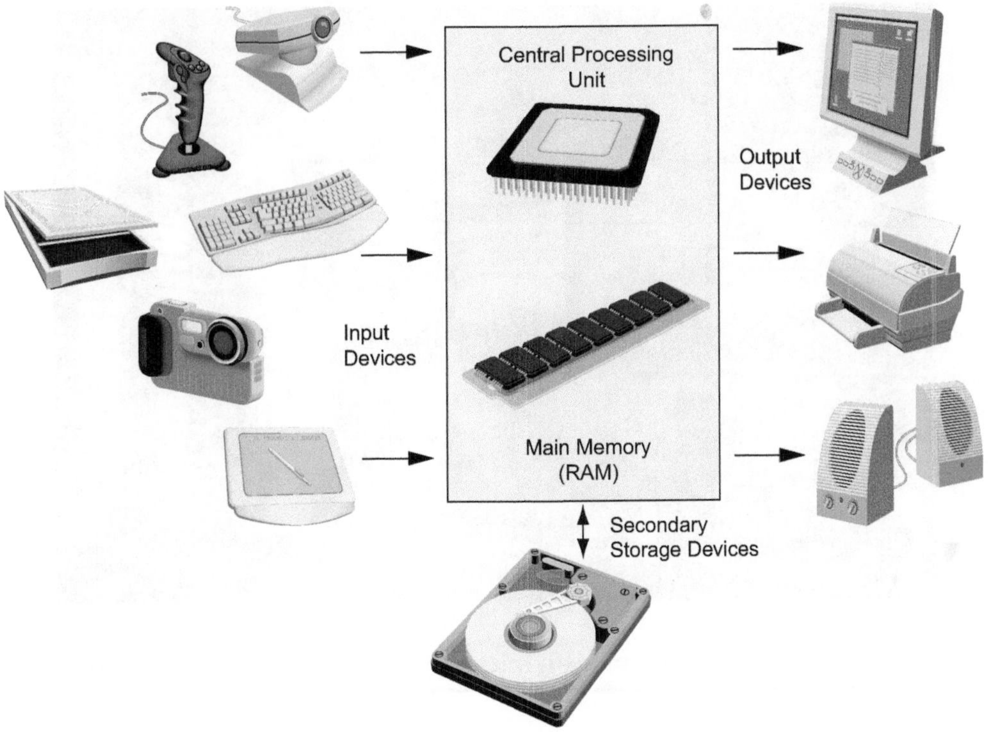

Let's take a closer look at each of these components.

The CPU

When a computer is performing the tasks that a program tells it to do, we say that the computer is *running* or *executing* the program. The *central processing unit,* or *CPU,* is the part of a computer that actually runs programs. The CPU is the most important component in a computer because without it, the computer could not run software.

In the earliest computers, CPUs were huge devices made of electrical and mechanical components such as vacuum tubes and switches. Figure 3 shows such a device. The two women in the photo are working with the historic ENIAC computer. The *ENIAC,* which is considered by many to be the world's first programmable electronic computer, was built in 1945 to calculate artillery ballistic tables for the U.S. Army. This machine, which was primarily one big CPU, was 8 feet tall, 100 feet long, and weighed 30 tons.

Today, CPUs are small chips known as *microprocessors.* Figure 4 shows a photo of a lab technician holding a modern microprocessor. In addition to being much smaller than the old electromechanical CPUs in early computers, microprocessors are also much more powerful.

Figure 3   The ENIAC computer (courtesy of U.S. Army Historic Computer Images)

Figure 4   A lab technician holds a modern microprocessor (photo courtesy of Intel Corporation)

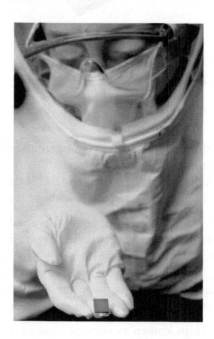

Main Memory

You can think of *main memory* as the computer's work area. This is where the computer stores a program while the program is running, as well as the data that the program is working with. For example, suppose you are using a word processing program to write an essay for one of your classes. While you do this, both the word processing program and the essay are stored in main memory.

Main memory is commonly known as *random-access memory,* or *RAM*. It is called this because the CPU is able to quickly access data stored at any random location in RAM. RAM is usually a *volatile* type of memory that is used only for temporary storage while a program is running. When the computer is turned off, the contents of RAM are erased. Inside your computer, RAM is stored in chips, similar to the ones shown in Figure 5.

Figure 5   Memory chips (photo courtesy of IBM Corporation)

Secondary Storage Devices

Secondary storage is a type of memory that can hold data for long periods of time, even when there is no power to the computer. Programs are normally stored in secondary memory and loaded into main memory as needed. Important data, such as word processing documents, payroll data, and inventory records, is saved to secondary storage as well.

The most common type of secondary storage device is the disk drive. A *disk drive* stores data by magnetically encoding it onto a circular disk. Most computers have a disk drive mounted inside their case. External disk drives, which connect to one of the computer's communication ports, are also available. External disk drives can be used to create backup copies of important data or to move data to another computer.

In addition to external disk drives, many types of devices have been created for copying data, and for moving it to other computers. For many years floppy disk drives were popular. A *floppy disk drive* records data onto a small floppy disk, which can be removed from the drive. Floppy disks have many disadvantages, however. They hold only a small amount of data, are slow to access data, and can be unreliable. The use of floppy disk drives has declined dramatically in recent years, in favor of superior devices such as USB drives. *USB drives* are small devices that plug into the computer's USB (universal serial bus) port, and appear to the system as a disk drive. These drives do not actually contain a disk, however. They store data in a special type of memory known as *flash memory*. USB drives, which are also known as *memory sticks* and *flash drives,* are inexpensive, reliable, and small enough to be carried in your pocket.

Optical devices such as the *CD* (compact disc) and the *DVD* (digital versatile disc) are also popular for data storage. Data is not recorded magnetically on an optical disc, but is encoded as a series of pits on the disc surface. CD and DVD drives use a laser to detect the pits and thus read the encoded data. Optical discs hold large amounts of data, and because recordable CD and DVD drives are now commonplace, they are good mediums for creating backup copies of data.

Input Devices

Input is any data the computer collects from people and from other devices. The component that collects the data and sends it to the computer is called an *input device*. Common input devices are the keyboard, mouse, scanner, microphone, and digital camera. Disk drives and optical drives can also be considered input devices because programs and data are retrieved from them and loaded into the computer's memory.

Output Devices

Output is any data the computer produces for people or for other devices. It might be a sales report, a list of names, or a graphic image. The data is sent to an *output device,* which formats and presents it. Common output devices are video displays and printers. Disk drives and CD recorders can also be considered output devices because the system sends data to them in order to be saved.

Software

If a computer is to function, software is not optional. Everything that a computer does, from the time you turn the power switch on until you shut the system down, is under the control of software. There are two general categories of software: system software and application software. Most computer programs clearly fit into one of these two categories. Let's take a closer look at each.

System Software

The programs that control and manage the basic operations of a computer are generally referred to as *system software*. System software typically includes the following types of programs:

> *Operating Systems* An *operating system* is the most fundamental set of programs on a computer. The operating system controls the internal operations of the computer's hardware, manages all of the devices connected to the computer, allows data to be saved to and retrieved from storage devices, and allows other programs to run on the computer. Figure 6 shows screens from three popular operating systems: Windows Vista, Mac OS X, and Linux.

Figure 6   Screens from the Windows Vista, Mac OS X, and Fedora Linux operating systems

Windows Vista   Mac OS X

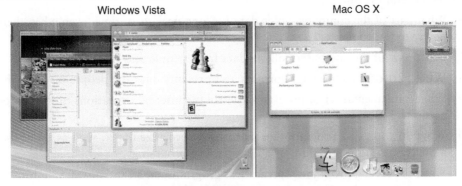

Fedora Linux

Utility Programs A *utility program* performs a specialized task that enhances the computer's operation or safeguards data. Examples of utility programs are virus scanners, file compression programs, and data backup programs.

Software Development Tools *Software development tools* are the programs that programmers use to create, modify, and test software. Assemblers, compilers, and interpreters are examples of programs that fall into this category.

Application Software

Programs that make a computer useful for everyday tasks are known as *application software*. These are the programs that people normally spend most of their time running on their computers. Figure 1, at the beginning of this chapter, shows screens from two commonly used applications: Microsoft Word, a word processing program, and Adobe Photoshop, an image editing program. Some other examples of application software are spreadsheet programs, email programs, web browsers, and game programs.

 Checkpoint

1 What is a program?

2 What is hardware?

3 List the five major components of a computer system.

4 What part of the computer actually runs programs?

5   What part of the computer serves as a work area to store a program and its data while the program is running?

6   What part of the computer holds data for long periods of time, even when there is no power to the computer?

7   What part of the computer collects data from people and from other devices?

8   What part of the computer formats and presents data for people or other devices?

9   What fundamental set of programs control the internal operations of the computer's hardware?

10 What do you call a program that performs a specialized task, such as a virus scanner, a file compression program, or a data backup program?

11 Word processing programs, spreadsheet programs, email programs, web browsers, and game programs belong to what category of software?

3   How Computers Store Data

CONCEPT: All data that is stored in a computer is converted to sequences of 0s and 1s.

A computer's memory is divided into tiny storage locations known as *bytes*. One byte is only enough memory to store a letter of the alphabet or a small number. In order to do anything meaningful, a computer has to have lots of bytes. Most computers today have millions, or even billions, of bytes of memory.

Each byte is divided into eight smaller storage locations known as bits. The term *bit* stands for *binary digit*. Computer scientists usually think of bits as tiny switches that can be either on or off. Bits aren't actual "switches," however, at least not in the conventional sense. In most computer systems, bits are tiny electrical components that can hold either a positive or a negative charge. Computer scientists think of a positive charge as a switch in the *on* position, and a negative charge as a switch in the *off* position. Figure 7 shows the way that a computer scientist might think of a byte of memory: as a collection of switches that are each flipped to either the on or off position.

Figure 7   Think of a byte as eight switches

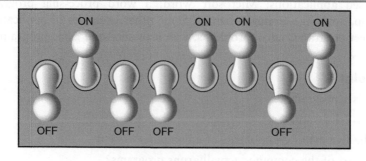

When a piece of data is stored in a byte, the computer sets the eight bits to an on/off pattern that represents the data. For example, the pattern shown on the left in Figure 8 shows how the number 77 would be stored in a byte, and the pattern on the right shows how the letter A would be stored in a byte. We explain below how these patterns are determined.

Figure 8   Bit patterns for the number 77 and the letter A

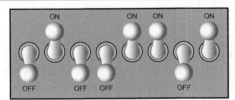
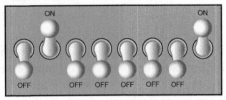

The number 77 stored in a byte.   The letter A stored in a byte.

Storing Numbers

A bit can be used in a very limited way to represent numbers. Depending on whether the bit is turned on or off, it can represent one of two different values. In computer systems, a bit that is turned off represents the number 0 and a bit that is turned on represents the number 1. This corresponds perfectly to the *binary numbering system*. In the binary numbering system (or *binary*, as it is usually called) all numeric values are written as sequences of 0s and 1s. Here is an example of a number that is written in binary:

    10011101

The position of each digit in a binary number has a value assigned to it. Starting with the rightmost digit and moving left, the position values are 2^0, 2^1, 2^2, 2^3, and so forth, as shown in Figure 9. Figure 10 shows the same diagram with the position values calculated. Starting with the rightmost digit and moving left, the position values are 1, 2, 4, 8, and so forth.

Figure 9   The values of binary digits as powers of 2

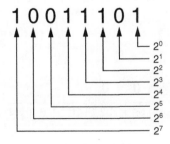

Figure 10   The values of binary digits

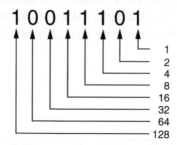

To determine the value of a binary number you simply add up the position values of all the 1s. For example, in the binary number 10011101, the position values of the 1s are 1, 4, 8, 16, and 128. This is shown in Figure 11. The sum of all of these position values is 157. So, the value of the binary number 10011101 is 157.

Figure 11   Determining the value of 10011101

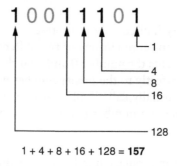

Figure 12 shows how you can picture the number 157 stored in a byte of memory. Each 1 is represented by a bit in the on position, and each 0 is represented by a bit in the off position.

Figure 12   The bit pattern for 157

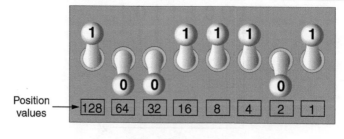

When all of the bits in a byte are set to 0 (turned off), then the value of the byte is 0. When all of the bits in a byte are set to 1 (turned on), then the byte holds the largest value that can be stored in it. The largest value that can be stored in a byte is $1 + 2 + 4 + 8 + 16 + 32 + 64 + 128 = 255$. This limit exists because there are only eight bits in a byte.

What if you need to store a number larger than 255? The answer is simple: use more than one byte. For example, suppose we put two bytes together. That gives us 16 bits. The position values of those 16 bits would be 2^0, 2^1, 2^2, 2^3, and so forth, up through 2^{15}. As shown in Figure 13, the maximum value that can be stored in two bytes is 65,535. If you need to store a number larger than this, then more bytes are necessary.

Figure 13 Two bytes used for a large number

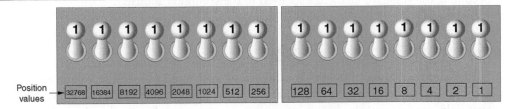

Position values → 32768 16384 8192 4096 2048 1024 512 256 128 64 32 16 8 4 2 1

32768 + 16384 + 8192 + 4096 + 2048 + 1024 + 512 + 256 + 128 + 64 + 32 + 16 + 8 + 4 + 2 + 1 = **65535**

TIP: In case you're feeling overwhelmed by all this, relax! You will not have to actually convert numbers to binary while programming. Knowing that this process is taking place inside the computer will help you as you learn, and in the long term this knowledge will make you a better programmer.

Storing Characters

Any piece of data that is stored in a computer's memory must be stored as a binary number. That includes characters, such as letters and punctuation marks. When a character is stored in memory, it is first converted to a numeric code. The numeric code is then stored in memory as a binary number.

Over the years, different coding schemes have been developed to represent characters in computer memory. Historically, the most important of these coding schemes is *ASCII,* which stands for the *American Standard Code for Information Interchange.* ASCII is a set of 128 numeric codes that represent the English letters, various punctuation marks, and other characters. For example, the ASCII code for the uppercase letter A is 65. When you type an uppercase A on your computer keyboard, the number 65 is stored in memory (as a binary number, of course). This is shown in Figure 14.

Figure 14 The letter A is stored in memory as the number 65

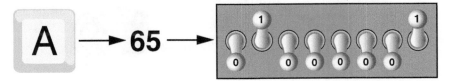

TIP: The acronym ASCII is pronounced "askee."

In case you are curious, the ASCII code for uppercase B is 66, for uppercase C is 67, and so forth.

The ASCII character set was developed in the early 1960s, and was eventually adopted by most all computer manufacturers. ASCII is limited however, because it defines codes for only 128 characters. To remedy this, the Unicode character set was developed in the early 1990s. *Unicode* is an extensive encoding scheme that is compatible with ASCII, but can also represent characters for many of the languages in the world. Today, Unicode is quickly becoming the standard character set used in the computer industry.

Advanced Number Storage

Earlier you read about numbers and how they are stored in memory. While reading that section, perhaps it occurred to you that the binary numbering system can be used to represent only integer numbers, beginning with 0. Negative numbers and real numbers (such as 3.14159) cannot be represented using the simple binary numbering technique we discussed.

Computers are able to store negative numbers and real numbers in memory, but to do so they use encoding schemes along with the binary numbering system. Negative numbers are encoded using a technique known as *two's complement,* and real numbers are encoded in *floating-point notation.* You don't need to know how these encoding schemes work, only that they are used to convert negative numbers and real numbers to binary format.

Other Types of Data

Computers are often referred to as digital devices. The term *digital* can be used to describe anything that uses binary numbers. *Digital data* is data that is stored in binary, and a *digital device* is any device that works with binary data. In this section we have discussed how numbers and characters are stored in binary, but computers also work with many other types of digital data.

For example, consider the pictures that you take with your digital camera. These images are composed of tiny dots of color known as *pixels.* (The term pixel stands for *picture element.*) As shown in Figure 15, each pixel in an image is converted to a numeric code that represents the pixel's color. The numeric code is stored in memory as a binary number.

Figure 15   A digital image is stored in binary format

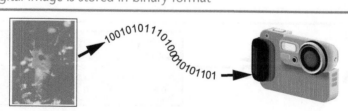

The music that you play on your CD player, iPod or MP3 player is also digital. A digital song is broken into small pieces known as *samples*. Each sample is converted to a binary number, which can be stored in memory. The more samples that a song is divided into, the more it sounds like the original music when it is played back. A CD quality song is divided into more than 44,000 samples per second!

Checkpoint

12   What amount of memory is enough to store a letter of the alphabet or a small number?

13   What do you call a tiny "switch" that can be set to either on or off?

14   In what numbering system are all numeric values written as sequences of 0s and 1s?

15   What is the purpose of ASCII?

16   What encoding scheme is extensive enough to represent the characters of many of the languages in the world?

17   What do the terms "digital data" and "digital device" mean?

4   How a Program Works

CONCEPT: A computer's CPU can only understand instructions that are written in machine language. Because people find it very difficult to write entire programs in machine language, other programming languages have been invented.

Earlier, we stated that the CPU is the most important component in a computer because it is the part of the computer that runs programs. Sometimes the CPU is called the "computer's brain," and is described as being "smart." Although these are common metaphors, you should understand that the CPU is not a brain, and it is not smart. The CPU is an electronic device that is designed to do specific things. In particular, the CPU is designed to perform operations such as the following:

- Reading a piece of data from main memory
- Adding two numbers
- Subtracting one number from another number
- Multiplying two numbers
- Dividing one number by another number
- Moving a piece of data from one memory location to another
- Determining whether one value is equal to another value

As you can see from this list, the CPU performs simple operations on pieces of data. The CPU does nothing on its own, however. It has to be told what to do, and that's the purpose of a program. A program is nothing more than a list of instructions that cause the CPU to perform operations.

Each instruction in a program is a command that tells the CPU to perform a specific operation. Here's an example of an instruction that might appear in a program:

```
10110000
```

To you and me, this is only a series of 0s and 1s. To a CPU, however, this is an instruction to perform an operation.[1] It is written in 0s and 1s because CPUs only understand instructions that are written in *machine language,* and machine language instructions always have an underlying binary structure.

A machine language instruction exists for each operation that a CPU is capable of performing. For example, there is an instruction for adding numbers, there is an instruction for subtracting one number from another, and so forth. The entire set of instructions that a CPU can execute is known as the CPU's *instruction set.*

> **NOTE:** There are several microprocessor companies today that manufacture CPUs. Some of the more well-known microprocessor companies are Intel, AMD, and Motorola. If you look carefully at your computer, you might find a tag showing a logo for its microprocessor.
>
> Each brand of microprocessor has its own unique instruction set, which is typically understood only by microprocessors of the same brand. For example, Intel microprocessors understand the same instructions, but they do not understand instructions for Motorola microprocessors.

The machine language instruction that was previously shown is an example of only one instruction. It takes a lot more than one instruction, however, for the computer to do anything meaningful. Because the operations that a CPU knows how to perform are so basic in nature, a meaningful task can be accomplished only if the CPU performs many operations. For example, if you want your computer to calculate the amount of interest that you will earn from your savings account this year, the CPU will have to perform a large number of instructions, carried out in the proper sequence. It is not unusual for a program to contain thousands or even millions of machine language instructions.

Programs are usually stored on a secondary storage device such as a disk drive. When you install a program on your computer, the program is typically copied to your computer's disk drive from a CD-ROM, or perhaps downloaded from a website.

Although a program can be stored on a secondary storage device such as a disk drive, it has to be copied into main memory, or RAM, each time the CPU executes it. For example, suppose you have a word processing program on your computer's disk. To execute the program you use the mouse to double-click the program's icon. This causes the program to be copied from the disk into main memory. Then, the computer's CPU executes the copy of the program that is in main memory. This process is illustrated in Figure 16.

---

[1] The example shown is an actual instruction for an Intel microprocessor. It tells the microprocessor to move a value into the CPU.

Figure 16   A program is copied into main memory and then executed

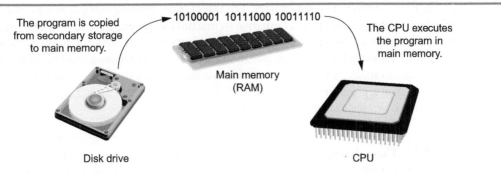

When a CPU executes the instructions in a program, it is engaged in a process that is known as the *fetch-decode-execute cycle*. This cycle, which consists of three steps, is repeated for each instruction in the program. The steps are:

1. **Fetch** A program is a long sequence of machine language instructions. The first step of the cycle is to fetch, or read, the next instruction from memory into the CPU.
2. **Decode** A machine language instruction is a binary number that represents a command that tells the CPU to perform an operation. In this step the CPU decodes the instruction that was just fetched from memory, to determine which operation it should perform.
3. **Execute** The last step in the cycle is to execute, or perform, the operation.

Figure 17 illustrates these steps.

Figure 17   The fetch-decode-execute cycle

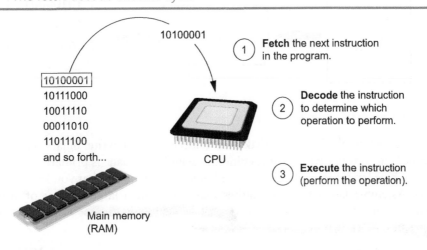

From Machine Language to Assembly Language

Computers can only execute programs that are written in machine language. As previously mentioned, a program can have thousands or even millions of binary instructions, and writing such a program would be very tedious and time consuming. Programming in machine language would also be very difficult because putting a 0 or a 1 in the wrong place will cause an error.

Although a computer's CPU only understands machine language, it is impractical for people to write programs in machine language. For this reason, *assembly language* was created in the early days of computing[2] as an alternative to machine language. Instead of using binary numbers for instructions, assembly language uses short words that are known as *mnemonics*. For example, in assembly language, the mnemonic add typically means to add numbers, mul typically means to multiply numbers, and mov typically means to move a value to a location in memory. When a programmer uses assembly language to write a program, he or she can write short mnemonics instead of binary numbers.

> **NOTE:** There are many different versions of assembly language. It was mentioned earlier that each brand of CPU has its own machine language instruction set. Each brand of CPU typically has its own assembly language as well.

Assembly language programs cannot be executed by the CPU, however. The CPU only understands machine language, so a special program known as an *assembler* is used to translate an assembly language program to a machine language program. This process is shown in Figure 18. The machine language program that is created by the assembler can then be executed by the CPU.

Figure 18   An assembler translates an assembly language program to a machine language program

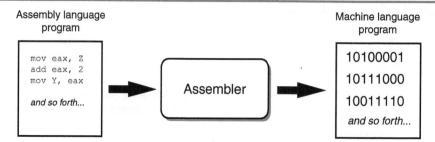

High-Level Languages

Although assembly language makes it unnecessary to write binary machine language instructions, it is not without difficulties. Assembly language is primarily a direct substitute for machine language, and like machine language, it requires that you know a lot about the CPU. Assembly language also requires that you write a large number of instructions for even the simplest program. Because assembly language is so close in nature to machine language, it is referred to as a *low-level language*.

In the 1950s, a new generation of programming languages known as *high-level languages* began to appear. A high-level language allows you to create powerful and complex programs without knowing how the CPU works, and without writing large numbers of low-level instructions. In addition, most high-level languages use words that are easy to understand. For example, if a programmer were using COBOL (which was one of the early high-level

---

[2] The first assembly language was most likely that developed in the 1940s at Cambridge University for use with a historic computer known as the EDSAC.

languages created in the 1950s), he or she would write the following instruction to display the message *Hello world* on the computer screen:

```
DISPLAY "Hello world"
```

Python is a modern, high-level programming language that we will use in this book. In Python you would display the message *Hello world* with the following instruction:

```
print 'Hello world'
```

Doing the same thing in assembly language would require several instructions, and an intimate knowledge of how the CPU interacts with the computer's output device. As you can see from this example, high-level languages allow programmers to concentrate on the tasks they want to perform with their programs rather than the details of how the CPU will execute those programs.

Since the 1950s, thousands of high-level languages have been created. Table 1 lists several of the more well-known languages.

Table 1   Programming languages

Language	Description
Ada	Ada was created in the 1970s, primarily for applications used by the U.S. Department of Defense. The language is named in honor of Countess Ada Lovelace, an influential and historic figure in the field of computing.
BASIC	Beginners All-purpose Symbolic Instruction Code is a general-purpose language that was originally designed in the early 1960s to be simple enough for beginners to learn. Today, there are many different versions of BASIC.
FORTRAN	FORmula TRANslator was the first high-level programming language. It was designed in the 1950s for performing complex mathematical calculations.
COBOL	Common Business-Oriented Language was created in the 1950s, and was designed for business applications.
Pascal	Pascal was created in 1970, and was originally designed for teaching programming. The language was named in honor of the mathematician, physicist, and philosopher Blaise Pascal.
C and C++	C and C++ (pronounced "c plus plus") are powerful, general-purpose languages developed at Bell Laboratories. The C language was created in 1972 and the C++ language was created in 1983.
C#	Pronounced "c sharp." This language was created by Microsoft around the year 2000 for developing applications based on the Microsoft .NET platform.
Java	Java was created by Sun Microsystems in the early 1990s. It can be used to develop programs that run on a single computer or over the Internet from a web server.
JavaScript	JavaScript, created in the 1990s, can be used in web pages. Despite its name, JavaScript is not related to Java.
Python	Python, the language we use in this book, is a general-purpose language created in the early 1990s. It has become popular in business and academic applications.
Ruby	Ruby is a general-purpose language that was created in the 1990s. It is increasingly becoming a popular language for programs that run on web servers.
Visual Basic	Visual Basic (commonly known as VB) is a Microsoft programming language and software development environment that allows programmers to create Windows-based applications quickly. VB was originally created in the early 1990s.

Key Words, Operators, and Syntax: an Overview

Each high-level language has its own set of predefined words that the programmer must use to write a program. The words that make up a high-level programming language are known as *key words* or *reserved words*. Each key word has a specific meaning, and cannot be used for any other purpose. You previously saw an example of a Python statement that uses the key word print to print a message on the screen. Table 2 shows all of the Python key words.

Table 2   The Python key words

and	del	from	not	while
as	elif	global	or	with
assert	else	if	pass	yiel
break	except	import	print	
class	exec	in	raise	
continue	finally	is	return	
def	for	lambda	try	

In addition to key words, programming languages have *operators* that perform various operations on data. For example, all programming languages have math operators that perform arithmetic. In Python, as well as most other languages, the + sign is an operator that adds two numbers. The following adds 12 and 75:

```
12 + 75
```

There are numerous other operators in the Python language, many of which you will learn about as you progress through this text.

In addition to key words and operators, each language also has its own *syntax,* which is a set of rules that must be strictly followed when writing a program. The syntax rules dictate how key words, operators, and various punctuation characters must be used in a program. When you are learning a programming language, you must learn the syntax rules for that particular language.

The individual instructions that you use to write a program in a high-level programming language are called *statements*. A programming statement can consist of key words, operators, punctuation, and other allowable programming elements, arranged in the proper sequence to perform an operation.

Compilers and Interpreters

Because the CPU understands only machine language instructions, programs that are written in a high-level language must be translated into machine language. Depending on the language that a program has been written in, the programmer will use either a compiler or an interpreter to make the translation.

A *compiler* is a program that translates a high-level language program into a separate machine language program. The machine language program can then be executed any time it is needed. This is shown in Figure 19. As shown in the figure, compiling and executing are two different processes.

Figure 19 Compiling a high-level program and executing it

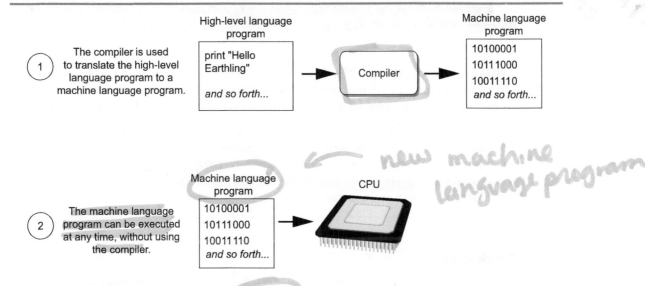

1 The compiler is used to translate the high-level language program to a machine language program.

2 The machine language program can be executed at any time, without using the compiler.

new machine language program

The Python language uses an *interpreter,* which is a program that both translates and executes the instructions in a high-level language program. As the interpreter reads each individual instruction in the program, it converts it to machine language instructions and then immediately executes them. This process repeats for every instruction in the program. This process is illustrated in Figure 20. Because interpreters combine translation and execution, they typically do not create separate machine language programs.

Figure 20 Executing a high-level program with an interpreter

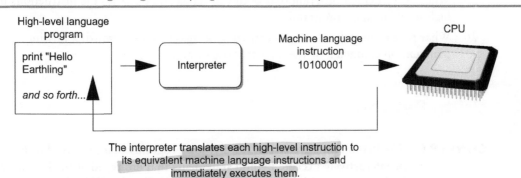

The interpreter translates each high-level instruction to its equivalent machine language instructions and immediately executes them.

This process is repeated for each high-level instruction.

The statements that a programmer writes in a high-level language are called *source code,* or simply *code.* Typically, the programmer types a program's code into a text editor and then saves the code in a file on the computer's disk. Next, the programmer uses a compiler to translate the code into a machine language program, or an interpreter to translate and execute the code. If the code contains a syntax error, however, it cannot be translated. A *syntax error* is a mistake such as a misspelled key word, a missing punctuation character, or the incorrect use of an operator. When this happens the compiler or interpreter displays an error message indicating that the program contains a syntax error. The programmer corrects the error and then attempts once again to translate the program.

NOTE: Human languages also have syntax rules. Do you remember when you took your first English class, and you learned all those rules about commas, apostrophes, capitalization, and so forth? You were learning the syntax of the English language.

Although people commonly violate the syntax rules of their native language when speaking and writing, other people usually understand what they mean. Unfortunately, compilers and interpreters do not have this ability. If even a single syntax error appears in a program, the program cannot be compiled or executed. When an interpreter encounters a syntax error, it stops executing the program.

Checkpoint

18   A CPU understands instructions that are written only in what language?

19   A program has to be copied into what type of memory each time the CPU executes it?

20   When a CPU executes the instructions in a program, it is engaged in what process?

21   What is assembly language?

22   What type of programming language allows you to create powerful and complex programs without knowing how the CPU works?

23   Each language has a set of rules that must be strictly followed when writing a program. What is this set of rules called?

24   What do you call a program that translates a high-level language program into a separate machine language program?

25   What do you call a program that both translates and executes the instructions in a high-level language program?

26   What type of mistake is usually caused by a misspelled key word, a missing punctuation character, or the incorrect use of an operator?

5   Using Python

CONCEPT: The Python interpreter can run Python programs that are saved in files, or interactively execute Python statements that are typed at the keyboard. Python comes with a program named IDLE that simplifies the process of writing, executing, and testing programs.

Installing Python

Before you can try any of the programs shown in this book, or write any programs of your own, you need to make sure that Python is installed on your computer and properly configured. If you are working in a computer lab, this has probably been done already.

The Python Interpreter

You learned earlier that Python is an interpreted language. When you install the Python language on your computer, one of the items that is installed is the Python interpreter. The *Python interpreter* is a program that can read Python programming statements and execute them. (Sometimes we will refer to the Python interpreter simply as the interpreter.)

You can use the interpreter in two modes: interactive mode and script mode. In *interactive mode,* the interpreter waits for you to type Python statements on the keyboard. Once you type a statement, the interpreter executes it and then waits for you to type another statement. In *script mode,* the interpreter reads the contents of a file that contains Python statements. Such a file is known as a *Python program* or a *Python script.* The interpreter executes each statement in the Python program as it reads it.

Interactive Mode

Once Python has been installed and set up on your system, you start the interpreter in interactive mode by going to the operating system's command line and typing the following command:

```
python
```

If you are using Windows, you can alternatively click the *Start* button, then *All Programs.* You should see a program group named something like *Python 2.5.* (The "2.5" is the version of Python that is installed. At the time this is being written, Python 2.5 is the latest version.) Inside this program group you should see an item named *Python (command line).* Clicking this menu item will start the Python interpreter in interactive mode.

When the Python interpreter starts in interactive mode, you will see something like the following displayed in a console window:

```
Python 2.5.1 (r251:54863, Apr 18 2007, 08:51:08) [MSC v.1310 32 bit
(Intel)] on win32
Type "help", "copyright", "credits" or "license" for more information.
>>>
```

The >>> that you see is a prompt that indicates the interpreter is waiting for you to type a Python statement. Let's try it out. One of the simplest statements that you can write in Python is a `print` statement, which causes a message to be displayed on the screen. For example, the following statement causes the message `Python programming is fun!` to be displayed:

```
print 'Python programming is fun!'
```

Notice that after the word `print`, we have written `Python programming is fun!` inside a set of single-quote marks. The quote marks are necessary, but they will not be displayed. They simply mark the beginning and the end of the text that we wish to display. Here is an example of how you would type this `print` statement at the interpreter's prompt:

```
>>> print 'Python programming is fun!'
```

After typing the statement you press the Enter key and the Python interpreter executes the statement, as shown here:

```
>>> print 'Python programming is fun!' [ENTER]
Python programming is fun!
>>>
```

After the message is displayed, the >>> prompt appears again, indicating that the interpreter is waiting for you to enter another statement. Let's look at another example. In the following sample session we have entered two `print` statements.

```
>>> print 'To be or not to be' [ENTER]
To be or not to be
>>> print 'That is the question.' [ENTER]
That is the question.
>>>
```

If you incorrectly type a statement in interactive mode, the interpreter will display an error message. This will make interactive mode useful to you while you learn Python. As you learn new parts of the Python language, you can try them out in interactive mode and get immediate feedback from the interpreter.

To quit the Python interpreter in interactive mode on a Windows computer, press Ctrl-Z (pressing both keys together) followed by Enter. On a Mac, Linux, or UNIX computer, press Ctrl-D.

Writing Python Programs and Running Them in Script Mode

Although interactive mode is useful for testing code, the statements that you enter in interactive mode are not saved as a program. They are simply executed and their results displayed on the screen. If you want to save a set of Python statements as a program, you save those statements in a file. Then, to execute the program, you use the Python interpreter in script mode.

For example, suppose you want to write a Python program that displays the following three lines of text:

```
Nudge nudge
Wink wink
Know what I mean?
```

To write the program you would use a simple text editor like Notepad (which is installed on all Windows computers) to create a file containing the following statements:

```
print 'Nudge nudge'
print 'Wink wink'
print 'Know what I mean?'
```

NOTE: It is possible to use a word processor to create a Python program, but you must be sure to save the program as a plain text file. Otherwise the Python interpreter will not be able to read its contents.

When you save a Python program, you give it a name that ends with the .py extension, which identifies it as a Python program. For example, you might save the program previously shown with the name test.py. To run the program you would go to the directory in which the file is saved and type the following command at the operating system command line:

```
python test.py
```

This starts the Python interpreter in script mode and causes it to execute the statements in the file test.py. When the program finishes executing, the Python interpreter exits.

The IDLE Programming Environment

The previous sections described how the Python interpreter can be started in interactive mode or script mode at the operating system command line. As an alternative, you can use an *integrated development environment*, which is a single program that gives you all of the tools you need to write, execute, and test a program.

Recent versions of Python include a program named *IDLE*, which is automatically installed when the Python language is installed. (IDLE stands for Integrated DeveLopment Environment.) When you run IDLE, the window shown in Figure 21 appears. Notice that the >>> prompt appears in the IDLE window, indicating that the interpreter is running in interactive mode. You can type Python statements at this prompt and see them executed in the IDLE window.

IDLE also has a built-in text editor with features specifically designed to help you write Python programs. For example, the IDLE editor "colorizes" code so that key words and other parts of a program are displayed in their own distinct colors. This helps make programs easier to read. In IDLE you can write programs, save them to disk, and execute them. Appendix B provides a quick introduction to IDLE, and leads you through the process of creating, saving, and executing a Python program.

Figure 21   IDLE

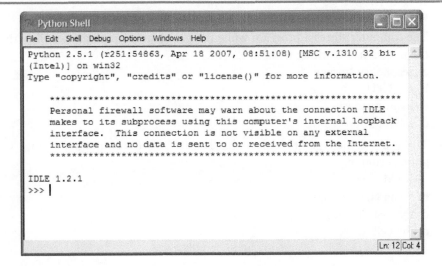

NOTE: Although IDLE is installed with Python, there are several other Python IDEs available. Your instructor might prefer that you use a specific one in class.

Review Questions

Multiple Choice

1. A(n) _____ is a set of instructions that a computer follows to perform a task.
   a. compiler
   b. program
   c. interpreter
   d. programming language

2. The physical devices that a computer is made of are referred to as _____.
   a. hardware
   b. software
   c. the operating system
   d. tools

3. The part of a computer that runs programs is called _____.
   a. RAM
   b. secondary storage
   c. main memory
   d. the CPU

4. Today, CPUs are small chips known as _____.
   a. ENIACs
   b. microprocessors
   c. memory chips
   d. operating systems

5. The computer stores a program while the program is running, as well as the data that the program is working with, in _____.
   a. secondary storage
   b. the CPU
   c. main memory
   d. the microprocessor

6. This is a volatile type of memory that is used only for temporary storage while a program is running.
   a. RAM
   b. secondary storage
   c. the disk drive
   d. the USB drive

7. A type of memory that can hold data for long periods of time, even when there is no power to the computer, is called _____.
   a. RAM
   b. main memory
   c. secondary storage
   d. CPU storage

8. A component that collects data from people or other devices and sends it to the computer is called _____.
   a. an output device
   b. an input device
   c. a secondary storage device
   d. main memory

9. A video display is a(n) _____ device.
   a. output device
   b. input device
   c. secondary storage device
   d. main memory

10. A _____ is enough memory to store a letter of the alphabet or a small number.
    a. byte
    b. bit
    c. switch
    d. transistor

11. A byte is made up of eight _____.
    a. CPUs
    b. instructions
    c. variables
    d. bits

12. In a(n) _____ numbering system, all numeric values are written as sequences of 0s and 1s.
    a. hexadecimal
    b. binary
    c. octal
    d. decimal

13. A bit that is turned off represents the following value: _____.
    a. 1
    b. –1
    c. 0
    d. "no"

14. A set of 128 numeric codes that represent the English letters, various punctuation marks, and other characters is _____.
    a. binary numbering
    b. ASCII
    c. Unicode
    d. ENIAC

15. An extensive encoding scheme that can represent characters for many languages in the world is _____.
    a. binary numbering
    b. ASCII
    c. Unicode
    d. ENIAC

16. Negative numbers are encoded using the _____ technique.
    a. twos compliment
    b. floating point
    c. ASCII
    d. Unicode

17. Real numbers are encoded using the _____ technique.
    a. two's complement
    b. floating point
    c. ASCII
    d. Unicode

18. The tiny dots of color that digital images are composed of are called _____.
    a. bits
    b. bytes
    c. color packets
    d. pixels

19. If you were to look at a machine language program, you would see _____.
    a. Python code
    b. a stream of binary numbers
    c. English words
    d. circuits

20. In the _____ part of the fetch-decode-execute cycle, the CPU determines which operation it should perform.
    a. fetch
    b. decode
    c. execute
    d. immediately after the instruction is executed

21. Computers can only execute programs that are written in _____.
    a. Java
    b. assembly language
    c. machine language
    d. Python

22. The _____ translates an assembly language program to a machine language program.
    a. assembler
    b. compiler
    c. translator
    d. interpreter

23. The words that make up a high-level programming language are called _____.
    a. binary instructions
    b. mnemonics
    c. commands
    d. key words

24. The rules that must be followed when writing a program are called _____.
    a. syntax
    b. punctuation
    c. key words
    d. operators

25. A(n) _____ program translates a high-level language program into a separate machine language program.
    a. assembler
    b. compiler
    c. translator
    d. utility

True or False

1. Today, CPUs are huge devices made of electrical and mechanical components such as vacuum tubes and switches.

2. Main memory is also known as RAM.

3. Any piece of data that is stored in a computer's memory must be stored as a binary number.

4. Images, like the ones you make with your digital camera, cannot be stored as binary numbers.

5. Machine language is the only language that a CPU understands.

6. Assembly language is considered a high-level language.

7. An interpreter is a program that both translates and executes the instructions in a high-level language program.

8. A syntax error does not prevent a program from being compiled and executed.

9. Windows Vista, Linux, UNIX, and Mac OSX are all examples of application software.

10. Word processing programs, spreadsheet programs, email programs, web browsers, and games are all examples of utility programs.

Short Answer

1. Why is the CPU the most important component in a computer?

2. What number does a bit that is turned on represent? What number does a bit that is turned off represent?

3. What would you call a device that works with binary data?

4. What are the words that make up a high-level programming language called?

5. What are the short words that are used in assembly language called?

6. What is the difference between a compiler and an interpreter?

7. What type of software controls the internal operations of the computer's hardware?

Exercises

1. To make sure that you can interact with the Python interpreter, try the following steps on your computer:

   - Start the Python interpreter in interactive mode.
   - At the >>> prompt type the following statement and then press Enter:

   ```
   print 'This is a test of the Python interpreter.' [ENTER]
   ```

   - After pressing the Enter key the interpreter will execute the statement. If you typed everything correctly, your session should look like this:

   ```
   >>> print 'This is a test of the Python interpreter.' [ENTER]
   This is a test of the Python interpreter.
   >>>
   ```

   - If you see an error message, enter the statement again and make sure you type it exactly as shown.
   - Exit the Python interpreter. (In Windows, press Ctrl-Z followed by Enter. On other systems press Ctrl-D.)

2. To make sure that you can interact with IDLE, try the following steps on your computer:

   - Start IDLE. To do this in Windows, click the *Start* button, then *All Programs*. In the Python program group click *IDLE (Python GUI)*.
   - When IDLE starts, it should appear similar to the window previously shown in Figure 21. At the >>> prompt type the following statement and then press Enter:

   ```
   print 'This is a test of IDLE.' [ENTER]
   ```

   - After pressing the Enter key the Python interpreter will execute the statement. If you typed everything correctly, your session should look like this:

   ```
   >>> print 'This is a test of IDLE.' [ENTER]
   This is a test of IDLE.
   >>>
   ```

   - If you see an error message, enter the statement again and make sure you type it exactly as shown.
   - Exit IDLE by clicking File, then Exit (or pressing Ctrl-Q on the keyboard).

3. Use what you've learned about the binary numbering system in this chapter to convert the following decimal numbers to binary:

   11

   65

   100

   255

4. Use what you've learned about the binary numbering system in this chapter to convert the following binary numbers to decimal:

   1101

   1000

   101011

5. Use the Internet to research the history of the Python programming language, and answer the following questions:

- Who was the creator of Python?
- When was Python created?
- In the Python programming community, the person who created Python is commonly referred to as the "BDFL." What does this mean?

13

Input, Processing, and Output

1 Designing a Program

CONCEPT: Programs must be carefully designed before they are written. During the design process, programmers use tools such as pseudocode and flowcharts to create models of programs.

The Program Development Cycle

You learned that programmers typically use high-level languages such as Python to create programs. There is much more to creating a program than writing code, however. The process of creating a program that works correctly typically requires the five phases shown in Figure 1. The entire process is known as the *program development cycle*.

Figure 1 The program development cycle

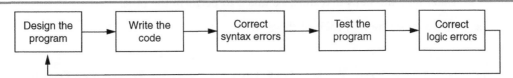

Let's take a closer look at each stage in the cycle.

1. **Design the Program** All professional programmers will tell you that a program should be carefully designed before the code is actually written. When programmers begin a new project, they never jump right in and start writing code as the first step. They start by creating a design of the program. There are several ways to design a program, and later in this section we will discuss some techniques that you can use to design your Python programs.

2. **Write the Code** After designing the program, the programmer begins writing code in a high-level language such as Python. Each language has its own rules, known as syntax, that must be followed when writing a program. A language's syntax rules dictate things such as how key words, operators, and punctuation characters can be used. A syntax error occurs if the programmer violates any of these rules.

3. **Correct Syntax Errors** If the program contains a syntax error, or even a simple mistake such as a misspelled key word, the compiler or interpreter will display an error message indicating what the error is. Virtually all code contains syntax errors when it is first written, so the programmer will typically spend some time correcting these. Once all of the syntax errors and simple typing mistakes have been corrected, the program can be compiled and translated into a machine language program (or executed by an interpreter, depending on the language being used).

4. **Test the Program** Once the code is in an executable form, it is then tested to determine whether any logic errors exist. A *logic error* is a mistake that does not prevent the program from running, but causes it to produce incorrect results. (Mathematical mistakes are common causes of logic errors.)

5. **Correct Logic Errors** If the program produces incorrect results, the programmer *debugs* the code. This means that the programmer finds and corrects logic errors in the program. Sometimes during this process, the programmer discovers that the program's original design must be changed. In this event, the program development cycle starts over, and continues until no errors can be found.

More About the Design Process

The process of designing a program is arguably the most important part of the cycle. You can think of a program's design as its foundation. If you build a house on a poorly constructed foundation, eventually you will find yourself doing a lot of work to fix the house! A program's design should be viewed no differently. If your program is designed poorly, eventually you will find yourself doing a lot of work to fix the program.

The process of designing a program can be summarized in the following two steps:

1. Understand the task that the program is to perform.
2. Determine the steps that must be taken to perform the task.

Let's take a closer look at each of these steps.

Understand the Task That the Program Is to Perform

It is essential that you understand what a program is supposed to do before you can determine the steps that the program will perform. Typically, a professional programmer gains this understanding by working directly with the customer. We use the term *customer* to describe the person, group, or organization that is asking you to write a program. This could be a customer in the traditional sense of the word, meaning someone who is paying you to write a program. It could also be your boss, or the manager of a department within your company. Regardless of whom it is, the customer will be relying on your program to perform an important task.

To get a sense of what a program is supposed to do, the programmer usually interviews the customer. During the interview, the customer will describe the task that the program should perform, and the programmer will ask questions to uncover as many details as possible about the task. A follow-up interview is usually needed because customers rarely mention everything they want during the initial meeting, and programmers often think of additional questions.

The programmer studies the information that was gathered from the customer during the interviews and creates a list of different software requirements. A *software requirement* is simply a single task that the program must perform in order to satisfy the customer. Once the customer agrees that the list of requirements is complete, the programmer can move to the next phase.

TIP: If you choose to become a professional software developer, your customer will be anyone who asks you to write programs as part of your job. As long as you are a student, however, your customer is your instructor! In every programming class that you will take, it's practically guaranteed that your instructor will assign programming problems for you to complete. For your academic success, make sure that you understand your instructor's requirements for those assignments and write your programs accordingly.

Determine the Steps That Must Be Taken to Perform the Task

Once you understand the task that the program will perform, you begin by breaking down the task into a series of steps. This is similar to the way you would break down a task into a series of steps that another person can follow. For example, suppose someone asks you how to boil water. You might break down that task into a series of steps as follows:

1. Pour the desired amount of water into a pot.
2. Put the pot on a stove burner.
3. Turn the burner to high.
4. Watch the water until you see large bubbles rapidly rising. When this happens, the water is boiling.

This is an example of an *algorithm,* which is a set of well-defined logical steps that must be taken to perform a task. Notice that the steps in this algorithm are sequentially ordered. Step 1 should be performed before step 2, and so on. If a person follows these steps exactly as they appear, and in the correct order, he or she should be able to boil water successfully.

A programmer breaks down the task that a program must perform in a similar way. An algorithm is created, which lists all of the logical steps that must be taken. For example, suppose you have been asked to write a program to calculate and display the gross pay for an hourly paid employee. Here are the steps that you would take:

1. Get the number of hours worked.
2. Get the hourly pay rate.

3. Multiply the number of hours worked by the hourly pay rate.
4. Display the result of the calculation that was performed in steps 3.

Of course, this algorithm isn't ready to be executed on the computer. The steps in this list have to be translated into code. Programmers commonly use two tools to help them accomplish this: pseudocode and flowcharts. Let's look at each of these in more detail.

Pseudocode

Because small mistakes like misspelled words and forgotten punctuation characters can cause syntax errors, programmers have to be mindful of such small details when writing code. For this reason, programmers find it helpful to write a program in pseudocode (pronounced "sue doe code") before they write it in the actual code of a programming language such as Python.

The word "pseudo" means fake, so *pseudocode* is fake code. It is an informal language that has no syntax rules, and is not meant to be compiled or executed. Instead, programmers use pseudocode to create models, or "mock-ups" of programs. Because programmers don't have to worry about syntax errors while writing pseudocode, they can focus all of their attention on the program's design. Once a satisfactory design has been created with pseudocode, the pseudocode can be translated directly to actual code. Here is an example of how you might write pseudocode for the pay calculating program that we discussed earlier:

> *Input the hours worked*
> *Input the hourly pay rate*
> *Calculate gross pay as hours worked multiplied by pay rate*
> *Display the gross pay*

Each statement in the pseudocode represents an operation that can be performed in Python. For example, Python can read input that is typed on the keyboard, perform mathematical calculations, and display messages on the screen.

Flowcharts

Flowcharting is another tool that programmers use to design programs. A *flowchart* is a diagram that graphically depicts the steps that take place in a program. Figure 2 shows how you might create a flowchart for the pay calculating program.

Notice that there are three types of symbols in the flowchart: ovals, parallelograms, and a rectangle. Each of these symbols represents a step in the program, as described here:

- The ovals, which appear at the top and bottom of the flowchart, are called *terminal symbols*. The *Start* terminal symbol marks the program's starting point and the *End* terminal symbol marks the program's ending point.

- Parallelograms are used as *input symbols* and *output symbols*. They represent steps in which the program reads input or displays output.
- Rectangles are used as *processing symbols*. They represent steps in which the program performs some process on data, such as a mathematical calculation.

The symbols are connected by arrows that represent the "flow" of the program. To step through the symbols in the proper order, you begin at the *Start* terminal and follow the arrows until you reach the *End* terminal.

Figure 2 Flowchart for the pay calculating program

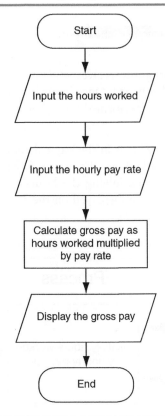

 Checkpoint

1 Who is a programmer's customer?

2 What is a software requirement?

3 What is an algorithm?

4 What is pseudocode?

5 What is a flowchart?

6 What do each of the following symbols mean in a flowchart?
- Oval
- Parallelogram
- Rectangle

 2 Input, Processing, and Output

CONCEPT: Input is data that the program receives. When a program receives data, it usually processes it by performing some operation with it. The result of the operation is sent out of the program as output.

Computer programs typically perform the following three-step process:

1. Input is received.
2. Some process is performed on the input.
3. Output is produced.

Input is any data that the program receives while it is running. One common form of input is data that is typed on the keyboard. Once input is received, some process, such as a mathematical calculation, is usually performed on it. The results of the process are then sent out of the program as output.

Figure 3 illustrates these three steps in the pay calculating program that we discussed earlier. The number of hours worked and the hourly pay rate are provided as input. The program processes this data by multiplying the hours worked by the hourly pay rate. The results of the calculation are then displayed on the screen as output.

Figure 3   The input, processing, and output of the pay calculating program

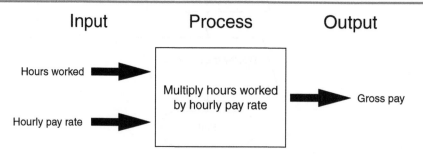

In this chapter we will discuss basic ways that you can perform input, processing, and output using Python.

Displaying Output with the print Statement

CONCEPT: You use the **print** statement to display output in a Python program.

Perhaps the most fundamental thing that a program can do is display a message on the computer screen. The print statement in Python displays output on the screen. Here is an example:

```
print 'Hello world'
```

The purpose of this statement is to display the message *Hello world* on the screen. Notice that after the word print, we have written Hello world inside single-quote marks. The quote marks will not be displayed when the statement executes. They simply mark the beginning and the end of the text that we wish to display.

Suppose your instructor tells you to write a program that displays your name and address on the computer screen. Program 1 shows an example of such a program, with the output that it will produce when it runs. (The line numbers that appear in a program listing in this book are *not* part of the program. We use the line numbers in our discussion to refer to parts of the program.)

Program 1   (output.py)

```
1   print 'Kate Austen'
2   print '123 Dharma Lane'
3   print 'Asheville, NC 28899'
```

Program Output

```
Kate Austen
123 Dharma Lane
Asheville, NC 28899
```

It is important to understand that the statements in this program execute in the order that they appear, from the top of the program to the bottom. When you run this program, the first statement will execute, followed by the second statement, and followed by the third statement.

Strings and String Literals

Programs almost always work with data of some type. For example, Program 1 uses the following three pieces of data:

```
'Kate Austen'
'123 Dharma Lane'
'Asheville, NC 28899'
```

These pieces of data are sequences of characters. In programming terms, a sequence of characters that is used as data is called a *string*. When a string appears in the actual code of a program it is called a *string literal*. In Python code, string literals must be enclosed in quote marks. As mentioned earlier, the quote marks simply mark where the string data begins and ends.

In Python you can enclose string literals in a set of single-quote marks(') or a set of double-quote marks ("). The string literals in Program 1 are enclosed in single-quote marks, but the program could also be written as shown in Program 2.

Program 2   (double_quotes.py)

```
1   print "Kate Austen"
2   print "123 Dharma Lane"
3   print "Asheville, NC 28899"
```

Program Output

```
Kate Austen
123 Dharma Lane
Asheville, NC 28899
```

If you want a string literal to contain either a single-quote or an apostrophe as part of the string, you can enclose the string literal in double-quote marks. For example, Program 3 prints two strings that contain apostrophes.

Program 3 (apostrophe.py)

```
1   print "Don't fear!"
2   print "I'm here!"
```

Program Output

```
Don't fear!
I'm here!
```

Likewise, you can use single-quote marks to enclose a string literal that contains double-quotes as part of the string. Program 4 shows an example.

Program 4 (display_quote.py)

```
1   print 'Your assignment is to read "Hamlet" by tomorrow.'
```

Program Output

```
Your assignment is to read "Hamlet" by tomorrow.
```

Python also allows you to enclose string literals in triple quotes (either """ or ' ' '). Triple-quoted strings can contain both single quotes and double quotes as part of the string. The following statement shows an example:

```
print """I'm reading "Hamlet" tonight."""
```

This statement will print

```
I'm reading "Hamlet" tonight.
```

Triple quotes can also be used to surround multiline strings, something for which single and double quotes cannot be used. Here is an example:

```
print """"One
Two
Three """
```

This statement will print

```
One
Two
Three
```

 **Checkpoint**

7   Write a print statement that displays your name.

8   Write a print statement that displays the following text:

    Python's the best!

9   Write a print statement that displays the following text:

    The cat said "meow."

4   Comments

CONCEPT: Comments are notes of explanation that document lines or sections of a program. Comments are part of the program, but the Python interpreter ignores them. They are intended for people who may be reading the source code.

Comments are short notes placed in different parts of a program, explaining how those parts of the program work. Although comments are a critical part of a program, they are ignored by the Python interpreter. Comments are intended for any person reading a program's code, not the computer.

In Python you begin a comment with the # character. When the Python interpreter sees a # character, it ignores everything from that character to the end of the line. For example, look at Program 5. Lines 1 and 2 are comments that briefly explain the program's purpose.

Program 5   (comment1.py)

```
1   # This program displays a person's
2   # name and address.
3   print 'Kate Austen'
4   print '123 Dharma Lane'
5   print 'Asheville, NC 28899'
```

Program Output

```
Kate Austen
123 Dharma Lane
Asheville, NC 28899
```

Programmers commonly write end-line comments in their code. An *end-line comment* is a comment that appears at the end of a line of code. It usually explains the statement that appears in that line. Program 6 shows an example. Each line ends with a comment that briefly explains what the line does.

Program 6   (comment2.py)

```
1  print "Kate Austen"        # Display the name
2  print "123 Dharma Lane"    # Display the street address
3  print "Asheville, NC 28899" # Display the city, state, and ZIP
```

Program Output

```
Kate Austen
123 Dharma Lane
Asheville, NC 28899
```

As a beginning programmer, you might be resistant to the idea of liberally writing comments in your programs. After all, it can seem more productive to write code that actually does something! It is crucial that you take the extra time to write comments, however. They will almost certainly save you and others time in the future when you have to modify or debug the program. Large and complex programs can be almost impossible easy to read and understand if they are not properly commented.

5   Variables

CONCEPT: A variable is a name that represents a value stored in the computer's memory.

Programs usually store data in the computer's memory and perform operations on that data. For example, consider the typical online shopping experience: you browse a website and add the items that you want to purchase to the shopping cart. As you add items to the shopping cart, data about those items is stored in memory. Then, when you click the checkout button, a program running on the website's computer calculates the cost of all the items you have in your shopping cart, applicable sales taxes, shipping costs, and the total of all these charges. When the program performs these calculations, it stores the results in the computer's memory.

Programs use variables to access and manipulate data that is stored in memory. A *variable* is a name that represents a value in the computer's memory. For example, a program that calculates the sales tax on a purchase might use the variable name `tax` to represent that value in memory. And a program that calculates the distance between two cities might use the variable name `distance` to represent that value in memory. When a variable represents a value in the computer's memory, we say that the variable *references* the value.

Creating Variables with Assignment Statements

You use an *assignment statement* to create a variable in Python. Here is an example of an assignment statement:

```
age = 25
```

After this statement executes, a variable named age will be created and it will reference the value 25. This concept is shown in Figure 4. In the figure, think of the value 25 as being stored somewhere in the computer's memory. The arrow that points from age to the value 25 indicates that the name age references the value.

Figure 4   The age variable references the value 25

age   ⟶   25

An assignment statement is written in the following general format:

```
variable = expression
```

The equal sign (=) is known as the *assignment operator*. In the general format, *variable* is the name of a variable and *expression* is a value, or any piece of code that results in a value. After an assignment statement executes, the variable listed on the left side of the = operator will reference the value given on the right side of the = operator.

In an assignment statement, the variable that is receiving the assignment must appear on the left side of the = operator. For example, the following statement will cause an error:

```
25 = age     # This is an error!
```

The code in Program 7 demonstrates a variable. Line 2 creates a variable named room and assigns it the value 503. The print statements in lines 3 and 4 display a message. Notice that line 4 displays the value that is referenced by the room variable.

Program 7   (variable_demo.py)

```
1   # This program demonstrates a variable.
2   room = 503
3   print 'I am staying in room number'
4   print room
```

Program Output

```
I am staying in room number
503
```

Notice that in line 4 there are no quotation marks around room. If quotation marks were placed around room, it would have indicated that we want to display the word "room" instead of the contents of the room variable. In other words, the following statement will display the contents of the room variable:

```
print room
```

This statement, however, will display the word "age":

```
print 'age'
```

Program 8 shows a sample program that uses two variables. Line 2 creates a variable named top_speed, assigning it the value 160. Line 3 creates a variable named distance, assigning it the value 300. This is illustrated in Figure 5.

Program 8   (variable_demo2.py)

```
1   # Create two variables: top_speed and distance.
2   top_speed = 160
3   distance = 300
4
5   # Display the values referenced by the variables.
6   print 'The top speed is'
7   print top_speed
8   print 'The distance traveled is'
9   print distance
```

Program Output

```
The top speed is
160
The distance traveled is
300
```

Figure 5   Two variables

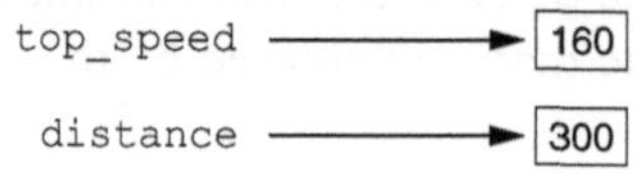

```
top_speed  ─────────▶  160

distance   ─────────▶  300
```

> **WARNING!** You cannot use a variable until you have assigned a value to it. An error will occur if you try to perform an operation on a variable, such as printing it, before it has been assigned a value.
>
> Sometimes a simple typing mistake will cause this error. One example is a misspelled variable name, as shown here:
>
> ```
>         temperature = 74.5 # Create a variable
>         print tempereture  # Error! Misspelled variable name
> ```
>
> In this code, the variable temperature is created by the assignment statement. The variable name is spelled differently in the print statement, however, which will cause an error. Another example is the inconsistent use of uppercase and lowercase letters in a variable name. Here is an example:
>
> ```
>         temperature = 74.5 # Create a variable
>         print Temperature  # Error! Inconsistent use of case
> ```
>
> In this code the variable temperature (in all lowercase letters) is created by the assignment statement. In the print statement, the name Temperature is spelled with an uppercase T. This will cause an error because variable names are case sensitive in Python.

Variable Naming Rules

Although you are allowed to make up your own names for variables, you must follow these rules:

- You cannot use one of Python's key words as a variable name.
- A variable name cannot contain spaces.
- The first character must be one of the letters a through z, A through Z, or an underscore character (_).
- After the first character you may use the letters a through z or A through Z, the digits 0 through 9, or underscores.
- Uppercase and lowercase characters are distinct. This means the variable name ItemsOrdered is not the same as itemsordered.

In addition to following these rules, you should always choose names for your variables that give an indication of what they are used for. For example, a variable that holds the temperature might be named temperature, and a variable that holds a car's speed might be named speed. You may be tempted to give variables names like x and b2, but names like these give no clue as to what the variable's purpose is.

Because a variable's name should reflect the variable's purpose, programmers often find themselves creating names that are made of multiple words. For example, consider the following variable names:

```
grosspay
payrate
hotdogssoldtoday
```

Unfortunately, these names are not easily read by the human eye because the words aren't separated. Because we can't have spaces in variable names, we need to find another way to separate the words in a multiword variable name, and make it more readable to the human eye.

One way to do this is to use the underscore character to represent a space. For example, the following variable names are easier to read than those previously shown:

```
gross_pay
pay_rate
hot_dogs_sold_today
```

This style of naming variables is popular among Python programmers and is the style we will use in this book. There are other popular styles, however, such as the *camelCase* naming convention. camelCase names are written in the following manner:

- The variable name begins with lowercase letters.
- The first character of the second and subsequent words is written in uppercase.

For example, the following variable names are written in camelCase:

```
grossPay
payRate
hotDogsSoldToday
```

NOTE: This style of naming is called camelCase because the uppercase characters that appear in a name may suggest a camel's humps.

Table 1 lists several sample variable names and indicates whether each is legal or illegal in Python.

Table 1   Sample variable names

Variable Name	Legal or Illegal?
`units_per_day`	Legal
`dayOfWeek`	Legal
`3dGraph`	Illegal. Variable names cannot begin with a digit.
`June1997`	Legal
`Mixture#3`	Illegal. Variable names may only use letters, digits, or underscores.

Displaying Multiple Items with the `print` Statement

If you refer to Program 7 you will see that we used the following two `print` statements in lines 3 and 4:

```
print 'I am staying in room number'
print room
```

We used two `print` statements because we needed to display two pieces of data. Line 3 displays the string literal `'I am staying in room number'`, and line 4 displays the value referenced by the `room` variable.

This program can be simplified, however, because Python allows us to display multiple items with one `print` statement. We simply have to separate the items with commas as shown in Program 9.

Program 9   (variable_demo3.py)

```
1   # This program demonstrates a variable.
2   room = 503
3   print 'I am staying in room number', room
```

Program Output

```
I am staying in room number 503
```

The `print` statement in line 4 displays two items: a string literal followed by the value referenced by the `room` variable. Notice that Python automatically printed a space between these two items. When multiple items are printed in one line of output, they will automatically be separated by a space.

Variable Reassignment

Variables are called "variable" because they can reference different values while a program is running. When you assign a value to a variable, the variable will reference that value until you assign it a different value. For example, look at Program 10. The statement in line 3 creates a variable named dollars and assigns it the value 2.75. This is shown in the top part of Figure 6. Then, the statement in line 8 assigns a different value, 99.95, to the dollars variable. The bottom part of Figure 6 shows how this changes the dollars variable. The old value, 2.75, is still in the computer's memory, but it can no longer be used because it isn't referenced by a variable. (The Python interpreter will eventually remove the unusable value from memory.)

Program 10   (variable_demo4.py)

```
1   # This program demonstrates variable reassignment.
2   # Assign a value to the dollars variable.
3   dollars = 2.75
4   print 'I have', dollars, 'in my account.'
5
6   # Reassign dollars so it references
7   # a different value.
8   dollars = 99.95
9   print 'But now I have', dollars, 'in my account!'
```

Program Output

```
I have 2.75 in my account.
But now I have 99.95 in my account!
```

Figure 6   Variable reassignment in Program 10

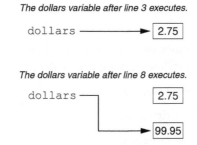

The dollars variable after line 3 executes.

dollars ──────────▶ 2.75

The dollars variable after line 8 executes.

dollars ──┐   2.75
          │
          └──────▶ 99.95

Numeric Data Types and Literals

Computers store data in memory and use a different technique for storing real numbers (numbers with a fractional part) than for storing integers. Not only are these types of numbers stored differently in memory, but similar operations on them are carried out in different ways.

Because different types of numbers are stored and manipulated in different ways, Python uses *data types* to categorize values in memory. When an integer is stored in memory, it is classified as an int, and when a real number is stored in memory, it is classified as a float.

Let's look at how Python determines the data type of a number. Several of the programs that you have seen so far have numeric data written into their code. For example, the following statement, which appears in Program 9, has the number 503 written into it.

```
room = 503
```

This statement causes the value 503 to be stored in memory, and it makes the room variable reference it. The following statement, which appears in Program 10, has the number 2.75 written into it.

```
dollars = 2.75
```

This statement causes the value 2.75 to be stored in memory, and it makes the dollars variable reference it. A number that is written into a program's code is called a *numeric literal*. When the Python interpreter reads a numeric literal in a program's code, it determines its data type according to the following rules:

- A numeric literal that is written as a whole number with no decimal point is considered an int. Examples are 7, 124, and −9.
- A numeric literal that is written with a decimal point is considered a float. Examples are 1.5, 3.14159, and 5.0.

So, the following statement causes the number 503 to be stored in memory as an int:

```
room = 503
```

And the following statement causes the number 2.75 to be stored in memory as a float:

```
dollars = 2.75
```

When you store an item in memory, it is important for you to be aware of the item's data type. As you will see, some operations behave differently depending on the type of data involved, and some operations can only be performed on values of a specific data type.

> **WARNING!** You cannot write currency symbols, spaces, or commas in numeric literals. For example, the following statement will cause an error:
>
> ```
> value = $4,567.99 # Error!
> ```
>
> This statement must be written as:
>
> ```
> value = 4567.99 # Correct
> ```

Storing Strings with the str Data Type

In addition to the int and float data types, Python also has a data type named str, which is used for storing strings in memory. The code in Program 11 shows how strings can be assigned to variables.

Program 11   (string_variable.py)

```
1   # Create variables to reference two strings.
2   first_name = 'Kathryn'
3   last_name = 'Marino'
4
5   # Display the values referenced by the variables.
6   print first_name, last_name
```

Program Output

Kathryn Marino

Checkpoint

10   What is a variable?

11   Which of the following are illegal variable names in Python, and why?

```
x
99bottles
july2009
theSalesFigureForFiscalYear
r&d
grade_report
```

12   Is the variable name Sales the same as sales? Why or why not?

13   Is the following assignment statement valid or invalid? If it is invalid, why?

```
72 = amount
```

14   What will the following code display?

```
val = 99
print 'The value is', 'val'
```

15   Look at the following assignment statements:

```
value1 = 99
value2 = 45.9
value3 = 7.0
value4 = 7
value5 = 'abc'
```

After these statements execute, what is the Python data type of the values referenced by each variable?

16   What will be displayed by the following program?

```
my_value = 99
my_value = 0
print my_value
```

6 ## Reading Input from the Keyboard

CONCEPT: Programs commonly need to read input typed by the user on the keyboard. We will use the Python functions to do this.

Most of the programs that you will write will need to read input, and then perform an operation on that input. In this section, we will discuss a basic input operation: reading data that has been typed on the keyboard. When a program reads data from the keyboard, usually it stores that data in a variable so it can be used later by the program.

In this book we will use two of Python's built-in functions to read input from the keyboard. A *function* is a piece of prewritten code that performs an operation and then returns a value back to the program. We will use the `input` function to read numeric data from the keyboard, and the `raw_input` function to read strings as input.

Reading Numbers with the `input` Function

Python's `input` function is useful for reading numeric input from the keyboard. You normally use the `input` function in an assignment statement that follows this general format:

```
variable = input(prompt)
```

In the general format, *prompt* is a string that is displayed on the screen. The string's purpose is to instruct the user to enter a value. *variable* is the name of a variable that will reference the data that was entered on the keyboard. Here is an example of a statement that uses the `input` function to read data from the keyboard:

```
hours = input('How many hours did you work? ')
```

When this statement executes, the following things happen:

- The string `'How many hours did you work? '` is displayed on the screen.
- The program pauses and waits for the user to type something on the keyboard, and then press the Enter key.
- When the Enter key is pressed, the data that was typed is assigned to the `hours` variable.

Program 12 shows a sample program that uses the `input` function.

Program 12   (input.py)

```
1   # This program gets input from the user.
2   age = input('How old are you? ')
3   print 'You said that you are', age, 'years old.'
```

Program Output (with input shown in bold)

```
How old are you? 28 [Enter]
You said that you are 28 years old.
```

The statement in line 2 uses the `input` function to read data that is typed on the keyboard. In the sample run, the user typed 28 and then pressed Enter. As a result, the integer value 28 was assigned to the `age` variable.

Take a closer look at the string we used as a prompt, in line 2:

```
'How old are you? '
```

Notice that the last character in the string, inside the quote marks, is a space. We put a space there because the input function does not automatically display a space after the prompt. When the user begins typing characters, they will appear on the screen immediately after the prompt. Making the last character in the prompt a space visually separates the prompt from the user's input on the screen.

When the user enters a number in response to the input function, Python determines the number's data type in the same way that it determines a numeric literal's data type: If the number contains no decimal point it is stored in memory as an int. If it contains a decimal point it is stored in memory as a float.

> **NOTE:** In this section, we mentioned the user. The *user* is simply any hypothetical person that is using a program and providing input for it. The user is sometimes called the *end user*.

Reading Strings with the `raw_input` Function

Although the input function works well for reading numbers, it is not convenient for reading strings. In order for the input function to read data as a string, the user has to enclose the data in quote-marks when he or she types it on the keyboard. Most users are not accustomed to doing this, so it's best to use another function: `raw_input`.

The `raw_input` function works like the input function, with one exception: the `raw_input` function retrieves all keyboard input as a string. There is no need for the user to type quote marks around the data that is entered. Program 13 shows a sample program that uses the `raw_input` function to read strings.

Program 13   (string_input.py)

```
1   # Get the user's first name.
2   first_name = raw_input('Enter your first name: ')
3
4   # Get the user's last name.
5   last_name = raw_input('Enter your last name: ')
6
7   # Print a greeting to the user.
8   print 'Hello', first_name, last_name
```

Program Output (with input shown in bold)
```
Enter your first name: Vinny [Enter]
Enter your last name: Brown [Enter]
Hello Vinny Brown
```

Checkpoint

17   You need the user of a program to enter the amount of sales for the week. Write a statement that prompts the user to enter this data and assigns the input to a variable.

18   You need the user of a program to enter a customer's last name. Write a statement that prompts the user to enter this data and assigns the input to a variable.

7   Performing Calculations

CONCEPT: Python has numerous operators that can be used to perform mathematical calculations.

Most real-world algorithms require calculations to be performed. A programmer's tools for performing calculations are *math operators*. Table 2 lists the math operators that are provided by the Python language.

Table 2   Python math operators

Symbol	Operation	Description
+	Addition	Adds two numbers
–	Subtraction	Subtracts one number from another
*	Multiplication	Multiplies one number by another
/	Division	Divides one number by another and gives the quotient
%	Remainder	Divides one number by another and gives the remainder
**	Exponent	Raises a number to a power

Programmers use the operators shown in Table 2 to create math expressions. A *math expression* performs a calculation and gives a value. The following is an example of a simple math expression:

```
12 + 2
```

The values on the right and left of the + operator are called *operands*. These are values that the + operator adds together. The value that is given by this expression is 14.

Variables may also be used in a math expression. For example, suppose we have two variables named `hours` and `pay_rate`. The following math expression uses the * operator to multiply the value referenced by the `hours` variable by the value referenced by the `pay_rate` variable:

```
hours * pay_rate
```

When we use a math expression to calculate a value, normally we want to save that value in memory so we can use it again in the program. We do this with an assignment statement. Program 14 shows an example.

Program 14   (simple_math.py)

```
 1   # Assign a value to the salary variable.
 2   salary = 2500.0
 3
 4   # Assign a value to the bonus variable.
 5   bonus = 1200.0
 6
 7   # Calculate the total pay by adding salary
 8   # and bonus. Assign the result to pay.
 9   pay = salary + bonus
10
11   # Display the pay.
12   print 'Your pay is', pay
```

Program Output

```
Your pay is 3700.0
```

Line 2 assigns 2500.0 to the salary variable, and line 5 assigns 1200.0 to the bonus variable. Line 9 assigns the result of the expression salary + bonus to the pay variable. As you can see from the program output, the pay variable holds the value 3700.0.

In the Spotlight:

Calculating a Percentage

Determining percentages is a common calculation in computer programming. In mathematics, the % symbol is used to indicate a percentage, but most programming languages, Python included, do not use the % symbol for this purpose. In a program, you usually have to convert a percentage to a decimal number. For example, 50 percent would be written as 0.5 and 2 percent would be written as 0.02.

Let's step through the process of writing a program that calculates a percentage. Suppose a retail business is planning to have a storewide sale where the prices of all items will be 20 percent off. We have been asked to write a program to calculate the sale price of an item after the discount is subtracted. Here is the algorithm:

1. *Get the original price of the item.*
2. *Calculate 20 percent of the original price. This is the amount of the discount.*
3. *Subtract the discount from the original price. This is the sale price.*
4. *Display the sale price.*

In step 1 we get the original price of the item. We will prompt the user to enter this data on the keyboard. In our program we will use the following statement to do this. Notice that the value entered by the user will be stored in a variable named original_price.

```
original_price = input("Enter the item's original price: ")
```

In step 2, we calculate the amount of the discount. To do this we multiply the original price by 20 percent. The following statement performs this calculation and assigns the result to the discount variable.

```
discount = original_price * 0.2
```

In step 3, we subtract the discount from the original price. The following statement does this calculation and stores the result in the sale_price variable.

```
sale_price = original_price - discount
```

Last, in step 4, we will use the following statement to display the sale price:

```
print 'The sale price is', sale_price
```

Program 15 shows the entire program, with example output.

Program 15   (sale_price.py)

```
 1   # This program gets an item's original price and
 2   # calculates its sale price, with a 20% discount.
 3
 4   # Get the item's original price.
 5   original_price = input("Enter the item's original price: ")
 6
 7   # Calculate the amount of the discount.
 8   discount = original_price * 0.2
 9
10   # Calculate the sale price.
11   sale_price = original_price - discount
12
13   # Display the sale price.
14   print 'The sale price is', sale_price
```

Program Output (with input shown in bold)

```
Enter the item's original price: 100.00 [Enter]
The sale price is 80.0
```

Integer Division

Be careful when dividing an integer by another integer. In Python, as well as many other languages, when an integer is divided by an integer the result will also be an integer. This behavior is known as *integer division*. For example, look at the following statement:

```
number = 3 / 2
```

What value will the `number` reference after this statement executes? You would probably assume that `number` would reference the value 1.5 because that's the result your calculator shows when you divide 3 by 2. However, that's not what will happen. Because the numbers 3 and 2 are both treated as integers, Python will throw away the fractional part of the result. (Throwing away the fractional part of a number is called *truncation*.) As a result, the statement will assign the value 1 to the `number` variable, not 1.5.

If you want to make sure that a division operation yields a real number, at least one of the operands must be a number with a decimal point or a `float` variable. For example, we could rewrite the statement as follows:

```
number = 3.0 / 2.0
```

Operator Precedence

You can write statements that use complex mathematical expressions involving several operators. The following statement assigns the sum of 17, the variable x, 21, and the variable y to the variable `answer`.

```
answer = 17 + x + 21 + y
```

Some expressions are not that straightforward, however. Consider the following statement:

```
outcome = 12.0 + 6.0 / 3.0
```

What value will be assigned to `outcome`? The number 6.0 might be used as an operand for either the addition or division operator. The `outcome` variable could be assigned either 6.0 or 14.0, depending on when the division takes place. Fortunately, the answer can be predicted because Python follows the same order of operations that you learned in math class.

First, operations that are enclosed in parentheses are performed first. Then, when two operators share an operand, the operator with the higher *precedence* is applied first. The precedence of the math operators, from highest to lowest, are:

1. Exponentiation: **
2. Multiplication, division, and remainder: * / %
3. Addition and subtraction: + −

Notice that the multiplication (*), division (/), and remainder (%) operators have the same precedence. The addition (+) and subtraction (−) operators also have the same precedence. When two operands with the same precedence share an operand, the operators execute from left to right.

Now, let's go back to the previous math expression:

```
outcome = 12.0 + 6.0 / 3.0
```

The value that will be assigned to `outcome` is 14.0 because the division operator has a higher *precedence* than the addition operator. As a result, the division takes place before the addition. The expression can be diagrammed as shown in Figure 7.

Figure 7   Operator precedence

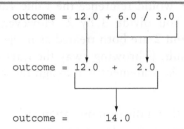

Table 3 shows some other sample expressions with their values.

Table 3   Some expressions

Expression	Value
5 + 2 * 4	13
10 / 2 − 3	2
8 + 12 * 2 − 4	28
6 − 3 * 2 + 7 − 1	6

Grouping with Parentheses

Parts of a mathematical expression may be grouped with parentheses to force some operations to be performed before others. In the following statement, the variables a and b are added together, and their sum is divided by 4:

```
result = (a + b) / 4
```

Without the parentheses, however, b would be divided by 4 and the result added to a. Table 4 shows more expressions and their values.

Table 4   More expressions and their values

Expression	Value
(5 + 2) * 4	28
10 / (5 − 3)	5
8 + 12 * (6 − 2)	56
(6 − 3) * (2 + 7) / 3	9

In the Spotlight:

Calculating an Average

Determining the average of a group of values is a simple calculation: add all of the values and then divide the sum by the number of values. Although this is a straightforward calculation, it is easy to make a mistake when writing a program that calculates an average. For example, let's assume that the variables a, b, and c each hold a value and we want to calculate the average of those values. If we are careless, we might write a statement such as the following to perform the calculation:

```
average = a + b + c / 3.0
```

Can you see the error in this statement? When it executes, the division will take place first. The value in c will be divided by 3, and then the result will be added to a + b. That is not the correct way to calculate an average. To correct this error we need to put parentheses around a + b + c, as shown here:

```
average = (a + b + c) / 3.0
```

Let's step through the process of writing a program that calculates an average. Suppose you have taken three tests in your computer science class, and you want to write a program that will display the average of the test scores. Here is the algorithm:

1. *Get the first test score.*
2. *Get the second test score.*
3. *Get the third test score.*
4. *Calculate the average by adding the three test scores and dividing the sum by 3.*
5. *Display the average.*

In steps 1, 2, and 3 we will prompt the user to enter the three test scores. We will store those test scores in the variables test1, test2, and test3. In step 4 we will calculate the average of the three test scores. We will use the following statement to perform the calculation and store the result in the average variable:

```
average = (test1 + test2 + test3) / 3.0
```

Last, in step 5, we display the average. Program 16 shows the program.

Program 16   (test_score_average.py)

```
 1  # Get three test scores and assign them to the
 2  # test1, test2, and test3 variables.
 3  test1 = input('Enter the first test score: ')
 4  test2 = input('Enter the second test score: ')
 5  test3 = input('Enter the third test score: ')
 6
 7  # Calculate the average of the three scores
 8  # and assign the result to the average variable.
 9  average = (test1 + test2 + test3) / 3.0
10
11  # Display the average.
12  print 'The average score is', average
```

Program Output (with input shown in bold)
```
Enter the first test score: 90 [Enter]
Enter the second test score: 80 [Enter]
Enter the third test score: 100 [Enter]
The average score is 90.0
```

The Exponent and Remainder Operators

In addition to the basic math operators for addition, subtraction, multiplication, and division, Python also provides an exponent operator and a remainder operator. Two asterisks written together (**) is the exponent operator, and its purpose it to raise a number to a power. For example, the following statement raises the length variable to the power of 2 and assigns the result to the area variable:

```
area = length**2
```

In Python, the % symbol is the remainder operator. (This is also known as the modulus operator.) The remainder operator performs division, but instead of returning the quotient, it returns the remainder. The following statement assigns 2 to leftover:

```
leftover = 17 % 3
```

This statement assigns 2 to leftover because 17 divided by 3 is 5 with a remainder of 2. You will not use the remainder operator frequently, but it is useful in some situations. It is commonly used in calculations that detect odd or even numbers, determine the day of the week, measure the passage of time, and other specialized operations.

Converting Math Formulas to Programming Statements

You probably remember from algebra class that the expression $2xy$ is understood to mean 2 times x times y. In math, you do not always use an operator for multiplication. Python, as well as other programming languages, requires an operator for any mathematical operation. Table 5 shows some algebraic expressions that perform multiplication and the equivalent programming expressions.

Table 5   Algebraic expressions

Algebraic Expression	Operation Being Performed	Programming Expression
$6B$	6 times B	6 * B
(3)(12)	3 times 12	3 * 12
$4xy$	4 times x times y	4 * x * y

When converting some algebraic expressions to programming expressions, you may have to insert parentheses that do not appear in the algebraic expression. For example, look at the following formula:

$$x = \frac{a + b}{c}$$

To convert this to a programming statement, $a + b$ will have to be enclosed in parentheses:

$$x = (a + b) / c$$

Table 6 shows additional algebraic expressions and their Python equivalents.

Table 6 Algebraic and programming expressions

Algebraic Expression	Python Statement
$y = 3\dfrac{x}{2}$	`y = 3 * x / 2`
$z = 3bc + 4$	`z = 3 * b * c + 4`
$a = \dfrac{x + 2}{b - 1}$	`a = (x + 2) / (b - 1)`

In the Spotlight:
Converting a Math Formula to a Programming Statement

Suppose you want to deposit a certain amount of money into a savings account, and then leave it alone to draw interest for the next 10 years. At the end of 10 years you would like to have $10,000 in the account. How much do you need to deposit today to make that happen? You can use the following formula to find out:

$$P = \frac{F}{(1 + r)^n}$$

The terms in the formula are as follows:

- P is the present value, or the amount that you need to deposit today.
- F is the future value that you want in the account. (In this case, F is $10,000.)
- r is the annual interest rate.
- n is the number of years that you plan to let the money sit in the account.

It would be convenient to write a computer program to perform the calculation, because then we can experiment with different values for the variables. Here is an algorithm that we can use:

1. *Get the desired future value.*
2. *Get the annual interest rate.*
3. *Get the number of years that the money will sit in the account.*
4. *Calculate the amount that will have to be deposited.*
5. *Display the result of the calculation in step 4.*

In steps 1 through 3, we will prompt the user to enter the specified values. We will assign the desired future value to a variable named `future_value`, the annual interest rate to a variable named `rate`, and the number of years to a variable named `years`.

In step 4, we calculate the present value, which is the amount of money that we will have to deposit. We will convert the formula previously shown to the following statement. The statement stores the result of the calculation in the present_value variable.

```
present_value = future_value / (1.0 + rate)**years
```

In step 5, we display the value in the present_value variable. Program 17 shows the program.

Program 17   (future_value.py)

```
 1   # Get the desired future value.
 2   future_value = input('Enter the desired future value: ')
 3
 4   # Get the annual interest rate.
 5   rate = input('Enter the annual interest rate: ')
 6
 7   # Get the number of years that the money will appreciate.
 8   years = input('Enter the number of years the money will grow: ')
 9
10   # Calculate the amount needed to deposit.
11   present_value = future_value / (1.0 + rate)**years
12
13   # Display the amount needed to deposit.
14   print 'You will need to deposit this amount:', present_value
```

Program Output (with input shown in bold)

```
Enter the desired future value: 10000.0 [Enter]
Enter the annual interest rate: 0.05 [Enter]
Enter the number of years the money will grow: 10 [Enter]
You will need to deposit this amount: 6139.13253541
```

NOTE: Unlike the output shown for this program, dollar amounts are usually rounded to two decimal places. Later in this chapter you will learn how to format numbers so they are rounded to a specified number of decimal places.

Data Type Conversion

When you perform a math operation on two operands, the data type of the result will depend on the data type of the operands. Python follows these rules when evaluating mathematical expressions:

- When an operation is performed on two int values, the result will be an int.
- When an operation is performed on two float values, the result will be a float.

- When an operation is performed on an int and a float, the int value will be temporarily converted to a float and the result of the operation will be a float. (An expression that uses an int and a float is called a *mixed-type expression*.)

The first two situations are straightforward: operations on ints produce ints, and operations on floats produce floats. Let's look at an example of the third situation, which involves mixed-type expressions:

```
my_number = 5 * 2.0
```

When this statement executes, the value 5 will be converted to a float (5.0) and then multiplied by 2.0. The result, 10.0, will be assigned to my_number.

The int to float conversion that takes place in the previous statement happens implicitly. In some situations, you want to explicitly make sure that a value is converted to a specific type. For example, look at Program 18.

Program 18   (books_per_month1.py)

```
1    # Get the number of books the user plans to read.
2    books = input('How many books do you want to read? ')
3
4    # Get the number of months it will take to read them.
5    months = input('How many months will it take? ')
6
7    # Calculate the number of books per month.
8    per_month = books / months
9
10   # Display the result.
11   print 'You will read', per_month, 'books per month.'
```

Program Output (with input shown in bold)
```
How many books do you want to read? 20 [Enter]
How many months will it take? 8 [Enter]
You will read 2 books per month.
```

This program asks the user for the number of books he or she plans to read, and the number of months it will take to read them. Line 8 divides books by months to calculate the number of books that the user must read per month. However, if the user has entered integer values for both books and months, this statement will perform integer division. This was what happened in the sample output. If you want the result to be completely accurate, you need to make sure that at least one of the operands in the division operation is a float. We can do that with Python's built-in float() function, as shown in Program 19.

Program 19   (books_per_month2.py)

```
1    # Get the number of books the user plans to read.
2    books = input('How many books do you want to read? ')
```

(program continues)

Program 19   *(continued)*

```
 3
 4   # Get the number of months it will take to read them.
 5   months = input('How many months will it take? ')
 6
 7   # Calculate the number of books per month.
 8   per_month = float(books) / months
 9
10   # Display the result.
11   print 'You will read', per_month, 'books per month.'
```

Program Output (with input shown in bold)
```
How many books do you want to read? 20 [Enter]
How many months will it take? 8 [Enter]
You will read 2.5 books per month.
```

In line 8 the expression `float(books)` converts the value referenced by `books` to a `float`. This ensures that when the division takes place, one of the operands will be a `float`, thus preventing integer division.

WARNING! Notice that in line 8 of Program 19, we did not put the entire expression `books / months` inside the parentheses of the `float` function, as shown here:

```
per_month = float(books / months)
```

This statement does not convert the value in `books` or `months` to a `float`, but converts the result of the expression `books / months`. If this statement were used in the program, an integer division operation would still have been performed. Here's why: The result of the expression `books / months` is 2 (because integer division takes place). The value 2 converted to a `float` is 2.0. To prevent the integer division from taking place, one of the operands must be converted to a `float`.

Python also has a built-in `int()` function that converts a value to an `int`. When a `float` is converted to an `int`, any fractional part is thrown away, or truncated. Here is an example:

```
x = 27.9
y = int(x)
```

After this code executes, the variable `y` will be assigned 27. Here is an example showing the `int` function converting a negative `float` value:

```
x = -12.9
y = int(x)
```

After this code executes, `y` will be assigned -12.

Breaking Long Statements into Multiple Lines

Most programming statements are written on one line. If a programming statement is too long, however, you will not be able to view all of it in your editor window without scrolling horizontally. In addition, if you print your program code on paper and one of the statements is too long to fit on one line, it will wrap around to the next line and make the code difficult to read.

Python allows you to break a statement into multiple lines by using the *line continuation character*, which is a backslash (\). You simply type the backslash character at the point you want to break the statement, and then press the Enter key. Here is a `print` statement that is broken into two lines with the line continuation character:

```
print 'We sold', units_sold, \
      'for a total of', sales_amount
```

The line continuation character that appears at the end of the first line tells the interpreter that the statement is continued on the next line. Here is a statement that performs a mathematical calculation and has been broken up to fit on two lines:

```
result = var1 * 2 + var2 * 3 + \
         var3 * 4 + var4 * 5
```

Here is one last example:

```
print "Monday's sales are", monday, \
      "and Tuesday's sales are", tuesday, \
      "and Wednesday's sales are", wednesday
```

This long `print` statement is broken into three lines. Notice that the first two lines end with a backslash.

Checkpoint

19 Complete the following table by writing the value of each expression in the Value column.

Expression	Value
6 + 3 * 5	_____
12 / 2 - 4	_____
9 + 14 * 2 - 6	_____
(6 + 2) * 3	_____
14 / (11 - 4)	_____
9 + 12 * (8 - 3)	_____
float(9) / 2	_____
float(9 / 2)	_____
int(9.0 / 3.0)	_____

20 What value will be assigned to `result` after the following statement executes?

```
result = 9 / 2
```

21 What value will be assigned to `result` after the following statement executes?

```
result = 9 % 2
```

 8 | # More About Data Output

So far we have discussed only basic ways to display data. Eventually, you will want to exercise more control over the way data appear on the screen. In this section, you will learn more details about the Python `print` statement, and you'll see techniques for formatting output in specific ways.

Suppressing the `print` Statement's Newline

The `print` statement normally displays a line of output. For example, the following three print statements will produce three lines of output:

```
print 'One'
print 'Two'
print 'Three'
```

Each of the `print` statements shown here displays a string and then prints a *newline character*. You do not see the newline character, but when it is displayed, it causes the output to advance to the next line. (You can think of the newline character as a special command that causes the computer to start a new line of output.)

If you do not want the `print` statement to start a new line of output when it finishes displaying its output, you can write a trailing comma at the end of the statement, as shown here:

```
print 'One',
print 'Two',
print 'Three'
```

Notice that the first two `print` statements end with a comma. The trailing commas prevent these two `print` statements from displaying a newline character at the end of their output. Instead, they display a space at the end of their output. Here is the output of these statements:

```
One Two Three
```

Escape Characters

An *escape character* is a special character that is preceded with a backslash (\), appearing inside a string literal. When a string literal that contains escape characters is printed, the escape characters are treated as special commands that are embedded in the string.

For example, \n is the newline escape character. When the \n escape character is printed, it isn't displayed on the screen. Instead, it causes output to advance to the next line. For example, look at the following statement:

```
print 'One\nTwo\nThree'
```

When this statement executes, it displays

```
One
Two
Three
```

Python recognizes several escape characters, some of which are listed in Table 7.

Table 7 Some of Python's escape characters

Escape Character	Effect
\n	Causes output to be advanced to the next line.
\t	Causes output to skip over to the next horizontal tab position.
\'	Causes a single quote mark to be printed.
\"	Causes a double quote mark to be printed.
\\	Causes a backslash character to be printed.

The \t escape character advances the output to the next horizontal tab position. (A tab position normally appears after every eighth character.) The following statements are illustrative:

```
print 'Mon\tTues\tWed'
print 'Thur\tFri\tSat'
```

This statement prints Monday, then advances the output to the next tab position, then prints Tuesday, then advances the output to the next tab position, then prints Wednesday. The output will look like this:

```
Mon    Tues   Wed
Thur   Fri    Sat
```

You can use the \' and \" escape characters to display quotation marks. The following statements are illustrative:

```
print "Your assignment is to read \"Hamlet\" by tomorrow."
print 'I\'m ready to begin.'
```

These statements display the following:

```
Your assignment is to read "Hamlet" by tomorrow.
I'm ready to begin.
```

You can use the \\ escape character to display a backslash, as shown in the following:

```
print 'The path is C:\\temp\\data.'
```

This statement will display

```
The path is C:\temp\data.
```

Displaying Multiple Items with the + Operator

Earlier in this chapter, you saw that the + operator is used to add two numbers. When the + operator is used with two strings, however, it performs *string concatenation*.

This means that it appends one string to another. For example, look at the following statement:

```
print 'This is ' + 'one string.'
```

This statement will print

```
This is one string.
```

String concatenation can be useful for breaking up a string literal so a long `print` statement can span multiple lines. Here is an example:

```
print 'Enter the amount of ' + \
      'sales for each day and ' + \
      'press Enter.'
```

This statement will display the following:

```
Enter the amount of sales for each day and press Enter.
```

Formatting Numbers

You might not always be happy with the way that numbers, especially floating-point numbers, are displayed on the screen. When a floating-point number is displayed by the `print` statement, it can appear with up to 12 significant digits. This is shown in the output of Program 20.

Program 20   (no_formatting.py)

```
1   # This program demonstrates how a floating-point
2   # number is displayed with no formatting.
3   amount_due = 5000.0
4   monthly_payment = amount_due / 12.0
5   print 'The monthly payment is', monthly_payment
```

Program Output

```
The monthly payment is 416.666666667
```

Because this program displays a dollar amount, it would be nice to see that amount rounded to two decimal places. Fortunately, Python gives us a way to do just that with the string format operator.

You previously learned that the `%` symbol is the remainder operator. That's true when both of its operands are numbers. When the operand on the left side of the `%` symbol is a string, however, it becomes the *string format operator*. Here is the general format of how we can use the string format operator with the `print` statement to format the way a number is displayed:

```
print string % number
```

In the general format, *string* is a string that contains text and/or a formatting specifier. A *formatting specifier* is a special set of characters that specify how a value should be formatted. In the general format, *number* is a variable or expression that gives a numeric value. The value of *number* will be formatted according to the formatting specifier in the *string*. Here is an example:

```
my_value = 7.23456
print 'The value is %.2f' % my_value
```

Figure 8 points out the important parts of the `print` statement. In the `print` statement, the formatting specifier is `%.2f`. When the statement executes, `%.2f` will not be displayed. Instead, the value referenced by `my_value` will be displayed in place of `%.2f`. Here is the way the output will appear:

```
The value is 7.23
```

The `f` in the formatting specifier indicates that we want to display a floating-point number. The `.2` that appears before the `f` indicates that the number should be rounded to two decimal places. Program 21 shows how we can modify Program 20 so that it formats its output using this technique.

Figure 8   Using the string format operator

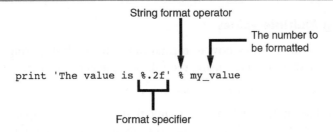

Program 21   (formatting.py)

```
1   # This program demonstrates how a floating-point
2   # number can be formatted.
3   amount_due = 5000.0
4   monthly_payment = amount_due / 12.0
5   print 'The monthly payment is %.2f' % monthly_payment
```

Program Output

```
The monthly payment is 416.67
```

You can round values to other numbers of decimal places. For example, the formatting specifier `%.3f` specifies three decimal places, and `%.6f` specifies six decimal places. In Program 22, a value is displayed rounded to one, two, three, four, five, and six decimal places.

Program 22   (decimal_places.py)

```
1   # This program demonstrates how a value can be
2   # formatted, rounded to different numbers of
```

(program continues)

Program 22   *(continued)*

```
 3   # decimal places.
 4   my_value = 1.123456789
 5   print '%.1f' % my_value # Rounded to 1 decimal place
 6   print '%.2f' % my_value # Rounded to 2 decimal places
 7   print '%.3f' % my_value # Rounded to 3 decimal places
 8   print '%.4f' % my_value # Rounded to 4 decimal places
 9   print '%.5f' % my_value # Rounded to 5 decimal places
10   print '%.6f' % my_value # Rounded to 6 decimal places
```

Program Output

```
1.1
1.12
1.123
1.1235
1.12346
1.123457
```

Formatting Multiple Values

The previous examples show how to format one value with the string formatting operator. You can format several values, using the following general format:

```
print string % (number, number, ...)
```

In the general format, *string* is a string that contains multiple formatting specifiers. (*number, number, ...*) is a list of variables or expressions enclosed in parentheses and separated by commas. The first value or expression in this list will be formatted according to the first formatting specifier in *string*, the second value or expression will be formatted according to the second formatting specifier in *string*, and so forth. Here is an example:

```
value1 = 6.7891234
value2 = 1.2345678
print 'The values are %.1f and %.3f' % (value1, value2)
```

In the print statement, the %.1f formatting specifier corresponds to the value1 variable and the %.3f formatting specifier corresponds to the value2 variable. When the code runs, it will produce the following output:

```
The values are 6.8 and 1.235
```

NOTE: You must have the same number of formatting specifiers as values to be formatted. Otherwise an error will occur.

Specifying a Minimum Field Width

A formatting specifier can also include a minimum field width, which is the minimum number of spaces that should be used to display the value.

```
my_value = 1.123456789
print 'The value is:%6.2f' % my_value
```

In the print statement, the formatting specifier is %6.2f. The 6 specifies that the number of spaces reserved on the screen for the value should be a minimum of 6. The output of the statement will be

```
The value is:   1.12
```

In this case, the number that is displayed is shorter than the field that it is displayed in. The number 1.12 uses only four spaces on the screen, but it is displayed in a field that is six spaces wide. When this is the case, the number will be right justified in the field. If a value is too large to fit in the specified field width, the field is automatically enlarged to accommodate it.

Field widths can help when you need to print values aligned in columns. For example, look at Program 23. Each of the variables is displayed in a field that is seven spaces wide,

Program 23   (columns.py)

```
 1    # This program displays the following
 2    # floating-point numbers in a column
 3    # with their decimal points aligned.
 4    num1 = 127.899
 5    num2 = 3465.148
 6    num3 = 3.776
 7    num4 = 264.821
 8    num5 = 88.081
 9    num6 = 799.999
10
11    # Display each number in a field of 7 spaces
12    # with 2 decimal places.
13    print '%7.2f' % num1
14    print '%7.2f' % num2
15    print '%7.2f' % num3
16    print '%7.2f' % num4
17    print '%7.2f' % num5
18    print '%7.2f' % num6
```

Program Output

```
 127.90
3465.15
   3.78
 264.82
  88.08
 800.00
```

Formatting Integers and Strings

In addition to floating-point values, Python provides formatting specifiers for integers and strings. For example, the following code shows how to use the %d formatting specifier to format an integer:

```
hours = 40
print 'I worked %d hours this week.' % hours
```

This code will display the following:

```
I worked 40 hours this week.
```

Here is an example that formats two integer values:

```
dogs = 2
cats = 3
print 'We have %d dogs and %d cats.' % (dogs, cats)
```

This code will display

```
We have 2 dogs and 3 cats.
```

Here is an example of how the %s formatting specifier can be used to format a string:

```
name = 'Ringo'
print 'Hello %s. Good to see you!' % name
```

This code will display the following:

```
Hello Ringo. Good to see you!
```

The following example shows how a string and a floating-point number can be formatted in the same statement:

```
day = 'Monday'
sales = 8450.55
print 'The sales on %s were $%.2f.' % (day, sales)
```

The output is

```
The sales on Monday were $8450.55.
```

You can also apply minimum field widths to the %d and %s formatting specifiers. For example, Program 24 prints a series of salesperson names and units sold in two columns. Each column uses a field width of 15 spaces.

Program 24   (names_and_sales.py)

```
1   # This program displays a set of salesperson
2   # names and units sold in two columns.
3
4   # Assign the names to variables.
5   salesperson1 = 'Graves'
6   salesperson2 = 'Harrison'
7   salesperson3 = 'Hoyle'
8   salesperson4 = 'Kramer'
9   salesperson5 = 'Smith'
10
11  # Assign the units sold to variables.
12  units1 = 1456.78
13  units2 = 2890.55
14  units3 = 946.77
15  units4 = 2678.91
```

```
16   units5 = 1287.87
17
18   # Display the data.
19   print '%15s %15s' % ('Salesperson', 'Units Sold')
20   print '%15s %15d' % (salesperson1, units1)
21   print '%15s %15d' % (salesperson2, units2)
22   print '%15s %15d' % (salesperson3, units3)
23   print '%15s %15d' % (salesperson4, units4)
24   print '%15s %15d' % (salesperson5, units5)
```

Program Output

```
Salesperson           Units Sold
Graves                1456
Harrison              2890
Hoyle                 946
Kramer                2678
Smith                 1287
```

Review Questions

Multiple Choice

1. A _____ error does not prevent the program from running, but causes it to produce incorrect results.
   a. syntax
   b. hardware
   c. logic
   d. fatal

2. A _____ is a single function that the program must perform in order to satisfy the customer.
   a. task
   b. software requirement
   c. prerequisite
   d. predicate

3. A(n) _____ is a set of well-defined logical steps that must be taken to perform a task.
   a. logarithm
   b. plan of action
   c. logic schedule
   d. algorithm

4. An informal language that has no syntax rules, and is not meant to be compiled or executed is called _____.
   a. faux code
   b. pseudocode
   c. Python
   d. a flowchart

5. A _____ is a diagram that graphically depicts the steps that take place in a program.
   a. flowchart
   b. step chart
   c. code graph
   d. program graph

6. A _____ is a sequence of characters.
   a. char sequence
   b. character collection
   c. string
   d. text block

7. A _____ is a name that references a value in the computer's memory.
   a. variable
   b. register
   c. RAM slot
   d. byte

8. A _____ is any hypothetical person using a program and providing input for it.
   a. designer
   b. user
   c. guinea pig
   d. test subject

9. A string literal in Python must be enclosed in
   a. parentheses
   b. single-quotes
   c. double-quotes
   d. either single-quotes or double-quotes

10. Short notes placed in different parts of a program explaining how those parts of the program work are called _____.
    a. comments
    b. reference manuals
    c. tutorials
    d. external documentation

11. A(n) _____ makes a variable reference a value in the computer's memory.
    a. variable declaration
    b. assignment statement
    c. math expression
    d. string literal

12. This symbol marks the beginning of a comment in Python.
    a. &
    b. *
    c. **
    d. #

13. Which of the following statements will cause an error?
  a. x = 17
  b. 17 = x
  c. x = 99999
  d. x = '17'

14. In the expression 12 + 7, the values on the right and left of the + symbol are called _____.
  a. operands
  b. operators
  c. arguments
  d. math expressions

15. This is an operator that raises a number to a power.
  a. %
  b. *
  c. **
  d. /

16. This operator performs division, but instead of returning the quotient it returns the remainder.
  a. %
  b. *
  c. **
  d. /

17. Suppose the following statement is in a program: price = 99.0. After this statement executes, the price variable will reference a value of this data type.
  a. int
  b. float
  c. currency
  d. str

18. This built-in function can be used to read a number that has been typed on the keyboard.
  a. input()
  b. get_num()
  c. read_number()
  d. keyboard()

19. This built-in function can be used to convert an int value to a float.
  a. int_to_float()
  b. float()
  c. convert()
  d. int()

20. This is the string format operator.
  a. %
  b. *
  c. &
  d. /

True or False

1. Programmers must be careful not to make syntax errors when writing pseudocode programs.
2. In a math expression, multiplication and division takes place before addition and subtraction.
3. Variable names can have spaces in them.
4. In Python the first character of a variable name cannot be a number.
5. If you print a variable that has not been assigned a value, the number 0 will be displayed.

Short Answer

1. What does a professional programmer usually do first to gain an understanding of a problem?
2. What is pseudocode?
3. Computer programs typically perform what three steps?
4. If a math expression adds a `float` to an `int`, what will the data type of the result be?
5. How can the following statement be modified to make sure integer division does not take place?

```
result = a / b
```

Algorithm Workbench

1. Write Python code that prompts the user to enter his or her height and assigns the user's input to a variable named `height`.
2. Write Python code that prompts the user to enter his or her favorite color and assigns the user's input to a variable named `color`.
3. Write assignment statements that perform the following operations with the variables a, b, and c.
   a. Adds 2 to a and assigns the result to b
   b. Multiplies b times 4 and assigns the result to a
   c. Divides a by 3.14 and assigns the result to b
   d. Subtracts 8 from b and assigns the result to a
4. Assume the variables `result`, w, x, y, and z are all integers, and that w = 5, x = 4, y = 8, and z = 2. What value will be stored in `result` after each of the following statements execute?
   a. `result = x + y`
   b. `result = z * 2`
   c. `result = y / x`
   d. `result = y - z`
5. Write a Python statement that assigns the sum of 10 and 14 to the variable `total`.
6. Write a Python statement that subtracts the variable `down_payment` from the variable `total` and assigns the result to the variable due.

7. Write a Python statement that multiplies the variable `subtotal` by 0.15 and assigns the result to the variable `total`.

8. What would the following display?

```
a = 5
b = 2
c = 3
result = a + b * c
print result
```

9. What would the following display?

```
num = 99
num = 5
print num
```

10. Assume the variable `sales` references a `float` value. Write a statement that displays the value rounded to two decimal points.

Programming Exercises

1. Personal Information

Write a program that displays the following information:

- Your name
- Your address, with city, state, and ZIP
- Your telephone number
- Your college major

2. Sales Prediction

A company has determined that its annual profit is typically 23 percent of total sales. Write a program that asks the user to enter the projected amount of total sales, and then displays the profit that will be made from that amount.

Hint: use the value 0.23 to represent 23 percent.

3. Land Calculation

One acre of land is equivalent to 43,560 square feet. Write a program that asks the user to enter the total square feet in a tract of land and calculates the number of acres in the tract.

Hint: divide the amount entered by 43,560 to get the number of acres.

4. Total Purchase

A customer in a store is purchasing five items. Write a program that asks for the price of each item, and then displays the subtotal of the sale, the amount of sales tax, and the total. Assume the sales tax is 6 percent.

5. Distance Traveled

Assuming there are no accidents or delays, the distance that a car travels down the interstate can be calculated with the following formula:

$$Distance = Speed \times Time$$

A car is traveling at 60 miles per hour. Write a program that displays the following:

- The distance the car will travel in 5 hours
- The distance the car will travel in 8 hours
- The distance the car will travel in 12 hours

6. Sales Tax

Write a program that will ask the user to enter the amount of a purchase. The program should then compute the state and county sales tax. Assume the state sales tax is 4 percent and the county sales tax is 2 percent. The program should display the amount of the purchase, the state sales tax, the county sales tax, the total sales tax, and the total of the sale (which is the sum of the amount of purchase plus the total sales tax).

Hint: use the value 0.02 to represent 2 percent, and 0.04 to represent 4 percent.

7. Miles-per-Gallon

A car's miles-per-gallon (MPG) can be calculated with the following formula:

$$MPG = Miles\ driven\ /\ Gallons\ of\ gas\ used$$

Write a program that asks the user for the number of miles driven and the gallons of gas used. It should calculate the car's miles-per-gallon and display the result.

8. Tip, Tax, and Total

Write a program that calculates the total amount of a meal purchased at a restaurant. The program should ask the user to enter the charge for the food, and then calculate the amount of a 15 percent tip and 7 percent sales tax. Display each of these amounts and the total.

9. Celsius to Fahrenheit Temperature Converter

Write a program that converts Celsius temperatures to Fahrenheit temperatures. The formula is as follows:

$$F = \frac{9}{5}C + 32$$

The program should ask the user to enter a temperature in Celsius, and then display the temperature converted to Fahrenheit.

10. Stock Transaction Program

Last month Joe purchased some stock in Acme Software, Inc. Here are the details of the purchase:

- The number of shares that Joe purchased was 1,000.
- When Joe purchased the stock, he paid $32.87 per share.
- Joe paid his stockbroker a commission that amounted to 2 percent of the amount he paid for the stock.

Two weeks later Joe sold the stock. Here are the details of the sale:

- The number of shares that Joe sold was 1,000.
- He sold the stock for $33.92 per share.
- He paid his stockbroker another commission that amounted to 2 percent of the amount he received for the stock.

Write a program that displays the following information:

- The amount of money Joe paid for the stock.
- The amount of commission Joe paid his broker when he bought the stock.
- The amount that Joe sold the stock for.
- The amount of commission Joe paid his broker when he sold the stock.
- Display the amount of money that Joe had left when he sold the stock and paid his broker (both times). If this amount is positive, then Joe made a profit. If the amount is negative, then Joe lost money.

14

Simple Functions

TOPICS

1	Introduction to Functions	4	Local Variables
2	Defining and Calling a Function	5	Passing Arguments to Functions
3	Designing a Program to Use Functions	6	Global Variables and Global Constants

1 Introduction to Functions

CONCEPT: A function is a group of statements that exist within a program for the purpose of performing a specific task.

In an algorithm for calculating an employee's pay, the number of hours worked is multiplied by an hourly pay rate. A more realistic payroll algorithm, however, would do much more than this. In a real-world application, the overall task of calculating an employee's pay would consist of several subtasks, such as the following:

- Getting the employee's hourly pay rate
- Getting the number of hours worked
- Calculating the employee's gross pay
- Calculating overtime pay
- Calculating withholdings for taxes and benefits
- Calculating the net pay
- Printing the paycheck

Most programs perform tasks that are large enough to be broken down into several subtasks. For this reason, programmers usually break down their programs into small manageable pieces known as functions. A *function* is a group of statements that exist within a program for the purpose of performing a specific task. Instead of writing a large program as one long sequence of statements, it can be written as several small functions, each one performing a specific part of the task. These small functions can then be executed in the desired order to perform the overall task.

This approach is sometimes called *divide and conquer* because a large task is divided into several smaller tasks that are easily performed. Figure 1 illustrates this idea by comparing two programs: one that uses a long complex sequence of statements to perform a task, and another that divides a task into smaller tasks, each of which is performed by a separate function.

When using functions in a program, you generally isolate each task within the program in its own function. For example, a realistic pay calculating program might have the following functions:

- A function that gets the employee's hourly pay rate
- A function that gets the number of hours worked
- A function that calculates the employee's gross pay
- A function that calculates the overtime pay
- A function that calculates the withholdings for taxes and benefits
- A function that calculates the net pay
- A function that prints the paycheck

Figure 1   Using functions to divide and conquer a large task

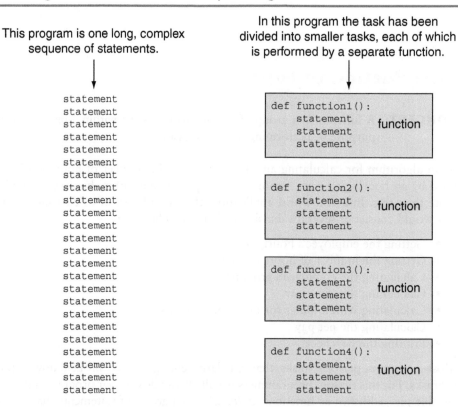

Benefits of Using Functions

A program benefits in the following ways when it is broken down into functions:

Simpler Code

A program's code tends to be simpler and easier to understand when it is broken down into functions. Several small functions are much easier to read than one long sequence of statements.

Code Reuse

Functions also reduce the duplication of code within a program. If a specific operation is performed in several places in a program, a function can be written once to perform that operation, and then be executed any time it is needed. This benefit of using functions is known as *code reuse* because you are writing the code to perform a task once and then reusing it each time you need to perform the task.

Better Testing

When each task within a program is contained in its own function, testing and debugging becomes simpler. Programmers can test each function in a program individually, to determine whether it correctly performs its operation. This makes it easier to isolate and fix errors.

Faster Development

Suppose a programmer or a team of programmers is developing multiple programs. They discover that each of the programs perform several common tasks, such as asking for a username and a password, displaying the current time, and so on. It doesn't make sense to write the code for these tasks multiple times. Instead, functions can be written for the commonly needed tasks, and those functions can be incorporated into each program that needs them.

Easier Facilitation of Teamwork

Functions also make it easier for programmers to work in teams. When a program is developed as a set of functions that each performs an individual task, then different programmers can be assigned the job of writing different functions.

 Checkpoint

    1 What is a function?

    2 What is meant by the phrase "divide and conquer?"

    3 How do functions help you reuse code in a program?

    4 How can functions make the development of multiple programs faster?

    5 How can functions make it easier for programs to be developed by teams of programmers?

2 Defining and Calling a Function

CONCEPT: The code for a function is known as a function definition. To execute the function, you write a statement that calls it.

Function Names

Before we discuss the process of creating and using functions, we should mention a few things about function names. Just as you name the variables that you use in a program, you also name the functions. A function's name should be descriptive enough so that anyone reading your code can reasonably guess what the function does.

Python requires that you follow the same rules that you follow when naming variables, which we recap here:

- You cannot use one of Python's key words as a function name.
- A function name cannot contain spaces.
- The first character must be one of the letters a through z, A through Z, or an underscore character (_).
- After the first character you may use the letters a through z or A through Z, the digits 0 through 9, or underscores.
- Uppercase and lowercase characters are distinct.

Because functions perform actions, most programmers prefer to use verbs in function names. For example, a function that calculates gross pay might be named `calculate_gross_pay`. This name would make it evident to anyone reading the code that the function calculates something. What does it calculate? The gross pay, of course. Other examples of good function names would be `get_hours`, `get_pay_rate`, `calculate_overtime`, `print_check`, and so on. Each function name describes what the function does.

Defining and Calling a Function

To create a function you write its *definition*. Here is the general format of a function definition in Python:

```
def function_name():
    statement
    statement
    etc.
```

The first line is known as the *function header*. It marks the beginning of the function definition. The function header begins with the key word `def`, followed by the name of the function, followed by a set of parentheses, followed by a colon.

Beginning at the next line is a set of statements known as a block. A *block* is simply a set of statements that belong together as a group. These statements are performed any time the function is executed. Notice in the general format that all of the statements in the block are indented. This indentation is required because the Python interpreter uses it to tell where the block begins and ends.

Let's look at an example of a function. Keep in mind that this is not a complete program. We will show the entire program in a moment.

```
def message():
    print 'I am Arthur,'
    print 'King of the Britons.'
```

This code defines a function named message. The message function contains a block with two print statements. Executing the function will cause these print statements to execute.

Calling a Function

A function definition specifies what a function does, but it does not cause the function to execute. To execute a function, you must *call* it. This is how we would call the message function:

```
message()
```

When a function is called, the interpreter jumps to that function and executes the statements in its block. Then, when the end of the block is reached, the interpreter jumps back to the part of the program that called the function, and the program resumes execution at that point. When this happens, we say that the function *returns*. To fully demonstrate how function calling works, we will look at Program 1.

Program 1   (function_demo.py)

```
1   # This program demonstrates a function.
2   # First, we define a function named message.
3   def message():
4       print 'I am Arthur,'
5       print 'King of the Britons.'
6
7   # Call the message function.
8   message()
```

Program Output

```
I am Arthur,
King of the Britons.
```

Let's step through this program and examine what happens when it runs. First, the interpreter ignores the comments that appear in lines 1 and 2. Then, it reads the def statement in line 3. This causes a function named message to be created in memory, containing the block of statements in lines 4 and 5. (Remember, a function definition creates a function, but it does not cause the function to execute.) Next, the interpreter encounters the comment in line 7, which is ignored. Then it executes the statement in line 8, which is a function call. This causes the message function to execute, which prints the two lines of output. Figure 2 illustrates the parts of this program.

Figure 2   The function definition and the function call

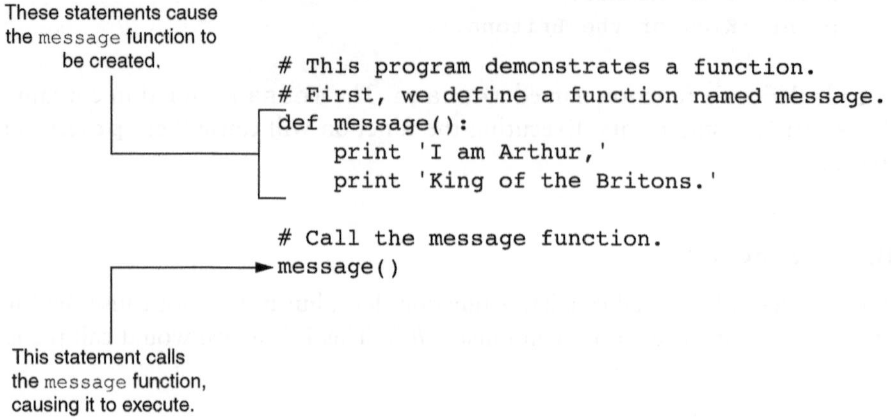

These statements cause
the message function to
be created.

```
# This program demonstrates a function.
# First, we define a function named message.
def message():
    print 'I am Arthur,'
    print 'King of the Britons.'

# Call the message function.
message()
```

This statement calls
the message function,
causing it to execute.

Program 1 has only one function, but it is possible to define many functions in a program. In fact, it is common for a program to have a main function that is called when the program starts. The main function then calls other functions in the program as they are needed. It is often said that the main function contains a program's *mainline logic,* which is the overall logic of the program. Program 2 shows an example of a program with two functions: main and message.

Program 2   (two_functions.py)

```
 1  # This program has two functions. First we
 2  # define the main function.
 3  def main():
 4      print 'I have a message for you.'
 5      message()
 6      print 'Goodbye!'
 7
 8  # Next we define the message function.
 9  def message():
10      print 'I am Arthur,'
11      print 'King of the Britons.'
12
13  # Call the main function.
14  main()
```

Program Output

```
I have a message for you.
I am Arthur,
King of the Britons.
Goodbye!
```

The definition of the main function appears in lines 3 through 6, and the definition of the message function appears in lines 9 through 11. The statement in line 14 calls the main function, as shown in Figure 3.

The first statement in the main function is the print statement in line 4. It displays the string 'I have a message for you'. Then, the statement in line 5 calls the message function. This causes the interpreter to jump to the message function, as shown in Figure 4 After the statements in the message function have executed, the interpreter returns to the main function and resumes with the statement that immediately follows the function call. As shown in Figure 5, this is the print statement that displays the string 'Goodbye!'.

Figure 3 Calling the main function

The interpreter jumps to the main function and begins executing the statements in its block.

```
# This program has two functions. First we
# define the main function.
def main():
    print 'I have a message for you.'
    message()
    print 'Goodbye!'

# Next we define the message function.
def message():
    print 'I am Arthur,'
    print 'King of the Britons.'

# Call the main function.
main()
```

Figure 4 Calling the message function

The interpreter jumps to the message function and begins executing the statements in its block.

```
# This program has two functions. First we
# define the main function.
def main():
    print 'I have a message for you.'
    message()
    print 'Goodbye!'

# Next we define the message function.
def message():
    print 'I am Arthur,'
    print 'King of the Britons.'

# Call the main function.
main()
```

Figure 5 The message function returns

When the message function ends, the interpreter jumps back to the part of the program that called it, and resumes execution from that point.

```
# This program has two functions. First we
# define the main function.
def main():
    print 'I have a message for you.'
    message()
    print 'Goodbye!'

# Next we define the message function.
def message():
    print 'I am Arthur,'
    print 'King of the Britons.'

# Call the main function.
main()
```

That is the end of the main function, so the function returns as shown in Figure 6. There are no more statements to execute, so the program ends.

Figure 6   The main function returns

```
# This program has two functions. First we
# define the main function.
def main():
    print 'I have a message for you.'
    message()
    print 'Goodbye!'

# Next we define the message function.
def message():
    print 'I am Arthur,'
    print 'King of the Britons.'

# Call the main function.
main()
```

When the main function ends, the interpreter jumps back to the part of the program that called it. There are no more statements, so the program ends.

NOTE: When a program calls a function, programmers commonly say that the *control* of the program transfers to that function. This simply means that the function takes control of the program's execution.

Indentation in Python

In Python, each line in a block must be indented. As shown in Figure 7, the last indented line after a function header is the last line in the function's block.

Figure 7   All of the statements in a block are indented

The last indented line is the last line in the block.

```
def greeting():
    print 'Good morning!'
    print 'Today we will learn about functions.'
```

These statements are not in the block.

```
print 'I will call the greeting function.'
greeting()
```

When you indent the lines in a block, make sure each line begins with the same number of spaces. Otherwise an error will occur. For example, the following function definition will cause an error because the lines are all indented with different numbers of spaces.

```
def my_function():
   print 'And now for'
print 'something completely'
     print 'different.'
```

In an editor there are two ways to indent a line: (1) by pressing the Tab key at the beginning of the line, or (2) by using the spacebar to insert spaces at the beginning of the line. You can use either tabs or spaces when indenting the lines in a block, but don't use both. Doing so may confuse the Python interpreter and cause an error.

IDLE, as well as most other Python editors, automatically indents the lines in a block. When you type the colon at the end of a function header, all of the lines typed afterward will automatically be indented. After you have typed the last line of the block you press the Backspace key to get out of the automatic indentation.

TIP: Python programmers customarily use four spaces to indent the lines in a block. You can use any number of spaces you wish, as long as all the lines in the block are indented by the same amount.

NOTE: Blank lines that appear in a block are ignored.

Checkpoint

6   A function definition has what two parts?

7   What does the phrase "calling a function" mean?

8   When a function is executing, what happens when the end of the function's block is reached?

9   Why must you indent the statements in a block?

3 Designing a Program to Use Functions

CONCEPT: Programmers commonly use a technique known as top-down design to break down an algorithm into functions.

Flowcharting a Program with Functions

Flowcharts are a tool for designing programs. In a flowchart, a function call is shown with a rectangle that has vertical bars at each side, as shown in Figure 8. The name of the function that is being called is written on the symbol.

Figure 8   Function call symbol

message( )

Programmers typically draw a separate flowchart for each function in a program. For example, Figure 9 shows how the main function and the message function in Program 2 would be flowcharted. When drawing a flowchart for a function, the starting terminal symbol usually shows the name of the function and the ending terminal symbol usually reads Return.

Figure 9   Flowchart for Program 2

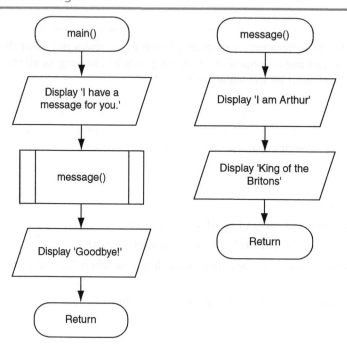

Top-Down Design

In this section, we have discussed and demonstrated how functions work. You've seen how control of a program is transferred to a function when it is called, and then returns to the part of the program that called the function when the function ends. It is important that you understand these mechanical aspects of functions.

Just as important as understanding how functions work is understanding how to design a program that uses functions. Programmers commonly use a technique known as *top-down design* to break down an algorithm into functions. The process of top-down design is performed in the following manner:

- The overall task that the program is to perform is broken down into a series of subtasks.
- Each of the subtasks is examined to determine whether it can be further broken down into more subtasks. This step is repeated until no more subtasks can be identified.
- Once all of the subtasks have been identified, they are written in code.

This process is called top-down design because the programmer begins by looking at the topmost level of tasks that must be performed, and then breaks down those tasks into lower levels of subtasks.

Hierarchy Charts

Flowcharts are good tools for graphically depicting the flow of logic inside a function, but they do not give a visual representation of the relationships between functions. Programmers commonly use *hierarchy charts* for this purpose. A hierarchy chart, which is also known as a *structure chart,* shows boxes that represent each function in a program. The boxes are connected in a way that illustrates the functions called by each function. Figure 10 shows an example of a hierarchy chart for a hypothetical pay calculating program.

Figure 10   A hierarchy chart

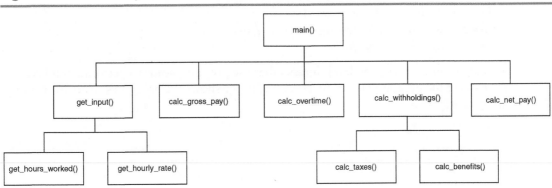

The chart shown in Figure 9 shows the main function as the topmost function in the hierarchy. The main function calls five other functions: get_input, calc_gross_pay, calc_overtime, calc_withholdings, and calc_net_pay. The get_input function calls two additional functions: get_hours_worked and get_hourly_rate. The calc_withholdings function also calls two functions: calc_taxes and calc_benefits.

Notice that the hierarchy chart does not show the steps that are taken inside a function. Because they do not reveal any details about how functions work, they do not replace flowcharts or pseudocode.

In the Spotlight:

Defining and Calling Functions

Professional Appliance Service, Inc. offers maintenance and repair services for household appliances. The owner wants to give each of the company's service technicians a small handheld computer that displays step-by-step instructions for many of the repairs that they perform. To see how this might work, the owner has asked you to develop a program that displays the following instructions for disassembling an Acme laundry dryer:

Step 1: Unplug the dryer and move it away from the wall.
Step 2: Remove the six screws from the back of the dryer.
Step 3: Remove the dryer's back panel.
Step 4: Pull the top of the dryer straight up.

During your interview with the owner, you determine that the program should display the steps one at a time. You decide that after each step is displayed, the user will be asked to press the Enter key to see the next step. Here is the algorithm in pseudocode:

Display a starting message, explaining what the program does.
Ask the user to press Enter to see step 1.
Display the instructions for step 1.
Ask the user to press Enter to see the next step.
Display the instructions for step 2.
Ask the user to press Enter to see the next step.
Display the instructions for step 3.
Ask the user to press Enter to see the next step.
Display the instructions for step 4.

This algorithm lists the top level of tasks that the program needs to perform, and becomes the basis of the program's main function. Figure 11 shows the program's structure in a hierarchy chart.

Figure 11   Hierarchy chart for the program

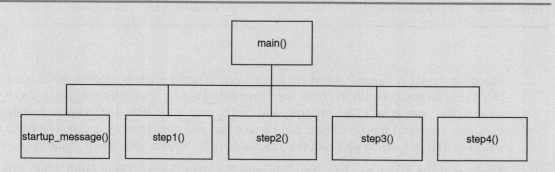

As you can see from the hierarchy chart, the main function will call several other functions. Here are summaries of those functions:

- startup_message—This function will display the starting message that tells the technician what the program does.
- step1—This function will display the instructions for step 1.
- step2—This function will display the instructions for step 2.
- step3—This function will display the instructions for step 3.
- step4—This function will display the instructions for step 4.

Between calls to these functions, the main function will instruct the user to press a key to see the next step in the instructions. Program 3 shows the code for the program.

Program 3   (acme_dryer.py)

```
1   # This program displays step-by-step instructions
2   # for disassembling an Acme dryer.
3   # The main function performs the program's main logic.
4   def main():
5       # Display the start-up message.
6       startup_message()
7       raw_input('Press Enter to see Step 1.')
8       # Display step 1.
9       step1()
10      raw_input('Press Enter to see Step 2.')
11      # Display step 2.
12      step2()
13      raw_input('Press Enter to see Step 3.')
14      # Display step 3.
15      step3()
16      raw_input('Press Enter to see Step 4.')
17      # Display step 4.
18      step4()
19
20  # The startup_message function displays the
21  # program's initial message on the screen.
22  def startup_message():
23      print 'This program tells you how to'
24      print 'disassemble an ACME laundry dryer.'
25      print 'There are 4 steps in the process.'
26      print                     # Print a blank line.
27
28  # The step1 function displays the instructions
29  # for step 1.
30  def step1():
31      print 'Step 1: Unplug the dryer and'
32      print 'move it away from the wall.'
33      print                     # Print a blank line.
34
35  # The step2 function displays the instructions
36  # for step 2.
37  def step2():
38      print 'Step 2: Remove the six screws'
39      print 'from the back of the dryer.'
40      print                     # Print a blank line.
41
42  # The step3 function displays the instructions
43  # for step 3.
44  def step3():
45      print 'Step 3: Remove the back panel'
```

(program continues)

Program 3   *(continued)*

```
46          print 'from the dryer.'
47          print                        # Print a blank line.
48
49   # The step4 function displays the instructions
50   # for step 4.
51   def step4():
52          print 'Step 4: Pull the top of the'
53          print 'dryer straight up.'
54
55   # Call the main function to begin the program.
56   main()
```

Program Output (with input shown in bold)

```
This program tells you how to
disassemble an ACME laundry dryer.
There are 4 steps in the process.

Press Enter to see Step 1. [Enter]
Step 1: Unplug the dryer and
move it away from the wall.

Press Enter to see Step 2. [Enter]
Step 2: Remove the six screws
from the back of the dryer.

Press Enter to see Step 3. [Enter]
Step 3: Remove the back panel
from the dryer.

Press Enter to see Step 4. [Enter]
Step 4: Pull the top of the
dryer straight up.
```

Pausing Execution Until the User Presses Enter

Sometimes you want a program to pause so the user can read information that has been displayed on the screen. When the user is ready for the program to continue execution, he or she presses the Enter key and the program resumes. In Python you can use the raw_input function to cause a program to pause until the user presses the Enter key. Line 7 in Program 3 is an example:

```
raw_input('Press Enter to see Step 1.')
```

This statement displays the prompt 'Press Enter to see Step 1.' and pauses until the user to presses the Enter key. The program also uses this technique in lines 10, 13, and 16.

4 **Local Variables**

CONCEPT: A local variable is created inside a function and cannot be accessed by statements that are outside the function. Different functions can have local variables with the same names because the functions cannot see each other's local variables.

Anytime you assign a value to a variable inside a function, you create a *local variable*. A local variable belongs to the function in which it is created, and only statements inside that function can access the variable. (The term *local* is meant to indicate that the variable can be used only locally, within the function in which it is created.)

An error will occur if a statement in one function tries to access a local variable that belongs to another function. For example, look at Program 4.

Program 4 (bad_local.py)

```
1   # Definition of the main function.
2   def main():
3       get_name()
4       print 'Hello', name      # This causes an error!
5
6   # Definition of the get_name function.
7   def get_name():
8       name = raw_input('Enter your name: ')
9
10  # Call the main function.
11  main()
```

This program has two functions: main and get_name. In line 8 the name variable is assigned a value that is entered by the user. This statement is inside the get_name function, so the name variable is local to that function. This means that the name variable cannot be accessed by statements outside the get_name function.

The main function calls the get_name function in line 3. Then, the print statement in line 4 tries to access the name variable. This results in an error because the name variable is local to the get_name function, and statements in the main function cannot access it.

Scope and Local Variables

A variable's *scope* is the part of a program in which the variable may be accessed. A variable is visible only to statements in the variable's scope. A local variable's scope is the function in which the variable is created. As you saw demonstrated in Program 4, no statement outside the function may access the variable.

In addition, a local variable cannot be accessed by code that appears inside the function at a point before the variable has been created. For example, look at the following function. It will cause an error because the print statement tries to access the val variable, but this statement appears before the val variable has been created. Moving the assignment statement to a line before the print statement will fix this error.

```
def bad_function():
    print 'The value is', val #     This will cause an error!
    val = 99
```

Because a function's local variables are hidden from other functions, the other functions may have their own local variables with the same name. For example, look at the Program 5. In addition to the main function, this program has two other functions: texas and california. These two functions each have a local variable named birds.

Program 5   (birds.py)

```
1    # This program demonstrates two functions that
2    # have local variables with the same name.
3
4    def main():
5        # Call the texas function.
6        texas()
7        # Call the california function.
8        california()
9
10   # Definition of the texas function. It creates
11   # a local variable named birds.
12   def texas():
13       birds = 5000
14       print 'texas has', birds, 'birds.'
15
16   # Definition of the california function. It also
17   # creates a local variable named birds.
18   def california():
19       birds = 8000
20       print 'california has', birds, 'birds.'
21
22   # Call the main function.
23   main()
```

Program Output

```
texas has 5000 birds.
california has 8000 birds.
```

Although there are two separate variables named birds in this program, only one of them is visible at a time because they are in different functions. This is illustrated in Figure 12. When the texas function is executing, the birds variable that is created in line 13 is visible. When the california function is executing, the birds variable that is created in line 19 is visible.

Figure 12   Each function has its own birds variable

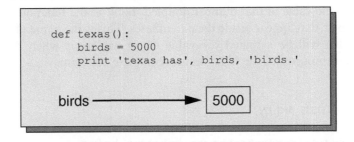

```
def texas():
    birds = 5000
    print 'texas has', birds, 'birds.'
```

birds ⟶ 5000

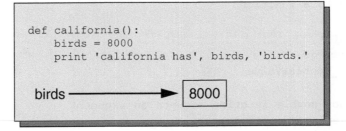

```
def california():
    birds = 8000
    print 'california has', birds, 'birds.'
```

birds ⟶ 8000

 Checkpoint

10   What is a local variable? How is access to a local variable restricted?

11   What is a variable's scope?

12   Is it permissible for a local variable in one function to have the same name as a local variable in a different function?

5   Passing Arguments to Functions

CONCEPT: An argument is any piece of data that is passed into a function when the function is called. A parameter is a variable that receives an argument that is passed into a function.

Sometimes it is useful not only to call a function, but also to send one or more pieces of data into the function. Pieces of data that are sent into a function are known as *arguments*. The function can use its arguments in calculations or other operations.

If you want a function to receive arguments when it is called, you must equip the function with one or more parameter variables. A *parameter variable,* often simply called a *parameter,* is a special variable that is assigned the value of an argument when a function is called. Here is an example of a function that has a parameter variable:

```
def show_double(number):
    result = number * 2
    print result
```

This function's name is `show_double`. Its purpose is to accept a number as an argument and display the value of that number doubled. Look at the function header and notice the word `number` that appear inside the parentheses. This is the name of a parameter variable. This variable will be assigned the value of an argument when the function is called. Program 6 demonstrates the function in a complete program.

Program 6   (pass_arg.py)

```
 1   # This program demonstrates an argument being
 2   # passed to a function.
 3
 4   def main():
 5       value = 5
 6       show_double(value)
 7
 8   # The show_double function accepts an argument
 9   # and displays double its value.
10   def show_double(number):
11       result = number * 2
12       print result
13
14   # Call the main function.
15   main()
```

Program Output

10

When this program runs, the `main` function is called in line 15. Inside the `main` function, line 5 creates a local variable named `value`, assigned the value 5. Then the following statement in line 6 calls the `show_double` function:

```
show_double(value)
```

Notice that `value` appears inside the parentheses. This means that `value` is being passed as an argument to the `show_double` function, as shown in Figure 13 When this statement executes, the `show_double` function will be called and the `number` parameter will be assigned the same value as the `value` variable. This is shown in Figure 14.

Figure 13 The value variable is passed as an argument

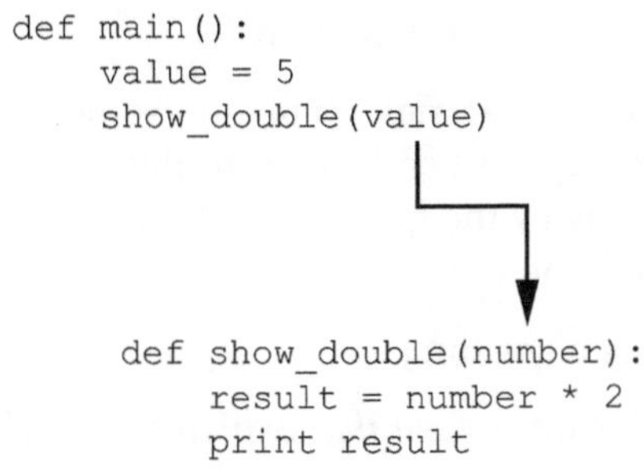

```
def main():
    value = 5
    show_double(value)


    def show_double(number):
        result = number * 2
        print result
```

Figure 14 The value variable and the number parameter reference the same value

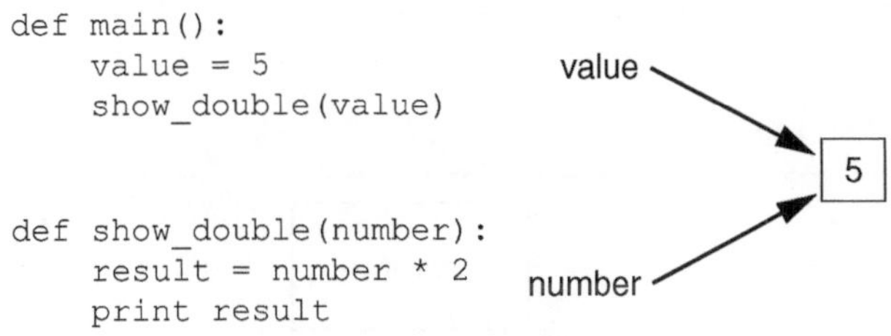

```
def main():
    value = 5                    value
    show_double(value)
                                       5
def show_double(number):
    result = number * 2      number
    print result
```

Let's step through the show_double function. As we do, remember that the number parameter variable will be assigned the value that was passed to it as an argument. In this program, that number is 5.

Line 11 assigns the value of the expression number * 2 to a local variable named result. Because number references the value 5, this statement assigns 10 to result. Line 12 displays the result variable.

The following statement shows how the show_double function can be called with a numeric literal passed as an argument:

```
show_double(50)
```

This statement executes the show_double function, assigning 50 to the number parameter. The function will print 100.

Parameter Variable Scope

Earlier in this chapter, you learned that a variable's scope is the part of the program in which the variable may be accessed. A variable is visible only to statements inside the variable's scope. A parameter variable's scope is the function in which the parameter is used. All of the statements inside the function can access the parameter variable, but no statement outside the function can access it.

In the Spotlight:

Passing an Argument to a Function

Your friend Michael runs a catering company. Some of the ingredients that his recipes require are measured in cups. When he goes to the grocery store to buy those ingredients, however, they are sold only by the fluid ounce. He has asked you to write a simple program that converts cups to fluid ounces.

You design the following algorithm:

1. *Display an introductory screen that explains what the program does.*
2. *Get the number of cups.*
3. *Convert the number of cups to fluid ounces and display the result.*

This algorithm lists the top level of tasks that the program needs to perform, and becomes the basis of the program's `main` function. Figure 15 shows the program's structure in a hierarchy chart.

Figure 15   Hierarchy chart for the program

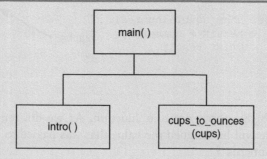

As shown in the hierarchy chart, the `main` function will call two other functions. Here are summaries of those functions:

- `intro`—This function will display a message on the screen that explains what the program does.
- `cups_to_ounces`—This function will accept the number of cups as an argument and calculate and display the equivalent number of fluid ounces.

In addition to calling these functions, the `main` function will ask the user to enter the number of cups. This value will be passed to the `cups_to_ounces` function. The code for the program is shown in Program 7.

Program 7   (cups_to_ounces.py)

```
1   # This program converts cups to fluid ounces.
2
3   def main():
4       # display the intro screen.
```

```
 5        intro()
 6        # Get the number of cups.
 7        cups_needed = input('Enter the number of cups: ')
 8        # Convert the cups to ounces.
 9        cups_to_ounces(cups_needed)
10
11   # The intro function displays an introductory screen.
12   def intro():
13        print 'This program converts measurements'
14        print 'in cups to fluid ounces. For your'
15        print 'reference the formula is:'
16        print ' 1 cup = 8 fluid ounces'
17        print
18
19   # The cups_to_ounces function accepts a number of
20   # cups and displays the equivalent number of ounces.
21   def cups_to_ounces(cups):
22        ounces = cups * 8
23        print 'That converts to', ounces, 'ounces.'
24
25   # Call the main function.
26   main()
```

Program Output (with input shown in bold)

```
This program converts measurements
in cups to fluid ounces. For your
reference the formula is:
    1 cup = 8 fluid ounces

Enter the number of cups: 4 [Enter]
That converts to 32 ounces.
```

Passing Multiple Arguments

Often it's useful to write functions that can accept multiple arguments. Program 8 shows a function named show_sum, that accepts two arguments. The function adds the two arguments and displays their sum.

Program 8   (multiple_args.py)

```
1    # This program demonstrates a function that accepts
2    # two arguments.
3
4    def main():
5        print 'The sum of 12 and 45 is'
```

(program continues)

Program 8   *(continued)*

```
 6        show_sum(12, 45)
 7
 8    # The show_sum function accepts two arguments
 9    # and displays their sum.
10    def show_sum(num1, num2):
11        result = num1 + num2
12        print result
13
14    # Call the main function.
15    main()
```

Program Output

```
The sum of 12 and 45 is
57
```

Notice that two parameter variable names, num1 and num2, appear inside the parentheses in the show_sum function header. This is often referred to as a *parameter list*. Also notice that a comma separates the variable names.

The statement in line 6 calls the show_sum function and passes two arguments: 12 and 45. These arguments are passed *by position* to the corresponding parameter variables in the function. In other words, the first argument is passed to the first parameter variable, and the second argument is passed to the second parameter variable. So, this statement causes 12 to be assigned to the num1 parameter and 45 to be assigned to the num2 parameter, as shown in Figure 16.

Figure 16   Two arguments passed to two parameters

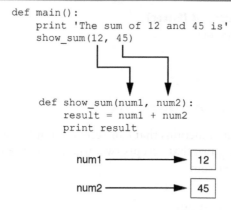

Suppose we were to reverse the order in which the arguments are listed in the function call, as shown here:

```
show_sum(45, 12)
```

This would cause 45 to be passed to the num1 parameter and 12 to be passed to the num2 parameter. The following code shows another example. This time we are passing variables as arguments.

```
    value1 = 2
    value2 = 3
    show_sum(value1, value2)
```

When the show_sum function executes as a result of this code, the num1 parameter will be assigned the value 2 and the num2 parameter will be assigned the value 3.

Program 9 shows one more example. This program passes two strings as arguments to a function.

Program 9   (string_args.py)

```
1   # This program demonstrates passing two string
2   # arguments to a function.
3
4   def main():
5       first_name = raw_input('Enter your first name: ')
6       last_name = raw_input('Enter your last name: ')
7       print 'Your name reversed is'
8       reverse_name(first_name, last_name)
9
10  def reverse_name(first, last):
11       print last, first
12
13  # Call the main function.
14  main()
```

Program Output (with input shown in bold)
```
Enter your first name: Matt [Enter]
Enter your last name: Hoyle [Enter]
Your name reversed is
Hoyle Matt
```

Making Changes to Parameters

When an argument is passed to a function in Python, the function parameter variable will reference the argument's value. However, any changes that are made to the parameter variable will not affect the argument. To demonstrate this look at Program 10.

Program 10   (change_me.py)

```
1   # This program demonstrates what happens when you
2   # change the value of a parameter.
3
```

(program continues)

Program 10 *(continued)*

```
 4  def main():
 5      value = 99
 6      print 'The value is', value
 7      change_me(value)
 8      print 'Back in main the value is', value
 9
10  def change_me(arg):
11      print 'I am changing the value.'
12      arg = 0
13      print 'Now the value is', arg
14
15  # Call the main function.
16  main()
```

Program Output

```
The value is 99
I am changing the value.
Now the value is 0
Back in main the value is 99
```

The `main` function creates a local variable named `value` in line 5, assigned the value 99. The `print` statement in line 6 displays `'The value is 99'`. The `value` variable is then passed as an argument to the `change_me` function in line 7. This means that in the `change_me` function the `arg` parameter will also reference the value 99. This is shown in Figure 17.

Figure 17 The value variable is passed to the `change_me` function

```
def main():
    value = 99
    print 'The value is', value
    change_me(value)
    print 'Back in main the value is', value


def change_me(arg):
    print 'I am changing the value.'
    arg = 0
    print 'Now the value is', arg
```

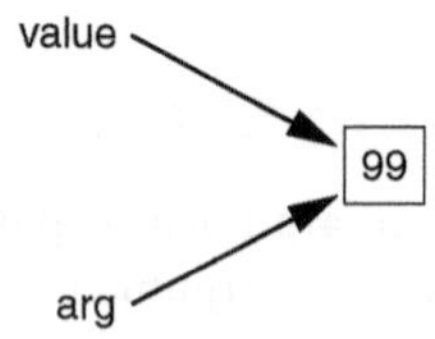

Inside the `change_me` function, in line 12, the `arg` parameter is assigned the value 0. This reassignment changes `arg`, but it does not affect the `value` variable in `main`. As shown in Figure 18, the two variables now reference different values in memory. The `print` statement in line 13 displays `'Now the value is 0'` and the function ends.

Figure 18   The value variable is passed to the change_me function

```
def main():
    value = 99
    print 'The value is', value
    change_me(value)                                value
    print 'Back in main the value is', value
                                                              99

def change_me(arg):
    print 'I am changing the value.'               arg          0
    arg = 0
    print 'Now the value is', arg
```

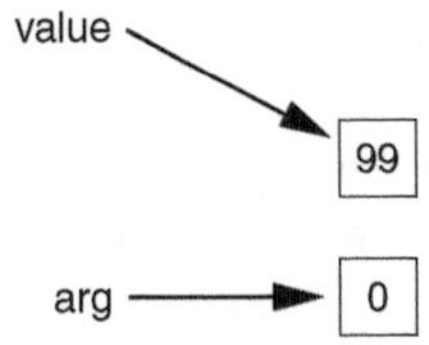

Control of the program then returns to the main function. The next statement to execute is the print statement in line 8. This statement displays 'Back in main the value is 99'. This proves that even though the parameter variable arg was changed in the change_me function, the argument (the value variable in main) was not modified.

The form of argument passing that is used in Python, where a function cannot change the value of an argument that was passed to it, is commonly called *pass by value*. This is a way that one function can communicate with another function. The communication channel works in only one direction, however. The calling function can communicate with the called function, but the called function cannot use the argument to communicate with the calling function.

Keyword Arguments

Programs 8 and 9 demonstrate how arguments are passed by position to parameter variables in a function. Most programming languages match function arguments and parameters this way. In addition to this conventional form of argument passing, the Python language allows you to write an argument in the following format, to specify which parameter variable the argument should be passed to:

   parameter_name=value

In this format, *parameter_name* is the name of a parameter variable and *value* is the value being passed to that parameter. An argument that is written in accordance with this syntax is known as a *keyword argument.*

Program 11 demonstrates keyword arguments. This program uses a function named show_interest that displays the amount of simple interest earned by a bank account for a number of periods. The function accepts the arguments principal (for the account principal), rate (for the interest rate per period), and periods (for the number of periods). When the function is called in line 7, the arguments are passed as keyword arguments.

Program 11   (keyword_args.py)

```
1   # This program demonstrates keyword arguments.
2
3   def main():
4       # Show the amount of simple interest, using 0.01 as
```

(program continues)

Program 11   *(continued)*

```
 5        # interest rate per period, 10 as the number of periods,
 6        # and $10,000 as the principal.
 7        show_interest(rate=0.01, periods=10, principal=10000.0)
 8
 9   # The show_interest function displays the amount of
10   # simple interest for a given principal, interest rate
11   # per period, and number of periods.
12
13   def show_interest(principal, rate, periods):
14       interest = principal * rate * periods
15       print 'The simple interest will be $%.2f.' % interest
16
17   # Call the main function.
18   main()
```

Program Output

```
The simple interest will be $1000.00.
```

Notice in line 7 that the order of the keyword arguments does not match the order of the parameters in the function header in line 13. Because a keyword argument specifies which parameter the argument should be passed into, its position in the function call does not matter.

Program 12 shows another example. This is a variation of the string_args program shown in Program 9. This version uses keyword arguments to call the reverse_name function.

Program 12   (keyword_string_args.py)

```
 1   # This program demonstrates passing two strings as
 2   # keyword arguments to a function.
 3
 4   def main():
 5       first_name = raw_input('Enter your first name: ')
 6       last_name = raw_input('Enter your last name: ')
 7       print 'Your name reversed is'
 8       reverse_name(last=last_name, first=first_name)
 9
10   def reverse_name(first, last):
11       print last, first
12
13   # Call the main function.
14   main()
```

Program Output (with input shown in bold)

```
Enter your first name: Matt [Enter]
Enter your last name: Hoyle [Enter]
Your name reversed is
Hoyle Matt
```

Mixing Keyword Arguments with Positional Arguments

It is possible to mix positional arguments and keyword arguments in a function call, but the positional arguments must appear first, followed by the keyword arguments. Otherwise an error will occur. Here is an example of how we might call the `show_interest` function of Program 10 using both positional and keyword arguments:

```
show_interest(10000.0, rate=0.01, periods=10)
```

In this statement, the first argument, `10000.0`, is passed by its position to the `principal` parameter. The second and third arguments are passed as keyword arguments. The following function call will cause an error, however, because a non-keyword argument follows a keyword argument:

```
# This will cause an ERROR!
show_interest(1000.0, rate=0.01, 10)
```

 Checkpoint

13 What are the pieces of data that are passed into a function called?

14 What are the variables that receive pieces of data in a function called?

15 What is a parameter variable's scope?

16 When a parameter is changed, does this affect the argument that was passed into the parameter?

17 The following statements call a function named `show_data`. Which of the statements passes arguments by position, and which passes keyword arguments?

```
a) show_data(name='Kathryn', age=25)
b) show_data('Kathryn', 25)
```

 6 ## Global Variables and Global Constants

CONCEPT: A global variable is accessible to all the functions in a program file.

You've learned that when a variable is created by an assignment statement inside a function, the variable is local to that function. Consequently, it can be accessed only by statements inside the function that created it. When a variable is created by an assignment statement that is written outside all the functions in a program file, the variable is *global*. A global variable can be accessed by any statement in the program file, including the statements in any function. For example, look at Program 13.

Program 13   (global1.py)

```
1   # Create a global variable.
2   my_value = 10
3
4   # The show_value function prints
5   # the value of the global variable.
```

(program continues)

Program 13   *(continued)*

```
 6   def show_value():
 7       print my_value
 8
 9   # Call the show_value function.
10   show_value()
```

Program Output

```
10
```

The assignment statement in line 2 creates a variable named my_value. Because this statement is outside any function, it is global. When the show_value function executes, the statement in line 7 prints the value referenced by my_value.

An additional step is required if you want a statement in a function to assign a value to a global variable. In the function you must declare the global variable, as shown in Program 14.

Program 14   (global2.py)

```
 1   # Create a global variable.
 2   number = 0
 3
 4   def main():
 5       global number
 6       number = input('Enter a number: ')
 7       show_number()
 8
 9   def show_number():
10       print 'The number you entered is', number
11
12   # Call the main function.
13   main()
```

Program Output (with input shown in bold)

```
Enter a number: 55 [Enter]
The number you entered is 55
```

The assignment statement in line 2 creates a global variable named number. Notice that inside the main function, line 5 uses the global key word to declare the number variable. This statement tells the interpreter that the main function intends to assign a value to the global number variable. That's just what happens in line 6. The value entered by the user is assigned to number.

Most programmers agree that you should restrict the use of global variables, or not use them at all. The reasons are as follows:

- Global variables make debugging difficult. Any statement in a program file can change the value of a global variable. If you find that the wrong value is being stored in a global variable, you have to track down every statement that accesses it to determine where the bad value is coming from. In a program with thousands of lines of code, this can be difficult.

- Functions that use global variables are usually dependent on those variables. If you want to use such a function in a different program, most likely you will have to redesign it so it does not rely on the global variable.
- Global variables make a program hard to understand. A global variable can be modified by any statement in the program. If you are to understand any part of the program that uses a global variable, you have to be aware of all the other parts of the program that access the global variable.

In most cases, you should create variables locally and pass them as arguments to the functions that need to access them.

Global Constants

Although you should try to avoid the use of global variables, it is permissible to use global constants in a program. A *global constant* is a global name that references a value that cannot be changed. Because a global constant's value cannot be changed during the program's execution, you do not have to worry about many of the potential hazards that are associated with the use of global variables.

Although the Python language does not allow you to create true global constants, you can simulate them with global variables. If you do not declare a global variable with the `global` key word inside a function, then you cannot change the variable's assignment inside that function. The following *In the Spotlight* section demonstrates how global variables can be used in Python to simulate global constants.

In the Spotlight:
Using Global Constants

Marilyn works for Integrated Systems, Inc., a software company that has a reputation for providing excellent fringe benefits. One of their benefits is a quarterly bonus that is paid to all employees. Another benefit is a retirement plan for each employee. The company contributes 5 percent of each employee's gross pay and bonuses to their retirement plans. Marilyn wants to write a program that will calculate the company's contribution to an employee's retirement account for a year. She wants the program to show the amount of contribution for the employee's gross pay and for the bonuses separately. Here is an algorithm for the program:

Get the employee's annual gross pay.
Get the amount of bonuses paid to the employee.
Calculate and display the contribution for the gross pay.
Calculate and display the contribution for the bonuses.

The code for the program is shown in Program 15.

Program 15   (retirement.py)

```
 1  # The following global variable represents
 2  # the contribution rate.
 3  CONTRIBUTION_RATE = 0.05
 4
 5  def main():
 6      gross_pay = input('Enter the gross pay: ')
 7      bonus = input('Enter the amount of bonuses: ')
 8      show_pay_contrib(gross_pay)
 9      show_bonus_contrib(bonus)
10
11  # The show_pay_contrib function accepts the gross
12  # pay as an argument and displays the retirement
13  # contribution for that amount of pay.
14  def show_pay_contrib(gross):
15      contrib = gross * CONTRIBUTION_RATE
16      print 'Contribution for gross pay: $%.2f' % contrib
17
18  # The show_bonus_contrib function accepts the
19  # bonus amount as an argument and displays the
20  # retirement contribution for that amount of pay.
21  def show_bonus_contrib(bonus):
22      contrib = bonus * CONTRIBUTION_RATE
23      print 'Contribution for bonuses: $%.2f' % contrib
24
25  # Call the main function.
26  main()
```

Program Output (with input shown in bold)
```
Enter the gross pay: 80000.00 [Enter]
Enter the amount of bonuses: 20000.00 [Enter]
Contribution for gross pay: $4000.00
Contribution for bonuses: $1000.00
```

First, notice the global variable that is created in line 3:

```
CONTRIBUTION_RATE = 0.05
```

This variable will be used as a global constant to represent the percentage of an employee's pay that the company will contribute to a retirement account. It is a common practice to write a constant's name in all uppercase letters. This serves as a reminder that the value referenced by the name is not to be changed in the program.

The CONTRIBUTION_RATE constant is used in the calculation in line 15 (in the show_pay_contrib function) and again in line 22 (in the show_bonus_contrib function).

Marilyn decided to use this global constant to represent the 5 percent contribution rate for two reasons:

- It makes the program easier to read. When you look at the calculations in lines 15 and 22 it is apparent what is happening.
- Occasionally the contribution rate changes. When this happens, it will be easy to update the program by changing the assignment statement in line 2.

 **Checkpoint**

18 What is the scope of a global variable?

19 Give one good reason that you should not use global variables in a program.

20 What is a global constant? Is it permissible to use global constants in a program?

Review Questions

Multiple Choice

1. A group of statements that exist within a program for the purpose of performing a specific task is a(n) _____.
   a. block
   b. parameter
   c. function
   d. expression

2. A design technique that helps to reduce the duplication of code within a program and is a benefit of using functions is _____.
   a. code reuse
   b. divide and conquer
   c. debugging
   d. facilitation of teamwork

3. The first line of a function definition is known as the _____.
   a. body
   b. introduction
   c. initialization
   d. header

4. You _____ the function to execute it.
   a. define
   b. call
   c. import
   d. export

5. A design technique that programmers use to break down an algorithm into functions is known as _____.
   a. top-down design
   b. code simplification

    c. code refactoring

    d. hierarchical subtasking

6. A _____ is a diagram that gives a visual representation of the relationships between functions in a program.

    a. flowchart

    b. function relationship chart

    c. symbol chart

    d. hierarchy chart

7. A _____ is a variable that is created inside a function.

    a. global variable

    b. local variable

    c. hidden variable

    d. none of the above; you cannot create a variable inside a function

8. A(n) _____ is the part of a program in which a variable may be accessed.

    a. declaration space

    b. area of visibility

    c. scope

    d. mode

9. A(n) _____ is a piece of data that is sent into a function.

    a. argument

    b. parameter

    c. header

    d. packet

10. A(n) _____ is a special variable that receives a piece of data when a function is called.

    a. argument

    b. parameter

    c. header

    d. packet

11. A variable that is visible to every function in a program file is a _____.

    a. local variable

    b. universal variable

    c. program-wide variable

    d. global variable

12. When possible, you should avoid using _____ variables in a program.

    a. local

    b. global

    c. reference

    d. parameter

True or False

1. The phrase "divide and conquer" means that all of the programmers on a team should be divided and work in isolation.

2. Functions make it easier for programmers to work in teams.

3. Function names should be as short as possible.

4. Calling a function and defining a function mean the same thing.

5. A flowchart shows the hierarchical relationships between functions in a program.

6. A hierarchy chart does not show the steps that are taken inside a function.

7. A statement in one function can access a local variable in another function.

8. Most languages do not allow you to write functions that accept multiple arguments.

9. In Python, you can specify which parameter an argument should be passed into a function call.

10. You cannot have both keyword arguments and non-keyword arguments in a function call.

Short Answer

1. How do functions help you to reuse code in a program?

2. Name and describe the two parts of a function definition.

3. When a function is executing, what happens when the end of the function block is reached?

4. What is a local variable? What statements are able to access a local variable?

5. What is a local variable's scope?

6. Why do global variables make a program difficult to debug?

Algorithm Workbench

1. Write a function named `times_ten`. The function should accept an argument and display the product of its argument multiplied times 10.

2. Examine the following function header, and then write a statement that calls the function, passing 12 as an argument.

   ```
   def show_value(quantity):
   ```

3. Look at the following function header:

   ```
   def my_function(a, b, c):
   ```

   Now look at the following call to `my_function`:

   ```
   myFunction(3, 2, 1)
   ```

   When this call executes, what value will be assigned to a? What value will be assigned to b? What value will be assigned to c?

4. What will the following program display?

   ```
   def main():
       x = 1
       y = 3.4
       print x, y
       change_us(x, y)
       print x, y

   def change_us(a, b):
       a = 0
       b = 0
       print a, b

   main()
   ```

5. Look at the following function definition:

```
def my_function(a, b, c):
    d = (a + c) / b
    print d
```

a. Write a statement that calls this function and uses keyword arguments to pass 2 into a, 4 into b, and 6 into c.
b. What value will be displayed when the function call executes?

Programming Exercises

1. Kilometer Converter

Write a program that asks the user to enter a distance in kilometers, and then converts that distance to miles. The conversion formula is as follows:

$$Miles = Kilometers \times 0.6214$$

2. Sale Tax Program Refactoring

Programming Exercise #6 was the Sales Tax program. For that exercise you were asked to write a program that calculates and displays the county and state sales tax on a purchase. If you have already written that program, redesign it so the subtasks are in functions. If you have not already written that program, write it using functions.

3. How Much Insurance?

Many financial experts advise that property owners should insure their homes or buildings for at least 80 percent of the amount it would cost to replace the structure. Write a program that asks the user to enter the replacement cost of a building and then displays the minimum amount of insurance he or she should buy for the property.

4. Automobile Costs

Write a program that asks the user to enter the monthly costs for the following expenses incurred from operating his or her automobile: loan payment, insurance, gas, oil, tires, and maintenance. The program should then display the total monthly cost of these expenses, and the total annual cost of these expenses.

5. Property Tax

A county collects property taxes on the assessment value of property, which is 60 percent of the property's actual value. For example, if an acre of land is valued at $10,000, its assessment value is $6,000. The property tax is then 64¢ for each $100 of the assessment value. The tax for the acre assessed at $6,000 will be $38.40. Write a program that asks for the actual value of a piece of property and displays the assessment value and property tax.

6. Body Mass Index

Write a program that calculates and displays a person's body mass index (BMI). The BMI is often used to determine whether a person with a sedentary lifestyle is overweight or underweight for his or her height. A person's BMI is calculated with the following formula:

$$BMI = weight \times 703 / height^2$$

where *weight* is measured in pounds and *height* is measured in inches.

7. Calories from Fat and Carbohydrates

A nutritionist who works for a fitness club helps members by evaluating their diets. As part of her evaluation, she asks members for the number of fat grams and carbohydrate grams that they consumed in a day. Then, she calculates the number of calories that result from the fat, using the following formula:

$$calories\ from\ fat = fat\ grams \times 9$$

Next, she calculates the number of calories that result from the carbohydrates, using the following formula:

$$calories\ from\ carbs = carb\ grams \times 4$$

The nutritionist asks you to write a program that will make these calculations.

8. Stadium Seating

There are three seating categories at a stadium. For a softball game, Class A seats cost $15, Class B seats cost $12, and Class C seats cost $9. Write a program that asks how many tickets for each class of seats were sold, and then displays the amount of income generated from ticket sales.

9. Paint Job Estimator

A painting company has determined that for every 115 square feet of wall space, one gallon of paint and eight hours of labor will be required. The company charges $20.00 per hour for labor. Write a program that asks the user to enter the square feet of wall space to be painted and the price of the paint per gallon. The program should display the following data:

- The number of gallons of paint required
- The hours of labor required
- The cost of the paint
- The labor charges
- The total cost of the paint job

10. Monthly Sales Tax

A retail company must file a monthly sales tax report listing the total sales for the month, and the amount of state and county sales tax collected. The state sales tax rate is 4 percent and the county sales tax rate is 2 percent. Write a program that asks the user to enter the total sales for the month. From this figure, the application should calculate and display the following:

- The amount of county sales tax
- The amount of state sales tax
- The total sales tax (county plus state)

15

Decision Structures and Boolean Logic

TOPICS

1 The if Statement
2 The if-else Statement
3 Comparing Strings
4 Nested Decision Structures and the if-elif-else Statement

5 Logical Operators
6 Boolean Variables

1   The if Statement

CONCEPT: The **if** statement is used to create a decision structure, which allows a program to have more than one path of execution. The **if** statement causes one or more statements to execute only when a Boolean expression is true.

A *control structure* is a logical design that controls the order in which a set of statements execute. So far in this book we have used only the simplest type of control structure: the sequence structure. A *sequence structure* is a set of statements that execute in the order that they appear. For example, the following code is a sequence structure because the statements execute from top to bottom.

```
name = raw_input('What is your name? ')
age = input('What is your age? ')
print 'Here is the data you entered:'
print 'Name:', name
print 'Age:', age
```

The following function is a sequence structure because the statements in its block execute in the order that they appear, from the beginning of the function to the end.

```
def show_double(value):
    result = value * 2
    print result
```

Although the sequence structure is heavily used in programming, it cannot handle every type of task. This is because some problems simply cannot be solved by performing a set of ordered steps, one after the other. For example, consider a pay calculating program that determines whether an employee has worked overtime. If the employee has worked more than 40 hours, he or she gets paid extra for all the hours over 40. Otherwise, the overtime calculation should be skipped. Programs like this require a different type of control structure: one that can execute a set of statements only under certain circumstances. This can be accomplished with a *decision structure*. (Decision structures are also known as *selection structures*.)

In a decision structure's simplest form, a specific action is performed only if a certain condition exists. If the condition does not exist, the action is not performed. The flowchart shown in Figure 1 shows how the logic of an everyday decision can be diagrammed as a decision structure. The diamond symbol represents a true/false condition. If the condition is true, we follow one path, which leads to an action being performed. If the condition is false, we follow another path, which skips the action.

Figure 1   A simple decision structure

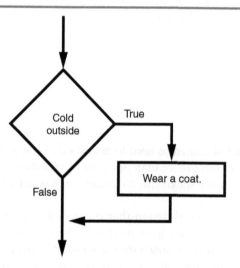

In the flowchart, the diamond symbol indicates some condition that must be tested. In this case, we are determining whether the condition Cold outside is true or false. If this condition is true, the action Wear a coat is performed. If the condition is false, the action is skipped. The action is *conditionally executed* because it is performed only when a certain condition is true.

Programmers call the type of decision structure shown in Figure 1 a *single alternative decision structure*. This is because it provides only one alternative path of execution. If the condition in the diamond symbol is true, we take the alternative path. Otherwise, we exit the structure. Figure 2 shows a more elaborate example, where three actions are taken only when it is cold outside. It is still a single alternative decision structure, because there is one alternative path of execution.

Figure 2   A decision structure that performs three actions if it is cold outside

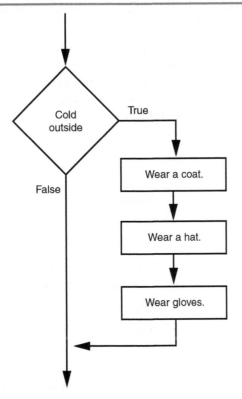

In Python we use the `if` statement to write a single alternative decision structure. Here is the general format of the `if` statement:

```
if condition:
    statement
    statement
    etc.
```

For simplicity, we will refer to the first line as the *if clause*. The `if` clause begins with the word `if`, followed by a `condition`, which is an expression that will be evaluated as either true or false. A colon appears after the `condition`. Beginning at the next line is a block of statements. (All of the statements in a block must be consistently indented. This indentation is required because the Python interpreter uses it to tell where the block begins and ends.)

When the `if` statement executes, the `condition` is tested. If the `condition` is true, the statements that appear in the block following the `if` clause are executed. If the condition is false, the statements in the block are skipped.

Boolean Expressions and Relational Operators

As previously mentioned, the `if` statement tests an expression to determine whether it is true or false. The expressions that are tested by the `if` statement are called *Boolean expressions*, named in honor of the English mathematician George Boole. In the 1800s Boole invented a system of mathematics in which the abstract concepts of true and false can be used in computations.

Typically, the Boolean expression that is tested by an `if` statement is formed with a relational operator. A *relational operator* determines whether a specific relationship exists between two values. For example, the greater than operator (>) determines whether one value is greater than another. The equal to operator (==) determines whether two values are equal. Table 1 lists the relational operators that are available in Python.

Table 1   Relational operators

Operator	Meaning
>	Greater than
<	Less than
>=	Greater than or equal to
<=	Less than or equal to
==	Equal to
!=	Not equal to

The following is an example of an expression that uses the greater than (>) operator to compare two variables, `length` and `width`:

```
length > width
```

This expression determines whether the value referenced by `length` is greater than the value referenced by `width`. If `length` is greater than `width`, the value of the expression is true. Otherwise, the value of the expression is false. The following expression uses the less than operator to determine whether `length` is less than `width`:

```
length < width
```

Table 2 shows examples of several Boolean expressions that compare the variables `x` and `y`.

Table 2   Boolean expressions using relational operators

Expression	Meaning
x > y	Is x greater than y?
x < y	Is x less than y?
x >= y	Is x greater than or equal to y?
x <= y	Is x less than or equal to y?
x == y	Is x equal to y?
x != y	Is x not equal to y?

The >= and <= Operators

Two of the operators, >= and <=, test for more than one relationship. The >= operator determines whether the operand on its left is greater than *or* equal to the operand on its right. The <= operator determines whether the operand on its left is less than *or* equal to the operand on its right.

For example, assume the following:

- a is assigned 4
- b is assigned 6
- c is assigned 4

These expressions are true:

```
b >= a
a >= c
a <= c
b <= 10
```

And these expressions are false:

```
a >= 5
b <= a
```

The == Operator

The == operator determines whether the operand on its left is equal to the operand on its right. If the values referenced by both operands are the same, the expression is true. Assuming that a is 4, the expression a == 4 is true and the expression a == 2 is false.

> **NOTE:** The equality operator is two = symbols together. Don't confuse this operator with the assignment operator, which is one = symbol.

The != Operator

The != operator is the not-equal-to operator. It determines whether the operand on its left is not equal to the operand on its right, which is the opposite of the == operator. As before, assuming a is 4, b is 6, and c is 4, both a != b and b != c are true because a is not equal to b and b is not equal to c. However, a != c is false because a is equal to c.

Putting It All Together

Let's look at the following example of the if statement:

```
if sales > 50000:
    bonus = 500.0
```

This statement uses the > operator to determine whether sales is greater than 50,000. If the expression sales > 50000 is true, the variable bonus is assigned 500.0. If the expression is false, however, the assignment statement is skipped. Figure 3 shows a flowchart for this section of code.

Figure 3   Example decision structure

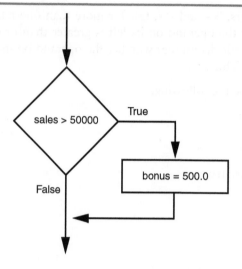

The following example conditionally executes three statements. Figure 4 shows a flowchart for this section of code.

```
if sales > 50000:
    bonus = 500.0
    commission_rate = 0.12
    print 'You met your sales quota!'
```

Figure 4   Example decision structure

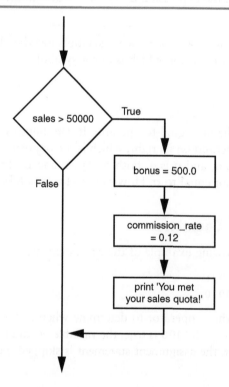

The following code uses the == operator to determine whether two values are equal. The expression balance == 0 will be true if the balance variable is assigned 0. Otherwise the expression will be false.

```
if balance == 0:
    # Statements appearing here will
    # be executed only if balance is
    # equal to 0.
```

The following code uses the != operator to determine whether two values are *not* equal. The expression choice != 5 will be true if the choice variable does not reference the value 5. Otherwise the expression will be false.

```
if choice != 5:
    # Statements appearing here will
    # be executed only if choice is
    # not equal to 5.
```

In the Spotlight:
Using the If-Then Statement

Kathryn teaches a science class and her students are required to take three tests. She wants to write a program that her students can use to calculate their average test score. She also wants the program to congratulate the student enthusiastically if the average is greater than 95. Here is the algorithm in pseudocode:

Get the first test score
Get the second test score
Get the third test score
Calculate the average
Display the average
If the average is greater than 95:
    Congratulate the user

Program 1 shows the code for the program.

Program 1   (test_average.py)

```
1   # This program prompts the user to enter three test
2   # scores. It displays the average of those scores
3   # and congratulates the user if the average is 95
4   # or greater.
5
6   def main():
7       # Get the three test scores.
8       test1 = input('Enter the score for test 1: ')
```

(program continues)

Program 1   *(continued)*

```
 9      test2 = input('Enter the score for test 2: ')
10      test3 = input('Enter the score for test 3: ')
11
12      # Calculate the average test score.
13      average = (test1 + test2 + test3) / 3.0
14
15      # Print the average.
16      print 'The average score is', average
17
18      # If the average is 95 or greater,
19      # congratulate the user.
20      if average >= 95:
21          print 'Congratulations!'
22          print 'That is a great average!'
23
24  # Call the main function.
25  main()
```

Program Output (with input shown in bold)

```
Enter the score for test 1: 82 [Enter]
Enter the score for test 2: 76 [Enter]
Enter the score for test 3: 91 [Enter]
The average score is 83.0
```

Program Output (with input shown in bold)

```
Enter the score for test 1: 93 [Enter]
Enter the score for test 2: 99 [Enter]
Enter the score for test 3: 96 [Enter]
The average score is 96.0
Congratulations!
That is a great score.
```

Nested Blocks

Program 1 is an example of a program that has a block inside a block. The main function has a block (in lines 7 through 22), and inside that block the if statement has a block (in lines 21 through 22). This is shown in Figure 5.

Python requires you to indent the statements in a block. When you have a block nested inside a block, the inner block must be further indented. As you can see in Figure 5, four spaces are used to indent the main function's block, and eight spaces are used to indent the if statement's block.

Figure 5   Nested blocks

```
def main():
    # Get the three test scores.
    test1 = input('Enter the score for test 1: ')        This is the main
    test2 = input('Enter the socre for test 2: ')        function's block.
    test3 = input('Enter the score for test 3: ')

    # Calculate the average test score.
    average = (test1 + test2 + test3) / 3.0

    # Print the average.
    print 'The average score is', average

    # If the average is 95 or greater,
    # congratulate the user.
    if average >= 95:
        print 'Congratulations!'                          This is the if
        print 'That is a great average!'                  statement's block.

# Call the main function.
main()
```

Checkpoint

1   What is a control structure?

2   What is a decision structure?

3   What is a single alternative decision structure?

4   What is a Boolean expression?

5   What types of relationships between values can you test with relational operators?

6   Write an `if` statement that assigns 0 to x if y is equal to 20.

7   Write an `if` statement that assigns 0.2 to `commission` if `sales` is greater than or equal to 10000.

2   The `if-else` Statement

CONCEPT: An `if-else` statement will execute one block of statements if its condition is true, or another block if its condition is false.

The previous section introduced the single alternative decision structure (the `if` statement), which has one alternative path of execution. Now we will look at the *dual alternative decision structure*, which has two possible paths of execution—one path is taken if a condition is true, and the other path is taken if the condition is false. Figure 6 shows a flowchart for a dual alternative decision structure.

The decision structure in the flowchart tests the condition `temperature < 40`. If this condition is true, the statement `print "A little cold, isn't it?"` is performed. If the condition is false, the statement `print "Nice weather we're having."` is performed.

Figure 6   A dual alternative decision structure

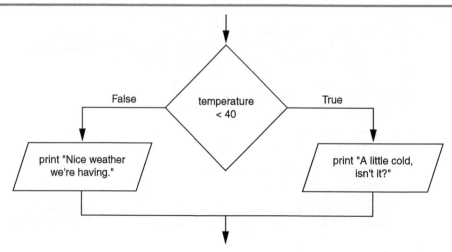

In code we write a dual alternative decision structure as an `if-else` statement. Here is the general format of the `if-else` statement:

```
if condition:
    statement
    statement
    etc.
else:
    statement
    statement
    etc.
```

When this statement executes, the *condition* is tested. If it is true, the block of indented statements following the `if` clause is executed, and then control of the program jumps to the statement that follows the `if-else` statement. If the condition is false, the block of indented statements following the `else` clause is executed, and then control of the program jumps to the statement that follows the `if-else` statement. This action is described in Figure 7.

Figure 7   Conditional execution in an `if-else` statement

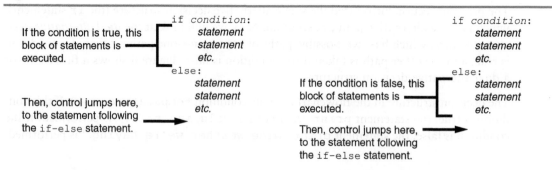

The following code shows an example of an `if-else` statement. This code matches the flowchart that was shown in Figure 5.

```
if temperature < 40:
    print "A little cold, isn't it?"
else:
    print "Nice weather we're having."
```

Indentation in the `if-else` Statement

When you write an `if-else` statement, follow these guidelines for indentation:

- Make sure the `if` clause and the `else` clause are aligned.
- The `if` clause and the `else` clause are each followed by a block of statements. Make sure the statements in the blocks are consistently indented.

This is shown in Figure 8.

Figure 8   Indentation with an `if-else` statement

Align the `if` and `else` clauses.

```
if temperature < 40:
    print "A little cold, isn't it?"
    print "Turn up the heat!"
else:
    print "Nice weather we're having."
    print "Pass the sunscreen."
```

The statements in each block must be indented consistently.

In the Spotlight:
Using the `if-else` Statement

Chris owns an auto repair business and has several employees. If any employee works over 40 hours in a week, he pays them 1.5 times their regular hourly pay rate for all hours over 40. He has asked you to design a simple payroll program that calculates an employee's gross pay, including any overtime wages. You design the following algorithm:

Get the number of hours worked.
Get the hourly pay rate.
If the employee worked more than 40 hours:
    Calculate and display the gross pay with overtime.
Else:
    Calculate and display the gross pay as usual.

Next, you go through the top-down design process and create the hierarchy chart shown in Figure 9. As shown in the hierarchy chart, there are three functions, summarized as follows:

- `main`—This function will be called when the program starts. It will get the number of hours worked and the hourly pay rate as input from the user. It will then call either the `calc_pay_with_OT` function or the `calc_regular_pay` function to calculate and display the gross pay.

- `calc_pay_with_OT`—This function will calculate and display an employee's pay with overtime.
- `calc_regular_pay`—This function will calculate and display the gross pay for an employee with no overtime.

Figure 9 Hierarchy chart

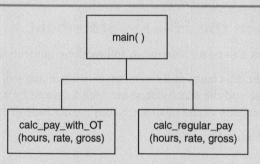

The code for the program is shown in Program 2. Notice that two global variables, which are used as constants, are created in lines 2 and 3. BASE_HOURS is assigned 40, which is the number of hours an employee can work in a week without getting paid overtime. OT_MULTIPLIER is assigned 1.5, which is the pay rate multiplier for overtime hours. This means that the employee's hourly pay rate is multiplied by 1.5 for all overtime hours.

Program 2   (auto_repair_payroll.py)

```
1   # Global constants
2   BASE_HOURS = 40      # Base hours per week
3   OT_MULTIPLIER = 1.5 # Overtime multiplier
4
5   # The main function gets the number of hours worked and
6   # the hourly pay rate. It calls either the calc_pay_with_OT
7   # function or the calc_regular_pay function to calculate
8   # and display the gross pay.
9   def main():
10      # Get the hours worked and the hourly pay rate.
11      hours_worked = input('Enter the number of hours worked: ')
12      pay_rate = input('Enter the hourly pay rate: ')
13
14      # Calculate and display the gross pay.
15      if hours_worked > BASE_HOURS:
16          calc_pay_with_OT(hours_worked, pay_rate)
17      else:
18          calc_regular_pay(hours_worked, pay_rate)
19
20  # The calc_pay_with_OT function calculates pay with
21  # overtime. It accepts the hours worked and the hourly
```

```
22    # pay rate as arguments. The gross pay is displayed.
23    def calc_pay_with_OT(hours, rate):
24        # Calculate the number of overtime hours worked.
25        overtime_hours = hours - BASE_HOURS
26
27        # Calculate the amount of overtime pay.
28        overtime_pay = overtime_hours * rate * OT_MULTIPLIER
29
30        # Calculate the gross pay.
31        gross_pay = BASE_HOURS * rate + overtime_pay
32
33        # Display the gross pay.
34        print 'The gross pay is $%.2f.' % gross_pay
35
36    # The calc_regular_pay function calculates pay with
37    # no overtime. It accepts the hours worked and the hourly
38    # pay rate as arguments. The gross pay is displayed.
39    def calc_regular_pay(hours, rate):
40        # Calculate the gross pay.
41        gross_pay = hours * rate
42
43        # Display the gross pay.
44        print 'The gross pay is $%.2f.' % gross_pay
45
46    # Call the main function.
47    main()
```

Program Output (with input shown in bold)

```
Enter the number of hours worked: 40 [Enter]
Enter the hourly pay rate: 20 [Enter]
The gross pay is $800.00.
```

Program Output (with input shown in bold)

```
Enter the number of hours worked: 50 [Enter]
Enter the hourly pay rate: 20 [Enter]
The gross pay is $1100.00.
```

Checkpoint use the word files as manuscript

8   How does a dual alternative decision structure work?

9   What statement do you use in Python to write a dual alternative decision structure?

10 .When you write an if-else statement, under what circumstances do the statements that appear after the else clause execute?

Comparing Strings

CONCEPT: Python allows you to compare strings. This allows you to create decision structures that test the value of a string.

You saw in the preceding examples how numbers can be compared in a decision structure. You can also compare strings. For example, look at the following code:

```
name1 = 'Mary'
name2 = 'Mark'
if name1 == name2:
    print 'The names are the same.'
else:
    print 'The names are NOT the same.'
```

The == operator compares name1 and name2 to determine whether they are equal. Because the strings 'Mary' and 'Mark' are not equal, the else clause will display the message 'The names are NOT the same.'

Let's look at another example. Assume the month variable references a string. The following code uses the != operator to determine whether the value referenced by month is not equal to 'October'.

```
if month != 'October':
    print 'This is the wrong time for Octoberfest!'
```

Program 3 is a complete program demonstrating how two strings can be compared. The program prompts the user to enter a password and then determines whether the string entered is equal to 'prospero'.

Program 3   (password.py)

```
1   # This program demonstrates how the == operator can
2   # be used to compare strings.
3
4   def main():
5       # Get a password from the user.
6       password = raw_input('Enter the password: ')
7
8       # Determine whether the correct password
9       # was entered.
10      if password == 'prospero':
11          print 'Password accepted.'
12      else:
13          print 'Sorry, that is the wrong password.'
14
15  # Call the main function.
16  main()
```

Program Output (with input shown in bold)

```
Enter the password: ferdinand [Enter]
Sorry, that is the wrong password.
```

Program Output (with input shown in bold)

```
Enter the password: prospero [Enter]
Password accepted.
```

String comparisons are case sensitive. For example, the strings 'saturday' and 'Saturday' are not equal because the "s" is lowercase in the first string, but uppercase in the second string. The following sample session with Program 3 shows what happens when the user enters Prospero as the password (with an uppercase P).

Program Output (with input shown in bold)

```
Enter the password: Prospero [Enter]
Sorry, that is the wrong password.
```

 TIP: You will learn how to manipulate strings so that case-insensitive comparisons can be performed.

Other String Comparisons

In addition to determining whether strings are equal or not equal, you can also determine whether one string is greater than or less than another string. This is a useful capability because programmers commonly need to design programs that sort strings in some order.

Computers do not actually store characters, such as A, B, C, and so on, in memory. Instead, they store numeric codes that represent the characters. ASCII (the American Standard Code for Information Interchange) is a commonly used character coding system.

- The uppercase characters A through Z are represented by the numbers 65 through 90.
- The lowercase characters a through z are represented by the numbers 97 through 122.
- When the digits 0 through 9 are stored in memory as characters, they are represented by the numbers 48 through 57. (For example, the string 'abc123' would be stored in memory as the codes 97, 98, 99, 49, 50, and 51.)
- A blank space is represented by the number 32.

In addition to establishing a set of numeric codes to represent characters in memory, ASCII also establishes an order for characters. The character "A" comes before the character "B", which comes before the character "C", and so on.

When a program compares characters, it actually compares the codes for the characters. For example, look at the following if statement:

```
if 'a' < 'b':
    print 'The letter a is less than the letter b.'
```

This code determines whether the ASCII code for the character `'a'` is less than the ASCII code for the character `'b'`. The expression `'a' < 'b'` is true because the code for `'a'` is less than the code for `'b'`. So, if this were part of an actual program it would display the message `'The letter a is less than the letter b.'`

Let's look at how strings containing more than one character are typically compared. Suppose a program uses the strings `'Mary'` and `'Mark'` as follows:

```
name1 = 'Mary'
name2 = 'Mark'
```

Figure 10 shows how the individual characters in the strings `'Mary'` and `'Mark'` would actually be stored in memory, using ASCII codes.

Figure 10   Character codes for the strings `'Mary'` and `'Mark'`

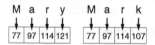

When you use relational operators to compare these strings, the strings are compared character-by-character. For example, look at the following code:

```
name1 = 'Mary'
name2 = 'Mark'
if name1 > name2:
    print 'Mary is greater than Mark'
else:
    print 'Mary is not greater than Mark'
```

The `>` operator compares each character in the strings `'Mary'` and `'Mark'`, beginning with the first, or leftmost, characters. This is shown in Figure 11.

Figure 11   Comparing each character in a string

Here is how the comparison takes place:

1. The `'M'` in `'Mary'` is compared with the `'M'` in `'Mark'`. Since these are the same, the next characters are compared.
2. The `'a'` in `'Mary'` is compared with the `'a'` in `'Mark'`. Since these are the same, the next characters are compared.
3. The `'r'` in `'Mary'` is compared with the `'r'` in `'Mark'`. Since these are the same, the next characters are compared.
4. The `'y'` in `'Mary'` is compared with the `'k'` in `'Mark'`. Since these are not the same, the two strings are not equal. The character `'y'` has a higher ASCII code (121) than `'k'` (107), so it is determined that the string `'Mary'` is greater than the string `'Mark'`.

If one of the strings in a comparison is shorter than the other, only the corresponding characters will be compared. If the corresponding characters are identical, then the shorter string is considered less than the longer string. For example, suppose the strings `'High'` and `'Hi'` were being compared. The string `'Hi'` would be considered less than `'High'` because it is shorter.

Program 4 shows a simple demonstration of how two strings can be compared with the `<` operator. The user is prompted to enter two names and the program displays those two names in alphabetical order.

Program 4   (password.py)

```
 1   # This program demonstrates how the < operator can
 2   # be used to compare strings.
 3
 4   def main():
 5       # Get two names from the user.
 6       name1 = raw_input('Enter a name (last name first): ')
 7       name2 = raw_input('Enter another name (last name first): ')
 8
 9       # Display the names in alphabetical order.
10       print 'Here are the names, listed alphabetically.'
11       if name1 < name2:
12           print name1
13           print name2
14       else:
15           print name2
16           print name1
17
18   # Call the main function.
19   main()
```

Program Output (with input shown in bold)
```
Enter a name (last name first): Jones, Richard [Enter]
Enter another name (last name first) Costa, Joan [Enter]
Here are the names, listed alphabetically:
Costa, Joan
Jones, Richard
```

Checkpoint

11 What would the following code display?

```
if 'z' < 'a':
    print 'z is less than a.'
else:
    p.rint 'z is not less than a.'
```

12 What would the following code display?

```
s1 = 'New York'
s2 = 'Boston'
```

```
if s1 > s2:
    print s2
    print s1
else:
    print s1
    print s2
```

4   Nested Decision Structures and the if-elif-else Statement

CONCEPT: To test more than one condition, a decision structure can be nested inside another decision structure.

In Section 1, we mentioned that a control structure determines the order in which a set of statements execute. Programs are usually designed as combinations of different control structures. For example, Figure 12 shows a flowchart that combines a decision structure with two sequence structures.

Figure 12   Combining sequence structures with a decision structure

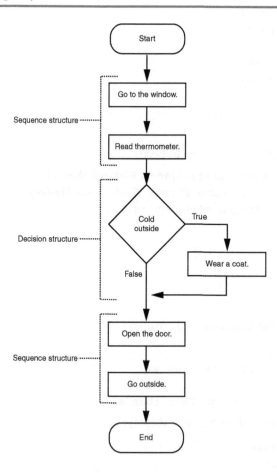

The flowchart in the figure starts with a sequence structure. Assuming you have an outdoor thermometer in your window, the first step is Go to the window, and the next step is Read thermometer. A decision structure appears next, testing the condition Cold outside. If this is true, the action Wear a coat is performed. Another sequence structure appears next. The step Open the door is performed, followed by Go outside.

Quite often, structures must be nested inside other structures. For example, look at the partial flowchart in Figure 13. It shows a decision structure with a sequence structure nested inside it. The decision structure tests the condition Cold outside. If that condition is true, the steps in the sequence structure are executed.

Figure 13   A sequence structure nested inside a decision structure

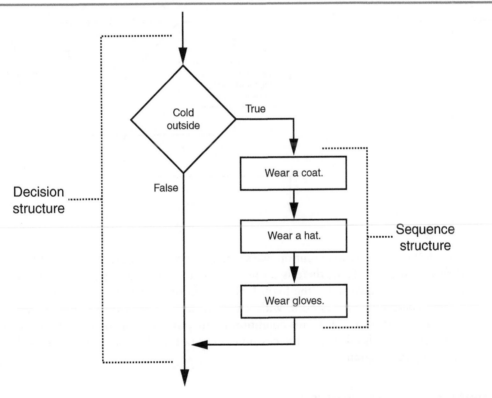

You can also nest decision structures inside other decision structures. In fact, this is a common requirement in programs that need to test more than one condition. For example, consider a program that determines whether a bank customer qualifies for a loan. To qualify, two conditions must exist: (1) the customer must earn at least $30,000 per year, and (2) the customer must have been employed at his or her current job for at least two years. Figure 14 shows a flowchart for an algorithm that could be used in such a program. Assume that the salary variable is assigned the customer's annual salary, and the years_on_job variable is assigned the number of years that the customer has worked on his or her current job.

Figure 14   A nested decision structure

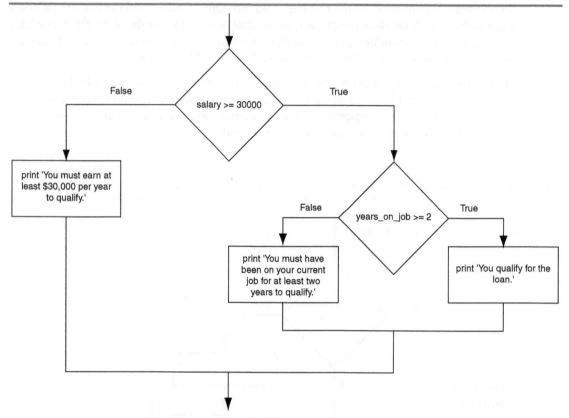

If we follow the flow of execution, we see that the condition `salary >= 30000` is tested. If this condition is false, there is no need to perform further tests; we know that the customer does not qualify for the loan. If the condition is true, however, we need to test the second condition. This is done with a nested decision structure that tests the condition `years_on_job >= 2`. If this condition is true, then the customer qualifies for the loan. If this condition is false, then the customer does not qualify. Program 5 shows the code for the complete program.

Program 5   (loan_qualifier.py)

```
1   # This program determines whether a bank customer
2   # qualifies for a loan.
3
4   def main():
5       # Get the customer's annual salary.
6       salary = input('Enter your annual salary: ')
7
8       # Get the number of years on the current job.
9       years_on_job = input('Enter the number of ' + \
10                             'years on your current job: ')
```

```
11
12          # Determine whether the customer qualifies.
13          if salary >= 30000.0:
14              if years_on_job >= 2:
15                  print 'You qualify for the loan.'
16              else:
17                  print 'You must have been on your current'
18                  print 'job for at least two years to qualify.'
19          else:
20              print 'You must earn at least $30,000 per year'
21              print 'to qualify.'
22
23      # Call the main function.
24      main()
```

Program Output (with input shown in bold)

```
Enter your annual salary: 35000 [Enter]
Enter the number of years on your current job: 1 [Enter]
You must have been on your current
job for at least two years to qualify.
```

Program Output (with input shown in bold)

```
Enter your annual salary: 25000 [Enter]
Enter the number of years on your current job: 5 [Enter]
You must earn at least $30,000
per year to qualify.
```

Program Output (with input shown in bold)

```
Enter your annual salary: 35000 [Enter]
Enter the number of years on your current job: 5 [Enter]
You qualify for the loan.
```

Look at the if-else statement that begins in line 13. It tests the condition salary >= 30000.0. If this condition is true, the if-else statement that begins in line 14 is executed. Otherwise the program jumps to the else clause in line 19 and executes the two print statements in lines 20 and 21. The program then leaves the decision structure and the main function ends.

It's important to use proper indentation in a nested decision structure. Not only is proper indentation required by the Python interpreter, but it also makes it easier for you, the human reader of your code, to see which actions are performed by each part of the structure. Follow these rules when writing nested if statements:

- Make sure each else clause is aligned with its matching if clause. This is shown in Figure 15.
- Make sure the statements in each block are consistently indented. The shaded parts of Figure 16 show the nested blocks in the decision structure. Notice that each statement in each block is indented the same amount.

Figure 15   Alignment of `if` and `else` clauses

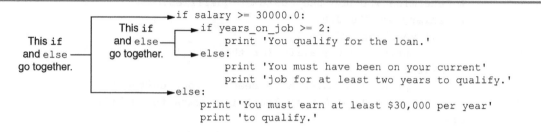

Figure 16   Nested blocks

```
if salary >= 30000.0:
    if years_on_job >= 2:
        print 'You qualify for the loan.'
    else:
        print 'You must have been on your current'
        print 'job for at least two years to qualify.'
else:
    print 'You must earn at least $30,000 per year'
    print 'to qualify.'
```

Testing a Series of Conditions

In the previous example you saw how a program can use nested decision structures to test more than one condition. It is not uncommon for a program to have a series of conditions to test, and then perform an action depending on which condition is true. One way to accomplish this it to have a decision structure with numerous other decision structures nested inside it. For example, consider the program presented in the following *In the Spotlight* section.

In the Spotlight:
Multiple Nested Decision Structures

Dr. Suarez teaches a literature class and uses the following 10 point grading scale for all of his exams:

Test Score	Grade
90 and above	A
80–89	B
70–79	C
60–69	D
Below 60	F

He has asked you to write a program that will allow a student to enter a test score and then display the grade for that score. Here is the algorithm that you will use:

1. Ask the user to enter a test score.

2. Determine the grade in the following manner:

If the score is less than 60, then the grade is F.
 Else, if the score is less than 70, then the grade is D.
  Else, if the score is less than 80, then the grade is C.
   Else, if the score is less than 90, then the grade is B.
    Else, the grade is A.

You decide that the process of determining the grade will require several nested decision structures, as shown in Figure 17. Program 6 shows the code for the program. The code for the nested decision structures is in lines 9 through 21.

Figure 17   Nested decision structure to determine a grade

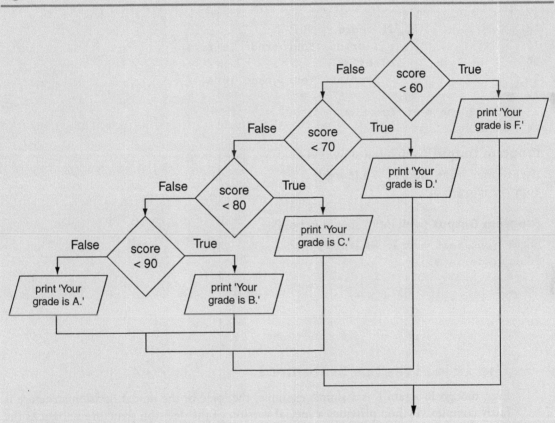

Program 6   (grader.py)

```
1   # This program gets a numeric test score from the
2   # user and displays the corresponding letter grade.
3
4   def main():
5       # Get a test score from the user.
6       score = input('Enter your test score: ')
```

(program continues)

Program 6   *(continued)*

```
 7
 8       # Determine the grade.
 9       if score < 60:
10           print 'Your grade is F.'
11       else:
12           if score < 70:
13               print 'Your grade is D.'
14           else:
15               if score < 80:
16                   print 'Your grade is C.'
17               else:
18                   if score < 90:
19                       print 'Your grade is B.'
20                   else:
21                       print 'Your grade is A.'
22
23   # Call the main function.
24   main()
```

Program Output (with input shown in bold)

```
Enter your test score: 78 [Enter]
Your grade is C.
```

Program Output (with input shown in bold)

```
Enter your test score: 84 [Enter]
Your grade is B.
```

The `if-elif-else` Statement

Even though Program 6 is a simple example, the logic of the nested decision structure is fairly complex. Python provides a special version of the decision structure known as the `if-elif-else` statement, which makes this type of logic simpler to write. Here is the general format of the `if-elif-else` statement:

```
if condition_1:
    statement
    statement
    etc.
elif condition_2:
    statement
    statement
    etc.
```

Insert as many `elif` *clauses as necessary . . .*

```
else:
    statement
    statement
    etc.
```

When the statement executes, `condition_1` is tested. If `condition_1` is true, the block of statements that immediately follow is executed, up to the `elif` clause. The rest of the structure is ignored. If `condition_1` is false, however, the program jumps to the very next `elif` clause and tests `condition_2`. If it is true, the block of statements that immediately follow is executed, up to the next `elif` clause. The rest the structure is then ignored. This process continues until a condition is found to be true, or no more `elif` clauses are left. If no condition is true, the block of statements following the `else` clause is executed.

The following is an example of the `if-elif-else` statement. This code works the same as the nested decision structure in lines 9 through 21 of Program 6.

```
if score < 60:
    print 'Your grade is F.'
elif score < 70:
    print 'Your grade is D.'
elif score < 80:
    print 'Your grade is C.'
elif score < 90:
    print 'Your grade is B.'
else:
    print 'Your grade is A.'
```

Notice the alignment and indentation that is used with the `if-elif-else` statement: The `if`, `elif`, and `else` clauses are all aligned, and the conditionally executed blocks are indented.

The `if-elif-else` statement is never required because its logic can be coded with nested `if-else` statements. However, a long series of nested `if-else` statements has two particular disadvantages when you are debugging code:

- The code can grow complex and become difficult to understand.
- Because of the required indentation, a long series of nested `if-else` statements can become too long to be displayed on the computer screen without horizontal scrolling. Also, long statements tend to "wrap around" when printed on paper, making the code even more difficult to read.

The logic of an `if-elif-else` statement is usually easier to follow than a long series of nested `if-else` statements. And, because all of the clauses are aligned in an `if-elif-else` statement, the lengths of the lines in the statement tend to be shorter.

Checkpoint

13 Convert the following code to an `if-elif-else` statement:

```
if number == 1:
    print 'One'
```

```
    else:
        if number == 2:
            print 'Two'
        else:
            if number == 3:
                print 'Three'
            else:
                print 'Unknown'
```

5 Logical Operators

CONCEPT: The logical **and** operator and the logical **or** operator allow you to connect multiple Boolean expressions to create a compound expression. The logical **not** operator reverses the truth of a Boolean expression.

Python provides a set of operators known as *logical operators*, which you can use to create complex Boolean expressions. Table 3 describes these operators.

Table 3   Logical operators

Operator	Meaning
and	The and operator connects two Boolean expressions into one compound expression. Both subexpressions must be true for the compound expression to be true.
or	The or operator connects two Boolean expressions into one compound expression. One or both subexpressions must be true for the compound expression to be true. It is only necessary for one of the subexpressions to be true, and it does not matter which.
not	The not operator is a unary operator, meaning it works with only one operand. The operand must be a Boolean expression. The not operator reverses the truth of its operand. If it is applied to an expression that is true, the operator returns false. If it is applied to an expression that is false, the operator returns true.

Table 4 shows examples of several compound Boolean expressions that use logical operators.

Table 4   Compound Boolean expressions using logical operators

Expression	Meaning
x > y and a < b	Is x greater than y AND is a less than b?
x == y or x == z	Is x equal to y OR is x equal to z?
not (x > y)	Is the expression x > y NOT true?

The and Operator

The and operator takes two Boolean expressions as operands and creates a compound Boolean expression that is true only when both subexpressions are true. The following is an example of an `if` statement that uses the and operator:

```
if temperature < 20 and minutes > 12:
    print 'The temperature is in the danger zone.'
```

In this statement, the two Boolean expressions `temperature < 20` and `minutes > 12` are combined into a compound expression. The `print` statement will be executed only if `temperature` is less than 20 and `minutes` is greater than 12. If either of the Boolean subexpressions is false, the compound expression is false and the message is not displayed.

Table 5 shows a truth table for the and operator. The truth table lists expressions showing all the possible combinations of true and false connected with the and operator. The resulting values of the expressions are also shown.

Table 5 Truth table for the and operator

Expression	Value of the Expression
true and false	false
false and true	false
false and false	false
true and true	true

As the table shows, both sides of the and operator must be true for the operator to return a true value.

The or Operator

The or operator takes two Boolean expressions as operands and creates a compound Boolean expression that is true when either of the subexpressions is true. The following is an example of an `if` statement that uses the or operator:

```
if temperature < 20 or temperature > 100:
    print 'The temperature is too extreme'
```

The `print` statement will execute only if `temperature` is less than 20 or `temperature` is greater than 100. If either subexpression is true, the compound expression is true. Table 6 shows a truth table for the or operator.

Table 6 Truth table for the or operator

Expression	Value of the Expression
true or false	true
false or true	true
false or false	false
true or true	true

All it takes for an or expression to be true is for one side of the or operator to be true. It doesn't matter if the other side is false or true.

Short-Circuit Evaluation

Both the and and or operators perform *short-circuit evaluation*. Here's how it works with the and operator: If the expression on the left side of the and operator is false, the expression on the right side will not be checked. Because the compound expression will be false if only one of the subexpressions is false, it would waste CPU time to check the remaining expression. So, when the and operator finds that the expression on its left is false, it short-circuits and does not evaluate the expression on its right.

Here's how short-circuit evaluation works with the or operator: If the expression on the left side of the or operator is true, the expression on the right side will not be checked. Because it is only necessary for one of the expressions to be true, it would waste CPU time to check the remaining expression.

The not Operator

The not operator is a unary operator that takes a Boolean expression as its operand and reverses its logical value. In other words, if the expression is true, the not operator returns false, and if the expression is false, the not operator returns true. The following is an if statement using the not operator:

```
if not(temperature > 100):
    print 'This is below the maximum temperature.'
```

First, the expression (temperature > 100) is tested and a value of either true or false is the result. Then the not operator is applied to that value. If the expression (temperature > 100) is true, the not operator returns false. If the expression (temperature > 100) is false, the not operator returns true. The previous code is equivalent to asking: "Is the temperature not greater than 100?"

 NOTE: In this example, we have put parentheses around the expression temperature > 100. This is to make it clear that we are applying the not operator to the value of the expression temperature > 100, not just to the temperature variable.

Table 7 shows a truth table for the not operator.

Table 7   Truth table for the not operator

Expression	Value of the Expression
not true	false
not false	true

The Loan Qualifier Program Revisited

In some situations the and operator can be used to simplify nested decision structures. For example, recall that the loan qualifier program in Program 5 uses the following nested if-else statements:

```
if salary >= 30000.0:
    if years_on_job >= 2:
        print 'You qualify for the loan.'
    else:
        print 'You must have been on your current'
        print 'job for at least two years to qualify.'
else:
        print 'You must earn at least $30,000 per year'
        print 'to qualify.'
```

The purpose of this decision structure is to determine that a person's salary is at least $30,000 and that he or she has been at their current job for at least two years. Program 7 shows a way to perform a similar task with simpler code.

Program 7   (loan_qualifier2.py)

```
 1   # This program determines whether a bank customer
 2   # qualifies for a loan.
 3
 4   def main():
 5       # Get the customer's annual salary.
 6       salary = input('Enter your annual salary: ')
 7
 8       # Get the number of years on the current job.
 9       years_on_job = input('Enter the number of ' + \
10                            'years on your current job: ')
11
12       # Determine whether the customer qualifies.
13       if salary >= 30000.0 and years_on_job >= 2:
14           print 'You qualify for the loan.'
15       else:
16           print 'You do not qualify for this loan.'
17
18   # Call the main function.
19   main()
```

Program Output (with input shown in bold)

```
Enter your annual salary: 35000 [Enter]
Enter the number of years on your current job: 1 [Enter]
You do not qualify for this loan.
```

Program Output (with input shown in bold)
```
Enter your annual salary: 25000 [Enter]
Enter the number of years on your current job: 5 [Enter]
You do not qualify for this loan.
```

Program Output (with input shown in bold)
```
Enter your annual salary: 35000 [Enter]
Enter the number of years on your current job: 5 [Enter]
You qualify for the loan.
```

The if-then-else statement in lines 13 through 16 tests the compound expression salary >= 30000 and years_on_job >= 2. If both subexpressions are true, the compound expression is true and the message "You qualify for the loan" is displayed. If either of the subexpressions is false, the compound expression is false and the message "You do not qualify for this loan" is displayed.

> **NOTE:** A careful observer will realize that Program 7 is similar to Program 5, but it is not equivalent. If the user does not qualify for the loan, Program 7 displays only the message "You do not qualify for this loan" whereas Program 5 displays one of two possible messages explaining why the user did not qualify.

Yet Another Loan Qualifier Program

Suppose the bank is losing customers to a competing bank that isn't as strict about whom it loans money to. In response, the bank decides to change its loan requirements. Now, customers have to meet only one of the previous conditions, not both. Program 8 shows the code for the new loan qualifier program. The compound expression that is tested by the if-else statement in line 13 now uses the or operator.

Program 8   (loan_qualifier3.py)

```
1   # This program determines whether a bank customer
2   # qualifies for a loan.
3
4   def main():
5       # Get the customer's annual salary.
6       salary = input('Enter your annual salary: ')
7
8       # Get the number of years on the current job.
9       years_on_job = input('Enter the number of ' + \
10                      'years on your current job: ')
11
12      # Determine whether the customer qualifies.
13      if salary >= 30000.0 or years_on_job >= 2:
```

```
14              print 'You qualify for the loan.'
15         else:
16              print 'You do not qualify for this loan.'
17
18    # Call the main function.
19    main()
```

Program Output (with input shown in bold)

```
Enter your annual salary: 35000 [Enter]
Enter the number of years on your current job: 1 [Enter]
You qualify for the loan.
```

Program Output (with input shown in bold)

```
Enter your annual salary: 25000 [Enter]
Enter the number of years on your current job: 5 [Enter]
You qualify for the loan.
```

Program Output (with input shown in bold)

```
Enter your annual salary 12000 [Enter]
Enter the number of years on your current job: 1 [Enter]
You do not qualify for this loan.
```

Checking Numeric Ranges with Logical Operators

Sometimes you will need to design an algorithm that determines whether a numeric value is within a specific range of values or outside a specific range of values. When determining whether a number is inside a range, it is best to use the and operator. For example, the following if statement checks the value in x to determine whether it is in the range of 20 through 40:

```
if x >= 20 and x <= 40:
    print 'The value is in the acceptable range.'
```

The compound Boolean expression being tested by this statement will be true only when x is greater than or equal to 20 and less than or equal to 40. The value in x must be within the range of 20 through 40 for this compound expression to be true.

When determining whether a number is outside a range, it is best to use the or operator. The following statement determines whether x is outside the range of 20 through 40:

```
if x < 20 or x > 40:
    print 'The value is outside the acceptable range.'
```

It is important not to get the logic of the logical operators confused when testing for a range of numbers. For example, the compound Boolean expression in the following code would never test true:

```
# This is an error!
if x < 20 and x > 40:
    print 'The value is outside the acceptable range.'
```

Obviously, x cannot be less than 20 and at the same time be greater than 40.

Checkpoint

14 What is a compound Boolean expression?

15 The following truth table shows various combinations of the values true and false connected by a logical operator. Complete the table by circling T or F to indicate whether the result of such a combination is true or false.

Logical Expression	Result (circle T or F)	
True and False	T	F
True and True	T	F
False and True	T	F
False and False	T	F
True or False	T	F
True or True	T	F
False or True	T	F
False or False	T	F
not True	T	F
not False	T	F

16 Assume the variables a = 2, b = 4, and c = 6. Circle the T or F for each of the following conditions to indicate whether its value is true or false.

```
a == 4 or b > 2          T    F
6 <= c and a > 3         T    F
1 != b and c != 3        T    F
a >= -1 or a <= b        T    F
not (a > 2)              T    F
```

17 Explain how short-circuit evaluation works with the and and or operators.

18 Write an if statement that displays the message "The number is valid" if the value referenced by speed is within the range 0 through 200.

19 Write an if statement that displays the message "The number is not valid" if the value referenced by speed is outside the range 0 through 200.

6 Boolean Variables

CONCEPT: A Boolean variable can reference one of two values: **True** or **False**. Boolean variables are commonly used as flags, which indicate whether specific conditions exist.

So far in this book we have worked with int, float, and str (string) variables. In addition to these data types, Python also provides a bool data type. The bool data type allows you to create variables that may reference one of two possible values: True or False. Here are examples of how we assign values to a bool variable:

```
hungry = True
sleepy = False
```

Boolean variables are most commonly used as flags. A *flag* is a variable that signals when some condition exists in the program. When the flag variable is set to `False`, it indicates the condition does not exist. When the flag variable is set to `True`, it means the condition does exist.

For example, suppose a salesperson has a quota of $50,000. Assuming `sales` references the amount that the salesperson has sold, the following code determines whether the quota has been met:

```
if sales >= 50000.0:
    sales_quota_met = True
else:
    sales_quota_met = False
```

As a result of this code, the `sales_quota_met` variable can be used as a flag to indicate whether the sales quota has been met. Later in the program we might test the flag in the following way:

```
if sales_quota_met:
    print 'You have met your sales quota!'
```

This code displays `'You have met your sales quota!'` if the `bool` variable `sales_quota_met` is `True`. Notice that we did not have to use the `==` operator to explicitly compare the `sales_quota_met` variable with the value `True`. This code is equivalent to the following:

```
if sales_quota_met == True:
    print 'You have met your sales quota!'
```

Checkpoint

20   What values can you assign to a `bool` variable?

21   What is a flag variable?

Review Questions

Multiple Choice

1. A _____ structure can execute a set of statements only under certain circumstances.
   a. sequence
   b. circumstantial
   c. decision
   d. Boolean

2. A _____ structure provides one alternative path of execution.
   a. sequence
   b. single alternative decision
   c. one path alternative
   d. single execution decision

3. A(n) _____ expression has a value of either true or false.
   a. binary
   b. decision
   c. unconditional
   d. Boolean

4. The symbols >, <, and == are all _____ operators.
   a. relational
   b. logical
   c. conditional
   d. ternary

5. A(n) _____ structure tests a condition and then takes one path if the condition is true, or another path if the condition is false.
   a. if statement
   b. single alternative decision
   c. dual alternative decision
   d. sequence

6. You use a(n) _____ statement to write a single alternative decision structure.
   a. test-jump
   b. if
   c. if-else
   d. if-call

7. You use a(n) _____ statement to write a dual alternative decision structure.
   a. test-jump
   b. if
   c. if-else
   d. if-call

8. and, or, and not are _____ operators.
   a. relational
   b. logical
   c. conditional
   d. ternary

9. A compound Boolean expression created with the _____ operator is true only if both of its subexpressions are true.
   a. and
   b. or
   c. not
   d. both

10. A compound Boolean expression created with the _____ operator is true if either of its subexpressions is true.
    a. and
    b. or
    c. not
    d. either

11. The _____ operator takes a Boolean expression as its operand and reverses its logical value.
   a. and
   b. or
   c. not
   d. either

12. A _____ is a Boolean variable that signals when some condition exists in the program.
   a. flag
   b. signal
   c. sentinel
   d. siren

True or False

1. You can write any program using only sequence structures.
2. A program can be made of only one type of control structure. You cannot combine structures.
3. A single alternative decision structure tests a condition and then takes one path if the condition is true, or another path if the condition is false.
4. A decision structure can be nested inside another decision structure.
5. A compound Boolean expression created with the and operator is true only when both subexpressions are true.

Short Answer

1. Explain what is meant by the term "conditionally executed."
2. You need to test a condition and then execute one set of statements if the condition is true. If the condition is false, you need to execute a different set of statements. What structure will you use?
3. Briefly describe how the and operator works.
4. Briefly describe how the or operator works.
5. When determining whether a number is inside a range, which logical operator is it best to use?
6. What is a flag and how does it work?

Algorithm Workbench

1. Write an if statement that assigns 20 to the variable y and assigns 40 to the variable z if the variable x is greater than 100.
2. Write an if statement that assigns 0 to the variable b and assigns 1 to the variable c if the variable a is less than 10.
3. Write an if-else statement that assigns 0 to the variable b if the variable a is less than 10. Otherwise, it should assign 99 to the variable b.
4. The following code contains several nested if-else statements. Unfortunately, it was written without proper alignment and indentation. Rewrite the code and use the proper conventions of alignment and indentation.

```
if score < 60:
print 'Your grade is F.'
```

```
else:
if score < 70:
print 'Your grade is D.'
else:
if score < 80:
print 'Your grade is C.'
else:
if score < 90:
print 'Your grade is B.'
else:
print 'Your grade is A.'
```

5. Write nested decision structures that perform the following: If amount1 is greater than 10 and amount2 is less than 100, display the greater of amount1 and amount2.

6. Write an if-else statement that displays 'Speed is normal' if the speed variable is within the range of 24 to 56. If the speed variable's value is outside this range, display 'Speed is abnormal'.

7. Write an if-else statement that determines whether the points variable is outside the range of 9 to 51. If the variable's value is outside this range it should display "Invalid points." Otherwise, it should display "Valid points."

Programming Exercises

1. Roman Numerals

Write a program that prompts the user to enter a number within the range of 1 through 10. The program should display the Roman numeral version of that number. If the number is outside the range of 1 through 10, the program should display an error message. The following table shows the Roman numerals for the numbers 1 through 10:

Number	Roman Numeral
1	I
2	II
3	III
4	IV
5	V
6	VI
7	VII
8	VIII
9	IX
10	X

2. Areas of Rectangles

The area of a rectangle is the rectangle's length times its width. Write a program that asks for the length and width of two rectangles. The program should tell the user which rectangle has the greater area, or if the areas are the same.

3. Mass and Weight

Scientists measure an object's mass in kilograms and its weight in newtons. If you know the amount of mass of an object in kilograms, you can calculate its weight in newtons with the following formula:

$$weight = mass \times 9.8$$

Write a program that asks the user to enter an object's mass, and then calculates its weight. If the object weighs more than 1000 newtons, display a message indicating that it is too heavy. If the object weighs less than 10 newtons, display a message indicating that it is too light.

4. Book Club Points

Serendipity Booksellers has a book club that awards points to its customers based on the number of books purchased each month. The points are awarded as follows:

- If a customer purchases 0 books, he or she earns 0 points.
- If a customer purchases 1 book, he or she earns 5 points.
- If a customer purchases 2 books, he or she earns 15 points.
- If a customer purchases 3 books, he or she earns 30 points.
- If a customer purchases 4 or more books, he or she earns 60 points.

Write a program that asks the user to enter the number of books that he or she has purchased this month and displays the number of points awarded.

5. Software Sales

A software company sells a package that retails for $99. Quantity discounts are given according to the following table:

Quantity	Discount
10–19	20%
20–49	30%
50–99	40%
100 or more	50%

Write a program that asks the user to enter the number of packages purchased. The program should then display the amount of the discount (if any) and the total amount of the purchase after the discount.

6. Shipping Charges

The Fast Freight Shipping Company charges the following rates:

Weight of Package	Rate per Pound
2 pounds or less	$1.10
Over 2 pounds but not more than 6 pounds	$2.20
Over 6 pounds but not more than 10 pounds	$3.70
Over 10 pounds	$3.80

Write a program that asks the user to enter the weight of a package and then displays the shipping charges.

7. Body Mass Index Program Enhancement

In programming Exercise #6 you were asked to write a program that calculates a person's body mass index (BMI). Recall from that exercise that the BMI is often used to determine whether a person with a sedentary lifestyle is overweight or underweight for their height. A person's BMI is calculated with the formula

$$BMI = weight \times 703 \,/\, height^2$$

where *weight* is measured in pounds and *height* is measured in inches. Enhance the program so it displays a message indicating whether the person has optimal weight, is underweight, or is overweight. A sedentary person's weight is considered to be optimal if his or her BMI is between 18.5 and 25. If the BMI is less than 18.5, the person is considered to be underweight. If the BMI value is greater than 25, the person is considered to be overweight.

8. Time Calculator

Write a program that asks the user to enter a number of seconds, and works as follows:

- There are 60 seconds in a minute. If the number of seconds entered by the user is greater than or equal to 60, the program should display the number of minutes in that many seconds.
- There are 3,600 seconds in an hour. If the number of seconds entered by the user is greater than or equal to 3,600, the program should display the number of hours in that many seconds.
- There are 86,400 seconds in a day. If the number of seconds entered by the user is greater than or equal to 86,400, the program should display the number of days in that many seconds.

16

Repetition Structures

TOPICS

1   Introduction to Repetition Structures

CONCEPT: A repetition structure causes a statement or set of statements to execute repeatedly.

Programmers commonly have to write code that performs the same task over and over. For example, suppose you have been asked to write a program that calculates a 10 percent sales commission for several sales people. Although it would not be a good design, one approach would be to write the code to calculate one sales person's commission, and then repeat that code for each sales person. For example, look at the following:

```
# Get a salesperson's sales and commission rate.
sales = input('Enter the amount of sales: ')
comm_rate = input('Enter the commission rate: ')

# Calculate the commission.
commission = sales * comm_rate

# Display the commission.
print 'The commission is $%.2f.' % commission

# Get another salesperson's sales and commission rate.
sales = input('Enter the amount of sales: ')
comm_rate = input('Enter the commission rate: ')

# Calculate the commission.
commission = sales * comm_rate
```

```
# Display the commission.
print 'The commission is $%.2f.' % commission

# Get another salesperson's sales and commission rate.
sales = input('Enter the amount of sales: ')
comm_rate = input('Enter the commission rate: ')

# Calculate the commission.
commission = sales * comm_rate

# Display the commission.
print 'The commission is $%.2f.' % commission
```

And this code goes on and on . . .

As you can see, this code is one long sequence structure containing a lot of duplicated code. There are several disadvantages to this approach, including the following:

- The duplicated code makes the program large.
- Writing a long sequence of statements can be time consuming.
- If part of the duplicated code has to be corrected or changed then the correction or change has to be done many times.

Instead of writing the same sequence of statements over and over, a better way to repeatedly perform an operation is to write the code for the operation once, and then place that code in a structure that makes the computer repeat it as many times as necessary. This can be done with a *repetition structure*, which is more commonly known as a *loop*.

Condition-Controlled and Count-Controlled Loops

In this chapter, we will look at two broad categories of loops: condition-controlled and count-controlled. A *condition-controlled loop* uses a true/false condition to control the number of times that it repeats. A *count-controlled loop* repeats a specific number of times. In Python you use the `while` statement to write a condition-controlled loop, and you use the `for` statement to write a count-controlled loop. In this chapter, we will demonstrate how to write both types of loops.

 Checkpoint

1   What is a repetition structure?
2   What is a condition-controlled loop?
3   What is a count-controlled loop?

The `while` Loop: a Condition-Controlled Loop

CONCEPT: A condition-controlled loop causes a statement or set of statements to repeat as long as a condition is true. In Python you use the ***while*** statement to write a condition-controlled loop.

The while loop gets its name from the way it works: *while a condition is true, do some task*. The loop has two parts: (1) a condition that is tested for a true or false value, and (2) a statement or set of statements that is repeated as long as the condition is true. Figure 1 shows the logic of a while loop.

Figure 1   The logic of a while loop

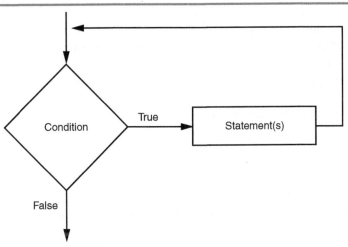

The diamond symbol represents the condition that is tested. Notice what happens if the condition is true: one or more statements are executed and the program's execution flows back to the point just above the diamond symbol. The condition is tested again, and if it is true, the process repeats. If the condition is false, the program exits the loop. In a flowchart, you will always recognize a loop when you see a flow line going back to a previous part of the flowchart.

Here is the general format of the while loop in Python:

```
while condition:
    statement
    statement
    etc.
```

For simplicity, we will refer to the first line as the *while clause*. The while clause begins with the word while, followed by a Boolean *condition* that will be evaluated as either true or false. A colon appears after the *condition*. Beginning at the next line is a block of statements. (All of the statements in a block must be consistently indented. This indentation is required because the Python interpreter uses it to tell where the block begins and ends.)

When the while loop executes, the *condition* is tested. If the *condition* is true, the statements that appear in the block following the while clause are executed, and then the loop starts over. If the *condition* is false, the program exits the loop. Program 1 shows how we might use a while loop to write the commission calculating program that was described at the beginning of this chapter.

Program 1   (commission.py)

```
1   # This program calculates sales commissions.
2   def main():
3       # Create a variable to control the loop.
4       keep_going = 'y'
5
6       # Calculate a series of commissions.
7       while keep_going == 'y':
8           # Get a salesperson's sales and commission rate.
9           sales = input('Enter the amount of sales: ')
10          comm_rate = input('Enter the commission rate: ')
11
12          # Calculate the commission.
13          commission = sales * comm_rate
14
15          # Display the commission.
16          print 'The commission is $%.2f.' % commission
17
18          # See if the user wants to do another one.
19          keep_going = raw_input('Do you want to calculate another ' + \
20                                  'commission (Enter y for yes): ')
21
22  # Call the main function.
23  main()
```

Program Output (with input shown in bold)
```
Enter the amount of sales: 10000.00 [Enter]
Enter the commission rate: 0.10 [Enter]
The commission is $1000.00.
Do you want to calculate another commission (Enter y for yes): y [Enter]
Enter the amount of sales: 20000.00 [Enter]
Enter the commission rate: 0.15 [Enter]
The commission is $3000.00.
Do you want to calculate another commission (Enter y for yes): y [Enter]
Enter the amount of sales: 12000.00 [Enter]
Enter the commission rate: 0.10 [Enter]
The commission is $1200.00.
Do you want to calculate another commission (Enter y for yes): n [Enter]
```

In line 4 we use an assignment statement to create a variable named `keep_going`. Notice that the variable is assigned the value `'y'`. This initialization value is important, and in a moment you will see why.

Line 7 is the beginning of a while loop, which starts like this:

```
while keep_going == 'y':
```

Notice the condition that is being tested: `keep_going == 'y'`. The loop tests this condition, and if it is true, the statements in lines 8 through 20 are executed. Then, the loop starts over at line 7. It tests the expression `keep_going == 'y'` and if it is true, the statements in lines 8 through 20 are executed again. This cycle repeats until the expression `keep_going == 'y'` is tested in line 7 and found to be false. When that happens, the program exits the loop. This is illustrated in Figure 2.

Figure 2   The while loop

```
                          This condition is tested.
                          ┌──────────┐
                                     │
        while keep_going == 'y':

                # Get a salesperson's sales and commission rate.
                sales = input('Enter the amount of sales: ')
If the condition is true,       comm_rate = input('Enter the commission rate: ')
these statements are
executed, and then the      # Calculate the commission.
loop starts over.           commission = sales * comm_rate

If the condition is false,      # Display the commission
these statements are        print 'The commission is $%.2f.' % commission
skipped and the
program exits the loop.         # See if the user wants to do another one.
                            keep_going = raw_input('Do you want to calculate another ' +
                                                   'commission (Enter y for yes): ')
```

In order for this loop to stop executing, something has to happen inside the loop to make the expression `keep_going == 'y'` false. The statement in lines 19 through 20 take care of this. This statement displays the prompt "Do you want to calculate another commission (Enter y for yes)." The value that is read from the keyboard is assigned to the `keep_going` variable. If the user enters y (and it must be a lowercase y), then the expression `keep_going == 'y'` will be true when the loop starts over. This will cause the statements in the body of the loop to execute again. But if the user enters anything other than lowercase y, the expression will be false when the loop starts over, and the program will exit the loop.

Now that you have examined the code, look at the program output in the sample run. First, the user entered 10000.00 for the sales and 0.10 for the commission rate. Then, the program displayed the commission for that amount, which is $1000.00. Next the user is prompted "Do you want to calculate another commission? (Enter y for yes)." The user entered y, and the loop started the steps over. In the sample run, the user went through this process three times. Each execution of the body of a loop is known as an *iteration*. In the sample run, the loop iterated three times.

Figure 3 shows a flowchart for the `main` function. In the flowchart we have a repetition structure, which is the `while` loop. The condition `keep_going == 'y'` is tested, and if it is true a series of statements are executed and the flow of execution returns to the point just above the conditional test.

Figure 3   Flowchart for Program 1

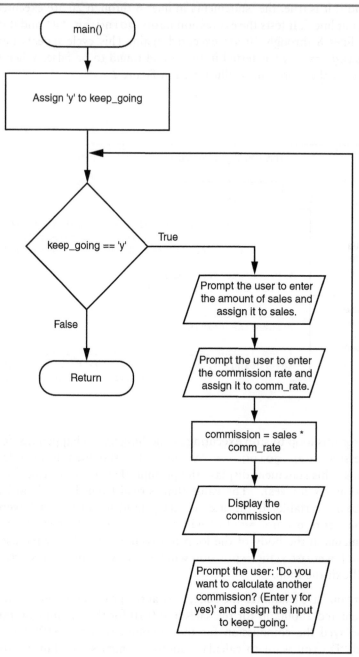

The while Loop is a Pretest Loop

The while loop is known as a *pretest* loop, which means it tests its condition *before* performing an iteration. Because the test is done at the beginning of the loop, you usually have to perform some steps prior to the loop to make sure that the loop executes at least once. For example, the loop in Program 1 starts like this:

```
while keep_going == 'y':
```

The loop will perform an iteration only if the expression `keep_going == 'y'` is true. This means that (a) the `keep_going` variable has to exist, and (b) it has to reference the value `'y'`. To make sure the expression is true the first time that the loop executes, we assigned the value `'y'` to the `keep_going` variable in line 4 as follows:

```
keep_going = 'y'
```

By performing this step we know that the condition `keep_going == 'y'` will be true the first time the loop executes. This is an important characteristic of the `while` loop: it will never execute if its condition is false to start with. In some programs, this is exactly what you want. The following *In the Spotlight* section gives an example.

In the Spotlight:
Designing a Program with a while Loop

A project currently underway at Chemical Labs, Inc. requires that a substance be continually heated in a vat. A technician must check the substance's temperature every 15 minutes. If the substance's temperature does not exceed 102.5 degrees Celsius, then the technician does nothing. However, if the temperature is greater than 102.5 degrees Celsius, the technician must turn down the vat's thermostat, wait 5 minutes, and check the temperature again. The technician repeats these steps until the temperature does not exceed 102.5 degrees Celsius. The director of engineering has asked you to write a program that guides the technician through this process.

Here is the algorithm:

1. Get the substance's temperature.
2. Repeat the following steps as long as the temperature is greater than 102.5 degrees Celsius:
   a. Tell the technician to turn down the thermostat, wait 5 minutes, and check the temperature again.
   b. Get the substance's temperature.
3. After the loop finishes, tell the technician that the temperature is acceptable and to check it again in 15 minutes.

After reviewing this algorithm, you realize that steps 2(a) and 2(b) should not be performed if the test condition (temperature is greater than 102.5) is false to begin with. The `while` loop will work well in this situation, because it will not execute even once if its condition is false. Program 2 shows the code for the program.

Program 2   (temperature.py)

```
 1   # This program assists a technician in the process
 2   # of checking a substance's temperature.
 3
 4   # MAX_TEMP is used as a global constant for
 5   # the maximum temperature.
 6   MAX_TEMP = 102.5
 7
 8   # The main function
 9   def main():
10       # Get the substance's temperature.
11       temperature = input("Enter the substance's Celsius temperature: ")
12
13       # As long as necessary, instruct the user to
14       # adjust the thermostat.
15       while temperature > MAX_TEMP:
16           print 'The temperature is too high.'
17           print 'Turn the thermostat down and wait'
18           print '5 minutes. Then take the temperature'
19           print 'again and enter it.'
20           temperature = input('Enter the new Celsius temperature: ')
21
22       # Remind the user to check the temperature again
23       # in 15 minutes.
24       print 'The temperature is acceptable.'
25       print 'Check it again in 15 minutes.'
26
27   # Call the main function.
28   main()
```

Program Output (with input shown in bold)

```
Enter the substance's Celsius temperature: 104.7 [Enter]
The temperature is too high.
Turn the thermostat down and wait
5 minutes. Take the temperature
again and enter it.
Enter the new Celsius temperature: 103.2 [Enter]
The temperature is too high.
Turn the thermostat down and wait
5 minutes. Take the temperature
again and enter it.
Enter the new Celsius temperature: 102.1 [Enter]
The temperature is acceptable.
Check it again in 15 minutes.
```

Program Output (with input shown in bold)

```
Enter the substance's Celsius temperature: 102.1 [Enter]
The temperature is acceptable.
Check it again in 15 minutes.
```

Infinite Loops

In all but rare cases, loops must contain within themselves a way to terminate. This means that something inside the loop must eventually make the test condition false. The loop in Program 1 stops when the expression `keep_going == 'y'` is false. If a loop does not have a way of stopping, it is called an infinite loop. An *infinite loop* continues to repeat until the program is interrupted. Infinite loops usually occur when the programmer forgets to write code inside the loop that makes the test condition false. In most circumstances you should avoid writing infinite loops.

Program 3 demonstrates an infinite loop. This is a modified version of the commission calculating program shown in Program 1. In this version, we have removed the code that modifies the `keep_going` variable in the body of the loop. Each time the expression `keep_going == 'y'` is tested in line 7, `keep_going` will reference the string 'y'. As a consequence, the loop has no way of stopping.

Program 3   (infinite.py)

```
1   # This program demonstrates an infinite loop.
2   def main():
3       # Create a variable to control the loop.
4       keep_going = 'y'
5
6       # Warning! Infinite loop!
7       while keep_going == 'y':
8           # Get a salesperson's sales and commission rate.
9           sales = input('Enter the amount of sales: ')
10          comm_rate = input('Enter the commission rate: ')
11
12          # Calculate the commission.
13          commission = sales * comm_rate
14
15          # Display the commission.
16          print 'The commission is $%.2f.' % commission
17
18  # Call the main function.
19  main()
```

Calling Functions in a Loop

Functions can be called from statements in the body of a loop. In fact, such code in a loop often improves the design. For example, in Program 1, the statements that get the amount of sales, calculate the commission, and display the commission can easily be placed in a function. That function can then be called in the loop. Program 4 shows how this might be done.

This program has a `main` function, which is called when the program runs, and a `show_commission` function that handles all of the steps related to calculating and displaying a commission. Figure 4 shows flowcharts for the `main` and `show_commission` functions.

Program 4   (commission2.py)

```
1   # This program calculates sales commissions.
2   def main():
3       # Create a variable to control the loop.
4       keep_going = 'y'
5
6       # Calculate a series of commissions.
7       while keep_going == 'y':
8           # Call the show_commission function to
9           # display a salesperson's commission.
10          show_commission()
11
12          # See if the user wants to do another one.
13          keep_going = raw_input('Do you want to calculate another ' + \
14                              'commission (Enter y for yes): ')
15
16  # The show_commission function gets the amount of
17  # sales and the commission rate, and then displays
18  # the amount of commission.
19  def show_commission():
20      # Get a salesperson's sales and commission rate.
21      sales = input('Enter the amount of sales: ')
22      comm_rate = input('Enter the commission rate: ')
23
24      # Calculate the commission.
25      commission = sales * comm_rate
26
27      # Display the commission.
28      print 'The commission is $%.2f.' % commission
29
30  # Call the main function.
31  main()
```

The output of this program is the same as that of Program 1

Figure 4 Flowcharts for the `main` and `show_commission` functions

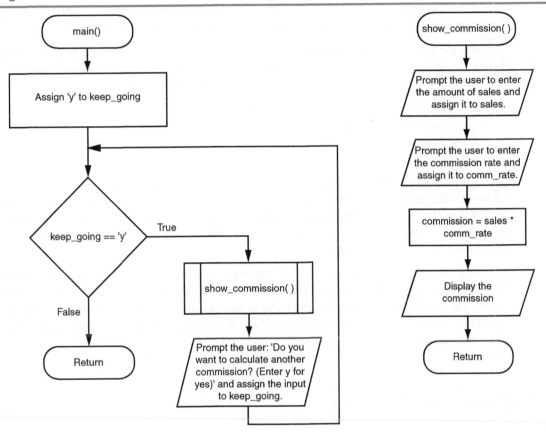

 Checkpoint

4 What is a loop iteration?

5 Does the `while` loop test its condition before or after it performs an iteration?

6 How many times will `'Hello World'` be printed in the following program?

```
count = 10
while count < 1:
        print 'Hello World'
```

7 What is an infinite loop?

The `for` Loop: a Count-Controlled Loop

CONCEPT: A count-controlled loop iterates a specific number of times. In Python you use the **for** statement to write a count-controlled loop.

As mentioned at the beginning of this chapter, a count-controlled loop iterates a specific number of times. Count-controlled loops are commonly used in programs. For example, suppose a business is open six days per week, and you are going to write a program that calculates the total sales for a week. You will need a loop that iterates exactly six times. Each time the loop iterates, it will prompt the user to enter the sales for one day.

You use the for statement to write a count-controlled loop. In Python, the for statement is designed to work with a sequence of data items. When the statement executes, it iterates once for each item in the sequence. Here is the general format:

```
for variable in [value1, value2, etc.]:
    statement
    statement
    etc.
```

We will refer to the first line as the *for clause*. In the for clause, *variable* is the name of a variable. Inside the brackets a sequence of values appears, with a comma separating each value. (In Python, a comma-separated sequence of data items that are enclosed in a set of brackets is called a *list*.) Beginning at the next line is a block of statements that is executed each time the loop iterates.

The for statement executes in the following manner: The *variable* is assigned the first value in the list, and then the statements that appear in the block are executed. Then, *variable* is assigned the next value in the list, and the statements in the block are executed again. This continues until *variable* has been assigned the last value in the list. Program 5 shows a simple example that uses a for loop to display the numbers 1 through 5.

Program 5 (simple_loop1.py)

```
1   # This program demonstrates a simple for loop
2   # that uses a list of numbers.
3
4   def main():
5       print 'I will display the numbers 1 through 5.'
6       for num in [1, 2, 3, 4, 5]:
7           print num
8
9   # Call the main function.
10  main()
```

Program Output
```
I will display the numbers 1 through 5.
1
2
3
4
5
```

The first time the for loop iterates, the num variable is assigned the value 1 and then the print statement in line 7 executes (displaying the value 1). The next time the loop iterates, num is assigned the value 2, and the print statement executes (displaying the value 2). This process continues, as shown in Figure 5, until num has been assigned the last value in the list. Because the list contains five values, the loop will iterate five times.

Python programmers commonly refer to the variable that is used in the for clause as the *target variable* because it is the target of an assignment at the beginning of each loop iteration.

Figure 5 The for loop

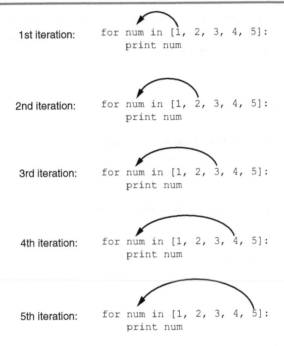

The values that appear in the list do not have to be a consecutively ordered series of numbers. For example, Program 6 uses a for loop to display a list of odd numbers. There are five numbers in the list, so the loop iterates five times.

Program 6   (simple_loop2.py)

```
1   # This program also demonstrates a simple for
2   # loop that uses a list of numbers.
3
4   def main():
5       print 'I will display the odd numbers 1 through 9.'
6       for num in [1, 3, 5, 7, 9]:
7           print num
8
9   # Call the main function.
10  main()
```

Program Output

```
I will display the odd numbers 1 through 9.
1
3
5
7
9
```

Program 7 shows another example. In this program the for loop iterates over a list of strings. Notice that the list (in line 5) contains the three strings 'Winken', 'Blinken', and 'Nod'. As a result, the loop iterates three times.

Program 7   (simple_loop3.py)

```
1   # This program also demonstrates a simple for
2   # loop that uses a list of numbers.
3
4   def main():
5       for name in ['Winken', 'Blinken', 'Nod']:
6           print name
7
8   # Call the main function.
9   main()
```

Program Output

```
Winken
Blinken
Nod
```

Using the range Function with the for Loop

Python provides a built-in function named range that simplifies the process of writing a count-controlled for loop. Here is an example of a for loop that uses the range function:

```
for num in range(5):
    print num
```

Notice that instead of using a list of values, we call to the range function passing 5 as an argument. In this statement the range function will generate a list of integers in the range of 0 up to (but not including) 5. This code works the same as the following:

```
for num in [0, 1, 2, 3, 4]:
    print num
```

As you can see, the list contains five numbers, so the loop will iterate five times. Program 8 uses the `range` function with a `for` loop to display "Hello world" five times.

Program 8   (simple_loop4.py)

```
1    # This program demonstrates how the range
2    # function can be used with a for loop.
3
4    def main():
5        # Print a message five times.
6        for x in range(5):
7            print 'Hello world!'
8
9    # Call the main function.
10   main()
```

Program Output

```
Hello world
Hello world
Hello world
Hello world
Hello world
```

If you pass one argument to the `range` function, as demonstrated in Program 8, that argument is used as the ending limit of the list. If you pass two arguments to the `range` function, the first argument is used as the starting value of the list and the second argument is used as the ending limit. Here is an example:

```
for num in range(1, 5):
    print num
```

This code will display the following:

```
1
2
3
4
```

By default, the `range` function produces a list of numbers that increase by 1 for each successive number in the list. If you pass a third argument to the `range` function, that argument is used as *step value*. Instead of increasing by 1, each successive number in the list will increase by the step value. Here is an example:

```
for num in range(1, 10, 2):
    print num
```

In this `for` statement, three arguments are passed to the `range` function:

- The first argument, 1, is the starting value for the list.
- The second argument, 10, is the ending limit of the list. This means that the last number in the list will be 9.

- The third argument, 2, is the step value. This means that 2 will be added to each successive number in the list.

This code will display the following:

```
1
3
5
7
9
```

Using the Target Variable Inside the Loop

In a `for` loop, the purpose of the target variable is to reference each item in a sequence of items as the loop iterates. In many situations it is helpful to use the target variable in a calculation or other task within the body of the loop. For example, suppose you need to write a program that displays the numbers 1 through 10 and their squares, in a table similar to the following:

Number	Square
1	1
2	4
3	9
4	16
5	25
6	36
7	49
8	64
9	81
10	100

This can be accomplished by writing a `for` loop that iterates over the values 1 through 10. During the first iteration, the target variable will be assigned the value 1, during the second iteration it will be assigned the value 2, and so forth. Because the target variable will reference the values 1 through 10 during the loop's execution, you can use it in the calculation inside the loop. Program 9 shows how this is done.

Program 9   (squares.py)

```
1  # This program uses a loop to display a
2  # table showing the numbers 1 through 10
3  # and their squares.
4
```

```
5   def main():
6       # Print the table headings.
7       print 'Number\tSquare'
8       print '--------------'
9
10      # Print the numbers 1 through 10
11      # and their squares.
12      for number in range(1, 11):
13          square = number**2
14          print number, '\t', square
15
16  # Call the main function.
17  main()
```

Program Output

```
Number  Square
--------------
1       1
2       4
3       9
4       16
5       25
6       36
7       49
8       64
9       81
10      100
```

First, take a closer look at line 7, which displays the table headings:

```
print 'Number\tSquare'
```

Notice that inside the string literal the \t escape sequence between the words Number and Square. The \t escape sequence is like pressing the Tab key; it causes the output cursor to move over to the next tab position. This causes the spaces that you see between the words Number and Square in the sample output.

The for loop that begins in line 12 uses the range function to produce a list containing the numbers 1 through 10. During the first iteration, number will reference 1, during the second iteration number will reference 2, and so forth, up to 10. Inside the loop, the statement in line 13 raises number to the power of 2 (recall that ** is the exponent operator), and assigns the result to the square variable. The statement in line 14 prints the value referenced by number, tabs over, and then prints the value referenced by square. (Tabbing over with the \t escape sequence causes the numbers to be aligned in two columns in the output.)

Figure 6 shows how we might draw a flowchart for this program.

Figure 6   Flowchart for Program 9

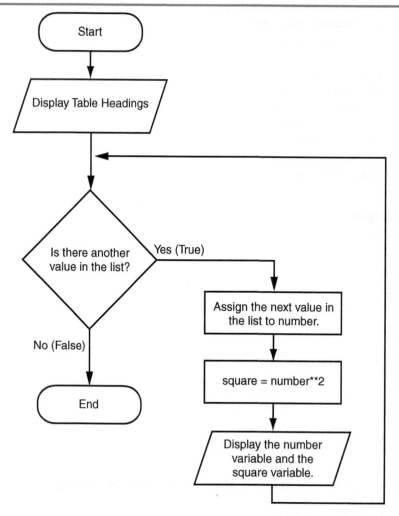

In the Spotlight:

Designing a Count-Controlled Loop with the `for` Statement

Your friend Amanda just inherited a European sports car from her uncle. Amanda lives in the United States, and she is afraid she will get a speeding ticket because the car's speedometer indicates kilometers per hour. She has asked you to write a program that displays a table of speeds in kilometers per hour with their values converted to miles per hour. The formula for converting kilometers per hour to miles per hour is:

$$MPH = KPH * 0.6214$$

In the formula, *MPH* is the speed in miles per hour and *KPH* is the speed in kilometers per hour.

The table that your program displays should show speeds from 60 kilometers per hour through 130 kilometers per hour, in increments of 10, along with their values converted to miles per hour. The table should look something like this:

KPH	MPH
60	37.284
70	43.498
80	49.712
etc. . . .	
130	80.782

After thinking about this table of values, you decide that you will write a for loop. The list of values that the loop will iterate over will be the kilometer-per-hour speeds. In the loop you will call the range function like this:

```
range(60, 131, 10)
```

The first value in the list will be 60. Notice that the third argument specifies 10 as the step value. This means that the numbers in the list will be 60, 70, 80, and so forth. The second argument specifies 131 as the list's ending limit, so the last number in the list will be 130.

Inside the loop you will use the target variable to calculate a speed in miles per hour. Program 10 shows the program.

Program 10   (speed_converter.py)

```
1   # This program converts the speeds 60 kph
2   # through 130 kph (in 10 kph increments)
3   # to mph.
4
5   def main():
6       # Print the table headings.
7       print 'kph\tmph'
8       print '----------------'
9
10      # Print the speeds.
11      for kph in range(60, 131, 10):
12          mph = kph * 0.6214
13          print kph, '\t', mph
14
15  # Call the main function.
16  main()
```

Program Output

```
kph       mph
----------------
60        37.284
70        43.498
80        49.712
90        55.926
100       62.14
110       68.354
120       74.568
130       80.782
```

Letting the User Control the Loop Iterations

In many cases, the programmer knows the exact number of iterations that a loop must perform. For example, recall Program 9, which displays a table showing the numbers 1 through 10 and their squares. When the code was written, the programmer knew that the loop had to iterate over the values 1 through 10.

Sometimes the programmer needs to let the user control the number of times that a loop iterates. For example, what if you want Program 9 to be a bit more versatile by allowing the user to specify the maximum value displayed by the loop? Program 11 shows how you can accomplish this.

Program 11   (user_squares.py)

```
1   # This program uses a loop to display a
2   # table of numbers and their squares.
3
4   def main():
5       # Get the ending limit.
6       print 'This program displays a list of numbers'
7       print '(starting at 1) and their squares.'
8       end = input('How high should I go? ')
9
10      # Print the table headings.
11      print 'Number\tSquare'
12      print '------------------'
13
14      # Print the numbers and their squares.
15      for number in range(1, end + 1):
16          square = number**2
17          print number, '\t', square
18
19  # Call the main function.
20  main()
```

Program Output (with input shown in bold)

```
This program displays a list of numbers
(starting at 1) and their squares.
How high should I go? 5 [Enter]
Number     Square
-----------------
1          1
2          4
3          9
4          16
5          25
```

This program asks the user to enter a value that can be used as the ending limit for the list. This value is assigned to the end variable in line 8. Then, the expression end + 1 is used in line 15 as the second argument for the range function. (We have to add one to end because otherwise the list would go up to, but not include, the value entered by the user.)

Program 12 shows an example that allows the user to specify both the starting value and the ending limit of the list.

Program 12   (user_squares2.py)

```
1   # This program uses a loop to display a
2   # table of numbers and their squares.
3
4   def main():
5       # Get the starting value.
6       print 'This program displays a list of numbers'
7       print 'and their squares.'
8       start = input('Enter the starting number: ')
9
10      # Get the ending limit.
11      end = input('How high should I go? ')
12
13      # Print the table headings.
14      print
15      print 'Number\tSquare'
16      print '--------------------'
17
18      # Print the numbers and their squares.
19      for number in range(start, end + 1):
20          square = number**2
21          print number, '\t', square
22
23  # Call the main function.
24  main()
```

Program Output (with input shown in bold)
```
This program displays a list of numbers
and their squares.
Enter the starting number: 5 [Enter]
How high should I go? 10 [Enter]
Number          Square
--------------------
5               25
6               36
7               49
8               64
9               81
10              100
```

Generating Lists that Range from Highest to Lowest

In the examples you have seen so far, the range function was used to generate a list with numbers that go from lowest to highest. Alternatively, you can use the range function to generate lists of numbers that go from highest to lowest. Here is an example:

```
range(10, 0, -1)
```

In this function call, the starting value is 10, the list's ending limit is 0, and the step value is −1. This expression will produce the following list:

```
[10, 9, 8, 7, 6, 5, 4, 3, 2, 1]
```

Here is an example of a for loop that prints the numbers 5 down to 1:

```
for num in range(5, 0, -1):
    print num
```

 Checkpoint

8 Rewrite the following code so it calls the range function instead of using the list [0,1, 2, 3, 4, 5].

```
for x in [0, 1, 2, 3, 4, 5]:
    print 'I love to program!'
```

9 What will the following code display?

```
for number in range(6):
    print number
```

10 What will the following code display?

```
for number in range(2, 6):
    print number
```

11 What will the following code display?

```
for number in range(0, 501, 100):
    print number
```

12 What will the following code display?

```
for number in range(10, 5, -1):
    print number
```

4 Calculating a Running Total

CONCEPT: A running total is a sum of numbers that accumulates with each itera-tion of a loop. The variable used to keep the running total is called an accumulator.

Many programming tasks require you to calculate the total of a series of numbers. For example, suppose you are writing a program that calculates a business's total sales for a week. The program would read the sales for each day as input and calculate the total of those numbers.

Programs that calculate the total of a series of numbers typically use two elements:

- A loop that reads each number in the series.
- A variable that accumulates the total of the numbers as they are read.

The variable that is used to accumulate the total of the numbers is called an *accumulator*. It is often said that the loop keeps a *running total* because it accumulates the total as it reads each number in the series. Figure 7 shows the general logic of a loop that calculates a running total.

Figure 7 Logic for calculating a running total

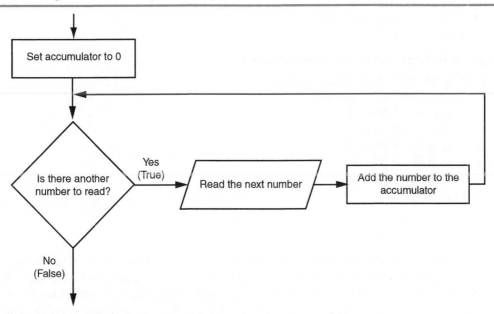

When the loop finishes, the accumulator will contain the total of the numbers that were read by the loop. Notice that the first step in the flowchart is to set the accumulator variable to 0. This is a critical step. Each time the loop reads a number, it adds it to the accumulator. If the accumulator starts with any value other than 0, it will not contain the correct total when the loop finishes.

Let's look at a program that calculates a running total. Program 13 allows the user to enter five numbers, and it displays the total of the numbers entered.

Program 13   (sum_numbers.py)

```
 1   # This program calculates the sum of
 2   # five numbers entered by the user.
 3
 4   def main():
 5       # Initialize an accumulator variable.
 6       total = 0.0
 7
 8       # Explain what we are doing.
 9       print 'This program calculates the sum of'
10       print 'five numbers you will enter.'
11
12       # Get five numbers and accumulate them.
13       for counter in range(5):
14           number = input('Enter a number: ')
15           total = total + number
16
17       # Display the total of the numbers.
18       print 'The total is', total
19
20   # Call the main function.
21   main()
```

Program Output (with input shown in bold)
```
This program calculates the sum of
five numbers you will enter.
Enter a number: 1 [Enter]
Enter a number: 2 [Enter]
Enter a number: 3 [Enter]
Enter a number: 4 [Enter]
Enter a number: 5 [Enter]
The total is 15.0
```

The total variable, created by the assignment statement in line 6, is the accumulator. Notice that it is initialized with the value 0.0. The for loop, in lines 13 through 15, does the work of getting the numbers from the user and calculating their total. Line 14 prompts the user to enter a number, and then assigns the input to the number variable. Then, the following statement in line 15 adds number to total:

```
total = total + number
```

After this statement executes, the value referenced by the number variable will be added to the value in the total variable. It's important that you understand how this statement works. First, the interpreter gets the value of the expression on the right side of the = operator, which is total + number. Then, that value is assigned by the = operator to the total variable. The effect of the statement is that the value of the number variable is added to the total variable. When the loop finishes, the total variable will hold the sum of all the numbers that were added to it. This value is displayed in line 18.

The Augmented Assignment Operators

Quite often, programs have assignment statements in which the variable that is on the left side of the = operator also appears on the right side of the = operator. Here is an example:

```
x = x + 1
```

On the right side of the assignment operator, 1 is added to x. The result is then assigned to x, replacing the value that x previously referenced. Effectively, this statement adds 1 to x. You saw another example of this type of statement in Program 14:

```
total = total + number
```

This statement assigns the value of total + number to total. As mentioned before, the effect of this statement is that number is added to the value of total. Here is one more example:

```
balance = balance - withdrawal
```

This statement assigns the value of the expression balance - withdrawal to balance. The effect of this statement is that withdrawal is subtracted from balance.

Table 1 shows other examples of statements written this way.

Table 1 Various assignment statements (assume x = 6 in each statement)

Statement	What It Does	Value of x after the Statement
x = x + 4	Add 4 to x	10
x = x - 3	Subtracts 3 from x	3
x = x * 10	Multiplies x by 10	60
x = x / 2	Divides x by 2	3
x = x % 4	Assigns the remainder of x / 4 to x	2

These types of operations are common in programming. For convenience, Python offers a special set of operators designed specifically for these jobs. Table 2 shows the *augmented assignment operators*.

Table 2 Augmented assignment operators

Operator	Example Usage	Equivalent To
+=	x += 5	x = x + 5
-=	y -= 2	y = y - 2
*=	z *= 10	z = z * 10
/=	a /= b	a = a / b
%=	c %= 3	c = c % 3

As you can see, the augmented assignment operators do not require the programmer to type the variable name twice. The following statement:

```
total = total + number
```

could be rewritten as

```
total += number
```

Similarly, the statement

```
balance = balance — withdrawal
```

could be rewritten as

```
balance —= withdrawal;
```

 Checkpoint

13 What is an accumulator?

14 Should an accumulator be initialized to any specific value? Why or why not?

15 What will the following code display?

```
total = 0
for count in range(1, 6):
    total = total + count
print total
```

16 What will the following code display?

```
number1 = 10
number2 = 5
number1 = number1 + number2
print number1
print number2
```

17 Rewrite the following statements using augmented assignment operators:

```
a) quantity = quantity + 1
b) days_left = days_left — 5
c) price = price * 10
d) price = price / 2
```

5   Sentinels

CONCEPT: A sentinel is a special value that marks the end of a sequence of values.

Consider the following scenario: You are designing a program that will use a loop to process a long sequence of values. At the time you are designing the program, you do not know the number of values that will be in the sequence. In fact, the number of values in the sequence could be different each time the program is executed. What is the best way to design such a loop? Here are some techniques that you have seen already in this chapter, along with the disadvantages of using them when processing a long list of values:

- Simply ask the user, at the end of each loop iteration, if there is another value to process. If the sequence of values is long, however, asking this question at the end of each loop iteration might make the program cumbersome for the user.
- Ask the user at the beginning of the program how many items are in the sequence. This might also inconvenience the user, however. If the sequence is very long, and the user does not know the number of items it contains, it will require the user to count them.

When processing a long sequence of values with a loop, perhaps a better technique is to use a sentinel. A *sentinel* is a special value that marks the end of a sequence of items. When a program reads the sentinel value, it knows it has reached the end of the sequence, so the loop terminates.

For example, suppose a doctor wants a program to calculate the average weight of all her patients. The program might work like this: A loop prompts the user to enter either a patient's weight, or 0 if there are no more weights. When the program reads 0 as a weight, it interprets this as a signal that there are no more weights. The loop ends and the program displays the average weight.

A sentinel value must be distinctive enough that it will not be mistaken as a regular value in the sequence. In the example cited above, the doctor (or her medical assistant) enters 0 to signal the end of the sequence of weights. Because no patient's weight will be 0, this is a good value to use as a sentinel.

In the Spotlight:
Using a Sentinel

The county tax office calculates the annual taxes on property using the following formula:

$$property\ tax = property\ value \times 0.0065$$

Every day, a clerk in the tax office gets a list of properties and has to calculate the tax for each property on the list. You have been asked to design a program that the clerk can use to perform these calculations.

In your interview with the tax clerk, you learn that each property is assigned a lot number, and all lot numbers are 1 or greater. You decide to write a loop that uses the number 0 as a sentinel value. During each loop iteration, the program will ask the clerk to enter either a property's lot number, or 0 to end. The code for the program is shown in Program 15.

Program 14   (property_tax.py)

```
1    # This program displays property taxes.
2
3    # TAX_FACTOR is used as a global constant
4    # for the tax factor.
5    TAX_FACTOR = 0.0065
6
7    # The main function.
8    def main():
```

(program continues)

Program 14   *(continued)*

```
 9        # Get the first lot number.
10        print "Enter the property's lot number"
11        print "or enter 0 to end."
12        lot = input("Lot number: ")
13
14        # Continue processing as long as the user
15        # does not enter lot number 0.
16        while lot != 0:
17            # Show the tax for the property.
18            show_tax()
19
20            # Get the next lot number.
21            print "Enter the next lot number or"
22            print "enter 0 to end."
23            lot = input("Lot number: ")
24
25    # The show_tax function gets a property's
26    # value and displays its tax.
27    def show_tax():
28        # Get the property value.
29        value = input("Enter the property's value: ")
30
31        # Calculate the property's tax.
32        tax = value * TAX_FACTOR
33
34        # Display the tax.
35        print "The property's tax is $%.2f." % tax
36
37    # Call the main function.
38    main()
```

Program Output (with input shown in bold)

```
Enter the property's lot number
or enter 0 to end.
Lot number: 100 [Enter]
Enter the property's value: 100000.00 [Enter]
The property's tax is $650.00.
Enter the next lot number or
enter 0 to end.
Lot number: 200 [Enter]
Enter the property's value: 5000.00 [Enter]
The property's tax is $32.50.
Enter the next lot number or
enter 0 to end.
Lot number: 0 [Enter]
```

Checkpoint

18   What is a sentinel?

19   Why should you take care to choose a distinctive value as a sentinel?

6   **Input Validation Loops**

CONCEPT: Input validation is the process of inspecting data that has been input to a program, to make sure it is valid before it is used in a computation. Input validation is commonly done with a loop that iterates as long as an input variable references bad data.

One of the most famous sayings among computer programmers is "garbage in, garbage out." This saying, sometimes abbreviated as *GIGO*, refers to the fact that computers cannot tell the difference between good data and bad data. If a user provides bad data as input to a program, the program will process that bad data and, as a result, will produce bad data as output. For example, look at the payroll program in Program 15 and notice what happens in the sample run when the user gives bad data as input.

Program 15   (gross_pay.py)

```
 1  # This program displays gross pay.
 2  def main():
 3      # Get the number of hours worked.
 4      hours = input('Enter the hours worked this week: ')
 5
 6      # Get the hourly pay rate.
 7      pay_rate = input('Enter the hourly pay rate: ')
 8
 9      # Calculate the gross pay.
10      gross_pay = hours * pay_rate
11
12      # Display the gross pay.
13      print 'The gross pay is $%.2f.' % gross_pay
14
15  # Call the main function.
16  main()
```

Program Output (with input shown in bold)
```
Enter the hours worked this week: 400 [Enter]
Enter the hourly pay rate: 20 [Enter]
The gross pay is $8000.00
```

Did you spot the bad data that was provided as input? The person receiving the paycheck will be pleasantly surprised, because in the sample run the payroll clerk entered 400 as the number of hours worked. The clerk probably meant to enter 40, because there are not 400 hours in a week. The computer, however, is unaware of this fact, and the program processed the bad data just as if it were good data. Can you think of other types of input that can be given to this program that will result in bad output? One example is a negative number entered for the hours worked; another is an invalid hourly pay rate.

Sometimes stories are reported in the news about computer errors that mistakenly cause people to be charged thousands of dollars for small purchases or to receive large tax refunds that they were not entitled to. These "computer errors" are rarely caused by the computer, however; they are more commonly caused by bad data that was read into a program as input.

The integrity of a program's output is only as good as the integrity of its input. For this reason, you should design your programs in such a way that bad input is never accepted. When input is given to a program, it should be inspected before it is processed. If the input is invalid, the program should discard it and prompt the user to enter the correct data. This process is known as *input validation*.

Figure 8 shows a common technique for validating an item of input. In this technique, the input is read, and then a loop is executed. If the input data is bad, the loop executes its block of statements. The loop displays an error message so the user will know that the input was invalid, and then it reads the new input. The loop repeats as long as the input is bad.

Figure 8   Logic containing an input validation loop

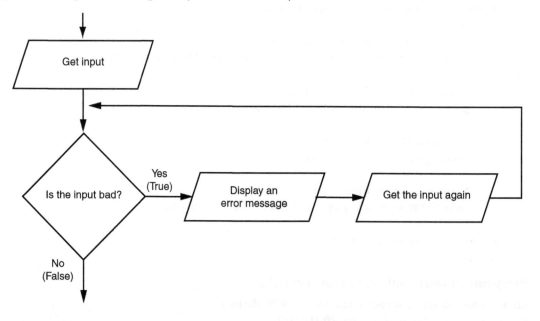

Notice that the flowchart in Figure 8 reads input in two places: first just before the loop and then inside the loop. The first input operation—just before the loop—is called a *priming read*, and its purpose is to get the first input value that will be tested by the validation loop. If that value is invalid, the loop will perform subsequent input operations.

Let's consider an example. Suppose you are designing a program that reads a test score and you want to make sure the user does not enter a value less than 0. The following code shows how you can use an input validation loop to reject any input value that is less than 0.

```
# Get a test score.
score = input('Enter a test score: ')

# Make sure it is not less than 0.
while score < 0:
    print 'ERROR: The score cannot be negative.'
    score = input ('Enter the correct score: ')
```

This code first prompts the user to enter a test score (this is the priming read), and then the while loop executes. Recall that the while loop is a pretest loop, which means it tests the expression score < 0 before performing an iteration. If the user entered a valid test score, this expression will be false and the loop will not iterate. If the test score is invalid, however, the expression will be true and the loop's block of statements will execute. The loop displays an error message and prompts the user to enter the correct test score. The loop will continue to iterate until the user enters a valid test score.

NOTE: An input validation loop is sometimes called an *error trap* or an *error handler*.

This code rejects only negative test scores. What if you also want to reject any test scores that are greater than 100? You can modify the input validation loop so it uses a compound Boolean expression, as shown next.

```
# Get a test score.
score = input('Enter a test score: ')

# Make sure it is not less than 0 or greater than 100.
while score < 0 or score > 100:
    print 'ERROR: The score cannot be negative'
    print 'or greater than 100.'
    score = input('Enter the correct score: ')
```

The loop in this code determines whether score is less than 0 or greater than 100. If either is true, an error message is displayed and the user is prompted to enter a correct score.

In the Spotlight:
Writing an Input Validation Loop

Samantha owns an import business and she calculates the retail prices of her products with the following formula:

$$retail\ price = wholesale\ cost \times 2.5$$

She currently uses the program shown in Program 16 to calculate retail prices.

Program 16   (retail_no_validation.py)

```
 1   # This program calculates retail prices.
 2
 3   # MARK_UP is used as a global constant for
 4   # the markup up percentage.
 5   MARK_UP = 2.5
 6
 7   # The main function
 8   def main():
 9       # Variable to control the loop.
10       another = 'y'
11
12       # Process one or more items.
13       while another == 'y' or another == 'Y':
14           # Display an item's retail price.
15           show_retail()
16
17           # Do this again?
18           another = raw_input('Do you have another item? ' + \
19                               '(Enter y for yes): ')
20
21   # The show_retail function gets an item's wholesale
22   # cost and displays the item's retail price.
23   def show_retail():
24       # Get the item's wholesale cost.
25       wholesale = input("Enter the item's wholesale cost: ")
26
27       # Calculate the retail price.
28       retail = wholesale * MARK_UP
29
30       # Display the retail price.
31       print 'The retail price is $%.2f.' % retail
32
33   # Call the main function.
34   main()
```

Program Output (with input shown in bold)

```
Enter the item's wholesale cost: 10.00 [Enter]
The retail price is $25.00.
Do you have another item? (Enter y for yes): y [Enter]
Enter the item's wholesale cost: 15.00 [Enter]
The retail price is $37.50.
Do you have another item? (Enter y for yes): y [Enter]
Enter the item's wholesale cost: 12.50 [Enter]
The retail price is $31.25.
Do you have another item? (Enter y for yes): n [Enter]
```

Samantha has encountered a problem when using the program, however. Some of the items that she sells have a wholesale cost of 50 cents, which she enters into the program as 0.50. Because the 0 key is next to the key for the negative sign, she sometimes accidentally enters a negative number. She has asked you to modify the program so it will not allow a negative number to be entered for the wholesale cost.

You decide to add an input validation loop to the show_retail function that rejects any negative numbers that are entered into the wholesale variable. Program 17 shows the revised program, with the new input validation code shown in lines 27 through 30.

Program 17   (retail_with_validation.py)

```
1   # This program calculates retail prices.
2
3   # MARK_UP is used as a global constant for
4   # the markup up percentage.
5   MARK_UP = 2.5
6
7   # The main function
8   def main():
9       # Variable to control the loop.
10      another = 'y'
11
12      # Process one or more items.
13      while another == 'y' or another == 'Y':
14          # Display an item's retail price.
15          show_retail()
16
17          # Do this again?
18          another = raw_input('Do you have another item? ' + \
19                          '(Enter y for yes): ')
20
21  # The show_retail function gets an item's wholesale
22  # cost and displays the item's retail price.
23  def show_retail():
24      # Get the item's wholesale cost.
25      wholesale = input("Enter the item's wholesale cost: ")
26
27      # Validate the wholesale cost.
28      while wholesale < 0:
29          print 'ERROR: the cost cannot be negative.'
30          wholesale = input('Enter the correct wholesale cost: ')
31
32      # Calculate the retail price.
33      retail = wholesale * MARK_UP
34
35      # Display the retail price.
36      print 'The retail price is $%.2f.' % retail
37
```

(program continues)

Program 17   *(continued)*

```
38  # Call the main function.
39  main()
```

Program Output (with input shown in bold)

Enter the item's wholesale cost: **-.50 [Enter]**
ERROR: the cost cannot be negative.
Enter the correct wholesale cost: **0.50 [Enter]**
The retail price is $1.25.
Do you have another item? (Enter y for yes): **n [Enter]**

 Checkpoint

20 What does the phrase "garbage in, garbage out" mean?

21 Give a general description of the input validation process.

22 Describe the steps that are generally taken when an input validation loop is used to validate data.

23 What is a priming read? What is its purpose?

24 If the input that is read by the priming read is valid, how many times will the input validation loop iterate?

7   Nested Loops

CONCEPT: A loop that is inside another loop is called a nested loop.

A nested loop is a loop that is inside another loop. A clock is a good example of something that works like a nested loop. The second hand, minute hand, and hour hand all spin around the face of the clock. The hour hand, however, only makes 1 revolution for every 12 of the minute hand's revolutions. And it takes 60 revolutions of the second hand for the minute hand to make 1 revolution. This means that for every complete revolution of the hour hand, the second hand has revolved 720 times. Here is a loop that partially simulates a digital clock. It displays the seconds from 0 to 59:

```
for seconds in range(60):
    print seconds
```

We can add a minutes variable and nest the loop above inside another loop that cycles through 60 minutes:

```
for minutes in range(60):
    for seconds in range(60):
        print minutes, ':', seconds
```

To make the simulated clock complete, another variable and loop can be added to count the hours:

```
for hours in range(24):
    for minutes in range(60):
        for seconds in range(60):
            print hours, ':', minutes, ':', seconds
```

This code's output would be:

```
0:0:0
0:0:1
0:0:2
```

(The program will count through each second of 24 hours.)

```
23:59:59
```

The innermost loop will iterate 60 times for each iteration of the middle loop. The middle loop will iterate 60 times for each iteration of the outermost loop. When the outermost loop has iterated 24 times, the middle loop will have iterated 1440 times and the innermost loop will have iterated 86,400 times! Figure 9 shows a flowchart for the complete clock simulation program previously shown.

Figure 9 Flowchart for a clock simulator

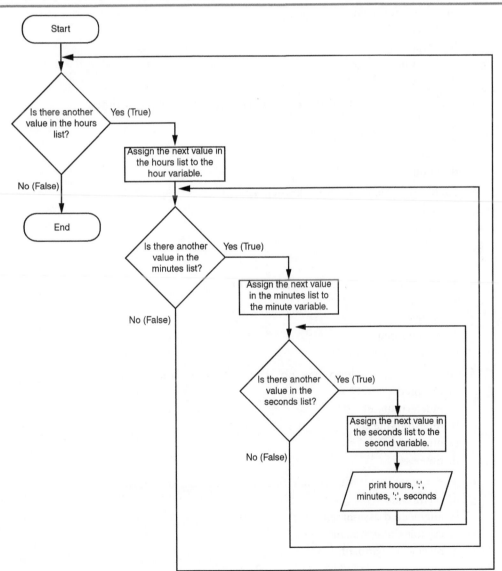

The simulated clock example brings up a few points about nested loops:

- An inner loop goes through all of its iterations for every single iteration of an outer loop.
- Inner loops complete their iterations faster than outer loops.
- To get the total number of iterations of a nested loop, multiply the number of iterations of all the loops.

Review Questions

Multiple Choice

1. A _____ -controlled loop uses a true/false condition to control the number of times that it repeats.
   a. Boolean
   b. condition
   c. decision
   d. count

2. A _____ -controlled loop repeats a specific number of times.
   a. Boolean
   b. condition
   c. decision
   d. count

3. Each repetition of a loop is known as a(n) _____.
   a. cycle
   b. revolution
   c. orbit
   d. iteration

4. The while loop is a _____ type of loop.
   a. pretest
   b. no-test
   c. prequalified
   d. post iterative

5. A(n) _____ loop has no way of ending and repeats until the program is interrupted.
   a. indeterminate
   b. interminable
   c. infinite
   d. timeless

6. The -= operator is an example of a(n) _____ operator.
   a. relational
   b. augmented assignment
   c. complex assignment
   d. reverse assignment

7. A(n) _____ variable keeps a running total.
   a. sentinel
   b. sum
   c. total
   d. accumulator

8. A(n) _____ is a special value that signals when there are no more items from a list of items to be processed. This value cannot be mistaken as an item from the list.
   a. sentinel
   b. flag
   c. signal
   d. accumulator

9. GIGO stands for
   a. great input, great output
   b. garbage in, garbage out
   c. GIGahertz Output
   d. GIGabyte Operation

10. The integrity of a program's output is only as good as the integrity of the program's
    a. compiler
    b. programming language
    c. input
    d. debugger

11. The input operation that appears just before a validation loop is known as the
    a. prevalidation read
    b. primordial read
    c. initialization read
    d. priming read

12. Validation loops are also known as
    a. error traps
    b. doomsday loops
    c. error avoidance loops
    d. defensive loops

True or False

1. A condition-controlled loop always repeats a specific number of times.

2. The `while` loop is a pretest loop.

3. The following statement subtracts 1 from x: `x = x - 1`

4. It is not necessary to initialize accumulator variables.

5. In a nested loop, the inner loop goes through all of its iterations for every single iteration of the outer loop.

6. To calculate the total number of iterations of a nested loop, add the number of iterations of all the loops.

7. The process of input validation works as follows: when the user of a program enters invalid data, the program should ask the user "Are you sure you meant to enter that?" If the user answers "yes," the program should accept the data.

Short Answer

1. What is a condition-controlled loop?
2. What is a count-controlled loop?
3. What is an infinite loop? Write the code for an infinite loop.
4. Why is it critical that accumulator variables are properly initialized?
5. What is the advantage of using a sentinel?
6. Why must the value chosen for use as a sentinel be carefully selected?
7. What does the phrase "garbage in, garbage out" mean?
8. Give a general description of the input validation process.

Algorithm Workbench

1. Write a `while` loop that lets the user enter a number. The number should be multiplied by 10, and the result assigned to a variable named `product`. The loop should iterate as long as `product` is less than 100.

2. Write a `while` loop that asks the user to enter two numbers. The numbers should be added and the sum displayed. The loop should ask the user if he or she wishes to perform the operation again. If so, the loop should repeat, otherwise it should terminate.

3. Write a `for` loop that displays the following set of numbers:

   `0, 10, 20, 30, 40, 50 . . . 1000`

4. Write a loop that asks the user to enter a number. The loop should iterate 10 times and keep a running total of the numbers entered.

5. Write a loop that calculates the total of the following series of numbers:

$$\frac{1}{30} + \frac{2}{29} + \frac{3}{28} + ... \frac{30}{1}$$

6. Rewrite the following statements using augmented assignment operators.
   a. `x = x + 1`
   b. `x = x * 2`
   c. `x = x / 10`
   d. `x = x - 100`

7. Write a set of nested loops that display 10 rows of # characters. There should be 15 # characters in each row.

8. Write code that prompts the user to enter a positive nonzero number and validates the input.

9. Write code that prompts the user to enter a number in the range of 1 through 100 and validates the input.

Programming Exercises

1. Bug Collector

A bug collector collects bugs every day for seven days. Write a program that keeps a running total of the number of bugs collected during the seven days. The loop should ask for the number of bugs collected for each day, and when the loop is finished, the program should display the total number of bugs collected.

2. Calories Burned

Running on a particular treadmill you burn 3.9 calories per minute. Write a program that uses a loop to display the number of calories burned after 10, 15, 20, 25, and 30 minutes.

3. Budget Analysis

Write a program that asks the user to enter the amount that he or she has budgeted for a month. A loop should then prompt the user to enter each of his or her expenses for the month, and keep a running total. When the loop finishes, the program should display the amount that the user is over or under budget.

4. Distance Traveled

The distance a vehicle travels can be calculated as follows:

$$distance = speed \times time$$

For example, if a train travels 40 miles per hour for three hours, the distance traveled is 120 miles. Write a program that asks the user for the speed of a vehicle (in miles per hour) and the number of hours it has traveled. It should then use a loop to display the distance the vehicle has traveled for each hour of that time period. Here is an example of the desired output:

```
What is the speed of the vehicle in mph? 40 [Enter]
How many hours has it traveled? 3 [Enter]
Hour              Distance Traveled
  1                      40
  2                      80
  3                     120
```

5. Average Rainfall

Write a program that uses nested loops to collect data and calculate the average rainfall over a period of years. The program should first ask for the number of years. The outer loop will iterate once for each year. The inner loop will iterate twelve times, once for each month. Each iteration of the inner loop will ask the user for the inches of rainfall for that month. After all iterations, the program should display the number of months, the total inches of rainfall, and the average rainfall per month for the entire period.

6. Celsius to Fahrenheit Table

Write a program that displays a table of the Celsius temperatures 0 through 20 and their Fahrenheit equivalents. The formula for converting a temperature from Celsius to Fahrenheit is

$$F = \frac{9}{5}C + 32$$

where F is the Fahrenheit temperature and C is the Celsius temperature. Your program must use a loop to display the table.

7. Pennies for Pay

Write a program that calculates the amount of money a person would earn over a period of time if his or her salary is one penny the first day, two pennies the second day, and continues to double each day. The program should ask the user for the number of days. Display a table showing what the salary was for each day, and then show the total pay at the end of the period. The output should be displayed in a dollar amount, not the number of pennies.

8. Sum of Numbers

Write a program with a loop that asks the user to enter a series of positive numbers. The user should enter a negative number to signal the end of the series. After all the positive numbers have been entered, the program should display their sum.

17

Value-Returning Functions and Modules

TOPICS

1 Introduction to Value-Returning Functions: Generating Random Numbers

CONCEPT: A value-returning function is a function that returns a value back to the part of the program that called it. Python, as well as most other programming languages, provides a library of prewritten functions that perform commonly needed tasks. These libraries typically contain a function that generates random numbers.

A simple function is a group of statements that exist within a program for the purpose of performing a specific task. When you need the function to perform its task, you call the function. This causes the statements inside the function to execute. When the function is finished, control of the program returns to the statement appearing immediately after the function call.

A *value-returning function* is a special type of function. It is like a simple function in the following ways.

- It is a group of statements that perform a specific task.
- When you want to execute the function, you call it.

When a value-returning function finishes, however, it returns a value back to the part of the program that called it. The value that is returned from a function can be used like any other value: it can be assigned to a variable, displayed on the screen, used in a mathematical expression (if it is a number), and so on.

Standard Library Functions

Python, as well as most other programming languages, comes with a *standard library* of functions that have already been written for you. These functions, known as *library functions,* make a programmer's job easier because they perform many of the tasks that programmers commonly need to perform. In fact, you have already used several of Python's library functions. Some of the functions that you have used are `input`, `raw_input`, and `range`. Python has many other library functions. Although we won't cover them all in this book, we will discuss library functions that perform fundamental operations.

Some of Python's library functions are built into the Python interpreter. If you want to use one of these built-in functions in a program, you simply call the function. This is the case with the `input`, `raw_input`, `range`, and other functions that you have already learned about. Many of the functions in the standard library, however, are stored in files that are known as *modules*. These modules, which are copied to your computer when you install Python, help organize the standard library functions. For example, functions for performing math operations are stored together in a module, functions for working with files are stored together in another module, and so on. In order to call a function that is stored in a module, you have to write an `import` statement at the top of your program. An `import` statement tells the interpreter the name of the module that contains the function.

Because you do not see the internal workings of library functions, many programmers think of them as *black boxes*. The term "black box" is used to describe any mechanism that accepts input, performs some operation (that cannot be seen) using the input, and produces output. Figure 1 illustrates this idea.

Figure 1   A library function viewed as a black box

This section demonstrates how functions work by looking at standard library functions that generate random numbers, and some interesting programs that can be written with them. Then you will learn to write your own value-returning functions and how to create your own modules. The last section in this chapter comes back to the topic of library functions and looks at several other useful functions in the Python standard library.

Generating Random Numbers

Random numbers are useful for lots of different programming tasks. The following are just a few examples.

- Random numbers are commonly used in games. For example, computer games that let the player roll dice use random numbers to represent the values of the dice. Programs that show cards being drawn from a shuffled deck use random numbers to represent the face values of the cards.
- Random numbers are useful in simulation programs. In some simulations, the computer must randomly decide how a person, animal, insect, or other living being will

behave. Formulas can be constructed in which a random number is used to determine various actions and events that take place in the program.

- Random numbers are useful in statistical programs that must randomly select data for analysis.
- Random numbers are commonly used in computer security to encrypt sensitive data.

Python provides several library functions for working with random numbers. These functions are stored in a module named `random` in the standard library. To use any of these functions you first need to write this `import` statement at the top of your program:

```
import random
```

This statement causes the interpreter to load the contents of the `random` module into memory. This makes all of the functions in the `random` module available to your program[1]

The first random-number generating function that we will discuss is named `randint`. Because the `randint` function is in the `random` module, we will need to use *dot notation* to refer to it in our program. In dot notation, the function's name is `random.randint`. On the left side of the dot (period) is the name of the module, and on the right side of the dot is the name of the function.

The following statement shows an example of how you might call the `randint` function.

```
number = random.randint(1, 100)
```

The part of the statement that reads `random.randint(1, 100)` is a call to the `randint` function. Notice that two arguments appear inside the parentheses: 1 and 100. These arguments tell the function to give an integer random number in the range of 1 through 100. (The values 1 and 100 are included in the range.) Figure 2 illustrates this part of the statement.

Figure 2   A statement that calls the random function

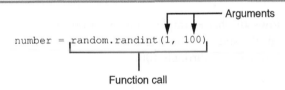

Notice that the call to the `randint` function appears on the right side of an = operator. When the function is called, it will generate a random number in the range of 1 through 100 and then *return* that number. The number that is returned will be assigned to the `number` variable, as shown in Figure 3.

Program 1 shows a complete program that uses the `randint` function. The statement in line 2 generates a random number in the range of 1 through 10 and assigns it to the `number` variable. (The program output shows that the number 7 was generated, but this value is arbitrary. If this were an actual program, it could display any number from 1 to 10.)

---

[1]There are several ways to write an `import` statement in Python, and each variation works a little differently. Many Python programmers agree that the preferred way to import a module is the way shown in this book.

Figure 3   The random function returns a value

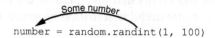

```
number = random.randint(1, 100)
```

A random number in the range of
1 through 100 will be assigned to
the number variable.

Program 1   (random_numbers.py)

```
 1  # This program displays a random number
 2  # in the range of 1 through 10.
 3  import random
 4
 5  def main():
 6      # Get a random number.
 7      number = random.randint(1, 10)
 8      # Display the number.
 9      print 'The number is', number
10
11  # Call the main function.
12  main()
```

Program Output

```
The number is 7
```

Program 2 shows another example. This program uses a for loop that iterates five times. Inside the loop, the statement in line 8 calls the randint function to generate a random number in the range of 1 through 100.

Program 2   (random_numbers2.py)

```
 1  # This program displays five random
 2  # numbers in the range of 1 through 100.
 3  import random
 4
 5  def main():
 6      for count in range(5):
 7          # Get a random number.
 8          number = random.randint(1, 100)
 9          # Display the number.
10          print number
11
12  # Call the main function.
13  main()
```

Program Output

```
89
7
16
41
12
```

Both Programs 1 and 2 call the `randint` function and assign its return value to the number variable. If you just want to display a random number, it is not necessary to assign the random number to a variable. You can send the `random` function's return value directly to the `print` statement, as shown here:

```
print random.randint(1, 10)
```

When this statement executes, the `randint` function is called. The function generates a random number in the range of 1 through 10. That value is returned and then sent to the `print` statement. As a result, a random number in the range of 1 through 10 will be displayed. Figure 4 illustrates this.

Figure 4   Displaying a random number

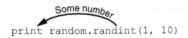

```
print random.randint(1, 10)
```

A random number in the range of
1 through 10 will be displayed.

Program 3 shows how you could simplify Program 2. This program also displays five random numbers, but this program does not use a variable to hold those numbers. The `randint` function's return value is sent directly to the `print` statement in line 7.

Program 3   (random_numbers3.py)

```
1   # This program displays five random
2   # numbers in the range of 1 through 100.
3   import random
4
5   def main():
6       for count in range(5):
7           print random.randint(1, 100)
8
9   # Call the main function.
10  main()
```

Program Output

```
89
7
16
41
12
```

In the Spotlight:
Using Random Numbers

Dr. Kimura teaches an introductory statistics class, and has asked you to write a program that he can use in class to simulate the rolling of dice. The program should randomly generate two numbers in the range of 1 through 6 and display them. In your interview with Dr. Kimura, you learn that he would like to use the program to simulate several rolls of the dice, one after the other. Here is the pseudocode for the program:

While the user wants to roll the dice:
  Display a random number in the range of 1 through 6
  Display another random number in the range of 1 through 6
  Ask the user if he or she wants to roll the dice again

You will `write` a while loop that simulates one roll of the dice, and then asks the user if another roll should be performed. As long as the user answers "y" for yes, the loop will repeat. Program 4 shows the program.

Program 4   (dice.py)

```
 1   # This program simulates the rolling of dice.
 2   import random
 3
 4   def main():
 5       # Create a variable to control the loop.
 6       again = 'y'
 7
 8       # Simulate rolling the dice.
 9       while again == 'y' or again == 'Y':
10           print 'Rolling the dice...'
11           print 'Their values are:'
12           print random.randint(1, 6)
13           print random.randint(1, 6)
14
15           # Do another roll of the dice?
16           again = raw_input('Roll them again? (y = yes): ')
17
18   # Call the main function.
19   main()
```

Program Output (with input shown in bold)
```
Rolling the dice...
Their values are:
3
1
Roll them again? (y = yes): y [Enter]
Rolling the dice...
```

```
Their values are:
1
1
Roll them again? (y = yes): y [Enter]
Rolling the dice...
Their values are:
5
6
Roll them again? (y = yes): y [Enter]
```

The randint function returns an integer value, so you can write a call to the function anywhere that you can write an integer value. You have already seen examples where the function's return value is assigned to a variable and where the function's return value is sent to the print statement. To further illustrate the point, here is a statement that uses the randint function in a math expression:

```
x = random.randint(1, 10) * 2
```

In this statement, a random number in the range of 1 through 10 is generated and then multiplied by 2. The result is a random integer from 2 to 20 assigned to the x variable. You can also test the return value of the function with an if statement, as demonstrated in the following In the Spotlight section.

In the Spotlight:
Using Random Numbers to Represent Other Values

Dr. Kimura was so happy with the dice rolling simulator that you wrote for him, he has asked you to write one more program. He would like a program that he can use to simulate ten coin tosses, one after the other. Each time the program simulates a coin toss, it should randomly display either "Heads" or "Tails".

You decide that you can simulate the tossing of a coin by randomly generating a number in the range of 1 through 2. You will write an if statement that displays "Heads" if the random number is 1, or "Tails" otherwise. Here is the pseudocode:

Repeat 10 times:
    If a random number in the range of 1 through 2 equals 1 then:
        Display 'Heads'
    Else:
        Display 'Tails'

Because the program should simulate 10 tosses of a coin you decide to use a for loop. The program is shown in Program 5.

Program 5   (coin_toss.py)

```
 1   # This program simulates 10 tosses of a coin.
 2   import random
 3
 4   def main():
 5       for toss in range(10):
 6           # Simulate the coin toss.
 7           if random.randint(1, 2) == 1:
 8               print 'Heads'
 9           else:
10               print 'Tails'
11
12   # Call the main function.
13   main()
```

Program Output

```
Tails
Tails
Heads
Tails
Heads
Heads
Heads
Tails
Heads
Tails
```

The `randrange`, `random`, and `uniform` Functions

The standard library's `random` module contains numerous functions for working with random numbers. In addition to the `randint` function, you might find the `randrange`, `random`, and `uniform` functions useful. (To use any of these functions you need to write `import random` at the top of your program.)

If you remember how to use the `range` function then you will immediately be comfortable with the `randrange` function. The `randrange` function takes the same arguments as the `range` function. The difference is that the `randrange` function does not return a list of values. Instead, it returns a randomly selected value from a sequence of values. For example, the following statement assigns a random number in the range of 0 through 9 to the number variable:

```
number = random.randrange(10)
```

The argument, in this case 10, specifies the ending limit of the sequence of values. The function will return a randomly-selected number from the sequence of values 0 up to, but not including, the ending limit. The following statement specifies both a starting value and an ending limit for the sequence:

```
number = random.randrange(5, 10)
```

When this statement executes, a random number in the range of 5 through 9 will be assigned to number. The following statement specifies a starting value, an ending limit, and a step value:

```
number = random.randrange(0, 101, 10)
```

In this statement the randrange function returns a randomly selected value from the following sequence of numbers:

```
[0, 10, 20, 30, 40, 50, 60, 70, 80, 90, 100]
```

Both the randint and the randrange functions return an integer number. The random function returns, however, returns a random floating-point number. You do not pass any arguments to the random function. When you call it, it returns a random floating point number in the range of 0.0 up to 1.0 (but not including 1.0). Here is an example:

```
number = random.random()
```

The uniform function also returns a random floating-point number, but allows you to specify the range of values to select from. Here is an example:

```
number = random.uniform(1.0, 10.0)
```

In this statement the uniform function returns a random floating-point number in the range of 1.0 through 10.0 and assigns it to the number variable.

Checkpoint

1   How does a value-returning function differ from simple functions?

2   What is a library function?

3   Why are library functions like "black boxes"?

4   What does the following statement do?
```
x = random.randint(1, 100)
```

5   What does the following statement do?
```
print random.randint(1, 20)
```

6   What does the following statement do?
```
print random.randrange(10, 20)
```

7   What does the following statement do?
```
print random.random()
```

8   What does the following statement do?
```
print random.uniform(0.1, 0.5)
```

2   Writing Your Own Value-Returning Functions

CONCEPT: A value-returning function has a return statement that returns a value back to the part of the program that called it.

You write a value-returning function in the same way that you write a simple function, with one exception: a value-returning function must have a `return` statement. Here is the general format of a value-returning function definition in Python:

```
def function_name():
    statement
    statement
    etc.
    return expression
```

One of the statements in the function must be a `return` statement, which takes the following form:

```
return expression
```

The value of the *expression* that follows the key word `return` will be sent back to the part of the program that called the function. This can be any value, variable, or expression that has a value (such as a math expression).

Here is a simple example of a value-returning function:

```
def sum(num1, num2):
    result = num1 + num2
    return result
```

Figure 5 illustrates various parts of the function.

Figure 5   Parts of the function

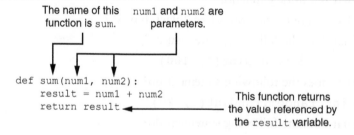

The purpose of this function is to accept two integer values as arguments and return their sum. Let's take a closer look at how it works. The first statement in the function's block assigns the value of num1 + num2 to the `result` variable. Next, the `return` statement executes, which causes the function to end execution and sends the value referenced by the `result` variable back to the part of the program that called the function. Program 6 demonstrates the function.

Program 6 (total_ages.py)

```
 1   # This program uses the return value of a function.
 2
 3   def main():
 4       # Get the user's age.
 5       first_age = input('Enter your age: ')
 6
 7       # Get the user's best friend's age.
 8       second_age = input("Enter your best friend's age: ")
 9
10       # Get the sum of both ages.
11       total = sum(first_age, second_age)
12
13       # Display the total age.
14       print 'Together you are', total, 'years old.'
15
16   # The sum function accepts two numeric arguments and
17   # returns the sum of those arguments.
18   def sum(num1, num2):
19       result = num1 + num2
20       return result
21
22   # Call the main function.
23   main()
```

Program Output (with input shown in bold)
```
Enter your age: 22 [Enter]
Enter your best friend's age: 24 [Enter]
Together you are 46 years old.
```

In the main function, the program gets two values from the user and stores them in the first_age and second_age variables. The statement in line 11 calls the sum function, passing first_age and second_age as arguments. The value that is returned from the sum function is assigned to the total variable. In this case, the function will return 46. Figure 6 shows how the arguments are passed into the function, and how a value is returned back from the function.

Figure 6 Arguments are passed to the sum function and a value is returned

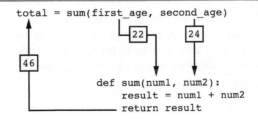

Making the Most of the `return` Statement

Look again at the sum function presented in Program 6:

```
def sum(num1, num2):
    result = num1 + num2
    return result
```

Notice that two things happen inside this function: (1) the value of the expression num1 + num2 is assigned to the `result` variable, and (2) the value of the `result` variable is returned. Although this function does what it sets out to do, it can be simplified. Because the `return` statement can return the value of an expression, you can eliminate the `result` variable and rewrite the function as:

```
def sum(num1, num2):
    return num1 + num2
```

This version of the function does not store the value of num1 + num2 in a variable. Instead, it takes advantage of the fact that the `return` statement can return the value of an expression. This version of the function does the same thing as the previous version, but in only one step.

How to Use Value-Returning Functions

Value-returning functions provide many of the same benefits as simple functions: they simplify code, reduce duplication, enhance your ability to test code, increase the speed of development, and ease the facilitation of teamwork.

Because value-returning functions return a value, they can be useful in specific situations. For example, you can use a value-returning function to prompt the user for input, and then it can return the value entered by the user. Suppose you've been asked to design a program that calculates the sale price of an item in a retail business. To do that, the program would need to get the item's regular price from the user. Here is a function you could define for that purpose:

```
def get_regular_price():
    price = input("Enter the item's regular price: ")
    return price
```

Then, elsewhere in the program, you could call that function, as shown here:

```
# Get the item's regular price.
reg_price = get_regular_price()
```

When this statement executes, the `get_regular_price` function is called, which gets a value from the user and returns it. That value is then assigned to the `reg_price` variable.

You can also use functions to simplify complex mathematical expressions. For example, calculating the sale price of an item seems like it would be a simple task: you calculate the discount and subtract it from the regular price. In a program, however, a statement that performs this calculation is not that straightforward, as shown in the following example. (Assume DISCOUNT_PERCENTAGE is a global constant that is defined in the program, and it specifies the percentage of the discount.)

```
sale_price = reg_price - (reg_price * DISCOUNT_PERCENTAGE)
```

This statement isn't easy to understand because it performs so many steps: it calculates the discount amount, subtracts that value from reg_price, and assigns the result to sale_price. You could simplify the statement by breaking out part of the math expression and placing it in a function. Here is a function named discount that accepts an item's price as an argument and returns the amount of the discount:

```
def discount(price):
    return price * DISCOUNT_PERCENTAGE
```

You could then call the function in your calculation:

```
sale_price = reg_price - discount(reg_price)
```

This statement is easier to read than the one previously shown, and it is clearer that the discount is being subtracted from the regular price. Program 7 shows the complete sale price calculating program using the functions just described.

Program 7   (sale_price.py)

```
1   # This program calculates a retail item's
2   # sale price.
3
4   # DISCOUNT_PERCENTAGE is used as a global
5   # constant for the discount percentage.
6   DISCOUNT_PERCENTAGE = 0.20
7
8   # The main function.
9   def main():
10      # Get the item's regular price.
11      reg_price = get_regular_price()
12
13      # Calculate the sale price.
14      sale_price = reg_price - discount(reg_price)
15
16      # Display the sale price.
17      print 'The sale price is $%.2f.' % sale_price
18
19  # The get_regular_price function prompts the
20  # user to enter an item's regular price and it
21  # returns that value.
22  def get_regular_price():
23      price = input("Enter the item's regular price: ")
24      return price
25
26  # The discount function accepts an item's price
27  # as an argument and returns the amount of the
28  # discount, specified by DISCOUNT_PERCENTAGE.
29  def discount(price):
```

(program continues)

Program 7   *(continued)*

```
30        return price * DISCOUNT_PERCENTAGE
31
32  # Call the main function.
33  main()
```

Program Output (with input shown in bold)

```
Enter the item's regular price: 100.00 [Enter]
The sale price is $80.00
```

Using IPO Charts

An IPO chart is a simple but effective tool that programmers sometimes use for designing and documenting functions. IPO stands for *input, processing,* and *output,* and an *IPO chart* describes the input, processing, and output of a function. These items are usually laid out in columns: the input column shows a description of the data that is passed to the function as arguments, the processing column shows a description of the process that the function performs, and the output column describes the data that is returned from the function. For example, Figure 7 shows IPO charts for the get_regular_price and discount functions that you saw in Program 7.

Figure 7   IPO charts for the getRegularPrice and discount functions

IPO Chart for the get_regular_price Function		
Input	Processing	Output
None	Prompts the user to enter an item's regular price	The item's regular price

IPO Chart for the discount Function		
Input	Processing	Output
An item's regular price	Calculates an item's discount by multiplying the regular price by the global constant DISCOUNT_PERCENTAGE.	The item's discount

Notice that the IPO charts provide only brief descriptions of a function's input, processing, and output, but do not show the specific steps taken in a function. In many cases, however, IPO charts include sufficient information so that they can be used instead of a flowchart. The decision of whether to use an IPO chart, a flowchart, or both is often left to the programmer's personal preference.

In the Spotlight:
Modularizing with Functions

Hal owns a business named Make Your Own Music, which sells guitars, drums, banjos, synthesizers, and many other musical instruments. Hal's sales staff works strictly on commission. At the end of the month, each salesperson's commission is calculated according to Table 1.

Table 1   Sales commission rates

Sales This Month	Commission Rate
Less than $10,000	10%
$10,000–14,999	12%
$15,000–17,999	14%
$18,000–21,999	16%
$22,000 or more	18%

For example, a salesperson with $16,000 in monthly sales will earn a 14 percent commission ($2240). Another salesperson with $18,000 in monthly sales will earn a 16 percent commission ($2880). A person with $30,000 in sales will earn an 18 percent commission ($5400).

Because the staff gets paid once per month, Hal allows each employee to take up to $2000 per month in advance. When sales commissions are calculated, the amount of each employee's advanced pay is subtracted from the commission. If any salesperson's commissions are less than the amount of their advance, they must reimburse Hal for the difference. To calculate a salesperson's monthly pay, Hal uses the following formula:

$$pay = sales \times commission\ rate - advanced\ pay$$

Hal has asked you to write a program that makes this calculation for him. The following general algorithm outlines the steps the program must take.

1. *Get the salesperson's monthly sales.*
2. *Get the amount of advanced pay.*
3. *Use the amount of monthly sales to determine the commission rate.*
4. *Calculate the salesperson's pay using the formula previously shown. If the amount is negative, indicate that the salesperson must reimburse the company.*

Program 8 shows the code, which is written using several functions. Rather than presenting the entire program at once, let's first examine the `main` function and then each function separately. Here is the `main` function:

Program 8   (commission_rate.py) main function

```
1   # This program calculates a salesperson's pay
2   # at Make Your Own Music.
3   def main():
4       # Get the amount of sales.
5       sales = get_sales()
6
7       # Get the amount of advanced pay.
8       advanced_pay = get_advanced_pay()
9
10      # Determine the commission rate.
11      comm_rate = determine_comm_rate(sales)
12
13      # Calculate the pay.
14      pay = sales * comm_rate - advanced_pay
15
16      # Display the amount of pay.
17      print 'The pay is $%.2f.' % pay
18
19      # Determine whether the pay is negative.
20      if pay < 0:
21          print 'The Salesperson must reimburse'
22          print 'the company.'
23
```

Line 5 calls the `get_sales` function, which gets the amount of sales from the user and returns that value. The value that is returned from the function is assigned to the `sales` variable. Line 8 calls the `get_advanced_pay` function, which gets the amount of advanced pay from the user and returns that value. The value that is returned from the function is assigned to the `advanced_pay` variable.

Line 11 calls the `determine_comm_rate` function, passing `sales` as an argument. This function returns the rate of commission for the amount of sales. That value is assigned to the `comm_rate` variable. Line 14 calculates the amount of pay, and then line 17 displays that amount. The `if` statement in lines 20 through 22 determines whether the pay is negative, and if so, displays a message indicating that the salesperson must reimburse the company. The `get_sales` function definition is next.

Program 8   (commission_rate.py) get_sales function

```
24  # The get_sales function gets a salesperson's
25  # monthly sales from the user and returns that value.
26  def get_sales():
```

```
27          # Get the amount of monthly sales.
28          monthly_sales = input('Enter the monthly sales: ')
29
30          # Return the amount entered.
31          return monthly_sales
32
```

The purpose of the get_sales function is to prompt the user to enter the amount of sales for a salesperson and return that amount. Line 28 prompts the user to enter the sales, and stores the user's input in the monthly_sales variable. Line 31 returns the amount in the monthly_sales variable. Next is the definition of the get_advanced_pay function.

Program 8   (commission_rate.py) get_advanced_pay function

```
33   # The get_advanced_pay function gets the amount of
34   # advanced pay given to the salesperson and returns
35   # that amount.
36   def get_advanced_pay():
37       # Get the amount of advanced pay.
38       print 'Enter the amount of advanced pay, or'
39       print 'enter 0 if no advanced pay was given.'
40       advanced = input('Advanced pay: ')
41
42       # Return the amount entered.
43       return advanced
44
```

The purpose of the get_advanced_pay function is to prompt the user to enter the amount of advanced pay for a salesperson and return that amount. Lines 38 and 39 tell the user to enter the amount of advanced pay (or 0 if none was given). Line 40 gets the user's input and stores it in the advanced variable. Line 43 returns the amount in the advanced variable. Defining the determine_comm_rate function comes next.

Program 8   (commission_rate.py) determine_comm_rate function

```
45   # The determine_comm_rate function accepts the
46   # amount of sales as an argument and returns the
47   # applicable commission rate.
48   def determine_comm_rate(sales):
49       # Determine the commission rate.
50       if sales < 10000.00:
51           rate = 0.10
52       elif sales >= 10000 and sales <= 14999.99:
53           rate = 0.12
54       elif sales >= 15000 and sales <= 17999.99:
55           rate = 0.14
```

(program continues)

Program 8   *(continued)*

```
56        elif sales >= 18000 and sales <= 21999.99:
57            rate = 0.16
58        else:
59            rate = 0.18
60
61        # Return the commission rate.
62        return rate
63
```

The determine_comm_rate function accepts the amount of sales as an argument, and it returns the applicable commission rate for that amount of sales. The if-elif-else state-ment in lines 50 through 59 tests the sales parameter and assigns the correct value to the local rate variable. Line 62 returns the value in the local rate variable.

Program Output (with input shown in bold)
```
Enter the monthly sales: 14650.00 [Enter]
Enter the amount of advanced pay, or
enter 0 if no advanced pay was given.
Advanced pay: 1000.00 [Enter]
The pay is $758.00.
```

Program Output (with input shown in bold)
```
Enter the monthly sales: 9000.00 [Enter]
Enter the amount of advanced pay, or
enter 0 if no advanced pay was given.
Advanced pay: 0 [Enter]
The pay is $900.00.
```

Program Output (with input shown in bold)
```
Enter the monthly sales: 12000.00 [Enter]
Enter the amount of advanced pay, or
enter 0 if no advanced pay was given.
Advanced pay: 2000.00 [Enter]
The pay is $-560.00.
The salesperson must reimburse
the company.
```

Returning Strings

So far you've seen examples of functions that return numbers. You can also write functions that return strings. For example, the following function prompts the user to enter his or her name, and then returns the string that the user entered.

```
def get_name():
    # Get the user's name.
```

```
name = raw_input('Enter your name: ')
# Return the name.
return name
```

Returning Boolean Values

Python allows you to write *Boolean functions,* which return either `True` or `False`. You can use a Boolean function to test a condition, and then return either `True` or `False` to indicate whether the condition exists. Boolean functions are useful for simplifying complex conditions that are tested in decision and repetition structures.

For example, suppose you are designing a program that will ask the user to enter a number, and then determine whether that number is even or odd. The following code shows how you can make that determination.

```
number = input('Enter a number: ')
if (number % 2) == 0:
    print 'The number is even.'
else:
    print 'The number is odd.'
```

Let's take a closer look at the Boolean expression being tested by this `if-else` statement:

```
(number % 2) == 0
```

This expression uses the `%` operator. This is called the remainder operator. It divides two numbers and returns the remainder of the division. So this code is saying, "If the remainder of `number` divided by 2 is equal to 0, then display a message indicating the number is even, or else display a message indicating the number is odd."

Because dividing an even number by 2 will always give a remainder of 0, this logic will work. The code would be easier to understand, however, if you could somehow rewrite it to say, "If the number is even, then display a message indicating it is even, or else display a message indicating it is odd." As it turns out, this can be done with a Boolean function. In this example, you could write a Boolean function named `is_even` that accepts a number as an argument and returns `True` if the number is even, or `False` otherwise. The following is the code for such a function.

```
def is_even(number):
    # Determine whether number is even. If it is,
    # set status to true. Otherwise, set status
    # to false.
    if (number % 2) == 0:
       status = True
    else:
        status = False
    # Return the value of the status variable.
    return status
```

Then you can rewrite the `if-else` statement so it calls the `is_even` function to determine whether number is even:

```
number = input('Enter a number: ')
if is_even(number):
    print 'The number is even.'
else:
    print 'The number is odd.'
```

Not only is this logic easier to understand, but now you have a function that you can call in the program anytime you need to test a number to determine whether it is even.

Using Boolean Functions in Validation Code

You can also use Boolean functions to simplify complex input validation code. For instance, suppose you are writing a program that prompts the user to enter a product model number and should only accept the values 100, 200, and 300. You could design the input algorithm as follows:

```
# Get the model number.
model = input('Enter the model number: ')

# Validate the model number.
while model != 100 and model != 200 and model != 300:
    print 'The valid model numbers are 100, 200 and 300.'
    model = input('Enter a valid model number: ')
```

The validation loop uses a long compound Boolean expression that will iterate as long as model does not equal 100 *and* model does not equal 200 *and* model does not equal 300. Although this logic will work, you can simplify the validation loop by writing a Boolean function to test the model variable and then calling that function in the loop. For example, suppose you pass the model variable to a function you write named `is_invalid`. The function returns `True` if model is invalid, or `False` otherwise. You could rewrite the validation loop as follows:

```
# Validate the model number.
while is_invalid(model):
    print 'The valid model numbers are 100, 200 and 300.'
    model = input('Enter a valid model number: ')
```

This makes the loop easier to read. It is evident now that the loop iterates as long as model is invalid. The following code shows how you might write the `is_invalid` function. It accepts a model number as an argument, and if the argument is not 100 and the argument is not 200 and the argument is not 300, the function returns `True` to indicate that it is invalid. Otherwise, the function returns `False`.

```
def is_invalid(mod_num):
    if mod_num != 100 and mod_num != 200 and mod_num != 300:
        status = True
    else:
        status = False
    return status
```

Returning Multiple Values

The examples of value-returning functions that we have looked at so far return a single value. In Python, however, you are not limited to returning only one value. You can specify multiple expressions separated by commas after the return statement, as shown in this general format:

```
return expression1, expression2, etc.
```

As an example, look at the following definition for a function named get_name. The function prompts the user to enter his or her first and last names. These names are stored in two local variables: first and last. The return statement returns both of the variables.

```
def get_name():
    # Get the user's first and last names.
    first = raw_input('Enter your first name: ')
    last = raw_input('Enter your last name: ')

    # Return both names.
    return first, last
```

When you call this function in an assignment statement, you need to use two variables on the left side of the = operator. Here is an example:

```
first_name, last_name = get_name()
```

The values listed in the return statement are assigned, in the order that they appear, to the variables on the left side of the = operator. After this statement executes, the value of the first variable will be assigned to first_name and the value of the last variable will be assigned to last_name. Note that the number of variables on the left side of the = operator must match the number of values returned by the function. Otherwise an error will occur.

Checkpoint

9   What is the purpose of the return statement in a function?

10 Look at the following function definition:

```
def do_something(number):
    return number * 2
```

a. What is the name of the function?

b. What does the function do?

c. Given the function definition, what will the following statement display?

```
print do_something(10)
```

11 What is a Boolean function?

3 The math Module

CONCEPT: The Python standard library's **math** module contains numerous functions that can be used in mathematical calculations.

The math module in the Python standard library contains several functions that are useful for performing mathematical operations. Table 2 lists many of the functions in the math module. These functions typically accept one or more values as arguments, perform a mathematical operation using the arguments, and return the result. For example, one of the functions is named sqrt. The sqrt function accepts an argument and returns the square root of the argument. Here is an example of how it is used:

```
result = math.sqrt(16)
```

This statement calls the sqrt function, passing 16 as an argument. The function returns the square root of 16, which is then assigned to the result variable. Program 9 demonstrates the sqrt function. Notice the import math statement in line 2. You need to write this in any program that uses the math module.

Program 9   (square_root.py)

```
 1   # This program demonstrates the sqrt function.
 2   import math
 3
 4   def main():
 5       # Get a number.
 6       number = input('Enter a number: ')
 7
 8       # Get the square root of the number.
 9       square_root = math.sqrt(number)
10
11       # Display the square root.
12       print 'The square root of', number, 'is', square_root
13
14   # Call the main function.
15   main()
```

Program Output (with input shown in bold)
```
Enter a number: 25 [Enter]
The square root of 25 is 5.0
```

Program 10 shows another example that uses the math module. This program uses the hypot function to calculate the length of a right triangle's hypotenuse.

Program 10   (hypotenuse.py)

```
 1   # This program calculates the length of a right
 2   # triangle's hypotenuse.
 3   import math
 4
 5   def main():
 6       # Get the length of the triangle's two sides.
 7       a = input('Enter the length of side A: ')
 8       b = input('Enter the length of side B: ')
 9
```

```
10          # Calculate the length of the hypotenuse.
11          c = math.hypot(a, b)
12
13          # Display the length of the hypotenuse.
14          print 'The length of the hypotenuse is', c
15
16   # Call the main function.
17   main()
```

Program Output (with input shown in bold)

```
Enter the length of side A: 5.0 [Enter]
Enter the length of side B: 12.0 [Enter]
The length of the hypotenuse is 13.0
```

Table 2   Many of the functions in the math module

math Module Function	Description
acos(x)	Returns the arc cosine of x, in radians.
asin(x)	Returns the arc sine of x, in radians.
atan(x)	Returns the arc tangent of x, in radians.
ceil(x)	Returns the smallest integer that is greater than or equal to x.
cos(x)	Returns the cosine of x in radians.
degrees(x)	Assuming x is an angle in radians, the function returns the angle converted to degrees.
exp(x)	Returns e^x
floor(x)	Returns the largest integer that is less than or equal to x.
hypot(x, y)	Returns the length of a hypotenuse that extends from (0, 0) to (x, y).
log(x)	Returns the natural logarithm of x.
log10(x)	Returns the base-10 logarithm of x.
radians(x)	Assuming x is an angle in degrees, the function returns the angle converted to radians.
sin(x)	Returns the sine of x in radians.
sqrt(x)	Returns the square root of x.
tan(x)	Returns the tangent of x in radians.

The math.pi and math.e Values

The math module also defines two variables, pi and e, which are assigned mathematical values for *pi* and *e*. You can use these variables in equations that require their values. For example, the following statement, which calculates the area of a circle, uses pi. (Notice that we use dot notation to refer to the variable.)

```
area = math.pi * radius**2
```

Checkpoint

12   What `import` statement do you need to write in a program that uses the `math` module.

13   Write a statement that uses a `math` module function to get the square root of 100 and assigns it to a variable.

14   Write a statement that uses a `math` module function to convert 45 degrees to radians and assigns the value to a variable.

4   Storing Functions in Modules

CONCEPT: A module is a file that contains Python code. Large programs are easier to debug and maintain when they are divided into modules.

As your programs become larger and more complex, the need to organize your code becomes greater. You have already learned that a large and complex program should be divided into functions that each performs a specific task. As you write more and more functions in a program, you should consider organizing the functions by storing them in modules.

A module is simply a file that contains Python code. When you break a program into modules, each module should contain functions that perform related tasks. For example, suppose you are writing an accounting system. You would store all of the account receivable functions in their own module, all of the account payable functions in their own module, and all of the payroll functions in their own module. This approach, which is called *modularization*, makes the program easier to understand, test, and maintain.

Modules also make it easier to reuse the same code in more than one program. If you have written a set of functions that are needed in several different programs, you can place those functions in a module. Then, you can import the module in each program that needs to call one of the functions.

Let's look at a simple example. Suppose your instructor has asked you to write a program that calculates the following:

- The area of a circle
- The circumference of a circle
- The area of a rectangle
- The perimeter of a rectangle

There are obviously two categories of calculations required in this program: those related to circles, and those related to rectangles. You could write all of the circle-related functions in one module, and the rectangle-related functions in another module. Program 11 shows the `circle` module. The module contains two function definitions: `area` (which returns the area of a circle) and `circumference` (which returns the circumference of a circle).

Program 11   (circle.py)

```
1    # The circle module has functions that perform
2    # calculations related to circles.
```

```
3   import math
4
5   # The area function accepts a circle's radius as an
6   # argument and returns the area of the circle.
7   def area(radius):
8       return math.pi * radius**2
9
10  # The circumference function accepts a circle's
11  # radius and returns the circle's circumference.
12  def circumference(radius):
13      return 2 * math.pi * radius
```

Program 12 shows the `rectangle` module. The module contains two function definitions: `area` (which returns the area of a rectangle) and `perimeter` (which returns the perimeter of a rectangle.)

Program 12   (rectangle.py)

```
1   # The rectangle module has functions that perform
2   # calculations related to rectangles.
3
4   # The area function accepts a rectangle's width and
5   # length as arguments and returns the rectangle's area.
6   def area(width, length):
7       return width * length
8
9   # The perimeter function accepts a rectangle's width
10  # and length as arguments and returns the rectangle's
11  # perimeter.
12  def perimeter(width, length):
13      return 2 * (width + length)
```

Notice that both of these files contain function definitions, but they do not contain code that calls the functions. That will be done by the program or programs that import these modules.

Before continuing, we should mention the following things about module names:

- A module's file name should end in `.py`. If the module's file name does not end in `.py` you will not be able to import it into other programs.
- A module's name cannot be the same as a Python key word. An error would occur, for example, if you named a module `for`.

To use these modules in a program, you import them with the `import` statement. Here is an example of how we would import the `circle` module:

```
import circle
```

When the Python interpreter reads this statement it will look for the file `circle.py` in the same folder as the program that is trying to import it. If it finds the file it will load it into memory. If it does not find the file, an error occurs.[2]

Once a module is imported you can call its functions. Assuming that `radius` is a variable that is assigned the radius of a circle, here is an example of how we would call the `area` and `circumference` functions:

```
my_area = circle.area(radius)
my_circum = circle.circumference(radius)
```

Program 13 shows a complete program that uses these modules.

Program 13   (geometry.py)

```
 1   # This program allows the user to choose various
 2   # geometry calculations from a menu. This program
 3   # imports the circle and rectangle modules.
 4
 5   import circle
 6   import rectangle
 7
 8   # The main function.
 9   def main():
10       # The choice variable controls the loop
11       # and holds the user's menu choice.
12       choice = 0
13
14       while choice != 5:
15           # display the menu.
16           display_menu()
17
18           # Get the user's choice.
19           choice = input('Enter your choice: ')
20
21           # Perform the selected action.
22           if choice == 1:
23               radius = input("Enter the circle's radius: ")
24               print 'The area is', circle.area(radius)
25           elif choice == 2:
26               radius = input("Enter the circle's radius: ")
27               print 'The circumference is', \
28                       circle.circumference(radius)
29           elif choice == 3:
30               width = input("Enter the rectangle's width: ")
31               length = input("Enter the rectangle's length: ")
32               print 'The area is', rectangle.area(width, length)
```

[2]Actually the Python interpreter is set up to look in various other predefined locations in your system when it does not find a module in the program's folder. If you choose to learn about the advanced features of Python, you can learn how to specify where the interpreter looks for modules.

```
33              elif choice == 4:
34                  width = input("Enter the rectangle's width: ")
35                  length = input("Enter the rectangle's length: ")
36                  print 'The perimeter is', \
37                        rectangle.perimeter(width, length)
38              elif choice == 5:
39                  print 'Exiting the program...'
40              else:
41                  print 'Error: invalid selection.'
42
43   # The display_menu function displays a menu.
44   def display_menu():
45       print '          MENU'
46       print '1) Area of a circle'
47       print '2) Circumference of a circle'
48       print '3) Area of a rectangle'
49       print '4) Perimeter of a rectangle'
50       print '5) Quit'
51
52   # Call the main function.
53   main()
```

Program Output (with input shown in bold)

```
          MENU
1) Area of a circle
2) Circumference of a circle
3) Area of a rectangle
4) Perimeter of a rectangle
5) Quit
Enter your choice: 1 [Enter]
Enter the circle's radius: 10
The area is 314.159265359
          MENU
1) Area of a circle
2) Circumference of a circle
3) Area of a rectangle
4) Perimeter of a rectangle
5) Quit
Enter your choice: 2 [Enter]
Enter the circle's radius: 10
The circumference is 62.8318530718
          MENU
1) Area of a circle
2) Circumference of a circle
3) Area of a rectangle
4) Perimeter of a rectangle
5) Quit
```

(program output continues)

Program Output   *(continued)*

```
Enter your choice: 3 [Enter]
Enter the rectangle's width: 5
Enter the rectangle's length: 10
The area is 50
        MENU
1) Area of a circle
2) Circumference of a circle
3) Area of a rectangle
4) Perimeter of a rectangle
5) Quit
Enter your choice: 4 [Enter]
Enter the rectangle's width: 5
Enter the rectangle's length: 10
The perimeter is 30
        MENU
1) Area of a circle
2) Circumference of a circle
3) Area of a rectangle
4) Perimeter of a rectangle
5) Quit
Enter your choice: 5 [Enter]
Exiting the program...
```

Menu Driven Programs

Program 13 is an example of a menu-driven program. A *menu-driven program* displays a list of the operations on the screen, and allows the user to select the operation that he or she wants the program to perform. The list of operations that is displayed on the screen is called a *menu*. When Program 13 is running, the user enters 1 to calculate the area of a circle, 2 to calculate the circumference of a circle, and so forth.

Once the user types a menu selection, the program uses a decision structure to determine which menu item the user selected. An if-elif-else statement is used in Program 13 (in lines 22 through 41) to carry out the user's desired action. The entire process of displaying a menu, getting the user's selection, and carrying out that selection is repeated by a while loop (which begins in line 14). The loop repeats until the user selects 5 (Quit) from the menu.

Review Questions

Multiple Choice

1. This is a prewritten function that is built into a programming language.
   a. standard function
   b. library function
   c. custom function
   d. cafeteria function

2. This term describes any mechanism that accepts input, performs some operation that cannot be seen on the input, and produces output.
   a. glass box
   b. white box
   c. opaque box
   d. black box

3. This standard library function returns a random integer within a specified range of values.
   a. `random`
   b. `randint`
   c. `random_integer`
   d. `uniform`

4. This standard library function returns a random floating-point number in the range of 0.0 up to 1.0 (but not including 1.0).
   a. `random`
   b. `randint`
   c. `random_integer`
   d. `uniform`

5. This standard library function returns a random floating-point number within a specified range of values.
   a. `random`
   b. `randint`
   c. `random_integer`
   d. `uniform`

6. This statement causes a function to end and sends a value back to the part of the program that called the function.
   a. `end`
   b. `send`
   c. `exit`
   d. `return`

7. This is a design tool that describes the input, processing, and output of a function.
   a. hierarchy chart
   b. IPO chart
   c. datagram chart
   d. data processing chart

8. This type of function returns either `True` or `False`.
   a. Binary
   b. `true_false`
   c. Boolean
   d. logical

9. This is `math` module function.
   a. `derivative`
   b. `factor`
   c. `sqrt`
   d. `differentiate`

10. A menu is a _____.
   a. case structure that selects an operation in a program
   b. group of modules that perform individual tasks
   c. list of operations displayed on the screen that the user may choose from
   d. table of Boolean choices

True or False

1. Some library functions are built into the Python interpreter.
2. You do not have to have an import statement in a program to use the functions in the random module.
3. Complex mathematical expressions can sometimes be simplified by breaking out part of the expression and putting it in a function.
4. A function in Python can return more than one value.
5. IPO charts provide only brief descriptions of a function's input, processing, and output, but do not show the specific steps taken in a function.

Short Answer

1. Suppose you want to select a random number from the following list:

   [0, 5, 10, 15, 20, 25, 30]

   What library function would you use?
2. What statement do you have to have in a value-returning function?
3. What three things are listed on an IPO chart?
4. What is a Boolean function?
5. What are the advantages of breaking a large program into modules?

Algorithm Workbench

1. Write a statement that generates a random number in the range of 1 through 100 and assigns it to a variable named rand.
2. The following statement calls a function named half, which returns a value that is half that of the argument. (Assume the number variable references a float value.) Write code for the function.

   ```
   result = half(number)
   ```
3. A program contains the following function definition:

   ```
   def cube(num):
   return num * num * num
   ```

   Write a statement that passes the value 4 to this function and assigns its return value to the variable result.
4. Write a function named times_ten that accepts a number as an argument. When the function is called, it should return the value of its argument multiplied times 10.
5. Write a function named get_first_name that asks the user to enter his or her first name, and returns it.

Programming Exercises

1. Feet to Inches

One foot equals 12 inches. Write a function named `feet_to_inches` that accepts a number of feet as an argument, and returns the number of inches in that many feet. Use the function in a program that prompts the user to enter a number of feet and then displays the number of inches in that many feet.

2. Math Quiz

Write a program that gives simple math quizzes. The program should display two random numbers that are to be added, such as:

```
  247
+ 129
```

The program should allow the student to enter the answer. If the answer is correct, a message of congratulations should be displayed. If the answer is incorrect, a message showing the correct answer should be displayed.

3. Maximum of Two Values

Write a function named `maximum` that accepts two integer values as arguments and returns the value that is the greater of the two. For example, if 7 and 12 are passed as arguments to the function, the function should return 12. Use the function in a program that prompts the user to enter two integer values. The program should display the value that is the greater of the two.

4. Falling Distance

The following formula can be used to determine the distance an object falls due to gravity in a specific time period, starting from rest:

$$d = \frac{1}{2}\,gt^2$$

The variables in the formula are as follows: d is the distance in meters, g is 9.8, and t is the amount of time in seconds, that the object has been falling.

Write a function named `falling_distance` that accepts an object's falling time in seconds as an argument. The function should return the distance in meters that the object has fallen during that time interval. Write a program that calls the function in a loop that passes the values 1 through 10 as arguments and displays the return value.

5. Kinetic Energy

In physics, an object that is in motion is said to have kinetic energy. The following formula can be used to determine a moving object's kinetic energy:

$$KE = \frac{1}{2}\,mv^2$$

The variables in the formula are as follows: KE is the kinetic energy in joules, m is the object's mass in kilograms, and v is the object's velocity in meters per second.

Write a function named `kinetic_energy` that accepts an object's mass in kilograms and velocity in meters per second as arguments. The function should return the amount of kinetic energy that the object has. Write a program that asks the user to enter values for mass and velocity, and then calls the `kinetic_energy` function to get the object's kinetic energy.

6. Test Average and Grade

Write a program that asks the user to enter five test scores. The program should display a letter grade for each score and the average test score. Write the following functions in the program:

- calc_average— This function should accept five test scores as arguments and return the average of the scores.
- determine_grade— This function should accept a test score as an argument and return a letter grade for the score, based on the following grading scale:

Score	Letter Grade
90–100	A
80–89	B
70–79	C
60–69	D
Below 60	F

7. Odd/Even Counter

In this chapter you saw an example of how to write an algorithm that determines whether a number is even or odd. Write a program that generates 100 random numbers, and keeps a count of how many of those random numbers are even and how many are odd.

8. Prime Numbers

A prime number is a number that is only evenly divisible by itself and 1. For example, the number 5 is prime because it can only be evenly divided by 1 and 5. The number 6, however, is not prime because it can be divided evenly by 1, 2, 3, and 6.

Write a Boolean function named is_prime which takes an integer as an argument and returns True if the argument is a prime number, or False otherwise. Use the function in a program that prompts the user to enter a number and then displays a message indicating whether the number is prime.

> **TIP:** Recall that the % operator divides one number by another and returns the remainder of the division. In an expression such as num1 % num2, the % operator will return 0 if num1 is evenly divisible by num2.

9. Prime Number List

This exercise assumes you have already written the is_prime function in Programming Exercise 8. Write another program that displays all of the prime numbers from 1 through 100. The program should have a loop that calls the is_prime function.

10. Rock, Paper, Scissors Game

Write a program that lets the user play the game of Rock, Paper, Scissors against the computer. The program should work as follows.

1. When the program begins, a random number in the range of 1 through 3 is generated. If the number is 1, then the computer has chosen rock. If the number is 2, then the com-

Value-Returning Functions and Modules   681

puter has chosen paper. If the number is 3, then the computer has chosen scissors. (Don't display the computer's choice yet.)
2. The user enters his or her choice of "rock", "paper", or "scissors" at the keyboard.
3. The computer's choice is displayed.
4. A winner is selected according to the following rules:

   - If one player chooses rock and the other player chooses scissors, then rock wins. (The rock smashes the scissors.)
   - If one player chooses scissors and the other player chooses paper, then scissors wins. (Scissors cuts paper.)
   - If one player chooses paper and the other player chooses rock, then paper wins. (Paper wraps rock.)
   - If both players make the same choice, the game must be played again to determine the winner.

Installing Python

Before you can run Python programs on your computer you will need to install the Python interpreter. You can download the latest version of the Python Windows installer from www.python.org/download. The website also provides downloadable versions of Python for several other operating systems.

Installing Python

When you execute the Python Windows installer, it's best to accept all of the default settings by clicking the Next button on each screen. (Answer "Yes" if you are prompted with any Yes/No questions.) As you perform the installation, take note of the directory where Python is being installed. It will be something similar to C:\Python25. (The 25 in the path name represents the Python version. At the time of this writing Python 2.5 is the most recent version.) You will need to remember this location after finishing the installation.

When the installer is finished, the Python interpreter, the IDLE programming environment, and the Python documentation will be installed on your system. When you click the Start button and look at your All Programs list you should see a program group named something like *Python 2.5*. The program group will contain the following items:

- IDLE (Python GUI)—When you click this item the IDLE programming environment will execute. IDLE is an integrated development environment that you can use to create, edit, and execute Python programs.
- Module Docs—This item launches a utility program that allows you to browse documentation for the modules in the Python standard library.
- Python Command Line—Clicking this item launches the Python interpreter in interactive mode.
- Python Manuals—This item opens the Python Manuals in your web browser. The manuals include tutorials, a reference section for the Python standard library, an in-depth reference for the Python language, and information on many advanced topics.
- Uninstall Python—This item removes Python from your system.

Adding the Python Directory to the Path Variable

If you plan to execute the Python interpreter from a command prompt window, you will probably want to add the Python directory to the existing contents of your system's Path variable. (You saw the name of the Python directory while installing Python. It is something similar to C:\Python25.) Doing this will allow your system to find the Python interpreter from any directory when you run it at the command-line.

Use the following instructions to edit the Path variable under Windows XP and Windows Vista.

Windows XP

- Open the Control Panel.
- Double-click the *System* icon. (If you are running Windows XP in Category View, click *Performance and Maintenance* in the Control Panel, and then click the *System* icon.)
- Click the *Advanced* tab.
- Click the *Environment Variables* button. In the *System Variables* list, scroll to the Path variable.
- Select the Path variable and click the *Edit* button. Add a semicolon to the end of the existing contents, and then add the Python directory path.
- Click the *OK* button.

Windows Vista
- Open the Control Panel.
- Select System and Maintenance.
- Select System.
- Select Advanced System Settings.
- Click the Environment Variables button.
- In the *System Variables* list, scroll to the Path variable.
- Select the Path variable and click the *Edit* button. Add a semicolon to the end of the existing contents, and then add the Python directory path.
- Click the *OK* button.

Introduction to IDLE

IDLE is an integrated development environment that combines several development tools into one program, including the following:

- A Python shell running in interactive mode. You can type Python statements at the shell prompt and immediately execute them. You can also run complete Python programs.
- A text editor that color codes Python keywords and other parts of programs.
- A "check module" tool that checks a Python program for syntax errors without running the program.
- Search tools that allow you to find text in one or more files.
- Text formatting tools that help you maintain consistent indentation levels in a Python program.
- A debugger that allows you to single-step through a Python program and watch the values of variables change as each statement executes.
- Several other advanced tools for developers.

The IDLE software is bundled with Python. When you install the Python interpreter, IDLE is automatically installed as well. This appendix provides a quick introduction to IDLE, and describes the basic steps of creating, saving, and executing a Python program.

Starting IDLE and Using the Python Shell

After Python is installed on your system a Python program group will appear in your Start menu's program list. One of the items in the program group will be titled *IDLE (Python GUI)*. Click this item to start IDLE and you will see the Python Shell window shown in Figure 1. Inside this window the Python interpreter is running in interactive mode, and at the top of the window is a menu bar that provides access to all of IDLE's tools.

Figure 1   IDLE shell window

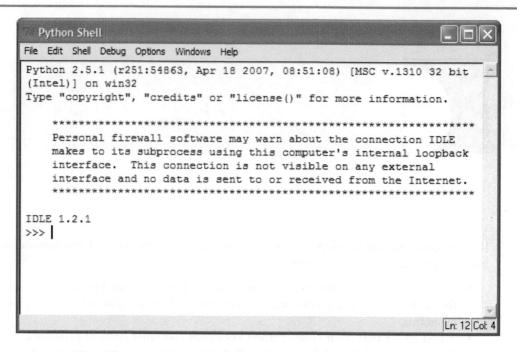

The >>> prompt indicates that the interpreter is waiting for you to type a Python statement. When you type a statement at the >>> prompt and press the Enter key, the statement is immediately executed. For example, Figure 2 shows the Python Shell window after three statements have been entered and executed.

Figure 2   Statements executed by the Python interpreter

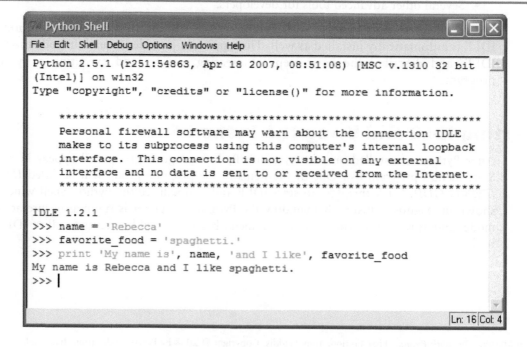

When you type the beginning of a multiline statement, such as an `if` statement or a loop, each subsequent line is automatically indented. Pressing the Enter key on an empty line indicates the end of the multiline statement and causes the interpreter to execute it. Figure 3 shows the Python Shell window after a `for` loop has been entered and executed.

Figure 3   A multiline statement executed by the Python interpreter

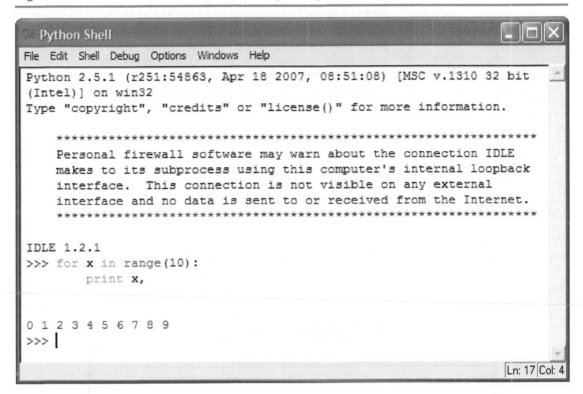

Writing a Python Program in the IDLE Editor

To write a new Python program in IDLE you open a new editing window. As shown in Figure 4 you click File on the menu bar, then click New Window. (Alternatively you can press Ctrl+N.) This opens a text editing window like the one shown in Figure 5.

Figure 4   The File menu

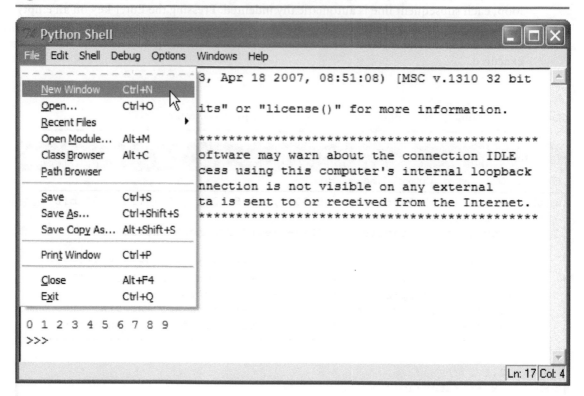

Figure 5   A text editing window

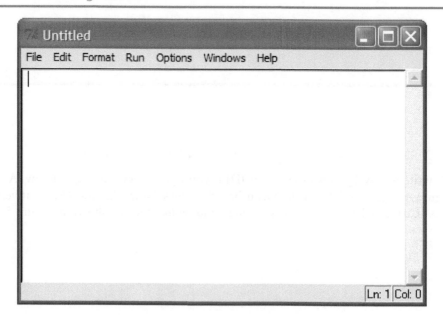

To open a program that already exists, click File on the menu bar, then Open. Simply browse to the file's location and select it, and it will be opened in an editor window.

Color Coding

Code that is typed into the editor window, as well as in the Python Shell window, is colorized as follows:

- Python keywords are displayed in orange.
- Comments are displayed in red.
- String literals are displayed in green.
- Defined names, such as the names of functions and classes, are displayed in blue.
- Built-in functions are displayed in purple.

Figure 6 shows an example of the editing window containing colorized Python code.

Figure 6   Colorized code in the editing window

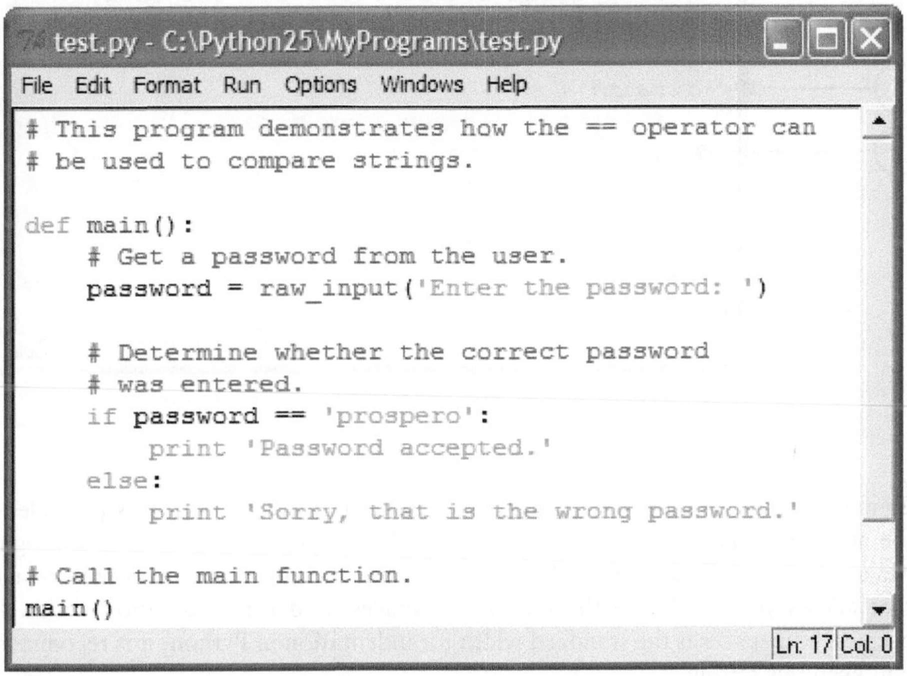

```
test.py - C:\Python25\MyPrograms\test.py
File  Edit  Format  Run  Options  Windows  Help

# This program demonstrates how the == operator can
# be used to compare strings.

def main():
    # Get a password from the user.
    password = raw_input('Enter the password: ')

    # Determine whether the correct password
    # was entered.
    if password == 'prospero':
        print 'Password accepted.'
    else:
        print 'Sorry, that is the wrong password.'

# Call the main function.
main()
                                              Ln: 17 Col: 0
```

 TIP: You can change IDLE's color settings by clicking Options on the menu bar, then clicking Configure IDLE. Select the Highlighting tab at the top of the dialog box, and you can specify colors for each element of a Python program.

Automatic Indentation

The IDLE editor has features that help you to maintain consistent indentation in your Python programs. Perhaps the most helpful of these features is automatic indentation. When you type a line that ends with a colon, such as an if clause, the first line of a loop, or a function header, and then press the Enter key, the editor automatically indents the lines that are entered next. For example, suppose you are typing the code shown in Figure 7. After you press the Enter key at the end of the line marked ①, the editor will automatically indent the lines that you type next. Then, after you press the Enter key at the end of the line marked ②, the editor indents again. Pressing the Backspace key at the beginning of an indented line cancels one level of indentation.

Figure 7   Lines that cause automatic indentation

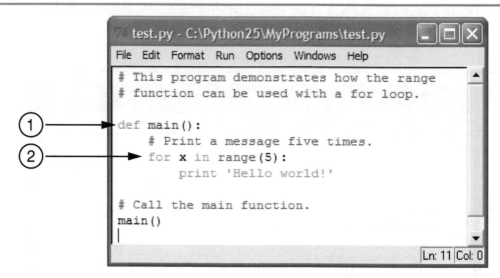

By default, IDLE indents four spaces for each level of indentation. It is possible to change the number of spaces by clicking Options on the menu bar, then clicking Configure IDLE. Make sure Fonts/Tabs is selected at the top of the dialog box, and you will see a slider bar that allows you to change the number of spaces used for indentation width. However, because four spaces is the standard width for indentation in Python, it is recommended that you keep this setting.

Saving a Program

In the editor window you can save the current program by performing any of these operations from the File menu:

- Save
- Save As
- Save Copy As

The Save and Save As operations work just as they do in any Windows application. The Save Copy As operation works like Save As, but it leaves the original program in the editor window.

Running a Program

Once you have typed a program into the editor, you can run it by pressing the F5 key, or as shown in Figure 8, by clicking Run on the editor window's menu bar, then Run Module. If the program has not been saved since the last modification was made, you will see the dialog box shown in Figure 9. Click OK to save the program. When the program runs you will see its output displayed in IDLE's Python Shell window, as shown in Figure 10.

Figure 8   The editor window's Run menu

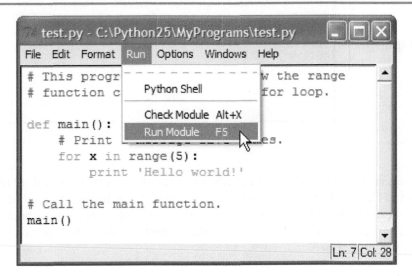

Figure 9   Save confirmation dialog box

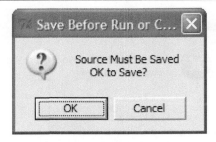

Figure 10   Output displayed in the Python Shell window

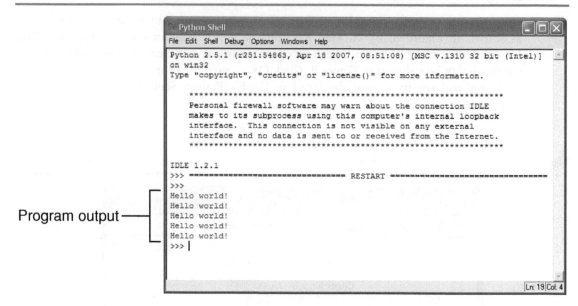

Program output

If a program contains a syntax error, when you run the program you will see the dialog box shown in Figure 11. After you click the OK button the editor will highlight the location of the error in the code. If you want to check the syntax of a program without trying to run it, you can click Run on the menu bar, then Check Module. Any syntax errors that are found will be reported.

Figure 11   Dialog box reporting a syntax error

Other Resources

This appendix has provided an overview for using IDLE to create, save, and execute programs. IDLE provides many more advanced features. To read about additional capabilities, see the official IDLE documentation at www.python.org/idle.

Index